Readings on the Development of Children

Readings
on the
Development
of
Children

Second Edition

EDITED BY

Mary Gauvain
University of California, Riverside

Michael Cole
University of California, San Diego

W. H. Freeman and Company
New York

Acquisitions Editor: Susan Finnemore Brennan

Project Editor: Christine Hastings

Cover Designer: Victoria Tomaselli

Illustration Coordinator: Susan Wein

Production Coordinator: Maura Studley

Composition: W. H. Freeman Electronic Publishing Center/Susan Cory

Manufacturing: Maple-Vail Book Manufacturing Group

Library of Congress Cataloging-in-Publication Data

Readings on the development of children /
        edited by Mary Gauvain, Michael Cole. —2nd ed.
                    p.   cm
    Includes bibliographical references.
    ISBN 0–7167–2860–5 (soft cover)
    1. Developmental psychology.   2. Child psychology.   3. Child development.
        I. Gauvain, Mary.   II. Cole, Michael, 1938–
BF713.R43   1997
155.4—dc20   96–31308
                                                                         CIP

Printed in the United States of America

First printing, 1996

Contents

Preface

Human development is a series of changes produced by the interaction of biological, social, and cultural factors over the lifespan that begins with conception. Developmental psychologists strive to explain this process of change by observing children, conducting experiments, and devising theories.

Students approach the subject of human development with a rich background based on their own experience of growing up as well as their observations of people of all ages. This background is a valuable resource when attempting to understand the scientific approaches to the study of human development encountered in textbooks. However, it has been our experience as instructors that textbooks alone, despite their great value as organized overviews of the field, often leave students puzzled about the process by which developmental psychologists construct their theories, collect their data, and draw conclusions. Textbooks, by their very nature, cannot devote sufficient space to the in-depth discussion of concepts or studies that form the basis of developmental theory.

The entries included in this book of readings have been selected with this problem in mind. Our intention has been to provide students with primary source material that introduces them to a broad range of scientific thinking about human development in all its diversity. We do not shy away from exposing students to classical contributions to the field simply because they do not carry an up-to-the-minute publication date; after all, physicists do not hesitate to teach about Newton's laws of motion although they were formulated several hundred years ago. On the other hand, human development is a rapidly developing discipline, so the bulk of our selection—especially research reports and literature reviews—were first published in the past few years.

The inspiration for this reader came from *The Development of Children*, Third Edition, by Michael Cole and Sheila R. Cole. Although typical of introductory texts in many ways, *The Development of Children* is unusual in the balanced emphasis it places on the biological, social, and cultural factors that make up development. We have not, however, specifically keyed these readings to any one textbook. Instead we have selected articles that provide a representative sample of the wide range of approaches to the study of human development.

The theoretical articles provide students direct access to important and provocative statements by acknowledged leaders in the field. For example, we pair selections by Jean Piaget and Lev Vygotsky discussing the relationship between learning and development. Each article was chosen for its power to capture the essence of each theorist's ideas in a brief, but compelling way. The articles focusing on research were selected to provoke thought and discussion about the ways researchers collect evidence on the process of development and how they interpret and draw conclusions from their data. We have taken special care to include articles about the development of children from many cultures in order to avoid the misrepresentation of middle-class Euro-Americans as the criterion against which the development of all children is measured.

All articles were selected with the undergraduate reader in mind. Because most of our selections were originally written for a professional audience, the text sometimes contains concepts which at first may be difficult to grasp. To alleviate this problem, we have provided brief introductory notes that should help orient the reader to the article's main points. To help students understand the important issues in the selections, we pose three questions at the end of each article. These questions are designed to help the student identify and summarize the key points of the articles, as well as provoke them to think critically about the issues that are raised. Finally, we would like to express our appreciation to the many colleagues who provided valuable feedback to us in the course of developing this reader.

M.G.
M.C.

Readings on the Development of Children

Introduction

1

The American Child and Other Cultural Inventions

WILLIAM KESSEN

According to William Kessen, the American child is a cultural invention. In other words, what it means to be a child, as well as the behavior and thinking of today's children, is shaped by the cultural conditions of life in the contemporary United States. In the following article, Kessen suggests that by considering cultural values and goals as critical components of the developmental process we may gain a better understanding of psychological development.

The theme of the child as a cultural invention can be recognized in several intellectual and social occasions. Ariès' (1962) commentary on the discovery and transformation of childhood has become common knowledge; there is an agitated sense that American children are being redefined by the present times (Lasch, 1978); there is a renewed appreciation of the complexity of all our children (Keniston, 1977); and ethnographic and journalistic reports tell us of the marvelous departures from our own ways of seeing children that exist in other lands (Kessen, 1975). In simple fact, we have recently seen a shower of books on childish variety across cultures and across the hierarchies of class and race.

We could have just as readily discovered commanding evidence of the shifting nature of childhood

Reprinted with permission from the author and *American Psychologist, 34,* 1979, 815–820.
Copyright 1979 by the American Psychological Association.

by a close look at our own history. Consider just three messages drawn haphazardly from the American past. To the parents of the late 18th century:

> The first duties of Children are in great measure mechanical: an obedient Child makes a Bow, comes and goes, speaks, or is silent, just as he is bid, before he knows any other Reason for so doing than that he is bid. (Nelson, 1753)

Or to our parents and grandparents:

> The rule that parents should not play with their children may seem hard but it is without doubt a safe one. (West, 1914)

Or hear a parent of the 1970s speak of her 6-year-old:

> LuAnn liked the school in California best—the only rules were no chemical additives in the food and no balling in the hallways. (Rothchild & Wolf, 1976)

And we cannot escape the implications of an unstable portrait of the child by moving from folk psychology to the professional sort. On the contrary, a clear-eyed study of what experts have said about the young—from Locke to Skinner, from Rousseau to Piaget, from Comenius to Erikson—will expose as bewildering a taxonomy as the one provided by preachers, parents, and poets. No other animal species has been cataloged by responsible scholars in so many wildly discrepant forms, forms that a perceptive extraterrestrial could never see as reflecting the same beast.

To be sure, most expert students of children continue to assert the truth of the positivistic dream—that we have not yet found the underlying structural simplicities that will reveal the child entire, that we have not yet cut nature at the joints—but it may be wise for us child psychologists in the International Year of the Child to peer into the abyss of the positivistic nightmare—that the child is essentially and eternally a cultural invention and that the variety of the child's definition is not the removable error of an incomplete science. For not only are American *children* shaped and marked by the larger cultural forces of political maneuverings, practical economics, and implicit ideological commitments (a new enough recognition), *child psychology* is itself a peculiar cultural invention that moves with the tidal sweeps of the larger culture in ways that we understand at best dimly and often ignore.

To accept the ambiguity of our task—to give up debates about the fundamental nature of the child—is not, however, a defeatist or unscientific move. Rather, when we seriously confront the proposition that we, like the children we study, are cultural inventions, we can go on to ask questions about the sources of our diversity and, perhaps more tellingly, about the sources of our agreements. It is surely remarkable that against the background of disarray in our definition of the child, a number of ideas are so widely shared that few scholars question their provenance and warrant. Paradoxically, the unexamined communalities of our commitment may turn out to be more revealing than our disagreements. Within the compass of the next several pages, I point toward disagreements that were present at the beginnings of systematic child study, and then turn in more detail to the pervasive and shared themes of American childhood in our time, themes that may require a more critical review than we have usually given them.

PRESENT AT THE BIRTH

When child psychology was born, in a longish parturition that ran roughly from Hall's first questionary studies of 1880 (Hall, 1883) to Binet's test of construction of 1905 (Binet & Simon, 1916), there were five determining spirits present. Four of them are familiar to us all; the fifth and least visible spirit may turn out to be the most significant. One of the familiars was in the line of Locke and Bain, and it appeared later for Americans as John Broadus Watson; the line has, then and now, represented behavior, restraint, clarity, simplicity, and good news. Paired in philosophical and theoretical opposition was the spirit that derived from Rousseau, Nietzsche, and Freud, the line that represented mind, impulse, ambiguity, complexity, and bad news. The great duel between the two lines has occupied students of children for just under 300 years.

The third magus at the beginning was the most fully American; William James can stand as the representative of the psychologists whose central concern was with sensation, perception, language, thought, and will—the solid, sensible folk who hid out in the years between the World Wars but who have returned in glory. It is of at least passing interest to note that the cognitivists participated lightly in the early development of child study; James and, even more, Munsterberg and, past all measure, Titchener found results from the study of children too messy for the precision they wanted from their methods.

The godfather of child psychology, the solidest spirit of them all, was Charles Darwin, foreshadowing his advocates and his exaggerators. His contemporary stand-in, G. Stanley Hall, was the first in a long and continuing line that has preached from animal analogues, has called attention to the biological in the child, and has produced a remarkably diverse progeny that includes Galton, Gesell, and the ethologists.

I rehearse (and oversimplify) the story of our professional beginnings to call attention to how persistent the lines have been, how little they have interpenetrated and modified one another, and how much their contributions to our understanding of the child rest on a network of largely implicit and undefended assumptions about the basis of human knowledge, social structures, and ethical ascriptions. The lines of the onlooking spirits are themselves historical and cultural constructions that grew, in ways that have rarely been studied analytically or biographically, from the matrix of the larger contemporaneous culture.[1]

And so to the fifth circumnatal spirit, the one that knew no technical psychology. In the middle 50 years of the 19th century, the years that prepared the United States for child psychology, dramatic and persistent changes took place in American society. I could sing the familiar litany of urbanization, industrialization, the arrival of the first millions of European immigrants (another strand of diversity among children that requires a closer look). We know that the Civil War transformed the lives of most American families, white and black (although we still know remarkably little about the daily lives of children during and after the war). The United States developed, and *developed* is the word of choice, from an isolated agricultural dependency to an aggressive and powerful state. Technology and science joined the industrial entrepreneurs to persuade the new Americans, from abroad and from the farm, that poverty was an escapable condition if one worked hard enough and was aggressively independent. But there were other changes that bore more immediately on the lives of American children; let me, as an example of cultural influences on children and child psychology rather than as a worked-through demonstration of my thesis, extract three interwoven strands of the changes that touched children.

The first, and the earliest, was the evolving separation of the domain of work from the domain of home. When women left or were excluded from the industrial work force in the 1830s and 1840s, the boundary marked by the walls of home became less and less penetrable. First for the white, the urban, the middle-class, the northeastern American, but enlisting other parts of the community as time went on, work (or *real work* as contrasted with *homework*, the activity of women and schoolchildren) was carried on in specialized spaces by specialized people, and home became the place where one (i.e., men) did not work (Cott, 1977; Lasch, 1977).

The second and entailed change was the radical separation of what a man was from what a woman was. Colonial and early Federal society, like all other cultures, had stable and divergent visions of the proper sphere of male and female. But in the half century under our present consideration, something of a moral metamorphosis occurred in the United States (and in large measure, in England, too) and one of modern history's most eccentric arrangements of human beings was put in place. The public world of men was seen as ugly, aggressive, corrupting, chaotic, sinful (not an altogether regretted characteristic), and irreligious. The increasingly private world of women was, in inevitable antithesis, sweet, chaste, calm, cultured, loving, protective, and godly. The muscular Christianity of the Mathers and Edwardses became the feminized Christianity of matrons and pastors; the caretaking of culture became the task of women's groups (Douglas, 1978). So dramatic a statement of the contrast is hardly an exaggeration of the facts. And the full story remains to be told; historians of medical practice, for example, are just beginning to reveal the systematic attempt to desex American and British women in the 19th century with methods that ranged from sermons to surgery (Barker-Benfield, 1977).

The third change in American life that set the cultural context for child psychology followed on the first two. Children continued to be cared for by women at home, and in consequence, they took on the coloration of mother, hearth, and heaven. The early American child, who was told, "consider that you may perish as young as you are; there are small Chips as well as great Logs, in the Fire of Hell" (18th-century primer, quoted by Johnson, 1904), became Little Eva, Huckleberry Finn, and eventually Peter Pan. The sentimentalization of children—caught for tombstones and psychology books best by Wordsworth's "Heaven lies about us in our infancy!"—had implications for family structure, education, and the definition of the child in expert writings that we have not yet, nearing the end of the 20th century, fully understood or confronted.

Thus it was that American child psychology began not only under the conflicting attention of Locke, Rousseau, James, and Darwin, but with the progressivist, sexist, and sentimental expectation of the larger culture standing by.

THE COMMON THEMES OF AMERICAN CHILD PSYCHOLOGY

Are we now free of our origins? It would be both unhistorical and undevelopmental to believe so, in spite of all we have learned about research and about children over the last 100 years. The positivist promise of pure objectivity and eternal science has been withdrawn. Therefore, it may be methodologically therapeutic to glance, however briefly, at several common themes of our field that seem dependent, in the usually complicated way of human history, on the story I have sketched thus far. All of the themes may be ready for a thoughtful new evaluation.

The Commitment to Science and Technology

The notable success of the physical sciences in the 19th century, the elation that followed on the Darwinian revolution, and the culture's high hopes for a technological utopia joined at the end of the 19th century to define child psychology as scientific and rational. The vagaries of casual stories about children, the eccentricities of folk knowledge, and the superstitions of grandmothers were all to be cleansed by the mighty brush of scientific method (Jacoby, 1914; Watson, 1928). The conviction that we are scientists remains one of the heart beliefs of child psychology, and in its humane and sensible forms, the commitment to a systematic analytic examination of the lives of children and their worlds is still the unique and continuing contribution of child psychology to American culture.

But some less obvious and perhaps less defensible consequences of the rational scientific commitment were pulled along into child psychology by the high hopes of its founders. Perhaps the one that we have had the most difficulty in handling as a profession is the implication *in all theories of the child* that lay folk, particularly parents, are in need of expert guidance. Critical examination and study of parental practices and child behavior almost inevitably slipped subtly over to advice about parental practices and child behavior. The scientific statement became an ethical imperative, the descriptive account became normative. And along the way, there have been unsettling occasions in which scraps of knowledge, gathered by whatever procedures were held to be proper science at the time, were given inordinate weight against poor old defenseless folk knowledge. Rigorously scheduled feedings of infants, separation of new mothers from their babies, and Mrs. West's injunction against playing with children can stand as examples of scientism that are far enough away not to embarrass us enlightened moderns.

More, I risk the guess that the sentimental view of the child that prevailed at the beginnings of child psychology—a vision which, let it be said, made possible humane and appropriate reforms in the treatment of children—was strongly influential in what can only be called a salvationist view of children. Child psychologists, again whatever their theoretical stripe, have taken the Romantic notion of childish innocence and openness a long way toward the several forms of "If only we could make matters right with the child, the world would be a better place." The child became the carrier of political progressivism and the optimism of reformers. From agitation for child labor reform in the 1890s to Head Start, American children have been saviors of the nation. The romantic inheritance of purity and perfectibility may, in fact, have misled us about the proper unit of developmental study and about the major forces influencing human growth and change. I will return to the consideration of our unit of study shortly.

There has often also been a socially hierarchical message in our scientific-normative interactions with the larger culture. Tolstoy said that there is no proletarian literature; there has been no proletarian child psychology either, and the ethically imperative forms of child psychology, our messages to practice, have ranged from pleas for equitable treatment of all children to recipes for forced assimilation to the expected forms of child behavior. Once a descriptive norm has been established, it is an antique cultural principle to urge adherence to it.

Finally, for some eras of child study, there has been an enthusiastic anticipation that all problems are reducible by the science of the moment; intellectual technology can succeed (and imitate) the 19th century's commercial and industrial technology in the progressive and ultimate betterment of humankind. The optimism of the founders of child study and their immediate successors is dimmer today— "The sky's the limit" may be replaced by "You win a few, you lose a few"—and serious questions have been posed even for the basic assumptions underlying the scientific analysis of human behavior (Barrett, 1978). Child psychology may soon have to face anew the question of whether or not a scientific account of human development can be given without bringing in its wake the false claims of scientism and the arrogance of an ethic based on current findings.

The Importance of Mothers, Early Experience, and Personal Responsibility

Strangely at odds with the theme of rational scientific inquiry has been the persistence of the commitment to home and mother in otherwise varying portraits of the child. Some child psychologists have been less than laudatory about the effectiveness of particular mothering procedures (Watson dedicated his directive book on child rearing to the first mother who raises a child successfully), but critics and praisers alike have rarely doubted the basic principle that children need home and mother to grow as they should grow (again, the normative injunction enters). I do not mean to dispute the assumption here; I want only to suggest its connection with the mid-19th-century ideology that long preceded systematic child psychology and to point out several riders on the assumption that have, in the past, been less vividly visible.

Two riders on the home-and-mother position are under active debate and study nowadays—the irrelevance of fathers and the critical role of early experience. The cases represent with the starkness of a line drawing the influence of contemporaneous cultural forces on the definition of psychology's child. It would be difficult to defend the proposition that the recent interest in the place of fathers or the possibilities of out-of-home child rearing grew either from a new theory of development or from striking new empirical discoveries. Rather, for reasons too elaborate to explore here, fewer and fewer American women have been willing or able to devote all of their work time to the rearing of children. It will be instructive to see how much the tasks assigned fathers and day-care centers reflect the old ascriptions to essential maternity. Psychology follows culture, but often at a discreet distance.

The blending of new social requirements into old ideology is precisely demonstrated by the incorporation of fathers and day-care workers into the premise that what happens to the child in the first hours, weeks, months of life holds an especially determining position in human development. Proclaimed on epistemological grounds by Locke, gathered into the American ethos in part because it so well fit the perfectionist argument, elevated to scientific status by evolutionary theory, the doctrine of the primacy of early experience has been an uncontested part of American culture and American child psychology throughout the history of both. Only in the last several years has the premise been called seriously into question (Kagan, Kearsley, & Zelazo,

1978) and, even then, at a time when ever more extravagant claims are being made about the practical necessity of safeguarding the child's first hours (Klaus & Kennell, 1976).

The assumption of essential maternity and the assumption of the determining role of early experience join to support yet another underdebated postulate of child psychology. If something goes wrong in the course of a child's development, it is the primary responsibility of the mother (or whoever behaves as mother), and once more in echo of the salvationist view, if a social problem is not repaired by modification of the child's first years, the problem is beyond repair. The working of the postulate has produced ways of blaming mothers that appear in all theoretical shapes and, more generally, ways of blaming other victims of social injustice because they are not readily transformed by the ministrations of the professionals (Ryan, 1971).

The tendency to assign personal responsibility for the successes and failures of development is an amalgam of the positivistic search for causes, of the older Western tradition of personal moral responsibility, and of the conviction that personal mastery and consequent personal responsibility are first among the goals of child rearing. It is difficult to imagine an American child psychology without a core commitment to the proposition that someone is responsible for what happens in the course of development.

The Belief in the Individual and Self-Contained Child

Hovering over each of the traditional beliefs mentioned thus far is the most general and, in my view, the most fundamental entanglement of technical child psychology with the implicit commitments of American culture. The child—like the Pilgrim, the cowboy, and the detective on television—is invariably seen as a free-standing isolable being who moves through development as a self-contained and complete individual. Other similarly self-contained people—parents and teachers—may influence the development of children, to be sure, but the proper unit of cultural analysis and the proper unit of developmental study is the child alone. The ubiquity of such radical individualism in our lives makes the consideration of alternative images of childhood extraordinarily difficult. We have never taken fully seriously the notion that development is, in large measure, a social construction, the child a modulated and modulating component in a shifting network of influences (Berger & Luckmann, 1966). The seminal thinkers about children over the past century have, in fact, been almost undeviating in their postulation of the child as container of self and of psychology. Impulses are in the child; traits are in the child; thoughts are in the child; attachments are in the child. In short, almost every major theory of development accepts the premises of individualism and takes the child as the basic unit of study, with all consequences the choice has for decisions that range from selecting a method of research to selecting a therapeutic maneuver.

Uniform agreement on the isolable child as the proper measure of development led to the research paradigms that have dominated child psychology during most of its history; basically, we have observed those parts of development that the child could readily transport to our laboratories or to our testing sites. The use of isolated preparations for the study of development has, happily, been productive of remarkable advances in our knowledge of children, but with the usual cost of uniform dogma, the commitment to the isolable child has occasionally led child psychology into exaggerations and significant omissions.

There are signals now aloft that the dogma of individualism, both in its claim of lifelong stability of personality and in its claim that human action can be understood without consideration of context or history, is under severe stress. The story that Vygotsky (1978) told 50 years ago, the story of the embeddedness of the developing mind in society, has finally been heard. The image of the child as an epigenetic and continuous creation of social and biological contexts is far more ambiguous and more difficult to paint than the relative simplicities of the traditional and culturally justified self-contained child; it may also illuminate our understanding of children and of our science.

THE PRESENT MOMENT

The cultural epigenesis that created the American child of the late 20th century continues, and so does the epigenesis that created child psychology. Necessarily, there is no end of the road, no equilibrium. Rather, the transformations of the past 100 years in both children and child psychology are a startling reminder of the eternal call on us to be scrupulous observers and imaginative researchers; they may also serve to force our self-critical recognition that we are both creators and performers in the cultural invention of the child.

Questions

1. According to Kessen, the child is "an invention of culture." Do you agree with this? Why or why not? What are two similarities and two differences in the cultural determinants of late 19th century America and modern America?

2. Kessen describes five "determining spirits" of child psychology. Which of these are still applicable in modern developmental psychology?

3. How does human growth maintain continuity across generations yet adapt to changing cultural influences?

References and Notes

1.   It has become a cliché to speak of psychoanalysis as an out-growth of Jewish intellectual culture in turn-of-the-century Vienna (a shallow summary at best), but no corresponding common saying exists for, say, Watson's growing up in postwar Carolina, or Hall's curious combination of *odium sexicum* and *odium theologicum* in Victorian times, or Binet's history as an apostate continental associationist.

Ariès, P. *Centuries of childhood: A social history of family life* (R. Baldick, Trans.). New York: Knopf, 1962.

Barker-Benfield, G. J. *Horrors of the half-known life.* New York: Harper & Row, 1977.

Barrett, W. *The illusion of technique.* Garden City, N.Y.: Doubleday, 1978.

Berger, P. L., & Luckmann, T. *The social construction of reality: A treatise in the sociology of knowledge.* Garden City, N.Y.: Doubleday, 1966.

Binet, A., & Simon, T. Upon the necessity of establishing a scientific diagnosis of inferior states of intelligence (E. S. Kite, Trans.). In A. Binet & T. Simon, *The development of intelligence in children.* Baltimore, Md.: Williams & Wilkins, 1916. (Originally published, 1905.)

Cott, N. F. *Bonds of womanhood: Women's sphere in New England, 1780–1835.* New Haven, Conn.: Yale University Press, 1977.

Douglas, A. *The feminization of American culture.* New York: Avon Books, 1978

Hall, G. S. The contents of children's minds. *Princeton Review,* 1883, *11,* 249–272.

Jacoby, G. W. *Child training as an exact science: A treatise based upon the principles of modern psychology, normal and abnormal.* New York: Funk & Wagnalls, 1914.

Johnson, C. *Old-time schools and schoolbooks.* New York: Macmillan, 1904.

Kagan, J., Kearsley, R. B., & Zelazo, P. R. (With the assistance of C. Minton). *Infancy: Its place in human development.* Cambridge, Mass.: Harvard University Press, 1978.

Keniston, K., & Carnegie Council on Children. *All our children: The American family under pressure.* New York: Harcourt Brace Jovanovich, 1977.

Kessen, W. (Ed.). *Childhood in China.* New Haven, Conn.: Yale University Press, 1975.

Klaus, M. H., & Kennell, J. H. *Maternal-infant bonding.* Saint Louis: Mosby, 1976.

Lasch, C. *Haven in a heartless world: The family besieged.* New York: Basic Books, 1977.

Lasch, C. *The culture of narcissism: American life in an age of diminishing expectations.* New York: Norton, 1978.

Nelson, J. *An essay on the government of children under three general heads: Viz., health, manners, and education.* London: (no publisher), 1753.

Rothchild, J., & Wolf, S. B. *The children of the counterculture.* Garden City, N.Y.: Doubleday, 1976.

Ryan, W. *Blaming the victim.* New York: Random House, 1971.

Vygotsky, L. S. *Mind in society: The development of higher psychological processes* (M. Cole, V. John-Steiner, S. Scribner, & E. Souberman, Eds.). Cambridge, Mass.: Harvard University Press, 1978.

Watson, J. B. *Psychological care of infant and child.* New York: Norton, 1928.

West, M. *Infant care* (Publication No. 8). Washington, D.C.: U.S. Children's Bureau, 1914.

2

Perspectives on Children's Development from Cultural Psychology

BARBARA ROGOFF AND GILDA MORELLI

Over the last few decades, psychologists have come to recognize the important role that culture plays in children's development. One important trend has been the gradual shift away from laboratory-based research that relies on manipulation and control of isolated variables toward studies of behaviors as they occur in children's everyday lives in the cultural communities in which they grow. However, understanding the importance of culture in development cannot result from changes in research methods alone. We must also adjust our ways of conceptualizing issues and reevaluate the theories on which we base our assumptions. In the following article Barbara Rogoff and Gilda Morelli discuss a contextual approach to development that focuses on the complex interaction between children's development and the cultural system in which their growth occurs.

This article summarizes how cultural research can inform mainstream psychology. It focuses on an organizing theme that has been explored in research in non-Western groups: the role of specific cultural practices in organizing human endeavors. This perspective has influenced the direction of mainstream research, encouraging the advancement of our ideas of the domain-specific nature of psychological processes, and their relation to sociocultural practices. The article provides a brief description of Vygotsky's theoretical approach, a perspective comfortable for many working within this tradition. Finally, a discussion of research on children in cultural groups in the United States

Reprinted with permission from the authors and *American Psychologist, 44*, 1989, 343–348. Copyright 1989 by the American Psychological Association.
    We thank Ana Estrada for her comments on this essay.

suggests that the cultural perspective can be useful in advancing research on issues involving American children with different cultural backgrounds.

Attention to the cultural context of child development has yielded important insights into the opportunities and constraints provided by the society in which children mature. Research with children of different cultures provides a broader perspective on human development than is available when considering human behavior in a single cultural group.

The purpose of this article is to indicate how cultural research can inform mainstream psychology. We discuss one organizing theme that has been explored in research in non-Western groups, the role of specific cultural practices in organizing all human endeavors. This perspective has influenced the direction of mainstream research, encouraging the advancement of our ideas of the domain-specific nature of psychological processes, and their relation to sociocultural practices. We provide a brief description of Vygotsky's theoretical approach, a perspective comfortable for many working within this tradition. Finally, we suggest that the cultural perspective can be useful in advancing research on issues involving American children varying in cultural background.

LESSONS LEARNED FROM CROSS-CULTURAL STUDIES OF DEVELOPMENT

Investigations of the role of culture in development have taken advantage of the impressive variations in the human condition, which occur around the world, to advance understanding of human adaptation. Reviews and discussion of cross-cultural developmental research appear in Bornstein (1980); Dasen (1977); Field, Sostek, Vietze, and Leiderman (1981); Laboratory of Comparative Human Cognition (1979, 1983); Leiderman, Tulkin, and Rosenfeld (1977); LeVine (in press); Munroe and Munroe (1975); Munroe, Munroe, and Whiting (1981); Rogoff, Gauvain, and Ellis (1984); Rogoff and Mistry (1985); Schieffelin and Ochs (1986); Serpell (1976); Super and Harkness (1980); Triandis and Heron (1981); Wagner and Stevenson (1982); Werner (1979); and Whiting and Edwards (1988).

Cross-cultural studies have focused especially on children in nontechnological (non-Western) societies because these children contrast in important ways with children from the United States and other Western nations. This first section thus describes lessons learned from cross-cultural studies involving children around the world; psychological research

on minorities in the United States has followed a somewhat different course, described later.

Perspectives Offered by Cross-cultural Research

An important function of cross-cultural research has been to allow investigators to look closely at the impact of their own belief systems (folk psychology) on scientific theories and research paradigms. When subjects and researchers are from the same population, interpretations of development may be constrained by implicit cultural assumptions. With subjects sharing researchers' belief systems, psychologists are less aware of their own assumptions regarding the world of childhood, the involvement of others in child development, and the physical and institutional circumstances in which development is embedded. Working with people from a quite different background can make one aware of aspects of human activity that are not noticeable until they are missing or differently arranged, as with the fish who reputedly is unaware of water until removed from it. Viewing the contrasts in life's arrangements in different cultures has enabled psychologists to examine very basic assumptions regarding developmental goals, the skills that are learned, and the contexts of development.

Cross-cultural research also allows psychologists to use cultural variation as a natural laboratory to attempt to disentangle variables that are difficult to tease apart in the United States and to study conditions that are rare in the United States. For example, one can examine how gender differences manifest themselves in differing cultural circumstances (Whiting & Edwards, 1988). Cross-cultural studies have examined the extent to which advances in intellectual skills are related to schooling versus children's age, a comparison that cannot be made in a country with compulsory schooling (Laboratory of Comparative Human Cognition, 1979; Rogoff, 1981). Other research examines conditions that are seen as normal in other cultures but carry connotations of being problematic in the United States. For example, studies have been made of gender roles in polygynous societies in which fathers are absent from the household because they have several wives (Munroe & Munroe, 1975), and of child care and infant psychological development in societies in which nonmaternal care (care by other adults or by child nurses) is valued and expected (Fox, 1977; Tronick, Morelli, & Winn, 1987; Zaslow, 1980).

Another function of cross-cultural studies is to examine the generality of theories of development that have been based on Western children. Examples include investigations of the universality of the stages of development proposed by Piaget, the family role relations emphasized by Freud, and patterns of mother-infant interaction taken to index security of attachment (Bretherton & Waters, 1985; Dasen, 1977; Dasen & Heron, 1981; Greenfield, 1976; Malinowski, 1927; Price-Williams, 1980). In such research, modifications to the assumptions of generality have often been suggested by cross-cultural findings. For example, findings that the highest stage of Piaget's theory, formal operations, seldom can be seen in non-Western cultures prompted Piaget to modify his theory in 1972 to suggest that the formal operational stage may not be universal but rather a product of an individual's expertise in a specific domain.

Research in a variety of cultures has also provided evidence of impressive regularities across cultures in developmental phenomena. For instance, there is marked similarity across cultures in the sequence and timing of sensorimotor milestones in infant development, smiling, and separation distress (Gewirtz, 1965; Goldberg, 1972; Konner, 1972; Super, 1981; Werner, 1988) and in the order of stages in language acquisition (Bowerman, 1981; Slobin, 1973).

An Emphasis on Understanding the Context of Development

An important contribution resulting from cultural challenges to researchers' assumptions is the conceptual restructuring emphasizing that human functioning cannot be separated from the contexts of their activities. Although there are other sources of contextual theorizing in the field of psychology, an important impetus has been the consistent findings that behavior and development vary according to cultural context.

Developmental researchers who have worked in other cultures have become convinced that human functioning cannot be separated from the cultural and more immediate context in which children develop. They observed that skills and behavior that did not appear in laboratory situations appeared in the same individuals in everyday situations. A subject whose logical reasoning or memory in a laboratory task seemed rudimentary could skillfully persuade the researcher or remind the researcher of promises outside the laboratory, or might be very skilled in a complex everyday task such as navigation or weaving (Cole, 1975; Cole, Hood, & McDermott, 1978; Gladwin, 1970; Laboratory of Comparative Human Cognition, 1979; Rogoff, 1981; Scribner, 1976). Such informal observations called into question

the widespread assumption that individuals' skills and behaviors have a generality extending across contexts.

Systematic studies noted the close relation between the skills or behavior exhibited by an individual and the contexts of elicitation and practice (Lave, 1977; Saxe, 1988). Children's nurturance and aggression varied as a function of the age and gender of the people with whom they interacted (Wenger, 1983; Whiting & Whiting, 1975). Perceptual modeling skills of Zambian and English children varied as a function of the cultural familiarity of the specific modeling activity (Serpell, 1979). Literacy provides practice with specific cognitive activities, leading to advances in particular skills rather than conferring general cognitive ability (Scribner & Cole, 1981). Such results point to the importance of considering the contexts in which people practice skills and behaviors, as well as those in which we as researchers observe them.

Many of the cognitive activities examined in developmental research, such as memory, perception, logical reasoning, and classification, have been found in cross-cultural studies to relate to children's experience of schooling (Lave, 1977; Rogoff, 1981; Sharp, Cole, & Lave, 1979). The extensive studies of the relation between school and cognitive skills call attention to a context of learning that is easily overlooked as an influence on cognitive development in the United States, where school is ubiquitous in the lives of children.

Remembering or classifying lists of unrelated objects may be unusual activities outside of literate or school-related activities (Goody, 1977; Rogoff & Waddell, 1982). The taxonomic categories seen as most appropriate in literate situations may not be valued in other circumstances, as is illustrated by Glick's (1975) report of Kpelle subjects' treatment of a classification problem. They sorted the 20 objects into functional groups (e.g., knife with orange, potato with hoe) rather than into categorical groups that the researcher considered more appropriate. When questioned, they often volunteered that that was the way a wise man would do things. "When an exasperated experimenter asked finally, 'How would a fool do it,' he was given back sorts of the type that were initially expected—four neat piles with food in one, tools in another, and so on" (p. 636).

People who have more schooling, such as older children and Western peoples, may excel on many kinds of cognitive tests because not only the skills but also the social situations of testing resemble the activities specifically practiced in school. In contrast with everyday life, where people classify and remember things in order to accomplish a functional goal, in schools and tests they perform in order to satisfy an adult's request to do so (Skeen, Rogoff, & Ellis, 1983; Super, Harkness, & Baldwin, 1977). Individuals with experience in school are likely to have more experience carrying out cognitive processes at the request of an adult without having a clear practical goal (Cazden & John, 1971; Rogoff & Mistry, in press).

Similar emphasis on contexts of development has come from other domains of cross-cultural research. In the area of infant sensorimotor development, Super (1981) and Kilbride (1980) have argued that the controversy over precocious development in African infants is best resolved by considering the practices of the cultural system in which the babies develop. African infants routinely surpass American infants in their rate of learning to sit and to walk, but not in learning to crawl or to climb stairs. African parents provide experiences for their babies that are apparently intended to teach sitting and walking—propping young infants in a sitting position supported by rolled blankets in a hole in the ground, exercising the newborn's walking reflex, and bouncing babies on their feet. But crawling is discouraged, and stair-climbing skills may be limited by the absence of access to stairs. Infant sensorimotor tests assess an aggregate of skills varying in rate of development according to the opportunity or encouragement to practice them.

Even infant sleep patterns vary as a function of culturally determined sleeping arrangements (Super, 1981). In the United States, the common developmental milestone of sleeping for eight uninterrupted hours by age four to five months is regarded as a sign of neurological maturity. In many other cultures, however, the infant sleeps with the mother and is allowed to nurse on demand with minimal disturbance of adult sleep. In such an arrangement, there is less parental motivation to enforce "sleeping through the night," and Super reported that babies continue to wake about every four hours during the night to feed, which is about the frequency of feeding during the day. Thus, it appears that this developmental milestone, in addition to its biological basis, is a function of the context in which it develops.

Cross-cultural studies demonstrating that individuals' behavior and skills are closely tied to specific activities have contributed to examination of important questions regarding the generality of the development of skills and behaviors, the structure of the ecology of development, and how to conceptualize the sociocultural context of practice of skills and behavior. These issues have recently pervaded the study of developmental psychology, with some large measure of influence from research on culture.

Conceptualizing the Sociocultural Context

Many researchers in the field of culture and development have found themselves comfortable with Vygotsky's theory, which focuses on the sociocultural context of development. Vygotsky's theory, developed in the 1930s in the Soviet Union, has gradually become more accessible to English-speaking researchers, with a rapid upsurge of interest following the publication of *Mind in Society* in 1978 (see also Laboratory of Comparative Human Cognition, 1983; Rogoff, 1982; Scribner & Cole, 1981; Wertsch, 1985a, 1985b). Although Vygotsky's theory focuses on cognitive development, it is gaining interest with researchers in emotional and social development as well, perhaps due to its integration of cognitive and social processes, as well as its emphasis on socialization (see, for example, Newson & Newson, 1975).

Vygotsky's theory offers a picture of human development that stresses how development is inseparable from human social and cultural activities. This contrasts with the image of the solitary little scientist provided by Piaget's theory. Vygotsky focused on how the development of higher mental processes such as voluntary memory and attention, classification, and reasoning involve learning to use inventions of society (such as language, mathematical systems, and memory devices) and how children are aided in development by guidance provided by people who are already skilled in these tools. Central to Vygotsky's theory is a stress on both the institutional and the interpersonal levels of social context.

THE INSTITUTIONAL LEVEL   Cultural history provides organizations and tools useful to cognitive activity (through institutions such as school and inventions such as the calculator or literacy) along with practices that facilitate socially appropriate solutions to problems (e.g., norms for the arrangement of grocery shelves to aid shoppers in locating or remembering what they need; common mnemonic devices). Particular forms of activity are practiced in societal institutions such as schools and political systems.

For example, Kohlberg's hierarchy of moral development can be tied to the political system of a society, with the bureaucratic systems' perspective (Stage Four) appropriate for people whose political frame of reference is a large industrialized society, but inappropriate for people in small traditional tribal societies: "The two types of social systems are very different (though of course both are valid working types of systems), and thus everyday social life in them calls forth different modes of moral problem solving whose adequacy must be judged relative to their particular contexts" (Edwards, 1981, p. 274). The political institutions of a society may channel individual moral reasoning by providing standards for the resolution of moral problems.

The cultural institution of Western schooling provides norms and strategies for performance that are considered advanced in cognitive tests. Goodnow (1976) has suggested that differences between cultural groups may be ascribed largely to the interpretation of what problem is being solved in the task and to different values regarding "proper" methods of solution (e.g., speed, reaching a solution with a minimum of moves or redundancy, physically handling materials versus mental shuffling). The cultural tools and techniques used in school involve specific conventions and genres, such as conventions for representing depth in two-dimensional pictures and story problem genres (similar to logical syllogisms) in which one must rely only on information given in the problem to reach the answer. Cross-cultural studies indicate that nonschooled subjects are unfamiliar with such conventions and genres. For example, they are uncomfortable having to answer questions for which they cannot verify the premises (Cole, Gay, Glick, & Sharp, 1971; Scribner, 1977).

THE INTERPERSONAL LEVEL   In Vygotsky's theory (1978), children develop skills in higher mental processes through the immediate social interactional context of activity, as social interaction helps structure individual activity. Information regarding tools and practices is transmitted through children's interaction with more experienced members of society during development, and patterns of interpersonal relations are organized by institutional conventions and the availability of cultural tools. For example, social aspects of experimental and observational situations relate to cultural practices. The relation between experimenter and subject may be rapidly grasped by Western children familiar with testing in school, but it may be highly discrepant from familiar adult–child interactions for non-Western children and young Western children. In some cultural settings, it is unusual for an adult who already knows an answer to request information from a child who may only partially know the subject matter, and it may be inappropriate for children to show off knowledge (Cazden & John, 1971; Irvine, 1978; Rogoff, Gauvain, & Ellis, 1984).

Similarly, in observational situations such as mother–child interaction, culturally varying agendas for public behavior may influence what people do in the presence of an observer (Zaslow & Rogoff, 1981). "It seems likely that one influence of the observer on parents is to produce a heightened frequency of behavior that the participants judge to be more socially desirable and inhibit behavior considered socially undesirable" (Pedersen, 1980, p. 181). Graves and Glick (1978) found that exchanges between middle-class mothers and their toddlers varied as a function of whether mothers thought that they were being videotaped. Mothers spoke more, used indirect directives more often, and spent more time in joint interactive focus with their children when they thought they were being observed. Clearly, peoples' interpretation of the goals of a task and cultural rules guiding social behavior influence the display of public behavior. Values regarding interpersonal relations may be inseparable from the activities observed for research purposes.

In addition to the cultural structuring of social interaction that has importance for research into human development, social interaction provides an essential context for development itself. Vygotsky stressed that interpersonal situations are important for guiding children in their development of the skills and behaviors considered important in their culture. Working within the "zone of proximal development," adults guide children in carrying out activities that are beyond the children's individual skills, and this joint problem solving provides children with information appropriate to stretch their individual skills. Cole (1981) argues that the zone of proximal development is "where culture and cognition create each other." Thus Vygotsky's conceptualization of how individual efforts are embedded in the interpersonal and institutional contexts of culture is proving useful for understanding the relation between culture and the individual.

RESEARCH ON CULTURE INVOLVING MINORITIES IN THE UNITED STATES

Historically, research on minorities in the United States has followed a different course than the cross-cultural investigations discussed earlier. For many years, researchers were intent on comparing the behavior and skills of minority children with mainstream children without taking into consideration the cultural contexts in which minority and mainstream children develop. This approach involved "deficit model" assumptions that mainstream skills and upbringing are normal and that variations observed with minorities are aberrations that produce deficits; intervention programs were designed to provide minority children with experiences to make up for their assumed deficits (Cole & Bruner, 1971; Hilliard & Vaughn-Scott, 1982; Howard & Scott, 1981; Ogbu, 1982).

The deficit model previously used in research on minority children contrasts sharply with the assumptions of the cross-cultural approach, which attempts to avoid ethnocentric evaluation of one group's practices and beliefs as being superior without considering their origins and functions from the perspective of the reality of that cultural group. With research in their own country, however, researchers have had more difficulty avoiding the assumption that the majority practices are proper (Ogbu, 1982). Variations have been assumed to account for the generally lower social status of the minority group members. It is only recently, and largely through the efforts of researchers with minority backgrounds, that deficit assumptions have been questioned in research on minority children.

The working model that appears to predominate in current minority research is one in which the positive features of cultural variation are emphasized. Although this is a valuable shift, we feel that research on minorities must move beyond reiterating the value of cultural diversity and begin more seriously to examine the source and functioning of the diversity represented in the United States to increase our understanding of the processes underlying development in cultural context.

Not only is the diversity of cultural backgrounds in our nation a resource for the creativity and future of the nation, it is also a resource for scholars studying how children develop. To make good use of this information, cultural research with minorities needs to focus on examining the processes and functioning of the cultural context of development. This requires "unpackaging" culture or minority status (Whiting, 1976) so as to disentangle the workings of the social context of development. This has become a central effort of cross-cultural research on non-Western populations.

Pioneering researchers of minorities are also beginning to look at the contexts in which children from different cultures develop, and these efforts provide a basis for a greater understanding of how culture channels development. (Examples include Brown & Reeve, 1985; Cazden, John, & Hymes, 1975; Chisholm, 1983; Erickson & Mohatt, 1982; Laboratory of Comparative Human Cognition, 1986; Ogbu, 1982.) It is notable that some of the most interesting efforts involve combining approaches from anthropology and education with those of psychology (see also recent issues of *Anthropology and Education Quarterly*).

The potential from research on cultural groups around the world as well as down the street lies in its challenge to our systems of assumptions and in the creative efforts of scholars to synthesize knowledge from observations of differing contexts of human development. Such challenge and synthesis is fruitful in the efforts to achieve a deeper and broader understanding of human nature and nurture.

Questions

1. According to Rogoff and Morelli, how does incorporation of culture in developmental psychology change our understanding of the process of human development?

2. Are there any developmental processes that are not influenced by culture? If so, what are they and why doesn't culture affect them?

3. Institutions of society, especially the availability and types of schools, play an important role in human development. What effect might inequalities in schooling within a society have on individual psychological development?

References

Bornstein, M. H. (1980). Cross-cultural developmental psychology. In M. H. Bornstein (Ed.), *Comparative methods in psychology* (pp. 231–281). Hillsdale, NJ: Erlbaum.

Bowerman, M. (1981). Language development. In H. C. Triandis & A. Heron (Eds.), *Handbook of cross-cultural psychology* (Vol. 4, pp. 93–185). Boston: Allyn & Bacon.

Bretherton, I., & Waters E. (Eds.). (1985). Growing points of attachment theory and research. *Monographs of the Society for Research in Child Development, 50* (1–2, Serial No. 209).

Brown, A. L., & Reeve, R. A. (1985). *Bandwidths of competence: The role of supportive contexts in learning and development* (Tech. Rep. No. 336). Champaign: University of Illinois at Urbana–Champaign, Center for the Study of Reading.

Cazden, C. B., John, V. P., & Hymes, D. (Eds.). (1975). *Functions of language in the classroom.* New York: Teachers College Press.

Cazden, C. B., & John, V. P. (1971). Learning in American Indian children. In M. L. Wax, S. Diamond, & F. O. Gearing (Eds.), *Anthropological perspectives in education* (pp. 252–272). New York: Basic Books.

Chisholm, J. S. (1983). *Navajo infancy: An ethological study of child development.* Hawthorne, NY: Aldine.

Cole, M. (1975). An ethnographic psychology of cognition. In R. W. Brislin, S. Bochner, & W. J. Lonner (Eds.), *Cross-cultural perspectives on learning* (pp. 157–175). New York: Wiley.

Cole, M. (1981, September). *The zone of proximal development: Where culture and cognition create each other* (Report No. 106). San Diego: University of California, Center for Human Information Processing.

Cole, M., & Bruner, J. S. (1971). Cultural differences and inferences about psychological processes. *American Psychologist, 26,* 867–876.

Cole, M., Gay, J., Glick, J. A., & Sharp, D. W. (1971). *The cultural context of learning and thinking.* New York: Basic Books.

Cole, M., Hood, L., & McDermott, R. P. (1978). Concepts of ecological validity: Their differing implications for comparative cognitive research. *The Quarterly Newsletter of the Institute for Comparative Human Development, 2,* 34–37.

Dasen, P. R. (Ed.). (1977). *Piagetian psychology: Cross-cultural contributions.* New York: Gardner Press.

Dasen, P. R., & Heron, A. (1981). Cross-cultural tests of Piaget's theory. In H. C. Triandis & A. Heron (Eds.), *Handbook of cross-cultural psychology* (Vol. 4, pp. 295–341). Boston: Allyn & Bacon.

Edwards, C. P. (1981). The comparative study of the development of moral judgment and reasoning. In R. H. Munroe, R. L. Munroe, & B. B. Whiting (Eds.), *Handbook of cross-cultural human development* (pp. 501–528). New York: Garland.

Erickson, F., & Mohatt, G. (1982). Cultural organization of participation structures in two classrooms of Indian students. In G. Spindler (Ed.), *Doing the ethnography of schooling* (pp.132–174). New York: Holt, Rinehart & Winston.

Field, T. M., Sostek, A. M., Vietze, P., & Leiderman, P. H. (Eds.). (1981). *Culture and early interactions.* Hillsdale, NJ: Erlbaum.

Fox, N. A. (1977). Attachment of kibbutz infants to mother and metapelet. *Child Development, 48,* 1228–1239.

Gewirtz. J. L. (1965). The course of infant smiling in four child-rearing environments in Israel. In B. M. Foss (Ed.), *Determinants of infant behavior* (Vol. 3, pp. 205–248). London, England: Methuen.

Gladwin, T. (1970). *East is a big bird.* Cambridge, MA: Belknap Press.

Glick, J. (1975). Cognitive development in cross-cultural perspective. In F. Horowitz (Ed.), *Review of child development research* (Vol. 4, pp. 595–654). Chicago: University of Chicago Press.

Goldberg, S. (1972). Infant care and growth in urban Zambia. *Human Development, 15,* 77–89.

Goodnow, J. J. (1976). The nature of intelligent behavior. Questions raised by cross-cultural studies. In L. B. Resnick (Ed.), *The nature of intelligence* (pp. 169–188). Hillsdale, NJ: Erlbaum.

Goody, J. (1977). *The domestication of the savage mind.* Cambridge, England: Cambridge University Press.

Graves, Z. R., & Glick, J. (1978). The effect of context on mother–child interaction. *The Quarterly Newsletter of the Institute for Comparative Human Development, 2,* 41–46.

Greenfield, P. M. (1976). Cross-cultural research and Piagetian theory: Paradox and progress. In K. R Riegel & J. A. Meacham (Eds.), *The developing individual in a changing world* (Vol. 1, pp. 322–345). Chicago: Aldine.

Hilliard, A. G., III, & Vaughn-Scott, M. (1982). The quest for the "minority" child. In S. G. Moore & C. R. Cooper (Eds.), *The young child: Reviews of research* (Vol. 3, pp. 175–189). Washington, DC: National Association for the Education of Young Children.

Howard, A., & Scott, R. A. (1981). The study of minority groups in complex societies. In R. H. Munroe, R. L. Munroe, & B. B. Whiting (Eds.), *Handbook of cross-cultural human development* (pp. 113–152). New York: Garland.

Irvine, J. T (1978). Wolof "magical thinking": Culture and conservation revisited. *Journal of Cross-Cultural Psychology, 9,* 300–310.

Kilbride, P. L. (1980). Sensorimotor behavior of Baganda and Samia infants. *Journal of Cross-Cultural Psychology, 11,* 131–152.

Konner, M. (1972). Aspects of the developmental ethology of a foraging people. In N. Blurton-Jones (Ed.), *Ethological studies of child behavior* (pp. 285–328). Cambridge, England: Cambridge University Press.

Laboratory of Comparative Human Cognition. (1979). Cross-cultural psychology's challenges to our ideas of children and development. *American Psychologist, 34,* 827–833.

Laboratory of Comparative Human Cognition. (1983). Culture and cognitive development. In W. Kessen (Ed.),

Handbook of Child Psychology: Vol. 1. History, theory, and methods (pp. 294–356). New York: Wiley.

Laboratory of Comparative Human Cognition. (1986). Contributions of cross-cultural research to educational practice. *American Psychologist, 41,* 1049–1058.

Lave, J. (1977). Tailor-made experiments and evaluating the intellectual consequences of apprenticeship training. *The Quarterly Newsletter of the Institute for Comparative Human Development, 1,* 1–3.

Leiderman, P. H., Tulkin, S. R., & Rosenfeld, A. (Eds.). (1977). *Culture and infancy.* New York: Academic Press.

LeVine, R. A. (in press). Environments in child development: An anthropological perspective. In W. Damon (Ed.), *Child development today and tomorrow.* San Francisco: Jossey-Bass.

Malinowski, B. (1927). *The father in primitive psychology.* New York: Norton.

Munroe, R. L., & Munroe, R. H. (1975). *Cross-cultural human devel*opment. Monterey, CA: Brooks/Cole.

Munroe, R. H., Munroe, R. L., & Whiting, B. B. (Eds.). (1981). *Handbook of cross-cultural human development.* New York: Garland.

Newson, J., & Newson, E. (1975). Intersubjectivity and the transmission of culture: On the social origins of symbolic functioning. *Bulletin of the British Psychological Society, 28,* 437–446.

Ogbu, J. U. (1982). Socialization: A cultural ecological approach. In K. M. Borman (Ed.), *The social life of children in a changing society* (pp. 253–267). Hillsdale, NJ: Erlbaum.

Pedersen, R A. (1980). *The father–infant relationship: Observational studies in the family setting.* New York: Praeger.

Piaget, J. (1972). Intellectual evolution from adolescence to adulthood. *Human Development, 15,* 1–12.

Price-Williams, D. R. (1980). Anthropological approaches to cognition and their relevance to psychology. In H. C. Triandis & W. Lonner (Eds.), *Handbook of cross-cultural psychology* (Vol. 3, pp. 155–184). Boston: Allyn & Bacon.

Rogoff, B. (1981). Schooling and the development of cognitive skills. In H. C. Triandis & A. Heron (Eds.), *Handbook of cross-cultural psychology* (Vol. 4, pp. 233–294). Boston: Allyn & Bacon.

Rogoff, B. (1982). Integrating context and cognitive development. In M. E. Lamb & A. L. Brown (Eds.), *Advances in developmental psychology* (Vol. 2, pp. 125–170). Hillsdale, NJ: Erlbaum.

Rogoff, B., Gauvain, M., & Ellis, S. (1984). Development viewed in its cultural context. In M. H. Bornstein & M. E. Lamb (Eds.), *Developmental Psychology* (pp. 533–571). Hillsdale, NJ: Erlbaum.

Rogoff, B., & Mistry, J. J. (1985). Memory development in cultural context. In M. Pressley & C. Brainerd (Eds.), *Progress in cognitive development* (pp. 117–142). New York: Springer-Verlag.

Rogoff, B., & Mistry, J. J. (in press). The social and motivational context of children's memory skills. In R. Fivish & J. Hudson (Eds.), *What young children remember and why.* Cambridge, England: Cambridge University Press.

Rogoff, B., & Waddell, K. J. (1982). Memory for information organized in a scene by children from two cultures. *Child Development, 53,* 1224–1228.

Saxe, G. B. (1988). *Mathematics in and out of school.* Unpublished manuscript, University of California at Los Angeles.

Schieffelin, B. B., & Ochs, E. (Eds.). (1986). *Language socialization across cultures.* Cambridge, England: Cambridge University Press.

Scribner, S. (1976). Situating the experiment in cross-cultural research. In K. F. Riegel & J. A. Meacham (Eds.), *The developing individual in a changing world* (Vol. 1, pp. 310–321). Chicago: Aldine.

Scribner, S. (1977). Modes of thinking and ways of speaking: Culture and logic reconsidered. In P. N. Johnson-Laird & P. C. Wason (Eds.), *Thinking* (pp. 483–500). Cambridge, England: Cambridge University Press.

Scribner, S., & Cole, M. (1981). *The psychology of literacy.* Cambridge, MA: Harvard University Press.

Serpell, R. (1976). *Culture's influence on behavior.* London, England: Methuen.

Serpell, R. (1979). How specific are perceptual skills? A cross-cultural study of pattern reproduction. *British Journal of Psychology, 70,* 365–380.

Sharp, D., Cole, M., & Lave, C. (1979). Education and cognitive development: The evidence from experimental research. *Monographs of the Society for Research in Child Development, 44* (1–2, Serial No. 178).

Skeen, J., Rogoff, B., & Ellis, S. (1983). Categorization by children and adults in communication contexts. *International Journal of Behavioral Development, 6,* 213–220.

Slobin, D. I. (1973). Cognitive prerequisites for the development of grammar. In C. A. Ferguson & D. I. Slobin (Eds.), *Studies of child language development* (pp. 175–200). New York: Holt, Rinehart & Winston.

Super, C. M. (1981). Behavioral development in infancy. In R. H. Munroe, R. L. Munroe, & B. B. Whiting (Eds.), *Handbook of cross-cultural human development* (pp. 181–270). New York: Garland.

Super, C. M., & Harkness, S. (Eds.), (1980). *Anthropological perspectives on child development.* San Francisco: Jossey-Bass.

Super, C. M., Harkness, S., & Baldwin, L. M. (1977). Category behavior in natural ecologies and in cognitive tests. *The Quarterly Newsletter of the Institute for Comparative Human Development, 1,* 4–7.

Triandis, H. C., & Heron, A. (Eds.). (1981). *Handbook of cross-cultural psychology* (Vol. 4). Boston: Allyn & Bacon.

Tronick, E. Z., Morelli, G. A., & Winn, S. (1987). Multiple

caretaking of Efe (pygmy) infants. *American Anthropologist, 89* (1), 96–106.

Vygotsky, L. S. (1978). *Mind in society.* Cambridge, MA: Harvard University Press.

Wagner, D. A., & Stevenson, H. W. (Eds.). (1982). *Cultural perspectives on child development.* San Francisco: Freeman.

Wenger, M. (1983). *Gender role socialization in East Africa: Social interactions between 2-to-3-year olds and older children, a social ecological perspective.* Unpublished doctoral dissertation, Harvard University, Cambridge, MA.

Werner, E. E. (1979). *Cross-Cultural child development.* Monterey, CA: Brooks/Cole.

Werner, E. E. (1988). A cross-cultural perspective on infancy. *Journal of Cross-Cultural Psychology, 19* (1), 96–113.

Wertsch, J. V. (Ed.). (1985a). *Culture, communication, and cognition: Vygotskian perspectives.* Cambridge, England: Cambridge University Press.

Wertsch, J. V. (1985b). *Vygotsky and the social formation of mind.* Cambridge, MA: Harvard University Press.

Whiting, B. B. (1976). The problem of the packaged variable. In K. F. Riegel & J. A. Meacham (Eds.), *The developing individual in a changing world.* Chicago: Aldine.

Whiting, B. B., & Edwards, C. P. (1988). *Children of different worlds.* Cambridge, MA: Harvard University Press.

Whiting, B. B., & Whiting, J. W. M. (1975). *Children of six cultures: A psycho-cultural analysis.* Cambridge, MA: Harvard University Press.

Zaslow, M. (1980). Relationships among peers in kibbutz toddler groups. *Child Psychiatry and Human Development, 10,* 178–189.

Zaslow, M., & Rogoff, B. (1981). The cross-cultural study of early interaction: Implications from research in culture and cognition. In T. Field, A. Sostek, P. Vietze, & H. Leiderman (Eds.), *Culture and early interactions* (pp. 237–256). Hillsdale, NJ: Erlbaum.

3

Development and Learning

JEAN PIAGET

This selection and the following paper were written by two of the most influential developmental psychologists of the twentieth century, Jean Piaget and Lev Vygotsky. Although written at different times and for different forums, these papers are similar in their attention to the relationship between two key psychological processes: learning and development.

Both Piaget and Vygotsky considered learning and development to be important and distinct psychological processes. However, they differed in how they viewed the relationship between these processes as well as the role that each played in organizing and guiding development. While exploring their different approaches, consider the types of educational programs that might be designed from each of these views. Such programs will differ in many aspects, including the ways that teachers and students interact with each other.

In his opening remarks Piaget makes a distinction between development and learning—development being a spontaneous process tied to embryogenesis, learning being provoked by external situations. He proceeds to discuss the concept of an operation as an interiorized action linked to other operations in a structure. Four stages of development are enumerated—sensori-motor, pre-operational, concrete operations, and formal operations. Factors explaining the development of one structure of operations from another are discussed—maturation, experience, social transmission, and equilibration. Equilibration is defended as the most fundamental factor. Commenting on the inadequacy of the stimulus-response approach to understanding learning, Piaget presents evidence negating the effectiveness of external reinforcement in hastening the development of operational structures. These operational structures can be learned only if one bases the learning on simpler, more elementary

This article was reprinted with permission from R. E. Ripple (ed. with V. N. Rockcastle) from *Piaget Rediscovered*, 1964 and 1972, 7–20.

structures—only if there is a natural relationship and development of structures. The learning of these structures is held to follow the same basic laws as does their natural development, i.e., learning is subordinated to development. Piaget concludes that the fundamental relation involved in development and learning is assimilation, not association.

My dear colleagues, I am very concerned about what to say to you, because I don't know if I shall accomplish the end that has been assigned to me. But I've been told that the important thing is not what you say, but the discussion which follows, and the answers to questions you are asked. So this morning I shall simply give a general introduction of a few ideas which seem to me to be important for the subject of this conference.

First I would like to make clear the difference between two problems: the problem of *development* in general, and the problem of *learning*. I think these problems are very different, although some people do not make this distinction.

The development of knowledge is a spontaneous process, tied to the whole process of embryogenesis. Embryogenesis concerns the development of the body, but it concerns as well the development of the nervous system, and the development of mental functions. In the case of the development of knowledge in children, embryogenesis ends only in adulthood. It is a total developmental process which we must resituate in its general biological and psychological context. In other words, development is a process which concerns the totality of the structures of knowledge.

Learning presents the opposite case. In general, learning is provoked by situations—provoked by a psychological experimenter; or by a teacher, with respect to some didactic point; or by an external situation. It is provoked, in general, as opposed to spontaneous. In addition, it is a limited process—limited to a single problem, or to a single structure.

So I think that development explains learning, and this opinion is contrary to the widely held opinion that development is a sum of discrete learning experiences. For some psychologists development is reduced to a series of specific learned items, and development is thus the sum, the cumulation of this series of specific items. I think this is an atomistic view which deforms the real state of things. In reality, development is the essential process and each element of learning occurs as a function of total development, rather than being an element which explains development. I shall begin, then, with a first part dealing with

development, and I shall talk about learning in the second part.

To understand the development of knowledge, we must start with an idea which seems central to me—the idea of an *operation*. Knowledge is not a copy of reality. To know an object, to know an event, is not simply to look at it and make a mental copy, or image, of it. To know an object is to act on it. To know is to modify, to transform the object, and to understand the process of this transformation, and as a consequence to understand the way the object is constructed. An operation is thus the essence of knowledge; it is an interiorised action which modifies the object of knowledge. For instance, an operation would consist of joining objects in a class, to construct a classification. Or an operation would consist of ordering, or putting things in a series. Or an operation would consist of counting, or of measuring. In other words, it is a set of actions modifying the object, and enabling the knower to get at the structures of the transformation.

An operation is an interiorised action. But in addition, it is a reversible action; that is, it can take place in both directions, for instance, adding or subtracting, joining or separating. So it is a particular type of action which makes up logical structures.

Above all, an operation is never isolated. It is always linked to other operations, and as a result it is always a part of a total structure. For instance, a logical class does not exist in isolation; what exists is the total structure of classification. An asymmetrical relation does not exist in isolation. Seriation is the natural, basic operational structure. A number does not exist in isolation. What exists is the series of numbers, which constitute a structure, an exceedingly rich structure whose various properties have been revealed by mathematicians.

These operational structures are what seem to me to constitute the basis of knowledge, the natural psychological reality, in terms of which we must understand the development of knowledge. And the central problem of development is to understand the formation, elaboration, organization, and functioning of these structures.

I should like to review the stages of development of these structures, not in any detail, but simply as a reminder. I shall distinguish four main stages. The first is a sensory-motor, pre-verbal stage, lasting approximately the first 18 months of life. During this stage is developed the practical knowledge which constitutes the substructure of later representational knowledge. An example is the construction of the schema of the permanent object. For an infant, during the first months, an object has no permanence. When it disappears from the perceptual field it no longer exists. No attempt is made to find it again. Later, the infant will try to find it, and he will find it by localizing it spatially. Consequently, along with the construction of the permanent object there comes the construction of practical, or sensory-motor, space. There is similarly the construction of temporal succession, and of elementary sensory-motor causality. In other words, there is a series of structures which are indispensable for the structures of later representational thought.

In a second stage, we have pre-operational representation—the beginnings of language, of the symbolic function, and therefore of thought, or representation. But at the level of representational thought, there must now be a reconstruction of all that was developed on the sensory-motor level. That is, the sensory-motor actions are not immediately translated into operations. In fact, during all this second period of pre-operational representations, there are as yet no operations as I defined this term a moment ago. Specifically, there is as yet no conservation which is the psychological criterion of the presence of reversible operations. For example, if we pour liquid from one glass to another of a different shape, the pre-operational child will think there is more in one than in the other. In the absence of operational reversibility, there is no conservation of quantity.

In a third stage the first operations appear, but I call these concrete operations because they operate on objects, and not yet on verbally expressed hypotheses. For example, there are the operations of classification, ordering, the construction of the idea of number, spatial and temporal operations, and all the fundamental operations of elementary logic of classes and relations, of elementary mathematics, of elementary geometry and even of elementary physics.

Finally, in the fourth stage, these operations are surpassed as the child reaches the level of what I call formal or hypothetic-deductive operations; that is, he can now reason on hypotheses, and not only on objects. He constructs new operations, operations of propositional logic, and not simply the operations of classes, relations, and numbers. He attains new structures which are on the one hand combinatorial, corresponding to what mathematicians call lattices; on the other hand, more complicated group structures. At the level of concrete operations, the operations apply within an immediate neighborhood: for instance, classification by successive inclusions. At the level of the combinatorial, however,

the groups are much more mobile. These, then, are the four stages which we identify, whose formation we shall now attempt to explain.

What factors can be called upon to explain the development from one set of structures to another? It seems to me that there are four main factors: first of all, *maturation,* in the sense of Gesell, since this development is a continuation of the embryogenesis; second, the role of *experience* of the effects of the physical environment on the structures of intelligence; third, *social transmission* in the broad sense (linguistic transmission, education, etc.); and fourth, a factor which is too often neglected but one which seems to me fundamental and even the principal factor. I shall call this the factor of *equilibration* or if you prefer it, of self-regulation.

Let us start with the first factor, maturation. One might think that these stages are simply a reflection of an interior maturation of the nervous system, following the hypotheses of Gesell, for example. Well, maturation certainly does play an indispensable role and must not be ignored. It certainly takes part in every transformation that takes place during a child's development. However, this first factor is insufficient in itself. First of all, we know practically nothing about the maturation of the nervous system beyond the first months of the child's existence. We know a little bit about it during the first two years but we know very little following this time. But above all, maturation doesn't explain everything, because the average ages at which these stages appear (the average chronological ages) vary a great deal from one society to another. The ordering of these stages is constant and has been found in all the societies studied. It has been found in various countries where psychologists in universities have redone the experiments but it has also been found in African peoples for example, in the children of the Bushmen, and in Iran, both in the villages and in the cities. However, although the order of succession is constant, the chronological ages of these stages vary a great deal. For instance, the ages which we have found in Geneva are not necessarily the ages which you would find in the United States. In Iran, furthermore, in the city of Teheran, they found approximately the same ages as we found in Geneva, but there is a systematic delay of two years in the children in the country. Canadian psychologists who redid our experiments, Monique Laurendeau and Father Adrien Pinard, found once again about the same ages in Montreal. But when they redid the experiments in Martinique, they found a delay of four years in all the experiments and this in spite of the fact that the children in Martinique go to a school set up according to the French system and the French curriculum and attain at the end of this elementary school a certificate of higher primary education. There is then a delay of four years, that is, there are the same stages, but systematically delayed. So you see that these age variations show that maturation does not explain everything.

I shall go on now to the role played by experience. Experience of objects, of physical reality, is obviously a basic factor in the development of cognitive structures. But once again this factor does not explain everything. I can give two reasons for this. The first reason is that some of the concepts which appear at the beginning of the stage of concrete operations are such that I cannot see how they could be drawn from experience. As an example, let us take the conservation of the substance in the case of changing the shape of a ball of plasticene. We give this ball of plasticene to a child who changes its shape into a sausage form and we ask him if there is the same amount of matter, that is, the same amount of substance as there was before. We also ask him if it now has the same weight and thirdly if it now has the same volume. The volume is measured by the displacement of water when we put the ball or the sausage into a glass of water. The findings, which have been the same every time this experiment has been done, show us that first of all there is conservation of the amount of substance. At about eight years old a child will say, "There is the same amount of plasticene." Only later does the child assert that the weight is conserved and still later that the volume is conserved. So I would ask you where the idea of the conservation of substance can come from. What is a constant and invariant substance when it doesn't yet have a constant weight or a constant volume? Through perception you can get at the weight of the ball or the volume of the ball but perception cannot give you an idea of the amount of substance. No experiment, no experience, can show the child that there is the same amount of substance. He can weigh the ball and that would lead to the conservation of weight. He can immerse it in water and that would lead to the conservation of volume. But the notion of substance is attained before either weight or volume. This conservation of substance is simply a logical necessity. The child now understands that when there is a transformation something must be conserved because by reversing the transformation you can come back to the point of departure and once again have the ball. He knows that something is conserved but he doesn't know what. It is not yet the weight, it is not yet the volume; it is simply a logical

form—a logical necessity. There, it seems to me, is an example of a progress in knowledge, a logical necessity for something to be conserved even though no experience can have led to this notion.

My second objection to the sufficiency of experience as an explanatory factor is that this notion of experience is a very equivocal one. There are, in fact, two kinds of experience which are psychologically very different and this difference is very important from the pedagogical point of view. It is because of the pedagogical importance that I emphasize this distinction. First of all, there is what I shall call physical experience, and secondly, what I shall call logical-mathematical experience.

Physical experience consists of acting upon objects and drawing some knowledge about the objects by abstraction from the objects. For example, to discover that this pipe is heavier than this watch, the child will weigh them both and find the difference in the objects themselves. This is experience in the usual sense of the term—in the sense used by empiricists. But there is a second type of experience which I shall call logical-mathematical experience where the knowledge is not drawn from the objects, but it is drawn by the actions effected upon the objects. This is not the same thing. When one acts upon objects, the objects are indeed there, but there is also the set of actions which modify the objects.

I shall give you an example of this type of experience. It is a nice example because we have verified it many times in small children under seven years of age, but it is also an example which one of my mathematician friends has related to me about his own childhood, and he dates his mathematical career from this experience. When he was four or five years old—I don't know exactly how old, but a small child—he was seated on the ground in his garden and he was counting pebbles. Now to count these pebbles he put them in a row and he counted them one, two, three, up to ten. Then he finished counting them and started to count them in the other direction. He began by the end and once again he found ten. He found this marvelous that there were ten in one direction and ten in the other direction. So he put them in a circle and counted them that way and found ten once again. Then he counted them in the other direction and found ten once more. So he put them in some other direction and found ten once more. So he put them in some other arrangement and kept counting them and kept finding ten. There was the discovery that he made.

Now what indeed did he discover? He did not discover a property of pebbles; he discovered a property of the action of ordering. The pebbles had no order. It was his action which introduced a linear order or a cyclical order, or any kind of an order. He discovered that the sum was independent of the order. The order was the action which he introduced among the pebbles. For the sum the same principle applied. The pebbles had no sum; they were simply in a pile. To make a sum, action was necessary—the operation of putting together and counting. He found that the sum was independent of the order, in other words, that the action of putting together is independent of the action of ordering. He discovered a property of actions and not a property of pebbles. You may say that it is in the nature of pebbles to let this be done to them and this is true. But it could have been drops of water, and drops of water would not have let this be done to them because two drops of water and two drops of water do not make four drops of water as you know very well. Drops of water then would not let this be done to them, we agree to that.

So it is not the physical property of pebbles which the experience uncovered. It is the properties of the actions carried out on the pebbles and this is quite another form of experience. It is the point of departure of mathematical deduction. The subsequent deduction will consist of interiorising these actions and then of combining them without needing any pebbles. The mathematician no longer needs his pebbles. He can combine his operations simply with symbols and the point of departure of this mathematical deduction is logical-mathematical experience and this is not at all experience in the sense of the empiricists. It is the beginning of the coordination of actions, but this coordination of actions before the stage of operations needs to be supported by concrete material. Later, this coordination of actions leads to the logical-mathematical structures. I believe that logic is not a derivative of language. The source of logic is much more profound. It is the total coordination of actions, actions of joining things together, or ordering things, etc. This is what logical-mathematical experience is. It is an experience of the actions of the subject, and not an experience of objects themselves. It is an experience which is necessary before there can be operations. Once the operations have been attained this experience is no longer needed and the coordinations of actions can take place by themselves in the form of deduction and construction for abstract structures.

The third factor is social transmission—linguistic transmission or educational transmission. This factor, once again, is fundamental. I do not deny the role of any one of these factors; they all play a part. But this factor is insufficient because the child can receive valuable information via language or via education directed by an adult only if he is in a state where he can understand this information. That is, to receive the information he must have a structure which enables him to assimilate this information. This is why you cannot teach higher mathematics to a five-year-old. He does not yet have structures which enable him to understand.

I shall take a much simpler example, an example of linguistic transmission. As my very first work in the realm of child psychology, I spent a long time studying the relation between a part and a whole in concrete experience and in language. For example, I used Burt's test employing the sentence, "Some of my flowers are buttercups." The child knows that all buttercups are yellow, so there are three possible conclusions: the whole bouquet is yellow, or part of the bouquet is yellow, or none of the flowers in the bouquet is yellow. I found that up until nine years of age (and this was in Paris, so the children certainly did understand the French language) they replied, "The whole bouquet is yellow or some of my flowers are yellow." Both of those mean the same thing. They did not understand the expression, "some *of* my flowers." They did not understand this *of* as a partitive genitive, as the inclusion of some flowers in my flowers. They understood some of my flowers to be my several flowers as if the several flowers and the flowers were confused as one and the same class. So there you have children who until nine years of age heard every day a linguistic structure which implied the inclusion of a sub-class in a class and yet did not understand this structure. It is only when they themselves are in firm possession of this logical structure, when they have constructed it for themselves according to the developmental laws which we shall discuss, that they succeed in understanding correctly the linguistic expression.

I come now to the fourth factor which is added to the three preceding ones but which seems to me to be the fundamental one. This is what I call the factor of equilibration. Since there are already three factors, they must somehow be equilibrated among themselves. That is one reason for bringing in the factor of equilibration. There is a second reason, however, which seems to me to be fundamental. It is that in the act of knowing, the subject is active, and consequently, faced with an external disturbance, he will react in order to compensate and consequently he will tend towards equilibrium. Equilibrium, defined by active compensation, leads to reversibility. Operational reversibility is a model of an equilibrated system where a transformation in one direction is compensated by a transformation in the other direction. Equilibration, as I understand it, is thus an active process. It's a process of self-regulation. I think that this self-regulation is a fundamental factor in development. I use this term in the sense in which it is used in cybernetics, that is, in the sense of processes with feedback and with feedforward, of processes which regulate themselves by a progressive compensation of systems. This process of equilibration takes the form of a succession of levels of equilibrium, of levels which have a certain probability which I shall call a sequential probability, that is, the probabilities are not established a priori. There is a sequence of levels. It is not possible to reach the second level unless equilibrium has been reached at the first level, and the equilibrium of the third level only becomes possible when the equilibrium of the second level has been reached, and so forth. That is, each level is determined as the most probable given that the preceding level has been reached. It is not the most probable at the beginning, but it is the most probable once the preceding level has been reached.

As an example, let us take the development of the idea of conservation in the transformation of the ball of plasticene into the sausage shape. Here you can discern four levels. The most probable at the beginning is for the child to think of only one dimension. Suppose that there is a probability of 0.8, for instance, that the child will focus on the length, and that the width has a probability of 0.2. This would mean that of ten children, eight will focus on the length alone without paying any attention to the width, and two will focus on the width without paying any attention to the length. They will focus only on one dimension or the other. Since the two dimensions are independent at this stage, focusing on both at once would have a probability of only 0.16. That is less than either one of the two. In other words, the most probable in the beginning is to focus only on one dimension and in fact the child will say, "It's longer, so there's more in the sausage." Once he has reached this first level, if you continue to elongate the sausage, there comes a moment when he will say, "No, now it's too thin, so there's less." Now he is thinking about the width, but he forgets the length, so you have come to a second level which becomes the most probable after the first level, but which is not the most probable at the point of departure. Once he has focused on the width, he will come back sooner or later to focus on the length. Here you will have a third level where he will oscillate between width and length and where he will discover that the two are related. When you elongate you make it more thin, and when you make it shorter, you make it thicker. He discovers that the two are

solidly related and in discovering this relationship, he will start to think in terms of the transformation and not only in terms of the final configuration. Now he will say that when it gets longer it gets thinner, so it's the same thing. There is more of it in length but less of it in width. When you make it shorter it gets thicker; there's less in length and more in width, so there is compensation—compensation which defines equilibrium in the sense in which I defined it a moment ago. Consequently, you have operations and conservation. In other words, in the course of these developments you will always find a process of self-regulation which I call equilibration and which seems to me the fundamental factor in the acquisition of logical-mathematical knowledge.

I shall go on now to the second part of my lecture, that is, to deal with the topic of learning. Classically, learning is based on the stimulus-response schema. I think the stimulus-response schema, while I won't say it is false, is in any case entirely incapable of explaining cognitive learning. Why? Because when you think of a stimulus-response schema, you think usually that first of all there is a stimulus and then a response is set off by this stimulus. For my part, I am convinced that the response was there first, if I can express myself in this way. A stimulus is a stimulus only to the extent that it is significant and it becomes significant only to the extent that there is a structure which permits its assimilation, a structure which can integrate this stimulus but which at the same time sets off the response. In other words, I would propose that the stimulus-response schema be written in the circular form—in the form of a schema or of a structure which is not simply one way. I would propose that above all, between the stimulus and the response there is the organism, the organism and its structures. The stimulus is really a stimulus only when it is assimilated into a structure and it is this structure which sets off the response. Consequently, it is not an exaggeration to say that the response is there first, or if you wish at the beginning there is the structure. Of course we would want to understand how this structure comes to be. I tried to do this earlier by presenting a model of equilibration or self-regulation. Once there is a structure, the stimulus will set off a response, but only by the intermediary of this structure.

I should like to present some facts. We have facts in great number. I shall choose only one or two and I shall choose some facts which our colleague, Smedslund, has gathered. (Smedslund is currently at the Harvard Center for Cognitive Studies.) Smedslund arrived in Geneva a few years ago convinced (he had published this in one of his papers) that the development of the ideas of conservation could be indefinitely accelerated through learning of a stimulus-response type. I invited Smedslund to come to spend a year in Geneva to show us this, to show us that he could accelerate the development of operational conservation. I shall relate only one of his experiments.

During the year that he spent in Geneva he chose to work on the conservation of weight. The conservation of weight is, in fact, easy to study since there is a possible external reinforcement, that is, simply weighing the ball and the sausage on a balance. Then you can study the child's reactions to these external results. Smedslund studied the conservation of weight on the one hand, and on the other hand, he studied the transitivity of weights, that is, the transitivity of equalities if A = B and B = C, then A = C, or the transitivity of the equalities if A is less than B, and B is less than C, then A is less than C.

As far as conservation is concerned, Smedslund succeeded very easily with five- and six-year-old children in getting them to generalize that weight is conserved when the ball is transformed into a different shape. The child sees the ball transformed into a sausage or into little pieces or into a pancake or into any other form, he weighs it, and he sees that it is always the same thing. He will affirm it will be the same thing, no matter what you do to it; it will come out to be the same weight. Thus Smedslund very easily achieved the conservation of weight by this sort of external reinforcement.

In contrast to this, however, the same method did not succeed in teaching transitivity. The children resisted the notion of transitivity. A child would predict correctly in certain cases but he would make his prediction as a possibility or a probability and not as a certainty. There was never this generalized certainty in the case of transitivity.

So there is the first example, which seems to me very instructive, because in this problem in the conservation of weight there are two aspects. There is the physical aspect and there is the logical-mathematical aspect. Note that Smedslund started his study by establishing that there was a correlation between conservation and transitivity. He began by making a statistical study on the relationships between the spontaneous responses to the questions about conservation and the spontaneous responses to the questions about transitivity, and he found a very significant correlation. But in the learning experiment, he obtained a learning of conservation and not of transitivity. Consequently, he was successful in obtaining learning of what I called earlier physical experience (this is not surprising; it is simply a question of noting facts about objects)

but he was not successful in obtaining a learning in the construction of the logical structure. This doesn't surprise me either, since the logical structure is not the result of physical experience. It cannot be obtained by external reinforcement. The logical structure is reached only through internal equilibration, by self-regulation, and the external reinforcement of seeing the balance did not suffice to establish this logical structure of transitivity.

I could give many other comparable examples, but it seems to me useless to insist upon these negative examples. Now I should like to show that learning is possible in the case of these logical-mathematical structures, but on one condition—that is, that the structure which you want to teach to the subjects can be supported by simpler, more elementary, logical-mathematical structures. I shall give you an example. It is the example of the conservation of number in the case of one-to-one correspondence. If you give a child seven blue tokens and ask him to put down as many red tokens, there is a pre-operational stage where he will put one red one opposite each blue one. But when you spread out the red ones, making them into a longer row, he will say to you, "Now, there are more red ones than there are blue ones."

Now how can we accelerate, if you want to accelerate, the acquisition of this conservation of number? Well, you can imagine an analogous structure but in a simpler, more elementary, situation. For example, with Mlle. Inhelder, we have been studying recently the notion of one-to-one correspondence by giving the child two glasses of the same shape and a big pile of beads. The child puts a bead into one glass with one hand and at the same time a bead into the other glass with the other hand. Time after time he repeats this action, a bead into one glass with one hand and at the same time a bead into the other glass with the other hand and he sees that there is always the same amount on each side. Then you hide one of the glasses. You cover it up. He no longer sees this glass but he continues to put one bead into it while putting at the same time one bead into the other glass which he can see. Then you ask him whether the equality has been conserved, whether there is still the same amount in one glass as in the other. Now you will find that very small children, about four years old, don't want to make a prediction. They will say, "So far, it has been the same amount, but now I don't know. I can't see anymore, so I don't know." They do not want to generalize. But the generalization is made from the age of about five and one-half years.

This is in contrast to the case of the red and blue tokens with one row spread out, where it isn't until seven or eight years of age that children will say there are the same number in the two rows. As one example of this generalization, I recall a little boy of five years and nine months who had been adding the beads to the glasses for a little while. Then we asked him whether, if he continued to do this all day and all night and all the next day, there would always be the same amount in the two glasses. The little boy gave this admirable reply, "Once you know, you know for always." In other words, this was recursive reasoning. So here the child does acquire the structure in this specific case. The number is a synthesis of class inclusion and ordering. This synthesis is being favored by the child's own actions. You have set up a situation where there is an iteration of one same action which continues and which is therefore ordered while at the same time being inclusive. You have, so to speak, a localized synthesis of inclusion and ordering which facilitates the construction of the idea of number in this specific case, and there you can find, in effect, an influence of this experience on the other experience. However, this influence is not immediate. We study the generalization from this recursive situation to the other situation where the tokens are laid on the table in rows, and it is not an immediate generalization but it is made possible through intermediaries. In other words, you can find some learning of this structure if you base the learning on simpler structures.

In this same area of the development of numerical structures, the psychologist Joachim Wohlwill, who spent a year at our Institute at Geneva, has also shown that this acquisition can be accelerated through introducing additive operations, which is what we introduced also in the experiment which I just described. Wohlwill introduced them in a different way but he too was able to obtain a certain learning effect. In other words, learning is possible if you base the more complex structure on simpler structures, that is, when there is a natural relationship and development of structures and not simply an external reinforcement.

Now I would like to take a few minutes to conclude what I was saying. My first conclusion is that learning of structures seems to obey the same laws as the natural development of these structures. In other words, learning is subordinated to development and not vice-versa as I said in the introduction. No doubt you will object that some investigators have succeeded in teaching operational structures. But, when I am faced with these facts, I always have three questions which I want to have answered before I am convinced.

The first question is, "Is this learning lasting? What remains two weeks or a month later?" If a structure develops spontaneously, once it has reached a state of equilibrium, it is lasting, it will continue throughout the child's entire life. When you achieve the learning by external reinforcement, is the result lasting or not and what are the conditions necessary for it to be lasting?

The second question is, "How much generalization is possible?" What makes learning interesting is the possibility of transfer of a generalization. When you have brought about some learning, you can always ask whether this is an isolated piece in the midst of the child's mental life, or if it is really a dynamic structure which can lead to generalizations.

Then there is the third question, "In the case of each learning experience what was the operational level of the subject before the experience and what more complex structures has this learning succeeded in achieving?" In other words, we must look at each specific learning experience from the point of view of the spontaneous operations which were present at the outset and the operational level which has been achieved after the learning experience.

My second conclusion is that the fundamental relation involved in all development and all learning is not the relation of association. In the stimulus-response schema, the relation between the response and the stimulus is understood to be one of association. In contrast to this, I think that the fundamental relation is one of assimilation. Assimilation is not the same as association. I shall define assimilation as the integration of any sort of reality into a structure, and it is this assimilation which seems to me fundamental in learning, and which seems to me the fundamental relation from the point of view of pedagogical or didactic applications. All of my remarks today represent the child and the learning subject as active. An operation is an activity. Learning is possible only when there is active assimilation. It is this activity on the part of the subject which seems to me underplayed in the stimulus-response schema. The presentation which I propose puts the emphasis on the idea of self-regulation, on assimilation. All the emphasis is placed on the activity of the subject himself, and I think that without this activity there is no possible didactic or pedagogy which significantly transforms the subject.

Finally, and this will be my last concluding remark, I would like to comment on an excellent publication by the psychologist Berlyne. Berlyne spent a year with us in Geneva during which he intended to translate our results on the development of operations into stimulus-response language, specifically into Hull's learning theory. Berlyne published in our series of studies of genetic epistemology a very good article on this comparison between the results of Geneva and Hull's theory. In the same volume, I published a commentary on Berlyne's results. Now the essence of Berlyne's results is this: our findings can very well be translated into Hullian language, but only on condition that two modifications are introduced. Berlyne himself found these modifications quite considerable, but they seemed to him to concern more the conceptualization than the Hullian theory itself. I'm not so sure about that. The two modifications are these. First of all, Berlyne wants to distinguish two sorts of responses in the S-R schema. First, responses in the ordinary, classical sense, which I shall call "copy responses," and secondly, what Berlyne called "transformation responses." Transformation responses consist of transforming one response of the first type into another response of the first type. These transformation responses are what I call operations, and you can see right away that this is a rather serious modification of Hull's conceptualization because here you are introducing an element of transformation and thus of assimilation and no longer the simple association of stimulus-response theory.

The second modification which Berlyne introduces into the stimulus-response language is the introduction of what he calls internal reinforcements. What are these internal reinforcements? They are what I call equilibration or self-regulation. The internal reinforcements are what enable the subject to eliminate contradictions, incompatibilities, and conflicts. All development is composed of momentary conflicts and incompatibilities which must be overcome to reach a higher level of equilibrium. Berlyne calls this elimination of incompatibilities internal reinforcements.

So you see that it is indeed a stimulus-response theory, if you will, but first you add operations and then you add equilibration. That's all we want!

Editor's note: A brief question and answer period followed Professor Piaget's presentation. The first question related to the fact that the eight-year-old child acquires conservation of substance prior to conservation of weight and volume. The question asked if this didn't contradict the order of emergence of the pre-operational and operational stages. Piaget's response follows:

The conservation of weight and the conservation of volume are not due only to experience. There is also involved a logical framework which is characterized by reversibility and the system of compensations.

I am only saying that in the case of weight and volume, weight corresponds to a perception. There is an empirical contact. The same is true of volume. But in the case of substance, I don't see how there can be any perception of substance independent of weight or volume. The strange thing is that this notion of substance comes before the two other notions. Note that in the history of thought, we have the same thing. The first Greek physicists, the pre-Socratic philosophers, discovered conservation of substance independently of any experience. I do not believe this is contradictory with the theory of operations. This conservation of substance is simply the affirmation that something must be conserved. The children don't know specifically what is conserved. They know that since the sausage can become a ball again there must be something which is conserved, and saying "substance" is simply a way of translating this logical necessity for conservation. But this logical necessity results directly from the discovery of operations. I do not think that this is contradictory with the theory of development.

Editor's note: The second question was whether or not the development of stages in children's thinking could be accelerated by practice, training, and exercise in perception and memory. Piaget's response follows:

I am not very sure that exercise of perception and memory would be sufficient. I think that we must distinguish within the cognitive function two very different aspects which I shall call the figurative aspect and the operative aspect. The figurative aspect deals with static configurations. In physical reality there are states, and in addition to these there are transformations which lead from one state to another. In cognitive functioning one has the figurative aspects—for example, perception, imitation, mental imagery, etc.

Secondly, there is the operative aspect, including operations and the actions which lead from one state to another. In children of the higher stages and in adults, the figurative aspects are subordinated to the operative aspects. Any given state is understood to be the result of some transformation and the point of departure for another transformation. But the pre-operational child does not understand transformations. He does not have the operations necessary to understand them so he puts all the emphasis on the static quality of the states. It is because of this, for example, that in the conservation experiments he simply compares the initial state and the final state without being concerned with the transformation.

In exercising perception and memory, I feel that you will reinforce the figurative aspect without touching the operative aspect. Consequently, I'm not sure that this will accelerate the development of cognitive structures. What needs to be reinforced is the operative aspect—not the analysis of states, but the understanding of transformations.

Questions

1. What, according to Piaget, are key differences between learning and development?

2. According to Piaget, what role do other people play in fostering cognitive development in children?

3. Suppose that you are asked to consult at an elementary school about children's understanding of scientific concepts, such as the conservation of weight and volume. Several second and third graders at this school are having difficulty with these concepts. What would you advise the teachers to do to help the children develop the skills needed to understand these concepts?

4

Interaction Between Learning and Development

LEV S. VYGOTSKY

Editor's Note: Please see the introduction to the previous article on Piaget for editorial comments on this related paper.

The problems encountered in the psychological analysis of teaching cannot be correctly resolved or even formulated without addressing the relation between learning and development in school-age children. Yet it is the most unclear of all the basic issues on which the application of child development theories to educational processes depends. Needless to say, the lack of theoretical clarity does not mean that the issue is removed altogether from current research efforts into learning; not one study can avoid this central theoretical issue. But the relation between learning and development remains methodologically unclear because concrete research studies have embodied theoretically vague, critically unevaluated, and sometimes internally contradictory postulates, premises, and peculiar solutions to the problem of this fundamental relationship; and these, of course, result in a variety of errors.

Essentially, all current conceptions of the relation between development and learning in children can be reduced to three major theoretical positions.

The first centers on the assumption that processes of child development are independent of learning. Learning is considered a purely external process that is not actively involved in development. It merely utilizes the achievements of development rather than providing an impetus for modifying its course.

In experimental investigations of the development of thinking in school children, it has been assumed that processes such as deduction and understanding, evolution of notions about the world, interpretation of physical causality, and mastery of logical forms of thought and abstract logic all occur by themselves, without any influence from school learning. An example of such a theory is Piaget's

This article is reprinted with permission of Harvard University Press, from L. S. Vygotsky, 1978, *Mind in Society*. Cambridge, MA: Harvard University Press, 79–91.

extremely complex and interesting theoretical principles, which also shape the experimental methodology he employs. The questions Piaget uses in the course of his "clinical conversations" with children clearly illustrate his approach. When a five-year-old is asked "why doesn't the sun fall?" it is assumed that the child has neither a ready answer for such a question nor the general capabilities for generating one. The point of asking questions that are so far beyond the reach of the child's intellectual skills is to eliminate the influence of previous experience and knowledge. The experimenter seeks to obtain the tendencies of children's thinking in "pure" form entirely independent of learning.[1]

Similarly, the classics of psychological literature, such as the works by Binet and others, assume that development is always a prerequisite for learning and that if a child's mental functions (intellectual operations) have not matured to the extent that he is capable of learning a particular subject, then no instruction will prove useful. They especially feared premature instruction, the teaching of a subject before the child was ready for it. All effort was concentrated on finding the lower threshold of learning ability, the age at which a particular kind of learning first becomes possible.

Because this approach is based on the premise that learning trails behind development, that development always outruns learning, it precludes the notion that learning may play a role in the course of the development or maturation of those functions activated in the course of learning. Development or maturation is viewed as a precondition of learning but never the result of it. To summarize this position: learning forms a superstructure over development, leaving the latter essentially unaltered.

The second major theoretical position is that learning is development. This identity is the essence of a group of theories that are quite diverse in origin.

One such theory is based on the concept of reflex, an essentially old notion that has been extensively revived recently. Whether reading, writing, or arithmetic is being considered, development is viewed as the mastery of conditioned reflexes; that is, the process of learning is completely and inseparably blended with the process of development. This notion was elaborated by James, who reduced the learning process to habit formation and identified the learning process with development.

Reflex theories have at least one thing in common with theories such as Piaget's: in both, development is conceived of as the elaboration and substitution of innate responses. As James expressed it, "Education, in short, cannot be better described than by calling it the organization of acquired habits of conduct and tendencies to behavior."[2] Development itself is reduced primarily to the accumulation of all possible responses. Any acquired response is considered either a more complex form of or a substitute for the innate response.

But despite the similarity between the first and second theoretical positions, there is a major difference in their assumptions about the temporal relationship between learning and developmental processes. Theorists who hold the first view assert that developmental cycles precede learning cycles; maturation precedes learning and instruction must lag behind mental growth. For the second group of theorists, both processes occur simultaneously; learning and development coincide at all points in the same way that two identical geometrical figures coincide when superimposed.

The third theoretical position on the relation between learning and development attempts to overcome the extremes of the other two by simply combining them. A clear example of this approach is Koffka's theory, in which development is based on two inherently different but related processes, each of which influences the other.[3] On the one hand is maturation, which depends directly on the development of the nervous system; on the other hand is learning, which itself is also a developmental process.

Three aspects of this theory are new. First, as we already noted, is the combination of two seemingly opposite viewpoints, each of which has been encountered separately in the history of science. The very fact that these two viewpoints can be combined into one theory indicates that they are not opposing and mutually exclusive but have something essential in common. Also new is the idea that the two processes that make up development are mutually dependent and interactive. Of course, the nature of the interaction is left virtually unexplored in Koffka's work, which is limited solely to very general remarks regarding the relation between these two processes. It is clear that for Koffka the process of maturation prepares and makes possible a specific process of learning. The learning process then stimulates and pushes forward the maturation process. The third and most important new aspect of this theory is the expanded role it ascribes to learning in child development. This emphasis leads us directly to an old pedagogical problem, that of formal discipline and the problem of transfer.

Pedagogical movements that have emphasized formal discipline and urged the teaching of classical languages, ancient civilizations, and mathematics have assumed that regardless of the irrelevance of these particular subjects for daily living, they were of the greatest value for the pupil's mental development. A variety of studies have called into question the soundness of this idea. It has been shown that learning in one area has very little influence on overall development. For example, reflex theorists Woodworth and Thorndike found that adults who, after special exercises, had achieved considerable success in determining the length of short lines, had made virtually no progress in their ability to determine the length of long lines. These same adults were successfully trained to estimate the size of a given two-dimensional figure, but this training did not make them successful in estimating the size of a series of other two-dimensional figures of various sizes and shapes.

According to Thorndike, theoreticians in psychology and education believe that every particular response acquisition directly enhances overall ability in equal measure.[4] Teachers believed and acted on the basis of the theory that the mind is a complex of abilities—powers of observation, attention, memory, thinking, and so forth—and that any improvement in any specific ability results in a general improvement in all abilities. According to this theory, if the student increased the attention he paid to Latin grammar, he would increase his abilities to focus attention on any task. The words "accuracy," "quick-wittedness," "ability to reason," "memory," "power of observation," "attention," "concentration," and so forth are said to denote actual fundamental capabilities that vary in accordance with the material with which they operate; these basic abilities are substantially modified by studying particular subjects, and they retain these modifications when they turn to other areas. Therefore, if someone learns to do any single thing well, he will also be able to do other entirely unrelated things well as a result of some secret connection. It is assumed that mental capabilities function independently of the material with which they operate, and that the development of one ability entails the development of others.

Thorndike himself opposed this point of view. Through a variety of studies he showed that particular forms of activity, such as spelling, are dependent on the mastery of specific skills and material necessary for the performance of that particular task. The development of one particular capability seldom means the development of others. Thorndike argued that specialization of abilities is even greater than superficial observation may indicate. For example, if, out of a hundred individuals we choose ten who display the ability to detect spelling errors or to measure lengths, it is unlikely that these ten will display better abilities regarding, for example, the estimation of the weight of objects. In the same way, speed and accuracy in adding numbers are entirely unrelated to speed and accuracy in being able to think up antonyms.

This research shows that the mind is not a complex network of general capabilities such as observation, attention, memory, judgment, and so forth, but a set of specific capabilities, each of which is, to some extent, independent of the others and is developed independently. Learning is more than the acquisition of the ability to think; it is the acquisition of many specialized abilities for thinking about a variety of things. Learning does not alter our overall ability to focus attention but rather develops various abilities to focus attention on a variety of things. According to this view, special training affects overall development only when its elements, material, and processes are similar across specific domains; habit governs us. This leads to the conclusion that because each activity depends on the material with which it operates, the development of consciousness is the development of a set of particular, independent capabilities or of a set of particular habits. Improvement of one function of consciousness or one aspect of its activity can affect the development of another only to the extent that there are elements common to both functions or activities.

Developmental theorists such as Koffka and the Gestalt School—who hold to the third theoretical position outlined earlier—oppose Thorndike's point of view. They assert that the influence of learning is never specific. From their study of structural principles, they argue that the learning process can never be reduced simply to the formation of skills but embodies an intellectual order that makes it possible to transfer general principles discovered in solving one task to a variety of other tasks. From this point of view, the child, while learning a particular operation, acquires the ability to create structures of a certain type, regardless of the diverse materials with which she is working and regardless of the particular elements involved. Thus, Koffka does not conceive of learning as limited to a process of habit and skill acquisition. The relationship he posits between learning and development is not that of an identity but of a more complex relationship. According to Thorndike, learning and development coincide at all points, but for Koffka, development is always a larger set than learning. Schematically, the relationship between the two processes could be depicted by two concentric circles, the smaller symbolizing the learning process and the larger the developmental process evoked by learning.

Once a child has learned to perform an operation, he thus assimilates some structural principle whose sphere of application is other than just the operations of the type on whose basis the principle was assimilated. Consequently, in making one step in learning, a child makes two steps in development, that is, learning and development do not coincide. This concept is the essential aspect of the third group of theories we have discussed.

ZONE OF PROXIMAL DEVELOPMENT: A NEW APPROACH

Although we reject all three theoretical positions discussed above, analyzing them leads us to a more adequate view of the relation between learning and development. The question to be framed in arriving at a solution to this problem is complex. It consists of two separate issues: first, the general relation between learning and development; and second, the specific features of this relationship when children reach school age.

That children's learning begins long before they attend school is the starting point of this discussion. Any learning a child encounters in school always has a previous history. For example, children begin to study arithmetic in school, but long beforehand they have had some experience with quantity—they have had to deal with operations of division, addition, subtraction, and determination of size. Consequently, children have their own preschool arithmetic, which only myopic psychologists could ignore.

It goes without saying that learning as it occurs in the preschool years differs markedly from school learning, which is concerned with the assimilation of the fundamentals of scientific knowledge. But even when, in the period of her first questions, a child assimilates the names of objects in her environment, she is learning. Indeed, can it be doubted that children learn speech from adults; or that, through asking questions and giving answers, children acquire a variety of information; or that, through imitating adults and through being instructed about how to act, children develop an entire repository of skills? Learning and development are interrelated from the child's very first day of life.

Koffka, attempting to clarify the laws of child learning and their relation to mental development, concentrates his attention on the simplest learning processes, those that occur in the preschool years. His error is that, while seeing a similarity between preschool and school learning, he fails to discern the difference—he does not see the specifically new elements that school learning introduces. He and others assume that the difference between preschool and school learning consists of non-systematic learning in one case and systematic learning in the other. But "systematicness" is not the only issue; there is also the fact that school learning introduces something fundamentally new into the child's development. In order to elaborate the dimensions of school learning, we will describe a new and exceptionally important concept without which the issue cannot be resolved: the zone of proximal development.

A well known and empirically established fact is that learning should be matched in some manner with the child's developmental level. For example, it has been established that the teaching of reading, writing, and arithmetic should be initiated at a specific age level. Only recently, however, has attention been directed to the fact that we cannot limit ourselves merely to determining developmental levels if we wish to discover the actual relations of the developmental process to learning capabilities. We must determine at least two developmental levels.

The first level can be called the *actual developmental level,* that is, the level of development of a child's mental functions that has been established as a result of certain already completed developmental cycles. When we determine a child's mental age by using tests, we are almost always dealing with the actual developmental level. In studies of children's mental development it is generally assumed that only those things that children can do on their own are indicative of mental abilities. We give children a battery of tests or a variety of tasks of varying degrees of difficulty, and we judge the extent of their mental development on the basis of how they solve them and at what level of difficulty. On the other hand, if we offer leading questions or show how the problem is to be solved and the child then solves it, or if the teacher initiates the solution and the child completes it or solves it in collaboration with other children—in short, if the child barely misses an independent solution of the problem—the solution is not regarded as indicative of his mental development. This "truth" was familiar and reinforced by common sense. Over a decade even the profoundest thinkers never questioned the assumption; they never entertained the notion that what children can do with the assistance of others might be in some sense even more indicative of their mental development than what they can do alone.

Let us take a simple example. Suppose I investigate two children upon entrance into school, both of whom are ten years old chronologically and eight years old in terms of mental development. Can I say that they are the same age mentally? Of course. What does this mean? It means that they can independently deal with tasks up to the degree of difficulty that has been standardized for the eight-year-old level. If I stop at this point, people would imagine that the subsequent course of mental development and of school learning for these children will be the same, because it depends on their intellect. Of course, there may be other factors, for example, if one child was sick for half a year while the other was never absent from school; but generally speaking, the fate of these children should be the same. Now imagine that I do not terminate my study at this point, but only begin it. These children seem to be capable of handling problems up to an eight-year-old's level, but not beyond that. Suppose that I show them various ways of dealing with the problem. Different experimenters might employ different modes of demonstration in different cases: some might run through an entire demonstration and ask the children to repeat it, others might initiate the solution and ask the child to finish it, or offer leading questions. In short, in some way or another I propose that the children solve the problem with my assistance. Under these circumstances it turns out that the first child can deal with problems up to a twelve-year-old's level, the second up to a nine-year-old's. Now, are these children mentally the same?

When it was first shown that the capability of children with equal levels of mental development to learn under a teacher's guidance varied to a high degree, it became apparent that those children were not mentally the same age and that the subsequent course of their learning would obviously be different. This difference between twelve and eight, or between nine and eight, is what we call *the zone of proximal development. It is the distance between the actual developmental level as determined by independent problem solving and the level of potential development as determined through problem solving under adult guidance or in collaboration with more capable peers.*

If we naively ask what the actual developmental level is, or, to put it more simply, what more independent problem solving reveals, the most common answer would be that a child's actual developmental level defines functions that have already matured, that is, the end products of development. If a child can do such-and-such independently, it means that the functions for such-and-such have matured in her. What, then, is defined by the zone of proximal development, as determined through problems that children cannot solve independently but only with assistance? The zone of proximal development defines those functions that have not yet matured but are in the process of maturation, functions that will mature tomorrow but are currently in an embryonic state. These functions could be termed the "buds" or "flowers" of development rather than the "fruits" of development. The actual developmental level characterizes mental development retrospectively, while the zone of proximal development characterizes mental development prospectively.

The zone of proximal development furnishes psychologists and educators with a tool through which the internal course of development can be understood. By using this method we can take account of not only the cycles and maturation processes that have already been completed but also those processes that are currently in a state of formation, that are just beginning to mature and develop. Thus, the zone of proximal development permits us to delineate the child's immediate future and his dynamic developmental state, allowing not only for what already has been achieved developmentally but also for what is in the course of maturing. The two children in our example displayed the same mental age from the viewpoint of developmental cycles already completed, but the developmental dynamics of the two were entirely different. The state of a child's mental development can be determined only by clarifying its two levels: the actual developmental level and the zone of proximal development.

I will discuss one study of preschool children to demonstrate that what is in the zone of proximal development today will be the actual developmental level tomorrow—that is, what a child can do with assistance today she will be able to do by herself tomorrow.

The American researcher Dorothea McCarthy showed that among children between the ages of three and five there are two groups of functions: those the children already possess, and those they can perform under guidance, in groups, and in collaboration with one another but which they have not mastered independently. McCarthy's study demonstrated that this second group of functions is at the actual developmental level of five-to-seven-year-olds. What her subjects could do only under guidance, in collaboration, and in groups at the age of three-to-five years they could do independently when they reached the age of five-to-seven years.[5] Thus, if we were to determine only mental age—that is, only functions that have matured—we would have but a summary of completed development while if we determine the maturing functions, we can predict what will happen to these children between five and seven, provided the same developmental conditions are maintained. The zone of proximal development can become a powerful concept in developmental research, one that can markedly enhance the effectiveness and utility of the application of diagnostics of mental development to educational problems.

A full understanding of the concept of the zone of proximal development must result in reevaluation of the role of imitation in learning. An unshakable tenet of classical psychology is that only the independent activity of children, not their imitative activity, indicates their level of mental development. This view is expressed in all current testing systems. In evaluating mental development, consideration is given to only those solutions to test problems which the child reaches without the assistance of others, without demonstrations, and without leading questions. Imitation and learning are thought of as purely mechanical processes. But recently psychologists have shown that a person can imitate only that which is within her developmental level. For example, if a child is having difficulty with a problem in arithmetic and the teacher solves it on the blackboard, the child may grasp the solution in an instant. But if the teacher were to solve a problem in higher mathematics, the child would not be able to understand the solution no matter how many times she imitated it.

Animal psychologists, and in particular Köhler, have dealt with this question of imitation quite well.[6] Köhler's experiments sought to determine whether primates are capable of graphic thought. The principal question was whether primates solved problems independently or whether they merely imitated solutions they had seen performed earlier, for example, watching other animals or humans use sticks and other tools and then imitating them. Köhler's special experiments, designed to determine what primates could imitate, reveal that primates can use imitation to solve only those problems that are of the same degree of difficulty as those they can solve alone. However, Köhler failed to take account of an important fact, namely, that primates cannot be taught (in the human sense of the word) through imitation, nor can their intellect be developed, because they have no zone of proximal development. A primate can learn a great deal through training by using its mechanical and mental skills, but it cannot be made more intelligent, that is, it cannot be taught to solve a variety of more advanced problems independently. For this reason animals are incapable of learning in the human sense of the term; *human learning presupposes a specific social nature and a process by which children grow into the intellectual life of those around them.*

Children can imitate a variety of actions that go well beyond the limits of their own capabilities. Using imitation, children are capable of doing much more in collective activity or under the guidance of adults. This fact, which seems to be of little significance in itself, is of fundamental importance in that it demands a radical alteration of the entire doctrine concerning the relation between learning and development in children. One direct consequence is a change in conclusions that may be drawn from diagnostic tests of development.

Formerly, it was believed that by using tests, we determine the mental development level with which education should reckon and whose limits it should not exceed. This procedure oriented learning toward yesterday's development, toward developmental stages already completed. The error of this view was discovered earlier in practice than in theory. It is demonstrated most clearly in the teaching of mentally retarded children. Studies have established that mentally retarded children are not very capable of abstract thinking. From this the pedagogy of the special school drew the seemingly correct conclusion that all teaching of such children should be based on the use of concrete, look-and-do methods. And yet a considerable amount of experience with this method resulted in profound disillusionment. It turned out that a teaching system based solely on concreteness—one that eliminated from teaching everything associated with abstract thinking—not only failed to help retarded children overcome their innate handicaps but also reinforced their handicaps by accustoming children exclusively to concrete thinking and thus suppressing the rudiments of any abstract thought that such children still have. Precisely because retarded children, when left to themselves, will never achieve well-elaborated forms of abstract thought, the school should make every effort to push them in that direction and to develop in them what is intrinsically lacking in their own development. In the current practices of special schools for retarded children, we can observe a beneficial shift away from this concept of concreteness, one that restores look-and-do methods to their proper role. Concreteness is now seen as necessary and unavoidable only as a stepping stone for developing abstract thinking—as a means, not as an end in itself.

Similarly, in normal children, learning which is oriented toward developmental levels that have already been reached is ineffective from the viewpoint of a child's overall development. It does not aim for a new stage of the developmental process but rather lags behind this process. Thus, the notion of a zone of proximal development enables us to propound a new formula, namely that the only "good learning" is that which is in advance of development.

The acquisition of language can provide a paradigm for the entire problem of the relation between learning and development. Language arises initially as a means of communication between the child and the people in his environment. Only subsequently, upon conversion to internal speech, does it come to organize the child's thought, that is, become an internal mental function. Piaget and others have shown that reasoning occurs in a children's group as an argument intended to prove one's own point of view before it occurs as an internal activity whose distinctive feature is that the child begins to perceive and check the basis of his thoughts. Such observations prompted Piaget to conclude that communication produces the need for checking and confirming thoughts, a process that is characteristic of adult thought.[7] In the same way that internal speech and reflective thought arise from the interactions between the child and persons in her environment, these interactions provide the source of development of a child's voluntary behavior. Piaget has shown that cooperation provides the basis for the development of a child's moral judgment. Earlier research established that a child first becomes able to subordinate her behavior to rules in group play and only later does voluntary self-regulation of behavior arise as an internal function.

These individual examples illustrate a general developmental law for the higher mental functions that we feel can be applied in its entirety to children's learning processes. We propose that an essential feature of learning is that it creates the zone of proximal development; that is, learning awakens a variety of internal developmental processes that are able to operate only when the child is interacting with people in his environment and in cooperation with his peers. Once these processes are internalized, they become part of the child's independent developmental achievement.

From this point of view, learning is not development; however, properly organized learning results in mental development and sets in motion a variety of developmental processes that would be impossible apart from learning. Thus, learning is a necessary and universal aspect of the process of developing culturally organized, specifically human, psychological functions.

To summarize, the most essential feature of our hypothesis is the notion that developmental processes do not coincide with learning processes. Rather, the developmental process lags behind the learning process; this sequence then results in zones of proximal development. Our analysis alters the traditional view that at the moment a child assimilates the meaning of a word, or masters an operation such as addition or written language, her developmental processes are basically completed. In fact, they have only just begun at that moment. The major consequence of analyzing the educational process in this manner is to show that the initial mastery of, for example, the four arithmetic operations provides the basis for the subsequent development of a variety of highly complex internal processes in children's thinking.

Our hypothesis establishes the unity but not the identity of learning processes and internal developmental processes. It presupposes that the one is converted into the other. Therefore, it becomes an important concern of psychological research to show how external knowledge and abilities in children become internalized.

Any investigation explores some sphere of reality. An aim of the psychological analysis of development is to describe the internal relations of the intellectual processes awakened by school learning. In this respect, such analysis will be directed inward and is analogous to the use of x-rays. If successful, it should reveal to the teacher how developmental processes stimulated by the course of school learning are carried through inside the head of each individual child. The revelation of this internal, subterranean developmental network of school subjects is a task of primary importance for psychological and educational analysis.

A second essential feature of our hypothesis is the notion that, although learning is directly related to the course of child development, the two are never accomplished in equal measure or in parallel. Development in children never follows school learning the way a shadow follows the object that casts it. In actuality, there are highly complex dynamic relations between developmental and learning processes that cannot be encompassed by an unchanging hypothetical formulation.

Each school subject has its own specific relation to the course of child development, a relation that varies as the child goes from one stage to another. This leads us directly to a reexamination of the problem of formal discipline, that is, to the significance of each particular subject from the viewpoint of overall mental development. Clearly, the problem cannot be solved by using any one formula; extensive and highly diverse concrete research based on the concept of the zone of proximal development is necessary to resolve the issue.

Questions

1. Consider the three theoretical views that, according to Vygotsky, have attempted to explain the relation between development and learning. Why does Vygotsky consider these unsatisfactory for explaining this relation?

2. What is the zone of proximal development? According to Vygotsky, what role does it play in learning and what role does it play in cognitive development?

3. If you were to design a new IQ test based on Vygotsky's ideas of the zone of proximal development, what would it be like? How might a child's score on such a test be used to organize his or her experiences in school?

Notes

1. J. Piaget, *The Language and Thought of the Child* (New York: Meridian Books, 1955).

2. William James, *Talks to Teachers* (New York: Norton, 1958), pp. 36–37.

3. Koffka, *The Growth of the Mind* (London: Routledge and Kegan Paul, 1924).

4. E. L. Thorndike, *The Psychology of Learning* (New York: Teachers College Press, 1914).

5. Dorothea McCarthy, *The Language Development of the Pre-school Child* (Minneapolis: University of Minnesota Press, 1930).

6. W. Köhler, *The Mentality of Apes* (New York: Harcourt, Brace, 1925).

7. Piaget, *Language and Thought*.

5

Ecological Models of Human Development

URIE BRONFENBRENNER

Urie Bronfenbrenner argues that in order to understand human development, one must consider the entire ecological system in which growth occurs. This system is composed of five socially organized subsystems that help support and guide human growth. They range from the microsystem, which refers to the relationship between a developing person and the immediate environment, such as school and family, to the macrosystem, which refers to institutional patterns of culture, such as the economy, customs, and bodies of knowledge.

Ecological models encompass an evolving body of theory and research concerned with the processes and conditions that govern the lifelong course of human development in the actual environments in which human beings live. Although most of the systematic theory-building in this domain has been done by Bronfenbrenner, his work is based on an analysis and integration of results from empirical investigations conducted over many decades by researchers from diverse disciplines, beginning with a study carried out in Berlin in 1870 on the effects of neighborhood on the development of children's

concepts (Schwabe and Bartholomai 1870). This entry consists of an exposition of Bronfenbrenner's theoretical system, which is also used as a framework for illustrating representative research findings.

1. THE EVOLUTION OF ECOLOGICAL MODELS

Bronfenbrenner's ecological paradigm, first introduced in the 1970s (Bronfenbrenner 1974, 1976, 1977, 1979), represented a reaction to the restricted

Reprinted with permission from the *International Encyclopedia of Education*, Vol. 3, 2nd ed., 1994, 1643–1647, Elsevier Sciences, Ltd., Oxford, England.

scope of most research then being conducted by developmental psychologists. The nature of both the restriction and the reaction is conveyed by this oft-quoted description of the state of developmental science at that time: "It can be said that much of developmental psychology is the science of the strange behavior of children in strange situations with strange adults for the briefest possible periods of time" (Bronfenbrenner 1977, p. 513).

In the same article, Bronfenbrenner presented a conceptual and operational framework (supported by the comparatively small body of relevant research findings then available) that would usefully provide the basis and incentive for moving the field in the desired direction. During the same period, he also published two reports pointing to the challenging implications of an ecological approach for child and family policy (1974) and educational practice (1976).

Within a decade, investigations informed by an ecological perspective were no longer a rarity. By 1986, Bronfenbrenner was able to write:

> Studies of children and adults in real-life settings, with real-life implications, are now commonplace in the research literature on human development, both in the United States and, as this volume testifies, in Europe as well. This scientific development is taking place, I believe, not so much because of my writings, but rather because the notions I have been promulgating are ideas whose time has come. (1986b p. 287).

At the same time, Bronfenbrenner continued his work on the development of a theoretical paradigm. What follows is a synopsis of the general ecological model as delineated in its most recent reformulations (Bronfenbrenner 1989, 1990, Bronfenbrenner and Ceci 1993).

2. THE GENERAL ECOLOGICAL MODEL

Two propositions specifying the defining properties of the model are followed by research examples illustrating both.

Proposition 1 states that, especially in its early phases, and to a great extent throughout the life course, human development takes place through processes of progressively more complex reciprocal interaction between an active, evolving biopsychological human organism and the persons, objects, and symbols in its immediate environment. To be effective, the interaction must occur on a fairly regular basis over extended periods of time. Such enduring forms of interaction in the immediate environment are referred to as *proximal processes*. Examples of enduring patterns of proximal process are found in parent-child and child-child activities, group or solitary play, reading, learning new skills, studying, athletic activities, and performing complex tasks.

A second defining property identifies the threefold source of these dynamic forces. Proposition 2 states that the form, power, content, and direction of the proximal processes effecting development vary systematically as a joint function of the characteristics of the developing person; of the environment—both immediate and more remote—in which the processes are taking place; and the nature of the developmental outcomes under consideration.

Propositions 1 and 2 are theoretically interdependent and subject to empirical test. A research design that permits their simultaneous investigation is referred to as a process-person-context model. A first example illustrating the model is shown in Figure 1. The data are drawn from a classic longitudinal study by Drillien (1963) of factors affecting the development of children of low birth weight compared to those of normal weight. The figure depicts the impact of the quality of mother-infant interaction at age 4 on the number of observed problems at age 4 as a joint function of birth weight and social class. As can be seen, a proximal process, in this instance mother-infant interaction across time, emerges as the most powerful predictor of developmental outcome. In all instances, good maternal treatment appears to reduce substantially the degree of behavioral disturbance exhibited by the child. Furthermore, as stipulated in Proposition 2, the power of the process varies systematically as a function of the environmental context (in this instance, social class) and of the characteristics of the person (in this case, weight at birth). Note also that the proximal process has the general effect of reducing or buffering against environmental differences in developmental outcome; specifically, under high levels of mother-child interaction, social class differences in problem behavior become much smaller.

Unfortunately, from the perspective of an ecological model the greater developmental impact of proximal processes in poorer environments is to be expected only for indices of developmental dysfunction, primarily during childhood. For outcomes reflecting developmental competence (e.g., mental ability, academic achievement, social skills) proximal processes are posited as having greater impact in more advantaged and stable environments throughout the life course. An example of this contrasting pattern is shown in Figure 2, which depicts the differential effects of parental monitoring on school

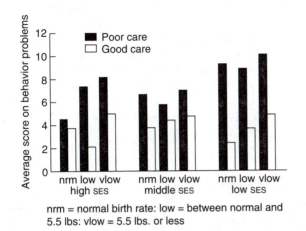

nrm = normal birth rate: low = between normal and
5.5 lbs: vlow = 5.5 lbs. or less

FIGURE 1   Problem behavior at age 4 (by birth weight,
mother's care, and social class).

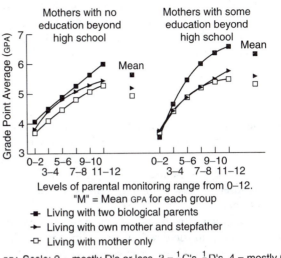

Levels of parental monitoring range from 0–12.
"M" = Mean GPA for each group
-■- Living with two biological parents
-▸- Living with own mother and stepfather
-□- Living with mother only

GPA Scale: 2 = mostly D's or less. 3 = $\frac{1}{2}$C's, $\frac{1}{2}$D's. 4 = mostly C's.
5 = $\frac{1}{2}$B's, $\frac{1}{2}$C's. 6 = mostly B's. 7 = $\frac{1}{2}$A's, $\frac{1}{2}$B's. 8 = mostly A's

FIGURE 2   Effect of parental monitoring on grades
in high school by family structure and mother's level of
education.

achievement for high school students living in the three most common family structures found in the total sample of over 4,000 cases. The sample is further stratified by two levels of mother's education, with completion of high school as the dividing point. Parental monitoring refers to the effort by parents to keep informed about, and set limits on, their children's activities outside the home. In the present analysis, it was assessed by a series of items in a questionnaire administered to adolescents in their school classes.

Once again, the results reveal that the effects of proximal processes are more powerful than those of the environmental contexts in which they occur. In this instance, however, the impact of the proximal process is greatest in what emerges as the most advantaged ecological niche, that is, families with two biological parents in which the mother has had some education beyond high school. The typically declining slope of the curve reflects the fact that higher levels of outcome are more difficult to achieve so that at each successive step, the same degree of active effort yields a somewhat smaller result.

3. ENVIRONMENTS AS CONTEXTS OF DEVELOPMENT

The foregoing example provides an appropriate introduction to another distinctive feature of the ecological model, its highly differentiated reconcep-

tualization of the environment from the perspective of the developing person. Based on Lewin's theory of psychological fields (Bronfenbrenner 1977; Lewin 1917, 1931, 1935), the ecological environment is conceived as a set of nested structures, each inside the other like a set of Russian dolls. Moving from the innermost level to the outside, these structures are defined as described below.

3.1 Microsystems

A microsystem is a pattern of activities, social roles, and interpersonal relations experienced by the developing person in a given face-to-face setting with particular physical, social, and symbolic features that invite, permit, or inhibit engagement in sustained, progressively more complex interaction with, and activity in, the immediate environment. Examples include such settings as family, school, peer group, and workplace.

It is within the immediate environment of the microsystem that proximal processes operate to produce and sustain development, but as the above definition indicates, their power to do so depends on the content and structure of the microsystem. Specific hypotheses regarding the nature of this content and structure, and the as yet limited research evidence on which they are based are documented in the work of Bronfenbrenner (1986a, 1986b, 1988, 1989, 1993). Most of the relevant studies of proximal processes have focused on the family, with all too few dealing with other key developmental settings, such as classrooms and schools. A notable exception in this regard is the work of Stevenson and his colleagues (Stevenson and Stigler 1992, see also Ceci 1990).

3.2 Mesosystems

The mesosystem comprises the linkages and processes taking place between two or more settings containing the developing person (e.g., the relations between home and school, school and workplace, etc.). In other words, a mesosystem is a system of microsystems.

An example in this domain is the work of Epstein (1983a, 1983b) on the developmental impact of two-way communication and participation in decision-making by parents and teachers. Elementary school pupils from classrooms in which such joint involvement was high not only exhibited greater initiative and independence after entering high school, but also received higher grades. The effects of family and school processes were greater than those attributable to socioeconomic status or race.

3.3 Exosystems

The exosystem comprises the linkages and processes taking place between two or more settings, at least one of which does not contain the developing person, but in which events occur that indirectly influence processes within the immediate setting in which the developing person lives (e.g., for a child, the relation between the home and the parent's workplace; for a parent, the relation between the school and the neighborhood peer group).

Especially since the early 1980s, research has focused on three exosystems that are especially likely to affect the development of children and youth indirectly through their influence on the family, the school, and the peer group. These are the parents' workplace (e.g., Eckenrode and Gore 1990), family social networks (e.g., Cochran et al. 1990), and neighborhood-community contexts (e.g., Pence 1988).

3.4 Macrosystems

The macrosystem consists of the overarching pattern of micro-, meso-, and exosystems characteristic of a given culture or subculture, with particular reference to the belief systems, bodies of knowledge, material resources, customs, life-styles, opportunity structures, hazards, and life course options that are embedded in each of these broader systems. The macrosystem may be thought of as a societal blueprint for a particular culture or subculture.

This formulation points to the necessity of going beyond the simple labels of class and culture to identify more specific social and psychological features at the macrosystem level that ultimately affect the particular conditions and processes occurring in the microsystem (see Bronfenbrenner 1986a, 1986b, 1988, 1989, 1993).

3.5 Chronosystems

A final systems parameter extends the environment into a third dimension. Traditionally in the study of human development, the passage of time was treated as synonymous with chronological age. Since the early 1970s, however, an increasing number of investigators have employed research designs in which time appears not merely as an attribute of the growing human being, but also as a property of the surrounding environment not only over the life course, but across historical time (Baltes and Schaie 1973, Clausen 1986, Elder 1974, Elder et al. 1993).

A chronosystem encompasses change or consistency over time not only in the characteristics of the person but also of the environment in which that person lives (e.g., changes over the life course in family structure, socioeconomic status, employment, place of residence, or the degree of hecticness and ability in everyday life).

An excellent example of a chronosystem design is found in Elder's classic study *Children of the Great Depression* (1974). The investigation involved a comparison of two otherwise comparable groups of families differentiated on the basis of whether the loss of income as a result of the Great Depression of the 1930s exceeded or fell short of 35 percent. The availability of longitudinal data made it possible to assess developmental outcomes through childhood, adolescence, and adulthood. Also, the fact that children in one sample were born eight years earlier than those in the other permitted a comparison of the effects of the Depression on youngsters who were adolescents when their families became economically deprived with the effects of those who were still young children at the time.

The results for the two groups presented a dramatic contrast. Paradoxically, for youngsters who were teenagers during the Depression years, the families' economic deprivation appeared to have a salutary effect on their subsequent development, especially in the middle class. As compared with the nondeprived who were matched on pre-Depression socioeconomic status, deprived boys displayed a greater desire to achieve and a firmer sense of career goals. Boys and girls from deprived homes attained greater satisfaction in life, both by their own and by societal standards. Though more pronounced for adolescents from middle-class backgrounds, these favorable outcomes were evident among their lower-class counterparts as well. Analysis of interview and observation protocols enabled Elder to identify what he regarded as a critical factor in investigating this favorable developmental trajectory: the loss of economic security forced the family to mobilize its own human resources, including its teenagers, who had to take on new roles and responsibilities both within and outside the home and to work together toward the common goal of getting and keeping the family on its feet. This experience provided effective training in initiative, responsibility, and cooperation.

4. GENETIC INHERITANCE IN ECOLOGICAL PERSPECTIVE

The most recent extension of the ecological paradigm involves a reconceptualization of the role of genetics in human development (Bronfenbrenner and Ceci 1993). The new formulation calls into question and replaces some of the key assumptions underlying the established "percentage-of-variance" model employed in behavior genetics. Specifically, in addition to incorporating explicit measures of the environment conceptualized in systems terms, and allowing for nonadditive, synergistic effects in genetics-environment interaction, the proposed "bioecological" model posits proximal processes as the empirically assessable mechanisms through which genotypes are transformed into phenotypes. It is further argued, both on theoretical and empirical grounds, that heritability, defined by behavioral geneticists as "the proportion of the total phenotypic variance that is due to additive genetic variation" (Cavalli-Storza and Bodmer 1971 p. 536), is in fact highly influenced by events and conditions in the environment. Specifically, it is proposed that heritability can be shown to vary substantially as a direct function of the magnitude of proximal processes and the quality of the environments in which they occur, potentially yielding values of heritability that, at their extremes, are both appreciably higher and lower than those hitherto reported in the research literature.

If this bioecological model sustains empirical testing, this would imply that many human beings may possess genetic potentials for development significantly beyond those that they are presently manifesting, and that such unrealized potentials might be actualized through social policies and programs that enhance exposure to proximal processes in environmental settings providing the stability and resources that enable such processes to be maximally effective.

Certainly, thus far it has by no means been demonstrated that this latest extension of the ecological paradigm has any validity. Nor is the validation of hypotheses the principal goal that ecological models are designed to achieve. Indeed, their purpose may be better served if the hypotheses that they generate are found wanting, for the primary scientific aim of the ecological approach is not to claim answers, but to provide a theoretical framework that, through its application, will lead to further progress in discovering the processes and conditions that shape the course of human development.

However, beyond this scientific aim lies a broader human hope. That hope was expressed in the first systematic exposition of the ecological paradigm:

> Species *Homo sapiens* appears to be unique in its capacity to adapt to, tolerate, and especially to create the ecologies in which it lives and grows. Seen in different contexts, human nature, which I had once thought of as a singular noun, turns out to be plural and pluralistic; for different environments produce discernible differences, not only across but within societies, in talent, temperament, human relations, and particularly in the ways in which each culture and subculture brings up the next generation. The process and product of making human beings human clearly varies by place and time. Viewed in historical as well as cross-cultural perspective, this diversity suggests the possibility of ecologies as yet untried that hold a potential for human natures yet unseen, perhaps possessed of a wiser blend of power and compassion than has thus far been manifested. (Bronfenbrenner 1979 p. xiii)

Questions

1.   What are the five subsystems of the ecological context that Bronfenbrenner discusses? Think of a particular process of psychological development and try to describe it from the perspective of each of these subsystems.

2.   What information about human development will an ecological systems approach add to the field of developmental psychology?

3.   In theory, the ecological systems approach is rich in the amount of new information it can provide about human development. But is it a practical or feasible approach? Which aspects of this approach lend themselves to study and which do not?

References

Baltes, P. B., Schaie, W. 1973. *Life-span Developmental Psychology: Personality and Socialization.* Academic Press, New York.

Bronfenbrenner, U. 1974. Developmental research, public policy, and the ecology of childhood. *Child Dev.* 45(1): 1–5.

Bronfenbrenner, U. 1976. The experimental ecology of education. *Teach. Coll. Rec.* 78(2): 157–204.

Bronfenbrenner, U. 1977. Toward an experimental ecology of human development. *Am. Psychol.* 32: 515–31.

Bronfenbrenner, U. 1979. *The Ecology of Human Development: Experiments by Nature and Design.* Harvard University Press, Cambridge, Massachusetts.

Bronfenbrenner, U. 1986a. Ecology of the family as a context for human development: Research perspectives. *Dev. Psychol.* 22(6): 723–42.

Bronfenbrenner, U. 1986b. Recent advances in the ecology of human development. In: Silbereisen, R. K., Eyferth, K., Rudinger, G. (eds.) 1986 *Development as Action in Context: Problem Behavior and Normal Youth Development.* Springer-Verlag, Berlin.

Bronfenbrenner, U. 1988. Interacting systems in human development: Research paradigms, present and future. In: Bolger, N., Caspi, A., Downey, G., Moorehouse, M. (eds.) 1988 *Persons in Context: Developmental Processes.* Cambridge University Press, Cambridge.

Bronfenbrenner, U. 1989. Ecological systems theory. In: Vasta, R. (ed.) 1989 *Six Theories of Child Development: Revised Formulations and Current Issues.* Vol. 6. JAI Press, Greenwich, Connecticut.

Bronfenbrenner, U. 1990. The ecology of cognitive development. *Zeitschrift für Sozialisationsforschung und Erziehungssoziologie (ZSE).* 10(2): 101–14.

Bronfenbrenner, U. 1993. The ecology of cognitive development: Research models and fugitive findings. In: Wozniak, R. H., Fischer, K. (eds.) 1993 *Thinking in Context.* Erlbaum, Hillsdale, New Jersey.

Bronfenbrenner, U., Ceci, S. J. 1993. Heredity, environment, and the question "how?": A new theoretical perspective for the 1990s. In: Plomin, R., McClearn, G. E. (eds.) 1993 *Nature, Nurture, and Psychology.* APA Books, Washington, DC.

Cavalli-Storza, L. L., Bodmer, W. F. 1971. *The Genetics of Human Populations.* W. H. Freeman, San Francisco, California.

Ceci, S. J. 1990. *On Intelligence . . . More or Less: A Bioecological Treatise on Intellectual Development.* Prentice-Hall, Englewood Cliffs, New Jersey.

Clausen, J. A. 1986. *The Life Course: A Sociological Perspective.* Prentice-Hall, Englewood Cliffs, New Jersey.

Cochran, M., Larner, M., Riley, D., Gunnarsson, L., Henderson, C. R., Jr. 1990. *Extending Families: The Social Networks of Parents and their Children.* Cambridge University Press, New York.

Drillien, C. M. 1963. *The Growth and Development of the Prematurely Born Infant.* E. and S. Livingston Ltd., Edinburgh.

Eckenrode, J., Gore, S. (eds.) 1990. *Stress between Work and Family.* Plenum Press, New York.

Elder, G. H., Jr. 1974. *Children of the Great Depression: Social Change in the Life Experience.* University of Chicago Press, Chicago, Illinois.

Elder, G. H., Jr., Modell, J., Parke, R. D. 1993. *Children in Time and Place: Individual, Historical and Developmental Insights.* Cambridge University Press, New York.

Epstein, J. L. 1983a. *Effects on Parents of Teacher Practices of Parent Involvement.* Center for the Social Organization of Schools, Johns Hopkins University, Baltimore, Maryland.

Epstein, J. L. 1983b. Longitudinal effects of family-school-person interactions on student outcomes. *Research in Sociology of Education and Socialization* 4: 101–27.

Lewin, K. 1917. Kriegslandschaft. *Zeitschrift für Angewandte Psychologie* 12: 440–47.

Lewin, K. 1931. Environmental forces in child behavior and development. In: Murchison, C. (ed.) 1931 *A Handbook of Child Psychology.* Clark University Press, Worcester, Massachusetts.

Lewin, K. 1935. *A Dynamic Theory of Personality.* McGraw-Hill, New York.

Pence, A. R. (ed.) 1988. *Ecological Research with Children and Families: From Concepts to Methodology.* Teachers College, Columbia University, New York.

Schwabe, H., Bartholomai, F. 1870. Der Vorstellungskreis der Berliner Kinder beim Eintritt in die Schule. In: *Berlin und seine Entwicklung: Städtisches Jahrbuch für Volkswirthschaft und Statistik Vierter Jahrgang.* Guttentag, Berlin.

Stevenson, H. W., Stigler, J. W. 1992. *The Learning Gap: Why Our Schools are Failing and What We Can Learn from Japanese and Chinese Education.* Summit Books, New York.

PART I

In the Beginning

6

The Genetic Basis of Complex Human Behaviors

ROBERT PLOMIN, MICHAEL J. OWEN, PETER MCGUFFIN

One basic goal of psychology as a scientific discipline is to understand individual variation. In this article, Robert Plomin, Michael Owen, and Peter McGuffin discuss the study of individual differences in development by examining genetic and environmental contributions to growth. An important point emphasized by Plomin is the complexity of the relations between genetic and environmental contributions to development. Individuals contribute to the environments in which their development occurs, and thus the psychological character of these situations is influenced by inherited characteristics.

Quantitative genetic research has built a strong case for the importance of genetic factors in many complex behavioral disorders and dimensions in the domains of psychopathology, personality, and cognitive abilities. Quantitative genetics can also provide an empirical guide and a conceptual framework for the application of molecular genetics. The success of molecular genetics in elucidating the genetic basis of behavioral disorders has largely relied on a reductionistic one gene, one disorder (OGOD) approach in which a single gene is necessary and sufficient to develop a disorder. In contrast, a quantitative trait loci (QTL) approach involves the search for multiple genes, each of which is neither necessary nor sufficient for the development of a trait. The OGOD and QTL approaches have both advantages and disadvantages for identifying genes that affect complex human behaviors.

The received wisdom of the behavioral sciences concerning the importance of "nature" (genetics) and "nurture" (environment) in the origins of behavioral differences among people has changed dramatically during the past few decades. Environmentalism, which attributes all that we are to nurture, peaked in the 1950s. A more balanced view that considers both nature and nurture swept into psychiatry in the 1960s and 1970s. Although this balanced view has been slower to reach some realms of psychology, there are signs that it has arrived. For example, at its centennial meeting in 1992, the American Psychological Association identified genetics as one of the themes that best represent the present and especially the future of psychology (*1*).

Behavioral genetic research began in the 1920s with inbred strain and selection studies of animal behavior and family, twin, and adoption studies of human behavior (*2*). These quantitative genetic designs assess the "bottom line" of transmissible genetic effects on behavior, regardless of the number of genes involved, the complexity of their interactions, or the influence of nongenetic factors. As discussed in the first part of this article, quantitative genetic research has built a strong case for the importance of genetic factors in many complex dimensions and disorders of human behavior.

Although more quantitative genetic research is needed, the future of behavioral genetics lies in harnessing the power of molecular genetics to identify specific genes for complex behaviors. In the second part of this paper, initial successes are described and research strategies are discussed. Although more powerful methods and results are available for the investigation of animal than human behavior, animal work is discussed in accompanying articles in this issue.

QUANTITATIVE GENETICS

The change from antipathy to acceptance of genetic factors in the behavioral sciences has occurred so rapidly and thoroughly, especially in psychiatry, that a reminder is warranted about how environmentalistic the behavioral sciences were, even in the 1960s. For example, the major explanation for schizophrenia was abnormal parenting.

Adoption studies were pivotal in leading psychiatrists to consider nature as well as nurture. Schizophrenia was known to run in families, with a risk of 13% for offspring of schizophrenic parents, 13 times the population rate of about 1% (*3*). Adoption experiments allow a determination of whether schizophrenia runs in families for reasons of nature or of

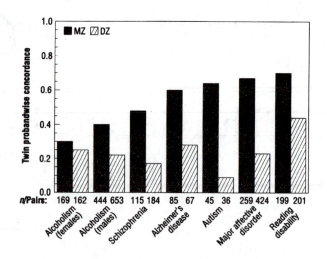

FIGURE 1   Identical twin [monozygotic (MZ)] and fraternal twin [dizygotic (DZ)] probandwise concordances for behavioral disorders. Average weighted concordances were derived from the references in (*60*).

nurture. In a classic study, Heston (*4*) examined the offspring of schizophrenic mothers who had been adopted at birth and compared their rate of schizophrenia to a control group of adopted offspring. Of the 47 adopted-away offspring of schizophrenic mothers, 5 were diagnosed as schizophrenic, as compared to none of the 50 control adoptees. Indeed, the risk of schizophrenia for the adopted-away offspring of schizophrenic mothers is the same as the risk for individuals reared by a schizophrenic parent.

These findings implicating substantial genetic influence in schizophrenia have been replicated and extended in other adoption studies, and they confirm the results of twin studies that show greater concordance for identical twins (about 45%) than fraternal twins (about 15%) (*3*). This twin method is a natural experiment in which the phenotypic resemblance for pairs of genetically identical individuals [identical, monozygotic (MZ) twins] is compared to the resemblance for pairs of individuals whose coefficient of genetic relationship is only 0.50 [fraternal, dizygotic (DZ) twins].

The convergence of evidence from family, twin, and adoption designs—each with distinct assumptions—provides the most convincing argument for the importance of genetic factors in behavioral traits.

Behavioral Disorders

Evidence for genetic influence has been found for nearly all behavioral disorders that have been inves-

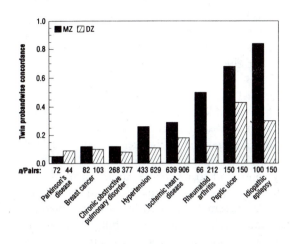

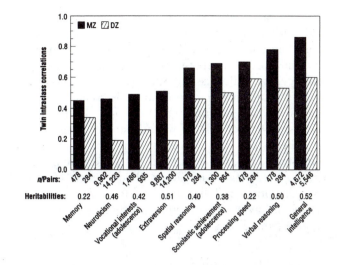

FIGURE 2 MZ and DZ probandwise concordances for common medical disorders. Average weighted concordances were derived from the references in (61).

FIGURE 3 MZ and DZ twin intraclass correlations for personality (neuroticism and extraversion), vocational interests in adolescence, scholastic achievement in adolescence (combined across similar results for English usage, mathematics, social studies, and natural science), specific cognitive abilities in adolescence (memory, spatial reasoning, processing speed, verbal reasoning), and general intelligence. Average weighted correlations were derived from the references in (62).

tigated (5). Figure 1 summarizes the results of twin studies for some of the best studied disorders. Genetic influence is substantial for schizophrenia, Alzheimer's disease, autism, major affective disorder, and reading disability (6). Not all behavioral disorders are influenced to the same degree by genetic factors. For example, diagnosed alcoholism has been assumed to be highly heritable, but new twin studies show only modest genetic influence for males and negligible genetic influence for females. Interestingly, the amount of alcohol consumed shows greater genetic influence than diagnosed alcoholism (7). In contrast to diagnosed alcoholism, autism, which until the 1970s was assumed to be environmental in origin, appears to be among the most heritable psychiatric disorders.

In addition to the examples in Figure 1, the following disorders have also shown some evidence of genetic influence: specific language disorder, panic disorder, eating disorders, antisocial personality disorder, and Tourette's syndrome. Some behavioral disorders such as mild mental retardation have not yet been analyzed by genetic research.

Figure 2 summarizes results from twin studies for some of the best studied common medical disorders. Like behavioral disorders, some medical disorders show substantial genetic influence—rheumatoid arthritis, peptic ulcers, and idiopathic epilepsy. Others show more modest genetic influence, such as hypertension and ischemic heart disease. Several common medical disorders show negligible genetic

influence. For example, twin studies suggest negligible heritability for breast cancer as a whole in the general population, even though a rare early on-set familial type is linked to markers on chromosome 17 (8). By comparing Figures 1 and 2, it appears that behavioral disorders on average show greater genetic influence than common medical disorders.

Behavioral Dimensions

Data on behavioral variability within the normal range also indicate widespread genetic influence. Figure 3 summarizes results of twin studies for personality (neuroticism and extraversion), vocational interests, scholastic achievement, and cognitive abilities (memory, spatial reasoning, processing speed, verbal reasoning, and general intelligence). For quantitative dimensions, the size of the genetic effect can be estimated roughly by doubling the difference between MZ and DZ correlations. This estimate is called heritability, which is a statistic that describes the proportion of phenotypic variance in a population that can be attributed to genetic influences. Heritabilities range from about 40 to 50% for personality, vocational interests, scholastic achievement, and general intelligence. For specific cognitive abilities, heritabilities are also in this range for spatial reasoning and verbal reasoning but lower for memory and processing speed. Recent research also suggests genetic influence for other cognitive measures such as information processing, electroencephalographic evoked potentials, and cerebral glucose metabolism (9). Examples of recently studied noncognitive behaviors that show genetic influence are self-esteem (10), social attitudes (11), and sexual orientation (12). Little is known about genetic effects for perception and learning and for many health-related behaviors (for example, responses to stress, exercise, and diet).

Beyond Heritability

Quantitative genetic research has gone beyond merely demonstrating the importance of genetics for complex human behaviors. Three new techniques are especially useful for this advancement, as can be seen most clearly in research on cognitive abilities, the most studied domain of behavior. First, developmental genetic analysis monitors change in genetic effects during development. For cognitive ability, genetic factors become increasingly important for general intelligence throughout the lifespan, reaching heritabilities as high as 80% later in life (13). This is the highest heritability reported for any behavioral dimension. In addition, with longitudinal genetic designs, it is possible to investigate the etiology of age-to-age change—that is, to what extent do genetic effects at one age overlap with genetic effects at another age? For general cognitive ability, longitudinal genetic analyses during childhood suggest that genetic effects do not completely overlap from age to age, indicating changes in genetic effects, especially at the early school years (14).

A second advance is multivariate genetic analysis, which assesses genetic contributions to covariance among traits rather than to the variance of each trait considered separately. Multivariate analyses of specific cognitive abilities suggest that genetic influences on all specific cognitive abilities overlap to a surprising degree, although some genetic effects are unique to each ability (15). This finding implies that genes associated with one cognitive ability are likely to be associated with other cognitive abilities as well. Multivariate analyses also indicate that genetic effects on scholastic achievement overlap completely with genetic effects on general cognitive ability (16). Such techniques can also be used to address the fundamental issues of heterogeneity and comorbidity

for psychiatric disorders, contributing to a nosology at the level of genetic effects rather than at the level of symptoms. Longitudinal and multivariate approaches have been facilitated by advances in analysis that test the fit between a model and observed data (17).

The third example, called extremes analysis, addresses genetic links between normal and abnormal behavior. If, as seems likely, multiple genes are responsible for genetic influences on behavioral dimensions and disorders, a continuum of genetic risk is likely to extend from normal to abnormal behavior. For example, is major depressive disorder merely the extreme of a continuous dimension of genetic and environmental variability? A quantitative genetic technique developed during the past decade investigates the extent to which a disorder is the etiological extreme of a continuous dimension (18). Preliminary research with this approach suggests that some common behavioral disorders such as depressive symptoms (19), phobias (20), and reading disability (21) represent the genetic extremes of continuous dimensions.

Nurture as well as Nature

Another way in which genetic research has gone beyond merely documenting genetic influence is to focus on the implications of genetic research for understanding environmental influences. Genetics research provides the best available evidence for the importance of nonheritable factors. Usually genetic factors do not account for more than about half of the variance for behavioral disorders and dimensions. Most of the disorders and dimensions summarized in Figures 1 and 3 show as much nonheritable as heritable influence. The current enthusiasm for genetics should not obscure the important contribution of nonheritable factors, even though these are more difficult to investigate. For environmental transmission, there is nothing comparable to the laws of hereditary transmission or to the gene as a basic unit of transmission. It should be noted that the "environmental" in quantitative genetics denotes all nonheritable factors, including nontransmissible stochastic DNA events such as somatic mutation, imprinting, and unstable DNA sequences (22).

Two specific discoveries from genetic research are important for understanding environmental influences. First, the way in which the environment influences behavioral development contradicts socialization theories from Freud onward. For example, the fact that psychopathology runs in families has reasonably, but wrongly, been interpreted to indicate that psychopathology is under environmental control. Research shows that genetics generally accounts for this familial resemblance. Environmental influences on most behavioral disorders and dimensions serve to make children growing up in the same family different, not similar (23). This effect, called nonshared environment, leads to the question of how children in the same family experience such different environments. For example, what are the nonshared experiences that make identical twins growing up in the same family so often discordant for schizophrenia?

The second genetic discovery about the environment concerns what has been called the nature of nurture (24). Many widely used measures of the environment show genetic influence in dozens of twin and adoption studies. Research with diverse twin and adoption experimental designs has found genetic influence on parenting, childhood accidents, television viewing, classroom environments, peer groups, social support, work environments, life events, divorce, exposure to drugs, education, and socioeconomic status (25). Although these results might seem paradoxical, what they mean is that ostensible measures of the environment appear to assess genetically influenced characteristics of individuals. To some extent, individuals create their own experiences for genetic reasons (26). In addition, genetic factors contribute to the prediction of developmental outcomes from environmental measures (25). For example, genetics is part of the reason why parenting behavior predicts children's cognitive development and why negative life events predict depression.

Quantitative Genetics and Molecular Genetics

Quantitative genetic research is needed to inform molecular genetic research. Most fundamentally, quantitative genetic research can steer molecular genetic research toward the most heritable syndromes and combinations of symptoms. Genes are less likely to be identified for complex behaviors that show little genetic influence in the population unless some aspect of the trait can be found that is more highly heritable, as in the case of breast cancer. Although genetic influence has been detected for many behavioral disorders and dimensions (Figures 1 and 3), little is known about the most heritable aspects within these domains.

Even more useful is quantitative genetic research that goes beyond heritability to take advantage of

new techniques mentioned above. For example, developmental genetic research shows that genetic influence increasingly affects cognitive abilities throughout the life-span. This suggests that molecular genetic research on cognitive abilities is most likely to be successful later in life when phenotype better represents genotype. Multivariate genetic research indicates that genes associated with one cognitive ability are likely to be associated with other cognitive abilities. The clue here is that molecular genetic research will profit from focusing on what cognitive abilities have in common. Quantitative genetic research suggests that common disorders represent the quantitative extremes of continuous dimensions. This suggests that genes associated with disorders can be found by investigating continuous dimensions and vice versa. Finally, quantitative genetic research suggests that nongenetic factors generally account for as much variance as genetic factors, that behavior-relevant environmental factors generally operate in a nonshared manner to make children growing up in the same family different, not similar, and that genetic factors play a role in individuals actively creating their own experience. Molecular genetic research will benefit from incorporating environmental measures, especially measures of nonshared environment.

MOLECULAR GENETICS

Quantitative genetic research leaves little room for doubt about the importance of genetic influence in behavior. The next step is to begin to identify some of these genes. This is obviously a more difficult step, especially in the case of complex traits, and some of the initial steps in this direction have faltered. However, the difficulty of identifying specific genes underlying complex traits should not obscure the evidence for the importance of genetic influence.

Many rare disorders such as Huntington's disease show simple Mendelian patterns of inheritance for which defects in a single gene are the necessary and sufficient cause of the disorder. Linkage analysis and the rapidly expanding map of the human genome guarantee that the underlying genes will be mapped and eventually cloned, as has already happened for scores of single-gene disorders. The new frontier for molecular genetics lies with common and complex dimensions, disorders, and diseases. The challenge is to use molecular genetic techniques to identify genes involved in such complex systems influenced by multiple genes as well as multiple nongenetic factors, especially when any single gene is neither necessary nor sufficient. Because this challenge is the same for complex behaviors as for common medical disorders, their futures will be intertwined.

One Gene, One Disorder?

Complex traits that show no simple Mendelian pattern of inheritance are unlikely to yield simple genetic answers. For this reason, it has often been assumed that complex disorders consist of a concatenation of several disorders, each caused by a single gene, or at least a gene of major effect that largely accounts for genetic influence. Indeed, one definition of the word "complex" is a composite of distinguishable constituents. This could be called the one gene, one disorder (OGOD) hypothesis. The OGOD hypothesis is more than a simple single-gene hypothesis. It does not look for a single gene for complex traits, but rather assumes that complex traits comprise several subtraits each influenced by a single gene. Even if single genes corresponding to subtypes of a disorder cannot be found throughout the population, the hope is that by analyzing linkage in large pedigrees, it may be possible to find a single gene responsible for a family's particular version of the disorder.

The OGOD strategy has already been successful for some complex behavioral disorders, especially severe mental retardation. A classic example is the distinct type of mental retardation, phenylketonuria (PKU), caused by recessive mutations in the phenylalanine hydroxylase (PAH) gene on chromosome 12 (27). Although its incidence is low (fewer than 1 in 10,000 births), PKU accounted for about 1% of institutionalized mentally retarded individuals before diets low in phenylalanine were implemented.

Recently, another distinct type of mental retardation was discovered, fragile X, which is caused by an unstable expansion of a CGG repeat in the *FMR-1* gene on the X chromosome (28). Its incidence is 1 in 1250 males and 1 in 2500 females, making it the single most important cause of mental retardation after Down syndrome. Another fragile site on the X chromosome has been linked to a less common form of mental retardation (29). In addition to these defects in single genes necessary and sufficient to develop distinct forms of mental retardation, more than 100 other rare single-gene disorders include mental retardation among their symptoms (30).

Another example of the success of the OGOD approach for behavior involves a common syndrome, dementia, which is marked by progressive memory loss and confusion. Dementia of the Alzheimer's disease (AD) type includes a rare, familial dementia that appears in middle age, shows a dominant Mendelian pattern of inheritance, but which accounts for fewer than 1% of AD cases. Mutations in the amyloid precursor protein gene on chromosome 21 segregate with the disease in some families with autosomal dominant AD (31). The majority of such cases are linked to chromosome 14 (32), although the gene is not yet identified.

An example of a successful OGOD approach outside the cognitive realm of retardation and dementia involves a particular type of violence. A point mutation in the monoamine oxidase A (MAOA) gene, which disrupts MAOA activity, has been linked to impulsive violence in one Dutch family (33).

The well-known false positive linkage results for bipolar affective disorder and schizophrenia (34) and the more recent failure to replicate reported X-linkage for bipolar affective disorder (35) were caused by procedural and interpretative problems rather than by faults with the analytic technology itself. If a single gene is responsible for genetic influence on a trait, linkage can detect it. Although the entire genome has not yet been screened for linkage with these disorders, it is possible that there are no genes of major effect to be found despite clear twin and adoption evidence for genetic influence. Conventional linkage analysis of extended pedigrees is unlikely to have sufficient power to detect a gene unless the gene accounts for most of the genetic variance. Newer linkage methods such as "affected-relative-pair" linkage designs are more robust than traditional pedigree studies because they do not depend on assumptions about mode of inheritance (36). These newer methods may be able to detect genes of somewhat smaller effect size if large samples (for example, several hundred sibling pairs) are used. They can also incorporate quantitative measures (37). Nonetheless, linkages found with these methods imply that a single gene explains most of the genetic effects on the trait, especially if sample sizes are not large.

Two behavioral examples involve linkages reported for sexual orientation and reading disability. For sexual orientation, linkage has been reported with markers on the X chromosome in a study of 40 homosexual brothers selected for pedigrees consistent with maternal transmission (38). Reading disability has been linked to markers on chromosome 15 and possibly to chromosome 6 in a family pedigree linkage analysis (39) as well as sib-pair linkage analyses of sibling pairs in these same families (40), although later reports show less evidence for chromosome 15 linkage.

Quantitative Trait Loci

Quantitative geneticists assume that genetic influences on complex, common behavioral disorders are the result of multiple genes of varying effect size. These multiple-gene effects can contribute additively and interchangeably, like risk factors, to vulnerability to a disorder. In this case, the word "complex" means "complicated" in the sense of multigenic and multifactorial rather than a composite of OGOD constituents. Any single gene in a multigene system is neither necessary nor sufficient to cause a disorder. In other words, genetic effects involve probabilistic propensities rather than predetermined programming.

Genes that contribute to genetic variance in quantitative traits are called quantitative trait loci (QTL) (41). One implication of a multigene system is that genotypes are distributed quantitatively (dimensionally) even when traits are assessed phenotypically by dichotomous diagnoses. For this reason, the term QTL is apropos for the liability to diagnosed disorders, not just quantitative traits. The term QTL replaces the word "polygenic," which literally means "multiple genes" but has come to connote many genes of such infinitesimal effect size that they are unidentifiable. QTL denote multiple genes of varying effect size. The hope is to be able to detect QTL of modest effect size. "Oligogenic" is another word that has been used as a substitute for polygenic, but it presupposes that only a few ("oligo") genes are involved.

QTL examples have been detected by allelic association, often called linkage disequilibrium. Allelic association refers to a correlation in the population between a phenotype and a particular allele, usually assessed as an allelic or genotypic frequency difference between cases and controls. Allelic association has often been used to pin down a single-gene effect, but it also provides the statistical power to detect small QTL effects, as discussed below. Allelic associations involving small genetic effects in multiple-gene systems could be called QTL associations. The best QTL example for a common medical disorder is provided by the associations between apolipoprotein genes and risk for cardiovascular disease, accounting for as much as a quarter of the genetic variance (42).

Two recent QTL associations from medical research are especially noteworthy in relation to complex behaviors. A deletion polymorphism in the angiotensin-converting enzyme (ACE) gene is associated with cardiovascular disease independent of effects on lipid metabolism (43). The frequency of individuals homozygous for the ACE deletion was 32% for patients with myocardial infarction and 27% for controls. This slightly increased relative risk of 1.3, which accounts for less than 1% of the liability for the disorder, is significant statistically because the sample was extremely large (610 cases and 733 controls). The second example involves longevity, which is only modestly heritable. Significant associations with longevity have recently been reported for both the ACE deletion and allele 4 of the apolipoprotein E (Apo-E) gene (44). Allelic frequencies for 325 centenarians differed from 20- to 70-year-old controls for the ACE deletion (62% as compared with 53%) and for Apo-E4 (5% as compared with 11%). Again, these modest allelic frequency differences are statistically significant because the sample size was so large. In addition, Apo-E2 was associated with increased longevity.

The best QTL example for a behavioral disorder is the recently discovered association between late onset AD and Apo-E4 (45). Unlike the rare, early onset, autosomal dominant form of dementia discussed above, the prevalence of AD increases steeply with age from less than 1% at age 65 years to 15% in the ninth decade (46). The frequency of the Apo-E4 allele is about 0.40 in individuals with AD as compared with 0.15 in control populations. The odds ratio, or approximate relative risk, is 6.4 for individuals with one or two Apo-E4 alleles (47). The Apo-E4 allele is neither necessary nor sufficient to develop the disorder: Many individuals with AD do not possess an Apo-E4 allele, and many individuals with an Apo-E4 allele do not develop AD. It has been estimated that Apo-E4 contributes approximately 17% to the population variance in liability to develop the disorder (47). Although this is a large effect for a QTL, it is much too small to qualify as a single-gene effect. A linkage study of 32 pedigrees found only relatively modest evidence of linkage for the Apo-E4 region of chromosome 19 (48). A QTL of this magnitude may be near the lower limit of detection by linkage analysis with realistic sample sizes, as discussed below.

We predict that QTL associations will soon be found for other complex human behaviors. For example, a weak association has been suggested for paranoid schizophrenia in seven of nine studies with the A9 allele of human leukocyte antigen (HLA), yielding a combined relative risk of 1.6, which accounts for about 1% of the liability to the

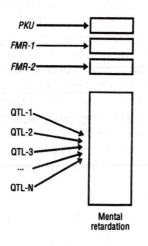

FIGURE 4   Complex behaviors such as mental retardation are likely to involve single genes, each responsible for a distinct subtype of the disorder, as well as QTL that contribute probabilistically and interchangeably to genetic risk.

disorder (49). Severe alcoholism (50) and other forms of drug abuse (51) have been reported in several studies to be associated with the *A1* allele of dopamine receptor D_2, but the association remains controversial (52). A QTL association study of general cognitive ability has found two suggestive but as yet unreplicated associations for DNA markers in or near neurally relevant genes (53). Thyroid receptor-gene has been associated with symptoms of attention deficit-hyperactivity disorder (54). However, because this allelic association was found in individuals hospitalized for resistance to thyroid hormone, it is possible that symptoms of hyperactivity were due to the disease itself.

As illustrated in Figure 4 for mental retardation, both the OGOD and QTL approaches are likely to contribute to the elucidation of the genetic basis of complex behaviors. Although we have emphasized the distinction between the OGOD and QTL approaches, we recognize that in fact there is a continuum of varying effect sizes. The relative contributions of single-gene effects at one end of the continuum and undetectably small effects at the other end are unknown. If genetic effects on complex behaviors are single-gene effects, traditional linkage approaches will detect them. If effects are

infinitesimal (for example, accounting for less than 0.1% of the variance), they will never be detected. In the middle of the continuum, QTL of large effect size (for example, genes accounting for 10% of the variance) might be detected by the newer linkage strategies. In the example of *Apo-E* and AD, linkage analysis suggested the possibility of a gene in this region of chromosome 19, and association analysis identified the gene. QTL of small effect size (for example, genes accounting for 1% of the variance) cannot be detected by linkage. Allelic association can detect such QTL, as in the example of *ACE* and myocardial infarction.

Of the few loci that have been implicated to date for complex behaviors (Table 1), most are genes of major effect rather than QTL, especially the indisputable linkages for PKU, fragile X, and early onset, dominant dementia. This may be the result of reliance on linkage approaches that are only able to detect genes of major effect. The replicated association between *Apo-E4* and AD makes it likely that more systematic association studies will be undertaken to identify QTL with modest effects on complex behaviors.

TABLE 1
Reported Linkages and Associations with Complex Behaviors

Behavior	Gene, chromosome	Reference
Mental Retardation		
Phenylketonuria	*PAH*, 12	(27)
Fragile X-1	*FMR-1*, X	(28)
Fragile X-e	*FRAX-E*, X	(29)
Alzheimer's Disease		
Early onset,		
dominant	*APP*, 21	(31)
	?, 14	(32)
Late onset	*APO-E*, 19	(43)
Violence	*MAOA*, X	(33)
Hyperactivity	Thyroid receptor–β,3	(54)
Paranoid		
schizophrenia	*HLA-A*, 6	(49)
Alcoholism,		
drug abuse	Dopamine receptor–D_2, 11	(50, 51)
Sexual orientation	?, X	(38)
Reading disability	?, 15	(39, 40)

Allelic Association

The advantage of linkage approaches is that they can identify genes without a priori knowledge of pathological processes in a systematic search of the genome by using a few hundred highly polymorphic DNA markers. Such systematic screens of the genome can also exclude the presence of genes of major effect. However, they cannot exclude small QTL effects, at least when realistic sample sizes are used. We predict that failure to find major gene effects by exclusion mapping for complex behaviors will by default provide the best evidence for QTL. The disadvantage of traditional linkage designs is that they are only able to detect single genes or genes largely responsible for the trait.

Although linkage remains the strategy of choice for detecting single-gene effects and for identifying the largest QTL effects, other strategies are needed to detect QTL of smaller effect size. Most likely, new techniques will soon be developed to reach this goal. For the present, allelic association represents an increasingly used strategy that is complementary to linkage (55). Allelic association can provide the statistical power needed to detect QTL of small effect size. As in the examples of allelic associations between myocardial infarction and the *ACE* deletion polymorphism and between longevity and *ACE* and *Apo-E*, statistical power can be increased to detect small QTL associations by increasing sample sizes of relatively easy-to-obtain unrelated subjects. Such small QTL effects could not be detected by linkage analysis with realistic sample sizes.

As noted above, allelic association refers to a correlation between a phenotype and a particular allele in the population. Loose linkage between two loci does not result in allelic associations in the population because alleles on the same chromosome at all but the tightest linked loci are separated by recombination with sufficient frequency that both sets of alleles quickly return to linkage equilibrium in the population. When allelic association depends on linkage disequilibrium between a DNA marker and the trait locus, the marker must be very close to the trait locus and both must have low rates of mutation. For example, when the marker and trait locus are separated by about one million base pairs (that is, a recombination fraction of 0.01), an allelic association would return halfway to equilibrium in about 70 generations or about 2000 years (56). For this reason, allelic association research on complex traits can use markers in or near relevant genes, be-

cause the markers are likely to be in linkage disequilibrium with any functional polymorphism in the gene.

Linkage disequilibrium is not the only cause of allelic association between a marker and a trait. Allelic association can also occur because the marker itself codes for a functional polymorphism that directly affects the phenotype (pleiotropy). Use of such functional polymorphisms greatly enhances the power of the allelic association approach to detect QTL (57). It is noteworthy that both the *Apo-E4* and *ACE* deletion markers show direct physiological effects. The new generation of complementary DNA markers and techniques to detect point mutations in coding sequences are rapidly producing markers of this type.

Another distinction between linkage and allelic association involves the issue of dimensions and disorders. As mentioned earlier, complex behaviors in multigene systems are likely to be distributed as continuous quantitative dimensions rather than as qualitative dichotomies. Quantitative dimensions cannot be easily analyzed by linkage, which is based on cosegregation between a DNA marker and a disorder, although a newly developed sib-pair linkage technique for use with quantitative measures employing interval mapping is promising (37). In contrast, allelic association is as easily applied to quantitative dimensions as to qualitative disorders.

Limitations of allelic association analysis include ethnic stratification and chance positive results when many markers are examined. The possibility that an allelic association might be the result of ethnic differences can be investigated by using within-family controls (58). False positives can best be addressed by replication (59). The major limitation to the use of allelic association analysis is that a systematic search of the genome would require thousands of DNA markers separated by about 500 kb or less and would detect only QTL with low mutation rates.

Until such massive genotyping is feasible, allelic association will be limited to screening functional polymorphisms or DNA markers in or near possible candidate genes. For complex behaviors, the problem is that few candidate genes are known that are as specific as the apolipoprotein genes associated with cardiovascular disease. Nonetheless, many genes expressed in the brain are likely to make very small contributions to the genetic variance for complex behaviors, which can be detected with large samples. A single very large representative sample could be used to screen functional polymorphisms for a multitude of common behavioral as well as medical dimensions and disorders. Inclusion of sib pairs would permit sib-pair linkage analyses as well as provide within-family control groups for allelic association analyses. Such a sample could serve as a cumulative and integrative resource for QTL allelic association research.

The goal of the genome project is to sequence the entire human genome. However, there is no single human genome. We need to determine the variability of genes between individuals and then to determine how this variation contributes to phenotypic differences between individuals. For complex traits (including behavior), this will be facilitated by a merger between quantitative genetics and molecular genetics.

CONCLUSIONS

Most of what is currently known about the genetics of complex human behavior comes from quantitative genetic research. Twin and adoption studies have documented ubiquitous genetic influence for most reliably measured behavioral dimensions and disorders. More quantitative genetic research is now needed that goes beyond merely documenting the presence of genetic influence. This will guide molecular genetic research by identifying the most heritable domains of behavior and the most heritable dimensions and disorders within domains. New quantitative genetic techniques can also track the developmental course of genetic contributions to behavior, identify genetic heterogeneity, and explore genetic links between the normal and abnormal. The same quantitative genetic data that document significant and substantial genetic influence for complex behavior also provide the best available evidence for the importance of nongenetic factors. Possible environmental factors need to be investigated in the context of genetically sensitive designs to follow up on the far-reaching findings of nonshared environment and genetic influences on experience and to explore the developmental processes of genotype-environment correlation and interaction by which genotypes become phenotypes. This research will in turn facilitate molecular genetic attempts to identify specific genes that contribute to genetic variance in complex behaviors. The confluence of quantitative genetics and molecular genetics will be synergistic for the elucidation of complex human behaviors.

Questions

1. Why have twin and adoption studies been used to assess the relative contributions of genetics and environment to development?

2. What is the "nonshared environment" and how does it help us understand why children in the same family can be so different from each other?

3. Considering both genetic and environmental contributions to development, what are the direct and indirect influences that parents have on their children's development?

References and Notes

1. R. Plomin and G. E. McClearn, Eds., *Nature, Nurture, and Psychology* (American Psychological Association, Washington, DC, 1993).

2. R. Plomin, J. C. DeFries, G. E. McClearn, *Behavioral Genetics: A Primer* (Freeman, New York, ed. 2, 1990).

3. I. I. Gottesman, *Schizophrenia Genetics: The Origins of Madness* (Freeman, New York, 1991). Resemblance for fraternal twins is often greater than for nontwin siblings. This suggests greater shared environment for twins, which may be a result of shared prenatal environment or growing up in the same family at exactly the same age. This does not affect the twin design's test of genetic influence, which compares the resemblance of fraternal twins to the resemblance of identical twins.

4. L. L. Heston, *Br. J. Psychiatry* 112, 819 (1966).

5. P. McGuffin, M. J. Owen, M. C. O'Donovan, A. Thapar, I. I. Gottesman, *Seminars in Psychiatric Genetics* (Gaskell, London, 1994).

6. Although the size of the difference between MZ and DZ twin concordances suggests the magnitude of the genetic effect, dichotomous concordance data present statistical problems in providing estimates of heritability, the statistic representing the effect size of genetic influence in a population. For this reason, concordances are usually converted to liability (tetrachoric) correlations, which assume that a continuous distribution of liability underlies the dichotomous data (5). Heritability estimates based on liability correlations estimate genetic influence on a

hypothetical construct of continuous liability that is derived from a dichotomous diagnosis; it is not the heritability of the disorder as diagnosed. Such estimates of the heritability of liability are often higher than the twin concordance data would suggest. For example, for schizophrenia, some estimates of the heritability of liability exceed 0.80, even though the MZ concordance is less than 0.50. Such high liability heritabilities might be misleading to molecular geneticists searching for specific genes when their research is based on the disorder as diagnosed. As discussed later, there is good reason to believe that multiple-gene influences on complex disorders result in continuous dimensions rather than dichotomous disorders. An important research direction that will increase the power of genetics research is to attempt to assess dimensions directly rather than to assume them from dichotomous diagnoses.

7. J. K. Kaprio *et al.*, *Alcohol. Clin. Exp. Res.* **11**, 249 (1987).

8. J. M. Hall *et al.*, *Science* **250**, 1684 (1990).

9. P. A. Vernon, Ed., *Biological Approaches to the Study of Human Intelligence* (Ablex, Norwood, NJ, 1993).

10. R. Plomin, *Social Dev.* **3**, 37 (1994).

11. L. J. Eaves, H. J. Eysenck, N. G. Martin, *Genes, Culture, and Personality: An Empirical Approach* (Academic Press, New York, 1989).

12. . M. Bailey and R. C. Pillard, *Arch. Gen. Psychiatry* **48**, 1089 (1991); ___, M. C. Neale, Y. Agyei, *ibid.* **50**, 217 (1993).

13. M. McGue, T. J. Bouchard Jr., W. G. Iacono, D. T. Lykken, in (*1*), pp. 59–76.

14. D. W. Fulker, S. S. Chemy, L. R. Cardon, in (*1*), pp. 77–97.

15. N. L. Pedersen, R. Plomin, G. E. McClearn, *Intelligence*, in press.

16. L. A. Thompson, D. K. Detterman, R. Plomin, *Psychol. Sci.* **2**, 158 (1991); S. J. Wadsworth, in *Nature and Nurture During Middle Childhood*, J. C. DeFries, R. Plomin, D. W. Fulker, Eds. (Blackwell, Cambridge, MA, 1994), pp. 86–101.

17. M. C. Neale and L. R. Cardon, *Methodology for Genetic Studies of Twins and Families* (Kluwer Academic, Norwell, MA, 1992).

18. C. DeFries and D. W. Fulker, *Behav. Gen.* **15**, 467 (1985).

19. R. Plomin, in *Biological Risk Factors for Psychosocial Disorders,* M. Rutter and P. Casaer, Eds. (Cambridge Univ. Press, Cambridge, 1991), pp. 101–138.

20. . Stevenson, N. Batten, M. Chemer, *J. Child Psychol. Psychiatry* **33**, 977 (1992).

21. J. C. DeFries and J. J. Gillis in (*1*), pp. 121–145.

22. P. McGuffin, P. Asherson, M. J. Owen, A. Farmer, *Br. J. Psychiatry* **164**, 593 (1994).

23. R. Plomin and D. Daniels *Behav. Brain Sci.* **10**, 1 (1987).

24. R. Plomin and C. S. Bergeman, *ibid.* **14**, 373 (1991).

25. R. Plomin, *Genetics and Experience: The Interplay Between Nature and Nurture* (Sage, Newbury Park, CA, 1994).

26. D. C. Rowe, *The Limits of Family Influence* (Guilford, New York, 1994); S. Scarr, *Child Dev.* **63**, 1 (1992).

27. S. L. C. Woo, in *Genes, Brain, and Behavior,* P. R. McHugh and V. A. McKusick, Eds. (Raven, New York, 1991), pp. 193-203.

28. A. J. Verkerk *et al., Cell* **65**, 905 (1991).

29. S. J. L. Knight *et al., ibid.* **74**, 127 (1993).

30. J. Walhsten, *J. Ment. Defic. Res.* **34**, 11 (1990).

31. A. Goate *et al., Nature* **349**, 704 (1991).

32. G. D. Schellenberg *et al., Science* **258**, 668 (1992).

33. H. G. Brunner, M. Nelen, X. 0. Breakefield, H. H. Ropers, B. A. van Oost, *ibid.* **262**, 578 (1993).

34. M. J. Owen and M. J. Mullan, *Trends Neurosci.* **13**, 29 (1990).

35. M. Baron *et al., Nature Genet.* **3**, 49 (1993).

36. N. Risch, *Am. J. Hum. Genet.* **46**, 229 (1990).

37. D. W. Fulker and L. R. Carbon, *ibid.*, in press.

38. D. H. Hamer, S. Hu, V. L. Magnuson, N. Hu, A. M. L. Pattatucci, *Science* **261**, 321 (1993).

39. S. D. Smith, W. J. Kimberling, B. F. Pennington, H. A. Lubs, *ibid.* **219**, 1345 (1993); S. D. Smith, B. F. Pennington, W. J. Kimberling, P. S. Ing, *J. Am. Acad. Child Adolesc. Psychiatry* **29**, 204 (1990).

40. S. D. Smith, W. J. Kimberling, B. F. Pennington, *Read. Writ. Interdiscipl. J.* **3**, 285 (1991); D. W. Fulker *et al., ibid.* **4**, 107 (1991).

41. H. Gelderman, *Theor. Appl. Genet.* **46**, 319 (1975); E. S. Lander and D. Botstein, *Genetics* **121**, 185 (1989).

42. S. E. Humphries, *Atherosclerosis* **72**, 89 (1988); C. F. Sing and E. A. Boerwinkle, in *Molecular Approaches to Human Polygenic Disease,* G. Bock and G. M. Collins, Eds. (Wiley, Chichester, UK, 1987), pp. 99–122.

43. F. Cambien *et al., Nature* **359**, 641 (1992).

44. F. Schächter *et al., Nature Genet.* **6**, 29 (1994).

45. E. H. Corder *et al., Science* **261**, 921 (1993).

46. I. Skoog, L. Nilsson, B. Palmertz, L. A. Andreasson, A. Svanborg, *N. Engl. J. Med.* **328**, 153 (1993).

47. M. J. Owen, M. Liddle, P. McGuffin, *Br. Med. J.* **308**, 672 (1994).

48. M. A. Pericak-Vance *et al., Am. J. Hum. Genet.* **48**, 1034 (1991).

49. P. McGuffin and E. Sturt, *Hum. Hered.* **36**, 65 (1986).

50. E. P. Noble, *Behav. Genet.* **23**, 119 (1993).

51. G. Uhl, K. Blum, E. P. Noble, S. Smith, *Trends Neurosci.* **16**, 83 (1993).

52. J. Gelrnter, D. Goldman, N. Risch, *J. Am. Med. Assoc.* **269**, 1673 (1993).

53. R. Plomin *et al.*, *Behav. Genet.* **24**, 107 (1994).

54. P. Hauser *et al.*, *N. Engl. J. Med.* **328**, 997 (1993).

55. M. J. Owen and P. McGuffin, *J. Med. Genet.* **30**, 638 (1993).

56. N. E. Morton, *Outline of Genetic Epidemiology* (Karger, Basel, Switzerland, 1982).

57. J. L. Sobell, L. L. Heston, S. S. Sommer, *Genomics* **12**,1 (1992).

58. C. T. Falk and P. Rubinstein, *Ann. Hum. Genet.* **51**, 227 (1987); J. D. Terwilliger and J. Ott, *Hum. Hered.* **42**, 337 (1992).

59. J. L. Sobell, L. L. Heston, S. S. Sommer, *Am J. Med. Genet. (Neuropsychiatr. Genet.)* **46**, 23 (1993).

60. Alcoholism: M. McGue, in (*1*), pp. 245–268; schizophrenia: I. I. Gottesman, *Schizophrenia Genetics: The Origins of Madness* (Freeman, New York, 1991); Alzheimer's disease: A. L. A. Bergem and E. Kringlen, *Psychiatr. Genet.* **2**, 9 (1991); A. F. Wright, in *The New Genetics of Mental Illness*, P. McGuffin and R. Murray, Eds. (Butterworth-Heinemann, London, 1991), pp. 259–273; autism: S. L. Smalley, R. F. Asamow, M. A. Spence, *Arch. Gen. Psychiatry* **45**, 953 (1988); major affective disorder: P. McGuffin and M. P. Sergeant, in *The New Genetics of Mental Illness*, P. McGuffin and R. Murray, Eds. (Butterworth-Heinemann, London, 1991), pp. 165–181; reading disability: J. C. DeFries and J. J. Gillis in (*1*), pp. 121–145.

61. Parkinson's disease: R. Eldridge and W. Rocca, in *The Genetic Basis of Common Diseases*, R. A. King, J. I. Rotter, A. G. Motulsky, Eds. (Oxford Univ. Press, New York, 1992), pp. 775–791; breast cancer: N. V. Holm, M. Hauge, 0. M. Jensen, *Cancer Surv.* **1**, 17 (1982); chronic obstructive pulmonary disease, hypertension, and ischemic heart disease: K. S. Kendler and C. D. Robinette, *Am. J. Psychiatry* **140**, 1551 (1983); rheumatoid arthritis: R. A. King, in *The Genetic Basis of Common Diseases*, R. A. King. J. I. Rotter, A. G. Motulsky, Eds. (Oxford Univ. Press. New York, 1992), pp. 596–624; peptic ulcer (diagnosed by x-ray): J. I. Rotter, T. Shohat, G. M. Petersen, in *ibid.*, pp. 240–278; epilepsy: T. B. Bird, in *ibid.*, pp. 732–752.

62. Neuroticism and extraversion: J. C. Loehlin. *Genes and Environment in Personality Development* (Sage, Newbury Park, CA 1992); vocational interests: J. C. Loehlin and R. C. Nichols *Heredity, Environment, and Personality* (Univ. of Texas Press, Austin, 1976); C.A. Roberts and C. B. Johansson, *J. Vocational Behav.* **4**, 237 (1974); scholastic achievement: J. C. Loehlin and R. C. Nichols, *Heredity, Environment, and Personality* (Univ. of Texas Press, Austin, 1976); specific cognitive abilities: L. F. Schoenfeldt, *Meas. Eval. Guid.* **1**, 130 (1968); M. Wictorin *Bidrag til Raknefardighetens Psykologi, en Tvillingundersokning* (Elanders, Göteborg, Sweden, 1952); general intelligence: T. J. Bouchard Jr. and M. McGue, *Science* **212**, 1055 (1981).

63. Supported by grant HD-27694 from the National Institutes of Child Health and Human Development. The article benefited from suggestions by J. C. Crabbe, J. C. DeFries, L. Rodriguez, and K. J. Saudino.

7

Neonatal Behavior Among Urban Zambians and Americans

T. BERRY BRAZELTON, BARBARA KOSLOWSKI, AND EDWARD TRONICK

One way in which psychologists study the contributions of biological and experiential factors in human development is by comparing behaviors and abilities across individuals reared in very different cultural settings. In the research described below, T. Berry Brazelton, Barbara Koslowski, and Edward Tronick compared newborns in Zambia and the United States. They were interested in infants' ability to regulate their emotional states and in how they react to the environment over the first ten days of life. They found differences in the rate that these skills developed in these two populations. But more interesting than the identification of these differences so early in life is how such differences developed. Brazelton and colleagues offer a thought-provoking hypothesis as to how genetic and nongenetic inheritance may be coordinated with child-rearing practices to produce particular patterns of human growth.

Geber's classic report of infant development in Africa (Geber and Dean, 1959) suggested that African babies are developmentally more advanced in their first year than are their Western European counterparts. Her tests reported precocity in motor development between the two groups, but did not document sensory or cognitive differences.

Studies of other cultures (Ainsworth, 1967; Brazelton et al., 1969; Freedman and Freedman, 1969; Goldberg, 1971; Schaffer, 1960) have supported

Reprinted with permission from *Journal of Child Psychiatry, 15*, 1976, 97–107. Copyright 1976 by Pergamon Press Ltd.

This research was supported in part by a grant from the National Early Childhood Research Council, Inc. (Edcom), Princeton, N.J., and was presented at the Biennial Meeting of the Society for Research in Child Development, Minneapolis, Minn., in 1971.

Reprints may be requested from Dr. Brazelton, 23 Hawthorn Street, Cambridge, Mass. 02138.

Geber's finding that developmental differences can be found early in a child's life—indeed, as early as the neonatal period. Several of these studies also suggested that infants in different cultural groups showed differences in behavior at birth that might influence the outcome of their subsequent development.

We wondered whether these observations might be relevant to observed Zambian-American differences in early childhood. Would these groups of infants differ during the neonatal period? Would these differences lie in interactive and perceptual abilities as well as in motor development?

PROCEDURE

Ten Zambian and 10 American infants were seen on days 1, 5, and 10 after birth. All mothers were reported to have had normal pregnancies terminated at 40 weeks, and no bleeding or infection was noted.

The U.S. babies were delivered via "natural childbirth": no anesthesia was administered to the mothers, and no more than one injection of Nisentil (a mild muscle relaxant, 30 mgm.) was given during the period of labor 6 hours prior to delivery. No other medication was administered. All the infants were firstborn and came from middle-class families. They were normal at birth. Apgars were above 8-9-9 at 1, 5, and 15 minutes (Apgar, 1953). Neurological and pediatric examinations were consistently normal. We evaluated all babies for neurological adequacy on the scale taught one of us (ET) by Prechtl (Prechtl and Beintema, 1964). In addition, we evaluated each baby with the Brazelton (1973) Neonatal Behavioral Assessment at 1, 5, and 10 days.

This Neonatal Behavioral Assessment Scale is a psychological scale for the newborn human infant. It assesses his reflexive and motor behavior, as well as his general physical state as he recovers from labor and delivery. It allows for an assessment of the infant's capabilities along dimensions that we think are relevant to his developing social relationships.

It reconceptualizes Prechtl's use of state[1] in such an assessment. State is no longer regarded as a static error variable, but serves to set a dynamic pattern which reflects the wholeness of the infant. Specifically, the examination tracks the pattern of state change over the course of the examination, its lability, and its directionality in response to external and internal stimuli. Thus, the variability of state becomes a dimension of assessment, pointing to the infant's initial abilities for self-organization.

An assessment of the infant's ability for self-organization is contained in the items which measure his capacity for self-quieting after exposure to aversive stimuli. This is contrasted to the infant's use of external stimuli to help him quiet after such stimulation. The latter item contains a graded series of examiner-administered procedures—talking to him, placing one's hand on his belly, rocking and holding him—maneuvers which are designed to calm the infant. The assessment results in an evaluation of how control is achieved by the infant. The infant's responsiveness to animate stimulation (voice and face, holding and cuddling, etc.) as well as to inanimate stimulation (rattle, bell, red ball, pinprick, temperature change, etc.) are quantified. Other items assess neuroreflexive adequacy and the vigor and attentional excitement exhibited by the infant throughout the exam. In all of this test, there is an attempt to elicit the infant's *best* performance in response to different kinds of stimulation.

The Zambian mothers were given no medication before or during delivery. These mothers had had several pregnancies in rapid succession at about 12- to 13-month intervals, among these several spontaneous abortions. But they all had more than three children living at home. There was historical evidence of low protein intake both before and during pregnancy, coupled with a high incidence of gastrointestinal infection in the mother during pregnancy. The resulting intrauterine conditions of a depleted uterus, low protein, and increased infections were a reflection of the conditions of recent urbanization as well as of a breakdown in traditional practices (Goldberg, 1970).

---

[1] "State" or "state of consciousness" is one of the most important variables in any observation period of neonatal behavior. Reactions to stimuli must be interpreted within the context of the present state of consciousness. We used a schema of six states (two sleep, three awake, and one intermediate state). State depends on physiological variables such as hunger, degree of hydration, time in the sleep-wake cycle. But each observable reaction is governed by the state within which it is perceived. The infant's state patterns and his use of state to govern his physiological and psychological reactions may be uniquely individual and may be the most important framework for observing all of his reactions.

The Zambian mothers we saw had recently moved to the urbanized slums of Lusaka because of the disruption of the economy in the country under an economic plan that stressed industrialization. In the country, the maternal grandmother dictated her daughter's diet and saw to it that protein was a daily requirement. In the urbanized group, the husband took over this prerogative. He set up a series of myths which we heard from our subjects: "If you eat fish, your baby will drown. If you eat meat, your baby will bleed to death. If you eat eggs, your baby will be born bald." The breakdown in dietary protection of pregnant women occurs in the city, where jobs and money are scarce and protein is expensive, and the family cannot afford to spend the little money they have on high-protein foods which might not satisfy hunger. The other powerful change in the urbanized groups around Lusaka had to do with birth control practices centered around pregnancy. In the country, a family is made up of several women and one man. A sexual relationship is maintained with a wife who is not pregnant and not nursing. This practice fosters a kind of birth control and recovery of the uterus in the postnatal period before subsequent pregnancy. In Lusaka, given the economic conditions, this pattern is impossible. A family is made up of a male and one female, and she suffers from the effects of rapidly repeated pregnancies.

All of the infants of the group examined lived in the semirural urbanized slum area which surrounds the city of Lusaka. Dwellings ranged from huts to small brick cottages. All families were reported to be recently (one generation) urbanized, and few had the advantage of extended families nearby (Goldberg, 1970, 1971).

Our study consisted of three examinations on days 1, 5, and 10 after birth for each infant. We all shared the examinations of the Zambians, although one (ET) was responsible for most of the examinations of U.S. controls. Interscorer reliability on the Brazelton scale had been tested in the United States and was retested in Africa, for we feared that we were becoming biased by our experience there. Repeated reliability tests were .85 or more on all items and between each pair of observers. The infants were scored on the 24 items listed in Table 1 as well as on 18 neurological items adapted from Prechtl and Beintema's (1964) neurological exam.

The first examination of the American infants was done in the hospital nurseries of the Boston

TABLE 1
Behavioral Measures in Neonatal Scale

Vigor	General tonus
Lability of states	Self-quieting activity
Tremulousness	Habituation to light in eyes
Amount of startling	Motor maturity
Amount of mouthing	Pulled-to-sit response
Hand to mouth activity	Passive movements
Motor activity	Following with eyes
Rapidity of buildup	Cuddliness
Defensive movements to cloth on face	Alertness
Tempo of activity at peak	Social interest in E
Irritability	Reactions to sound
Consolability	Reactivity to stimulation

Hospital for Women and Cambridge City Hospital, and on the Zambian infants in the University Hospital of Lusaka. On the first day the examination was administered two hours after feeding. The examinations on days 5 and 10 were carried out in the homes. An attempt was made to control conditions, e.g., to have the baby fed and comfortable; to include the mother, but exclude the other members of the family; and to standardize light, temperature, and noise as much as possible. This was difficult in the home examinations.

An estimate of the infants' pediatric, neurological, and nutritional status[2] was made in each case, and two infants were excluded because of possibly abnormal reactions. None of the babies in either group was found to be abnormal on any examination, including neurological evaluations. All babies in each group were being breastfed.

RESULTS

In the Zambian group, observations in the neonatal nursery on day 1 demonstrated pediatric evidence of intrauterine depletion in each of these infants. The average birth weight was 6 pounds, and the length was an average of 19 1/2 inches. The infants' skin was dry and scaly; their faces were wrinkled. The stumps of their umbilical cords were somewhat dried and yellow at birth. In short, the infants

---

[2]Pediatric and nutritional assessments for evidences of prematurity and dysmaturity according to Dubowitz et al. (1970) and Clifford (1954).

demonstrated the signs of dysmaturity which indicate recent depletion of nutrients in utero (Clifford, 1954). Their weight and size suggested placental dysfunction, and suggested that the infants had been affected by their mothers' inadequate protein diet and their stressed uteri with placentae inadequate to feed them—especially in the period just prior to birth. On this first examination, the Zambian infants' muscle tone was very poor. Little resistance was evidenced to passive extension or flexion of their limbs. Head control on being pulled to sit was extremely poor. And, lastly, when held, the Zambian infants made no active attempt to mold or adjust themselves to being held. They were essentially limp and unresponsive in the motor sphere.

The American infants were not depleted. They averaged 7.6 pounds, 20 1/4 inches in length, and showed no clinical evidence of dysmaturity or prematurity. They were active and responsive on the first day in all spheres of behavior.

On days 5 and 10 the Zambian infants were no longer clinically dehydrated. Because the mothers were multiparous and had nursed infants before, their milk came in rapidly, and nursing was uniformly successful. By day 5, the Zambian infants were filled out, dry skin was peeling away, and their eyes and mouths were moist. Their skin and subcutaneous tissue were normal again. Their energy level had considerably increased, as was reflected in their performance (see Table 2).

The performance of the two groups of infants on the Brazelton scale was compared item by item for each day of the examination with the Mann-Whitney U Test. The most striking differences were found on the 1st-day (6 items) and 10th-day (8 items) examinations, with only 2 items differentiating the two groups on the 5th-day examination.

Before describing these differences, we wish to note a certain stability and lack of change discernible in the United States babies. The scores of the American infants in this sample stayed within an average range on all three days. This is in contrast to results obtained in other groups of American infants who typically score below the average on day 1 and who recover by day 5 (Brazelton, 1970). These latter groups were obtained from mothers who were medicated during delivery and whose infants demonstrated a resulting depression in all behavior. Note that the infants in the present sample were delivered with a minimal use of drugs, and by "natural" childbirth.

On the day 1 examination, there were 6 items on which the two groups of infants were significantly different. The Zambian infants scored lower on following with eyes ($p < .05$), motor activity ($p < .02$), tempo at height ($p < .10$), irritability ($p < .05$), rapidity of buildup ($p < .10$), and cuddliness ($p < .10$). On the day 5 examination, only 2 items differentiated the groups, with Americans scoring lower on rapidity of buildup ($p < .10$) and on alertness ($p < .10$).

TABLE 2

Mean Scores for Zambians and for Americans on Day 1, 5, and 10 for All Measures that Distinguished between Groups on at Least One Day[a]

Measures	Day 1 Zamb.	Day 1 Amer.	Day 5 Zamb.	Day 5 Amer.	Day 10 Zamb.	Day 10 Amer.
Motor activity	3.00	4.90	5.89	5.50	4.60	5.90
Tempo at height	3.20	5.77	5.90	5.50	4.40	6.44
Rapidity of buildup	3.22	4.80	5.62	4.50	3.50	5.50
Irritability	2.50	4.40	4.40	4.70	3.80	5.00
Consolability	6.60	5.56	5.00	4.63	6.12	4.75
Social interest	4.20	4.29	6.20	5.22	6.70	4.33
Alertness	3.40	4.20	6.30	5.11	7.40	4.80
Follow with eyes	2.40	4.16	4.60	4.70	4.67	5.11
Reactivity to stimulation	3.35	4.38	5.30	4.71	6.14	4.67
Defensive movements	3.20	4.38	5.11	5.50	4.90	6.11
Cuddliness	3.30	4.40	5.22	5.60	6.30	5.12

[a]Scores in italics indicate that the difference between them was significant.

The 10th-day examination comparisons found 8 items which distinguished the two groups. The Zambian infants scored lower on reactivity to stimulation ($p < .07$), defensive movements ($p < .05$), motor activity ($p < .05$), rapidity of buildup ($p < .05$), and tempo at height ($p < .02$). The Zambians scored higher on consolability ($p < .06$), social interest ($p < .02$), and alertness ($p < .02$). By day 10, also, muscle tone was better than average, in contrast to day 1. No longer were the Zambians limp. Their head control was good; passive resistance of limbs to flexion and extension normal; and they actively responded upon being held (scores on cuddliness were above average). Reference to Table 2 emphasizes again that it is the Zambian group which is changing, not the American group.

To summarize: the Americans remained approximately within the average range on all three days. On day 1, the Zambians scored lower than the Americans on items that seemed to reflect reactivity. By day 10, however, although (or maybe, because) the Zambians were still scoring low on items which measured motor reactivity, they were scoring higher on items which measured social attentiveness.

DISCUSSION

One of the questions we had been interested in was whether behavioral differences existed between cultural groups during the neonatal period. This question was certainly answered in the affirmative.

The most striking feature of the results is the difference in the pattern of increase in the scores of the Zambian and American infants. On the day 1 examination the Zambian infants scored low relative to the American infants and to their own later performance on behaviors related to activity and to alertness. They were not very irritable and did not invest much energy in being upset (as indicated by their scores on irritability, tempo, and rapidity of buildup). They also lacked energy for relating to the social and inanimate environment (as demonstrated by poor responses to being cuddled and to visual stimulation).

By the 10th day, there had been a dramatic change. They were alert, controlled in motor activities, and oriented toward their social environment. Their high scores on alertness and social interest were coupled with a high degree of consolability and low scores on overreactiveness—motor activity, rapidity of buildup, and tempo at height of disturbance. Their scores in defensive reactions and reactivity to inanimate stimulation seemed to indicate that their energy was directed toward and invested in the social environment. In contrast, the American infants' scores remained stable throughout the first 10 days.

Interesting though these differences may be, the real question is: what accounts for them?

We suggest that these differences are compatible with a view of some so-called "cultural" differences as resulting from a combination of the effects of genetic and nongenetic inheritance, operating in conjunction with certain child-rearing practices.

We start with the nongenetic inherited factors. We know that nongenetic inheritance certainly plays a role in determining the characteristics of children under some circumstances. The effects of changes in nongenetic inheritance are exemplified in a number of situations: Down's syndrome (which results from chromosomal changes that are highly correlated with mother's age); changes in the infant that result either from drugs ingested by the mother in early pregnancy or from hormonal imbalance during pregnancy (Baker, 1960; Brazelton, 1970; Money et al., 1968). Additionally, there are the nongenetic but inherited effects of protein malnutrition (Schaffer, 1960; Zamenhof et al., 1968); of infections suffered by the mother during pregnancy (Klein et al., 1971); and of depletion of the uterus, a depletion that results from a series of pregnancies following so closely upon one another that there is no opportunity for the uterus to recover. We know that the last three factors affect the infant's gain in body weight and growth in length in the uterus. Might they not also be responsible for behavioral differences between the neonates of different cultures?

The differences between Zambians and Americans on day 1 were differences in behavior that are usually associated with sheer physical energy. That the lack of energy was, in fact, the primary cause of the Zambian infants' low scores is made more credible by what we know of these infants' physical state. We could see that they were dehydrated. We also knew that their mothers had had low protein intake during pregnancy as well as a series of closely spaced pregnancies. These facts made it clear that the day 1 differences could easily reflect the effects of a stressed intrauterine environment. This environment was inherited, but nongenetic, and its effects were dramatic. Once their mothers began to nurse them, thereby both rehydrating them and providing them with needed nutrients, the Zambian infants became much more reactive.

An additional and complementary argument is also possible. Behavioral differences after birth are rapidly affected by factors other than inheritance. They are quickly molded by social factors, especially by such divergent child-rearing practices as these two groups were exposed to.

The change in behavior that was evident by day 10 was of a different quality from the changes that took place between days 1 and 5. First, the change involved more than simple recovery from a poor physiological environment. The behaviors that improved from day 1 to day 5 were behaviors that seemed to require a certain level of physical energy: the behaviors that changed from day 5 to day 10 were those commonly seen as requiring a certain level of social interest.

The changes from day 1 to day 5 seemed to be primarily attributable to the rehydration and nutrition that resulted from nutrients. We thought that the changes from day 5 to day 10 resulted primarily from certain child-rearing practices, and that these were of the sort that facilitate the development of muscle tone, alertness, and social responsivity.

The kind of motoric stimulation that the infants received seemed to put a premium on developing muscle tone. When asked to rouse their babies, the Zambian mothers picked them up under the arms and tossed them up and down in the air. All cries were first responded to with nursing. However, if this did not quiet the infant, the mother resorted to vigorous activity and bouncing. Goldberg (1971) has noted that from as early as 24 hours after delivery, the Zambian mother secures her infant to her body with a *dashica,* a long piece of cloth, in such a way that the infant essentially rides on the mother's hip. In this position, the infant's body has no support from the armpits up. Since his head is not supported, the infant must maintain a strong shoulder girdle response to keep his head steady. The mother places the infant in her *dashica* either by holding him by the arm or by holding his trunk under the arm and then swinging him over her shoulder. In short, this active handling of the infant seems to encourage the development of muscle tone.

But in addition to favoring the development of muscle tone, carrying the infant in a *dashica* seems to encourage alertness as well (Korner, 1970). In this position, an infant is able to see more than he would in other positions. Long periods of being carried also provide more opportunities for the infant to be tactually stimulated. This tactile stimulation by another person encourages social responsiveness on the part of the infant, but other practices also seem to facilitate social responsivity. Breast feeding is frequent and in response to any indication from the infant that he is either hungry or fussy. There is little attempt to make him wait (Goldberg, 1970, 1971).

When the infants are not being carried about, they are left uncovered on a bed in a family room where everyone, including siblings and visitors, can admire, play with, and hold the tiny infant. At night, the infant is swaddled loosely next to his mother in the same bed.

Since at birth the Zambian infants were very limp and quite unresponsive, one might wonder at their mothers's willingness to provide the infants with vigorous, stimulating experiences. We concluded that the mothers' practices were based on their expectancies of how their infants would develop. Assuming that the infants in our sample were not atypical of the population, one can infer that the Zambian mothers in our sample had seen other Zambian infants recover shortly after birth. One can also infer that these mothers thus had reason to expect that their infants, too, would recover in the same way. Individually, each mother's expectations were probably also reinforced by the dramatic change in muscle tone and responsivity that took place in her infant from day 1 to day 5, which she could easily have interpreted as evidence that her infant would continue to show improvement.

These expectations were based both on the Zambian mother's observation of her own and other infants' recovery from their state on day 1. The infants' ability to recover must reflect genetic capacities to respond to these practices. Such rapid recovery seems to point to inherited potential which is not incapacitated by conditions of intrauterine deprivation.

Contrast the Zambian caretaker practices with those of our American mothers. The American infants' behavior reflected very different inherited (genetic and nongenetic) potential at birth. In addition, they remained in the hospital environment for a minimum of 4 days. Five of the babies roomed in with their mothers after 48 hours, and it is presumed that their cries were responded to with nursing or handling by their mothers. The 5 infants who were kept in the nursery were fed every 4 hours, day and night, on hospital schedules. The rooming-in mothers were urged to feed the babies on a similar schedule, and because of their inexperience and the delay in getting breast milk (4 to 5 days in a primiparous mother), it is obvious that there was less feeding and handling than there was among Zambian mothers. When these American mothers went home, they followed the cultural emphasis in the United States on quieting the infant and protecting him from external stimulation. There is no care practice that even approximates the Zambian mother's almost constant contact with her infant. From our observation of them in their homes, it was quite obvious that these American mothers provided a very different early environment for their infants. The unchanging behavior over the 10 days reflects a different inheritance as well as the relatively nonstimulating environment to which the babies were exposed in this period.

SUMMARY

The abilities of an infant and the changes in those abilities reflect inherited factors—both genetic and nongenetic—cultural practices and expectations. An understanding of the recovery of the Zambian infants and the pattern of performance of the American infants reflects all three. The Zambian infants recovered rapidly from an intrauterine (inherited) environment which had been physiologically inadequate. Their rapid recovery reflected the infants' genetic abilities as well as the supportive child-rearing practices and the cultural expectations for early precocious development. The American infants reflected an adequate intrauterine environment with their more unchanging behavioral patterns. The protective, relatively nonstimulating child-rearing practices were suited to genetic capabilities as well as to cultural expectations of a "prolonged" and protected infancy.

Questions

1. What is the Neonatal Behavioral Assessment Scale and why is it useful for examining abilities early in life?

2. What specific cultural practices of the mothers in these two communities influenced early infant development? Can you think of similar variations in cultural styles within North America that might influence the way in which infants develop in the first few weeks of life?

3. Do you agree with Brazelton, Koslowski, and Tronick about the importance of culture in organizing emotional states in the first few days of life? Why or why not?

References

Ainsworth, M. D. S. (1967), *Infancy in Uganda: Infant Care and the Growth of Love.* Baltimore: Johns Hopkins Press.

Apgar, V. (1953), A proposal for a new method of evaluation of the newborn infant. *Curr. Res. Anesth. Analges.,* 32:260–283.

Baker, J. B. E. (1960), The effects of drugs on the fetus. *Pharmacol. Rev.,* 12:37–90.

Brazelton, T. B. (1970), Effect of prenatal drugs on the behavior of the neonate. *Amer. J. Psychiat.* 126:1261–1266.

——— (1973), *Neonatal Behavioral Assessment Scale.* London: Heinemann.

———, Koloslowski, B., & Main, M. (1973), Origins of reciprocity: mother and infant interaction. In: *Origins of Behavior,* Vol. I, ed. M. Lewis & L. Rosenblum. New York: Wiley, pp. 49–76.

———, Robey, J. S., & Collier, G. A. (1969), Infant development in the Zinacanteco Indians of Southern Mexico. *Pediatrics,* 44:274–290.

Clifford, S. H. (1954), Postmaturity with placental dysfunction: clinical syndrome and pathologic findings. *J. Pediat.,* 44:1–13.

Dubowitz, L. M. S., Dubowitz, V., & Goldberg, C. (1970), Clinical assessment of gestational age in the newborn infant. *J. Pediat.,* 77:1–10.

Freedman, D. G. & Freedman, N. (1969), Behavioral differences between Chinese-American and American newborns. *Nature,* 224:1227.

Gerber, M. & Dean, R. F. A. (1959), The state of development of newborn African children. *Lancet,* 1: 1216.

Goldberg, S. A. (1970), Infant care in Zambia: Measuring maternal behavior. HDRU Reports No. 13, Lusaka, Zambia.

——— (1971), Infant care and growth in urban Zambia. Presented at the meetings of the Society for Research in Child Development, Minneapolis, Minn., April 4.

Klein, R. E., Habicht, J. P., & Yarbrough, C. (1971), Effect of protein-calorie malnutrition on mental development. Incap (Institute of Nutrition of Central America, Panama) publication no. I-571, Guatemala, CA.

Korner, A. (1970) Visual alertness in neonates: individual differences and their correlates. Percept. *Mot. Skills,* 31:499–509.

Money, J., Ehrhardt, A. A., & Masica, D. N. (1968), Fetal feminization induced by androgen insensitivity in the Testicular Feminizing Syndrome. *Johns Hopkins Med. J.,* 123:105–114.

Prechtl, H. & Beintema, O. (1964), *The Neurological Examination of the Full Term Newborn Infant.* London: Heinemann.

Schaffer, A. J. (1960), *Diseases of the Newborn.* Philadelphia: Saunders, p. 628.

Zamenhof, S., Van Marthens, E., & Margolis, F. L. (1968), DNA and protein in neonatal brain: alteration by maternal dietary restriction. *Science,* 160:322–323.

8

Of Human Bonding: Newborns Prefer Their Mothers' Voices

ANTHONY J. DECASPER AND WILLIAM P. FIFER

Over the past two decades there has been a huge increase in developmental research describing infant capabilities, such as perception, emotional regulation, and social behavior. This increase is due in part to technical innovations that allow researchers to study infant behavior during the early days and months of life. But it also reflects a shift in psychologists' conception of infancy. Whereas infants were once seen as having few inherent capabilities, they are now considered to be quite capable. The following article describes one of these early capabilities: the neonate's ability to discriminate the sounds of particular human voices. The adaptive benefits of this ability are immense and its presence in newborns attests to the complex biological preparedness of the human infant—a preparedness that helps even very young babies play an active role in their own development.

By sucking on a nonnutritive nipple in different ways, a newborn human could produce either its mother's voice or the voice of another female. Infants learned how to produce the mother's voice and produced it more often than the other voice. The neonate's preference for the maternal voice suggests *that the period shortly after birth may be important for initiating infant bonding to the mother.*

Human responsiveness to sound begins in the third trimester of life and by birth reaches sophisticated levels (1), especially with respect to speech (2). Early auditory competency probably subserves a variety of developmental functions such as language acquisition (*1, 3*) and mother-infant bonding (*4, 5*). Mother-infant bonding would best be served by (and may even require) the ability of a newborn to discriminate its mother's voice from that of other females. However, evidence for differential sensitivity to or discrimination of the maternal voice is available only for older infants for whom the bonding process is well advanced (*6*). Therefore, the role of maternal voice discrimination in formation of the mother-infant bond is unclear. If the newborn's sensitivities to speech subserves bonding, discrimination of and preference for the maternal voice should be evident near birth. We now report that a newborn infant younger than 3 days of age can not only discriminate its mother's voice but also will work to produce her voice in preference to the voice of another female.

The subjects were ten Caucasian neonates (five male and five female) (*7*). Shortly after delivery we tape-recorded the voices of mothers of infants selected for testing as they read Dr. Seuss's *To Think That I Saw It On Mulberry Street*. Recordings were edited to provide 25 minutes of uninterrupted prose, and testing of whether infants would differentially produce their mothers' voices began within 24 hours of recording. Sessions began by coaxing the infant to a state of quiet alertness (*8*). The infant was then placed supine in its basinette, earphones were secured over its ears, and a nonnutritive nipple was placed in its mouth. An assistant held the nipple loosely in place; she was unaware of the experimental condition of the individual infant and could neither hear the tapes nor be seen by the infant. The nipple was connected, by way of a pressure transducer, to the solid-state programming and recording equipment. The infants were then allowed 2 minutes to adjust to the situation. Sucking activity was recorded during the next 5 minutes, but voices were never presented. This baseline period was used to determine the median interburst interval (IBI) or time elapsing between the end of one burst of sucking and the beginning of the next (*9*). A burst was defined as a series of individual sucks separated from one another by less than 2 seconds. Testing with the voices began after the baseline had been established.

For five randomly selected infants, sucking burst terminating IBI's equal to or greater than the baseline median (*t*) produced only his or her mother's voice (IBI ≥ *t*), and bursts terminating intervals less than the median produced only the voice of another infant's mother (*10*). Thus, only one of the voices was presented, stereophonically, with the first suck of a burst and remained on until the burst ended,

that is, until 2 seconds elapsed without a suck. For the other five infants, the conditions were reversed. Testing lasted 20 minutes.

A preference for the maternal voice was indicated if the infant produced it more often than the nonmaternal voice. However, unequal frequencies not indicative of preference for the maternal voice per se could result either because short (or long) IBI's were easier to produce or because the acoustic qualities of a particular voice, such as pitch or intensity, rendered it a more effective form of feedback. The effects of response requirements and voice characteristics were controlled (i) by requiring half the infants to respond after short IBI's to produce the mother's voice and half to respond after long ones and (ii) by having each maternal voice also serve as the nonmaternal voice for another infant.

Preference for the mother's voice was shown by the increase in the proportion of IBI's capable of producing her voice; the median IBI's shifted from their baseline values in a direction that produced the maternal voice more than half the time. Eight of the ten medians were shifted in a direction of the maternal voice (mean = 1.90 seconds, a 34 percent increase) (sign test, *P* = .02), one shifted in the direction that produced the nonmaternal voice more often, and one median did not change from its baseline value (Figure 1).

If these infants were working to gain access to their mother's voice, reversing the response requirements should result in a reversal of their IBI's. Four infants, two from each condition, who produced their mother's voice more often in session 1 were able to complete a second session 24 hours later, in which the response requirements were reversed (*11*). Differential feedback in session 2 began immediately after the 2-minute adjustment period. The criterion time remained equal to the baseline median of the first session. For all four infants, the median IBI's shifted toward the new criterion values and away from those which previously produced the maternal voice. The average magnitude of the difference between the medians of the first and reversal sessions was 1.95 seconds.

Apparently the infant learned to gain access to the mother's voice. Since specific temporal properties of sucking were required to produce the maternal voice, we sought evidence for the acquisition of temporally differentiated responding. Temporal discrimination within each condition was ascertained by constructing the function for IBI per opportunity: IBI's were collected into classes equal to one-fifth the baseline median, and the frequency of each class was divided by the total frequency of classes having equal

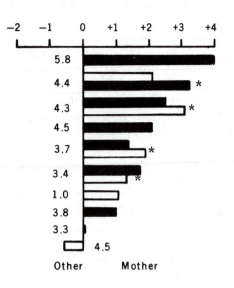

FIGURE 1   For each subject, signed difference scores between the median IBI's without vocal feedback (baseline) and with differential vocal feedback (session1). Differences of the four reversal sessions (*) are based on medians with differential feedback in sessions 1 and 2. Positive values indicate a preference for the maternal voice and negative values a preference for the nonmaternal voice. Filled bars indicate that the mother's voice followed IBI's of less than the baseline median; open bars indicate that her voice followed intervals equal to or greater than the median. Median IBI's of the baseline (in seconds) are shown opposite the bars.

infants, a sucking burst initiated during a tone period turned off the tone and produced the Dr. Seuss story read by the infant's mother, whereas sucking bursts during a no-tone period produced the nonmaternal voice. The elicited voice remained until the sucking burst ended, at which time the tone-no-tone alternation began anew. The discriminative stimuli were reversed for the other eight neonates. Testing with the voices began immediately after the 2-minute adjustment period and lasted 20 minutes. Each maternal voice also served as a nonmaternal voice.

During the first third of the testing session, the infants were as likely to suck during a stimulus period correlated with the maternal voice as during one correlated with the nonmaternal voice (Table 1). However, in the last third of the session the infants sucked during stimulus periods associated with their mother's voice approximately 24 percent more often than during those associated with the nonmaternal voice, a significant increase [$F(1, 14) = 8.97$, $P < .01$]. Thus, at the beginning of testing there was no indication of stimulus discrimination or voice preference. By the end of the 20-minute session, feedback from the maternal voice produced clear evidence of an auditory discrimination; the probability of sucking during tone and no-tone periods was greater when sucking produced the maternal voice.

The infants in these studies lived in a group nursery; their general care and night feedings were handled by a number of female nursery personnel.

and larger values (*12*). When IBI's less than the baseline median were required, the likelihood of terminating interburst intervals was highest for classes less than the median (Figure 2), whereas when longer intervals were required, the probability of terminating an IBI was maximal for intervals slightly longer than the median. Feedback from the maternal voice effectively differentiated the temporal character of responding that produced it: the probability of terminating IBI's was highest when termination resulted in the maternal voice.

Repeating the experiment with 16 female neonates and a different discrimination procedure confirmed their preference for the maternal voice (*13*). The discriminative stimuli were a 400-Hz tone of 4 seconds duration (tone) and a 4-second period of silence (no tone). Each IBI contained an alternating sequence of tone-no-tone periods, and each stimulus was equally likely to begin a sequence. For eight

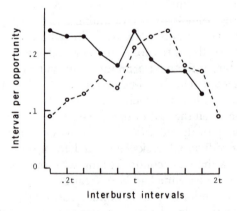

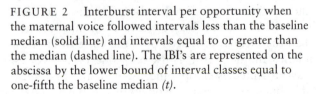

FIGURE 2   Interburst interval per opportunity when the maternal voice followed intervals less than the baseline median (solid line) and intervals equal to or greater than the median (dashed line). The IBI's are represented on the abscissa by the lower bound of interval classes equal to one-fifth the baseline median (*t*).

TABLE 1

Mean ($\overline{X}$) and Standard Deviation (S.D.) of the Relative Frequency of Sucking During a Stimulus Associated with the Maternal Voice Divided by the Relative Frequency of Sucking During a Stimulus Associated with the Nonmaternal Voice

Stimulus associated with maternal voice	First third		Last third	
	$\overline{X}$	S.D.	$\overline{X}$	S.D.
Tone	0.97	.33	1.26	.33
No tone	1.04	.31	1.22	.19
Last: Combined	1.00[a]	.32	1.24	.27

[a] A ratio of 1.0 indicates no preference.

They were fed in their mothers' rooms by their mothers at 9:30 a.m. and at 1:30, 5:00, and 8:30 p.m. At most, they had 12 hours of postnatal contact with their mothers before testing. Similarly reared infants prefer the human voice to other acoustically complex stimuli (*14*). But, as our data show, newborns reared in group nurseries that allow minimal maternal contact can also discriminate between their mothers and other speakers and, moreover, will work to produce their mothers' voices in preference to those of other females. Thus, within the first 3 days of postnatal development, newborns prefer the human voice, discriminate between speakers, and demonstrate a preference for their mothers' voices with only limited maternal exposure.

The neonate's capacity to rapidly acquire a stimulus discrimination that controls behavior (*15*) could provide the means by which limited postnatal experience with the mother results in preference for her voice. The early preference demonstrated here is possible because newborns have auditory competencies adequate for discriminating individual speakers: they are sensitive to rhythmicity (*16*), intonation (*17*), frequency variation (*1, 13*), and phonetic components of speech (*18*). Their general sensory competency may enable other maternal cues, such as her odor (*19*) and the manner in which she handles her infant (*20*), to serve as supporting bases for discrimination and vocal preference. Prenatal (intrauterine) auditory experience may also be a factor. Although the significance and nature of intrauterine auditory experience in humans is not known, perceptual preferences and proximity-seeking responses of some infrahuman infants are profoundly affected by auditory experience before birth (*21*).

Questions

1. What is the logic of the method the authors use to study the capabilities of newborns? Why might they have chosen this method rather than another?

2. Why might infants prefer their mother's voice? Do you think that prenatal exposure may play a role in formulating this preference?

3. What other early sensory capabilities may also prepare infants to interact socially?

References and Notes

1. R. B. Eisenberg, *Auditory Competence in Early Life: The Roots of Communicative Behavior* (University Park Press, Baltimore, 1976.)

2. P. D. Eimas, in *Infant Perception: From Sensation to Cognition*, L. B. Cohen and P. Salapatek, Eds. (Academic Press, New York, 1975), vol. 2., p. 193.

3. B. Friedlander, *Merrill-Palmer Q.*, 16, 7 (1970).

4. R. Bell, in *The Effect of the Infant on Its Caregiver*, M. Lewis and L. A. Rosenblum, Eds. (Wiley, New York, 1974), p. 1; T. B. Brazelton, E. Tronick, L. Abramson, H. Als, S. Wise, *Ciba Found. Symp.*, 33, 137 (1975).

5. M. H. Klaus and J. H. Kennel, *Maternal Infant Bonding* (Mosby, St. Louis, 1976); P. DeChateau, *Birth Family J.*, 41, 10 (1977).

6. M. Miles and E. Melvish, *Nature (London) 252*, 123 (1974); J. Mehler, J. Bertoncini, M. Baurière, D. Jassik-Gershenfeld, *Perception, 7, 491* (1978).

7. The infants were randomly selected from those meeting the following criteria: (i) gestation, full term; (ii) delivery, uncomplicated; (iii) birth weight, between 2500 and 3850 grams; and (iv) APGAR score, at least eight at 1 and 5 minutes after birth. If circumsized, males were not observed until at least 12 hours afterward. Informed written consent was obtained from the mother, and she was invited to observe the testing procedure. Testing sessions began between 2.5 and 3.5 hours after the 6 a.m. or 12 p.m. feeding. All infants were bottle-fed.

8. P. H. Wolff, *Psychol. Issues, 5,* 1 (1966). The infants were held in front of the experimenter's face, spoken to, and then presented with the nonnutritive nipple. Infants failing to fixate visually on the experimenter's face or to suck on the nipple were returned to the nursery. Once begun, a session was terminated only if the infant cried or stopped sucking for two consecutive minutes. The initial sessions of two infants were terminated because they cried for 2 minutes. Their data are not reported. Thus, the results are based on 10 of 12 infants meeting the behavioral criteria for entering and remaining in the study.

9. With quiet and alert newborns, nonnutritive sucking typically occurs as bursts of individual sucks, each separated by a second or so, while the bursts themselves are separated by several seconds or more. Interburst intervals tend to be unimodally distributed with modal values differing among infants. [K. Kaye, in *Studies in Mother-Infant Interaction,* H. R. Schaffer, Ed. (Academic Press, New York, 1977)]. A suck was said to occur when the negative pressure exerted on the nipple reached 20 mm-Hg. This value is almost always exceeded during nonnutritive sucking by healthy infants, but is virtually never produced by nonsucking mouth movement.

10. The tape reels revolved continuously, and one or the other of the voices was electronically switched to the earphones when the response threshold was met. Because the thresholds were detected electronically, voice onset occurred at the moment the negative pressure reached 20 mm-Hg.

11. Two infants were not tested a second time, because we could not gain access to the testing room, which served as an auxiliary nursery and as an isolation room. The sessions of two infants who cried were terminated. Two other infants were tested a second time, but in their first session one had shown no preference and the other had shown only a slight preference for the nonmaternal voice. Their performance may have been affected by inconsistent feedback. Because their peak sucking pressures were near the threshold of the apparatus, very similar sucks would sometimes produce feedback and sometimes not, and sometimes feedback would be terminated in the midst of a sucking burst. Consequently, second session performances of these two infants, which were much like their initial performances, were uninterpretable.

12. D. Anger, *J. Exp. Psychol., 52,* 145 (1956).

13. Three other infants began testing with the voices, but their sessions were terminated because they cried. Their data are not included. This study is part of a doctoral thesis submitted by W.P.F.

14. E. Butterfield and G. Siperstein, in *Oral Sensation and Perception: The Mouth of the Infant,* J. Bosma, Ed. (Thomas, Springfield, Ill., 1972).

15. E. R. Siqueland and L. P. Lipsitt, *J. Exp. Child. Psychol. 3,* 356 (1966); R. E. Kron, in *Recent Advances in Biological Psychiatry,* J. Wortis, Ed. (Plenum, New York, 1967), p. 295.

16. W. S. Condon and L. W. Sander, *Science, 183,* 99 (1974).

17. R. B. Eisenberg, D. B. Cousins, N. Rupp, *J. Aud. Res., 7,* 245 (1966); P. A. Morse, *J. Exp. Child. Psychol., 14,* 477 (1972).

18. E. C. Butterfield and G. F. Cairns, in *Language Perspectives: Acquisition, Retardation and Intervention,* R. L. Schiefelbusch and L. L. Lloyd, Eds. (University Park Press, Baltimore, 1974), p. 75; A. J. DeCasper, E. C. Butterfield, G. F. Cairns, paper presented at the fourth biennial conference on Human Development, Nashville. April 1976.

19. A. MacFarlane, *Ciba Found. Symp., 33,* 103 (1975).

20. P. Burns, L. W. Sander, G. Stechler, H. Julia. *J. Am. Acad. Child Psychiatry, 11,* 427 (1972), E. B. Thoman, A. F. Korner, L. Bearon-Williams, *Child Dev., 48,* 563 (1977).

21. G. Gottlieb, *Development of Species Identification in Birds: An Inquiry into the Prenatal Determinants of Perception* (Univ. of Chicago Press, Chicago, 1971); E. H. Hess. *Imprinting* (Van Nostrand-Reinhold, New York, 1973).

22. Supported by Research Council grant 920. We thank the infants, their mothers, and the staff of Moses Cane Hospital, where this work was performed, and A. Carstens for helping conduct the research.

PART II

Infancy

9

Early Rule Structure: The Case of "Peekaboo"

JEROME S. BRUNER AND V. SHERWOOD

Humans are social animals and we create and participate in many social activities that are governed by rules. From the beginning of life infants participate in some social activities that are structured by adults. For these activities to be successful, they must be coordinated with the emerging skills and capabilities of the infants involved. A common activity involving adults and young children is peekaboo, a game that draws on the infant's emerging skills of responsiveness, anticipation, and object knowledge. The adult helps coordinate the infant's skills with the rule structure of the game. In the following article, Bruner and Sherwood describe this social synchronization and suggest that development occurs through participation in such activities.

Peekaboo surely must rank as one of the most universal forms of play between adults and infants. It is rich indeed in the mechanisms it exhibits. For in point of fact, the game depends upon the infant's capacity to integrate a surprisingly wide range of phenomena. For one, the very playing of the game depends upon the child having some degree of mastery of object permanence, the capacity to recognize the continued existence of an object when it is out of sight (e.g. Piaget, 1954). Charlesworth (1966) has shown, moreover, that the successful playing of the game is dependent in some measure on the child being able to keep track of the location in which a face has disappeared, the child showing more persistent effects when the reappearance of a face varied unexpectedly with respect to its prior position. Greenfield (1970) has also indicated that the initial effect of the game depends upon the presence not only of the reappearing face, but also of an accompanying vocalization by the mother, although with repetition the role of vocalization declined. She also found that the voice was increasingly important the less familiar the setting in which the game was played. It is quite plain, then, that complex expectancies are built up in the infant in the course of playing the game, and that these expectancies are characterized by considerable spatio-temporal structuring.

Another way of saying the same thing is to note that the child very soon becomes sensitive to the 'rules of the game' as he plays it. That is to say, he expects disappearance and reappearance to be in a certain place, at a certain time, accompanied by certain vocalizations, in certain general settings. The bulk of the studies reported in the literature suggest that these 'conventions', though they may rest upon certain preadapted readinesses to respond to disappearance and reappearance, are soon converted into rules for defining the pattern of play. If this were the case, one would expect that not only would the child have learned procedures, but would have learned them in a way that is characteristic of rule learning— i.e. in a general form, with assignable roles, with permissible substitutions of moves, etc.

The present study is concerned specifically with the conversion of peekaboo procedures into rule structures and, without intending to minimize the importance of preadapted patterns of response in making the game possible, we shall concentrate upon this aspect of the matter.

The study is based upon an intensive investigation of six infants over a period of 10 months, from seven to 17 months of age. The infants and their mothers were seen once a fortnight at our laboratory for an hour, and among the instructions given to the mothers was one asking them to show us the games that they and their infants most enjoyed playing. Our observations of peekaboo are all based upon behaviour spontaneously produced by the mothers in play, all but one of them including peekaboo in the play they exhibited. All sessions were videotaped and analysis was carried out on the video records. Partly for convenience of reporting and partly because each pair developed somewhat different procedures, we shall concentrate on a single mother-infant dyad over the 10-month period. The corpus of such play for this dyad consisted of 22 episodes of peekaboo, the first at 10 months, the last at 15 months. Peekaboo starts earlier than our initial age and goes on later, but the sample of games over the five-month period suffices to illustrate the points we wish to make. Though the other infant-mother dyads show some differences from the one we are reporting, they are in no sense different in pattern.

OBSERVATIONS

The first thing to be noted in the one mother–daughter (Diane) dyad on which we shall concentrate is that all instances of the game are quite notably constrained with respect to their limits. That is to say, the game always starts after the two players have made an explicit contact. This is the opening move, but it should be noted immediately that here, as in other features of the game, variation prevails. In most instances, initial contact is by face-to-face mutual looking. Where this does not occur, the mother may use either vocalization to contact the child or make the hiding 'instrument' conspicuous. The following table gives the frequencies of opening moves.

Face-to-face contact	16 (of 21 episodes in which orientation could be ascertained)
Vocalization	9 (of 22)
Highlighting of instrument	3 (of 22)

Typically, vocalization and face-to-face contact go together, with seven out of nine episodes of vocalization being accompanied by face-to-face contact. Interestingly enough, the mother will sometimes use a chance event as a 'starter' as when, inadvertently, her smock hides the child's face and the mother uses this as a start for a round of peekaboo. Also, there is what might best be called the 'opportunistic start', in which the mother when drying the child's hair after a bath 'lightens' the occasion by turning the drying with towel into an episode of peekaboo—a pattern also used by mothers to divert a fretting baby.

As Garvey (in press) has put it, social games can be described in terms of (a) the nature of the format, (b) the turns of each player and (c) the rounds in which the turns are sequenced. In the peekaboo situation, the initial round is a mutual attention-focusing episode that seems invariant although its form, as we have seen, may vary from one instance of the peekaboo format to the next.

The second round of peekaboo is the actual act of hiding and its accompaniments. Note first that there are four alternatives possible: mother can be hidden, or child, and the act of hiding can be initiated by the mother or the infant. The four alternatives and their frequencies are as follows.

M initiated, M hidden	8
C initiated, C hidden	2
M initiated, C hidden	11
C initiated, M hidden	0
[Ambiguous	1]

We may note that whilst there are at most three instances of the child initiating the hiding act, and all of these came at 15 months, they indicate that the child is by no means always a passive participant. We shall have more to say of this later in discussing role reversal. One of the striking features of what is hidden is that it is about equally distributed between the mother's face being masked and the child's—one of the forms of variation that the mother uses in order to keep uncertainty operative within the game. The child seems readily to accept this variation in the format and, indeed, seems to take a certain delight in it.

What is very notable is that there is virtually complete openness with regard to the instrument and mode used for hiding. The game when first observed was carried out exclusively with a nappy and hiding was controlled by the mother, and this occurred six times, hiding herself four times and the child twice. Thereafter, the distribution of the remaining episodes was five times nappy, five times clothing, three times a towel, two times a chair, and once with the child averting her head. In short, the nature of the hiding instrument and the masking act might almost be called optional in constrast to certain obligatory features, such as the requirement of initial contact.

During the period of hiding, and we shall discuss the limits on its length below, there is a further ancillary feature of the game—a mode of sustaining contact during hiding. This occurs both on the mother's side and on the child's. In 16 of the 22 episodes, mother uses either the rising intonation pattern of the typical Where question ('Where's Diane?' or 'Where's baby?' or 'Where's mummy?') or employs an extended 'Ahhhh', sometimes with a rising intonation pattern. In one sense, this act on the part of the mother can be thought of as helping the child sustain attention and bridging any uncertainty concerning the mother's 'conservation' behind the hiding instrument. The child's responses during

hiding seem, on the other hand, to be expressions of excitement or anticipation, though they help the mother control her own output of bridging vocalizations to keep the child at an appropriate activation level. There are 13 in 19 episodes involving a hiding cloth where the child actively seeks to remove the hiding mask from the mother's or her own face. It is to these initiatives that the mother often responds with vocalization as if to control the child's activation. This part of the game is characteristically 'non-rule bound' and seems to be an instance, rather, of the mother providing a scaffold for the child.

We come now to a crucial round in the game: uncovering and reappearance. Note first a point already made—hiding time is very constrained: 19 of the 22 episodes range between two and seven seconds, with only one being above seven (at 10 months) and two at one second. It is only at 15 months, when the child consistently controls reappearance, that there is a fairly homogeneous and rapid hiding time: five episodes in a row ranging from one to two seconds. But note that at this age the child has virtually given up 'static' peekaboo for an ambulatory version, so that variation is now in format rather than in timing. The five uniformly fast episodes were all with a nappy—an old and familiar game that is much less exciting for the child than the ambulatory game we shall describe below. One of these episodes, a one-second instance, was completely controlled by the child, and between two was an instance where the child demanded the game vocatively after she had failed to cover her own face successfully. We believe that the constraint on time of hiding is a reflection of the appreciation of the child's limited attention span by both members of the pair—the mother reacting to signs of the child's impatience, the child responding directly to his own.

The actual act of uncovering is open to considerable variation. We find instances where it is controlled by the child, others where the mother controls uncovering. Occasionally, the mother, by drawing near and vocalizing, provokes the child into removing the mask from her face, as if to stimulate more control from the infant. Indeed, one even encounters partial, 'tempting' uncovering by the mother to provoke the child into completion, where the mother exposes a corner of her eye. In terms of control of unmasking, we note that before 12 months, nine of 12 of the episodes of unmasking are controlled by the mother. From 12 on, none are, and six in 10 are controlled by the child alone—a phenomenon seen only once before this age.

Following uncovering, there is again a rather standard ritual: remaking contact. In the 19 episodes where we were able to determine it 14 uncoverings were accompanied by face-to-face contact immediately or shortly after. In all instances of uncovering but one, mother sought to establish such conduct, though in four she failed to do so. Moreover, in 16 of 22 episodes, mother vocalized upon uncovering, usually with a 'Boo' or a 'Hello' or an 'Ahhh'. Obviously, there is considerable release of tension at this point, since laughter accompanies the above 15 times for the child (and indeed 12 for the mother, always in accompaniment with the child).

At 15 months, the child invents and controls a new variation of the game, as already noted. It consists of her moving behind a chair, out of sight of her mother, then reappearing and saying 'Boo'. She has now become the agent in the play, mother being recipient of her action. The format has been revised by the child and the prior role of agent and recipient reversed. This variation in agency has, of course, appeared before in the more static form of the game involving a hiding instrument. But it is important to note that the child has now extended the rules under her own control to a new, but formally identical format—again involving initial face-to-face contact, hiding and reappearing by self-initiated movement, and reestablishing contact. From there on out, peekaboo is a game embedded in self-directed movement by the child that produces disappearance and reappearance. The child has not only learned to conform to the rules of the static game as initiated by mother and by child, but also to use the rules for the initiation of a variant of the old format. At this point, the range of possible games incorporating the basic rules of peekaboo becomes almost limitless, and what provides unity is the agreement of mother and infant to maintain a skeleton rule structure with new instruments for hiding and new settings in which to play. We can say that at this point the child is no longer performance-bound, but rather has achieved a proper 'competence' for generating new versions of an old game.

But we must turn now to the question of what brought the child to a full realization of the 'syntax' of the game of peekaboo so that he can henceforth be fully 'generative' in his disappearance-reappearance play. Before we do so, however, we must examine briefly three of the other children on whom we have sufficient data for analysis.

In the case of Lynn and her mother, the pattern is much the same as described, save for the fact that she begins to take over the active role of initiator of the game and controller of the mask as early as 10 months. She too, at 10 months, begins to use a stationary object, a chair, as a hiding mask behind which she moves, looking through the legs to effect reappearance. But she is still quite confused about it, and when mother says 'Boo' to herald her reappearance hides again rather than remaking contact. But she is on the way towards mastering the ambulatory variant.

Where Nan is concerned, the game is rather more sophisticated in an important respect. She and her mother share control. For example, at 11 months Nan lifts her petticoat over her face and leaves it in place until her mother says 'Boo' and then lowers it. This joint feature is a very consistent aspect of their games, but it must be regarded as a variant, for instances occur without joint control as well. Their turn-taking is also much more precisely segmented. For example, Nan raises her petticoat over her face, then lowers it after a few seconds, and waits for mother to say 'Boo' before showing any reaction herself—then usually responding to the mother's vocalizations with laughter. There is, in this instance, a separation between unmasking and vocalization, with a further timing element between the two.

Sandy and his mother are instances of a failure to develop workable rules because of excessive variation and some misreading by the mother. But the failure is instructive. Too often, the mother starts the game without having enlisted Sandy's attention. In other instances, when Sandy is having difficulty in hiding his own face behind a cloth, the mother takes the cloth (and the initiative) away from him and tries to do the masking herself. Interestingly, the game does not develop, and in its place there emerges a game in which Sandy crawls away from mother, she in pursuit, with excitement being exhibited by both when she catches him. He never serves as agent in this game. They are an instructive failure, and the disappearance of the game is reminiscent of the failures reported by Nelson (1973) that occur when mother attempts to correct the child's linguistic usage or insists upon an interpretation of the child's utterance that does not accord with his own. Under the circumstances, the lexical items in question disappear from the child's lexicon, just as peekaboo disappears from the game repertory of this pair.

DISCUSSION

When peekaboo first appears, our mothers often report, it is an extension or variation of a looming game in which the mother approaches the child from a distance of a meter or so, looms towards him almost to face-to-face contact, accompanying the close approach with a 'Boo' or a rising intonation. We know from the work of Bower (1971), Ball and Tronick (1971) and White (1963) that such looming produces considerable excitement and, indeed, when the loom is directly towards the face, a real or incipient avoidance response. The play may start by substituting disappearance of the face at a close point at which excitement has already been aroused. But this is not necessary. The only point one would wish to make is that, at the start, peekaboo involves an arousal of responses that are either innate or fairly close to innate. For even without the link to the looming game, disappearance and reappearance are 'manipulations' of object permanence, which is itself either innate or maturing through very early experience along the lines indicated by Piaget (1954). At least one can say unambiguously that, at the outset, peekaboo is not a game in the sense of it being governed by rules and conventions that are, in any respect, arbitrary. It is, rather, an exploitation by the mother of very strong, preadapted response tendencies in the infant, an exploitation that is rewarded by the child's responsiveness and pleasure.

William James (1890) comments in the *Principles* that an instinct is a response that only occurs once, thereafter being modified by experience. And surely one could say the same for the interaction involved in peekaboo. For once it has occurred, there rapidly develops a set of reciprocal anticipations in mother and child that begin to modify it and, more importantly, to conventionalize it. At the outset, this conventionalization is fostered by a quite standard or routine set of capers on the part of the mother—as we have noted, the early version involves a very limited range of hiding instruments, masking acts, vocalizations and time variations. At the outset, it is also very important for mother to keep the child's activation level at an appropriate intensity, and one is struck by the skill of mothers in knowing how to keep the child in an anticipatory mood, neither too sure of outcome nor too upset by a wide range of possibilities.

But what is most striking thereafter is precisely the systematic introduction of variations constrained by set rules. The basic rules are:

Initial contact

Disappearance

Reappearance

Reestablished contact

Within this rule context, there can be variations in degree and kind of vocalization for initial contact, in kind of mask, in who controls the mask, in whose face is masked, in who uncovers, in the form of vocalization upon uncovering, in the relation between uncovering and vocalization, and in the timing of the constituent elements (though this last is strikingly constrained by a capacity variable). What the child appears to be learning is not only the basic rules of the game, but the range of variation that is possible within the rule set. It is this emphasis upon patterned variation within a constraining rule set that seems crucial to the mastery of competence and generativeness. The process appears much as in concept attainment, in which the child learns the regularity of a concept by learning the variants in terms of which it expresses itself. What is different in peekaboo is that the child is not only learning such variants, but obviously getting great pleasure from the process and seeking it out.

It is hard to imagine any function for peekaboo aside from practice in the learning of rules in converting 'gut play' into play with conventions. But there may be one additional function. As Garvey (in press) has noted, one of the objectives of play in general is to give the child opportunity to explore the boundary between the 'real' and the 'make-believe'. We have never in our sample of peekaboo games seen a child exhibit the sort of separation pattern noted by Ainsworth (1964) when mother *really* leaves the scene. Mothers often report, moreover, that they frequently start their career of playing peekaboo by hiding their own faces rather than the infant's for fear of his being upset. Eight of the nine mothers asked about this point reported behaving in this way (Scaife, 1974). This suggests a sensitivity on the part of mothers to where the line may be between 'real' and 'make-believe' for the child. This function doubtless dwindles in time. Yet the game continues in its formal pattern, sustained in its attractiveness by being incorporated into new formats involving newly emergent behaviours (such as crawling or walking). An old pattern seems, then, to provide a framework for the pleasurable expression of new behaviour and allows the new behaviour to be quickly incorporated into a highly skilled, rule-governed pattern.

Questions

1.   What types of actions need to be coordinated in order for the infant and the adult to be successful at peekaboo?

2.   What roles do emotional arousal and emotional regulation play in the infants' ability to sustain play in games like peekaboo?

3.   What other games that adults play with infants might encourage the development of infants' motor, perceptual and social skills?

References

Ainsworth, M. D. S. (1964). Patterns of attachment behaviour shown by the infant in interaction with his mother. *Merrill-Palmer Quarterly, 10,* 51.

Ball, W., and Tronick, E. (1971). 'Infant responses to impending collision: optical and real', *Science, 171,* 818.

Bower, T. G. R. (1971). 'The object in the world of the infant', *Scientific American, 225,* 30.

Charlesworth, W. R. (1966). 'Persistence of orienting, and attending behaviour in infants as a function of stimulus-locus uncertainty', *Child Development, 37,* 473.

Garvey, C. (In press). 'Some properties of social play', *Merrill-Palmer Quarterly.*

Greenfield, P. M. (1970). 'Playing peekaboo with a four-month-old: a study of the role of speech and nonspeech sounds in the formation of a visual schema', Unpublished manuscript.

James, W. (1890). *The Principles of Psychology,* New York, Henry Holt.

Nelson, K. (1973). 'Structure and strategy in learning to talk', *Monographs of The Society for Research in Child Development, 38,* 1.

Piaget, J. (1954). *The Construction of Reality in the Child,* New York, Basic Books.

Scaife, M. (1974). Personal communication, Department of Experimental Psychology, Oxford University, Oxford.

White, B. L. (1963). 'Plasticity in perceptual development during the first six months of life', Paper presented to the American Association for the Advancement of Science, Cleveland, Ohio, 30 December.

10

How Do Infants Learn About the Physical World?

RENÉE BAILLARGEON

A recent major accomplishment in the field of developmental psychology has been the better understanding of cognitive development in infancy. For many years, developmentalists have believed that newborn infants must construct or learn about the physical properties of the world into which they are born. Recently, this belief has been called into question as researchers such as Renée Baillargeon have devised new methods for exploring infants' knowledge of the physical world. This article reviews this research and raises important questions about both the timing and origins of object knowledge.

Until recently, young infants were assumed to lack even the most fundamental of adults' beliefs about objects. This conclusion was based largely on analyses of young infants' performance in object manipulation tasks. For example, young infants were said to be unaware that an object continues to exist when masked by another object because they consistently failed tasks that required them to search for an object hidden beneath or behind another object.[1]

In time, however, researchers came to realize that young infants might fail tasks such as search tasks not because of limited physical knowledge, but because of difficulties associated with the planning and execution of action sequences. This concern led investigators to seek alternative methods for exploring young infants' physical knowledge, methods that did not depend on the manipulation of objects.

Reprinted with permission from the author and *Current Directions in Psychological Science, Vol. 3,* 1994, 133–140. Published by Cambridge University Press, New York. Copyright 1994 by the American Psychological Society.

This research was supported by grants from the Guggenheim Foundation, the University of Illinois Center for Advanced Study, and the National Institute of Child Health and Human Development (HD-21104). I would like to think Jerry DeJong, for his support and insight, and Susan Carey, Noam Chomsky, Judy DeLoache, Cindy Fischer, John Flavell, Laura Kotovsky, Brian Ross, and Bob Wyer, for many helpful comments and suggestions.

Infants' well-documented tendency to look longer at novel than at familiar events[2] suggested one alternative method for investigating young infants' beliefs about objects. In a typical experiment, infants are presented with two test events: a possible and an impossible event. The possible event is consistent with the expectation or belief examined in the experiment; the impossible event, in contrast, violates this expectation. The rationale is that if infants possess the belief being tested, they will perceive the impossible event as more novel or surprising than the possible event, and will therefore look reliably longer at the impossible than at the possible event.

Using this violation-of-expectation method, investigators have demonstrated that even very young infants possess many of the same fundamental beliefs about objects as adults do.[3,4] For example, infants aged 2.5 to 3.5 months are aware that objects continue to exist when masked by other objects, that objects cannot remain stable without support, that objects move along spatially continuous paths, and that objects cannot move through the space occupied by other objects.

The repeated demonstration of sophisticated physical knowledge in early infancy has led investigators in recent years to focus their efforts in a new direction. In addition to exploring what infants know about the physical world, researchers have become interested in the question of how infants attain their physical knowledge.

My colleagues and I have begun to build a model of the development of young infants' physical reasoning.[5–7] The model is based on the assumption that infants are born not with substantive beliefs about objects (e.g., intuitive notions of impenetrability, continuity, or force), as researchers such as Spelke[8] and Leslie[9] have proposed, but with highly constrained mechanisms that guide the development of infants' reasoning about objects. The model is derived from findings concerning infants' intuitions about different physical phenomena (e.g., support, collision, and unveiling phenomena). Comparison of these findings points to two developmental patterns that recur across ages and phenomena. We assume that these patterns reflect, at least indirectly, the nature and properties of infants' learning mechanisms. In this review, I describe the patterns and summarize some of the evidence supporting them.

FIRST PATTERN: IDENTIFICATION OF INITIAL CONCEPT AND VARIABLES

The first developmental pattern is that, when learning about a new physical phenomenon, infants first form a preliminary, all-or-none concept that captures the essence of the phenomenon but few of its details. With further experience, this *initial concept* is progressively elaborated. Infants slowly identify discrete and continuous *variables* that are relevant to the initial concept, study the effects of those variables, and incorporate this accrued knowledge into their reasoning, resulting in increasingly accurate predictions over time.

To illustrate the distinction between initial concepts and variables, I summarize experiments on the development of young infants' reasoning about support phenomena (conducted with Amy Needham, Julie DeVos, and Helen Raschke), collision phenomena (conducted with Laura Kotovsky), and unveiling phenomena (conducted with Julie DeVos).[3,5–7]

Support Phenomena

Our experiments on young infants' ability to reason about support phenomena have focused on simple problems involving a box and a platform. Our results indicate that by 3 months of age, if not before, infants expect the box to fall if it loses all contact with the platform and to remain stable otherwise. At this stage, any contact between the box and the platform is deemed sufficient to ensure the box's stability. At least two developments take place between 3 and 6.5 months of age. First, infants become aware that the locus of contact between the box and the platform must be taken into account when judging the box's stability. Infants initially assume that the

FIGURE 1   Paradigm for studying infants' understanding of support phenomena. In both events, a gloved hand pushes a box from left to right along the top of a platform. In the possible event (top), the box is pushed until its leading edge reaches the end of the platform. In the impossible event (bottom), the box is pushed until only the left 15% of its bottom surface rests on the platform.

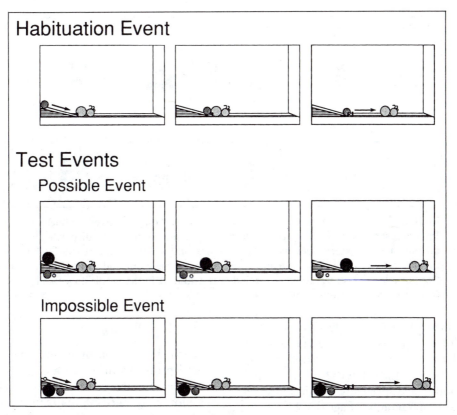

FIGURE 2   Paradigm for studying infants' understanding of collision phenomena. First, infants are habituated to (i.e., repeatedly shown) an event in which a blue, medium-size cylinder rolls down a ramp and hits a bug resting on one end of a track; the bug then rolls to the middle of the track. In the test events, two new cylinders are introduced, and the bug now rolls to the end of the track. The cylinder used in the possible event is a yellow cylinder larger than the habituation cylinder; the cylinder used in the impossible event is an orange cylinder smaller than the habituation cylinder.

box will remain stable if placed either on the top or against the side of the platform. By 4.5 to 5.5 months of age, however, infants come to distinguish between the two types of contact and recognize that only the former ensures support. The second development is that infants begin to appreciate that the amount of contact between the box and the platform affects the box's stability. Initially, infants believe that the box will be stable even if only a small portion (e.g., the left 15%) of its bottom surface rests on the platform (see Figure 1). By 6.5 months of age, however, infants expect the box to fall unless a significant portion of its bottom surface lies on the platform.

These results suggest the following developmental sequence. When learning about the support relation between two objects, infants first form an initial concept centered on a distinction between contact and no contact. With further experience, this initial concept is progressively revised. Infants identify first a discrete (locus of contact) and later a continuous (amount of contact) variable and incorporate these variables into their initial concept, resulting in more successful predictions over time.

Collision Phenomena

Our experiments on infants' reasoning about collision events have focused on simple problems involving a moving object (a cylinder that rolls down a ramp) and a stationary object (a large, wheeled toy bug resting on a track at the bottom of the ramp). Adults typically expect the bug to roll down the track when hit by the cylinder. When asked how far the bug will be displaced, adults are generally reluctant to hazard a guess (they are aware that the length of the bug's trajectory depends on a host of factors about which they have no information). After observing that the bug rolls to the middle of the track when hit by a medium-size cylinder, however, adults readily predict that the bug will roll farther with a larger cylinder and less far with a smaller cylinder made of identical material.

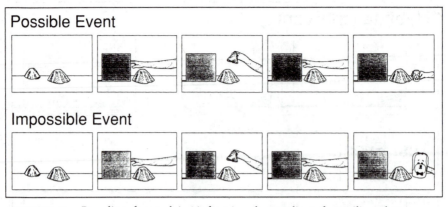

FIGURE 3   Paradigm for studying infants' understanding of unveiling phenomena. Infants first see two identical covers placed side by side; both covers display a small protuberance. Next, a screen hides the left cover, and a gloved hand reaches behind the screen twice in succession, reappearing first with the cover and then with a small (top) or a large (bottom) toy dog. Each dog is held next to the visible cover, so that their sizes can be readily compared.

Our experiments indicate that by 2.5 months of age, infants already possess clear expectations that the bug should remain stationary when not hit (e.g., when a barrier prevents the cylinder from contacting the bug) and should be displaced when hit. However, it is not until 5.5 to 6.5 months of age that infants are able to judge, after seeing that the medium cylinder causes the bug to roll to the middle of the track, that the bug should roll farther with the larger but not the smaller cylinder (see Figure 2). Younger infants are not surprised to see the bug roll to the end of the track when hit by either the larger or the smaller cylinder, even though all three of the cylinders are simultaneously present in the apparatus, so that their sizes can be readily compared, and even though the infants have no difficulty remembering (as shown in other experiments) that the bug rolled to the middle of the track with the medium cylinder. These results suggest that prior to 5.5 to 6.5 months of age, infants are unaware that the size of the cylinder can be used to reason about the length of the bug's trajectory.

One interpretation of these findings is that when learning about collision events between a moving and a stationary object, infants first form an initial concept centered on a distinction between impact and no impact. With further experience, infants begin to identify variables that influence this initial concept. By 5.5 to 6.5 months of age, infants realize that the size of the moving object can be used to predict how far the stationary object will be displaced. After seeing how far a stationary object travels with a moving object of a given size, infants readily use this information to calibrate their predictions about how far the stationary object will travel with moving objects of different sizes.

Unveiling Phenomena

Our experiments on unveiling phenomena have involved problems in which a cloth cover is removed to reveal an object. Our results indicate that by 9.5 months of age, infants realize that the presence (or absence) of a protuberance in the cover signals the presence (or absence) of an object beneath the cover. Infants are surprised to see a toy retrieved from under a cover that lies flat on a surface, but not from under a cover that displays a marked protuberance.

At this stage, however, infants are not yet aware that the size of the protuberance in the cover can be used to infer the size of the object beneath the cover. When shown a cover with a small protuberance, they are not surprised to see either a small or a large toy retrieved from under the cover. Furthermore, providing infants with a reminder of the protuberance's size has no effect on their performance. In one experiment, for example, infants saw two identical covers placed side by side; both covers displayed a small protuberance (see Figure 3). After a few seconds, a screen hid the left cover; the right cover remained visible to the right of the screen. Next, a hand reached behind the screen's right edge twice in succession, reappearing first with the cover and then with a small (possible event) or a large (impossible event) toy dog. Each dog was held next to the visible cover, so that their sizes could be readily compared. At 9.5 months of age, infants judged that either dog could have been hidden under the cover behind the screen. At 12.5 months of age, however, infants showed reliable surprise at the large dog's retrieval.

Together, these results suggest the following developmental sequence. When learning about unveiling phenomena, infants first form an initial concept centered on a distinction between protuberance and no protuberance. Later on, infants identify a continuous variable that affects this concept: They begin to appreciate that the size of the protuberance in the cover can be used to infer the size of the object under the cover.

Comments

How can the developmental sequences described in this section be explained? As I mentioned earlier, we assume that these sequences reflect not the gradual unfolding of innate beliefs, but the application of highly constrained, innate learning mechanisms to available data. In this approach, the problem of explaining the age at which specific initial concepts and variables are understood is that of determining (a) what data—observations or manipulations—are necessary for learning and (b) when these data become available to infants.

For example, one might propose that 3-month-old infants have already learned that objects fall when released in midair because this expectation is consistent with countless observations (e.g., watching their caretakers drop peas in pots, toys in baskets, clothes in hampers) and manipulations (e.g., noticing that their pacifiers fall when they open their mouths) available virtually from birth. Furthermore, one might speculate that it is not until 6.5 months that infants begin to appreciate how much contact is needed between objects and their supports because it is not until this age that infants have available pertinent data from which to abstract such a variable. Researchers have reported that the ability to sit without support emerges at about 6 months of age; infants then become able to sit in front of tables (e.g., on a parent's lap or in a high chair) with their upper limbs and hands relieved from the encumbrance of postural maintenance and thus free to manipulate objects.[10] For the first time, infants may have the opportunity to deposit objects on tables and to note that objects tend to fall unless significant portions of their bottom surfaces are supported. In the natural course of events, infants would be unlikely to learn about such a variable from observation alone because caretakers rarely deposit objects on the edges of surfaces. There is no a priori reason, however, to assume that infants could not learn such a variable if given appropriate observations (e.g., seeing that a box falls when released on the edge of a platform). We are currently conducting a "teaching" experiment to investigate this possibility; our preliminary results are extremely encouraging and suggest that very few observations may be necessary to set infants on the path to learning.

SECOND PATTERN: USE OF QUALITATIVE AND QUANTITATIVE STRATEGIES

In the previous section, I proposed that when learning about a novel physical phenomenon, infants first develop an all-or-none initial concept and later identify discrete and continuous variables that affect this concept. The second developmental pattern suggested by current evidence concerns the strategies infants use when reasoning about continuous variables. Following the terminology used in computational models of everyday physical reasoning,[11] a strategy is said to be *quantitative* if it requires infants to encode and use information about absolute quantities (e.g., object A is "this" large or has traveled "this" far from object B, where "this" stands for some absolute measure of A's size or distance from B). In contrast, a strategy is said to be *qualitative* if it requires infants to encode and use information about relative quantities (e.g., object A is larger than or has traveled farther than object B). After identifying a continuous variable, infants appear to succeed in reasoning about the variable qualitatively before they succeed in doing so quantitatively.

To illustrate the distinction between infants' use of qualitative and quantitative strategies, I report experiments on the development of infants' ability to reason about collision phenomena (conducted with Laura Kotovsky), unveiling phenomena (conducted with Julie DeVos), and barrier phenomena.[3, 5–7]

Collision Phenomena

As I explained earlier, 5.5- to 6.5-month-old infants are surprised, after observing that a medium-size cylinder causes a bug to roll to the middle of a track, to see the bug roll farther when hit by a smaller but not a larger cylinder. Such a finding suggests that by 5.5 to 6.5 months of age, infants are aware that the size of the cylinder affects the length of the bug's trajectory.

In these initial experiments, the small, medium, and large cylinders were placed side by side at the start of each event, allowing infants to compare their sizes directly. In subsequent experiments, only one cylinder was present in the apparatus in each test event. Under these conditions, 6.5-month-old infants were no longer surprised when the small cylinder caused the bug to roll to the end of the track; only

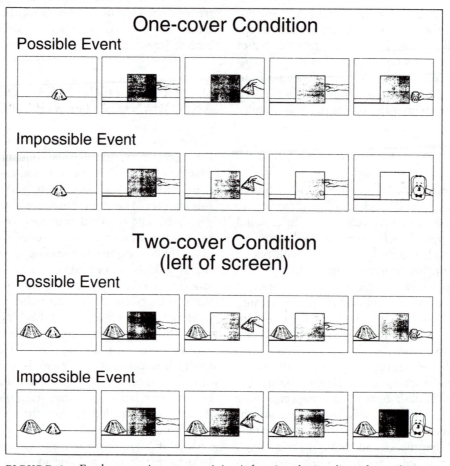

FIGURE 4   Further experiments examining infants' understanding of unveiling phenomena. These test events are identical to those depicted in Figure 3 except that only one cover is used (top) or the second, identical cover is placed to the left of the screen (bottom). In the latter condition, infants can no longer compare in a single glance the height of the dog to that of the second cover.

older, 7.5 month-old infants showed surprise at this event.

Our interpretation of these results is that at 5.5 to 6.5 months of age, infants are able to reason about the cylinder's size only qualitatively: They can predict the effect of modifications in the cylinder's size only when they are able to encode such modifications in relative terms (e.g., "this cylinder is smaller than the one used in the last trial"). When infants are forced to encode and compare the absolute sizes of the cylinders, because the cylinders are never shown side by side, they fail the task. By 7.5 months of age, however, infants have already overcome this initial limitation and succeed in the task even when they must rely on their representation of the absolute size of each cylinder to do so.[12]

Unveiling Phenomena

In the previous section, I reported that 9.5-month-old infants are not surprised to see either a small or a large toy dog retrieved from under a cover with a small protuberance, even when a second, identical cover is present. Unlike these younger infants, however, 12.5-month-old infants *are* surprised when the large dog is brought into view. This last finding suggests that by 12.5 months of age, infants are aware that the size of the protuberance in a cloth cover can be used to infer the size of the object under the cover.

In our initial experiment, 12.5 month-old infants were tested with the second cover present to the right of the screen (see Figure 3). Subsequent

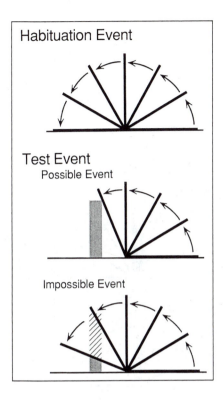

FIGURE 5 Paradigm for studying infants' understanding of barrier phenomena. Infants are first habituated to a screen that rotates through a 180° arc, in the manner of a drawbridge. Next, a large box is placed behind the screen. In the possible event, the screen stops when it encounters the box (112° arc); in the impossible event, the screen stops after rotating through the top 80% of the space occupied by the box (157° arc).

experiments were conducted without the second cover (see Figure 4, top panel) or with the second cover placed to the left, rather than to the right, of the screen (see Figure 4, bottom panel); in the latter condition, infants could no longer compare in a single glance the size of the dog to that of the cover. Our results indicated that 12.5-month-old infants fail both of these conditions: They no longer show surprise when the large dog is retrieved from behind the screen. By 13.5 months of age, however, infants are surprised by the large dog's retrieval even when no second cover is present.

These results suggest that at 12.5 months of age, infants are able to reason about the size of the protuberance in the cover only qualitatively: They can determine which dog could have been hidden under the cover only if they are able to compare, in a single glance, the size of the dog with that of a second, identical cover (e.g., "the dog is bigger than the

cover"). When infants are forced to represent the absolute size of the protuberance in the cover, they fail the task. By 13.5 months of age, however, infants have already progressed beyond this initial limitation; they no longer have difficulty representing the absolute size of the protuberance and comparing it with that of each dog.

Barrier Phenomena

Our experiments on barrier phenomena have focused on problems involving a moving object (a rotating screen) and a stationary barrier (a large box). In the test events, infants first see the screen lying flat against the apparatus floor; the box stands clearly visible behind the screen. Next, the screen rotates about its distant edge, progressively occluding the box. At 4.5 months of age, infants expect the screen to stop when it reaches the occluded box; they are surprised if the screen rotates unhindered through a full 180° arc. However, infants are initially poor at predicting at what point the screen should encounter the box and stop. When shown a possible event in which the screen stops against the box (112° arc) and an impossible event in which the screen stops after rotating through the top 80% of the space occupied by the box (157° arc), 6.5-month-old infants give evidence of detecting this 80% violation, but 4.5-month-old infants do not: They judge both the 112° and the 157° stopping points to be consistent with the box's height and location (see Figure 5).

In subsequent experiments, we examined whether 4.5-month-old infants would succeed in detecting the 80% violation if provided with a second, identical box. In one condition, this second box was placed to the right of and in the same frontoparallel plane as the box behind the screen (see Figure 6, left panel). In the possible event, the screen stopped when aligned with the top of the second box; in the impossible event, the screen rotated past the top of the second box. In another condition, the second box was placed to the right of but slightly in front of the box behind the screen (see Figure 6, right panel). In this condition, the screen rotated past the top of the second box in each test event. The infants succeeded in detecting the 80% violation in the first but not the second condition.

These results suggest that at 4.5 months of age, infants are able to reason about the box's height and location only qualitatively: They can predict the screen's stopping point only when they are able to rely on a simple alignment strategy (e.g., "the screen

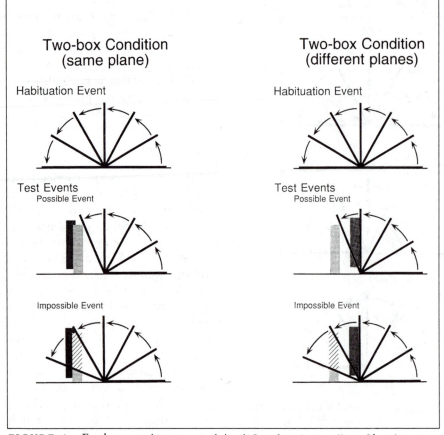

FIGURE 6   Further experiments examining infants' understanding of barrier phenomena. These events are identical to those depicted in Figure 5 except that a second, identical box stands to the right of and in the same fronto-parallel plane as the box behind the screen (left) or to the right and in front of the box behind the screen (right).

is aligned with the top of the visible box"). By 6.5 months of age, however, infants have already progressed beyond this point; they can use their representations of the occluded box's height and distance from the screen to estimate, within broad limits, at what point the screen will stop.

Comments

How should the developmental sequences described in this section be explained? We think it unlikely that these sequences reflect the maturation of infants' general quantitative reasoning or information processing because the same pattern recurs at different ages for different phenomena. What phenomenon-specific changes could account for the findings reported here? At least two hypotheses can be advanced. On the one hand, it could be that when first

reasoning about a continuous variable, infants either do not spontaneously encode information about this variable or do not encode this information swiftly enough or precisely enough for it to be of use in the tasks examined here (e.g., infants do not encode the size of the protuberance in the cover and hence are unable to judge which dog could have been hidden beneath it). On the other hand, infants could encode the necessary quantitative information but have difficulty accessing or processing this information in the context of deriving new and unfamiliar predictions (e.g., infants encode the protuberance's size and realize that they must compare it with that of the dog, but are thwarted in performing this comparison by the added requirement of having to retrieve part of the information from memory). Future research will no doubt help determine which, if either, of these hypotheses is correct.

CONCLUDING REMARKS

I have argued that in learning to reason about a novel physical phenomenon, infants first form an all-or-none concept and then add to this initial concept discrete and continuous variables that are discovered to affect the phenomenon. Furthermore, I have proposed that after identifying continuous variables, infants succeed in reasoning first qualitatively and only later quantitatively about the variables.

This sketchy description may suggest a rather static view of development in which accomplishments, once attained, are retained in their initial forms. Nothing could be further from the truth, however. Our data suggest that the variables infants identify evolve over time, as do the qualitative and quantitative strategies infants devise. When judging whether a box resting on a platform is stable, for example, infants initially focus exclusively on the amount of contact between the box's bottom surface and the platform, and as a consequence treat symmetrical and asymmetrical boxes alike. By the end of the 1st year, however, infants appear to have revised their definition of this variable to take into account the shape (or weight distribution) of the box.[5] Similarly, evidence obtained with the rotating-screen paradigm suggests that infants' quantitative reasoning continues to improve over time (e.g., 6.5-month-old infants can detect 80% but not 50% violations, whereas 8.5-month-old infants can detect both), as does their qualitative reasoning (e.g., 6.5 month-old infants will make use of a second box to detect a violation even if this second box differs markedly in color from the box behind the screen, whereas 4.5-month-old infants will not).[3]

The model of the development of infants' physical reasoning proposed here suggests many questions for future research. In particular, what are the innate constraints that guide this development? Are infants born with core principles (e.g., intuitive notions of impenetrability and continuity) that direct their interpretations of physical events? Or are infants, as I suggested earlier, equipped primarily with learning mechanisms that are capable, when applied to coherent sets of observations, of producing appropriate generalizations? What evidence would help distinguish between these two views?

Some insight into this question may be gained by considering two predictions that proponents of the innate-principles view might offer. The first prediction is that when reasoning about a physical event involving a core principle, infants should succeed at about the same age at detecting all equally salient violations of the principle. Thus, researchers who deem impenetrability a likely core principle might expect infants who realize that a small object cannot pass through a gapless surface to understand also that a large object cannot pass through a small gap; provided that the two situations violate the impenetrability principle to a similar degree, they would be expected to yield identical interpretations. The second prediction is that infants should succeed at about the same age at reasoning about different physical events that implicate the same underlying core principle. Thus, it might be proposed that infants who are successful at reasoning about objects' passage through gaps should be just as adept at reasoning about objects' entry into containers, because both phenomena would trigger the application of the impenetrability principle.

The model presented here departs systematically from the two predictions just described. First, the model predicts explicitly that when reasoning about physical events, infants succeed in detecting certain types of violations before others. Thus, in contrast to the innate-principles view, the model would expect infants to recognize that a small object cannot pass through a gapless surface before they recognize that a large object cannot pass through a smaller gap. This developmental sequence would be cast in terms of the formation of an initial concept centered on a distinction between gap and no gap, followed by the identification of size as a continuous variable relevant to the phenomenon.

Second, the present model also diverges from the prediction that different physical events that implicate the same core principle should be understood at about the same age. The results summarized in the preceding sections and elsewhere[6] —such as the finding that unveiling tasks yield the same developmental patterns as rotating-screen tasks, but at much later ages—suggest that infants respond to physical events not in terms of abstract underlying principles, but in terms of concrete categories corresponding to specific ways in which objects behave or interact. Thus, according to our model, it would not be at all surprising to find that infants succeed in reasoning about gaps several weeks or months before they do containers; the order of acquisition of the two categories would be expected to depend on the content of infants' daily experiences. The model does not rule out the possibility that infants eventually come to realize that superficially distinct events—such as those involving gaps and containers, or rotating screens and cloth covers—can be deeply related; unlike the innate-principles view, however, the model considers such a realization a product, rather than a point of departure, of learning.

One advantage of the view that infants process physical events in terms of concrete categories focusing on specific types of interactions between objects is that this view makes it possible to explain incorrect interpretations that appear to stem from miscategorizations of events. Pilot data collected in our laboratory suggest that young infants expect a moving object to stop when it encounters a tall, thin box but not a short, wide box, even when the latter is considerably larger in volume than the former. We suspect that infants are led by the dominant vertical axis of the tall box to perceive it as a wall-like, immovable object, and hence categorize the event as an instance of a barrier phenomenon; in contrast, infants tend to view the wide box as a movable object, and hence categorize the event as an instance of a collision phenomenon, resulting in incorrect predictions.

The foregoing discussion highlighted several types of developmental sequences that would be anticipated in an innate-mechanisms view but not

(without considerable elaboration) in an innate-principles view. To gain further insight into the nature and origins of these developmental sequences, we have adopted a dual research strategy. First, we are examining the development of infants' understanding of additional physical phenomena (e.g., gap, containment, and occlusion phenomena) to determine how easily these developments can be captured in terms of the patterns described in the model and to compare more closely the acquisition time lines of phenomena that are superficially distinct but deeply related. Second, as was alluded to earlier, we are attempting to teach infants initial concepts and variables to uncover what kinds of observations, and how many observations, are required for learning. We hope that the pursuit of these two strategies will eventually allow us to specify the nature of the learning mechanisms that infants bring to the task of learning about the physical world.

Questions

1. What are the major changes in object understanding that Piaget believed occur over infancy and how does evidence from recent studies by Baillargeon challenge this view?

2. What, according to Baillargeon, gives rise to the development of object knowledge in infants?

3. Try to think of an alternative explanation for the infant behavior observed in one of the studies discussed in this article. Whose explanation, Piaget's, Baillargeon's, or yours, is the most persuasive and why?

Notes

1. J. Piaget, *The Construction of Reality in the Child* (Basic Books, New York, 1954).

2. E. S. Spelke, Preferential looking methods as tools for the study of cognition in infancy, in *Measurement of Audition and Vision in the First Year of Postnatal Life,* G. Gottlieb and N. Krasnegor, Eds. (Ablex, Norwood, NJ, 1985).

3. R. Baillargeon, The object concept revisited: New directions in the investigation of infants' physical knowledge, in *Visual Perception and Cognition in Infancy,* C. E. Granrud, Ed. (Erlbaum, Hillsdale, NJ, 1993).

4. E. S. Spelke, K. Breinlinger, J. Macomber, and K. Jacobson, Origins of knowledge, *Psychological Review, 99,* 605–632 (1992).

5. R. Baillargeon, L. Kotovsky, and A. Needham, The acquisition of physical knowledge in infancy, in *Causal Understandings in Cognition and Culture,* G. Lewis, D. Premack, and D. Sperber, Eds. (Oxford University Press, Oxford, in press).

6. R. Baillargeon, A model of physical reasoning in infancy, in *Advances in Infancy Research,* Vol. 9, C. Rovee-Collier and L. Lipsitt, Eds. (Ablex, Norwood, NJ, in press).

7. R. Baillargeon, Physical reasoning in infants, in *The Cognitive Neurosciences,* M.S. Gazzaniga, Ed. (MIT Press, Cambridge, MA, in press).

8. E. S. Spelke, Physical knowledge in infancy: Reflections on Piaget's theory, in *The Epigenesis of Mind: Essays on Biology and Cognition,* S. Carey and R. Gelman, Eds. (Erlbaum, Hillsdale, NJ, 1991).

9. A. M. Leslie, ToMM, ToBy, and Agency: Core architecture and domain specificity, in *Causal Understandings in Cognition and Culture,* G. Lewis, D. Premack, and D. Sperber, Eds. (Oxford University Press, Oxford, in press).

10. P. Rochat and A. Bullinger, Posture and functional action in infancy, in *Francophone Perspectives on Structure and Process in Mental Development,* A. Vyt, H. Bloch, and M. Bornstein, Eds. (Erlbaum, Hillsdale, NJ, in press).

11. K. D. Forbus, Qualitative process theory, *Artificial Intelligence, 24,* 85–168 (1984).

12. This example focused exclusively on the size of the cylinder, but what of the distance traveled by the bug in each event? It seems likely that infants encode this information not in quantitative terms (e.g., "the bug traveled x as opposed to y distance"), but rather in qualitative terms, using as their point of reference the track itself (e.g., "the bug rolled to the middle of the track"), their own spatial position (e.g., "the bug stopped in front of me"), or the brightly decorated back wall of the apparatus (e.g., "the bug stopped in front of such-and-such section of the back wall").

11

Early Experience and Emotional Development: The Emergence of Wariness of Heights

JOSEPH J. CAMPOS, BENNETT I. BERTENTHAL, AND ROSANNE KERMOIAN

The existence of gravity affects all life on earth including the life of the human embryo and the newborn child. At birth, a newborn, when allowed to fall, exhibits characteristic grasping reflexes and a primary emotion, fear. How does this emotion develop and play a role in organizing children's behavior early in life? In the following article, Joseph Campos, Bennett Bertenthal, and Rosanne Kermoian discuss the relation between early locomotor experience and the development of fear.

Because of its biological adaptive value, wariness of heights is widely believed to be innate or under maturational control. In this report, we present evidence contrary to this hypothesis, and show the importance of locomotor experience for emotional development. Four studies bearing on this conclusion have shown that (1) when age is held constant, locomotor experience accounts for wariness of heights; (2) "artificial" experience locomoting in a walker generates evidence of wariness of heights; (3) an orthopedically handicapped infant tested longitudinally did not show wariness of heights so long as he had no locomotor experience; and (4) regardless of the age when infants begin to crawl, it is the duration of locomotor experience and not age that predicts avoidance of heights. These findings suggest that when infants begin to crawl, experiences generated by locomotion make possible the development of wariness of heights.

Reprinted with permission from the authors and *Psychological Science, Vol. 3*, 1992, 61–64. Published by Cambridge University Press, New York. Copyright 1992 by the American Psychological Society.

This research was supported by grants from the National Institutes of Health (HD–16195, HD–00695, and HD–25066) and from the John D. and Catherine T. MacArthur Foundation.

Between 6 and 10 months of age, major changes occur in fearfulness in the human infant. During this period, some fears are shown for the first time, and many others show a step-function increase in prevalence (Bridges, 1932; Scarr & Salapatek, 1970; Sroufe, 1979). These changes in fearfulness occur so abruptly, involve so many different elicitors, and have such biologically adaptive value that many investigators propose maturational explanations for this developmental shift (Emde, Gaensbauer, & Harmon, 1976; Kagan, Kearsley, & Zelazo, 1978). For such theorists, the development of neurophysiological structures (e.g., the frontal lobes) precedes and accounts for changes in affect.

In contrast to predominantly maturational explanations of developmental changes, Gottlieb (1983, 1991) proposed a model in which different types of experiences play an important role in developmental shifts. He emphasized that new developmental acquisitions, such as crawling, generate experiences that, in turn, create the conditions for further developmental changes. Gottlieb called such "bootstrapping" processes probabilistic epigenesis. In contrast to most current models of developmental transition, Gottlieb's approach stresses the possibility that, under some circumstances, psychological function may precede and account for development of neurophysiological structures.

There is evidence in the animal literature that a probabilistic epigenetic process plays a role in the development of wariness of heights. Held and Hein (1963), for instance, showed that dark-reared kittens given experience with active self-produced locomotion in an illuminated environment showed avoidance of heights, whereas dark-reared littermates given passive experience moving in the same environment manifested no such avoidance. In these studies, despite equivalent maturational states in the two groups of kittens, the experiences made possible by correlated visuomotor responses during active locomotion proved necessary to elicit wariness of heights.

So long as they are prelocomotor, human infants, despite their visual competence and absence of visual deprivation, may be functionally equivalent to Held and Hein's passively moved kittens. Crawling may generate or refine skills sufficient for the onset of wariness of heights. These skills may include improved calibration of distances, heightened sensitivity to visually specified self-motion, more consistent coordination of visual and vestibular stimulation, and increased awareness of emotional signals from significant others (Bertenthal & Campos, 1990; Campos, Hiatt, Ramsay, Henderson, & Svejda, 1978).

There is anecdotal evidence supporting a link between locomotor experience and development of wariness of heights in human infants. Parents commonly report that there is a phase following the acquisition of locomotion when infants show no avoidance of heights, and will go over the edge of a bed or other precipice if the caretaker is not vigilant. Parents also report that this phase of apparent fearlessness is followed by one in which wariness of heights becomes quite intense (Campos et al., 1978).

In sum, both the kitten research and the anecdotal human evidence suggest that wariness of heights is not simply a maturational phenomenon, to be expected even in the absence of experience. From the perspective of probabilistic epigenesis, locomotor experience may operate as an organizer of emotional development, serving either to induce wariness of heights (i.e., to produce a potent emotional state that would never emerge without such experience) or to facilitate its emergence (i.e., to bring it about earlier than it otherwise would appear). The research reported here represents an attempt to determine whether locomotor experience is indeed an organizer of the emergence of wariness of heights.

Pinpointing the role of locomotion in the emergence of wariness of heights in human infants requires solution of a number of methodological problems. One is the selection of an ecologically valid paradigm for testing wariness of heights. Another is the determination of an outcome measure that can be used with both prelocomotor and locomotor infants. A third is a means of determining whether locomotion is playing a role as a correlate, an antecedent, an inducer, or a facilitator of the onset of wariness of heights.

The ecologically valid paradigm we selected for testing was the visual cliff (Walk, 1966; Walk & Gibson, 1961)—a large, safety-glass-covered table with a solid textured surface placed immediately underneath the glass on one side (the "shallow" side) and a similar surface placed some 43 in. underneath the glass on the floor below on the other side (the "deep" side).

To equate task demands for prelocomotor and locomotor infants, we measured the infants' wariness reactions while they were slowly lowered toward either the deep or the shallow side of the cliff. This descent procedure not only allowed us to assess differences in wariness reactions as a function of locomotor experience in both prelocomotor and locomotor infants but also permitted us to assess an index of depth perception, that is, a visual placing response (the extension of the arms and hands in anticipation of contact with the shallow, but not the deep, surface of the cliff [Walters, 1981]).

To assess fearfulness with an index appropriate to both pre- and postlocomoting infants, we measured heart rate (HR) responses during the 3-s period of descent onto the surface of the cliff. Prior work had shown consistently that heart rate decelerates in infants who are in a state of nonfearful attentiveness, but accelerates when infants are showing either a defensive response (Graham & Clifton, 1966) or a precry state (Campos, Emde, Gaensbauer, & Henderson, 1975).

To relate self-produced locomotion to fearfulness, we used a number of converging research operations. One was an *age-held-constant design,* contrasting the performance of infants who were locomoting with those of the same age who were not yet locomoting; the second was an analog of an experiential *enrichment* manipulation, in which infants who were otherwise incapable of crawling or creeping were tested after they had a number of hours of experience moving about voluntarily in walker devices; the third was an analog of an experiential *deprivation* manipulation, in which an infant who was orthopedically handicapped, but otherwise normal, was tested longitudinally past the usual age of onset of crawling and again after the delayed acquisition of crawling; and the fourth was a *cross-sequential lag design* aimed at teasing apart the effects of age of onset of locomotion and of duration of locomotor experience on the infant's avoidance of crossing the deep or the shallow side of the cliff to the mother.

EXPERIMENT 1: HR RESPONSES OF PRELOCOMOTOR AND LOCOMOTOR INFANTS

In the first study, a total of 92 infants, half locomoting for an average of 5 weeks, were tested at 7.3 months of age. Telemetered HR, facial expressions (taped from a camera under the deep side of the cliff), and the visual placing response were recorded. Each infant was lowered to each side of the cliff by a female experimenter, with the mother in another room.

As predicted from the work of Held and Hein (1963), locomotor infants showed evidence of wariness of heights, and prelocomotor infants did not. Only on deep trials did the HR of locomotor infants accelerate significantly from baselevels (by 5 beats/min), and differ significantly from the HR responses of prelocomotor infants. The HR responses of prelocomotor infants did not differ from baselevels on either the deep or shallow sides. Surprisingly, facial expressions did not differentiate testing conditions,

perhaps because the descent minimized the opportunity to target these expressions to social figures.

In addition, every infant tested, regardless of locomotor status, showed visual placing responses on the shallow side, and no infant showed placing responses on the deep side of the cliff. Thus, all infants showed evidence for depth perception on the deep side, but only locomotor infants showed evidence of fear-related cardiac acceleration in response to heights.

EXPERIMENT 2: ACCELERATION OF LOCOMOTOR EXPERIENCE

Although correlated, the development of locomotion and the emergence of wariness of heights may be jointly determined by a third factor that brings about both changes. Disambiguation of this possibility required a means of providing "artificial" locomotor experience to infants who were not yet able to crawl. This manipulation was achieved by providing wheeled walkers to infants and testing them after their mothers had reported at least 32 hr of voluntary forward movement in the device.

Infants who received walkers were divided into two groups: prelocomotor walkers (N = 9M, 9F, Mean Age = 224 days, Walker Experience = 47 hr of voluntary forward movement) and locomotor walkers (N = 9M, 7F, Mean Age = 222 days, Walker Experience = 32 hr). The performance of infants in these two groups was compared with the performance of age-matched subjects, also divided into two groups: prelocomotor controls (N = 9M, 9F, Mean Age = 222 days) and locomotor controls (N = 9M, 7F, Mean Age = 222 days). The average duration of crawling experience was only 5 days in the locomotor walker and the locomotor control groups. All infants were tested using the same procedure as in the prior study. No shallow trials were administered in order to minimize subject loss due to the additional testing time required for such trials.

As revealed in Figure 1, the three groups of infants with any type of locomotor experience showed evidence of cardiac acceleration, whereas the prelocomotor control infants did not. It is noteworthy that all 16 infants in the locomotor walker group (who had a "double dosage" of locomotor experience consisting of walker training and some crawling) showed HR accelerations upon descent to the cliff. Planned comparisons revealed significant differences between (1) all walker infants and all controls, (2) all spontaneously locomoting infants and prelocomotor controls, and (3) prelocomotor walkers and prelocomotor controls. These findings show that the

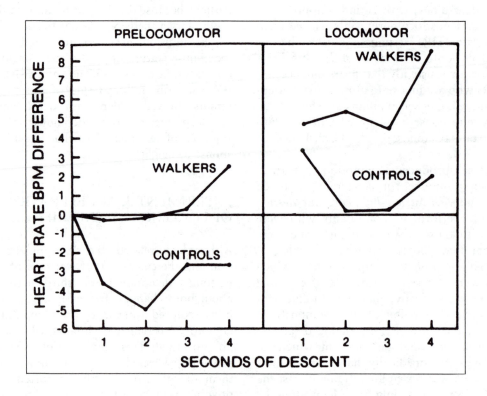

FIGURE 1   Heart rate response while the infant is lowered toward the deep side
of the visual cliff as a function of locomotor experience. The left panel contrasts the
performance of prelocomotor infants with and without "artificial" walker experience.
The right panel contrasts the performance of crawling infants with and without
"artificial" walker experience. Heart rate is expressed as difference from baseline in
beats/min.

provision of "artificial" locomotor experience may
facilitate or induce wariness of heights, even for infants who otherwise have little or no crawling experience. Locomotor experience thus appears to be an
antecedent of the emergence of wariness.

EXPERIMENT 3: DEPRIVATION OF LOCOMOTOR EXPERIENCE

Although Experiment 2 showed that training in
locomotion accelerates the onset of wariness
of heights, it is possible that this response would
eventually develop even in the absence of locomotor
experience. To determine whether the delayed acquisition of crawling precedes the delayed emergence of wariness of heights, we longitudinally tested
an infant with a peripheral handicap to locomotion.
This infant was neurologically normal and had a

Bayley Developmental Quotient of 126, but was born
with two congenitally dislocated hips. After an early
operation, he was placed in a full body cast. The infant was tested on the visual cliff monthly between 6
and 10 months of age using the procedures described
above. While the infant was in the cast, he showed no
evidence of crawling. At 8.5 months of age (i.e., 1.5
months after the normative age of onset of locomotion), the cast was removed, and the infant began
crawling soon afterward.

This infant showed no evidence of differential
cardiac responsiveness on the deep versus shallow
side of the cliff until 10 months of age, at which
time his HR accelerated markedly on the deep side,
and decelerated on the shallow. Although we cannot
generalize from a single case study, these data provide further support for the role of self-produced locomotion as a facilitator or inducer of wariness of
heights.

EXPERIMENT 4: AGE OF ONSET OF LOCOMOTION VERSUS LOCOMOTOR EXPERIENCE

In the studies described so far, HR was used as an imperfect index of wariness. However, we felt that a study using behavioral avoidance was needed to confirm the link between locomotor experience and wariness of heights. We thus used the locomotor crossing test on the visual cliff, in which the infant is placed on the center of the cliff, and the mother is instructed to encourage the infant to cross to her over either the deep or the shallow side. In this study, we also assessed separately the effects of age of onset of crawling (early, normative, or late) and of duration of locomotor experience (11 or 41 days), as well as their interaction, using a longitudinal design.

The results of this study demonstrated a clear effect of locomotor experience independent of the age when self-produced locomotion first appeared. This effect of experience was evident with both nominal data (the proportion of infants who avoided descending onto the deep side of the cliff on the first test trial) and interval data (the latency to descend from the center board of the visual cliff onto the deep side on deep trials minus the latency to descend onto the shallow side on shallow trials). At whatever age the infant had begun to crawl, only 30% to 50% of infants avoided the deep side after 11 days of locomotor experience. However, after 41 days of locomotor experience, avoidance increased to 60% to 80% of infants. The latency data revealed a significant interaction of side of cliff with locomotor experience, but not a main effect of age, nor of the interaction of age with experience. The results of this study further suggest that locomotor experience paces the onset of wariness of heights.

PROCESSES UNDERLYING THE DEVELOPMENT OF WARINESS OF HEIGHTS

The pattern of findings obtained in these four studies, taken together with the animal studies by Held and Hein (1963), demonstrates a consistent relation between locomotor experience and wariness of heights. We propose the following interpretations for our findings.

We believe that crawling initially is a goal in itself, with affect solely linked to the success or failure of implementing the act of moving. Locomotion is initially not context dependent, and infants show no wariness of heights because the goal of moving is not coordinated with other goals, including the avoidance of threats. However, as a result of locomotor experience, infants acquire a sense of both the efficacy and the limitations of their own actions. Locomotion stops being an end in itself, and begins to be goal corrected and coordinated with the environmental surround. As a result, infants begin to show wariness of heights once locomotion becomes context dependent (cf. Bertenthal & Campos, 1990).

The context-dependency of the infants' actions may come about from falling and near-falling experiences that locomotion generates. Near-falls are particularly important because they are frequent, they elicit powerful emotional signals from the parent, and they set the stage for long-term retention of negative affect in such contexts.

There is still another means by which the infant can acquire a sense of wariness of depth with locomotion. While the infant moves about voluntarily, visual information specifying self-movement becomes more highly correlated with vestibular information specifying the same amount of self-movement (Bertenthal & Campos, 1990). Once expectancies related to the correlation of visual and vestibular information are formed, being lowered toward the deep side of the cliff creates a violation of the expected correlation. This violation results from the absence of visible texture near the infant when lowered toward the deep side of the cliff, relative to the shallow side. As a consequence, angular acceleration is not detected by the visual system, whereas it is detected by the vestibular system. This violation of expectation results in distress proportional to the magnitude of the violation. A test of this interpretation requires assessment of the establishment of visual-vestibular coordination as a function of locomotor experience and confirmation that wariness occurs in contexts that violate visual-vestibular coordination.

LOCOMOTOR EXPERIENCE AND OTHER EMOTIONAL CHANGES

The consequences of the development of self-produced locomotion for emotional development extend far beyond the domain of wariness of heights. Indeed, the onset of locomotion generates an entirely different emotional climate in the family. For instance, as psychoanalytic theories predict (e.g., Mahler, Pine, & Bergman, 1975), the onset of locomotion brings about a burgeoning of both positive and negative affect—positive affect because of the child's new levels of self-efficacy; negative affect because of the increases in frustration resulting from thwarting of the child's goals and because of the affective resonance that comes from increased parental expressions of prohibition (Campos, Kermoian, & Zumbahlen, in press). Locomotion is also crucial for the development of attachment (Ainsworth, Blehar, Waters, & Wall, 1978; Bowlby, 1973), because it makes physical proximity to the caregiver possible. With the formation of specific attachments, locomotion increases in significance as the child becomes better able to move independently toward novel and potentially frightening environments. Infants are also more sensitive to the location of the parent, more likely to show distress upon separation, and more likely to look to the parent in ambiguous situations.

Locomotion also brings about emotional changes in the parents. These changes include the increased pride (and sometimes sorrow) that the parents experience in their child's new mobility and independence and the new levels of anger parents direct at the baby when the baby begins to encounter forbidden objects. It seems clear from the findings obtained in this line of research that new levels of functioning in one behavioral domain can generate experiences that profoundly affect other developmental domains, including affective, social, cognitive, and sensorimotor ones (Kermoian & Campos, 1988). We thus propose that theoretical orientations like probabilistic epigenesis provide a novel, heuristic, and timely perspective for the study of emotional development.

Questions

1. Why did Campos, Bertenthal and Kermoian go to so much trouble to try to distinguish the development of knowledge of heights from the development of wariness of heights?

2. If you were caring for two 6-month-old infants, one who had been using a walker for a month or more and one who had no experience with walkers, might you have different concerns about their behavior? How does this issue relate to the article you just read?

3. If an infant were deprived of the ability to crawl or squirm from one place to another, do you think he or she would develop wariness of heights?

References

Ainsworth, M. D. S., Blehar, M., Waters, E., & Wall, S. (1978). *Patterns of attachment.* Hillsdale, NJ: Erlbaum.

Bertenthal, B., & Campos, J. J. (1990). A systems approach to the organizing effects of self-produced locomotion during infancy. In C. Rovee-Collier & L. P. Lipsitt (Eds.), *Advances in infancy research* (Vol. 6, pp. 1–60). Norwood, NJ: Ablex.

Bowlby, J. (1973). *Attachment and loss: Vol. 2. Separation.* New York: Basic Books.

Bridges, K. M. (1932). Emotional development in early infancy. *Child Development, 3,* 324–341.

Campos, J. J., Emde, R. N., Gaensbauer, T. J., & Henderson, C. (1975). Cardiac and behavioral interrelationships in the reactions of infants to strangers. *Developmental Psychology, 11,* 589–601.

Campos, J. J., Hiatt, S., Ramsay, D., Henderson, C., & Svejda, M. (1978). The emergence of fear of heights. In M. Lewis & L. Rosenblum (Eds.), *The development of affect* (pp. 149–182). New York: Plenum Press.

Campos, J. J., Kermoian, R., & Zumbahlen, R. M. (In press). In N. Eisenberg (Ed.), *New directions for child development.* San Francisco: Jossey-Bass.

Emde, R. N., Gaensbauer, T. J., & Harmon, R. J. (1976). Emotional expression in infancy: A biobehavioral study. *Psychological Issues* (Vol. 10, No. 37). New York: International Universities Press.

Gottlieb, G. (1983). The psychobiological approach to developmental issues. In P. Mussen (Ed.), *Handbook of child psychology: Vol. II. Infancy and developmental psychobiology* (4th ed.) (pp. 1–26). New York: Wiley.

Gottlieb, G. (1991). Experiential canalization of behavioral development: Theory. *Developmental Psychology, 27,* 4–13.

Graham, F. K., & Clifton, R. K. (1966). Heartrate change as a component of the orienting response. *Psychological Bulletin, 65,* 305–320.

Held, R. & Hein, A. (1963). Movement-produced stimulation in the development of visually guided behavior. *Journal of Comparative and Physiological Psychology, 56,* 872–876.

Kagan, J., Kearsley, R., & Zelazo, P. R. (1978). *Infancy: Its place in human development.* Cambridge, MA: Harvard University Press.

Kermoian, R., & Campos, J. J. (1988). Locomotor experience: A facilitator of spatial cognitive development. *Child Development, 59,* 908–917.

Mahler, M., Pine, F., & Bergman, A. (1975). *The psychological birth of the human infant.* New York: Basic Books.

Scarr, S., & Salapatek, P. (1970). Patterns of fear development during infancy. *Merrill-Palmer Quarterly, 16,* 53–90.

Sroufe, L. A. (1979). Socioemotional development. In J. Osofsky (Ed.), *Handbook of infant development* (pp. 462–516). New York: Wiley.

Walk, R. (1966). The development of depth perception in animals and human infants. *Monographs of the Society for Research in Child Development, 31* (Whole No. 5).

Walk, R., & Gibson, E. (1961). A comparative and analytical study of visual depth perception. *Psychological Monographs, 75* (15, Whole No. 5).

Walters, C. (1981). Development of the visual placing response in the human infant. *Journal of Experimental Child Psychology, 32,* 313–329.

12

Patterns of Attachment in Two- and Three-Year-Olds in Normal Families and Families with Parental Depression

MARIAN RADKE-YARROW, E. MARK CUMMINGS, LEON KUCZYNSKI, AND MICHAEL CHAPMAN

Aunique and universal characteristic of the human species is that human children have a lengthy period of dependence on adults. The theory of early social attachment focuses on the relationship between young children and their primary caregivers, and considers this process critical for organizing and supporting early socioemotional development. In the following article a team of developmental psychologists used an experimental procedure known as the Strange Situation to explore attachment between depressed mothers and their children. Since depression interferes with the normal flow of interaction, depressed mothers and their children may be at risk for developing an unhealthy attachment relationship. Depressed mothers may also be modeling a depressive style of behavior that may then affect the development of the child's style of interacting with her and others.

Reprinted with permission from *Child Development, 56,* 1985, 884–893. Copyright 1985 by the Society for Research in Child Development.

This work was supported by the National Institute of Mental Health, Bethesda, MD, and by the John D. and Catherine T. MacArthur Foundation, Research Network Award on the Transition from Infancy to Early Childhood, Chicago, IL. We wish to acknowledge the assistance of Judy Stillwell, Barbara Hollenbeck, Jonita Conners, Christine Kirby, Anne Mayfield, Wendy Rozario, and Rita Dettmers in the many phases of the research process. Requests for reprints should be sent to Marian Radke-Yarrow, Laboratory of Developmental Psychology, National Institute of Mental Health, Bldg. 15K, 9000 Rockville Pike, Bethesda, MD 20205.

Patterns of attachment were examined in normal and depressed mothers. Mother's diagnosis (bipolar, major unipolar, or minor depression, or no psychiatric disorder), self-reported current mood states, and affective behavior in interaction with the child were considered. A modified version of Ainsworth and Wittig's Strange Situation was used to assess attachment. Insecure (A, C, and A/C patterns) attachments were more common among children of mothers with a major depression (bipolar or unipolar) than among children of mothers with minor depression or among children of normal mothers. Insecure attachment was more frequent in children of mothers with bipolar depression than in children of mothers with unipolar depression. A/C attachments were associated with histories of most severe depression in the mother. In families in which mothers were depressed, depression in the father did not increase the likelihood of anxious attachment between mother and child. However, if mothers with a major affective disorder were without a husband in the household, risk of an insecure mother-child attachment was significantly increased. The mothers' expressed emotions (positive vs. negative) in interaction with their children in situations other than the Strange Situation, and independent of diagnosis, predicted patterns of attachment: mothers of insecurely attached children expressed more negative and less positive emotion. Mothers' self-reports of moods on the days they were observed were unrelated to attachment. Results are discussed in terms of the transmission of social and emotional disorders in relation to mothers' affective functioning.

Depression is known to aggregate in families, to be transmitted from one generation to the next. Significantly higher frequencies of psychopathology have been reported among children of parents with affective disorders than among children of normal parents, with a variety of mechanisms proposed as explanations (see reviews by Akisal & McKinney, 1975; Beardslee, Bemporad, Keller, & Klerman, 1983; Cytryn, McKnew, Zahn-Waxler, & Gershon, in press; Rutter & Garmezy, 1983). The likelihood of a genetic predisposition has been emphasized; and particularly for manic-depression, there is considerable evidence for biologically or genetically based transmission (see review by Meyersberg & Post, 1979). Although few investigators would rule out influences of environmental factors, such influences have not been extensively studied. Moreover, when the environment has been considered, both the conceptualizations and the methods used to assess its qualities have been inadequate. These deficiencies

impose serious limitations on what is known about the role of environment and the interaction of genetic and environmental factors in the development of the offspring of depressed parents.

The depressed parent *is* the primary environment of the young child. The conditions of care and rearing that the parent provides must, of necessity, reflect the symptomatic behaviors of depression, the impairments that constitute the illness (emotional unavailability, sad affect, hopelessness, irritability, confusion, etc.). Although depressive illness does not present a homogeneous pattern of behaviors in every parent, the behaviors and mental status of the depressed person are all potentially interfering with the functions and responsibilities of a caregiver and with the development of a good affective relationship with the child. The present study focuses on the quality of the affective bond that forms between mother and child under such conditions.

The quality of attachment between mother and child has been associated with the young child's adaptive and maladaptive behaviors in an impressively consistent succession of studies. Insecurely attached children, compared with those securely attached, have been found to be less competent in their relationships with peers and adults, more fearful of strangers, more prone to behavior problems, including social withdrawal and anxiety, and more dependent on adults (Arend, Gove, & Sroufe, 1979; Erickson, Sroufe, & Egeland, in press; LaFreniere & Sroufe, in press; Lieberman, 1977; Londerville & Main, 1981; Matas, Arend, & Sroufe, 1978; Pastor, 1981; Sroufe, Fox, & Pancake, 1983; Waters, Wippman, & Sroufe, 1979).

The literature on attachment identifies certain characteristics of mothering that are associated with the infant's secure attachment. These include the mother's responsivity, her emotional availability, and warm and accepting attitude toward the child (Ainsworth, Blehar, Waters, & Wall, 1978; Belsky, Rovine, & Taylor, 1984; Blehar, Lieberman, & Ainsworth, 1976; Londerville & Main, 1981; Main, Tomasini, & Tolan, in press; Stayton & Ainsworth, 1973; Tracy & Ainsworth, 1981). However, knowledge of the rearing environment at a level of detail and directness that allows examination of the processes through which a secure or insecure relationship develops and is maintained is very incomplete. This is particularly the case with regard to our understanding of the role of affective aspects of the environment in which the child is reared.

In the present study we have used parents' diagnoses of affective disorders (depression and manic-depression) and parental reports and expressions of their emotions and moods as indices of the affective quality of the child's rearing environment. How do attachment patterns in families with parental depression differ from patterns in normal families?

Research findings and theory support an expectation of increased attachment disturbances in the depressed families. A recent study of toddler-age offspring of manic-depressive parents shows attachment disturbances and early behavior problems (Gaensbauer, Harmon, Cytryn, & McKnew, 1984; Zahn-Waxler, Cummings, & McKnew, 1984; Yarrow, 1984). Bowlby (1969, 1973), Bretherton (in press), and Main, Kaplan, and Cassidy (in press) have hypothesized that early insecure attachment relationships result in children developing a fundamental view or working model of themselves as unlovable, and of others as rejecting and unresponsive. Some findings supportive of these expectations have been reported by Main and her colleagues (Cassidy & Main, 1983; Main, Kaplan, & Cassidy, in press). Moreover, since the depressed parent is likely to be self-deprecating, it is quite possible that such views are conveyed to the child and extend to perceptions of the child.

If disturbed attachment patterns are characteristic of the offspring of affectively ill parents, a number of important research questions follow: (a) Within depressed and normal families, what are the parental behaviors that promote or interfere with the development of a secure attachment relationship? (b) Are the links between attachment patterns and child's (outcome) behavioral characteristics in the clinical population similar to the links found in nonclinical populations, or is the developmental course of the offspring of depressed parents more preprogrammed for maladaptive affective, cognitive, and social characteristics (i.e., more independent of environmental variables) than is the case for children of normal parents? (c) How may discordances (secure attachment and poor psychosocial development, or the obverse case) be explained?[1]

METHOD

Sample

The sample consists of 99 children: 14 offspring of bipolar depressive (manic-depressive) mothers, 42 of mothers with major unipolar depression, 12 of mothers with minor depression, and 31 of mothers with no history of affective disturbance.

Families (normal and depressed) were recruited by advertising for participants in a study of child rearing and development in healthy families and families in which the mother is depressed. Of the mothers who responded to announcements, approximately two-thirds wished to participate after learning more about the study. All volunteers were given a standard psychiatric interview, the Schedule for Affective Disorders and Schizophrenia (SADS) (Spitzer & Endicott, 1977). On the basis of the interview, families were selected who met specific diagnostic criteria, as well as criteria of SES, race, age, and sex of children. For a family to be selected for the normal group, both parents had to be present and had to be without a history of affective disorder. In families in which the mother had a diagnosis of depression, father's psychiatric status varied. Fathers could be with or without a diagnosis of depression; however, schizophrenic, alcoholic, and antisocial personalities were excluded. In eight families with major maternal depression, there was no father in the household. Of the families given psychiatric interviews, about half were screened out by us because they did not meet diagnostic requirements, or because their cell within the design was complete. Table 1 provides more information on the characteristics of the sample.

Families differed in terms of the percent of the child's lifetime in which the mother had episodes of depression. For bipolar mothers, the mean percent of the child's lifetime was 39.8 (range, 0%–100%); for mothers with unipolar depression, the mean percent was 61.6 (range, 0%–100%); and for mothers with minor depression, the mean percent was 13.7 (range, 0%–47%). (0 indicates mother's depression occurred before the child was born.)

Each mother who received a psychiatric diagnosis was rated on the severity of psychopathology on the Global Assessment Scale (GAS) (Spitzer, Gibbon, & Endicott, 1978). The mother is rated on her poorest functioning during the child's lifetime, on a continuous scale of 0 (needing continuous care and supervision) to 100 (superior functioning). The mean score for bipolar mothers was 47.6 (range, 15–65), for mothers with unipolar depression, 54.2 (range, 30–70), and for mothers with minor depression, 76.3 (range, 60–79). Mothers whose depression

---

[1]Data addressing these questions are being gathered in an ongoing study involving observations of parental and child behaviors at two periods in the child's life—at 2–3 years and at 5–6 years. The data reported here are from the first phase of this study.

TABLE 1

Comparisons of Diagnostic Groups
on Age, Sex, and Race

| | Diagnostic Group | | Major Affective Disorder | |
	Normal (N = 31)	Minor Depression (N = 12)	Unipolar Depression (N = 42)	Bipolar Depression (N = 14)
Demographic Characteristics				
Age[a] (months)	31.9	31.4	30.4	36.0
Sex:				
Boys	13	7(1)[b]	24(4)[b] (2)[c]	3(2)[b]
Girls	18	5(2)[b]	18(3)[b] (3)[c]	11(4)[b] (3)[c]
Race:				
White	24	12(3)[b]	34(6)[b] (1)[c]	12(6)[b] (3)[c]
Black	7	0	8(0)[b] (4)[c]	2(0)[b]
Hollingshead SES[d]	52.9	47.6	46.1	51.1

[a] Ranges in age are 25–39 months, 25–34 months, 16–44 months, and 30–47 months for the diagnostic groups, respectively.

[b] Number of families in which the father had a diagnosis of major depression.

[c] Number of families in which the father was not present.

[d] Ranges in SES in each of the groups, from low to high status, are 17–66, 34–64, 11–64.5, and 33.5–64, respectively.

occurred before the child was born and could be rated for poorest functioning in their own lifetime (N = 6) had a mean rating of 43.7 (range, 1–65). Normal mothers are not given ratings. Treatments that mothers had received for affective illness were as follows: Seven had been hospitalized (three in the lifetime of their child), 25 were on drug treatment at some time (four currently), and 51 had sought professional help (19 were currently seeing a mental health professional).

PROCEDURE

The Strange Situation, developed by Ainsworth and Wittig (1969), was used in the present study to assess quality of attachment. The families came to the laboratory, an informal homelike apartment, for a series of half-days over a period of several weeks. Their behavior was observed (videotaped) over a variety of conditions constructed to approximate a range of natural rearing situations and demands. The Strange Situation was introduced in their first visit to the apartment. The procedure involves eight brief episodes in which the child's reactions to two separations from and reunions with the mother and to the presence of a stranger are observed. The sequence of episodes according to the individuals present is: (1) mother, child, and experimenter; (2) mother and child; (3) stranger, mother, and child; (4) stranger and child (separation from the mother); (5) mother and child (reunion with the mother); (6) child alone (separation from the mother); (7) stranger and child; and (8) mother and child (reunion with the mother). The traditional version of the Strange Situation was followed with two exceptions: (*a*) episode 3 was allowed to continue for 7 minutes instead of the usual 3, and the mother and also the stranger were asked to approach the child in a series of graded steps; (*b*) when the mother returned in episode 8, she brought with her a small case of toys, rather than returning empty-handed. The modifications were adaptations consistent with objectives of the larger study, in which (*a*) the child's capacities in familiar and unfamiliar interpersonal situations, and (*b*) the child's approach to a novel nonpersonal situation, were of interest.

Mother's current moods and emotions were assessed by self-report. An inventory of mood ratings, the Profile of Mood States (McNair, Lorr, & Droppleman, 1971), was filled out by the mother at the time of arrival for each laboratory visit.

Finally, the mothers' expressed affect was coded "live" during the Strange Situation and during subsequent half-day observations of mother-child interaction. The predominant emotions expressed were recorded on a minute-to-minute basis. Approximately 6 hours of the mother's affective behavior in the presence of her child was rated ($\overline{X}$ = 356.7 min, SD = 3.8).

Measures

ASSESSMENT OF THE QUALITY OF ATTACHMENT
Ratings were made of interactive behaviors, including contact maintaining and proximity seeking, avoidance, resistance, search, and distance interaction. Two coders were given intensive training by one of the investigators, with whom reliability checks were also done. The mean Pearson product-moment reliability coefficient for ratings of interactive behaviors in the Strange Situation was .86 (range, .66–1.00) based on 50 Strange Situations coded by two independent observers. The percentage of interobserver agreement for classification of the quality of attachment was 96%. Coders of the attachment relationship did not take part in other aspects of the study and were blind to family diagnoses.

Quality of attachment was classified based on criteria outlined in Ainsworth et al. (1978). Consistent with the work of others, judgments of quality of attachment heavily emphasized responses to the two reunions with the mother. On the basis of studies of age changes in attachment behavior (Maccoby & Feldman, 1972; Marvin, 1972, 1977), we expected our 2–3-year-olds to show less proximity seeking and contact maintaining, but comparable levels of avoidance and resistance vis-à-vis the 12–18-month-olds on which this system was based. Accordingly, to obtain distributions of classifications as close to Ainsworth's as possible, avoidance and resistance were stressed in classification decisions. Children were classified as securely attached (B); insecurely attached, either insecure-ambivalent (C) or insecure-avoidant (A); or (3) insecurely attached, manifesting both ambivalence and avoidance (A/C).

The first three categories closely follow from Ainsworth et al. Secure children respond promptly to the mother on reunion, either by seeking proximity or physical contact with her, or by greeting her across a distance. Insecure-avoidant children ignore or avoid the mother on reunion. Insecure-ambivalent children resist contact with the mother on reunion, but may alternate this with proximity seeking. The fourth category (A/C), is not reported by Ainsworth et al., but is similar, although not identical, to Crittenden's A/C (1983) classification and Main and Weston's (1981) Unclassified category. These children showed moderate to high avoidance and moderate to high resistance during reunion, which served as the basis for classification, and most also displayed one or more of the following: "Affectless or sad with signs of depression," "Odd or atypical body posture or movement," and "Moderate to high proximity seeking." These responses were reported by those making attachment classifications, and by independent observers carefully reviewing the A/C tapes. Finally, one child of a mother diagnosed for current major depression could not be classified because his mother, responding to his protests, could not leave in either separation episode.

Analyses were conducted to determine the extent to which differences within the sample in age, sex, SES, and race might influence the interpretation of findings. The only age difference in interactive behaviors in the present study was a decline with age in contact-maintaining behavior during the two reunions with the mother: in episodes 5, $r(89) = -.25$, $p < .05$, and episode 8, $r(89) = -.50$, $p < .01$. There were no differences as a function of age in classifications (B, A, C, or A/C) of the quality of attachment. This is consistent with the findings from other research on age changes in attachment; children seldom show evidence of entering into qualitatively different forms of attachment relationships before 3 years of age (Marvin & Greenberg, 1982). Quality of attachment did not vary as a function of Hollingshead SES, whether calculated on a continuum or as a function of categories of status structure. Within the five categories of SES status structure, disregarding diagnostic classifications, there was insecure attachment in four of the 10 families in the lowest two categories, in 16 of the 40 families in the middle two categories, and in 23 of the 48 families in the highest categories. Other studies have also failed to find differences in patterns of attachment as a function of social class (Schneider-Rosen & Cicchetti, 1984; Vaughn, Egeland, Sroufe, & Waters, 1979). Boys and girls and blacks and whites also did not differ significantly in the distribution of classifications of attachment. Subjects were collapsed across age, sex, race, and SES in further analyses.

MOTHERS' SELF-REPORT OF MOODS ON THE POMS
Six mood scales from mothers' responses on the POMS were: (1) agreeable–hostile, (2) elated–depressed, (3) energetic–tired, (4) clearheaded–confused, (5) composed–anxious, and (6) confident–unsure. Scores were derived for each scale for each of 3 days in the laboratory apartment.

MOTHERS' EXPRESSED EMOTIONS OBSERVED IN ACTIONS AND REACTIONS IN THE APARTMENT
Mothers' affects were scored, on a minute-by-minute basis, as cheerful–happy, tender–loving, tense–anxious, irritable–angry, sad–tearful, neutral–positive, or neutral–negative. The mean interobserver reliability, using the Kappa statistic (Bartko & Carpenter, 1976), which corrects for chance agreement, was .78. Because coders were not blind to mothers' diagnoses, a subset of sessions ($N = 21$) was coded from the videotapes by a coder who was blind to mothers' diagnoses. There was a high level of agreement; the mean intercoder reliability was Kappa = .79. Scores were derived for each of the affect categories by summing the number of minutes in which the emotion was observed, dividing by the total number of minutes of observation. Overall scores for any type of positive and any type of negative affect were also derived.

RESULTS

Maternal Depression and Quality of Attachment

Distributions of attachment patterns by diagnostic groups are shown in Table 2. Insecure attachments were relatively infrequent in both the normal and minor depression groups (25%–30% of cases), and are comparable to rates reported in other studies of normal populations among younger children (e.g.,

Ainsworth et al., 1978; Waters, 1978). By contrast, insecure attachments were relatively frequent in families with major affective disorders (55% of cases), particularly among children of bipolar mothers (79%). Compared by means of tests of proportions (Hays, 1963), the difference between children of normal mothers and children of mothers with minor depression in incidence of insecure attachments was not significant, $z < 1$. There was a greater incidence of insecure attachments in families with major affective disorders than in normal families, $z = 2.33$, $p < .05$, or in families with minor depression, $z = 1.89$, $p < .10$ (all reported p values are two-tailed). Within the major affective disorders groups, insecure attachment was more frequent among children of bipolar mothers and among children of mothers with unipolar depression, $z = 2.08$, $p < .05$.

In 18 of the two-parent families with maternal depression, the father, too, had a diagnosis of depression. Forty-two percent of children in this group were insecurely attached, and 50% of the children within the depression group in which only the mother was depressed were insecurely attached, $z < 1$. Thus, whether mother only or both mother and father were depressed made no difference in the number of children with insecure attachments to mother. However, father's absence or presence did make a difference in the security of attachment to the mother. Because the number of families in which fathers were absent was small ($N < 10$), groups were compared by means of Fisher Exact Tests (Siegel, 1956). In the eight families (six girls and two boys) with major maternal depression and no father pre-

TABLE 2
Maternal Diagnostic Status and Quality of Attachment Relationship

Diagnostic Group	N	Attachment (%)			
		Secure	Insecure		
		B	A	C	A/C
Normal	31	71 (22)[a]	29 (9)	0	0
Minor depression	12	75 (9)	17 (2)	8(1)	0
Major affective disorder	55	45 (25)	31 (18)	4(2)	20 (10)
Unipolar depression[b]	41	53 (22)	27 (11)	2(1)	17 (7)
Bipolar	14	21 (3)	43 (7)	7(1)	29 (3)

[a] Number of children receiving the classification.
[b] One child could not be classified, because his mother, responding to his extreme protests, would not leave in either separation episode.

sent, anxious attachment characterized seven of the children, a proportion higher than in families with major depression in which both parents were present, Fisher Exact Test, $p < .06$.

As noted earlier, a subgroup of children were classified as A/C. This classification occurred significantly more often among children of mothers with major affective disorders, Fisher Exact Test, $p < .01$. In fact, this pattern was observed only in children of mothers with a major affective disorder. Also, a disproportionate number of A/C's ($N = 4$) were in the single-parent major depression group.

In further analyses of attachment and mother's depression, the percent of the child's lifetime in which the mother was ill, the severity (GAS) of her worst depressive episode, and her history of treatment for affective illness (number of forms of treatments received from among hospitalization, drug therapy, and psychotherapy) were considered. Analyses of variance with one between-subjects factor (attachment group) were performed for these indices: For the percent of the child's lifetime in which the mother was depressed, $F(2,91) = 8.96$, $p < .001$; for the severity of the mother's worst depressive episode, $F(2,56) = 4.68$, $p < .05$; and for the index of treatment history, $F(2,91) = 6.00$, $p < .005$. These relationships are shown in Table 3. Post-hoc Tukey tests were conducted to compare groups. Mothers of A/C children compared with mothers of children with B classifications or with A or C classifications had histories indicative of significantly more serious depression (all

comparisons, $p < .05$). Mothers of B classification children and mothers of children with traditional insecure classifications (A or C) did not differ.

Next we examined the extent to which variables pertaining to mothers' depression contributed nonredundantly to prediction of attachment classification. For this analysis, three groups were distinguished: B, A or C, and A/C. The multiple correlation between attachment classification and maternal depression variables was $R = .38$, thus accounting for 15% of the variance in attachment classification. Stepwise multiple regression analyses indicated that mother's diagnosis was the best predictor, and the severity of her worst depressive episode was the second best predictor. Adding whether the father was absent into the analysis increased R to .47 and R^2 to 22%.

Mothers' Current Affect and Quality of Attachment

To examine relations between mother's current emotions (disregarding diagnosis) and child's security of attachment, one-way analyses of variance with attachment group as the between-subjects factor were conducted for mother's self-assessed moods and for her expressed affect in interaction. There were no significant findings involving mothers' self-assessed moods. However, mothers' expressed emotions in interaction with their children during half-days in the apartment differentiated groups. Composite scores of positive and negative emotions showed that mothers of securely attached children expressed positive affect more often, and negative affect less often, than mothers of insecurely attached children (positive affect appeared in 80% and 69% of the minutes and negative affect in 18% and 31% of the minutes, respectively), F's$(1,80) \geq 4.02$, p's $< .05$. There were no significant differences between groups in expression of specific emotions.

Mothers' expressions of emotions and their diagnoses independently predicted attachment classification: Correlations between the percent of minutes rated positive or negative in affect and mother's diagnoses were nonsignificant. Multiple regression analyses indicated that mothers' general affective tone added significantly (5%) to the variance accounted for in attachment classification.

TABLE 3
Mothers' Affective Functioning in the Child's Lifetime and Quality of Attachment Relationship

| | Attachment | | |
| | Secure | Insecure | |
Index	B	A or C	A/C
Percent of the child's lifetime mother is ill	26.5	25.9	79.7
Severity of mother's illness[a]	58.3	58.2	44.5
Treatment history[b]	.65	.73	1.60

[a]GAS scores varied from 0 (needing continuous care and supervision) to 100 (superior functioning); normal mothers are not given ratings.

[b] Number of forms of treatment received: hospitalization, drug therapy, psychotherapy; maximum score equals 3.

DISCUSSION

That affective illness of the mother may interfere with her ability to relate to her child in ways that promote a secure attachment is documented in these data. Depression decreased the likelihood of secure attachment between mother and child, at least as this is reflected in the child's responses to the mother in reunions after separation in the Strange Situation. Also, A/C patterns appear in children of mothers with major depression. The similarities with Crittenden's (1983) and Main and Weston's (1981) "unclassifiable" patterns observed among younger children are of interest. Crittenden's A/C's showed moderate to high avoidance and resistance, and most also showed some stereotypic or maladaptive behaviors, including "huddling on the floor," which might be interpreted as sadness. Main and Weston's "U's" showed extreme avoidance and distress, behaved "oddly" during the Strange Situation, and were affectless with signs of depression. Another interesting parallel is that Crittenden's A/C's and those in the present study were found only among children of mothers with psychopathology: In Crittenden's study mothers were highly abusing, while our mothers were severely depressed. Mothers of Main and Weston's U's were unscreened for maternal psychopathology, so it is unclear whether psychopathology was a factor. These studies suggest that Ainsworth's classification system may not describe the entire range of patterns of attachment, and that important new patterns may be found in atypical samples. Another implication is that there is more than a dichotomy between security and insecurity; it may be necessary to distinguish between secure, insecure, and very insecure (A/C) patterns, or introduce more divisions along a dimension of anxiety (Crittenden, in press; Main, Kaplan, & Cassidy, in press). External validation is required, however, before any firm conclusions about the significance of new patterns can be drawn. The search for very insecure patterns may be complicated by the fact that they may vary as a function of the mothers' particular psychopathology or the age of the child.

The children of unipolar and bipolar depressed mothers had different patterns of attachment. Although children of mothers with major unipolar depression were more likely to be insecurely attached than children of mothers with no history of affective disturbance (47% vs. 29%), the difference in incidence of insecure attachment is not as great as with bipolar depression. Children of mothers with bipolar depression were more than twice as likely to be insecurely attached as children of normal mothers. This greater vulnerability in the bipolar families is consistent with existing evidence of a strong genetic component determining offspring develop- ment, as well as with an environmental interpreta- tion that takes into account the difficulties posed not only by the severity of symptoms but also by the contrasting extremes and alternations in behavior in bipolar parents.

We know from the responses of depressed moth- ers on the SADS interview that their children had been exposed to episodes of maternal sad affect, hopelessness and helplessness, irritability, confu- sions, and, in bipolar depression, to these episodes alternating with periods of euphoria and grandiosity. It would be desirable to know the effects on the child of each of these patterns of behavior. We have suggestive evidence on the importance of various ele- ments within these patterns. There is indication that, regardless of diagnosis, mothers' negative affective expression in interaction is associated with insecure attachment. Amount of exposure to disturbed affect was also associated with increased probability of a poor mother-child relationship. The significant rela- tion between severity of disturbance and attachment classification suggests that mother's own ability to cope or to function well despite her disorder is one factor to be considered.

One can speculate concerning the effect of other depression-related behaviors. Consistent and posi- tively responsive mothering has been repeatedly shown to be beneficial to the child in the literature of child development. To some degree, major depres- sion precludes consistency of mothering, since de- pression is episodic (both unipolar and bipolar). Depressed mothers are likely, therefore, to be experi- enced by their children as unpredictable or inconsis- tent. Since confusion and preoccupations with self are conditions of depression, young children of de- pressed mothers are also likely to find their mothers unresponsive as well as physically and emotionally unavailable.

The hopeless and self-deprecating outlook of the parent who is severely depressed raises ques- tions concerning another kind of possible impact on the child: How is this dimension of depression conveyed to the child, and with what effects? The research of Cummings, Zahn-Waxler, and Radke- Yarrow (1981), Klinnert, Campos, Sorce, Emde, and Svejda (1983), Radke-Yarrow and Zahn-Waxler (1984), and others has documented very young chil- dren's keen awareness of affective signals in others (in facial expressions, body language, and speech), whether or not the affect is directed to the child. What are the consequences of the exaggerated as well as the flat affect of depressed mothers for the cognitive and social-emotional aspects of the child's relationship with her? An important next step is to observe each of these aspects of maternal affect in interaction with the child in order to assess the child's responses to these encounters on a day-to-day basis.

We have been discussing the present findings as group differences between normal and depressed mothers. Not all mother-child pairs conform to the group difference. Normal mothers and mothers with a diagnosis of minor depression did not differ in frequencies of secure attachment (roughly three-fourths of the pairs were securely attached). The drop in the secure attachments to 53% in unipolar depression and 21% in bipolar depression, although impressive, still leaves "discordant" cases. Conditions outside the mother's illness-based behavior are surely contributory to the mother-child relationship. The attachment relationship, we assume, has contributions from the child. Since the present study provides information primarily on the mother component, the child's characteristics and coping mechanisms are unknowns.

One might assume that the father's relationship with the mother, his relationship with the child, and specifically his functioning when the mother is ill would be important. Although the present study has limited information concerning the father's role, the significance of father absence in increasing the frequency of insecure attachments throws some light on these questions. It suggests an interpretation in terms of the availability of an alternative attachment figure when the mother is ill. Bowlby (1969) has suggested that the effect of physical separation on attachment relationships depends in part on the physical availability of acceptable alternative figures during separation. In the case of maternal depression, when the mother may be emotionally unavailable, an available alternative paternal attachment figure appears to be important. In a related vein, the social supports available to the mother have been shown to be important in the quality of attachment relationship with the mother (Crockenberg, 1981). Social supports from father or others are likely to be important for depressed mothers in determining their ability to cope with their depression and with their role as parent. However, the findings suggest that whether the father has psychopathology may not be a critical factor in the social support provided by the father.

The father's illness was anticipated to be a factor influencing the child's relationship with the mother. It might be expected to influence the mother-child bond by virtue of its effects on both the mother's and child's well-being, as well as by its possible genetic contribution to the child's makeup. The expected effect of father's illness was not observed. It is possible that father's illness affected the child in other ways, which our data did not explore.

Research on the specific qualities of the rearing environment created for the child by parental pathology and on the conditions that moderate or modify the pathogenic aspects of parental rearing has a number of implications. If there are identifiably different rearing conditions associated with secure and insecure attachment in depressed families and with correspondingly good and poor child development, then there are implications for interpretations of epidemiological data. Questions could be raised as to the soundness of giving depressed parents specific probability statements about the likelihood of pathology in their children. Also, such data on rearing would provide instructive bases for interventions that would enhance the chances for adaptive development in the offspring of depressed parents.

Questions

1. Why is secure attachment with a primary caregiver important for healthy development?

2. Why do you think children of depressed mothers are more likely to be insecurely attached to their mothers than children of mothers who are not depressed?

3. How do you think that experience with an alternative caregiver who is not depressed, such as in a day care center, might help or hurt a child with a depressed mother?

References

Ainsworth, M. D. S., Blehar, M. C., Waters, E., & Wall, S. (1978). *Patterns of attachment: A psychological study of the strange situation.* Hillsdale, NJ: Erlbaum.

Ainsworth, M. D. S., & Wittig, B. A. (1969). Attachment and exploratory behavior of one-year-olds in a Strange Situation. In B. M. Foss (Ed.), *Determinants of infant behavior* (Vol. 4, pp. 111–136). London: Methuen.

Akisal, H., & McKinney, W. (1975). Overview of recent research in depression: Integration of ten conceptual models into a comprehensive clinical frame. *Archives of General Psychiatry, 32,* 285–305.

Arend, R., Gove, F. L, & Sroufe, L. A. (1979). Continuity of individual adaptation from infancy to kindergarten: A predictive study of egoresiliency and curiosity in preschoolers. *Child Development, 50,* 950–959.

Bartko, J. J., & Carpenter, W. T. (1976). On the methods and theory of reliability. *Journal of Nervous and Mental Disease, 1976, 163,* 307–317.

Beardslee, W., Bemporad J., Keller, M., & Klerman G. (1983). Children of parents with major affective disorder: A review. *American Journal of Psychiatry,* 140(7), 825–832.

Belsky, J., Rovine, M., & Taylor, D. (1984). The Pennsylvania Infant and Family Development Project: III. The origins of individual differences in infant-mother attachment: Maternal and infant contributions. *Child Development, 55,* 718–728.

Blehar, M. C., Lieberman, A. F., & Ainsworth, M. D. S. (1976). Early face-to-face interaction and its relation to later infant-mother attachment. *Child Development, 48,* 182–194.

Bowlby, J. (1969). *Attachment and loss: Vol. 1. Attachment.* London: Hogarth.

Bowlby, J. (1973). *Attachment and loss: Vol. 2. Separation: Anxiety and anger.* New York: Basic.

Bretherton, I. (in press). Attachment theory: Retrospect and prospect. In I. Bretherton & E. Waters (Eds.), Growing points in attachment theory and research. *Monographs of the Society for Research in Child Development.*

Cassidy, J., & Main, M. (1983, March). *Secure attachment in infancy as a precursor of the ability to tolerate a brief laboratory separation at six years.* Paper presented at the Second World Congress of Infant Psychiatry, Cannes, France.

Crittenden, P. M. (1983, April). *Maltreated infants: Vulnerability and resilience.* Paper presented at the meeting of the Society for Research in Child Development, Detroit.

Crittenden, P. M. (in press). Social networks, quality of child-rearing, and child development. *Child Development.*

Crockenberg, S. B. (1981). Infant irritability, mother responsiveness, and social support influences on the security of infant-mother attachment. *Child Development, 52,*857–865.

Cummings, E. M., Zahn-Waxler, C., & Radke-Yarrow, M. (1981). Young children's responses to expressions of anger and affection by others in the family. *Child Development, 52,* 1274–1282.

Cytryn, L., McKnew, D. H., Zahn-Waxler, C., & Gershon, E. S. (in press). Developmental issues in risk research: The offspring of affectively ill parents. In M. Rutter, C. E. Izard, & P. B. Read (Eds.), *Depression in children: Developmental perspectives.* New York: Guilford.

Erickson, M. F., Sroufe, L., & Egeland, B. (in press). The relationship between quality of attachment and behavior problems in preschool in a high risk sample. In I. Bretherton & E. Waters (Eds.), Growing points in attachment theory and research. *Monographs of the Society for Research in Child Development.*

Gaensbauer, T. J., Harmon, R. J., Cytryn, L., & McKnew, D. H. (1984). Social and affective development in children with a manic-depressive parent. *American Journal of Psychiatry, 141,* 223–229.

Hays, W. L (1963). *Statistics.* New York: Holt, Rinehart & Winston.

Klinnert, M., Campos, J., Sorce, J., Emde, R., & Svejda, M. (1983). Emotions as behavior regulators: Social referencing in infancy. In R. Plutchek & H. Kellerman (Eds.), *Emotions in early development: Vol. 2. The emotions.* New York: Academic Press.

LaFreniere, P., & Sroufe, L. A. (in press). Profiles of peer competence in the preschool: Interrelations among measures, influence of social ecology, and relation to attachment history. *Developmental Psychology.*

Lieberman, A. F. (1977). Preschoolers' competence with a peer: Influence of attachment and social experience. *Child Development, 48,* 1277–1287.

Londerville, S., & Main, M. (1981). Security of attachment, compliance, and maternal training methods in the second year of life. *Developmental Psychology, 17,* 289–299.

Maccoby, E., & Feldman, S. (1972). Mother-attachment and stranger-reactions in the third year of life. *Monographs of the Society for Research in Child Development, 37* (1, Serial No. 146).

Main, M., Kaplan, N., & Cassidy, J. (in press). Security in infancy, childhood, and adulthood: A move to the level of representation. In I. Bretherton & E. Waters (Eds.), Growing points in attachment theory and research. *Monographs of the Society for Research in Child Development.*

Main, J., Tomasini L., & Tolan, W. (in press). Differences among mothers of infants judged to differ in security. *Infant Behavior and Development.*

Main, M., & Weston, D. R. (1981). The quality of the toddlers' relationship to mother and father: Related to conflict behavior and the readiness to establish new relationships. *Child Development, 52,* 932–940.

Marvin, R. S. (1972). *Attachment and cooperative behavior in two-, three-, and four-year olds.* Unpublished doctoral dissertation, University of Chicago.

Marvin, R. S. (1977). An ethological-cognitive model for the attenuation of mother-child attachment behavior. In T. M. Alloway & L. Kramer (Eds.), *Advances in the study of communication and affect: Vol. 3. The development of social attachments* (pp. 25–29). New York: Plenum.

Marvin, R. S., & Greenberg, M. T. (1982). Preschoolers' changing conceptions of their mothers: A social-cognitive study of mother-child attachment. In D. Forbes & M. T. Greenberg (Eds.), *New directions in child development: Vol. 14. Developing plans for behavior* (pp. 47–60). San Francisco: Jossey-Bass.

Matas, L., Arend, R. E., & Sroufe, L. A. (1978). Continuity of adaptation in the second year: The relationship between quality of attachment and later competence. *Child Development, 49,* 547–556.

McNair, D. M., Lorr, M., & Droppleman, L. F. (1971). *POMS—Profile of mood states.* San Diego, CA: Educational and Industrial Testing Service.

Meyersberg, M. A., & Post, R. M. (1979). An holistic developmental view of neural and psychological processes: A neurobiological-psychoanalytic integration. *British Journal of Psychiatry, 135,* 139–155.

Pastor, D. L. (1981). The quality of mother-infant attachment and its relationship to toddlers' initial sociability with peers. *Developmental Psychology, 17,* 326–335.

Radke-Yarrow, M., & Zahn-Waxler, C. (1984). Roots, motives, and patternings in children's prosocial behavior. In E. Staub, D. Bar-Tal, J. Karylowski, & J. Reykowski (Eds.), *The development and maintenance of prosocial behavior. International perspectives on positive morality.* New York: Plenum.

Rutter, M., & Garmezy, N. (1983). Developmental psychopathology. In E. M. Hetherington (Ed.), P. H. Mussen (Series Ed.), *Handbook of child psychology: Vol. 4. Socialization, personality, and social development* (pp. 775–911). New York: Wiley.

Schneider-Rosen, K., & Cicchetti, D. (1984). The relationships between affect and cognition in maltreated infants: Quality of attachment and the development of self recognition. *Child Development, 55,* 648–658.

Siegel, S. (1956). *Nonparametric statistics.* New York: McGraw Hill.

Spitzer, R. L., & Endicott, J. (1977). *The schedule for affective disorders and schizophrenia: Lifetime version.* New York: New York State Psychiatric Institute, Biometrics Research.

Spitzer, R. L., Gibbon, M., & Endicott, J. (1978). *Global assessment scale.* New York: New York State Psychiatric Institute, Biometrics Research.

Sroufe, L. A., Fox, N. E., & Pancake, V. R. (1983). Attachment and dependency in developmental perspective. *Child Development, 54,* 1615–1627.

Stayton, D. J., & Ainsworth, M. D. S. (1973). Individual differences in infant responses to brief everyday separations as related to other infant and maternal behavior. *Developmental Psychology, 9,* 226–235.

Tracy, R., & Ainsworth, M. D. S. (1981). Maternal affectionate behavior and infant-mother attachment patterns. *Child Development, 52,* 1341–1343.

Vaughn, B., Egeland, B., Sroufe, L. A., & Waters, E. (1979). Individual differences in infant-mother attachment at twelve and eighteen months: Stability and change in families under stress. *Child Development, 50,* 971–975.

Waters, E. (1978). The reliability and stability of individual differences in infant-mother attachment. *Child Development, 49,* 483–494.

Waters, E., Wippman, J., & Sroufe, L. A. (1979). Attachment, positive affect, and competence in the peer group: Two studies in construct validation. *Child Development, 50,* 821–829.

Zahn-Waxler, C., Cummings, E. M., McKnew, D. H., & Radke-Yarrow, M. (1984). Affective arousal and social interactions in young children of manic-depressive parents. *Child Development, 55,* 112–122.

13

Children of the Garden Island

EMMY E. WERNER

Does exposure to problematic and stressful experiences in early life lead to the development of an unhealthy personality? Are some individuals more resilient than others to developmental difficulties such as birth complications or poverty? The best technique available in developmental psychology for addressing this issue is the longitudinal research design: the same individuals are observed over time to determine if and how their early experiences are related to their later development. A classic longitudinal investigation of the long-term effects of early developmental difficulties was conducted on the Hawaiian island of Kauai by Emmy Werner and her colleagues. This study took place over a thirty-year period and involved a group of approximately 700 individuals. The research team found a number of children who, despite experiential barriers to healthy development, were resistant to these barriers and developed into healthy adults. Resilient children such as these challenge the traditional assumption that there is a simple and direct link between early experiences and later development.

In 1955, 698 infants on the Hawaiian island of Kauai became participants in a 30-year study that has shown how some individuals triumph over physical disadvantages and deprived childhoods.

Kauai, the Garden Island, lies at the northwest end of the Hawaiian chain, 100 miles and a half-hour flight from Honolulu. Its 555 square miles encompass mountains, cliffs, canyons, rain forests and sandy beaches washed by pounding surf. The first Polynesians who crossed the Pacific to settle there in the eighth century were charmed by its beauty, as were the generations of sojourners who visited there after Captain James Cook "discovered" the island in 1778.

The 45,000 inhabitants of Kauai are for the most part descendants of immigrants from Southeast Asia and Europe who came to the island to work on the sugar plantations with the hope of finding a better life for their children. Thanks to the islanders' unique spirit of cooperation, my colleagues Jessie M. Bierman and Fern E. French of the University of California at Berkeley, Ruth S. Smith, a clinical psychologist on Kauai, and I have been able to carry out a longitudinal study on Kauai that has lasted for more than three decades. The study has had two principal goals: to assess the long-term consequences of prenatal and perinatal stress and to document the effects of adverse early rearing conditions on children's physical, cognitive and psychosocial development.

The Kauai Longitudinal Study began at a time when the systematic examination of the development of children exposed to biological and psychosocial risk factors was still a bit of a rarity. Investigators attempted to reconstruct the events that led to physical or psychological problems by studying the history of individuals in whom such problems had already surfaced. This retrospective approach can create the impression that the outcome is inevitable, since it takes into account only the "casualties," not the "survivors." We hoped to avoid that impression by monitoring the development of all the children born in a given period in an entire community.

We began our study in 1954 with an assessment of the reproductive histories of all the women in the community. Altogether 2,203 pregnancies were reported by the women of Kauai in 1954, 1955 and 1956; there were 240 fetal deaths and 1,963 live births. We chose to study the cohort of 698 infants born on Kauai in 1955, and we followed the development of these individuals at one, two, 10, 18 and 31 or 32 years of age. The majority of the individuals in the birth cohort—422 in all—were born without complications, following uneventful pregnancies, and grew up in supportive environments.

But as our study progressed we began to take a special interest in certain "high risk" children who, in spite of exposure to reproductive stress, discordant and impoverished home lives and uneducated, alcoholic or mentally disturbed parents, went on to develop healthy personalities, stable careers and strong interpersonal relations. We decided to try to identify the protective factors that contributed to the resilience of these children.

Finding a community that is willing or able to cooperate in such an effort is not an easy task. We chose Kauai for a number of reasons, not the least of which was the receptivity of the island population to our endeavors. Coverage by medical, public-health, educational and social services on the island was comparable to what one would find in communities of similar size on the U.S. mainland at that time. Furthermore, our study would take into account a variety of cultural influences on childbearing and child rearing, since the population of Kauai includes

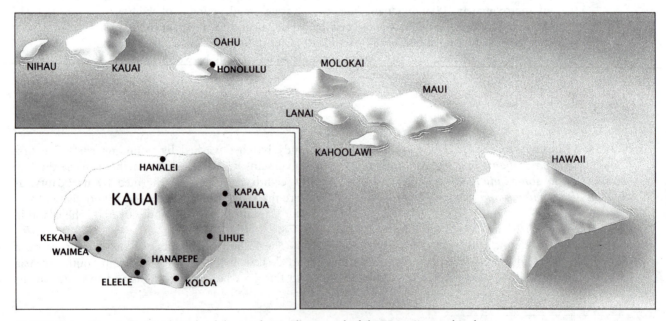

FIGURE 1   Kauai, the Garden Island, lies at the northwest end of the Hawaiian archipelago. The towns that participated in the Kauai Longitudinal Study are shown in the inset. Lihue is the county seat; it is about 100 miles from Honolulu, the capital of Hawaii.

individuals of Japanese, Philipino, Portuguese, Chinese, Korean and northern European as well as of Hawaiian descent.

We also thought the population's low mobility would make it easier to keep track of the study's participants and their families. The promise of a stable sample proved to be justified. At the time of the two-year follow-up, 96 percent of the living children were still on Kauai and available for study. We were able to find 90 percent of the children who were still alive for the 10-year follow-up, and for the 18-year follow-up we found 88 percent of the cohort.

In order to elicit the cooperation of the island's residents, we needed to get to know them and to introduce our study as well. In doing so we relied on the skills of a number of dedicated professionals from the University of California's Berkeley and Davis campuses, from the University of Hawaii and from the island of Kauai itself. At the beginning of the study five nurses and one social worker, all residents of Kauai, took a census of all households on the island, listing the occupants of each dwelling and recording demographic information, including a reproductive history of all women 12 years old or older. The interviewers asked the women if they were pregnant; if a woman was not, a card with a postage-free envelope was left with the request that she mail it to the Kauai Department of Health as soon as she thought she was pregnant.

Local physicians were asked to submit a monthly list of the women who were coming to them for prenatal care. Community organizers spoke to women's groups, church gatherings, the county medical society and community leaders. The visits by the census takers were backed up with letters, and milk cartons were delivered with a printed message urging mothers to cooperate. We advertised in newspapers, organized radio talks, gave slide shows and distributed posters.

Public-health nurses interviewed the pregnant women who joined our study in each trimester of pregnancy, noting any exposure to physical or emotional trauma. Physicians monitored any complications during the prenatal period, labor, delivery and the neonatal period. Nurses and social workers interviewed the mothers in the postpartum period and when the children were one and 10 years old; the interactions between parents and offspring in the home were also observed. Pediatricians and psychologists independently examined the children at two and 10 years of age, assessing their physical, intellectual and social development and noting any handicaps or behavior problems. Teachers evaluated the children's academic progress and their behavior in the classroom.

From the outset of the study we recorded information about the material, intellectual and emotional aspects of the family environment, including stressful life events that resulted in discord or disruption of the family unit. With the parents' permission we also were given access to the records of public-health, educational and social-service agencies and to the files of the local police and the family court. My collaborators and I also administered a wide range of aptitude, achievement and personality tests in the elementary grades and in high school. Last but not least, we gained the perspectives of the young people themselves by interviewing them at the age of 18 and then again when they were in their early 30's.

Of the 698 children in the 1955 cohort, 69 were exposed to moderate prenatal or perinatal stress, that is, complications during pregnancy, labor or delivery. About 3 percent of the cohort—23 individuals in all—suffered severe prenatal or perinatal stress; only 14 infants in this group lived to the age of two. Indeed, nine of the 12 children in our study who died before reaching two years of age had suffered severe perinatal complications.

Some of the surviving children became "casualties" of a kind in the next two decades of life. One out of every six children (116 children in all) had physical or intellectual handicaps of perinatal or neonatal origin that were diagnosed between birth and the age of two and that required long-term specialized medical, educational or custodial care. About one out of every five children (142 in all) developed serious learning or behavior problems in the first decade of life that required more than six months of remedial work. By the time the children were 10 years old, twice as many children needed some form of mental-health service or remedial education (usually for problems associated with reading) as were in need of medical care.

By the age of 18, 15 percent of the young people had delinquency records and 10 percent had mental health problems requiring either in- or outpatient care. There was some overlap among these groups. By the time they were 10, all 25 of the children with long-term mental-health problems had learning problems as well. Of the 70 children who had mental health problems at 18, 15 also had a record of repeated delinquencies.

As we followed these children from birth to the age of 18 we noted two trends: the impact of reproductive stress diminished with time, and the developmental outcome of virtually every biological risk condition was dependent on the quality of the rearing environment. We did find some correlation between moderate to severe degrees of perinatal

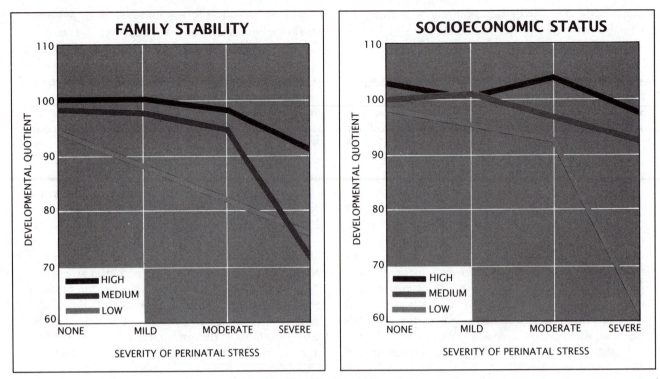

FIGURE 2 Influence of environmental factors such as family stability *(left)* or socioeconomic status *(right)* appears in infancy. The "developmental quotients" derived from tests given at 20 months show that the rearing environment can buffer or worsen the stress of perinatal complications. Children who had suffered severe perinatal stress but lived in stable, middle-class families scored as well as or better than children in poor, unstable households who had not experienced such stress.

trauma and major physical handicaps of the central nervous system and of the musculo-skeletal and sensory systems; perinatal trauma was also correlated with mental retardation, serious learning disabilities and chronic mental-health problems such as schizophrenia that arose in late adolescence and young adulthood.

But overall rearing conditions were more powerful determinants of outcome than perinatal trauma. The better the quality of the home environment was, the more competence the children displayed. This could already be seen when the children were just two years old: toddlers who had experienced severe perinatal stress but lived in middle-class homes or in stable family settings did nearly as well on developmental tests of sensory-motor and verbal skills as toddlers who had experienced no such stress.

Prenatal and perinatal complications were consistently related to impairment of physical and psychological development at the ages of 10 and 18 only when they were combined with chronic poverty, family discord, parental mental illness or other persistently poor rearing conditions. Children who were raised in middle-class homes, in a stable

family environment and by a mother who had finished high school showed few if any lasting effects of reproductive stress later in their lives.

How many children could count on such a favorable environment? A sizable minority could not. We designated 201 individuals—30 percent of the surviving children in this study population—as being high-risk children because they had experienced moderate to severe perinatal stress, grew up in chronic poverty, were reared by parents with no more than eight grades of formal education or lived in a family environment troubled by discord, divorce, parental alcoholism or mental illness. We termed the children "vulnerable" if they encountered four or more such risk factors before their second birthday. And indeed, two-thirds of these children (129 in all) did develop serious learning or behavior problems by the age of 10 or had delinquency records, mental-health problems or pregnancies by the time they were 18.

Yet one out of three of these high-risk children—72 individuals altogether—grew into competent young adults who loved well, worked well and played well. None developed serious learning or behavior problems in childhood or adolescence. As far as we could tell from interviews and from their record in the community, they succeeded in school, managed home and social life well and set realistic educational and vocational goals and expectations for themselves when they finished high school. By the end of their second decade of life they had developed into competent, confident and caring people who expressed a strong desire to take advantage of whatever opportunity came their way to improve themselves.

They were children such as Michael, a boy for whom the odds on paper did not seem very promising. The son of teen-age parents, Michael was born prematurely, weighing four pounds five ounces. He spent his first three weeks of life in a hospital, separated from his mother. Immediately after his birth his father was sent with the U.S. Army to Southeast Asia, where he remained for two years. By the time Michael was eight years old he had three siblings and his parents were divorced. His mother had deserted the family and had no further contact with her children. His father raised Michael and his siblings with the help of their aging grandparents.

Then there was Mary, born after 20 hours of labor to an overweight mother who had experienced several miscarriages before that pregnancy. Her father was an unskilled farm laborer with four years of formal education. Between Mary's fifth and 10th birthdays her mother was hospitalized several times for repeated bouts of mental illness, after having inflicted both physical and emotional abuse on her daughter.

Surprisingly, by the age of 18 both Michael and Mary were individuals with high self-esteem and sound values who cared about others and were liked by their peers. They were successful in school and looked forward to the future. We looked back at the lives of these two youngsters and the 70 other resilient individuals who had triumphed over their circumstances and compared their behavioral characteristics and the features of their environment with those of the other high-risk youths who developed serious and persistent problems in childhood and adolescence.

We identified a number of protective factors in the families, outside the family circle and within the resilient children themselves that enabled them to resist stress. Some sources of resilience seem to be constitutional: resilient children such as Mary and Michael tend to have characteristics of temperament that elicit positive responses from family members and strangers alike. We noted these same qualities in adulthood. They include a fairly high activity level, a low degree of excitability and distress and a high degree of sociability. Even as infants the resilient individuals were described by their parents as "active," "affectionate," "cuddly," "easygoing" and "even tempered." They had no eating or sleeping habits that were distressing to those who took care of them.

The pediatricians and psychologists who examined the resilient children at 20 months noted their alertness and responsiveness, their vigorous play and their tendency to seek out novel experiences and to ask for help when they needed it. When they entered elementary school, their classroom teachers observed their ability to concentrate on their assignments and noted their problem-solving and reading skills. Although they were not particularly gifted, these children used whatever talents they had effectively. Usually they had a special hobby they could share with a friend. These interests were not narrowly sex-typed; we found that girls and boys alike excelled at such activities as fishing, swimming, horseback riding and hula dancing.

We could also identify environmental factors that contributed to these children's ability to withstand stress. The resilient youngsters tended to come from families having four or fewer children, with a space of two years or more between themselves and the next sibling. In spite of poverty, family discord or parental mental illness, they had the opportunity to establish a close bond with at least one caretaker from whom they received positive attention during the first years of life.

The nurturing might come from substitute parents within the family (such as grandparents, older siblings, aunts or uncles) or from the ranks of regular baby-sitters. As the resilient children grew older they seemed to be particularly adept at recruiting such surrogate parents when a biological parent was unavailable (as in the case of an absent father) or incapacitated (as in the case of a mentally ill mother who was frequently hospitalized).

Maternal employment and the need to take care of younger siblings apparently contributed to the pronounced autonomy and sense of responsibility noted among the resilient girls, particularly in households where the father had died or was permanently absent because of desertion or divorce. Resilient boys, on the other hand, were often first-born sons who did not have to share their parents' attention with many additional children in the household. They also had some male in the family who could serve as a role model (if not the father, then a grandfather or an uncle). Structure and rules in the household and assigned chores were part of the daily routine for these boys during childhood and adolescence.

Resilient children also seemed to find a great deal of emotional support outside their immediate family. They tended to be well liked by their classmates and had at least one close friend, and usually several. They relied on an informal network of neighbors, peers and elders for counsel and support in times of crisis and transition. They seem to have made school a home away from home, a refuge from a disordered household. When we interviewed them at 18, many resilient youths mentioned a favorite teacher who had become a role model, friend and confidant and was particularly supportive at times when their own family was beset by discord or threatened with dissolution.

For others, emotional support came from a church group, a youth leader in the YMCA or YWCA or a favorite minister. Participation in extracurricular activities—such as 4-H, the school band or a cheerleading team which allowed them to be part of a cooperative enterprise—was also an important source of emotional support for those children who succeeded against the odds.

With the help of these support networks, the resilient children developed a sense of meaning in their lives and a belief that they could control their fate. Their experience in effectively coping with and mastering stressful life events built an attitude of hopefulness that contrasted starkly with the feelings of helplessness and futility that were expressed by their troubled peers.

In 1985, 12 years after the 1955 birth cohort had finished high school, we embarked on a search for the members of our study group. We managed to find 545 individuals—80 percent of the cohort—through parents or other relatives, friends, former classmates, local telephone books, city directories and circuit-court, voter-registration and motor-vehicle registration records and marriage certificates filed with the State Department of Health in Honolulu. Most of the young men and women still lived on Kauai, but 10 percent had moved to other islands and 10 percent lived on the mainland; 2 percent had gone abroad.

We found 62 of the 72 young people we had characterized as "resilient" at the age of 18. They had finished high school at the height of the energy crisis and joined the work force during the worst U.S. recession since the Great Depression. Yet these 30-year-old men and women seemed to be handling the demands of adulthood well. Three out of four (46 individuals) had received some college education

and were satisfied with their performance in school. All but four worked full time, and three out of four said they were satisfied with their jobs.

Indeed, compared with their low-risk peers from the same cohort, a significantly higher proportion of high-risk resilient individuals described themselves as being happy with their current life circumstances (44 percent versus 10 percent). The resilient men and women did, however, report a significantly higher number of health problems than their peers in low-risk comparison groups (46 percent versus 15 percent). The men's problems seemed to be brought on by stress: back problems, dizziness and fainting spells, weight gain and ulcers. Women's health problems were largely related to pregnancy and childbirth. And although 82 percent of the women were married, only 48 percent of the men were. Those who were married had strong commitments to intimacy and sharing with their partners and children. Personal competence and determination, support from a spouse or mate, and a strong religious faith were the shared qualities that we found characterized resilient children as adults.

We were also pleasantly surprised to find that many high-risk children who had problems in their teens were able to rebound in their twenties and early thirties. We were able to contact 26 (90 percent) of the teen-age mothers, 56 (80 percent) of the individuals with mental-health problems and 74 (75 percent) of the former delinquents who were still alive at the age of 30.

Almost all the teen-age mothers we interviewed were better off in their early thirties than they had been at 18. About 60 percent (16 individuals) had gone on to additional schooling and about 90 percent (24 individuals) were employed. Of the delinquent youths, three-fourths (56 individuals) managed to avoid arrest on reaching adulthood. Only a minority (12 individuals) of the troubled youths were still in need of mental-health services in their early thirties. Among the critical turning points in the lives of these individuals were entry into military service, marriage, parenthood and active participation in a church group. In adulthood, as in their youth, most of these individuals relied on informal rather than formal sources of support: kith and kin rather than mental-health professionals and social-service agencies.

Our findings appear to provide a more hopeful perspective than can be had from reading the extensive literature on "problem" children that come to the attention of therapists, special educators and social-service agencies. Risk factors and stressful environments do not inevitably lead to poor adaptation. It seems clear that, at each stage in an individual's development from birth to maturity, there is a shifting balance between stressful events that heighten vulnerability and protective factors that enhance resilience.

As long as the balance between stressful life events and protective factors is favorable, successful adaptation is possible. When stressful events outweigh the protective factors, however, even the most resilient child can have problems. It may be possible to shift the balance from vulnerability to resilience through intervention, either by decreasing exposure to risk factors or stressful events or by increasing the number of protective factors and sources of support that are available.

It seems clear from our identification of risk and protective factors that some of the most critical determinants of outcome are present when a child is very young. And it is obvious that there are large individual differences among high-risk children in their responses to both negative and positive circumstances in their caregiving environment. The very fact of individual variation among children who live in adverse conditions suggests the need for greater assistance to some than to others.

If early intervention cannot be extended to every child at risk, priorities must be established for choosing who should receive help. Early-intervention programs need to focus on infants and young children who appear most vulnerable because they lack—permanently or temporarily—some of the essential social bonds that appear to buffer stress. Such children may be survivors of neonatal intensive care, hospitalized children who are separated from their families for extended periods of time, the young offspring of addicted or mentally ill parents, infants and toddlers whose mothers work full time and do not have access to stable child care, the babies of single or teen-age parents who have no other adult in the household and migrant and refugee children without permanent roots in a community.

Assessment and diagnosis, the initial steps in any early intervention, need to focus not only on the risk factors in the lives of the children but also on the protective factors. These include competencies and informal sources of support that already exist and that can be utilized to enlarge a young child's communication and problem-solving skills and to enhance his or her self-esteem. Our research on resilient children has shown that other people in a child's life—grandparents, older siblings, day-care providers or teachers—can play a supportive role if a parent is incapacitated or unavailable. In many situations it might make better sense and be less costly as well to strengthen such available informal ties to kin and community than it would to introduce additional layers of bureaucracy into delivery of services.

Finally, in order for any intervention program to be effective, a young child needs enough consistent nurturing to trust in its availability. The resilient children in our study had at least one person in their lives who accepted them unconditionally, regardless of temperamental idiosyncrasies or physical or mental handicaps. All children can be helped to become more resilient if adults in their lives encourage their independence, teach them appropriate communication and self-help skills and model as well as reward acts of helpfulness and caring.

Thanks to the efforts of many people, several community-action and educational programs for high-risk children have been established on Kauai since our study began. Partly as a result of our findings, the legislature of the State of Hawaii has funded special mental-health teams to provide services for troubled children and youths. In addition the State Health Department established the Kauai Children's Services, a coordinated effort to provide services related to child development, disabilities, mental retardation and rehabilitation in a single facility.

The evaluation of such intervention programs can in turn illuminate the process by which a chain of protective factors is forged that affords vulnerable children an escape from adversity. The life stories of the resilient individuals on the Garden Island have taught us that competence, confidence and caring can flourish even under adverse circumstances if young children encounter people in their lives who provide them with a secure basis for the development of trust, autonomy and initiative.

Questions

1.   Why is longitudinal research important for studying resilience in children?

2.   What types of protective factors contribute to a favorable environment for child development?

3.   What do these findings suggest about the long-term prognosis for children and adolescents who are identified as at risk? Do you think that intervention programs in the schools or the community for these at risk children or adolescents are worthwhile? Why or why not?

Further Reading

Kauai's Children Come of Age. Emmy E. Werner and Ruth S. Smith. The University of Hawaii Press, 1977.

Vulnerable But Invincible: A Longitudinal Study of Resilient Children and Youth. Emmy E. Werner and Ruth S. Smith. McGraw-Hill Book Company, 1982.

Longitudinal Studies in Child Psychology and Psychiatry: Practical Lessons from Research Experience. Edited by A. R. Nichol. John Wiley & Sons, Inc., 1985.

High Risk Children in Young Adulthood: A Longitudinal Study from Birth to 32 Years. Emmy E. Werner in *American Journal of Orthopsychiatry,* Vol. 59, No. 1, pages 72–81; January, 1989.

14

Facts, Fantasies and the Future of Child Care in the United States

SANDRA SCARR, DEBORAH PHILLIPS, AND KATHLEEN MCCARTNEY

O ver the past twenty years, women have entered the labor force in great numbers, with the majority of these women having young children in need of supervision and care while their mothers are at work. What effects might early and repeated separations of the parent and infant or young child have on the development of this early social relationship? Sandra Scarr, Deborah Phillips and Kathleen McCartney review research on this issue, focusing on how day care may effect psychological development and what social policy needs to address in this area.

Psychologists in both family practice and developmental research may be puzzled about the scientific status of research on child care as it affects children, parents, and caregivers. What conclusions can be reached about mothers in the labor force, about the advisability of various child care arrangements, about their short and long-term consequences, and what advice do we as psychologists have to offer in the public interest to parents of infants and young children? In this article, we review research on child care, and discuss its implications for the nation and for psychology as a research enterprise and a helping profession.

Child care is now as essential to family life as the automobile and the refrigerator. As of 1986, the majority of families, including those with infants, require child care to support parental employment. Yet most families find it far easier to purchase quality cars and refrigerators than to buy good care for their children.

Contemporary realities about the need for child care, captured in statistics about family income,

Reprinted with permission from the authors and *Psychological Science, Vol. 1,* 1990, 26–35.
Published by Cambridge University Press, New York. Copyright 1990 by the American
Psychological Society.

mens' wages, maternal employment, and labor force needs, have not produced a coherent national policy on parental leaves or on child care services for working parents (Kahn & Kamerman, 1987; Scarr, Phillips, & McCartney, 1989a). Instead, our society remains ambivalent about mothers who work and about children whose care is shared, part-time, with others (McCartney & Phillips, 1988). The cost of our reluctance to shed fantasies about children's needs and parents' obligations, particularly mothers' obligations, is the failure to develop constructive social policies.

Facts and fantasies about child care arrangements influence the thinking of psychologists, other experts, parents, and those who make child care policy. It is thus imperative to reassess our ideas about children's needs and maternal roles, based especially on research. The social and demographic facts that are affecting the growing reliance on child care are now well known. They encompass documentation of declines in family income (Greenstein, 1987), dramatic changes in family structure (Cherlin, 1988), rapid increases in maternal employment and projected continuations of this trend (Hofferth & Phillips, 1987), and converging patterns of employment among mothers of all races and marital statuses (Kahn & Kamerman, 1987; Phillips, 1989). In this article we aim to dispel some of the fantasies that have prevented our nation from making appropriate provisions for the care of infants and young children, and to present research facts about child care. In conclusion, we take a brief look at current policy debates and at the future of child care that could emerge if we proceeded from facts about infants, mothers, and child care.

FANTASIES ABOUT MOTHERS

Science is, in part, a social construction (Scarr, 1985). As such, we sometimes construct fantasies about child development, the uses and implications of which can endure long beyond the time when conflicting evidence becomes available. This is most likely to occur when prior scientific results support strongly-held social values. We argue here that the field of psychology has constructed fantasies about the role of mothers in infant development that have impact on our views of child care. We label these beliefs *fantasies* because they are not supported by contemporary scientific evidence. Such fantasies can be found in thinking about mother-infant attachment, maternal deprivation, and the role of early

experience for later development. The end result is that some of our fantasies about the mothers and infant development have contributed to our national ambivalence about child care as an acceptable child-rearing environment.

Fantasies about Mother-Infant Attachment

Prevailing views about mother-infant attachment have their roots in psychoanalytic theory, Bowlby's theory (1951), and ethology. In some way, all these theories espouse "monotropism" (Smith, 1980), the idea that a single relationship with a special caregiver, typically the mother, is critical for physical and social nourishment. Psychiatrists and others from a psychoanalytic tradition have most often objected to the use of child care, especially in infancy, for this reason (Fraiberg, 1977; Goldstein, Freud, & Solnit, 1973). Yet, research reveals that infants can and do develop multiple attachment relationships: with fathers (Lamb, 1980), with other family members and close friends of the family (Schaffer, 1977), and with caregivers (Ainslie & Anderson, 1984; Farran & Ramey, 1977; Howes, Rodning, Galluzzo, & Myers, 1988). Moreover, we know that most infants become securely attached to their parents, even when they live with a full-time caregiver in a kibbutz (Fox, 1977). Some research has shown that a secure attachment with a caregiver can buttress a child who otherwise might be at risk (Howes, Rodning, Galluzzo & Myers, 1988). Nevertheless, little is known about children's relationships with their caregivers, whose roles in children's lives must differ from those of parents, especially because of the high turnover rates of caregivers in the United States. An enduring child-adult relationship requires at least moderate stability in caregiving.

A number of studies have compared attachment relationships between infants and their mothers as a function of maternal employment or use of child care. Currently, there is a controversy concerning whether extensive child care during infancy is a risk to infants' attachments to their mothers (Belsky, 1988). But most infants require care while their mothers work. Should we view as a "risk factor" a small mean difference in attachment security (8%; Clarke-Stewart, 1989) between children as a function of maternal employment status or child care use? When children in child care seem to fare less well, child care is said to be a risk. When children in child care fare better on assessments of social competence, independence, or school readiness (e.g., Clarke-Stewart, 1984; Gunnarsson, 1978; Howes &

Olenick, 1986; Howes & Stewart, 1987), no one is prepared to call care by mothers a risk factor. All forms of care have their strengths and weaknesses, although the effect sizes are likely to be small (for a thorough review of infant care, see Clarke-Stewart, 1989).

Few would disagree that maternal employment and child care are contextual issues (Bronfenbrenner, 1979, 1986), with many "ifs, ands, and buts" that depend upon the family and the child care situation. Unfortunately, expert advice to parents often fails to mention the size of effects, fails to acknowledge known moderators of effects, and fails to speculate on the possibility, indeed probability, of unknown moderators (Gerson, Alpert, & Richardson, 1984). A notable exception comes from Maurer & Maurer (1989):

> Developmental psychology knows much more about babies now than it knew even ten years ago. . . . Consider, for instance, the effect upon the baby of the mother's going back to work. . . . Studies on the topic abound, and every new one yields a flurry of pronouncements, either dire or reassuring depending on the results. But look at some of the factors involved here. A baby may be cared for in his own home, or in somebody else's home, or in a day care center, by either a relative or a stranger. The caretaker may be trained or untrained, and may be looking after one baby or several babies. The mother may be an overbearing woman and the caretaker easy-going, or vice versa. The mother may be happy about going to work and relaxed about giving over her baby in the morning, or she may be distressed at having to leave him with someone else: either way she may communicate her emotions to the child. At home in the evening, the mother may not have time to play with the baby because she is swamped with housework, or the babysitter or her husband may do the housework, leaving her evenings free. Her husband may be unhappy about her returning to work, so their evenings with the child become tense, or her husband may support her. And, of course, babies differ in temperament from one to another, so they react differently to all these factors. Clearly, no one study can take all of this into account (pp. 207–208).

No study to date has taken into account this full complement of possible influences on children's development and family functioning.

Fantasies about Early Experience

The "romance of early experience" (Scarr & Arnett, 1987) has given us the assumption that infancy provides more potent and pervasive influences than does later human experience. Although evidence for modest relations between early experience and later development exists (Caspi, Elder, & Bem, 1987; Erickson, Sroufe, & Egeland, 1985; Fagan, 1984; Funder, Block, & Block, 1983; Sigman, Cohen, Beckwith, & Parmelee, 1986), we agree with Kagan's (1979) interpretation of the data, namely that continuity does not imply inevitability. The human organism is surprisingly resilient in the face of deleterious experiences and sufficiently malleable to "bounce back" given constructive inputs. Only the most pervasive and continuous detrimental experiences have lasting, negative effects on development (Clarke & Clarke, 1976; Ernst, 1988; Lerner, 1984). Although this fact is encouraging for developmentalists, it is discouraging for interventionists, because even the most intensive early interventions appear to require some follow-up services or lasting environmental changes to assure long-term gains (Rutter, 1979; Scarr & McCartney, 1988; Valentine & Stark, 1979).

As a consequence of growing evidence for malleability, the search for critical periods has shifted toward efforts to examine relations between early and later experience, and to elucidate the mechanisms by which individuals and their environments interact to promote continuities and discontinuities in development (Brim & Kagan, 1980; Lerner, 1984; Scarr & Weinberg, 1983; Wachs & Gruen, 1982). Research on the developmental implications of child care would benefit greatly from adopting this perspective.

Fantasies about Maternal Deprivation

Images about child care include for some the notion of deprivation of maternal care. Research on "maternal deprivation" reached an emotional climax in the 1950s, when Spitz (1945), Bowlby (1951), and others claimed that institutionalized infants were retarded intellectually and socially for lack of mothering. Reanalyses and reinterpretation of the evidence (Yarrow, 1961) found that it was, in fact, lack of sensory and affective stimulation in typical institutions that led to detrimental outcomes for the orphans. Infants need someone consistently there with whom to interact and to develop a trusting relationship, but that person does not have to be the child's biological mother.

Critics of child care sometimes write as though working parents abandon their infants as orphans. For example, the term, "maternal absence," was used to describe employed mothers in the title of a recent article in the prestigious journal, *Child Development* (Barglow, Vaughn & Molitor, 1987). The terms "maternal absence" and "maternal deprivation" seem uncomfortably close and both conjure up negative images. Some seem to forget that employed mothers are typically with their babies in the mornings, evenings, weekends, and holidays, which for most fully-employed workers constitutes about half of the child's waking time.[1] And, when the child is ill, mothers are more likely than other family members to stay at home with the child (Hughes & Galinsky, 1986).

There are moderators of effects in the maternal deprivation literature as well. In his comprehensive review, Rutter (1979) concluded that it is not separation alone but separation in conjunction with other risk factors, for example, family stress, that leads to later antisocial behavior in children. A recent study by Ernst (1988) in Switzerland demonstrates Rutter's point nicely. Ernst's longitudinal study of 137 children who spent their first years in residential nurseries showed no differences between these children and the general population in IQ and in popularity. These children were two to three times more likely to develop behavior and social disorders, however. Ernst's careful analyses revealed that it was not nursery status alone that accounted for the difference. Rather, risk was associated with psychosocial factors in the environment such as parental discord, psychosocial disorder in parents, and abuse.

Early deprivation often indicates that an unfavorable situation will continue. For example, one research team has conducted a retrospective study and found that care during infancy is associated with negative outcomes at age 8 (Vandell & Corasaniti, in press). Infant care was atypical 8 years ago from a demographic perspective (Hofferth & Phillips, 1987). Thus, we must ask the follow-up questions Ernst thought to ask about psychosocial factors in the environment that might be continuous. Was the use of infant child care 8 years ago an indicator of unfavorable circumstances that continue in childhood? A search for these moderators is most likely to advance our knowledge of any identified child care effects. The quality of maternal care, just like other child care arrangements, depends on many aspects of the home situation and mothers' mental health. The fantasy that mothers at home with young children provide the best possible care neglects the observation that some women at home full-time are lonely, depressed, and not functioning well (see Crosby, 1987; Scarr, Phillips & McCartney, 1989b). Although, surely, most mothers at home are well motivated to provide good and stimulating care, they have many responsibilities other than direct child care. Time-use studies show that mothers at home full-time with preschool children spend very little time in direct interaction with them. They spend less time playing educational games and talking with the children than in many other household activities (Hill & Stafford, 1978; Hoffman, 1984; Nock & Kingston, in press; Ziegler, 1983). Child caregivers, on the other hand, usually have a majority of their time to give to their charges, although they usually have more children to care for than a mother at home. There are trade-offs: Neither home care nor out-of-home care promises quality child care. In fact, employed mothers of infants and young children spend less time in total home activities than non-employed mothers (715 versus 930 minutes, summed across one workday and a Sunday), but their actual time with their *children* is much closer to that of non-employed mothers. The largest difference in time with young children is the distribution of time between weekdays and weekends, with employed mothers concentrating their child-time on the weekends. Employed mothers scrimp on housework and on their own leisure time, rather than on time with their children (Nock & Kingston, in press). Fathers with employed wives spend more time with their infants and preschool children than fathers with non-employed wives (580 versus 521 minutes; Nock & Kingston, in press). Thus, working parents do spend considerable time in both direct and indirect activities with their children. In addition, children of working parents have the attention of caregivers while their parents work.

RESEARCH FACTS ABOUT CHILD CARE AND CHILD DEVELOPMENT

Child care arrangements, like families, vary enormously in their abilities to promote children's development, to provide support for working families, and to give caregivers rewarding adult roles. In the research literature, however, child care is still cast as nonmaternal care by investigators who, in fact, rarely study variation in child care settings. Similarly, home care is treated uniformly as though all families were alike, and is assumed to be preferred to other child care arrangements. Thus studies often ignore the facts that families vary from abusive and neglectful of children's needs to supportive and loving systems that promote optimal development, and so do other child care arrangements. Actual child care arrangements vary from hiring a trained nanny or untrained babysitter in one's own home, to family day care in another person's home, to centers that care for more than 100 infants and children. Diversity in the quality of child care, at home and in other settings, is what matters for children. High-quality day care settings have in fact been shown to compensate for poor family environments (McCartney, Scarr, Phillips, & Grajek, 1985; Ramey, Bryant & Suarez, 1985) and, for low-income children, to promote better intellectual and social development than they would have experienced in their own homes.

Developmental Effects of Child Care

Fears about the effects of child care have centered on possible interference with infants' attachment to their mothers, on their later social development, and on their intellectual development.

ATTACHMENT RESEARCH The earliest research on child care asked whether or not caregivers replaced mothers as children's primary attachment figures. Concerns that daily prolonged separations from mother might weaken the mother-child bond were a direct heritage of the work on children in orphanages. But child care was not found to be a milder form of full-time institutionalization. Attachment was not adversely affected by enrollment in the university-based child care centers that provided the early child care samples. Bonds formed between children and their caregivers did not replace the mother-child attachment relationship (Belsky & Steinberg, 1978; Etaugh, 1980).

Now, almost twenty years later, the emergence of infant day care as a middle-class phenomenon among parents who themselves were reared at home by their mothers, has spawned an active debate about infant day care. The central issue here is whether full-time child care in the first year of life increases the probability of insecure attachments between mothers and infants. Some researchers have presented evidence that supports this claim (Belsky, 1986; Belsky, 1988; Belsky & Rovine, in press).

Other researchers have highlighted the many limitations of this new literature on infant day care (Clarke-Stewart, in press; Clarke-Stewart & Fein, 1983; McCartney & Galanopoulos, 1988; Phillips, McCartney, Scarr, & Howes, 1987). The main limi-tation concerns the exclusive use of the Strange Situation (Ainsworth & Wittig, 1969) to assess attachment. Critics question whether this experimental laboratory procedure of separation from and re-union with mother is equally stressful for children with and without child care experience, because children with child care experience have daily experience with the supposed stressful procedure. Furthermore, studies with an attachment Q-sort measure (Waters & Deane, 1985) have failed to show differences between children in child care and children at home with mother (Belsky, personal communication, to K. McCartney, November 6, 1987; Weinraub, Jaeger, & Hoffman, in press). Finally, the practical significance of differences reported in the Strange Situation between child care and non-child care samples is minimal, despite press reports to the contrary (Clarke-Stewart, 1989).

SOCIAL DEVELOPMENT Although some studies have reported no differences in social behavior (Golden, Rosenbluth, Grossi, Policare, Freeman, & Brownlees, 1978; Kagan, Kearsley & Zelaso, 1978), others find that children who have attended child care are more socially competent (Clarke-Stewart, 1984; Gunnarsson, 1978; Howes & Olenick, 1986; Howes & Stewart, 1987; Ruopp, et al., 1979), and still others suggest lower levels of social competence (Haskins, 1985; Rubenstein, Howes, & Boyle, 1983). Positive outcomes include teacher and parent ratings of considerateness and sociability (Phillips, McCartney, & Scarr, 1987), observations of compliance and self regulation (Howes & Olenick, 1986), and observations of involvement and positive interactions with teachers (McCartney, 1984; Ruopp, Travers, Glantz, & Coelen, 1979; Vandell & Powers, 1983).

Negative outcomes of day care experience have emphasized aggression. For example, Haskins' (1985) study of graduates from the Abecedarian project, a high-quality intervention day care program, showed that teachers in the early elementary grades rated these children higher on scales of aggression than a control group that was not enrolled in the program. However, a subgroup of the control children who were enrolled in an equivalent amount of community-based child care were found to be among the least aggressive children in the study, thereby demonstrating that the effect was not due to child care per se. A change in the curriculum of the Abecedarian project decreased aggression by 80% (Finkelstein, 1982), and by third grade, all early effects had dissipated for the initial group (Bryant, personal communication, February 1988). Here again, the story of day care effects will eventually be told through an examination of moderators, such as quality, and of trends in behavior over time.

Senate approval in June [1989] of the Act for Better Child Care (ABC) represents the first major effort by the federal government to address the nation's child care crisis since 1971 when President Nixon vetoed the Child Development Act. It is the first of several bills in progress that deal with the long-neglected issue.

—from *Child Behavior and Development Letter* (Brown University), 1989, *5*, 1.

INTELLECTUAL AND COGNITIVE DEVELOPMENT

Differences in intelligence between children in varying forms of day care and children cared for by their mothers have not been reported in most studies (Carew, 1980; Doyle & Somers, 1978; Kagan, Kearsley, & Zelaso, 1978; Robertson, 1982; Stith & Davis, 1984). Two studies, however, have reported that children in center care score higher on tests of cognitive competence (Clarke-Stewart, 1984; Rubenstein, Howes, & Boyle, 1981) than children in other types of child care settings. Similar evidence is provided by evaluations of early intervention programs (Lee, Brooks-Gunn, & Schnur, 1988; McCartney, Scarr, Phillips & Grajek, 1985; McKey, Condelli, Ganson, Barrett, McConkey & Plantz, 1985; Ramey & Haskins, 1981; Schweinhart & Weikart, 1980; Seitz, Apel, Rosenbaum, & Zigler, 1983), which indicate that carefully designed group programs can have substantial, and, in some cases lasting, positive effects on children's patterns of achievement.

In sum, there is near consensus among developmental psychologists and early childhood experts that child care per se does not constitute a risk factor in children's lives; rather, poor quality care and poor family environments can conspire to produce poor developmental outcomes (National Center for Clinical Infant Programs, 1988).

Child Care as a Heterogeneous Environment

Contemporary developmental research has recognized the vast heterogeneity of child care and turned to the question of "what is *quality?*" in child care. Reliable indices of child care quality include caregiver-child ratio, group size, and caregiver training and experience. These variables, in turn, facilitate constructive and sensitive interactions among caregivers and children, which promote positive social and cognitive development (Phillips, 1987; Ruopp et al., 1979).

The caregiver-child ratio is related to decreased exposure to danger (Ruopp et al., 1979) and to increased language interactions in the child care setting. Both Bruner (1980) and Howes and Rubenstein (1985) report that children in centers with more adults per child engage in more talking and more playing. Another study (McCartney, 1984) has documented a link between verbal interaction with caregivers and children's language competence. Results of the National Day Care Study suggest that adequate ratios are particularly important for infants, with experts citing 1:4 as the threshold for good quality care.

Research on group size has revealed that the larger the group, the more management is necessary; the smaller the group, the more education and social interaction is possible. As first demonstrated in the National Day Care Study (Ruopp et al., 1979), caregivers in larger groups provide less social interaction and cognitive stimulation. Children in larger groups were found to be more apathetic and more distressed. These findings have since been replicated in other studies (Bruner, 1980; Howes, 1983; Howes & Rubenstein, 1985).

The research on caregiver training and education is particularly consistent. Not surprisingly, years of child-related education are associated with increased caregiver responsivity, positive affect, and ability to provide socially- and intellectually-stimulating experiences (Clarke-Stewart & Gruber, 1984; Howes, 1983; Ruopp et al., 1979; Stallings & Porter, 1980). These findings do not simply represent the effects of self-selection. Two intervention studies show that training leads to caregiver improvement (Arnett, 1989; Kaplan & Conn, 1984). Experience working with children cannot replace child-related training. Although Howes (1983) found an association between years of experience and responsiveness to children, the National Day Care Study (Ruopp et al., 1979) found that day care experience was associated with less social interaction and more apathy. Other studies have not found any important effects of experience per se (Phillips, McCartney, Scarr, & Howes, 1987; Stallings & Porter, 1980).

Research has also shown that many aspects of quality are correlated and that a good center is essentially one with good caregivers. Good caregivers are caring, able to read a baby's signals, and responsive to babies signals (McCartney, 1987). In fact, preschoolers perceive caregivers to provide the same caregiving functions as their mothers (Tephly & Elardo, 1984). The vast literature on mother-child interaction can also inform us of caregiving behaviors that are important. Although these behaviors are not legislatable, they are trainable.

Among the most recent indicators of quality to emerge from research is the stability of children's child care arrangements (Cummings, 1980; Howes & Olenick, 1986; Howes & Stewart, 1987). Children who experience multiple changes in caregivers and settings develop less optimally in social and language areas than children with stable child care, with effects lasting into the early school years (Howes, 1988). The importance of stable care stands in stark contrast with the alarmingly high turnover rates among child care workers. Between 1980 and 1990, 42% of all non-household child care workers will need to be replaced each year, just to maintain the current supply of child care providers ("New Occupational," 1984). Low pay, lack of benefits, and stressful working conditions are the major reasons cited by child care workers who leave their jobs (Jorde-Bloom, 1987; Kontos & Stremmel, 1988; Whitebook, Howes, Darrah, & Friedman, 1982). Infants and young children cannot develop stable relationships with caregivers if they are faced with new caregivers every few weeks.

Relations Between Home and Child Care

In studies of typical child care, researchers can neither assign children randomly to child care nor assign parents to varying employment patterns. As a consequence, efforts to decipher the "effects" of child care are a methodological conundrum. Pre-existing family differences—in background, traits, and beliefs—are confounded with child care arrangements.

Recent research suggests that there may be interaction effects between family characteristics and child care arrangements in maternal anxiety (Hock, DeMeis & McBride, 1987), marital status and living arrangements (Scarr, Lande, & McCartney, 1989), such that good child care can compensate for poor home environments. There is also increasing evidence that the lowest income and most disorganized families (among the middle class) end up in the lowest quality child care programs (Howes & Olenick, 1986; Howes & Stewart, 1987; Lamb, Huang, Brookstein, Broberg, Hult, & Frodi, 1988). A number of other family variables might reasonably moderate effects, especially those related to family stress (Kontos & Wells, 1986).

A number of relationships may affect children's sense of security and thereby their adjustment. Belsky found that daughters with unemployed mothers were more likely to be insecurely attached to their fathers than daughters of employed mothers (Belsky & Rovine, in press). Using the attachment Q-sort (Waters & Deane, 1985), Howes and her colleagues (Howes, et al., 1988) have shown recently that both attachment security at home with mother and attachment security with the caregiver at day care are predictors of the child's positive interaction with caregivers and peers in day care. Interactions between family characteristics and child care have been found to affect development in the first 2 years of life. For example, Scarr, Lande, and McCartney (1989) reported negative main effects for typical center care (but not family day care) in the first 2 years of life on both intellectual and social/emotional ratings. The same children were also disadvantaged by being reared in single mother-headed households (but not in extended families with single mothers). Further, they found important interactions between households and center care, such that infants from single mother-headed households benefited from group care more than similar children in other kinds of care, including maternal care. By the age of 4 years, there were no effects of child care in the first 2 years or in the second 2 years on any child development outcome. Other research (McBride & Belsky, 1988; Weinraub, Jaeger & Hoffman, in press) has found that relations between maternal employment and attachment vary according to maternal satisfaction with child care arrangements, role satisfaction, and coping skills. Studies such as these suggest that child care must be seen in the context of the child's family life before one can interpret any effects of child care per se.

FACTS ABOUT CHILD CARE POLICY

For the first time in a decade, child care is on the national agenda. In 1988, more than 40 bills containing provisions for child care were introduced in the U.S. Congress (Robins, 1988). Driven largely by escalating rates of employment among non-poor, married mothers (Kahn & Kamerman, 1987), federal child care policies have come under intense scrutiny and numerous proposals for restructuring the federal role have surfaced. These range from "supply side" proposals that emphasize improvements in the current system of child care to "demand side" proposals that offer families additional tax subsidies for purchasing child care. Parental leave policies are also being debated. In addition, the majority of states are now moving towards limited funding for school-based child care programs that typically are targeted at poor and/or disadvantaged families (Marx & Seligson, 1988).

The same demographic trends that are influencing child care policy are also creating new goals for welfare reform effects. For low-income mothers, prevailing beliefs about maternal care have traditionally led us to favor policies that enable them to stay home with their babies, through child support and public assistance (e.g., Aid to Families with Dependent Children). But the new welfare reform bill (Family Support Act of 1988: P.L. 100–483), emphasizes training, employment and women's attainment of economic independence rather than support for full-time mothering (Phillips, in press). This shift in purpose is due largely to policymakers' recognition that the majority of mothers with preschool-age children are now in the labor force. Under these circumstances, it is difficult to justify the prior exemption from training and employment programs for AFDC-eligible mothers with children under age 6. Unfortunately, even in the best of circumstances, the child care subsidies included in the Family Support Act are continued for only one year after mothers achieve the minimum wage jobs for which they are being trained.

The policy debate about child care is no longer about whether there will be support for child care or whether families will continue to rely on child care (Martinez, 1989). Instead, it has focused on relatively pragmatic questions about delivery systems, target populations, and financing. These questions, however, are not uncontroversial. For example, the high cost of market forms of child care and fears about nationalizing our child care system have generated strong resistance to legislation that ties government subsidies to use of licensed programs (i.e., centers and regulated family day care homes) or that mandates federal day care standards. For these reasons, we are unlikely ever to see child care and leave policies in the United States that resemble European or Canadian policies (see Scarr, Phillips, & McCartney, 1989a). Considerations of "who should provide child care?" are now mired in an acrimonious debate involving the schools, community-based child care programs, and church-housed programs. And, on-going debates about whether government child care benefits should be reserved for the poor or also assist the non-poor, and about whether these benefits should purchase good quality child care (as in the Head Start program) or disregard consideration of quality are far from resolved.

The child care policies that result from today's debate will constitute some adaptation to the realities of working parents. However, the effects of our national ambivalence about working mothers will undoubtedly be felt, as well. Prevailing beliefs that mothers of very young children belong at home and that child care problems are best solved privately will assure that any new child care policy is likely to remain fragmented, marginal, and modestly funded. At a minimum, any generous policy that might actually create an incentive for those mothers who have a choice about working to use child care, will be avoided.

This is the political and social context on which research on child care has a bearing. The ways in which research questions are framed and the values that underlie our questions can challenge the assumptions that guide policy and promote policies that are based more on facts and less on fantasies.

THE FUTURE

Research on Child Care

Future research on child care influences will need to place more emphasis on the contexts in which families use child care services (Bronfenbrenner, 1986; McCartney & Galanopoulis, 1988). The ecology of child care includes the family, its choice of child care arrangements, its ability to pay for quality care, and its independent effects on child development. Contemporary researchers recognize the necessity of taking into account not only the quality of child care, but also the quality of the home environment, individual differences in children, and the history of children's experience with child care. Life is complicated, and thus requires complex models.

As part of the ecology of child care, research needs to examine the effects of the *un*availability of child care, particularly of the unavailability of good quality, consistent care. Similarly, we have no understanding of the effects of the virtual absence of parental leave policies in the United States (Scarr, Phillips, & McCartney, 1989b). What are the effects on children and families when parents do not have choices about when they return to work, and about the type and quality of the child care they offer their children?

Research on child care has also sampled a relatively narrow range of care types, with licensed centers and regulated family day care homes dominating the empirical literature. Even among center-based arrangements, we have neglected for-profit chains and centers that are exempted from state regulation (e.g., church-run centers in several states). Unregulated family day care homes and other types of care that are not covered by state licensing (e.g., nannies) are virtually unstudied. As a consequence, it is entirely possible that we have not sampled programs that represent the poorest quality care offered in this country.

Longitudinal research is necessary to determine which effects of child care are transitory and which represent enduring influences on development. So far, there are conflicting findings on the long term correlates of early child care arrangements (Scarr, Lande & McCartney, 1989; Scarr & McCartney, in preparation; Vandell & Corasaniti, in press; Vandell, Henderson & Wilson, in press).

At the very least, research is needed on: (1) the family and other mediators of development that correlate, augment, and interact with child care arrangements; (2) range of types and qualities of child care; and (3) longitudinal research on short and long term effects of child care on development, on families, and on caregivers. For these reasons, we can make few definitive statements at this time about the direct effects of child care on children. Rather, we have documented effects that appear to be caused by child care, but may be attributable to children's case histories, temperaments, families, or to complex interactions among these and other circumstances.

Conclusions

The discussion of fantasies about the nature of child care suggests that we need a closer look at the facts about children's, parents', and care providers' experiences in our current child care system—their discomforts and their satisfactions—to orient our research to the most pressing issues. As one of the reviewers of the article said,

. . . in the circumstances prevailing in contemporary society, day care—far more often than not—plays an essential and crucial role as a support system that enables families to function and can provide important supplementary developmental experiences for children. To be sure, there are probably some circumstances, not yet fully understood, that involve some measure of risk, especially for very young children, and these risks need to be weighed, but they are hardly comparable in their probability and magnitude to those to which many children are exposed, through the unavailability of quality child care for thousands of families that desperately want and need it. (Bronfenbrenner, personal communication, December 1988)

For children, the most pressing issue is quality of care—care that will encourage and support all aspects of child development.

For parents, the most pressing issues are affordability and availability of consistent and dependable child care, and employment options that make the task of combining worker and parent roles less stressful.

For child care providers, the most pressing issues are staff wages and working conditions and public support for a system of high quality care that will meet the diverse needs of the working poor, minority families, middle income families, and even yuppie parents who want "the best."

For policy makers, at federal and state levels, the most pressing issues are how to fund a system of quality child care, regulate those aspects of quality that can be legislated and enforced, and coordinate efforts with the private sector and at all levels of government.

Questions

1.   Which conventional views of childhood do Scarr, Phillips and McCartney call fantasies? What are their reasons for doing so?

2.   How does the social and cognitive development of children who have been in child care differ from children who are raised at home by their parents?

3.   What role can and should developmental psychologists play in the formulation and review of social policy regarding child care in the United States? What aspects of the issue should they not get involved with?

Note

1.   Consider 5 working days/weeks for 49 weeks of the year: 1.5 hours in the morning, 3 hours of the child's waking time in the late afternoon and evening, for a sum of 4.5 of the approximately 14 hours of the child's daily waking time. The caregiver accounts for approximately 9 hours of which 2 hours are typically spent in a nap. (A half hour is allocated for transportation.) The sum of the work-week hours for parents employed full-time is 1102; for caregivers, 1715.

To the parental sum, add week-ends (2 days/work week) for 49 weeks, sum of 1274. To that add 3 weeks of vacation time, and 10 days of personal and sick leave (for self and child) during the work week, a sum of 455.

By these calculations, typical, fully-employed parents spend 2831 hours with the child; caregivers spent approximately 1715.

References

Ainslie, R. C., & Anderson, C. W. (1984). Day care children's relationships to their mothers and caregivers: An inquiry into the conditions for the development of attachment. In R. C. Ainslie (Ed.), *The child and the day care setting*. New York: Praeger.

Ainsworth, M., & Wittig, B. A. (1969). Attachment and exploratory behavior of one-year olds in a strange situation. In B. M. Foss (Ed.), *Determinants of infant behavior*, Vol. 4. London: Methuen.

Arnett, J. (1989). Issues and obstacles in the training of caregivers. In J. Lande, S. Scarr, & N. Gunzenhauser (Eds.), *Caring for children: Challenge to America* (pp. 241–256). Hillsdale, NJ: Erlbaum.

Barglow, P., Vaughn, B. E., & Molitor, N. (1987). Effects of maternal absence due to employment on the quality of infant-mother attachment in a low-risk sample. *Child Development, 58*, 945–954.

Belsky, J. (1986). Infant day care: A cause for concern? *Zero to Three, 6*(5), 1–9.

Belsky, J. (1988). The "effects" of infant day care reconsidered. *Early Childhood Research Quarterly, 3*, 235–272.

Belsky, J., & Rovine, M. J. (in press). Nonmaternal care in the first year of life and the security of infant-parent attachment. *Child Development*.

Belsky, J., & Steinberg, L. D. (1978). The effects of daycare: A critical review. *Child Development, 49*, 929–949.

Bowlby, J. (1951). *Maternal care and mental health*. Geneva: World Health Organization.

Bronfenbrenner, U. (1979). *The ecology of human development: Experiments by nature and design*. Cambridge, MA: Harvard University Press.

Bronfenbrenner, U. (1986). Ecology of the family as a context for human development: Research perspectives. *Developmental Psychology, 22*, 723–742.

Brim, O. G., & Kagan, J. (1980). *Constancy and change in human development*. Cambridge, MA: Harvard University Press.

Bruner, J. (1980). *Under five in Britain*. London: Methuen.

Carew, J. (1980). Experience and the development of intelligence in young children. *Monographs of the Society for Research in Child Development, 45*, 6–7 (Serial No. 187).

Caspi, A., Elder, G. H., Jr., & Bem, D. J. (1987). Moving against the world: Life course patterns of explosive children. *Developmental Psychology, 23*, 308–313.

Cherlin, A. J. (Ed.). (1988). *The changing American family and public policy*. Washington, DC: The Urban Institute Press.

Clarke, A.M., & Clarke, A. D. B. (1976). *Early experience: Myth and evidence*. London: Open Books.

Clarke-Stewart, A. (1984). Day care: A new context for research and development. In M. Perlmutter (Ed.), *The Minnesota Symposia on Child Psychology: Vol. 27. Parent-child interaction and parent-child relations in child development* (pp. 61–100). Hillsdale, NJ: Erlbaum.

Clarke-Stewart, A. (1989). Infant day care: Malignant or maligned? *American Psychologist*.

Clarke-Stewart, A., & Fein, G. (1983). Early childhood programs. In P. H. Mussen (Series Ed.) & M. Haith and J. Campos (Vol. Eds.), *Handbook of child psychology: Vol. II. Infancy and developmental psychobiology* (pp. 917–1000). New York: Wiley.

Clarke-Stewart, A., & Gruber, C. (1984). Day care forms and features. In R. C. Ainslie (Ed.), *The child and the day care setting* (pp. 35-62). New York: Praeger.

Crosby, F. J. (Ed.). (1987). *Spouse, parent, worker: On gender and multiple roles.* New Haven: Yale University Press.

Cummings, E. H. (1980). Caregiver stability and day care. *Developmental Psychology, 16,* 31–37.

Doyle, A., & Somers, K. (1978). The effects of group and family day care on infant attachment behaviors. *Canadian Journal of Behavioral Science, 10,* 38–45.

Erickson, M. F., Sroufe, L. A., & Egeland, B. (1985). The relationship between quality of attachment and behavior problems in preschool in a high-risk sample. In I. Bertherton & E. Waters (Eds.), Growing points in attachment theory and research. *Monographs of the Society for Research in Child Development, 50,* 147–166.

Ernst, D. (1988). Are early childhood experiences overrated? A reassessment of maternal deprivation. *European Archives of Psychiatry and Neurological Sciences, 237,* 80–90.

Etaugh, C. (1980). Effects of nonmaternal care on children: Research evidence and popular views. *American Psychologist, 35,* 309–319.

Fagan, J. F. (1984). The intellectual infant: Theoretical implications. *Intelligence, 8,* 1–9.

Farran, D., & Ramsey, C. (1977). Infant day care and attachment behaviors toward mothers and teachers. *Child Development, 48,* 1112–1116.

Finkelstein, N. (1982). Aggression: Is it stimulated by day care? *Young Children, 37,* 3–9.

Fox, N. (1977). Attachment of kibbutz infants to mothers and metapelet. *Child Development, 48,* 1228–1239.

Fraiberg, S. (1977). *Every child's birthright: In defense of mothering.* New York: Basic Books.

Funder, D., Block, J. H., & Block, J. (1983). Delay of gratification: Some longitudinal personality correlates. *Journal of Personality and Social Psychology, 44,* 1198–1213.

Gerson, J., Alpert, J. L., & Richardson, M. (1984). Mothering: The view from psychological research. *Signs, 9,* 434–453.

Golden, M., Rosenbluth, L., Grossi, M. T., Policare, H. J., Freeman, H., Jr., & Brownlee, E. M. (1978). *The New York City infant day care study.* New York: Medical and Health Research Association of New York City.

Goldstein, J., Freud, A., & Solnit, A. J. (1973). *Beyond the best interests of the child.* New York: Free Press.

Greenstein, R. (1987). Testimony presented before the Income Security Task Force Committee on the Budget, U.S. House of Representatives, Washington, D.C., November 9, 1987.

Gunnarsson, L. (1978). *Children in day care and family care in Sweden* (Research Bulletin, No. 21). Gothenburg, Sweden: University of Gothenburg.

Haskins, R. (1985). Public school aggression among children with varying day care experience. *Child Development, 56,* 689–703.

Hill, C. R., & Stafford, F. P. (1978). Parental care of children: Time diary estimates of quantity, predictability, and variety. *Institute for Social Research Working Paper Series.* Ann Arbor: University of Michigan.

Hock, E., DeMeis, D., & McBride, S. (1987). Maternal separation anxiety: Its role in the balance of employment and motherhood in mothers of infants. In A. Gottfried, & A. Gottfried (Eds.), *Maternal employment and children's development: Longitudinal research (pp. 191–229).* New York: Plenum.

Hofferth, S. L., & Phillips, D. A. (1987). Child care in the United States, 1970 to 1995. *Journal of Marriage and the Family, 49,* 559–571.

Hoffman, L.W. (1984). Maternal employment and the child. In M. Perlmutter (Ed.), *The Minnesota Symposia on Child Psychology: Vol. 17. Parent child interaction and parent-child relations in development* (pp. 101–127). Hillsdale, NJ: Erlbaum.

Howes, C. (1983). Caregiver behavior in center and family day care. *Journal of Applied Developmental Psychology, 4,* 99–107.

Howes, C. (1988). Relations between early child care and schooling. *Developmental Psychology, 24,* 53–57.

Howes, C., and Olenick, M. (1986). Child care and family influences on compliance. *Child Development, 57,* 202–216.

Howes, C., Rodning, C., Galluzzo, D., & Myers, L. (1988). Attachment and child care: Relationships with mother and caregiver. *Early Childhood Research Quarterly, 3,* 403–416.

Howes, C., & Rubenstein, J. (1985). Determinants of toddlers' experience in daycare: Age of entry and quality of setting. *Child Care Quarterly, 14,* 140–151.

Howes, C., & Stewart, P. (1987). Child's play with adults, toys, and peers: An examination of family and child-care influences. *Developmental Psychology, 23,* 423–430.

Hughes, D., & Galinsky, E. (1986). Maternity, paternity, and parenting policies: How does the United States compare. In S. A. Hewlett, A. S. Ilchman, & J. J. Sweeney (Eds.), *Family and work: Bridging the gap* (pp. 53–66). Cambridge, MA: Ballinger.

Jorde-Bloom, P. (1987, April). *Factors influencing overall job commitment and facet satisfaction in early childhood work environments.* Paper presented at the meeting of the American Education Research Association, Washington, D.C.

Kagan, J. (1979). Family experience and the child's development. *American Psychologist, 34,* 886–891.

Kagan, J., Kearsley, R. B., & Zelaso, P. R. (1978). *Infancy: Its place in human development.* Cambridge, MA: Harvard University Press.

Kahn, A. J., & Kamerman, S. B. (1987). *Child care: Facing the hard choices.* Dover, MA; Auburn House.

Kaplan, M., & Conn, J. (1984). The effects of caregiver training on classroom setting and caregiver performance in eight community day care centers. *Child Study Journal, 14,* 79–93.

Kontos, S., & Stremmel, A. J. (1988). Caregivers' perceptions of working conditions in a child care environment. *Early Childhood Research Quarterly, 3,* 77–90.

Kontos, S., & Wells, W. (1986). Attitudes of caregivers and the day care experiences of families. *Early Childhood Research Quarterly, 1,* 47–67.

Lamb, M. (1980). The development of parent-infant attachments in the first two years of life. In F. Pederson (Ed.), *The father-infant relationship: Observational studies in the family setting.* New York: Praeger.

Lamb, M., Hwang, C., Bookstein, F. L., Broberg, A., Hult, G., & Frodi, M. (1988). Determinants of social competence in Swedish preschoolers. *Developmental Psychology, 24,* 58–70.

Lee, V. E., Brooks-Gunn, J., & Schnur, E. (1988). Does Head Start work? A 1-year follow-up comparison of disadvantaged children attending Head Start, no preschool, and other preschool programs. *Developmental Psychology, 24,* 210–222.

Lerner, R. M. (1984). *On the nature of human plasticity.* New York: Cambridge University Press.

Martinez, S. (1989). Child care and federal policy. In J. Lande, S. Scarr, & N. Gunzenhauser (Eds.), *Caring for children: Challenge to America* (pp. 111–124). Hillsdale, NJ: Erlbaum.

Marx, F., & Seligson, M. (1988). *The public school early childhood study. The state survey.* New York: Bank Street College of Education.

Maurer, C., & Maurer, D. (1988). *World of the newborn.* New York: Basic.

McBride, S., & Belsky, J. (1988). Characteristics, determinants, and consequences of maternal separation anxiety. *Developmental Psychology, 24,* 407–414.

McCartney, K. (1984). The effect of quality of day care environment upon children's language development. *Developmental Psychology, 20,* 244–260.

McCartney, K. (1987, July/August). Quality: A child's point of view. *Child Care Action News,* Newsletter of the Child Care Action Campaign, 4(4).

McCartney, K., & Galanopoulis, A. (1988). Child care and attachment: A new frontier the second time around. *American Journal of Orthopsychiatry, 58,* 16–24.

McCartney, K., & Phillips, D. (1988). Motherhood and child care. In B. Birns & D. Hay (Eds.), *Different faces of motherhood* (pp. 157–183). New York: Plenum Press.

McCartney, K., Scarr, S., Phillips, D., & Grajek, S. (1985). Day care as intervention: Comparisons of varying quality programs. *Journal of Applied Development Psychology, 6,* 247–260.

McKey, R. H., Condelli, L., Ganson, H., Barrett, B. J., McConkey, C., & Plantz, M. C. (1985). *The impact of Head Start on children, families, and communities: Final report of the Head Start evaluation, synthesis, and utilization project.* Washington, D.C.: CSR Inc.

National Center for Clinical Infant Programs. (1988). *Infants, Families and Child Care.* Washington, D.C.: Author. Brochure.

New occupational separation data improve estimates of job replacement needs. (1984, March). *Monthly Labor Review, 107(3),* 3–10.

Nock, S. L., & Kingston, P. W. (in press). Time with children: The impact of couples' work-time commitments. *Social Forces.*

Phillips, D. (Ed.). (1987). *Quality in child care: What does research tell us?* Washington, D.C.: National Association for the Education of Young Children.

Phillips, D. (1989). Future directions and need for child care in the United States. In J. S. Lande, S. Scarr, & N. Gunzenhauser (Eds.), *Caring for children: Challenge to America* (pp. 257–275). Hillsdale, NJ: Erlbaum.

Phillips, D. (in press). With a little help: Children in poverty and child care. In A. Huston (Ed.), *Children and Poverty.* New York: Cambridge University Press.

Phillips, D., McCartney, K., & Scarr, S. (1987). Child-care quality and children's social development. *Developmental Psychology, 23,* 537–543.

Phillips, D., McCartney, K., Scarr, S., & Howes, C. (1987, February). Selective view of infant day care research: A cause for concern! *Zero to Three, 7,* 18–21.

Ramey, C. T., Bryant, D. M., & Suarez, T. M. (1985). Preschool compensatory education and the modifiability of intelligence: A critical review. In D. Detterman (Ed.), *Current topics in human intelligence* (pp. 247–296). Norwood, NJ: Ablex.

Ramey, C. T., & Haskins, R. (1981). The causes and treatment of school failure: Insights from the Carolina Abecedarian Project. In M. J. Begab, H. C. Haywood, & H. L. Garber (Eds.), *Psychosocial influences in retarded performance: Strategies for improving competence.* Baltimore: University Park Press.

Robertson, A. (1982). Day care and children's response to adults. In E. Zigler & E. W. Gordon (Eds.), *Day care: Scientific and social policy issues* (pp. 152–173). Boston: Auburn House.

Robins, P. (1988). Child care and convenience: The effects of labor market entry cost on economic self-sufficiency among public housing residents. *Social Science Quarterly, 69,* 122–136.

Rubenstein, J., Howes, C., & Boyle, P. (1981). A two year follow-up of infants in community based day care. *Journal of Child Psychology and Psychiatry, 22,* 209–218.

Ruopp, R., Travers, J., Glantz, F., & Coelen, C. (1979). *Children at the center: Final results of the National Day Care Study.* Boston: Abt. Associates.

Rutter, M. (1979). Maternal deprivation, 1972-1978: New findings, new concepts, new approaches. *Child Development, 50,* 283–291.

Scarr, S. (1985). Constructing psychology: Making facts and fables for our times. *American Psychologist, 40,* 499–512.

Scarr, S., & Arnett, J. (1987). Malleability: Lessons from intervention and family studies. In J. J. Gallagher (Ed.), *The malleability of children* (pp. 71–84). New York: Brooke.

Scarr, S., Lande, J., & McCartney, K. (1989). Child care and the family: Cooperation and interaction. In J. Lande, S. Scarr, & N. Gunzenhauser (Eds.), *Caring for children: The future of child care in the United States* (pp. 1–21). Hillsdale, NJ: Erlbaum.

Scarr, S., & McCartney, K. (in preparation). Follow-up studies of early child care experiences at school age.

Scarr, S., & McCartney, K. (1988). Far from home: An experimental evaluation of the mother-child home program in Bermuda. *Child Development, 59,* 531–543.

Scarr, S., Phillips, D., & McCartney, K. (1989a). Dilemmas of child care in the United States: Employed mothers and children at risk. *Canadian Psychology, 30(2),* 126–139.

Scarr, S., Phillips, D., & McCartney, K. (1989b). Working mothers and their families. *American Psychologist,* June.

Scarr, S., & Weinberg, R. A. (1983). The Minnesota adoption studies: Genetic differences and malleability. *Child Development, 54,* 260–267.

Schaffer, H. R. (1977). *Attachments.* Cambridge, MA: Harvard University Press.

Schweinhart, L., & Weikart, D. (1980). The effects of the Perry Preschool Program on youths through age 15. *Monographs of the High/Scope Educational Research Foundation No. 7.*

Seitz, V., Apfel, N., Rosenbaum, L., & Zigler, E. (1983). Long term effects of Projects Head Start and Follow Through: The New Haven Project. In Consortium for Longitudinal Studies, *As the twig is bent. Lasting effects of preschool programs* (pp. 299–332). Hillsdale, NJ: Erlbaum.

Sigman, M., Cohen, S. E., Beckwith, L., & Parmelee, A. H. (1986). Infant attention in relation to intellectual abilities in childhood. *Developmental Psychology, 22,* 788–792.

Smith, P. K. (1980). Shared care of young children: Alternative models to monotropism. *Merrill-Palmer Quarterly, 26,* 371–389.

Spitz, R. (1945). Hospitalism: An inquiry into the genesis of psychiatric conditions in early childhood. *Psychoanalytic Study of the Child, 1,* 53–74.

Stallings, J., & Porter, A. (1980, June). *National Day Care Home Study: Observation component* (Final Report of the National Day Care Home Study, Vol. III). Washington, DC: Dept of Health, Education and Welfare.

Stith, S., & Davis, A. (1984). Employed mothers and family day care substitute caregivers. *Child Development, 55,* 1340–1348.

Tephly, J., & Elardo, R. (1984). Mothers and day care teachers: Young children's perceptions. *British Journal of Developmental Psychology, 2,* 251–256.

Valentine, J., & Stark, E. (1979). The social context of parent involvement in Head Start. In E. Zigler, & J. Valentine (Eds.), *Project Head Start: A legacy of the War on Poverty.* (pp. 291–314). New York: Free Press.

Vandell, D. L., & Corsaniti, M. A. (in press). Child care in the family: Complex contributions to child development. In K. McCartney (Ed.), *New directions in child development research, Vol. 20: The social ecology of child care.* New York: Jossey-Bass.

Vandell, D. L., Henderson, V. K., & Wilson, K. S. (in press). A longitudinal study of children with varying quality day care experiences. *Child Development.*

Vandell, D. L., & Powers, C. P. (1983). Day care quality and children's free play activities. *American Journal of Orthopsychiatry, 53,* 493–500.

Wachs, T. D., & Gruen, G. E. (1982). *Early experience and human development.* New York: Plenum Press.

Waters, E., & Deane, K. E. (1985). Defining and assessing individual differences in attachment relationships: Q-methodology and the organization of behaviors in infancy and childhood. In I. Bertherton & E. Waters (Eds.), Growing points in attachment theory and research. *Monographs of the Society for Research in Child Development, 50,* 41–65.

Weinraub, M., Jaeger, E., & Hoffman, L. (in press). Predicting infant outcome in families of employed and non-employed mothers. *Early Childhood Research Quarterly.*

Whitebook, M., Howes, C., Darrah, R., & Friedman, J. (1982). Caring for the caregivers: Staff burnout in child care. In L. Katz (Ed.), *Current topics in early childhood education* (Vol. 4, pp. 211–235). Norwood, NJ: Ablex.

Yarrow, L. (1961). Maternal deprivation: Toward an empirical and conceptual evaluation. *Psychological Bulletin, 58,* 459–490.

Ziegler, M. E. (1983). *Assessing parents' and children's time together.* Paper presented at the annual meeting of the Society for Research in Child Development, Detroit, Michigan.

PART III

Early Childhood

15

From Communicating to Talking

JEROME S. BRUNER

Language is a uniquely human capability that develops rapidly in the early years of life. In the following selection, Bruner discusses children's transformation from nontalking communicative companions to talkers in their own right. Bruner argues that culture provides the medium through which this critical transition occurs. Using this framework, he offers a provocative examination of infant capabilities, human action, and social experience, with language and culture as the connecting pieces that give these processes both form and direction.

If we are to consider the transition from prelinguistic communication to language, particularly with a concern for possible continuities, we had better begin by taking as close a look as we can at the so-called "original endowment" of human beings. Might that endowment affect the acquisition and early use of language? I do not mean simply the prelinguistic precursors of grammar or an "innate capacity" for language. The question must be a more general one. What predisposes a living being to use language and be changed by its use? Suppose we grant that there is some innate capacity to master language as a symbolic system, as Noam Chomsky urged, or even to be predisposed toward particular linguistic distinctions, as Derek Bickerton has recently proposed? Why is language used? After all, chimpanzees have some of the same capacities and they don't use them.

The awkward dilemma that plagues questions about the original nature and later growth of human faculties inheres in the unique nature of human competence. For human competence is both biological in origin and cultural in the means by which it finds expression. While the *capacity* for intelligent action has deep biological roots and a discernible evolutionary history, the *exercise* of that capacity depends upon man appropriating to himself modes of acting and thinking that exist not in his genes but in his culture. There is obviously something in "mind" or in "human nature" that mediates between the genes and the culture that makes it possible for the latter to be a prosthetic device for the realization of the former.

When we ask then about the endowment of human beings, the question we put must be twofold. We must ask not only about capacities, but also about how humans are aided in expressing them in the medium of culture. The two questions, of course, are inseparable, since human intellectual capacity necessarily evolved to fit man for using the very prosthetic devices that a culture develops and accumulates for the enablement of its members.

There is some point in studying early human capacities and their development in seemingly culture-less laboratories, as if they were simply expressions of man's biological dispositions and endowment. But we must also bear in mind that the idealization of this endowment depends on the tool kit of the culture, whatever we choose to do in the laboratory. The main trend of the last quarter century has been to look increasingly at the contexts that enable human beings to act as they do; increasingly, we can see the futility of considering human nature as a set of autonomous dispositions.

I can easily outline what seems to me, at least, to be "infant endowment" in the so-called cognitive sphere. But to do so relevantly I must focus on those aspects that fit and perhaps even compel human beings to operate in the culture. For I think that it is the requirement of *using* culture as a necessary form of coping that forces man to master language. Language is the means for interpreting and regulating the culture. The interpreting and negotiating start the moment the infant enters the human scene. It is at this stage of interpretation and negotiation that language acquisition is acted out. So I shall look at "endowment" from the point of view of how it equips the infant to come on stage in order to acquire the means for taking his place in culture.

INITIAL COGNITIVE ENDOWMENT

Let me begin with some more or less "firm" conclusions about perception, skill, and problem solving in the prelinguistic infant and consider how they might conceivably predispose the child to acquire "culture" through language.

The first of these conclusions is that much of the cognitive processing going on in infancy appears to operate in support of goal-directed activity. From the start, the human infant is *active* in seeking out regularities in the world about him. The child is active in a uniquely human way, converting experience into species-typical means-end structures. Let me begin with the unlikely example of nonnutritive sucking.

The human infant, like mammals generally, is equipped with a variety of biological processes that ensure initial feeding, initial attachment to a caretaker, initial sensory contact with the world—all quite well buffered to prevent the infant from overreacting. Nonnutritive sucking, an example of one of these buffering mechanisms, has the effect of relaxing large muscle groups, stilling movements of the gut, reducing the number of eye movements in response to excessively patterned visual fields, and in general assuring the maintenance of a moderate level of arousal in the face of even a demanding environment. That much is probably "hard-wired."

But such sucking soon comes under the child's own control. Infants as young as five to six weeks are quite capable, we found, of sucking on a pacifier nipple in order to bring a visual display from blur into focus—increasing their rate of sucking well above baseline when the picture's focus is made contingent on speed of sucking. Sucking and looking, moreover, are coordinated to assure a good view. When babies suck to produce clarity, they suck as they look, and when they stop they soon learn to look away. The same infants, when their sucking in a later session produces blur, suck while looking away from the blurred picture their sucking is producing and desist from sucking while looking at the picture. (We should note, by the way, that infants do not like blurred pictures.)

The Czech pediatrician Hanus Papousek has reported the same capacity for coordination of action in another domain, head turning. He taught six-to-ten-week-old babies to turn their heads to the right (or the left) in order to activate an attractive set of flashing lights. The infants soon learned the required response and, indeed, could even be taught to turn twice to each side for the desired lights. With mastery, their reactions became quite economical: They turned just enough to bring on the lights. But more interesting still, as the experiment progressed and the light display became familiar, they looked at it only briefly, just enough of a glance to confirm that the lights had gone on as expected (following which there was often a smile) and would then begin visually exploring other features of the situation. Successful prediction seems finally to have been the rewarding feature of the situation. With habituation, performance deteriorated—prediction was no longer interesting.

The point is not that infants are cleverer than was suspected before. Rather, it is that their behavior from early on is guided by active means-end readiness and by search. To put it another way, more in keeping with our general point, the infant from the start is tuned to the coordinative requirements of action. He seems able to appreciate, so to speak, the structure of action and particularly the manner in which means and ends must be combined in achieving satisfactory outcomes—even such arbitrary means as sucking to produce changes in the visual world. He seems, moreover, to be sensitive to the requirements of prediction and, if Papousek's interpretation of the "smile of predictive pleasure" is to be taken seriously, to get active pleasure from successful prediction. Anyone who has bothered to ponder the pleasure infants derive from achieving repetitive, surefire prediction will appreciate this point.

To say that infants are also "social" is to be banal. They are geared to respond to the human voice, to the human face, to human action and gesture. Their means-end readiness is easily and quickly brought into coordination with the actions of their caretakers. The pioneering work of Daniel Stern and Berry Brazelton and their colleagues underlines how early and readily activated infants are by the adults with whom they interact and how quickly their means-end structuring encompasses the actions of another. The infant's principal "tool" for achieving his ends is another familiar human being. In this respect, human infants seem more socially interactive than any of the Great Apes, perhaps to the same degree that Great Apes are more socially interactive than Old or New World Monkeys, and this may be a function of their prolonged and uniquely dependent form of immaturity, as I have argued elsewhere.

Infants are, in a word, tuned to enter the world of human action. Obvious though the point may seem, we shall see that it has enormous consequences for the matter at hand. This leads directly to the second conclusion about infant "endowment."

It is obvious that an enormous amount of the activity of the child during the first year and a half of life is extraordinarily social and communicative. Social interaction appears to be both self-propelled and self-rewarding. Many students of infant behavior, like Tom Bower, have found that a social response to the infant is the most powerful reinforcer one can use in ordinary learning experiments. And withholding social response to the child's initiatives is one of the most disruptive things one can do to an infant—e.g., an unresponding face will soon produce tears. Even in the opening weeks of life the infant has the capacity to imitate facial and manual gestures (as Andrew Meltzoff has shown); they respond with distress if their mothers are masked during feeding; and, they show a sensitivity to expression in the mother by turn taking in vocalization when their level of arousal is moderate and by simultaneous expression when it is high.

While the child's attachment to the mother (or caretaker) is initially assured by a variety of innate response patterns, there very quickly develops a reciprocity that the infant comes to anticipate and count on. For example, if during play the mother assumes a sober immobile face, the infant shows fewer smiles and turns his head away from the mother more frequently than when the mother responds socially, as Edward Tronick and his colleagues have shown. The existence of such reciprocity—buttressed by the mother's increasing capacity to differentiate an infant's "reasons" for crying as well as by the infant's capacity to anticipate these consistencies—soon creates a form of mutual attention, a harmony or "intersubjectivity," whose importance we shall take up later.

In any case, a pattern of inborn initial social responses in the infant, elicited by a wide variety of effective signs from the mother—her heartbeat, the visual configuration of her face and particularly her eyes, her characteristic smell, the sound and rhythms of her voice—is soon converted into a very complex joint anticipatory system that converts initial biological attachment between mother and child into something more subtle and more sensitive to individual idiosyncracies and to forms of cultural practice.

The third conclusion is that much of early infant action takes place in constrained, familiar situations and shows a surprisingly high degree of order and "systematicity." Children spend most of their time doing a very limited number of things. Long periods are spent in reaching and taking, banging and looking, etc. Within any one of these restricted domains, there is striking "systematicity." Object play provides an example. A single act (like banging) is applied successively to a wide range of objects. Everything on which the child can get his hands is banged. Or the child tries out on a single object all the motor routines of which he or she is capable—grasping the object, banging it, throwing it to the floor, putting it in the mouth, putting it on top of the head, running it through the entire repertory.

Nobody has done better than Jean Piaget in characterizing this systematicity. The older view that pictured the infant as "random" in his actions and saw growth as consisting of becoming "coordinated" can no longer stand up to the evidence. Given the limits of the child's range of action, what occurs within that range is just as orderly and systematic as is adult behavior. There may be differences of

opinion concerning the "rules" that govern this orderly behavior, but there can be no quarrel about its
systematicity. Whether one adopts a Piagetian view
of the matter or one more tuned to other theories,
like Heinz Werner's, is, in light of the more general
issues, quite irrelevant.

It is not the least surprising, in light of this conclusion, that infants enter the world of language and
of culture with a readiness to find or invent syst3m-
atic ways of dealing with social requirements and
linguistic forms. The child reacts "culturally" with
characteristic hypotheses about what is required and
enters language with a readiness for order. We shall,
of course, have much more to say about this later.

There are two important implications that follow from this. The first is obvious, though I do not
recall ever having encountered the point. It is that
from the start, the child becomes readily attuned to
"making a lot out of a little" by combination. He
typically works on varying a small set of elements to
create a larger range of possibilities. Observations of
early play behavior and of the infant's communicative efforts certainly confirm this "push" to generativeness, to combinatorial and variational efforts.
Indeed, Ruth Weir's classic study of the child's spontaneous speech while alone in his crib after bedtime
speaks volumes on this combinatorial readiness, as
does Melissa Bowerman's on children's spontaneous
speech errors.

The second implication is more social. The acquisition of prelinguistic and linguistic communication takes place, in the main, in the highly constrained settings to which we are referring. The child
and his caretaker readily combine elements in these
situations to extract meanings, assign interpretations, and infer intentions. A decade ago there was
considerable debate among developmental linguists
on whether in writing "grammars" of child speech
one should use a method of "rich interpretation"—
taking into account not only the child's actual speech
but also the ongoing actions and other elements of
the context in which speech was occurring. Today
we take it for granted that one must do so. For it is
precisely the combining of all elements in constrained situations (speech and nonspeech alike) that
provides the road to communicative effectiveness. It
is for this reason that I shall place such heavy emphasis on the role of "formats" in the child's entry
into language.

*A fourth conclusion about the nature of infant
cognitive endowment is that its systematic character
is surprisingly abstract.* Infants during their first year
appear to have rules for dealing with space, time,

and even causation. A moving object that is transformed in appearance while it is moving behind a
screen produces surprise when it reappears in a new
guise. Objects that seem to be propelled in ways that
we see as unnatural (e.g., without being touched by
an approaching object) also produce surprise reactions in a three-month-old as well. Objects explored
by touch alone are later recognized by vision alone.
The infant's perceptual world, far from being a
blooming, buzzing confusion, is rather orderly and
organized by what seem like highly abstract rules.

Again, it was Piaget who most compellingly
brought this "abstractness" to our attention in describing the logical structure of the child's search for
invariance in his world—the search for what remains
unchanged under the changing surface of appearance. And again, it is not important whether the
"logic" that he attributed to this systematic action is
correct or not. What is plain is that, whether
Piagetian logical rules characterize early "operational behavior" or whether it can be better described by some more general logical system, we
know that cognitively and communicatively there is
from the start a capacity to "follow" abstract rules.

It is *not* the case that language, when it is encountered and then used, is the first instance of abstract rule following. It is not, for example, in language alone that the child makes such distinctions as
those between specific and nonspecific, between
states and processes, between "punctual" acts and
recurrent ones, between causative and noncausative
actions. These abstract distinctions, picked up with
amazing speed in language acquisition, have analogues in the child's way of ordering his world of experience. Language will serve to specify, amplify, and
expand distinctions that the child has already about
the world. But these abstract distinctions are already
present, even without language.

These four cognitive "endowments"—means-end
readiness, transactionality, systematicity, and abstractness—provide foundation processes that aid the
child's language acquisition. None of them "generates" language, for language involves a set of phono-
logical, syntactic, semantic, and illocutionary rules
and maxims that constitute a problem space of their
own. But linguistic or communicative hypotheses depend upon these capacities as enabling conditions.
Language does not "grow out of" prior protophono-
logical, protosyntactic, protosemantic, or protoprag-
matic knowledge. It requires a unique sensitivity to a
patterned sound system, to grammatical constraints,
to referential requirements, to communicative intentions, etc. Such sensitivity grows in the process of ful-

filling certain general, nonlinguistic functions—predicting the environment, interacting transactionally, getting to goals with the aid of another, and the like. These functions are first fulfilled primitively if abstractly by prelinguistic communicative means. Such primitive procedures, I will argue, must reach requisite levels of functioning before *any* Language Acquisition Device (whether innate or acquired) can begin to generate "linguistic hypotheses."

ENTRY INTO LANGUAGE

We can turn now to the development of language per se. Learning a native language is an accomplishment within the grasp of any toddler, yet discovering how children do it has eluded generations of philosophers and linguists. Saint Augustine believed it was simple. Allegedly recollecting his own childhood, he said, "When they named any thing, and as they spoke turned towards it, I saw and remembered that they called what one would point out by the name they uttered. . . . And thus by constantly hearing words, as they occurred in various sentences, I collected gradually for what they stood; and having broken in my mouth to these signs, I thereby gave utterance to my will." But a look at children as they actually acquire language shows Saint Augustine to be far, far off target. Alas, he had a powerful effect both on his followers and on those who set out to refute him.

Developmental linguistics is now going through rough times that can be traced back to Saint Augustine as well as to the reactions against him. Let me recount a little history. Saint Augustine's view, perhaps because there was so little systematic research on language acquisition to refute it, prevailed for a long time. It was even put into modern dress. Its most recent "new look" was in the form of behaviorist "learning theory." In this view's terms, nothing particularly linguistic needed to be said about language. Language, like any other behavior, could be "explained" as just another set of responses. Its principles and its research paradigms were not derived from the phenomena of language but from "general behavior." Learning tasks, for example, were chosen to construct theories of learning so as to ensure that the learner had no predispositions toward or knowledge of the material to be learned. All was as if *ab initio,* transfer of response from one stimulus to another was assured by the similarity between stimuli. Language learning was assumed to be much like, say, nonsense syllable learning, except that it might be aided by imitation, the learner imi-

tating the performance of the "model" and then being reinforced for correct performance. Its emphasis was on "words" rather than on grammar. Consequently, it missed out almost entirely in dealing with the combinatorial and generative effect of having a syntax that made possible the routine construction of sentences never before heard and that did not exist in adult speech to be imitated. A good example is the Pivot-Open class, P(0), construction of infant speech in which a common word or phrase is combined productively with other words as in *all-gone mummy, all-gone apple,* and even *all-gone bye-bye* (when mother and aunt finally end a prolonged farewell).

It is one of the mysteries of Kuhnian scientific paradigms that this empiricist approach to language acquisition persisted in psychology (if not in philosophy, where it was overturned by Frege and Wittgenstein) from its first enunciation by Saint Augustine to its most recent one in B. F. Skinner's *Verbal Behavior.* It would be fair to say that the persistence of the mindless behavioristic version of Augustinianism finally led to a readiness, even a reckless readiness, to be rid of it. For it was not only an inadequate account, but one that damped inquiry by its domination of "common sense." It set the stage for the Chomskyan revolution.

It was to Noam Chomsky's credit that he boldly proclaimed the old enterprise bankrupt. In its place he offered a challenging, if counterintuitive hypothesis based on nativism. He proposed that the acquisition of the *structure* of language depended upon a Language Acquisition Device (LAD) that had as its base a universal grammar or a "linguistic deep structure" that humans know innately and without learning. LAD was programmed to recognize in the surface structure of any natural language encountered its deep structure or universal grammar by virtue of the kinship between innate universal grammar and the grammar of any and all natural languages. LAD abstracted the grammatical realization rules of the local language and thus enabled the aspirant speaker potentially to generate all the well-formed utterances possible in the language and none that were ill-formed. The universal grammatical categories that programmed LAD were in the innate structure of the mind. No prior nonlinguistic knowledge of the world was necessary, and no privileged communication with another speaker was required. Syntax was independent of knowledge of the world, of semantic meaning, and of communicative function. All the child needed was exposure to language, however fragmentary and uncontextualized his samples of it might be. Or more correctly, the acquisition of syntax could be conceived of as progressing with the assistance of whatever *minimum* world knowledge or privileged communication proved necessary. The only constraints on rate of linguistic development were psychological limitations on *performance*: the child's limited but growing attention and memory span, etc. Linguistic competence was there from the start, ready to express itself when performance constraints were extended by the growth of requisite skills.

It was an extreme view. But in a stroke it freed a generation of psycholinguists from the dogma of association-cum-imitation-cum-reinforcement. It turned attention to the problem of rule learning, even if it concentrated only on syntactic rules. By declaring learning theory dead as an explanation of language acquisition (one of the more premature obituaries of our times), it opened the way for a new account.

George Miller put it well. We now had *two* theories of language acquisition: one of them, empiricist associationism, was impossible; the other, nativism, was miraculous. But the void between the impossible and the miraculous was soon to be filled in, albeit untidily and partially.

To begin with, children in fact had and *needed* to have a working knowledge of the world before they acquired language. Such knowledge gave them semantic targets, so to speak, that "corresponded" in some fashion to the distinctions they acquired in their language. A knowledge of the world, appropriately organized in terms of a system of concepts, might give the child hints as to where distinctions could be expected to occur in the language, might even alert him to the distinctions. There were new efforts to develop a generative semantics out of which syntactical hypotheses could presumably be derived by the child. In an extreme form, generative semantics could argue that the concepts in terms of which the world was organized are the same as those that organize language. But even so, the *linguistic* distinctions still had to be mastered. These were not about the *world* but about morphology or syntax or whatever else characterized the linguistic *code*.

The issue of whether rules of *grammar* can somehow be inferred or generalized from the structure of our knowledge of the world is a very dark one. The strong form of the claim insists that syntax can be derived directly from nonlinguistic categories of knowledge in some way. Perhaps the best claim can be made for a case grammar. It is based on the reasonable claim that the concepts of action are innate and primitive. The aspiring language learner already knows the so called arguments of action: who performed the action, on what object, toward whom, where, by what instrument, and so on. In Charles Fillmore's phrase, "meanings are relativized to scenes," and this involves an "assignment of perspective." Particular phrases impose a perspective on the scene and sentence decisions are perspective decisions. If, for example, the agent of action is perspectively forefronted by some grammatical means such as being inserted as head word, the placement of the nominal that represents agency must be the "deep subject" of the sentence. This leaves many questions unanswered about how the child gets to the point of being able to put together sentences that assign his intended action perspectives to scenes.

The evidence for the semantic account was nonetheless interesting. Roger Brown pointed out, for example, that at the two-word stage of language acquisition more than three-quarters of the child's utterances embody only a half dozen semantic relations that are, at base, case or caselike relations—Agent-Action, Action-Object, Agent-Object, Possession, etc. Do these semantic relations generate the grammar of the language? Case notions of this kind, Fillmore tells us, "comprise a set of universal, presumably innate, concepts which identify certain types of judgments human beings are capable of making about the events that are going on around them . . . who did it, who it happened to, and what got changed." The basic structures are alleged to be these arguments of action, and different languages go about realizing them in different ways: by function words, by inflectional morphemes as in the case endings of Latin, by syntactic devices like passivization, and so on. Grammatical forms might then be the surface structures of language, depending for their acquisition on a prior understanding of deep semantic, indeed even protosemantic, concepts about action.

Patrica Greenfield then attempted to show that the earliest *one-word* utterances, richly interpreted in context, could also be explained as realizations of caselike concepts. And more recently Katherine Nelson has enriched the argument that children acquire language already equipped with concepts related to action: "The functional core model (FCM) essentially proposed that the child came to language with a store of familiar concepts of people and objects that were organized around the child's experience with these things. Because the child's experience was active, the dynamic aspects would be the most potent part of what the child came to know about the things experienced. It could be expected that the child would organize knowledge around what he could do with things and what they could do. In other words, knowledge of the world would be functionally organized from the child's point of view." To this earlier view she has now added a temporal dimension—the child's mastery of "scripts for event structures," a sequential structure of "causally and temporally linked acts with the actors and objects specified in the most general way." These scripts provide the child with a set of syntagmatic formats that permit him to organize his concepts sequentially into sentencelike forms such as those reported by Roger Brown. The capacity to do this rests upon a basic form of representation that the child uses from the start and gradually elaborates. In effect, it is what guides the formation of utterances beyond the one-word stage.

The role of world knowledge in generating or supporting language acquisition is now undergoing intensive study. But still another element has now been added—the pragmatic. It is the newest incursion into the gap between "impossible" and "miraculous" theories of language acquisition. In this view, the central idea is communicative intent: we communicate with some end in mind, some function to be fulfilled. We request or indicate or promise or threaten. Such functionalism had earlier been a strong thread in linguistics, but had been elbowed aside by a prevailing structuralism that, after Ferdinand de Saussure's monumental work, became the dominant mode.

New developments revived functionalism. The first was in the philosophy of language spearheaded by Ludwig Wittgenstein's use-based theory of meaning, formulated in his *Philosophical Investigations,* and then by the introduction of speech acts in Austin's *How to Do Things with Words.* Austin's argument (as already noted) was that an utterance cannot be analyzed out of the context of its use and its use must include the intention of the speaker and interpretation of that intention by the addressee in the light of communication conventions. A speaker may make a request by many alternative linguistic means, so long as he honors the conventions of his linguistic community. It may take on interrogative construction ("What time is it?"), or it may take the declarative form ("I wonder what time it is").

Roger Brown notes an interesting case with respect to this issue: in the protocols of Adam, he found that Adam's mother used the interrogative in two quite different ways, one as a request for action, the other as a request for information: "Why don't you . . . (e.g., play with your ball now)," and "Why are you playing with your ball?" Although Adam answered informational *why* questions with *Because,*

there was no instance of his ever confusing an action and an information-seeking *why* question. He evidently recognized the differing intent of the two forms of utterance quite adequately from the start. He must have been learning speech acts rather than simply the *why* interrogative form.

This raises several questions about acquisition. It puts pragmatics into the middle of things. Is intent being decoded by the child? It would seem so. But linguistics usually defines its domain as "going from sound to sense." But what is "sense?" Do we in fact go from sound to intention, as John Searle proposed? A second question has to do with shared or conventional presuppositions. If children are acquiring notions about how to interpret the intentions encoded in utterances, they must be taking into account not only the structure of the utterance, but also the nature of the conditions that prevail just at the time the utterance is made. Speech acts have at least three kinds of conditions affecting their appropriateness or "felicity": a preparatory condition (laying appropriate ground for the utterance); an essential condition (meeting the logical conditions for performing a speech act, like, for example, being uninformed as a condition for asking for information related to a matter); and sincerity conditions (wishing to have the information that one asks for). They must also meet affiliative conditions: honoring the affiliation or relation between speaker and hearer, as in requesting rather than demanding when the interlocutor is not under obligation.

Paradoxically, the learning of speech acts may be easier and less mysterious than the learning either of syntax or semantics. For the child's syntactic errors are rarely followed by corrective feedback, and semantic feedback is often lax. But speech acts, on the contrary, get not only immediate feedback but also correction. Not surprising, then, that prelinguistic communicative acts precede lexico-grammatical speech in their appearance. Not surprising, then, that such primitive "speech act" patterns may serve as a kind of matrix in which lexico-grammatical achievements can be substituted for earlier gestural or vocal procedures.

In this view, entry into language is an entry into discourse that requires both members of a dialogue pair to interpret a communication and its intent. Learning a language, then, consists of learning not only the grammar of a particular language but also learning how to realize one's intentions by the appropriate use of that grammar.

The pragmatician's stress on intent requires a far more active role on the part of the adult in aiding the child's language acquisition than that of just being a "model." It requires that the adult be a consenting partner, willing to negotiate with the child. The negotiation has to do, probably, least with syntax, somewhat more with the semantic scope of the child's lexicon, and a very great deal with helping make intentions clear and making their expression fit the conditions and requirements of the "speech community," i.e., the culture.

And the research of the last several years—much of it summarized in Catherine Snow and Charles Ferguson's *Talking to Children*—does indeed indicate that parents play a far more active role in language acquisition than simply modeling the language and providing, so to speak, input for a Language Acquisition Device. The current phrase for it is "fine tuning." Parents speak at the level where their children can comprehend them and move ahead with remarkable sensitivity to their child's progress. The dilemma, as Roger Brown puts it, is how do you teach children to talk by talking baby talk with them at a level that they already understand? And the answer has got to be that the important thing is to keep communicating with them, for by so doing one allows them to learn how to extend the speech that they have into new contexts, how to meet the conditions on speech acts, how to maintain topics across turns, how to know what's worth talking about—how indeed to regulate language use.

So we can now recognize two ways of filling the gap between an impossible empiricist position and a miraculous nativist one. The child must master the conceptual structure of the world that language will map—the social world as well as the physical. He must also master the conventions for making his intentions clear by language.

SUPPORT FOR LANGUAGE ACQUISITION

The development of language, then, involves two people negotiating. Language is not encountered willy-nilly by the child; it is shaped to make communicative interaction effective—fine-tuned. If there is a Language Acquisition Device, the input to it is not a shower of spoken language but a highly interactive affair shaped, as we have already noted, by some sort of an adult Language Acquisition Support System.

After all, it is well known from a generation of research on another "innate" system, sexual behavior, that much experiential priming is necessary before innate sexual responses can be evoked by "appropriate" environmental events. Isolated animals are seriously retarded. By the same token, the recog-

nition and the production of grammatical universals may similarly depend upon prior social and conceptual experience. Continuities between prelinguistic communication and later speech of the kind I alluded to earlier may, moreover, need an "arranged" input of adult speech if the child is to use his growing grasp of conceptual distinctions and communicative functions as guides to language use. I propose that this "arranging" of early speech interaction requires routinized and familiar settings, formats, for the child to comprehend what is going on, given his limited capacity for processing information. These routines constitute what I intend by a Language Acquisition Support System.

There are at least four ways in which such a Language Acquisition Support System helps assure continuity from prelinguistic to linguistic communication. Because there is such concentration on familiar and routine transactional formats, it becomes feasible for the adult partner to highlight those features of the world that are already salient to the child and that have a basic or simple grammatical form. Slobin has suggested, for example, that there are certain prototypical ways in which the child experiences the world: e.g., a "prototypical transitive event" in which "an animate agent is seen willfully . . . to bring about a physical and perceptible change of state or location in a patient by means of direct body contact." Events of this kind, we shall see, are a very frequent feature of mother-child formats, and it is of no small interest that in a variety of languages, as Slobin notes, they "are encoded in consistent grammatical form by age two." Slobin offers the interesting hypothesis "that [these] prototypical situations are encoded in the most basic grammatical forms available in a language." We shall encounter formats built around games and tasks involving both these prototypical means-end structures and canonical linguistic forms that seem almost designed to aid the child in spotting the referential correspondence between such utterances and such events.

Or to take another example, Bickerton has proposed that children are "bioprogrammed" to notice certain distinctions in real world events and to pick up (or even to invent) corresponding linguistic distinctions in order to communicate about them. His candidates are the distinctions (a) between specific and nonspecific events, (b) between state and process, (c) between "punctual" and continuous events, and (d) between causative and noncausative actions. And insofar as the "fine tuning" of adult interaction with a child concentrates on these distinctions—both in reality and in speech—the child is aided in moving from their conceptual expression to an appreciation of their appropriate linguistic representation. Again, they will be found to be frequent in the formats of the children we shall look at in detail.

A second way in which the adult helps the child through formatting is by encouraging and modeling lexical and phrasal substitutes for familiar gestural and vocal means for effecting various communicative functions. This is a feature of the child's gradual mastery of the request mode.

H. P. Grice takes it as a hallmark of mature language that the speaker not only has an intention to communicate, but that he also has *conventionalized* or "nonnatural" means for expressing his intention. The speaker, in his view, presupposes that his interlocutor will accept his means of communication and will infer his intention from them. The interlocutor presupposes the same thing about the speaker. Grice, concerned with adults, assumes all this to be quite conscious, if implicit.

An infant cannot at the prelinguistic outset be said to be participating in a conscious Gricean cycle when signaling conventionally in his games with his mother. That much selfconsciousness seems unlikely. But what we will find in the following chapters is that the mother acts as if he did. The child in turn soon comes to operate with some junior version of the Gricean cycle, awaiting his mother's "uptake" of his signaling.

In Katherine Nelson's terms, the young child soon acquires a small library of scripts and communicative procedures to go with them. They provide steady frameworks in which he learns effectively, by dint of interpretable feedback, how to make his communicative intentions plain. When he becomes "conscious" enough to be said to be operating in a Gricean cycle is, I think, a silly question.

What is striking is how early the child develops means to signal his focus of attention and his requests for assistance—to signal them by conventionalized means in the limited world of familiar formats. He has obviously picked up the gist of "nonnatural" or conventionalized signaling of his intentions before ever he has mastered the formal elements of lexico-grammatical speech. I think the reader will agree, in reading later chapters, that the functional framing of communication starts the child on his way to language proper. Thirdly, it is characteristic of play formats particularly that they are made of stipulative or constitutive "events" that are created by language and then recreated on demand by language. Later these formats take on the character of "pretend" situations. They are a rich source of opportunity for language learning and language use.

Finally, once the mother and child are launched into routinized formats, various psychological and linguistic processes are brought into play that generalize from one format to another. Naming, for example, appears first in indicating formats and then transfers to requesting formats. Indeed, the very notion of finding linguistic parallels for conceptual distinctions generalizes from one format to another. So too do such "abstract" ideas as segmentation, interchangeable roles, substitutive means—both in action and in speech.

These are the mundane procedures and events that constitute a Language Acquisition Support System, along with the elements of fine tuning that comprise "baby talk" exchanges.

Questions

1. What role does language play in how children are socialized into a culture?

2. What early capabilities help set the stage for infants to be social and communicative beings?

3. What role do parents play in children's learning of language?

16

Looking for Big Bird: Studies of Memory in Very Young Children

JUDY S. DELOACHE AND ANN L. BROWN

For most of this century, psychological descriptions of the cognitive abilities of preschool children emphasized their limitations when compared with children a few years older. Preschoolers appeared to have a difficult time thinking logically, planning their course of action, and remembering.

One of the reasons for this rather negative assessment of preschool cognition was the tradition of investigating preschooler's mental abilities on the psychologist's home turf—in a school room or a laboratory setting. Yet, such settings may overwhelm young children and lead to inaccurate assessments of their abilities. In the following study, DeLoache and Brown investigated young children's memory in the familiar settings of their own homes. Furthermore, they made sure that the children were well motivated to remember by using toys to which the children had formed a close attachment. The picture that emerges from this rather simple change in procedure challenges earlier ideas about young children's ability to remember.

The period between one and three years of age is one of the most fascinating eras in human development: in no other comparable span of time do so many revolutionary changes occur. Cognitive processes undergo an extraordinary degree of reorganization as the child acquires language and makes the transition from sensorimotor to symbolic, representational thought. In spite of the importance of this early period, it has been relatively neglected by developmental psychologists until quite recently. One of the main reasons for this neglect has been the fact that young children are notoriously intractable research

Reprinted with permission from *The Quarterly Newsletter of the Laboratory of Comparative Human Cognition, 1,* 1979, 53–57. Copyright 1979 by The Laboratory of Comparative Human Cognition.

This research was supported in part by Grants HD 05951 and HD 06864 and Research Career Development Award HD 00111 from the National Institutes of Child Health and Human Development.

subjects; it is difficult to enlist their cooperation in the relatively artificial, unfamiliar tasks traditionally favored by psychologists, and even when they do seem to cooperate, their performance tends to be quite low (see, for example, Myers & Perlmutter, 1978). Although most parents recount numerous instances of their toddler remembering personally experienced events over days or even months, we are aware of no memory studies of young children where retention intervals of longer than 30 seconds have been used. It seems reasonable to infer from this discrepancy that the procedures commonly used to study early cognitive development are inadequate.

In this paper we will report an ongoing research project on young children's memory for object location that is aimed at studying the emergence and early refinement of various self-regulatory skills. We have made extensive efforts to avoid artificial experimental formats and to develop naturalistic, meaningful situations. The basic task that we have selected for our current research involves memory for object location (i.e., remembering where something is in space so one can retrieve it later). This is a variant of the delayed response task introduced by Hunter (1917) and used by him to study memory in a variety of species, ranging from rats to his 1-year-old daughter, Thayer. The essential feature of the delayed response problem is that the subject watches while an object is concealed in one of several potential containers. After a specified delay interval, during which the child's attention is typically distracted from the containers, he or she is allowed to find the hidden object.

This general format has been used in several recent studies with children between 1½ and 3 years of age (e.g., Daehler, Bukatko, Benson, & Myers, 1976; Horn & Myers, 1978; Loughlin & Daehler, 1973). In the standard task 2-year-olds, for example, have been found to retrieve the object with no errors on slightly less than 50% of the trials (Daehler et al., 1976; Horn & Myers, 1978). The addition of visual and verbal cues to the spatial cues already present has sometimes increased the level of correct responding, to 66% with labeled pictures (Horn & Myers, 1978) and as high as 69% with containers differing in size (Daehler et al., 1976); but in other studies visual cues have not been helpful (Babska, 1965; Loughlin & Daehler, 1973). Thus, 2-year-old children generally perform above chance (Myers & Ratner, in press) in the standard delayed response task. Getting them to be correct more than half the time, however, requires the addition of carefully engineered cues. Furthermore, we wish to emphasize that in none of the above experiments was the delay interval longer than 25 seconds.

In our research our preliminary goals included devising a task in which we could ask very young children to remember something for more than half a minute. Accordingly, we have attempted to transform the basic delayed response task into a relatively natural situation. It takes the form of a hide-and-seek game that the child plays with a small stuffed animal. Several days before the experiment, each subject is given a toy (Mickey Mouse, Big Bird). Then, following our instructions, the parents teach their child the hide-and-seek game. The children are told that Mickey Mouse is going to hide and that they have to remember where he is hiding so they will be able to find him later. On each trial the child watches while his or her mother (or father) hides the toy in some natural location in their home, with a different location used for each trial. The specific locations obviously depend on the particular home, but include places like behind or under chairs and couches, under pillows, behind curtains, inside desk drawers. A kitchen timer is set for a specified interval and the child is taught to wait for the bell to ring. When it does, the child is allowed to go retrieve the "hiding" toy. The children very readily learn the rules of the hide-and-seek game and show obvious delight and excitement in playing it.

While we hoped that the hide-and-seek task would elicit performance from young children that would more accurately reflect their memorial competence, it was also designed to enable us to study very early forms of self-regulatory skills. These skills are the various processes by which people organize their thoughts and actions (Brown, 1978; Brown & DeLoache, 1978), including activities such as: *planning* ahead, *predicting* the outcome of some action (what will happen if?), *monitoring* ongoing activity (how am I doing?), *checking* on the results of actions (did that work, did it achieve my goal?), *correcting* errors or inadequacies (since what I just did didn't work, what would be a reasonable thing to try now?). These skills are the basic characteristics of efficient thought throughout life, and one of their most important properties is that they are transsituational. They apply to a whole range of problem-solving activities, from artificial experimental settings to everyday life. It is equally important to exercise these skills whether you're reading a textbook or a recipe; whether you're trying to remember who the seventh President of the United States was or where you left your car keys.

What we are referring to here as self-regulatory skills have often been described as a form of metacognition, and they are subsumed under Flavell's (1978) definition of metacognition as "knowledge that takes as its object or regulates any aspect of any cognitive endeavor." However, it is worthwhile noting that this definition comprises two (not necessarily separate) clusters—*knowledge* about cognition and *regulation* of cognition. The first concerns the relatively stable information individuals have about cognitive processes, tasks, strategies, and so forth, in general, as well as the knowledge they have about themselves engaged in those activities and tasks. We would not expect very young children to be capable of this sort of metacognitive activity, i.e., conscious knowledge about cognition. Indeed, Wellman (1977) has demonstrated the very meager extent of such information possessed by 3-year-old children.

It is the second cluster of metacognitive activities included in Flavell's statement, the self-regulatory skills, that we are interested in here. These might be expected to be exhibited by very young children as they attempt to learn or solve problems. However, unlike the activities in the first cluster, whether or not the self-regulatory mechanisms appear depends critically on the nature of the task and the expertise of the child.

One of the prerequisites to observing very early examples of self-regulatory activities is the existence of an appropriate task, one that challenges young children (so that planning, monitoring, and so forth might be helpful), yet that falls within their general competence. Otherwise, even if they have, or are at the point of developing, any rudimentary self-regulatory skills, they may be too overwhelmed by the novelty and difficulty of the task to exercise those skills (Shatz, 1978).

Several features of our hide-and-seek task should increase the likelihood of finding self-regulatory behavior in very young children. The task requires retrieval to be manifested in overt action—finding an object in the environment—rather than the purely internal retrieval of information from memory. In this situation, external cues can be used, and the desired goal state (as well as success or failure in attaining it) is obvious, even to a young child. In addition, the task takes place in the home and with parents, and there is evidence that self-regulation occurs earlier in natural and familiar settings than in artificial, unfamiliar ones (Istomina, 1977). This naturalism of the hide-and-seek task helped us avoid some of the common problems associated with testing children between 1 and 3 years of age. A frequent problem is that one is often not really sure whether the child completely understands the task. The extensive pretraining provided by their parents ensures us that our subjects clearly understand the task before being observed. Also, the children typically enjoy the hide-and-seek game enormously, so

they are motivated to participate fully. This is critical, because getting young children to *want* to do whatever it is you want them to do is one of the most difficult aspects of working with them.

We have now completed three studies involving 41 subjects between 18 and 30 months of age.[1] The children participated in a total of four to eight trials of the basic hide-and-seek task for one or two observation days. Except for the first two trials in Study I, the delay intervals were either three or five minutes. (Notice that these are exceptionally long intervals for use with this age group. As stated before, the standard delayed response studies with toddlers have used intervals of less than 30 seconds.)

In all three studies the children's baseline performance was excellent. They went directly (with no errors of any kind) to the hidden toy from 71 to 84% of the trials. For purposes of comparison the subjects in each study were divided into older (25-30 months, mean age = approximately 27 months) and younger (18-24 months, mean age = approximately 20 months) groups. The older children generally did somewhat better (with between 83 and 96% errorless retrievals) than the younger ones (58 to 71% correct).[2]

Although the three- and five-minute intervals we used were much longer than any in the developmental literature, they did not appear to give our subjects much difficulty. In order to examine their performance at much longer intervals, we recruited most of the mothers of subjects in Study I to serve as surrogate experimenters. Each mother made five observations of her own child in the hide-and-seek game—two with 30-minute intervals, two at 60 minutes, and one overnight. They were cautioned to put the toy somewhere the child would not happen upon it by chance. Since the mothers had been given extensive instructions about how to conduct the game with their children, and since we had observed all of them playing with the children, we were fairly confident of their ability to make objective and accurate observations for us. However, as a partial check on their data, one of the regular experimenters was present for one of the 30- or 60-minute observations for each child.

The children did surprisingly well at these longer intervals. They found their toy (with no errors) 88% of the time after a 30-minute wait, and 69% after an hour. After the overnight interval, they scored 77% errorless retrievals. (Several children, after the overnight hiding, retrieved their toy before their parents got up in the morning. One long-suffering mother informed us that her child woke her at 5 A.M. wanting to go downstairs and get Big Bird.) On the occasions we formally observed, the children *always* found their toy, so it seems reasonable to assume that the mothers' reports were not exaggerated.

Most of the children were also given a more complex task on later observation days in Study I. The same basic procedure was followed, except that on each trial three toys were hidden, each one in a different place. After an interval of either three or five minutes, the child was instructed which of the three toys to retrieve (with each serial position during hiding tested equally often). The child was then encouraged to find the other two toys as well. This multiple hiding procedure might be expected to produce a great deal of interference, since each trial involved three different toys hidden in three different locations, and sometimes a location was used more than once over trials. However, performance was again surprisingly good. On 67% of the trials the subjects retrieved the specific toy requested. Overall, they found 70% of the hidden toys, with a mean of 2.1 toys found per trial. These figures were closely replicated in a similar task in Study II.

The data reported so far argue forcefully that if freed from the artificial constraints and demands of standard laboratory tasks, very young children may be willing to demonstrate more of their cognitive competence than they have heretofore done. Given that our young subjects did so well in the standard hide-and-seek task, it seemed reasonable to think that variations in it might elicit some simple forms of the self-regulatory skills in which we are interested. In fact, we believe that in Studies II and III we have evidence showing the appearance of one such skill, intelligent self-correction, during the age period between 18 and 30 months.

A major goal of these two experiments was to examine what can be considered a rudimentary form of metamemory: we wanted to assess how confident our subjects were of their own memory. Only a few studies have examined metamemory in children as young as three. Wellman (1977) investigated 3- to 5-year-olds' knowledge of the effect of various task variables on memory difficulty, and Wellman, Ritter, & Flavell (1975) observed the use of primitive precursors of deliberate memory strategies by 3-year-olds but not 2-year-olds. No form of metamemory has to date been noted for children under three.

An extremely simple form of metamemory would be the assessment of how well or how certainly one knows something. Since our subjects' performance was generally so high, one would expect that they would be quite confident that they remembered correctly, even if they were incapable of ver-

balizing that confidence. A standard way of assessing certainty in preverbal infants and young children is to present a surprise trial (Charlesworth, 1969; Gelman, 1972), where the experimenter does something to disconfirm the subject's expectations. The degree of surprise shown is used as an index of how strong the expectation was.

Each subject received two surprise trials on which the toy was hidden as usual, but was surreptitiously moved by the experimenter while the child was out of the room on some pretext. The surprise trials were embedded (as Trials 2 and 5) in a series of six or seven standard hide-and-seek trials (i.e., ones in which the toy was not moved). The surprise trials were administered on a separate day following the standard hide-and-seek testing described earlier.

In Study II two observers independently recorded and coded the subjects' behavior upon looking for and not finding the toy where it had been hidden. To be conservative, we have included only behaviors noted by both observers on the surprise trials. In Study III, the subjects were videotaped while participating in the game in their homes, so data from that study have been scored from the tapes. The figures that follow reflect the combined data from the two studies.

The experimenters' subjective impressions were that the children were very surprised indeed not to find their toy on the surprise trials. Several behaviors indicative of surprise were coded and analyzed (including verbalizations and negative emotional reactions), and they substantiate the experimenters' impressions. In this paper we will discuss in detail one of our surprise measures—the patterns of searching other locations after failing to find the toy in the correct place.

We should first mention that in general, the children almost never searched a location that had not been used previously, either on that day of testing or on a previous day. This was true for both age groups, and for both surprise trials and those trials on which subjects happened to make errors. Thus, the children had some general recollection of the set of hiding locations used.

The older and younger groups displayed different patterns of searching after failing to find their toy on surprise trials. The older children generally behaved in an intelligent fashion, much as an older child or an adult would do. After looking in the correct location and not finding the toy, they usually (on 88% of the surprise trials) searched somewhere else for it, and on the majority of the trials (76%) their searches fell into one or more of the following categories: (1) an adjacent location—if the toy had been hidden under one couch cushion, they might look under the next cushion; (2) a nearby or related location—if the toy had been put in a chair, they might look under or behind the chair; (3) an analogous location—if the toy had been hidden under a pillow at one end of the couch, they might look under the pillow at the other end of the couch; and (4) on the second surprise trial only, they sometimes looked in the place to which the experimenter had moved the toy on the first surprise trial.

The younger children were much less likely to conduct additional searches after failing to find their toy. On slightly over half the surprise trials (54%), they did not look in any other location after searching the correct one. They would often wander around in the middle of the room or stand near their mothers, apparently at a loss for what to do next. Some of the younger subjects returned to the correct location and searched there again, sometimes repeatedly. On only 26% of the surprise trials did the younger children search in the kind of related areas favored by the older subjects. They were just as likely, when they searched somewhere, to go to a place where the toy had been hidden on an earlier trial (especially the immediately preceding one). This tendency to search a prior location is reminiscent of the Stage IV error in object permanence (Harris, 1975) and the perseverative errors frequently observed for toddlers in memory and problem solving tasks (Webb, Massar, & Nadolny, 1972).

The older children's tendency to search additional locations on surprise trials reveals a form of certainty of memory in that they concentrated their searching in areas that were nearby or logically related to the correct location. They looked in places where the toy might reasonably be. They seemed to allow for the possibility that they misremembered some detail ("maybe it's under this cushion instead of that one") or that some fairly plausible event intervened ("maybe the toy fell out of the chair"). One subject verbalized exactly this: he looked in the desk drawer in which his toy had been hidden, said "Did Mickey Mouse fall out?", and then proceeded to search behind the desk. The children were also alert to the possibility that the experimenter was tricking them a second time.

To summarize, both the younger and older children seem certain of their memory for the correct location, but they differ in their ability to re-evaluate the situation after failing to find the toy and in their flexibility in initiating alternative measures. The younger children most often do nothing at all. When they do, they are as likely to simply go to a prior hiding place as to search in a related location. The older children are more flexible and logical in their attempt to deal with the disconfirmation of their expectations. They are able to reflect on the situation and consider where the toy *must* be, given it is not where they remembered. To account for its absence, they appear to consider plausible physical or mental explanations: something happened to the toy, or some detail of their memory must be faulty.

These examples of logical searching on the part of the older children (and a few of the younger ones) represent the exercise of a self-regulatory skill—thoughtful correction of errors. When the children fail to find the toy, they can only assume that they are in error (at least on the first surprise trial). They then try to correct that supposed error by thinking about where the toy is most likely to be. They proceed to conduct the same sort of organized, logical search that an adult might do. If you remembered that you had left your car keys on top of the kitchen counter but then couldn't find them, you would probably look for them behind the cookie jar on the counter and on the floor around the counter.

In conclusion, these very young children performed very competently in our basic hide-and-seek game, which they completely understood and thoroughly enjoyed playing. Even when the game was modified to be presumably more difficult, with multiple hidings and delay intervals extended to as long as an hour, they maintained an excellent level of performance. Furthermore, they showed what is probably the earliest evidence yet observed of self-regulation by the logical search procedures they employed on the surprise trials. The competent and sophisticated behavior of our young subjects suggests that if tasks are made more comprehensible and meaningful to young children, they will be more enthusiastic research participants and provide us with more valid data.

Questions

1. What evidence suggests that young children have poor memories?

2. Why do you think a familiar context, like home, helped children to remember? Do you think familiar settings facilitate memory in people of any age or is this effect limited to young children? Explain your reasoning.

3. Why did the experimenters use a procedure that involved surprise trials? What can such trials tell us about children's memory?

Footnotes

1. The number of subjects and their mean ages in the three studies were as follows: Study I—17 Subjects, mean age = 23 months (Older = 27 months, Younger = 20 months); Study II—12 Subjects, mean age = 24 months (Older = 27 months, Younger = 22 months); Study III—12 Subjects, mean age = 24 months (Older = 28 months, Younger = 21 months).

2. The complete data on errorless retrievals in the three studies were as follows: Study I—76% correct over-all (Older = 85%, Younger = 67%), Study II—84% correct overall (Older = 96%, Younger = 71%); Study III—71% correct overall (Older = 83%, Younger = 58%).

References and Notes

Babska, Z. The formation of the conception of identity of visual characteristics of objects seen successively. In P. H. Mussen (Ed.), European research in cognitive development. *Monographs of the Society for Research in Child Development,* 1965, 30(2, Serial No. 100), 112–124.

Brown, A. L. Knowing when, where, and how to remember: A problem of metacognition. In R. Glaser (Ed.), *Advances in instructional psychology.* Hillsdale, N.J.: Erlbaum, 1978.

Brown, A. L., & DeLoache, J. S. Skills, plans, and self-regulation. In R. Siegler (Ed.), *Children's thinking: What develops.* Hillsdale, N.J.: Erlbaum, 1978.

Charlesworth, W. R. Surprise and cognitive development. In D. Elkind & J. H. Flavell (Eds.), *Studies in cognitive development: Essays in honor of Jean Piaget.* New York: Oxford University Press, 1969.

Daehler, M., Bukatko, D., Benson, K., & Myers, N. The effects of size and color cues on the delayed response of very young children. *Bulletin of the Psychonomic Society,* 1976, 7, 65–68.

Flavell, J. H. Metacognitive development. In J. M. Scandura & C. J. Brainerd (Eds.), *Structural-process theories of complex human behavior.* Leyden, The Netherlands: Sijthoff, 1978.

Gelman, R. Logical capacity of very young children: Number invariance rules. *Child Development,* 1972, 43, 75–90.

Harris, P. L. Development of search and object permanence during infancy. *Psychological Bulletin,* 1975, 82, 332–344.

Horn, H. A. & Myers, N. A. Memory for location and picture cues at ages two and three. *Child Development,* 1978, 49, 845–856.

Hunter, W. S. The delayed reaction in a child. *Psychological Review,* 1917, 24, 74–87.

Istomina, Z. M. The development of voluntary memory in preschool-age children. In M. Cole (Ed.), *Soviet developmental psychology: An anthology.* White Plains, N.Y.: Sharpe, 1977.

Loughlin, K. A., & Daehler, M. A. The effects of distraction and added perceptual cues on the delayed reaction of very young children. *Child Development,* 1973, 44, 384–388.

Myers, N., & Ratner, H. H. Memory of very young children in delayed response tasks. In J. Sidowski (Ed.), *Cognition, conditioning, and methodology: Contemporary issues in experimental psychology.* Hillsdale, N.J.: Erlbaum, in press.

Myers, N.A., & Perlmutter, M. Memory in the years from two to five. In P.A. Ornstein (Ed.), *Memory development in children.* Hillsdale, N.J.: Erlbaum, 1978.

Shatz, M. The relationship between cognitive processes and the development of communication skills. In B. Keasey (Ed.), *Nebraska Symposium on Motivation.* Lincoln: University of Nebraska Press, 1978.

Webb, R. A., Massar, B., & Nadolny, T. Information and strategy in the young child's search for hidden objects. *Child Development*, 1972, *43*, 91–104.

Wellman, M. Preschoolers' understanding of memory-relevant variables. *Child Development*, 1977, *48*, 1720–1723.

Wellman, H. M., Ritter, R., & Flavell, J. H. Deliberate memory behavior in the delayed reactions of very young children. *Developmental Psychology*, 1975, *11*, 780–787.

17

Emotional Development in the Preschool Child

MICHAEL LEWIS

It has long been believed that infants are born with a small set of basic emotions, such as anger, surprise, disgust, and perhaps fear and sadness. Within a few years, the set of emotions increases to include disappointment, embarrassment and many others. The study of how the basic set of emotions develops in children is a relatively recent but fast-growing area of study among developmental psychologists. In the following article, Michael Lewis summarizes current themes in the study of socioemotional development, paying particular attention to the role of cognition in the development and organization of emotionality.

This article explores children's emotional development in the first three years of life. The discussion is divided into three parts: (1) the role of emotion in children's lives; (2) the development of emotions over the first three years of life; and (3) individual differences in emotion or emotionality.

ROLE OF EMOTIONS

Darwin viewed emotion as part of the biological apparatus of humans.[1] He saw emotions as a set of action patterns that enable children to behave in specific ways. For example, anger is not only a set of expressions but includes vocal growling and gross motor patterns, which enable the child to try to overcome a frustrating event. Darwin and those after him elaborated a system of scoring facial expression using the neuromusculature of the face.[2-4] This coding system allows developmental investigators to map out emotion.

Although clinicians recognize the importance of children's motor, sensory, and cognitive development, relatively little attention has been paid to children's emotional life. This is surprising because children's emotions play such a central role, both for the parent and the clinician. Consider, for example, a child who looks at an object, decreases his or her activity level, and smiles. On one hand we consider this an accurate marker for central nervous system integrity; that is, the child who is able to attend for long periods is not at risk for subsequent attentional disorders. The same behaviors that index attention also index the emotion of interest. Thus, from a clinical point of view, interest (an emotion) has important implications.

Many other examples of our use of emotions to mark children's ability can be found. Surprise is an emotion that has an important function in assessing development. A child who shows surprise when something unusual occurs has knowledge about the environment. In a series of studies, children as young as 6 months of age were placed in the company of different people.[5–6] We observed that when the infants were placed in the presence of children, the infants smiled and moved toward them. When the infants were placed in the presence of an adult, they showed some wariness (itself an emotion). When the children were placed in the presence of a midget (a small adult) they showed surprise.[6] This emotional response is used as a marker of cognitive ability, as surprise can be interpreted to mean that the infant understands that the midget is an unusual social stimuli. Thus, by 6 months of age the normal infant has already learned something about people.

Emotional behavior as a clinical tool is important. Testing for language acquisition begins with items related to hearing. When testing for hearing loss, children's emotional behavior is assessed. For example, one item in the test asks, "When the infant hears a human voice and sees a human face does it brighten?" This brightening response has to do with changes in emotional expression. The knowledge of children's emotional development aids in the assessment of children's abilities and provides a basis for understanding the normal and dysfunctional development of the young child.

From parents' point of view, the emotional behavior of the child is the first signal parents have to indicate that they are acting appropriately. It is important for the mother to know that the care of a crying child results in the child's smiling. She interprets this signal as an indication that she has solved her child's distress. Careful analysis reveals, therefore, that the emotional life of a child plays a significant role in the ability of adults to determine the child's internal state.

DEVELOPMENT OF EMOTIONS

Emotional differentiation moves from the general to the specific (Figure 1).[7] The first emotions that emerge are the most general; they are characterized as positive or negative emotions. This division between a positive and negative emotion soon undergoes differentiation. Joy and interest become differentiated within the positive side, and fear, sadness, anger, and disgust within the negative side. These emotions are called the primary emotions and all emerge within the first 6 months of life.

In terms of the positive emotions, interest appears present at birth. Joy shows a developmental path. Smiling, at least in the first few months of life, is related to a reflex action, in particular the reduction of tension. Smiling as a reflex has less to do with environmental conditions than with simple physiologic changes. At approximately 2 to 3 months of life, smiling as an emotion emerges (joy appears). The smiling response now becomes tied to social events associated with happy situations. For example, at this time children start to smile at facial stimuli, the presence of soothing sounds, and human-like faces. The smiling response becomes further differentiated over the next 6 to 8 months. Smiling becomes increasingly related to external events of a social nature. By 8 months children no longer smile in response to just any social stimulus, the smiles are now restricted to familiar people and events.[8]

Interest is evident at the beginning of life. Children show interest in response to changes in stimulus intensity and complexity. The interest response grows over the first 6 to 8 months of life but, even in the earliest period, interest expressions

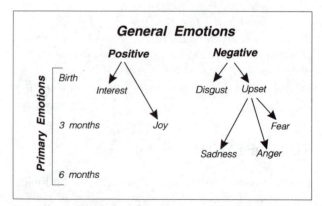

FIGURE 1   Emotional development in the preschool child.

are tied to autonomic nervous system responses associated with taking in and processing information.[9]

The early negative emotions are also undifferentiated at birth. General upset (characterized by crying and fretting behavior) is the most prevalent, although the disgust emotion appears soon after birth. Disgust is associated with the expelling of noxious tastes and smells and appears early in the child's life, certainly sometime during the first month. This response is quite different from the general upset or distress response, which is related to any uncomfortable or painful stimulus event.

The three negative emotions—sadness, fear, and anger—appear to differentiate themselves from the general upset emotion. Fear occurs early, although it may be seen as a reflex-like response to certain events, such as falling or loud noises.[10] By 6 months, loss of control evokes fear.[11] Sadness also does not appear to emerge before the third or fourth month of life. Sadness occurs to the loss of social interaction. Anger has still another pattern related to specific cognitive abilities. The anger response is evolutionarily programmed as an attempt to overcome an obstacle. Prior to 4 months the child is unable to understand the relationship between the cause of a frustration and the response needed to overcome it. For this reason, prior to 4 months frustration does not produce anger, but general distress. At about 4 months and older, frustration produces anger. For example, a 2-month-old when physically restrained by an experimenter will show general distress. However, by 4 to 6 months when this constraint is applied the child shows anger. In addition to anger, the infant is able to focus attention on the source of frustration. This integration of cognition with emotion to produce anger is only one of the examples of the interface between emotion and cognition.[12]

By the middle of the first year of life, the undifferentiated emotions that existed at birth have become differentiated. By this time *joy* is seen under two conditions: when the child comes in contact with a significant social other, such as the caretaker, mother, father, or other family members; and when the child is able to demonstrate mastery over particular events. *Interest* is observed when the child is confronted with novel events or events that require elaborated attention to be understood. *Fear*, wariness, or suspicion is often observed in situations that involve violation of expectation or being introduced to strange and unusual people. *Sadness* is observed over the loss of the mother or significant other, either if the mother moves away from the child or terminates an interaction. *Anger* emerges in frustrat-

ing situations; for example, when the child is unable to reach for something it wishes to obtain. *Disgust* appears early, particularly around noxious tastes and smells.

Secondary emotions emerge after the primary emotions, typically after the first 18 months of life. These emotions are sometimes called *self-conscious emotions,* for their emergence is dependent on the development of a particular important cognitive capacity: self-awareness. Self-awareness or self-consciousness is the human capacity reflected in statements such as "I am," "I am hungry," or "I know you know I am hungry." At about this time the child develops personal pronouns such as "me" or "mine," and the child seems to know it has a specific location in time and space.[13] We often recognize this cognitive milestone as the "terrible twos." It is at this time that the child demonstrates a "will" of its own; parental directions are ignored and the child follows its own desires rather than parental direction.

This cognitive milestone allows for the development of the self-conscious emotions. This large class of emotions requires a self-system, in particular self-awareness.[14] Consider the emotions of embarrassment, empathy, guilt, shame, and pride. They all require a self-system. Exposure of the self, produced by public attention being drawn to the self, elicits embarrassment.[15] Empathy requires that the young child place itself in the role of the other.[16] However, for emotions such as shame, pride, and guilt to be felt the child must not only be self-aware, but a standard of behavior against which the self can evaluate its own action must be understood. Shame and guilt are elicited when the standard of behavior is not attained; the child evaluates its own behavior and finds it lacking. In the case of pride, the child evaluates itself against the standard and finds that its behavior exceeds the standard. All of these emotions require that the child has a self-system capable of referring to itself, a self-referential concept called *consciousness.*

Figure 2 describes the general developmental model this article presents.[17] In stage 1 the primary emotional states appear. In stage 2, self-consciousness appears. This is the last phase of the self-system, which has been developing during the first two years of life.[18] The appearance and consolidation of this cognitive skill—consciousness—provides the underpinning of all the secondary emotions.

The first class of self-conscious or secondary emotions to appear includes embarrassment, empathy, and perhaps envy; these emerge during the

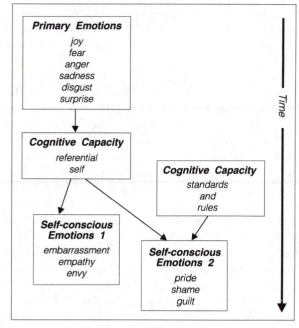

FIGURE 2   Model for the development of emotions.

last half of the second year of life. In addition to developing self-consciousness, the child is learning about other aspects of its social world, including how and when to express emotions as well as particular rules of conduct. The development of these standards is a life-long process that begins as the child's cognitive representation of social reality emerges.

Because of this cognitive support, a second class of self-conscious emotions—self-conscious evaluative emotions—becomes possible: emotions such as guilt, shame, and pride. Whereas the first class of self-conscious emotions appears by 18 to 24 months, the self-conscious evaluative emotions appear later because more cognitive capacity is required. This second class of self-conscious emotions emerges sometime after the second half of the third year of life.

The development of these primary and secondary emotions takes place in the first three years of life. The process begins with the undifferentiated emotions of pleasure and pain. Reorganization and differentiation ultimately lead to the complex emotions that are species specific. Their emergence involves the socialization of standards and rules, the cognitive capacities to recognize the nature of environmental stimuli, and the development of self-consciousness. Failure in the emergence of any of these capacities results in distortion of the developmental process. Thus, failures of self-consciousness in autistic children result in their inability to develop the self-conscious evaluative emotions.

INDIVIDUAL DIFFERENCES

The progression of the normal sequence of emotional development is dependent on a complex set of variables. Individual differences in rate of development as well as in intensity of expression are observed by parents and clinicians. Differences in individual rates of emotional development are dependent on the child's cognitive capacities. In terms of anger for example (one of the primary emotions), children who are able to acquire an understanding of the means to achieve a particular goal are more likely to express this emotion earlier than children who have not obtained this cognitive milestone. Likewise children who have not attained a mental age of 15 or 18 months are unlikely to develop self-consciousness.[18]

The rate at which this cognitive capacity is acquired affects all the emotions associated with it. Down's syndrome children who have not attained a mental age of 15 to 18 months do not show self-consciousness and therefore lack self-conscious emotions.[18] Autistic children also show a delay in self-consciousness and, therefore, a delay in secondary emotion development. Individual differences in the parent-child relationship may also affect emotional development.[19, 20] How parents help regulate their child's expressive behavior can lead to differential emotions.

Individual differences in the intensity of emotional expression also have been studied under the general category of temperament, a topic first introduced and made popular by Thomas and Chess[21] and by Carey.[22] Individual differences in temperament appear to be stable over the first few months of life.[23] Temperament relates to three aspects of a child's emotional response to stimulation: (1) level of threshold, (2) ease of dampening the response once it occurs, and (3) patterns of habituation to repeated exposure.[24] Individual differences in temperament are important for both parents and clinicians. Temperament acts on the parent-child interaction.[25] A child with a difficult temperament is most likely to cause parent-child interactive problems, as the parent is unable to soothe the child. Parents of these children are more likely to appear at the pediatrician's office for help. In general, differences in children's emotionality are related to particular features of temperament and are best understood in that context.

CONCLUSION

Emotional development in the young child has received relatively little attention in both the psychological and pediatric literature; in part, because the focus has been on sensory, motor, and cognitive development. Nevertheless, the emotional life of a child is important. A child's emotions are an evolving developmental system progressing from an undifferentiated to a highly differentiated state. This system interacts with other domains of competence and bears upon the child's social life.

Questions

1.   Why might the emotion of interest be present at the beginning of life?

2.   What internal, or biological, processes and external, or social-experiential, processes might contribute to increased differentiation of the primary emotions over the first year of life?

3.   According to Lewis, what role does cognition play in the development of emotions?

References

1. Darwin C: *The Expressions of Emotions in Man and Animals.* Chicago, University of Chicago Press, 1872.

2. Tomkins SS: *Affect, Imagery, Consciousness*, Vol. 2: The Negative Affects. New York, Springer, 1963.

3. Ekman P, Friessen WV: *The Facial Action Coding System (FACS)*, Palo Alto, CA. Consulting Psychologists Press, 1978.

4. Izard, CE. *The Face of Emotion.* New York, Appleton, 1971.

5. Lewis M, Brooks J: Self, other, and fear: Infant's reactions to people, in Lewis M, Rosenblum L (eds): *The Origins of Fear: The Origins of Behavior*, ed 2, New York, John Wiley & Sons, 1974.

6. Brooks J, Lewis M: Infants' responses to strangers: Midget, adult and child. *Child Dev* 1976; 47:323–332.

7. Bridges KMB: Emotional development in early infancy. *Child Dev* 1932; 3:324–334.

8. Wolff PH: Observations on early development of smiling, in Foss BM (ed): *Determinants of Infant Behavior.* New York, John Wiley & Sons, 1963, vol. 2.

9. Berk WK, Berg KM: Psychophysiological development in infancy: State, sensory function and attention, in Osofsky JD (ed): *Handbook of Infant Development.* New York, John Wiley & Sons, 1979.

10. Watson JB, Rayner R: Conditioned emotional reactions. *J Exp. Psychol* 1920; 3:1–14.

11. Gunnar MR: Control, warning signals and distress in infancy. *Developmental Psychology* 1980; 16:281–289.

12. Stenberg C, Campos J, Emde R: The facial expression of anger in seven-month-old infants. *Child Dev* 1983; 54:178–184.

13. Lewis M: Origins of self knowledge and individual differences in early self recognition, in Greenwald AG, Suls J (eds): *Psychological Perspective on the Self*, ed 3, Hillsdale, NJ, L. Erlbaum Associates, 1986; pp 55–78.

14. Lewis M, Sullivan MW, Stanger C, et al: Self development and self-conscious emotions. *Child Dev* 1989, 60:146–156.

15. Buss AH: *Self Consciousness and Social Anxiety.* San Francisco, W. H. Freeman, 1980.

16. Hoffman ML: Altruistic behavior and the parent-child relationship, *J.Pers Soc Psychol* 1975; 31:937–943(a).

17. Lewis M: Thinking and feeling—The elephant's tail, in Maher CA, Schwebel M, Fagley NS, (eds): *Psychological Perspective on the Self*, ed 3, Hillsdale, NJ, L. Erlbaum Associates, in press.

18. Lewis M, Brooks-Gunn J: *Social Cognition and the Acquisition of Self.* New York, Plenum Press, 1979.

19. Brooks-Gunn J, Lewis M: Affective exchanges between normal and handicapped infants and their mothers, in Field T, Fogel A (eds): *Emotion and Early Interaction.* Hillsdale, NJ, L. Erlbaum Associates, 1982, pp. 161–188.

20. Field T, Fogel A (eds): *Emotion and Interaction: Normal and High Risk Infants.* Hillsdale, NJ, L. Erlbaum Associates, 1976.

21. Thomas A, Chess S: *Temperament and Development.* New York, Bruner-Mazel, 1977.

22. Carey WB: Clinical applications of infant temperament. *J Pediatr* 1972; 81:823–828.

23. Worobey J, Lewis M: Individual differences in the reactivity of young infants. *Dev Psychol*, in press.

24. Lewis M: The development of attention and perception in the infant and young child, in Cruickshank WM, Hallahan DP (eds): *Perceptual and Learning Disabilities in Children*, ed 2, Syracuse, NY, University Press, 1975.

25. Crockenberg SB: Infant irritability, mother responsiveness and social support, influence on the security of infant-mother attachment. *Child Dev* 1981; 52:857–865.

18

Gender and Relationships: A Developmental Account

Questions about gender-related differences in human behavior have preoccupied psychologists for generations. What is the source of the gender-related patterns that are so often observed? The behavior of young children provides one of the best sources of evidence for grappling with such questions. By observing young children, especially in the preschool and early school-age years when many aspects of gender-related behaviors begin to appear, psychologists seek insight into how such behaviors are developed and maintained. This article by Eleanor Maccoby explores the role of social experience in the development of gender-related behaviors and suggests that peers play a central role in this process.

This article argues that behavioral differentiation of the sexes is minimal when children are observed or tested individually. Sex differences emerge primarily in social situations, and their nature varies with the gender composition of dyads and groups. Children find same-sex play partners more compatible, and they segregate themselves into same-sex groups, in which distinctive interaction styles emerge. These styles are described. As children move into adolescence, the patterns they developed in their childhood same-sex groups are carried over into cross-sex encounters in which girls' styles put them at a disadvantage. Patterns of mutual influence can become more symmetrical in intimate male-female dyads, but the distinctive styles of the two sexes can still be seen in such dyads and are subsequently manifested in the roles and relationships of parenthood. The implications of these continuities are considered.

Historically, the way we psychologists think about the psychology of gender has grown out of our

Reprinted with permission from the author and *American Psychologist*, 45, 1990, 513–520.
Copyright 1990 by the American Psychological Association.

thinking about individual differences. We are accustomed to assessing a wide variety of attributes and skills and giving scores to individuals based on their standing relative to other individuals in a sample population. On most psychological attributes, we see wide variation among individuals, and a major focus of research has been the effort to identify correlates or sources of this variation. Commonly, what we have done is to classify individuals by some antecedent variable, such as age or some aspect of their environment, to determine how much of the variance among individuals in their performance on a given task can be accounted for by this so-called *antecedent* or *independent* variable. Despite the fact that hermaphrodites exist, almost every individual is either clearly male or clearly female. What could be more natural for psychologists than to ask how much variance among individuals is accounted for by this beautifully binary factor?

Fifteen years ago, Carol Jacklin and I put out a book summarizing the work on sex differences that had come out of the individual differences perspective (Maccoby & Jacklin, 1974). We felt at that time that the yield was thin. That is, there were very few attributes on which the average values for the two sexes differed consistently. Furthermore, even when consistent differences were found, the amount of variance accounted for by sex was small, relative to the amount of variation within each sex. Our conclusions fitted in quite well with the feminist zeitgeist of the times, when most feminists were taking a minimalist position, urging that the two sexes were basically alike and that any differences were either illusions in the eye of the beholder or reversible outcomes of social shaping. Our conclusions were challenged as having both overstated the case for sex differences (Tieger, 1980) and for having understated it (Block, 1976).

In the last 15 years, work on sex differences has become more methodologically sophisticated, with greater use of meta analyses to reveal not only the direction of sex differences but quantitative estimates of their magnitude. In my judgment, the conclusions are still quite similar to those Jacklin and I arrived at in 1974: There are still some replicable sex differences, of moderate magnitude, in performance on tests of mathematical and spatial abilities, although sex differences in verbal abilities have faded. Other aspects of intellectual performance continue to show gender equality. When it comes to attributes in the personality–social domain, results are particularly sparse and inconsistent. Studies continue to find that men are more often agents of aggression than are women (Eagly, 1987; Huston,

1985; Maccoby & Jacklin, 1980). Eagly (1983, 1987) reported in addition that women are more easily influenced than men and that men are more altruistic in the sense that they are more likely to offer help to others. In general, however, personality traits measured as characteristics of individuals do not appear to differ systematically by sex (Huston, 1985). This no doubt reflects in part the fact that male and female persons really are much alike, and their lives are governed mainly by the attributes that all persons in a given culture have in common. Nevertheless, I believe that the null findings coming out of comparisons of male and female individuals on personality measures are partly illusory. That is, they are an artifact of our historical reliance on an individual differences perspective. Social behavior, as many have pointed out, is never a function of the individual alone. It is a function of the interaction between two or more persons. Individuals behave differently with different partners. There are certain important ways in which gender is implicated in social behavior—ways that may be obscured or missed altogether when behavior is summed across all categories of social partners.

An illustration is found in a study of social interaction between previously unacquainted pairs of young children (mean age, 33 months; Jacklin & Maccoby, 1978). In some pairs, the children had same-sex play partners; in others, the pair was made up of a boy and a girl. Observers recorded the social behavior of each child on a time-sampling basis. Each child received a score for total social behavior directed toward the partner. This score included both positive and negative behaviors (e.g., offering a toy and grabbing a toy; hugging and pushing; vocally greeting, inviting, protesting, or prohibiting). There was no overall sex difference in the amount of social behavior when this was evaluated without regard to sex of partner. But there was a powerful interaction between sex of the subject and that of the partner: Children of each sex had much higher levels of social behavior when playing with a same-sex partner than when playing with a child of the other sex. This result is consistent with the findings of Wasserman and Stern (1978) that when asked to approach another child, children as young as age three stopped farther away when the other child was of the opposite sex, indicating awareness of gender similarity or difference, and wariness toward the other sex.

The number of time intervals during which a child was simply standing passively watching the partner play with the toys was also scored. There was no overall sex difference in the frequency of this behavior, but the behavior of girls was greatly affected by the sex of the partner. With other girls, passive behavior seldom occurred; indeed, in girl–girl pairs it occurred less often than it did in boy–boy pairs. However when paired with boys, girls frequently stood on the sidelines and let the boys monopolize the toys. Clearly, the little girls in this study were not more passive than the little boys in any overall, trait-like sense. Passivity in these girls could be understood only in relation to the characteristics of their interactive partners. It was a characteristic of girls in cross-sex dyads. This conclusion may not seem especially novel because for many years we have known that social behavior is situationally specific. However, the point here is that interactive behavior is not just situationally specific, but that it depends on the gender category membership of the participants. We can account for a good deal more of the behavior if we know the gender mix of dyads, and this probably holds true for larger groups as well.

An implication of our results was that if children at this early age found same-sex play partners more compatible, they ought to prefer same-sex partners when they entered group settings that included children of both sexes. There were already many indications in the literature that children do have same-sex playmate preferences, but there clearly was a need for more systematic attention to the degree of sex segregation that prevails in naturally occurring children's groups at different ages. As part of a longitudinal study of children from birth to age six, Jacklin and I did time-sampled behavioral observation of approximately 100 children on their preschool playgrounds, and again two years later when the children were playing during school recess periods (Maccoby & Jacklin, 1987). Same-sex playmate preference was clearly apparent in preschool when the children were approximately 4½. At this age, the children were spending nearly 3 times as much time with same-sex play partners as with children of the other sex. By age 6½, the preference had grown much stronger. At this time, the children were spending 11 times as much time with same-sex as with opposite-sex partners.

Elsewhere we have reviewed the literature on playmate choices (Maccoby, 1988; Maccoby & Jacklin, 1987), and here I will simply summarize what I believe the existing body of research shows:

1. Gender segregation is a widespread phenomenon. It is found in all the cultural settings in which children are in social groups large enough to permit choice.

2. The sex difference in the gender of preferred playmates is large in absolute magnitude, compared to sex differences found when children are observed or tested in nonsocial situations.

3. In a few instances, attempts have been made to break down children's preferences for interacting with other same-sex children. It has been found that the preferences are difficult to change.

4. Children choose same-sex playmates spontaneously in situations in which they are not under pressure from adults to do so. In modern co-educational schools, segregation is more marked in situations that have not been structured by adults than in those that have (e.g., Eisenhart & Holland, 1983). Segregation is situationally specific, and the two sexes can interact comfortably under certain conditions, for example, in an absorbing joint task, when structures and roles are set up by adults, or in non-public settings (Thorne, 1986).

5. Gender segregation is not closely linked to involvement in sex-typed activities. Preschool children spend a great deal of their time engaged in activities that are gender neutral, and segregation prevails in these activities as well as when they are playing with dolls or trucks.

6. Tendencies to prefer same-sex playmates can be seen among three-year-olds and at even earlier ages under some conditions. But the preferences increase in strength between preschool and school and are maintained at a high level between the ages of 6 and at least age 11.

7. The research base is thin, but so far it appears that a child's tendency to prefer same-sex playmates has little to do with that child's standing on measures of individual differences. In particular, it appears to be unrelated to measures of masculinity or femininity and also to measures of gender schematicity (Powlishta, 1989).

Why do we see such pronounced attraction to same-sex peers and avoidance of other-sex peers in childhood? Elsewhere I have summarized evidence pointing to two factors that seem to be important in the preschool years (Maccoby, 1988). The first is the rough-and-tumble play style characteristic of boys and their orientation toward issues of competition and dominance. These aspects of male–male interaction appear to be somewhat aversive to most girls. At least, girls are made wary by male play styles. The second factor of importance is that girls find it difficult to influence boys. Some important work by Serbin and colleagues (Serbin, Sprafkin, Elman, & Doyle, 1984) indicates that between the ages of 3½ and 5½, children greatly increase the frequency of their attempts to influence their play partners. This indicates that children are learning to integrate their activities with those of others so as to be able to carry out coordinated activities. Serbin and colleagues found that the increase in influence attempts by girls was almost entirely an increase in making polite suggestions to others, whereas among boys the increase took the form of more use of direct demands. Furthermore, during this formative two-year period just before school entry, boys were becoming less and less responsive to polite suggestions, so that the style being progressively adopted by girls was progressively less effective with boys. Girls' influence style was effective with each other and was well adapted to interaction with teachers and other adults.

These asymmetries in influence patterns were presaged in our study with 33-month-old children: We found then that boys were unresponsive to the vocal prohibitions of female partners (in that they did not withdraw), although they would respond when a vocal prohibition was issued by a male partner. Girls were responsive to one another and to a male partner's prohibitions. Fagot (1985) also reported that boys are "reinforced" by the reactions of male peers—in the sense that they modify their behavior following a male peer's reaction—but that their behavior appears not to be affected by a female's response.

My hypothesis is that girls find it aversive to try to interact with someone who is unresponsive and that they begin to avoid such partners. Students of power and bargaining have long been aware of the importance of reciprocity in human relations. Pruitt (1976) said, "Influence and power are omnipresent in human affairs. Indeed, groups cannot possibly function unless their members can influence one another" (p. 343). From this standpoint, it becomes clear why boys and girls have difficulty forming groups that include children of both sexes.

Why do little boys not accept influence from little girls? Psychologists almost automatically look to the nuclear family for the origins of behavior patterns seen in young children. It is plausible that boys

may have been more reinforced for power assertive behavior by their parents, and girls more for politeness, although the evidence for such differential socialization pressure has proved difficult to come by. However, it is less easy to imagine how or why parents should reinforce boys for being unresponsive to *girls*. Perhaps it is a matter of observational learning: Children may have observed that between their two parents, their fathers are more influential than their mothers. I am skeptical about such an explanation. In the first place, mothers exercise a good deal of managerial authority within the households in which children live, and it is common for fathers to defer to their judgment in matters concerning the children. Or, parents form a coalition, and in the eyes of the children they become a joint authority, so that it makes little difference to them whether it is a mother or a father who is wielding authority at any given time. Furthermore, the asymmetry in children's cross-sex influence with their peers appears to have its origins at quite an early age—earlier, I would suggest, than children have a very clear idea about the connection between their own sex and that of the same-sex parent. In other words, it seems quite unlikely that little boys ignore girls' influence attempts because little girls remind them of their mothers. I think we simply do not know why girls' influence styles are ineffective with boys, but the fact that they are has important implications for a variety of social behaviors, not just for segregation.

Here are some examples from recent studies. Powlishta (1987) observed preschool-aged boy–girl pairs competing for a scarce resource. The children were brought to a playroom in the nursery school and were given an opportunity to watch cartoons through a movie-viewer that could only be accessed by one child at a time. Powlishta found that when the two children were alone together in the playroom, the boys got more than their share of access to the movie-viewer. When there was an adult present, however, this was no longer the case. The adult's presence appeared to inhibit the boys' more power-assertive techniques and resulted in girls having at least equal access.

This study points to a reason why girls may not only avoid playing with boys but may also stay nearer to a teacher or other adult. Following up on this possibility, Greeno (1989) brought four-child groups of kindergarten and first-grade children into a large playroom equipped with attractive toys. Some of the quartets were all-boy groups, some all-girl groups, and some were made up of two boys and two girls. A female adult sat at one end of the room, and halfway through the play session, moved to a seat at the other end of the room. The question posed for this study was: Would girls move closer to the teacher when boys were present than when they were not? Would the sex composition of a play group make any difference to the locations taken up by the boys? The results were that in all-girl groups, girls actually took up locations *farther* from the adult than did boys in all-boy groups. When two boys were present, however, the two girls were significantly closer to the adult than were the boys, who tended to remain at intermediate distances. When the adult changed position halfway through the session, boys' locations did not change, and this was true whether there were girls present or not. Girls in all-girl groups tended to move in the opposite direction when the adult moved, maintaining distance between themselves and the adult; when boys were present, however, the girls tended to move *with* the adult, staying relatively close. It is worth noting, incidentally, that in all the mixed-sex groups except one, segregation was extreme; both boys and girls behaved as though there was only one playmate available to them, rather than three.

There are some fairly far-reaching implications of this study. Previous observational studies in preschools had indicated that girls are often found in locations closer to the teacher than are boys. These studies have been done in mixed-sex nursery school groups. Girls' proximity seeking toward adults has often been interpreted as a reflection of some general affiliative trait in girls and perhaps as a reflection of some aspect of early socialization that has bound them more closely to caregivers. We see in the Greeno study that proximity seeking toward adults was *not* a general trait in girls. It was a function of the gender composition of the group of other children present as potential interaction partners. The behavior of girls implied that they found the presence of boys to be less aversive when an adult was nearby. It was as though they realized that the rough, power-assertive behavior of boys was likely to be moderated in the presence of adults, and indeed, there is evidence that they were right.

We have been exploring some aspects of girls' avoidance of interaction with boys. Less is known about why boys avoid interaction with girls, but the fact is that they do. In fact, their cross-sex avoidance appears to be even stronger. Thus, during middle childhood both boys and girls spend considerable portions of their social play time in groups of their own sex. This might not matter much for future relationships were it not for the fact that fairly distinctive styles of interaction develop in all-boy and all-girl groups. Thus, the segregated play groups

constitute powerful socialization environments in which children acquire distinctive interaction skills that are adapted to same-sex partners. Sex-typed modes of interaction become consolidated, and I wish to argue that the distinctive patterns developed by the two sexes at this time have implications for the same-sex and cross-sex relationships that individuals form as they enter adolescence and adulthood.

It behooves us, then, to examine in somewhat more detail the nature of the interactive milieus that prevail in all-boy and all-girl groups. Elsewhere I have reviewed some of the findings of studies in which these two kinds of groups have been observed (Maccoby, 1988). Here I will briefly summarize what we know.

The two sexes engage in fairly different kinds of activities and games (Huston, 1985). Boys play in somewhat larger groups, on the average, and their play is rougher (Humphreys & Smith, 1987) and takes up more space. Boys more often play in the streets and other public places; girls more often congregate in private homes or yards. Girls tend to form close, intimate friendships with one or two other girls, and these friendships are marked by the sharing of confidences (Kraft & Vraa, 1975). Boys' friendships, on the other hand, are more oriented around mutual interests in activities (Erwin, 1985). The breakup of girls' friendships is usually attended by more intense emotional reactions than is the case for boys.

For our present purposes, the most interesting thing about all-boy and all-girl groups is the divergence in the interactive styles that develop in them. In male groups, there is more concern with issues of dominance. Several psycholinguists have recorded the verbal exchanges that occur in these groups, and Maltz and Borker (1983) summarized the findings of several studies as follows: Boys in their groups are more likely than girls in all-girl groups to interrupt one another; use commands, threats, or boasts of authority; refuse to comply with another child's demand; give information; heckle a speaker; tell jokes or suspenseful stories; top someone else's story; or call another child names. Girls in all-girl groups, on the other hand, are more likely than boys to express agreement with what another speaker has just said, pause to give another girl a chance to speak, or when starting a speaking turn, acknowledge a point previously made by another speaker. This account indicates that among boys, speech serves largely egoistic functions and is used to establish and protect an individual's turf. Among girls, conversation is a more socially binding process.

In the past five years, analysts of discourse have done additional work on the kinds of interactive processes that are seen among girls, as compared with those among boys. The summary offered by Maltz and Borker has been both supported and extended. Sachs (1987) reported that girls soften their directives to partners, apparently attempting to keep them involved in a process of planning a play sequence, while boys are more likely simply to tell their partners what to do. Leaper (1989) observed children aged five and seven and found that verbal exchanges among girls more often take the form of what he called "collaborative speech acts" that involve positive reciprocity, whereas among boys, speech acts are more controlling and include more negative reciprocity. Miller and colleagues (Miller, Danaher, & Forbes, 1986) found that there was more conflict in boys' groups, and given that conflict had occurred, girls were more likely to use "conflict mitigating strategies," whereas boys more often used threats and physical force. Sheldon (1989) reported that when girls talk, they seem to have a double agenda: to be "nice" and sustain social relationships, while at the same time working to achieve their own individual ends. For boys, the agenda is more often the single one of self-assertion. Sheldon (1989) has noted that in interactions among themselves, girls are *not* unassertive. Rather, girls do successfully pursue their own ends, but they do so while toning down coercion and dominance, trying to bring about agreement, and restoring or maintaining group functioning. It should be noted that boys' confrontational style does not necessarily impede effective group functioning, as evidenced by boys' ability to cooperate with teammates for sports. A second point is that although researchers' own gender has been found to influence to some degree the kinds of questions posed and the answers obtained, the summary provided here includes the work of both male and female researchers, and their findings are consistent with one another.

As children move into adolescence and adulthood, what happens to the interactive styles that they developed in their largely segregated childhood groups? A first point to note is that despite the powerful attraction to members of the opposite sex in adolescence, gender segregation by no means disappears. Young people continue to spend a good portion of their social time with same-sex partners. In adulthood, there is extensive gender segregation in workplaces (Reskin, 1984), and in some societies and some social-class or ethnic groups, leisure time also is largely spent with same-sex others even after marriage. The literature on the nature of the interac-

tions that occur among same-sex partners in adolescence and adulthood is quite extensive and cannot be reviewed here. Suffice it to say in summary that there is now considerable evidence that the interactive patterns found in sex-homogeneous dyads or groups in adolescence and adulthood are very similar to those that prevailed in the gender-segregated groups of childhood (e.g., Aries, 1976; Carli, 1989; Cowan, Drinkard, & MacGavin, 1984; Savin-Williams, 1979).

How can we summarize what it is that boys and girls, or men and women, are doing in their respective groups that distinguishes these groups from one another? There have been a number of efforts to find the major dimensions that best describe variations in interactive styles. Falbo and Peplau (1980) have factor analyzed a battery of measures and have identified two dimensions: one called direct versus indirect, the other unilateral versus bilateral. Hauser et al. (1987) have distinguished what they called *enabling* interactive styles from *constricting* or *restrictive* ones, and I believe this distinction fits the styles of the two sexes especially well. A restrictive style is one that tends to derail the interaction—to inhibit the partner or cause the partner to withdraw, thus shortening the interaction or bringing it to an end. Examples are threatening a partner, directly contradicting or interrupting, topping the partner's story, boasting, or engaging in other forms of self-display. Enabling or facilitative styles are those, such as acknowledging another's comment or expressing agreement, that support whatever the partner is doing and tend to keep the interaction going. I want to suggest that it is because women and girls use more enabling styles that they are able to form more intimate and more integrated relationships. Also I think it likely that it is the male concern for turf and dominance—that is, with not showing weakness to other men and boys—that underlies their restrictive interaction style and their lack of self-disclosure.

Carli (1989) has recently found that in discussions between pairs of adults, individuals are more easily influenced by a partner if that partner has just expressed agreement with them. In this work, women were quite successful in influencing one another in same-sex dyads, whereas pairs of men were less so. The sex difference was fully accounted for by the fact that men's male partners did not express agreement as often. Eagly (1987) has summarized data from a large number of studies on women's and men's susceptibility to influence and has found women to be somewhat more susceptible. Carli's work suggests that this tendency may not be a general female personality trait of "suggestibility" but may reflect the fact that women more often interact with other women who tend to express reciprocal agreement. Carli's finding resonates with some work with young children interacting with their mothers. Mary Parpal and I (Parpal & Maccoby, 1985) found that children were more compliant to a mother's demands if the two had previously engaged in a game in which the child was allowed to give directions that the mother followed. In other words, maternal compliance set up a system of reciprocity in which the child also complied. I submit that the same principle applies in adult interactions and that among women, influence is achieved in part by being open to influence from the partner.

Boys and men, on the other hand, although less successful in influencing one another in dyads, develop group structures—well-defined roles in games, dominance hierarchies, and team spirit—that appear to enable them to function effectively in groups. One may suppose that the male directive interactive style is less likely to derail interaction if and when group structural forces are in place. In other words, men and boys may *need* group structure more than women and girls do. However, this hypothesis has yet to be tested in research. In any case, boys and men in their groups have more opportunity to learn how to function within hierarchical structures than do women and girls in theirs.

We have seen that throughout much of childhood and into adolescence and adulthood as well, people spend a good deal of their social time interacting with others of their own gender, and they continue to use distinctive interaction styles in these settings. What happens, then, when individuals from these two distinctive "cultures" attempt to interact with one another? People of both sexes are faced with a relatively unfamiliar situation to which they must adapt. Young women are less likely to receive the reciprocal agreement, opportunities to talk, and so on that they have learned to expect when interacting with female partners. Men have been accustomed to counter-dominance and competitive reactions to their own power assertions, and they now find themselves with partners who agree with them and otherwise offer enabling responses. It seems evident that this new partnership should be easier to adapt to for men than for women. There is evidence that men fall in love faster and report feeling more in love than do women early in intimate relationships (Huston & Ashmore, 1986). Furthermore, the higher rates of depression in females have their onset in adolescence, when rates of cross-sex interaction rise (Nolen-Hoeksema, in press).

Although these phenomena are no doubt multi-determined, the asymmetries in interaction styles may contribute to them.

To some degree, men appear to bring to bear much the same kind of techniques in mixed-sex groups that they are accustomed to using in same-sex groups. If the group is attempting some sort of joint problem solving or is carrying out a joint task, men do more initiating, directing, and interrupting than do women. Men's voices are louder and are more listened to than women's voices by both sexes (West & Zimmerman, 1985); men are more likely than women to lose interest in a taped message if it is spoken in a woman's rather than a man's voice (Robinson & MacArthur, 1982). Men are less influenced by the opinions of other group members than are women. Perhaps as a consequence of their greater assertiveness, men have more influence on the group process (Lockheed, 1985; Pugh & Wahrman, 1983), just as they did in childhood. Eagly and colleagues (Eagly, Wood, & Fishbaugh, 1981) have drawn our attention to an important point about cross-sex interaction in groups: The greater resistance of men to being influenced by other group members is found only when the men are under surveillance, that is, if others know whether they have yielded to their partners' influence attempts. I suggest that it is especially the monitoring by other *men* that inhibits men from entering into reciprocal influence with partners. When other men are present, men appear to feel that they must guard their dominance status and not comply too readily lest it be interpreted as weakness.

Women's behavior in mixed groups is more complex. There is some work indicating that they adapt by becoming more like men—that they raise their voices, interrupt, and otherwise become more assertive than they would be when interacting with women (Carli, 1989; Hall & Braunwald, 1981). On the other hand, there is also evidence that they carry over some of their well-practiced female-style behaviors, sometimes in exaggerated form. Women may wait for a turn to speak that does not come, and thus they may end up talking less than they would in a women's group. They smile more than the men do, agree more often with what others have said, and give nonverbal signals of attentiveness to what others—perhaps especially the men—are saying (Duncan & Fiske, 1977). In some writings this female behavior has been referred to as "silent applause."

Eagly (1987) reported a meta-analysis of behavior of the two sexes in groups (mainly mixed-sex groups) that were performing joint tasks. She found a consistent tendency for men to engage in more task behavior—giving and receiving information, suggestions, and opinions (see also Aries, 1982)—whereas women are more likely to engage in socioemotional behaviors that support positive affective relations within the group. Which style contributes more to effective group process? It depends. Wood, Polek, and Aiken (1985) have compared the performance of all-female and all-male groups on different kinds of tasks, finding that groups of women have more success on tasks that require discussion and negotiation, whereas male groups do better on tasks where success depends on the volume of ideas being generated. Overall, it appears that *both* styles are productive, though in different ways.

There is evidence that women feel at a disadvantage in mixed-sex interaction. For example, Hogg and Turner (1987) set up a debate between two young men taking one position and two young women taking another. The outcomes in this situation were contrasted with a situation in which young men and women were debating against same-sex partners. After the cross-sex debate, the self-esteem of the young men rose, but that of the young women declined. Furthermore, the men liked their women opponents better after debating with them, whereas the women liked the men less. In other words, the encounter in most cases was a pleasurable experience for the men, but not for the women. Another example comes from the work of Davis (1978), who set up get-acquainted sessions between pairs of young men and women. He found that the men took control of the interaction, dictating the pace at which intimacy increased, whereas the women adapted themselves to the pace set by the men. The women reported later, however, that they had been uncomfortable about not being able to control the sequence of events, and they did not enjoy the encounter as much as the men did.

In adolescence and early adulthood, the powerful forces of sexual attraction come into play. When couples are beginning to fall in love, or even when they are merely entertaining the possibility of developing an intimate relationship, each is motivated to please the other, and each sends signals implying "Your wish is my command." There is evidence that whichever member of a couple is more attractive, or less in love, is at an advantage and is more able to influence the partner than vice versa (Peplau, 1979). The influence patterns based on the power of interpersonal attraction are not distinct in terms of gender; that is, it may be either the man or the woman in a courting relationship who has the influence advantage. When first meeting, or in the early stages

of the acquaintance process, women still may feel at some disadvantage, as shown in the Davis study, but this situation need not last. Work done in the 1960s indicated that in many couples, as relationships become deeper and more enduring, any overall asymmetry in influence diminishes greatly (Heiss, 1962; Leik, 1963; Shaw & Sadler, 1965). Most couples develop a relationship that is based on communality rather than exchange bargaining. That is, they have many shared goals and work jointly to achieve them. They do not need to argue over turf because they have the same turf. In well-functioning married couples, both members of the pair strive to avoid conflict, and indeed there is evidence that the men on average are even more conflict-avoidant than the women (Gottman & Levenson, 1988; Kelley et al., 1978). Nevertheless, there are still carry-overs of the different interactive styles males and females have acquired at earlier points in the life cycle. Women seem to expend greater effort toward maintaining harmonious moods (Huston & Ashmore, 1986, p. 177). With intimate cross-sex partners, men use more direct styles of influence, and women use more indirect ones. Furthermore, women are more likely to withdraw (become silent, cold, and distant) and/or take unilateral action in order to get their way in a dispute (Falbo & Peplau, 1980), strategies that we suspect may reflect their greater difficulty in influencing a male partner through direct negotiation.

Space limitations do not allow considering in any depth the next set of important relationships that human beings form: that between parents and children. Let me simply say that I think there is evidence for the following: The interaction styles that women have developed in interaction with girls and other women serve them well when they become mothers. Especially when children are young, women enter into deeper levels of reciprocity with their children than do men (e.g., Gleason, 1987; Maccoby & Jacklin, 1983) and communicate with them better. On the other hand, especially after the first two years, children need firm direction as well as warmth and reciprocity, and fathers' styles may contribute especially well to this aspect of parenting. The relationship women develop with young children seems to depend very little on whether they are dealing with a son or a daughter; it builds on maternal response to the characteristics and needs of early childhood that are found in both boys and girls to similar degrees. Fathers, having a less intimate relationship with individual children, treat young boys and girls in a somewhat more gendered way (Siegal, 1987). As children approach middle childhood and interact with same-sex other children, they develop the interactive styles characteristic of their sex, and their parents more and more interact with them as they have always done with same-sex or opposite-sex others. That is, mothers and daughters develop greater intimacy and reciprocity; fathers and sons exhibit more friendly rivalry and joking, more joint interest in masculine activities, and more rough play. Nevertheless, there are many aspects of the relationships between parents and children that do not depend on the gender of either the parent or the child.

Obviously, as the scene unfolds across generations, it is very difficult to identify the point in the developmental cycle at which the interactional styles of the two sexes begin to diverge, and more important, to identify the forces that cause them to diverge. In my view, processes within the nuclear family have been given too much credit—or too much blame—for this aspect of sex-typing. I doubt that the development of distinctive interactive styles

has much to do with the fact that children are parented primarily by women, as some have claimed (Chodorow, 1978; Gilligan, 1982), and it seems likely to me that children's "identification" with the same-sex parent is more a consequence than a cause of children's acquisition of sex-typed interaction styles. I would place most of the emphasis on the peer group as the setting in which children first discover the compatibility of same-sex others, in which boys first discover the requirements of maintaining one's status in the male hierarchy, and in which the gender of one's partners becomes supremely important. We do not have a clear answer to the ultimate question of why the segregated peer groups function as they do. We need now to think about how it can be answered. The answer is important if we are to adapt ourselves successfully to the rapid changes in the roles and relationships of the two sexes that are occurring in modern societies.

Questions

1. Why are children's behaviors more sex-typed when they play with a child of the same sex than with a child of the other sex?

2. What patterns of gender segregation appear in children between the ages of 4 and 6 years?

3. What consequences do you think might result from children playing mostly with children of the same sex during the years of childhood?

References

Aries, E. (1976). Interaction patterns and themes of male, female, and mixed groups. *Small Group Behavior, 7,* 7–18.

Aries, E. J. (1982). Verbal and nonverbal behavior in single-sex and mixed-sex groups: Are traditional sex roles changing? *Psychological Reports, 51,* 127–134.

Block, J. H. (1976). Debatable conclusions about sex differences. *Contemporary Psychology, 21,* 517–522.

Carli, L. L. (1989). Gender Differences in interaction style and influence. *Journal of Personality and Social Psychology, 56,* 565–576.

Chodorow, N. (1978). *The reproduction of mothering.* Berkeley, CA: University of California Press.

Cowan, C., Drinkard, J., & MacGavin, L. (1984). The effects of target, age and gender on use of power strategies. *Journal of Personality and Social Psychology, 47,* 1391–1398.

Davis, J. D. (1978). When boy meets girl: Sex roles and the negotiation of intimacy in an acquaintance exercise. *Journal of Personality and Social Psychology, 36,* 684–692.

Duncan, S., Jr., & Fiske, D. W. (1977). *Face-to-face interaction: Research, methods and theory.* Hillsdale, NJ: Erlbaum.

Eagly, A. H. (1983). Gender and social influence. *American Psychologist, 38,* 971–981.

Eagly, A. H. (1987). *Sex differences in social behavior: A social role interpretation.* Hillsdale, NJ: Erlbaum.

Eagly, A. H., Wood, W., & Fishbaugh, L. (1981). Sex differences in conformity: Surveillance by the group as a determinant of male non-conformity. *Journal of Personality and Social Psychology, 40,* 384–394.

Eisenhart, M. A., & Holland, D. C. (1983). Learning gender from peers: The role of peer group in the cultural transmission of gender. *Human Organization, 42,* 321–332.

Erwin, P. (1985). Similarity of attitudes and constructs in children's friendships. *Journal of Experimental Child Psychology, 40,* 470–485.

Fagot, B. I. (1985). Beyond the reinforcement principle: Another step toward understanding sex roles. *Developmental Psychology, 21,* 1097–1104.

Falbo, T. & Peplau, L. A. (1980). Power strategies in intimate relationships. *Journal of Personality and Social Psychology, 38,* 618–628.

Gilligan, C. (1982). *In a different voice: Psychological theory and women's development.* Cambridge, MA: Harvard University Press.

Gleason, J. B. (1987). Sex differences in parent-child interaction. In S. U. Phillips, S. Steele, & C. Tanz (Eds.), *Language, gender and sex in comparative perspective* (pp. 189–199). Cambridge, England: Cambridge University Press.

Gottman, J. M., & Levenson, R. W. (1988). The social psycho-physiology of marriage. In P. Roller & M. A. Fitzpatrick (Eds.), *Perspectives on marital interaction* (pp. 182–200). New York: Taylor & Francis.

Greeno, C. G. (1989). *Gender differences in children's proximity to adults.* Unpublished doctoral dissertation, Stanford University, Stanford, CA.

Hall, J. A., & Braunwald, K. G. (1981). Gender cues in conversation. *Journal of Personality and Social Psychology, 40,* 99–110.

Hauser, S. T., Powers, S. I., Weiss-Perry, B., Follansbee, D. J., Rajapark, D., & Greene, W. M. (1987). *The constraining and enabling coding system manual.* Unpublished manuscript.

Heiss, J. S. (1962). Degree of intimacy and male-female interaction. *Sociometry, 25,* 197–208.

Hogg, M. A., & Turner, J. C. (1987). Intergroup behavior, self stereotyping and the salience of social categories. *British Journal of Social Psychology, 26,* 325–340.

Humphreys, A. P., & Smith, P. K. (1987). Rough and tumble friendship and dominance in school children: Evidence for continuity and change with age in middle childhood. *Child Development, 58,* 201–212.

Huston, A. C. (1985). The development of sex-typing: Themes from recent research. *Developmental Review, 5,* 1-17.

Huston, T. L., & Ashmore, R. D. (1986). Women and men in personal relationship. In R. D. Ashmore & R. K. Del Boca (Eds.), *The social psychology of female-male relations.* New York: Academic Press.

Jacklin, C. N., & Maccoby, E. E. (1978). Social behavior at 33 months in same-sex and mixed-sex dyads. *Child Development, 49,* 557–569.

Kelley, H. H., Cunningham, J. D., Grisham, J. A., Lefebvre, L. M., Sink, C. R., & Yablon, G. (1978). Sex differences in comments made during conflict in close relationships. *Sex Roles, 4,* 473–491.

Kraft, L. W., & Vraa, C. W. (1975). Sex composition of groups and pattern of self-disclosure by high school females. *Psychological Reports, 37,* 733–734.

Leaper, C. (1989). *The sequencing of power and involvement in boys' and girls' talk.* Unpublished manuscript (under review), University of California, Santa Cruz.

Leik, R. K. (1963). Instrumentality and emotionality in family interaction. *Sociometry, 26,* 131–145.

Lockheed, M. E. (1985). Sex and social influence: A meta-analysis guided by theory. In J. Berger & M. Zelditch (Eds.), *Status, attributions, and rewards* (pp. 406–429). San Francisco, CA: Jossey-Bass.

Maccoby, E. E. (1988). Gender as a social category. *Developmental Psychology, 26,* 755–765.

Maccoby, E. E., & Jacklin, C. N. (1974). *The psychology of sex differences.* Stanford, CA: Stanford University Press.

Maccoby, E. E., & Jacklin, C. N. (1980). Sex differences in aggression: A rejoinder and reprise. *Child Development, 51,* 964–980.

Maccoby, E. E., & Jacklin, C. N. (1983). The "person" characteristics of children and the family as environment. In D. Magnusson & V. L. Allen (Eds.), *Human development: An interactional perspective* (pp. 76–92). New York: Academic Press.

Maccoby, E. E., & Jacklin, C. N. (1987). Gender segregation in childhood. In H. W. Reese (Ed.), *Advances in child development and behavior.* (Vol. 20, pp. 239–288). New York: Academic Press.

Maltz, D. N., & Borker, R. A. (1983). A cultural approach to male-female miscommunication. In John A. Gumperz (Ed.), *Language and social identity* (pp. 195–216). New York: Cambridge University Press.

Miller, P., Danaher, D., & Forbes, D. (1986). Sex-related strategies for coping with interpersonal conflict in children aged five and seven. *Developmental Psychology, 22,* 543–548.

Nolen-Hoeksema, S. (in press). *Sex differences in depression.* Stanford, CA: Stanford University Press.

Parpal, M., & Maccoby, E. E. (1985). Maternal responsiveness and subsequent child compliance. *Child Development, 56,* 1326–1334.

Peplau, A. (1979). Power in dating relationships. In J. Freeman (Ed.), *Women: A feminist perspective* (pp. 121–137). Palo Alto, CA: Mayfield.

Powlishta, K. K. (1987, April). *The social context of cross-sex interactions.* Paper presented at biennial meeting of the Society for Research in Child Development, Baltimore, MD.

Powlishta, K. K. (1989). *Salience of group membership: The case of gender.* Unpublished doctoral dissertation, Stanford University, Stanford, CA.

Pruitt, D. G. (1976). Power and bargaining. In B. Seidenberg & A. Snadowsky (Eds.), *Social psychology: An introduction* (pp. 343–375). New York: Free Press.

Pugh, M. D., & Wahrman, R. (1983). Neutralizing sexism in mixed-sex groups: Do women have to be better than men? *American Journal of Sociology, 88,* 746–761.

Reskin, B. F. (Ed.). (1984). *Sex segregation in the workplace: Trends, explanations and remedies.* Washington, DC: National Academy Press.

Robinson, J., & McArthur, L. Z. (1982). Impact of salient vocal qualities on causal attribution for a speaker's behavior. *Journal of Personality and Social Psychology, 43,* 236–247.

Sachs, J. (1987). Preschool boys' and girls' language use in pretend play. In S. U. Phillips, S. Steele, & C. Tanz (Eds.), *Language, gender and sex in comparative perspective* (pp. 178–188). Cambridge, England: Cambridge University Press.

Savin-Williams, R. C. (1979). Dominance hierarchies in groups of early adolescents, *Child Development, 50,* 923–935.

Serbin, L. A., Sprafkin, C., Elman, M., & Doyle, A. (1984). The early development of sex differentiated patterns of social influence. *Canadian Journal of Social Science, 14,* 350–363.

Shaw, M. E., & Sadler, 0. W. (1965). Interaction patterns in heterosexual dyads varying in degree of intimacy. *Journal of Social Psychology, 66,* 345–351.

Sheldon, A. (1989, April). *Conflict talk: Sociolinguistic challenges to self-assertion and how young girls meet them.* Paper presented at the biennial meeting of the Society for Research in Child Development, Kansas City.

Siegal, M. (1987). Are sons and daughters treated more differently by fathers than mothers? *Developmental Review, 7,* 183-209.

Thorne, B. (1986). Girls and boys together, but mostly apart. In W. W. Hartup & L. Rubin (Eds.), *Relationships and development* (pp. 167–184). Hillsdale, NJ: Erlbaum.

Tieger, T. (1980). On the biological basis of sex differences in aggression. *Child Development, 51,* 943–963.

Wasserman, G. A., & Stern, D. N. (1978). An early manifestation of differential behavior toward children of the same and opposite sex. *Journal of Genetic Psychology, 133,* 129–137.

West, C., & Zimmerman, D. H. (1985). Gender, language and discourse. In T. A. van Dijk (Ed.), *Handbook of discourse analysis: Vol. 4. Discourse analysis in society* (pp. 103–124). London: Academic Press.

Wood, W., Polek, D., & Aiken, C. (1985). Sex differences in group task performance. *Journal of Personality and Social Psychology, 48,* 63–71.

PART IV

Middle Childhood

19

Cognitive Variability:
A Key to Understanding
Cognitive Development

ROBERT S. SIEGLER

Researchers who adopt an information processing approach to cognitive development emphasize the ways in which children gradually overcome limitations imposed by their immature bodies and lack of experience. Research based on this perspective focuses largely on the development of particular cognitive processes such as memory, perception, or problem solving. This approach has yielded important insights into how the mind is organized and how cognitive development occurs. In the following article, Robert Siegler discusses findings from research using an information processing approach and argues that, at every level of cognitive development, children's thinking is much more varied or diverse than stage-like approaches have assumed.

Among the most remarkable characteristics of human beings is how much our thinking changes with age. When we compare the thinking of an infant, a toddler, an elementary school student, and an adolescent, the magnitude of the change is immediately apparent. Accounting for how these changes occur is perhaps the central goal of researchers who study cognitive development.

Alongside this agreement about the importance of the goal of determining how change occurs,

Reprinted with permission from the author and *Current Directions in Psychological Science, Vol. 3,* 1994, 1–5. Published by Cambridge University Press, New York. Copyright 1994 by the American Psychological Society.

Preparation of this article was made possible by grants from the Spencer Foundation, the National Institutes of Health, and the Mellon Foundation to the author. Special thanks go to Kevin Crowley for his careful readings and excellent suggestions regarding the article.

however, is agreement that we traditionally have not done very well in meeting it. In most models of cognitive development, children are depicted as thinking or acting in a certain way for a prolonged period of time, then undergoing a brief, rather mysterious, transition, and then thinking or acting in a different way for another prolonged period. For example, on the classic conservation-of-liquid quantity problem, children are depicted as believing for several years that pouring water into a taller, thinner beaker changes the amount of water; then undergoing a short period of cognitive conflict, in which they are not sure about the effects of pouring the water; and then realizing that pouring does not affect the amount of liquid. How children get from the earlier to the later understanding is described only superficially.

Critiques of the inadequacy of such accounts have been leveled most often at stage models such as Piaget's. The problem, however, is far more pervasive. Regardless of whether the particular approach describes development in terms of stages, rules, strategies, or theories; regardless of whether the focus is on reasoning about the physical or the social world; regardless of the age group of central interest, most theories place static states at center stage and change processes either in the wings or offstage altogether. Thus, 3-year-olds are said to have nonrepresentational theories of mind and 5-year-olds representational ones; 5-year-olds to have absolute views about justice and 10-year-olds relativistic ones; 10-year-olds to be incapable and 15-year-olds capable of true scientific reasoning. The emphasis in almost all cognitive-developmental theories has been on identifying sequences of one-to-one correspondences between ages and ways of thinking or acting, rather than on specifying how the changes occur.

If developmentalists are so interested in change processes, why would the topic be given such cursory treatment in most contemporary theories? Part of the problem is that studying change is inherently difficult. It poses all the conceptual and methodological demands of studying performance at any one time, and imposes the added demands of determining what is changing and how the change is being accomplished.

An additional part of the difficulty, however, may be self-imposed. In our efforts to describe differences among age groups in as simple, dramatic, and memorable terms as possible, we may unwittingly have made understanding change more difficult than it needs to be. In particular, portraying children's thinking and knowledge as monolithic for several years at a time creates a need to explain the wide gulfs between the successive hypothesized understandings—even though such gulfs may not exist. The typical depictions make change a rare, almost exotic, event that demands an exceptional explanation. If children of a given age have for several years had a particular understanding, why would they suddenly form a different understanding, and why would they regularly form it at a particular age? The problem is exacerbated by the fact that for many of the competencies of interest, generally relevant experience is available at all ages and specifically relevant experience at none. Children see liquids poured into containers of different dimensions at all ages—and are not ordinarily told at any age that the amount of liquid remains the same after pouring as before. Why, then, would they consistently have one concept of liquid quantity conservation at age 5 and a different one at age 7?

Recognition of the unwelcome side effects of the one-to-one depictions of cognitive growth has led to a new generation of research that focuses directly on changes in children's thinking. This research has documented large-scale variability in children's thinking and suggests that the variability contributes directly to cognitive growth.

PERVASIVE VARIABILITY

Variability in children's thinking exists at every level—not just between children of different ages, or between different children of the same age, but also within an individual solving a set of related problems, within an individual solving the same problem twice, and even within an individual on a single trial.

Variability Within an Individual Solving Related Problems

Detailed analyses of tasks on which one-to-one correspondences between age and way of thinking have been postulated indicate that children's thinking is generally much more variable than past depictions have suggested. To cite an example from language development, rather than young children passing through a stage in which they always overregularize past tense forms (e.g., saying "goed" and "eated" rather than "went" and "ate"), children at all ages between 2½ and 5 years produce both substantial numbers of overregularized forms and substantial numbers of correct ones. The variability throughout this age range is present for a single child followed throughout the period, as well as for groups of children sampled at a single age. Adding to the variability, children often produce more than one incorrect form of a given verb; on different occasions, a given child will say, "I ate it," "I eated it," and "I ated it."[1]

Similar variability has been found in the development of memory strategies. Contrary to the widely cited model that 5-year-olds do not rehearse and 8-year-olds do, trial-by-trial assessments indicate that the majority of children of both ages sometimes do and sometimes do not rehearse.[2] The percentage of trials on which they rehearse increases with age, but, again, there is variability throughout the age range.

Conceptual development evidences the same pattern. Despite claims that 5-year-olds think of number conservation solely in terms of the lengths of the rows, trial-by-trial assessments indicate that most 5-year-olds sometimes rely on the lengths of the rows, sometimes rely on the type of transformation, and sometimes use other strategies such as counting or pairing.[3] Again, the frequency of reliance on these ways of thinking changes with age, but most 5-year-olds' judgments and verbal explanations indicate several different ways of thinking about the concept.

Development of problem-solving skills provides yet more evidence for such within-subject cognitive variability. Contradicting models in which preschoolers are said to use the sum strategy (counting from 1) to solve simple addition problems and in which first through third graders are said to use the min strategy (counting from the larger addend, as when solving 3 + 6 by counting "6, 7, 8, 9") to solve them, children of all these ages use a variety of strategies. In one study, most children presented a set of addition problems used at least three different strategies on different problems, and most children examined in a more extensive microlongitudinal study used at least five distinct strategies.[4]

Variability Within an Individual Solving a Single Problem Twice

The variability within individual children cannot be reduced to children using different strategies on different problems. Even presented the identical problem twice within a single session, or on 2 successive days, children use different strategies on roughly one third of the pairs of trials in addition, timetelling, and block-building tasks.[5] This variability within individuals within problems cannot be explained by learning; in these studies, children used the strategy that appeared more advanced

almost as often for the first presentation of a problem as for the second (roughly 45% vs. 55%).

Variability Within a Single Trial

In the limiting case, variability has been found even within an individual solving a particular problem on a single trial. This type of variability has been reported by investigators interested in the relation between children's hand gestures and verbal explanations. In these studies, children often express one type of understanding through the gestures and a quite different understanding through the explanations.[6] For example, on number conservation problems, children may express a reliance on relative lengths of the rows in their hand gestures, while at the same time verbally expressing reliance on the type of transformation, or vice versa.

These findings suggest that cognitive change is better thought of in terms of changing distributions of ways of thinking than in terms of sudden shifts from one way of thinking to another. The types of descriptions of change that emerge from such analyses are illustrated in Figures 1 and 2. Figure 1 shows changes in 3 children's addition strategies over a 3-month period;[4] Figure 2 shows changes in a child's map-drawing strategies over a 2-year period.[7] Similar changes in distributions of strategies have been found in studies of conceptual understanding, memory strategies, problem solving, and language. In all these domains, cognitive development involves changing distributions of approaches, rather than discontinuous movements from one way of thinking to another.

VARIABILITY AND COGNITIVE CHANGE

Variability is not just an incidental feature of thinking; it appears to play a critical role in promoting cognitive change. Several types of evidence converge on this conclusion. One comes from observations of children in the process of discovering new strategies. Both the trials immediately before a discovery and the trial on which the discovery is made frequently involve especially variable behavior—disfluencies, unclear references, long pauses, and unusual gestures.[4] A second type of empirical evidence linking variability to cognitive change involves analyses of which children are most likely to make discoveries. Children whose verbal explanations and gestures reflect different initial misunderstandings of number conservation and of numerical equivalence problems (a + b + c = __ + c) are more likely to make

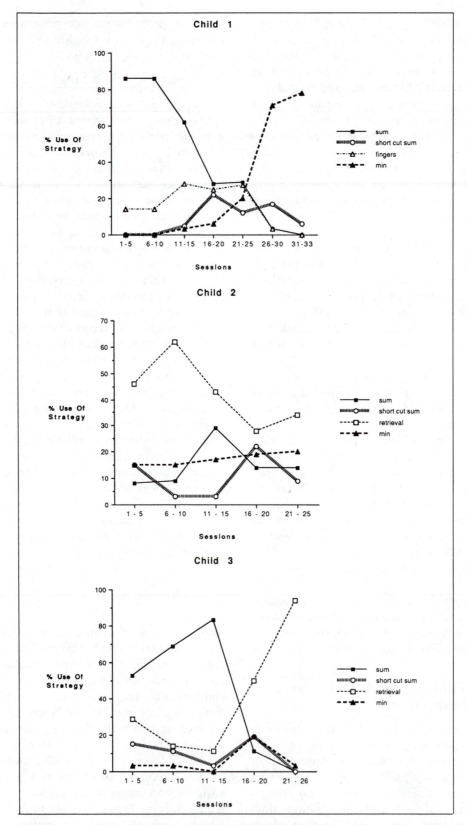

FIGURE 1   Changes in distributions of addition strategies of 3 children over roughly 30 sessions conducted over a 3-month period. Notice the variability that is present within each child's performance within each block of sessions, as well as the changes in distributions of strategy use over the course of the study (data from Siegler and Jenkins[4]).

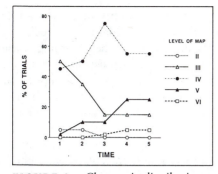

FIGURE 2 Changes in distributions of map-drawing approaches across five sessions, conducted over a 2-year period. Higher numbers indicate more advanced levels of map drawing; thus, Level IV maps are more advanced than Level III ones (data from Feldman[7]).

discoveries subsequently than are children whose explanations and gestures reflect the same initial misunderstanding.[6] Similarly, children whose pretest explanations reflect varied ways of thinking are more likely to learn from instruction regarding the meaning of the equal sign in mathematics than are children whose pretest explanations reflect crisp, specific misunderstandings.[8]

A different type of evidence for the contribution of variability to cognitive change comes from formal models of development. Theorists who differ in many particular assumptions have found that modeling change requires both mechanisms that produce variability and mechanisms that produce adaptive choices among the variants. Connectionist models of development are based on connection strengths among processing units varying at all points in learning, from initial, randomly varying strengths to final, asymptotic levels; change occurs through redistributions of the varying connection strengths. Dynamic systems models also treat variability as a fundamental property of development; they aim to explain how local variability gives rise to global regularities. Similarly, recent symbolic-processing models of development focus on how varying strategies, analogies, and other higher order units come to be used increasingly in the situations in which they are most effective. At a less formal level, operant conditioning models, evolutionarily based models, and generate-and-test models are all based on the assumption that change occurs through selection processes operating on omnipresent, spontaneously produced variability in behavior.[9]

A striking empirical finding about the variability in children's thinking, and one that is important for its ability to contribute to cognitive development, is the constrained quality of the variations that children generate. Far from conforming to a trial-and-error model, in which all types of variations might be expected, the new approaches that children attempt consistently conform to the principles that define legal strategies in the domain (except when children are forced to solve problems for which they do not possess any adequate strategy). For example, in a 30-session study of preschoolers' discovery of new addition strategies, none of the children ever attempted strategies that violated the principles underlying addition.[4] They invented legitimate new strategies, such as the min strategy, but never illegitimate ones, such as adding the smaller addend to itself or counting from the larger addend the number of times indicated by the first addend. The question is how they limit their newly generated strategies to legal forms.

One possibility is that even before discovering new strategies, children often understand the goals that legitimate strategies in the domain must satisfy. Such understanding would allow them, without trial and error, to discriminate between legitimate new strategies that meet the essential goals and illegitimate strategies that do not. A very recent study revealed that children possessed such knowledge in both of the domains that were examined—simple addition and tic-tac-toe.[10] In simple addition, children who had not yet discovered the min strategy nonetheless judged that strategy (demonstrated by the experimenter) to be as smart as the strategy they themselves most often used—counting from 1—and significantly smarter than an equally novel but illegitimate strategy that the experimenter demonstrated. In tic-tac-toe, children rated a novel strategy that they did not yet use—forking—as even smarter than the strategy they themselves usually employed—trying to complete a single row or column. Ability to anticipate the value of untried strategies may promote cognitive growth by filtering out unpromising possibilities and thus channeling innovations in potentially useful directions.

CONCLUSIONS

Thinking is far more variable than usually depicted. In the past, researchers have usually ignored such variability or viewed it as a bother. This stance has led to subjects being given practice periods, not so the especially variable behavior in those periods can be studied, but so that it can be discarded, in order that it not obscure the more orderly patterns in later performance. When such variability has been explicitly noted at all, it has usually been viewed as an unfortunate limitation of human beings, a kind of design defect, something to be overcome through practice. Computers, robots, and other machines not subject to this flaw can perform many tasks more accurately than people can. Presumably, people's performance would also be enhanced if it were less variable.

This view of variability as detracting from efficient performance misses at least half the story, though. The variability of cognition and action allows us to discover a great deal about the environments toward which the thinking and action are directed. Our difficulty in reproducing the way we pronounced a word in an unfamiliar foreign language may lead to some even less adequate pronunciations in the short run, but in the longer run may lead us to generate and then learn better pronunciations. Likewise, our inability to give a colloquium in the same words twice, even when we want to, may lead to some parts being less clear than in the best of our previous presentations, but it also allows us to observe audience reaction to new lines of argument and to learn which ones are best received. In general, cognitive variability may lead to performance never incorporating on any one occasion all the best features of previous performance, but also may be critical to our becoming increasingly proficient over time.

If cognitive variability does indeed facilitate learning, it would be adaptive if such variability were most pronounced when learning, rather than efficient performance, is most important—that is, in infancy and early childhood. This appears to be the case. Across many domains, expertise brings with it decreasingly variable performance. To the extent that young children are "universal novices," their lack of expertise alone would lead to their performance being more variable than that of older children and adults. A number of cognitive neuroscientists have hypothesized that above and beyond such effects of practice, the process of synaptogenesis, which results in children from roughly birth to age 7 having far more synaptic connections than older children and adults, may contribute both to the high variability of early behavior and to young children's special ability to acquire language, perceptual skills, and other competencies under abnormal organismic and environmental conditions.[11] That is, young children's greater variability at the neural level seems to allow them to learn useful behaviors under a greater range of circumstances. The general lesson seems to be that explicitly recognizing the great variability of infants' and young children's thinking, and attempting to explain how it is generated and constrained, will advance our understanding of the central mystery about cognitive development—how change occurs.

Questions

1. Why, according to Siegler, has it been difficult for cognitive developmental psychologists to study the process of mental change?

2. What evidence does Siegler use to support his claim that variability in mental development is more the norm than the exception?

3. If variability is characteristic of mental functioning at any particular point in development, what is the best way, according to Siegler, to describe cognitive change?

Notes

1. S. A. Kuczaj, The acquisition of regular and irregular past tense forms, *Journal of Verbal Learning and Verbal Behavior, 16,* 589–600 (1977).

2. K. McGilly and R. S. Siegler, The influence of encoding and strategic knowledge on children's choices among serial recall strategies, *Developmental Psychology, 26,* 939–941 (1990).

3. R. S. Siegler, *A microgenetic study of number conservation,* manuscript in preparation, Carnegie Mellon University, Pittsburgh (1993).

4. R. S. Siegler and E. Jenkins, *How Children Discover New Strategies* (Erlbaum, Hillsdale, NJ, 1989).

5. R. S. Siegler and K. McGilly, Strategy choices in children's time-telling, in *Time and Human Cognition: A Life Span Perspective,* I. Levin and D. Zakay, Eds. (Elsevier Science, Amsterdam, 1989); R. S. Siegler and J. Shrager, Strategy choices in addition and subtraction: How do children know what to do? in *The Origins of Cognitive Skills,* C. Sophian, Ed. (Erlbaum, Hillsdale, NJ, 1984); A.C. Wilkinson, Partial knowledge and self-correction: Developmental studies of a quantitative concept, *Developmental Psychology, 18,* 876–893 (1982).

6. R. B. Church and S. Goldin-Meadow, The mismatch between gesture and speech as an index of transitional knowledge, *Cognition, 23,* 43–71 (1986);

S. Goldin-Meadow and M. W. Alibali, Transitions in concept acquisition: Using the hand to read the mind, *Psychological Review* (in press).

7. D. H. Feldman, *Beyond Universals in Cognitive Development* (Ablex, Norwood, NJ, 1980).

8. T. Graham and M. Perry, Indexing transitional knowledge, *Developmental Psychology, 29, 779–788* (1993).

9. For examples of these perspectives, see D. T. Campbell, Evolutionary epistemology, in *The Philosophy of Karl Popper,* Vol. 14, P. A. Schilpp, Ed. (Open Court, La Salle, IL, 1974); J. L. McClelland and E. Jenkins, Nature, nurture, and connections: Implications of connectionist models for cognitive development, in *Architectures for Intelligence,* K. Van Lehn, Ed. (Erlbaum, Hillsdale, NJ, 1991); L. B. Smith and E. Thelen, Eds., *Dynamical Systems in Development: Applications* (Bradford Books, Cambridge, MA, in press); B. F. Skinner, Selection by consequences, *Science, 213,* 509–504 (1981).

10. R. S. Siegler and K. Crowley, Goal sketches constrain children's strategy discoveries, *Cognitive Psychology* (in press).

11. P. S. Goldman-Rakic, Development of cortical circuitry and cognitive function, Child Development, 58, 609–622 (1987); W. T. Greenough, J. E. Black, and C. Wallace, Experience and brain development, *Child Development, 58,* 539–559 (1987).

20

Culture and Testing

DALTON MILLER-JONES

Of the many individual differences that distinguish one person from another, none has produced a stormier and more prolonged debate than intelligence. During the entire twentieth century, psychologists have sought valid measures of children's intelligence that would not be influenced by family background or cultural origins. However, the goal of creating a "culture-free" test has eluded psychologists. Dalton Miller-Jones discusses this issue, focusing on the performance of African American children. He concludes that a contextualist approach to intelligence testing is more accurate in assessing the intellectual competencies of children from diverse ethnic backgrounds.

The accurate assessment of cognitive abilities in individuals not from mainstream Anglo-American backgrounds is encumbered by several factors. Chief among these is the difficulty of inferring underlying cognitive processes from performances on standardized tests. Recent developments in contextualist analyses of cognitive performance, such as cultural practice theory, argue (a) that skills are acquired in specific learning activity contexts and therefore tests of generalized cognitive functioning will inevitably provide a less than accurate portrayal of individuals' capacities; and (b) that appropriate assessment requires an understanding of the constraints that govern access to a person's knowledge and regulate the deployment of concepts and reasoning processes.

In this article I examine recent research and theory concerning the assessment of cognitive abilities in culturally distinct populations, particularly Afro-

---

Reprinted with permission from the author and *American Psychologist, 44,* 1989, 343–348.
Copyright 1989 by the American Psychological Association.

American children, in order to provide a better understanding of variation in performance on tests of ability and academic achievement. Most tests of ability and achievement have been specifically designed to reveal individual differences in performances. The question is, where do such differences come from, or to what causes do we attribute variations in cognitive performance? Any satisfactory answer to this question must perforce involve an examination of our conceptions of those processes that constitute competence in the particular domain of knowledge that a test purports to measure as well as the way we characterize individuals along dimensions of experience and group membership. Cross-cultural research and studies of ethnic groups within the United States over the past two decades have revealed the critical role that situational contexts play in governing performance.

We are limited in discussing cultural differences in test performance by two facts: (a) There is controversy over the exact nature of the processes constituting mental abilities; and (b) there is little agreement on how best to represent the concept of "culture." In the sections that follow, I first discuss issues of the validity in test content and procedures because these have direct consequences for the question of cultural influences on test performance. This discussion is followed by a review of cross-cultural research in which it has been argued that competencies are acquired within and tied to specific task and interpersonal event contexts. Within this framework, culture is thought to exert its influence on cognition by determining the kinds of activities or practices an individual typically engages in. In this view it is the individual's interpretation of the task itself that influences the performance; and this interpretation is related to both the features of the task *and* previous cultural experiences. Finally, I discuss the implications of this research and make recommendations for assessment.

TESTING ISSUES

Arguments Supportive of Standardized Tests

Tests of ability and achievement are widely used for a variety of reasons, including their widespread public and professional acceptance (Snyderman & Rothman, 1987) and their relative cost-efficiency in administration and reporting. Testing has developed into a major commercial enterprise that subserves several institutionalized functions, including *accountability* in assessing the effectiveness of teachers, schools, and school districts; *selection and sorting* of students for placement in special programs or ability groupings; and *curricular decisions* such as determining which subject areas teachers should emphasize in classroom instruction (though this may lead to "teaching to the test").

In all of these areas it is assumed that we know what abilities are being assessed, that abilities and knowledge can be represented by a numerical score, and that a particular score means the same thing for any individual taking the test. Critics question the veracity of test performances and the utility of test scores as an aid to instructional practice. For example, tests of ability and achievement are administered at intervals that make it difficult for any useful diagnostic feedback to influence the teaching process for the particular set of children taking the test.

Whereas claims of efficiency and economy are not disputed, it is in the areas of selecting and sorting of students and guiding instructional practices that the use of tests is most often questioned (for an overview of the nature of tests and the role of testing see the *American Psychologist's* special issue on testing, Glaser & Bond, 1981; and Tyler & White, 1979).

Arguments Critical of Standardized Tests

Criticisms of standardized tests of achievement and ability are primarily directed at how well these tests meet the following underlying premises: (a) that the structure of a knowledge domain is sufficiently understood such that it can be adequately represented in a sample of items; (b) that the processes underlying such knowledge are adequately reflected in the item's content and keyed alternatives to yield valid inferences from differential performances; (c) that such items are not *biased* and can be written and illustrated in ways that *do not favor a particular sociocultural experience over any other*—that is, one wants a set of items that reduce the chances of nonrandom extraneous influences to a minimum; and finally (d) that items, especially for achievement tests, will be *fair*—that is, the content sampled by items needs to reflect the kind of coverage of subject matter likely to be encountered by most students.

The problems of inferring cognitive processes from test performance and eliminating extraneous influences on performance arising from aspects of the testing situation pose particular problems for tests as indicators of the amount of learning accomplished.

Inferring Cognitive Processes

One of the fundamental problems for tests of mental ability is the lack of theoretical consensus concerning the exact nature of cognitive processes underlying the items themselves (Frederiksen, 1986; Neisser, 1976, 1985, 1986). Neisser (1986), for example, suggested that one of the most compelling reasons to avoid entering a debate about culture and testing of mental abilities is "the confusion surrounding the concept of intelligence itself" (p. 13). Theorists have proposed various subdivisions of intelligence, such as Thurstone's six or more primary factors; Cattell's two or three higher-order factors; Guilford's 120 factors along three dimensions; and Gardner's (1983) distinct domains of "intelligences"—language, mathematics, music, spatial representation, bodily movement, and personal relationships.

So there is confusion about the *definition* of intellectual abilities. But the problem and the concern go deeper than this. I argue that we do not know *which* intellectual skill is being assessed by any particular set of items or subtests. Farnham-Diggory (1970), commenting on Jensen's (1969) Level I (associative-learning) and Level II (conceptual-learning) abilities, observed, "Many Level II tasks are such jumbles of psychological functions that a defective performance tells us very little about the systematic nature of the defect itself" (p. 2). Even with tests that are supposed to be specific measures of factors, such as Thurstone's Primary Mental Abilities Test (PMA), Farnham-Diggory (1970) noted, "Each test is clearly a conglomerate of functions, and we have no way of knowing which mental operation is in fact more difficult for Black children" (p. 2). Thorndike (1927) pointed to three fundamental defects of standardized intelligence tests:

> Just what they measure is not known; how far it is proper to add, subtract, multiply, divide, and compute ratios with the measures obtained is not known; just what the measures obtained signify concerning intellect is not known. We may refer to these defects in order as ambiguity in content, arbitrariness in units, and ambiguity in significance. (p. 28)

An inspection of the item content of ability tests reveals problems in defining which cognitive processes are being assessed as well as inconsistencies in criteria invoked across questions. The following example from the Stanford-Binet Intelligence Scale, Form L-M (Terman & Merrill, 1973, pp. 79, 138–139) for four- to six-year-olds illustrates this point[1]:

	Correct	Incorrect
What is a *house* made of?	Wood. Boards. Bricks. Cement. Stucco. Shingles. Stone. Lumber. Blocks. Rocks.	Sticks. Nails. Walls.
What is a *book* made of?	Paper. Cloth. Leather. Plastic. Pages are made of paper and the outside is made of something hard.	Pictures. Pages. Cards. Pastings. Made out of pictures and covers.

What cognitive principle is measured by these items and what intellectual distinction is made between acceptable and unacceptable responses? What is being discerned, for example, by accepting "A house is made of wood" and *not* accepting "A house is made of walls" or "Books are made of pictures and pages"? It can be concluded that, in general, the accepted responses do not incorporate all reasonably intelligent responses to the question. The only discernible criterion for not accepting some of the alternative responses is that by considering these responses as incorrect a significant proportion of children at a particular age in the standard sample "pass" the item while a critical number of younger children "fail" it; the decision is based on differentiation by age norms for items, not on logical soundness. This is one reason why, if given a choice, "criterion" referenced tests (i.e., tests based on theoretically defined criteria of skill attainment) are preferred over "norm" referenced tests based on average age or grade performance.

The Testing Situation

In addition to the lack of theoretical specificity, another difficulty in determining competence using standardized tests is that the constraints imposed in test construction and administration for the purposes of test reliability do not provide for adjustments in procedures to account for possible response biases in children. It is axiomatic that the test must be administered using a constant format that precludes test administrators from providing any feedback to individuals to help clarify the question being asked (Frederiksen, 1986). Such constraints do not permit one to distinguish between performance and capacity (Cole & Bruner, 1971). In almost every case the tester is *not* permitted to probe, answer questions, or encourage individuals to try an alternative answer. Consequently, such procedures may underestimate children's skills. Because some responses are more frequently used and therefore have priority of access for the child, the tests measure the first response that occurs to the child, his or her first approximation. This may be a simple association, which is *not* what the test-maker is looking for. A five-year-old lower middle class Afro-American provides examples:

Similarities
Tester: "How are wood and coal alike? How are they the same?"
Child: "They're hard."
Tester: "An apple and a peach?"
Child: "They taste good."
Tester: "A ship and an automobile?"
Child: "They're hard."
Tester: "Iron and silver?"
Child: "They're hard."

Because no feedback is permitted, the child must guess what the tester wants, and the child appears to have decided that anything she says will be acceptable. Earlier in the testing session the child provided evidence that she was seeking some definition of the task situation by providing her own evaluative feedback ("I'm good at this one!") and by inquiring about the tester's behavior:

Picture Identification
Tester: "Show me what we cook on . . . Show me the one that catches mice."
Child: [Points correctly, then comments] "You forgot the clock."
Tester: "I know. We're not using all the pictures."

Picture Vocabulary
Tester: "What's this? What do you call it?"
Child: "Leaf."
Tester: [Writes child's response in test booklet]
Child: "Now you got to write in script, right? *Leaves.*"

Definitions
Tester: "Pat, what is a ball?"
Child: "You kick balls."
Tester: "What is a hat?"
Child: "You put it on your head."

Tester: "What is a stove?"
Child: "You cook. That's what you writing down?"
Tester: "Yeah. I'm writing down what you say so I can remember it later."
Child: [Incredulously] "Cause you don't know what it's for?"

These examples illustrate how decrements in performance may result from the interpersonal aspects of the testing situation rather than from the absence of a particular competence (Canady, 1936; Labov, 1972; Rogoff & Mistry, 1985; Seymour & Miller-Jones, 1981). Children may not share the same understanding of the social context or the nature of the format in testing situations. Attempts to interpret and establish a task's *meaning*, such as those illustrated above, are undoubtedly related to a person's prior culturally contexted activities.

In addition, these social-cultural experiences may stress sets of competencies and cognitive organizations different from those expected in assessment situations (Goodnow, 1976; Seymour & Miller-Jones, 1981). The child in the examples just cited gave primarily *functional-relational* classifications of objects; that is, she showed she has the capacity to spontaneously classify according to *conceptual category* (e.g., when asked what an orange was, she replied, "a fruit"). The issue then is not one of whether the person has the capacity for this kind of intellectual operation. We must ask, instead, what are the contextually imposed constraints that govern access to knowledge within a domain and regulate the deployment of the cognitive schema or structure under investigation (Mistry & Rogoff, 1985).

The proposition that children have many culturally determined problem-solving and information-organizing strategies available to them, if true, poses a more serious problem for ability and achievement test construction than the more commonly cited concern for cultural and gender biases in the language and content of specific items (Block & Dworkin, 1976). For example, test publishers such as the Educational Testing Service (1987) have instituted item review procedures for modifying or eliminating items that have differential error rates for women and ethnic groups or that have insensitive or offensive language and content. However, the possibility that differences in test performance result more from preferences in or differential access to cognitive modes requires modifying test administration formats and developing more flexible testing procedures. If ability tests are to achieve more veridical assessments of children whose experiences are different from those of mainstream Anglo-Americans, an important item on the testing research agenda will have to be systematic determination of the contingencies governing the use of these processing repertoires.

It is important to note that Jensen (1980) dismissed criticisms based on selective anecdotal scrutiny of items, as presented here. Relying on Spearman's original unitary concept of intelligence, or "g" factor, Jensen argued that

> in an intelligence test the specific content of the items is unessential, so long *as it is apprehended or perceived in the same way by all persons taking the test. . . .* The content of the items is a mere vehicle for the essential elements of intelligence test items. (italics added, p. 127)

It is precisely the issue of determining uniform item apprehension that is at the center of the concern for cultural influences on testing. By not accepting responsibility for item integrity, in terms of underlying processes, the position stated in the above quote can lead tests of ability and achievement to cognitive bankruptcy.

CULTURE AND ASSESSMENT OF COGNITIVE ABILITIES

If experiences within particular social-cultural contexts significantly influence cognitive performance, how does one define such contexts and specify the processes by which influence is exerted? In this section I review two closely related approaches to the investigation of differential performance between and within cultural and subcultural groups: analyses based on cultural practices and social-cognitive ecology. Both approaches represent a form of contextualism (Pepper, 1942) because they emphasize that an understanding of performances "requires knowledge of the situation in which they occur and the purpose of the actions they include" (Kendler, 1986, p. 87).

An alternative view, the universalist approach, has as its conceptual goal the description of the development of abstract logically necessary thinking, the structures of which are constructed through the person's mental reflections on his or her actions in the world (Dasen, 1977; Piaget, 1974). Universalist theories such as Piaget's are inherently *acultural* in the sense that structures of knowledge may be constrained by cultural experiences but are not determined by it (Glick, 1985). Research in several cultures on the attainment of Piagetian logical struc-

tures has provided only partial support for the universalist position. On the one hand, there is evidence that individuals in most cultures display cognitive operations characteristic of Piaget's early stages, that is, preoperational and early concrete operational thinking. On the other hand, there is great variation in the age or rate of attainment and many people never demonstrate reasoning associated with later stages, that is, late concrete and formal logical operations (Dasen, 1977; Laboratory of Comparative Human Cognition, 1983). Both the forms of reasoning in these latter stages and the measures used to assess them appear to be highly specific to and sensitive to cultural experience (Glick, 1985).

Cultural Practice Perspective

Research investigating cognitive operations such as memory or classification in diverse cultural groups has found evidence for commonly held cognitive abilities (Cole, Gay, Glick, & Sharp, 1971). It is significant that demonstrations of these competencies required adjustments in experimental task content and procedures to render them more culturally appropriate (Cole & Scribner, 1973). However, equating tasks or items for cultural appropriateness or familiarity is extremely difficult. The Laboratory for Comparative Human Cognition (LCHC, 1982) asked,

> If we change the instructions, do we change the task or the context? If we are working in a culture where adults do not ask children known-answer questions, or where one-to-one dialogue with a strange adult is unknown, or where sleight of hand is a culturally valued practice, how are we to make the task familiar when it is, *because of differences in culturally organized contexts for thinking,* an unfamiliar form of interaction? (p. 688)

Furthermore, when attempting to achieve task and stimulus equivalence, simple "objective" descriptive equivalence is insufficient. Tasks and items need to be "functionally equivalent" or similar from the point of view of the cultural subject (LCHC, 1982). Establishing task equivalence is exceedingly difficult. However, when exhaustive efforts are made to achieve these conditions (i.e., using familiar and culturally relevant situations, procedures, and materials), the people are more likely to perform competently. Such observations led Cole et al. (1971) to conclude that "cultural differences in cognition reside more in the situations to which particular cognitive processes are applied than in the existence of a process in one cultural group, and its absence in another" (p. 233).

In formulating a theory of cultural practice, Scribner and Cole (1981; LCHC, 1982, 1983) rejected the notion of a central cognitive processor that operates across several knowledge domains. They argued instead that learning is *predominantly* context- or task-specific. The evidence cited for rejecting the concept of a generalized cognitive processor is primarily based on the findings that abilities manifested in one task context do not transfer or generalize to other domains of assessment (LCHC, 1982; Rogoff & Gauvain, 1984; Scribner & Cole, 1981). It has been argued that some cultures may provide systematic practice in thinking outside the context of one's daily experience; for example, it is claimed that Euro-American school experiences have been shown to produce somewhat more generalized thinking (Price-Williams, 1975). However, other research has challenged this claim, finding instead that skills are tied to the specific context in which they are practiced (see reviews by Rogoff, 1981; Sharp, Cole, & Lave, 1979).

Scribner and Cole (1981) compared the performances of four groups literate in school-taught English, Vai script (an indigenous African language), Qur'anic (based on memorization of the Koran), and Arabic on a variety of cognitive tasks. They reported differences in performances associated with skills practiced in each of the literacy contexts. For example, experiences with Qur'anic recitation were associated with superior performance on serial recall tasks, and school-English literates ranked highest in the ability to provide better verbal explanations of their logic, grammatical rules, and criteria for sorting. Scribner and Cole found no significant effect of schooling in tasks considered to tap the use of more generalized cognitive skills, such as taxonomic clustering in free recall or in grouping objects by class membership.

A cultural practice analysis derives from the observation that tests of ability and achievement are in fact context-specific assessment environments with culturally specific content. Appropriate assessment involves a determination of how well any particular assessment situation matches the function-specific practices individuals experience as part of their culturally contexted activities (Rogoff, 1982). To apply this context-specific approach to individual difference testing would require the development of something like a theory of contexts, which would permit a determination of task equivalence for the purpose of testing transfer of abilities.

There is, then, a need to reintegrate a conceptualization of the individual's reasoning processes and knowledge representations with an emphasis on cognitive processes being tied to task activities and on locating tasks in relation to culturally organized activities. It may be impossible to achieve task or context equivalence between highly divergent cultures; however, an understanding of factors leading to the application of processing strategies across situations (intersituational generalization) may be within our reach. It is toward this end that the construct of social-cognitive ecology is offered.

Social-Cognitive Ecology

A social-cognitive ecology analysis focuses on the possibility of more generalized cognitive operations or approaches to solving problems that transfer across specific task boundaries. It has been proposed that children have organized repertoires of possible responses to a question and that culture determines the availability or priority of access to any one of them, including those the test-maker has in mind. The social-cognitive ecology form of contextualism (Miller-Jones, 1981; Ogbu, 1985) suggests that some cognitive processes may be more functionally adaptive and more frequently used and thus have higher priority than others.

An ecological analysis of the impact of culture on children's developing information organizations, knowledge systems, and processes of acquisition leans heavily on analogies drawn from the conception of the role of environment in evolution theory (Miller-Jones, 1981, in press). Critical to the concept of adaptation is the proposition that an organism's ecology—the dynamic sets of relationships between organic and physical processes—operates as a critical selection force determining the adaptive fitness of organisms and as such constitutes a central construct in evolution theory. From this perspective, children's social-cultural ecologies pose problems and tasks that function to organize intellectual processes (Ogbu, 1985, 1986). Furthermore, the meaning taken in a given task situation will reflect cultural values for interpreting the situation. Accordingly, these values are acquired often implicitly through the dynamics of social interactions.

Several studies of Afro-American children attempt to elucidate the nature of logical processes and cognitive skills from the perspective of adaptations to the task demands characteristic of their social-cognitive ecologies. Boykin (1978, 1982) referred to aspects of Black cultural-physical ecology in suggesting that the high ambient levels of stimulation experienced by many urban Black children may lead to higher levels of activation and needs for stimulus variation in both affective and cognitive domains. Evidence for this "vervistic" quality in Black children's cognitive systems is seen in their superior performance on tasks that vary in format—essentially, the more changing the format, the better their performance compared to that of Anglo children. Consequently, testing might benefit from using multiple task formats.

Social-cognitive patterning within the home and neighborhood environment may exert a determining influence on the child's cognitive processes (Sigel, 1970). For example, Cohen (1971) reported that relational conceptual styles, as opposed to analytic styles, are associated with families that have flexible interchangeable functional roles (e.g., who does child-care, cooks meals). This social-cognitive patterning relates to what Ogbu (1985) referred to as the "opportunity structure." Essentially, these patterns are dictated by the highly contingent circumstances typical of the under-resourced life space of the urban poor. Sigel (1970) found that lower class children may use more relational categories in classification sorting tasks and that this reflected differences in representational competence produced by the lack of "distancing experiences" in lower class homes. Distancing experiences are considered those parental practices that provide the opportunity for differentiation and abstraction, and middle-class homes typically have more of these.

Several investigations support the view that children have the capacity for the various kinds of intellectual operations and knowledge organizations that we are typically interested in assessing but that some of these operations and organizations occupy lower levels of probability of occurrence than others within a child's repertoire of problem-solving heuristics (Franklin, 1978; Simmons, 1979). I argue that the child's interpretation of the *meaning* of a task or situation determines which reasoning processes he or she will deploy and that such "meanings" are the product of the interaction between the child's knowledge (i.e., his or her internal representation of past experiences) and the properties of the task (i.e., external features) at hand (Miller-Jones, in press).

RECOMMENDATIONS FOR ASSESSMENT

It is important to consider children's repertoires of cognitive processes and the contingencies affecting their use in order to improve success in assessing the competencies of children from diverse ethnic backgrounds. What does this mean for testing? At the moment the implications are general:

1. For any knowledge domain one must specify the possible processes that may be involved or elicited by tasks and stimuli (LCHC, 1982). In this, cross-cultural psychology agrees with the approach typically associated with information-processing methods of task analysis (Glaser, 1981).

2. One should use multiple tasks, with a variety of different materials, with the same individual or population, and not assume generality from a single measure. Furthermore, one has to demonstrate that "the range of tasks used to sample a hypothetical domain of intellectual activity actually covers the domain in a representative manner" (LCHC, 1982, p. 654).

3. It is critical that "the tasks used to sample the domain in question do so for the culture in question" (LCHC, 1982, p. 654).

4. Validation procedures need to better establish the relationship between cognitive operations tested and the acquisition of school concepts and skills such as reading, mathematics, writing, and science.

5. Because representations of knowledge may be configured and accessed differently by individuals varying in cultural background, it is important to develop assessment procedures that permit and direct examiners to probe for the reasoning behind a child's response to an item. It is often not a failure to a use a self-generated cognitive strategy that accounts for poor test performance. Rather it is the inconsistent application of an approach or the failure to recognize the cognitive operation the task calls for.

Cultural practice theory has moved us away from a conception of cognitive skills as stable trait-like personal qualities and offered in its place the idea that competencies develop in the context of culturally based activities or practices. The social-cognitive ecology model adds the possibility of enduring or *transcontextual* knowledge and cognitive abilities. The model also is a call to incorporate more aspects of culture into this formulation, to incorporate culture as a symbol system that permits interpretation of task meaning through dialogue, or language in interaction.

Questions

1.   What is the problem caused by the use of standardized tests to assess the intelligence of minority children in the US?

2.   When children take intelligence tests in school the situation can often be very stressful. How do you think stress affects children's performance and do you think it has a differential effect on minority and nonminority children?

3.   Recently, Murray and Herrnstein published a book entitled *The Bell Curve* where they argued that ethnic differences in IQ are based on biological differences in intellectual capability. Given Miller-Jones' argument, do you agree with this claim?

References and Notes

1. Although the examples cited here are taken from tests of mental ability or aptitude, the same qualifications and concerns hold for standardized achievement tests as well. Although one can distinguish between tests of ability and achievement *in principle*, this conceptual distinction is not easy to operationalize. Schwartz (1975) observed that group achievement and ability tests "are sufficiently similar that without the labels one has difficulty telling which is which" (p. 39). It is hardly surprising then that tests of mental ability attain reasonably high correlations with school success (their predictive validity) as measured by achievement tests!

Block, N., & Dworkin, G. (Eds.). (1976). *The IQ controversy*. New York: Pantheon.

Boykin, A. W. (1978). Psychological/behavioral verve as a differentiating factor in the task/academic performance of Afro-Americans and whites: Pretheoretical considerations. *Journal of Negro Education, 47,* 343–354.

Boykin, A. W. (1982). Population differences in the effect of format variability on task performance. *Journal of Black Studies, 12,* 469–485.

Canady, H. G. (1936). The effects of "rapport" on the IQ: A new approach to the problem of racial psychology. *Journal of Negro Education, 5,* 209–219.

Cohen, R. (1971). The influence of conceptual rule-sets on measures of learning ability. In C. L. Bracc, G. R. Gamble, & J. T. Bond (Eds.), *Race and intelligence* (pp. 41–57). Washington, DC: American Anthropological Association.

Cole, M., & Bruner, J. (1971). Cultural differences and inferences about psychological processes. *American Psychologist, 26,* 867–876.

Cole, M., Gay, J., Glick, J., & Sharp, D. W. (1971). *The cultural context of learning and thinking*. New York: Basic Books.

Cole, M., & Scribner, S. (1973). Cognitive consequences of formal and informal education. *Science, 182,* 553–559.

Dasen, P. R. (Ed.). (1977). *Piagetian psychology: Cross-cultural contributions*. New York: Gardner Press.

Educational Testing Service. (1987). *ETS sensitivity review process*. Princeton, NJ: Author.

Farnham-Diggory, S. (1970). Cognitive synthesis in Negro and white children. *Monographs of the Society for Research in Child Development, 35(2,* Serial No. 135).

Franklin, A. J. (1978). Sociolinguistic structure of word lists and ethnic group differences in categorical recall. *Institute for Comparative Human Development Newsletter, 2,* 30–34.

Frederiksen, N. (1986). Toward a broader conception of human intelligence. *American Psychologist, 41,* 445–452,

Gardner, H. (1983). *Frames of mind: The theory of multiple intelligences*. New York: Basic Books.

Glaser, R. (1981). The future of testing. *American Psychologist, 36,* 923–936.

Glaser, R., & Bond, L. (Eds.). (1981). Testing: Concepts, policy, practice, and research [Special issue]. *American Psychologist, 36(10)*.

Glick, J. (1985). Culture and cognition revisited. In E. D. Neimark & R. De Lisi (Eds.), *Moderators of competence* (pp. 99–144). Hillsdale, NJ: Erlbaum.

Goodnow, J. J. (1976). The nature of intelligent behavior: Questions raised by cross-cultural studies. In L. B. Resnick (Ed.), *The nature of intelligence* (pp. 169–188). Hillsdale, NJ: Erlbaum.

Jensen, A. R. (1969). How much can we boost IQ and scholastic achievement? *Harvard Educational Review, 39,* 1–123.

Jensen, A. R. (1980). *Bias in mental testing*. New York: Free Press.

Kendler, T. S. (1986). World views and the concept of development: A reply to Lerner and Kauffman. *Developmental Review, 6,* 80–95.

Laboratory of Comparative Human Cognition. (1982). Culture and intelligence. In R. J. Sternberg (Ed.), *Handbook of human intelligence* (pp. 642–722). New York: Cambridge University Press.

Laboratory of Comparative Human Cognition. (1983). Culture and cognitive development. In W. Kessen (Ed.), *Mussen handbook of child development* (Vol. 1, pp. 295–356). New York: Wiley.

Labov, W. (1972). *Language in the inner city.* Philadelphia: University of Pennsylvania Press.

Miller-Jones, D. (1981). Differences in social and cognitive information processing between high and low achieving five-year old black children. In J. McAdoo & W. Cross (Eds.), *Proceedings of the Fifth Conference on Empirical Research in Black Psychology* (pp. 76–107). Ithaca, NY: Africana Studies and Research Center, Cornell University.

Miller-Jones, D. (in press). Informal reasoning in inner-city children. In J. Voss, D. Perkins, & J. Segal (Eds.), *Informal reasoning in education.* Hillsdale, NJ: Erlbaum.

Mistry, J. J., & Rogoff, B. (1985). A cultural perspective on the development of talent. In F. D. Horowitz & M. O'Brien (Eds.), *The gifted and talented: Developmental perspectives* (pp. 125–144). Washington, DC: American Psychological Association.

Neisser, U. (1976). General, academic, and artificial intelligence. In L. B. Resnick (Ed.), *The nature of intelligence* (pp. 135–144). Hillsdale, NJ: Erlbaum.

Neisser, U. (1985). Toward an ecologically oriented cognitive science. In T. M. Schlechter & M. P. Toglia (Eds.), *New directions in cognitive science* (pp. 17–32). Norwood, NJ: Ablex.

Neisser, U. (Ed.). (1986). *The school achievement of minority children: New perspectives.* Hillsdale, NJ: Erlbaum.

Ogbu, J. U. (1985). A cultural ecology of competence among inner-city blacks. In M. B. Spencer, G. K. Brookins, & W. R. Allen (Eds.), Beginnings: *The social and affective development of black children* (pp. 45–66). Hillsdale, NJ: Erlbaum.

Ogbu, J. U. (1986). The consequences of the American caste system. In U. Neisser (Ed.), *The school achievement of minority children: New perspectives* (pp. 19–56). Hillsdale, NJ: Erlbaum.

Pepper, S. C. (1942). *World hypotheses.* Berkeley: University of California Press.

Piaget, J. (1974). Need and significance of cross-cultural studies in genetic psychology. In J. W. Berry & P. R. Dasen (Eds.), *Culture and cognition: Readings in cross-cultural psychology* (pp. 299–310). London: Methuen.

Price-Williams, D. R. (Ed.). (1975). *Explorations in cross-cultural psychology.* San Francisco: Chandler & Sharp.

Rogoff, B. (1981). Schooling and the development of cognitive skills. In H. Triandis & A. Heron (Eds.), *Handbook of cross-cultural psychology* (Vol. 4, pp. 233–294). Rockleigh, NJ: Allyn & Bacon.

Rogoff, B. (1982). Integrating context and cognitive development. In M. E. Lamb & A. L. Brown (Eds.), *Advances in developmental psychology* (Vol. 2, pp. 125–170). Hillsdale, NJ: Erlbaum.

Rogoff B., & Gauvain, M. (1984). The cognitive consequences of specific experiences: Weaving versus schooling among the Navajo. *Journal of Cross-Cultural Psychology, 15,* 453–475.

Rogoff, B., & Mistry, J. (1985). Memory development in cultural context. In M. Pressley & C. Brainerd (Eds.), *Cognitive learning and memory in children* (pp. 117–142). New York: Springer-Verlag.

Schwartz, J. L. (1975). A is to B as C is to anything at all: The illogic of I.Q. tests. *National Elementary Principal, 54,* 38–41.

Scribner, S., & Cole, M. (1981). *The psychology of literacy.* Cambridge, MA: Harvard University Press.

Seymour, H., & Miller-Jones, D. (1981). Language and cognitive assessment of black children. In N. Lass (Ed.), *Speech and language: Advances in basic research and practice* (Vol. 6, pp. 203–263). New York: Academic Press.

Sharp, D., Cole, M., & Lave, C. (1979). Education and cognitive development: The evidence from experimental research. *Monographs of the Society for Research in Child Development, 44,* (1–2, Serial No. 178).

Sigel, I. E. (1970). The distancing hypothesis: A causal hypothesis for the acquisition of representational thought. In M. R. Jones (Ed.), *Miami Symposium on the Prediction of Behavior, 1986: Effects of early experience* (pp. 73–86). Coral Gables, FL: University of Miami Press.

Simmons, W. (1979). The role of cultural salience in ethnic and social class difference in cognitive performance. In W. Cross, Jr. & A. Harrison (Eds.), *Proceedings of the Fourth Conference on Empirical Research in Black Psychology* (pp. 85–98). Ithaca, NY: Africana Studies and Research Center, Cornell University.

Snyderman, M., & Rothman, S. (1987). Survey of expert opinion on intelligence and aptitude testing. *American Psychologist, 42,* 137–144.

Thorndike, E. L. (1927). *The measurement of intelligence.* New York: Teachers College Bureau of Publications.

Tyler, R., & White, S. (Eds.). (1979). *Testing, teaching and learning.* Washington, DC: U.S. Department of Health, Education and Welfare and National Institute of Education.

Terman, L. M., & Merrill, M. A. (1973). *Stanford-Binet Intelligence Scale.* Chicago: Riverside Publishing.

21

How Asian Teachers Polish Each Lesson to Perfection

JAMES W. STIGLER AND HAROLD W. STEVENSON

Much attention has been directed recently to the educational performance of children in the United States relative to that of children in other societies. James W. Stigler and Harold W. Stevenson have examined the practices and goals of schooling in China, Japan, and the United States. Their observations indicate that both the processes and outcomes of schooling in these three societies reflect deeply held cultural values. These values influence the experiences that children have in school. Their observations suggest that modeling U.S. classrooms after those in other cultures will not necessarily benefit children in the absence of the supporting cultural context from which these practices derive meaning and direction.

Although there is no overall difference in intelligence, the differences in mathematical achievement of American children and their Asian counterparts are staggering.[1]

Let us look first at the results of a study we conducted in 120 classrooms in three cities: Taipei (Taiwan); Sendai (Japan); and the Minneapolis met-ropolitan area. First and fifth graders from representative schools in these cities were given a test of mathematics that required computation and problem solving. Among the one hundred first graders in the three locations who received the lowest scores, fifty-eight were American children; among the one hundred lowest-scoring fifth graders, sixty-seven

Reprinted with permission from the authors and *American Educator*, Spring, 1992, 12–20, 43–47. Copyright 1992 by the American Federation of Teachers. This article is an excerpt from H. S. Stevenson and J. S. Stigler, *The Learning Gap: Why Our Schools Are Failing and What We Can Learn from Japanese and Chinese Education*, New York: Summit Books, 1992.

A thirty-four-minute cassette depicting Japanese and Chinese classroom scenes that illustrate the techniques described in this article is available for $35. Called *The Polished Stones*, it can be ordered from Catherine A. Smith, 300 North Ingalls, 10th floor, University of Michigan, Ann Arbor, Michigan 48109. Checks should be made payable to the university.

were American children. Among the top one hundred first graders in mathematics, there were only fifteen American children. And only one American child appeared among the top one hundred fifth graders. The highest-scoring American classroom obtained an average score lower than that of the lowest-scoring Japanese classroom and of all but one of the twenty classrooms in Taipei. In whatever way we looked at the data, the poor performance of American children was evident.

These data are startling, but no more so than the results of a study that involved 40 first- and 40 fifth-grade classrooms in the metropolitan area of Chicago—a very representative sample of the city and the suburbs of Cook County—and twenty-two classes in each of these grades in metropolitan Beijing (China). In this study, children were given a battery of mathematics tasks that included diverse problems, such as estimating the distance between a tree and a hidden treasure on a map, deciding who won a race on the basis of data in a graph, trying to explain subtraction to visiting Martians, or calculating the sum of nineteen and forty-five. There was no area in which the American children were competitive with those from China. The Chinese children's superiority appeared in complex tasks involving the application of knowledge as well as in the routines of computation. When fifth graders were asked, for example, how many members of a stamp club with twenty-four members collected only foreign stamps if five-sixths of the members did so, 59 percent of Beijing children, but only 9 percent of the Chicago children produced the correct answer. On a computation test, only 2.2 percent of the Chinese fifth graders scored at or below the mean for their American counterparts. All of the twenty Chicago area schools had average scores on the fifth-grade geometry test that were below those of the Beijing schools. The results from all these tasks paint a bleak picture of American children's competencies in mathematics.[2]

The poor performance of American students compels us to try to understand the reasons why. We have written extensively elsewhere about the cultural differences in attitudes toward learning and toward the importance of effort vs. innate ability and about the substantially greater amounts of time Japanese and Chinese students devote to academic activities in general and to the study of math in particular.[3] Important as these factors are, they do not tell the whole story. For that we have to take a close look inside the classrooms of Japan, China, and the United States to see how mathematics is actually taught in the three cultures.

LESSONS NOT LECTURES

If we were asked briefly to characterize classes in Japan and China, we would say that they consist of coherent lessons that are presented in a thoughtful, relaxed, and nonauthoritarian manner. Teachers frequently rely on students as sources of information. Lessons are oriented toward problem solving rather than rote mastery of facts and procedures and utilize many different types of representational materials. The role assumed by the teacher is that of knowledgeable guide, rather than that of prime dispenser of information and arbiter of what is correct. There is frequent verbal interaction in the classroom as the teacher attempts to stimulate students to produce, explain, and evaluate solutions to problems. These characteristics contradict stereotypes held by most Westerners about Asian teaching practices. Lessons are not rote; they are not filled with drill. Teachers do not spend large amounts of time lecturing but attempt to lead the children in productive interactions and discussions. And the children are not the passive automata depicted in Western descriptions but active participants in the learning process.

We begin by discussing what we mean by the coherence of a lesson. One way to think of a lesson is by using the analog of a story. A good story is highly organized; it has a beginning, a middle, and an end; and it follows a protagonist who meets challenges and resolves problems that arise along the way. Above all, a good story engages the reader's interest in a series of interconnected events, which are best understood in the context of the events that precede and follow it.

Such a concept of a lesson guides the organization of instruction in Asia. The curricula are defined in terms of coherent lessons, each carefully designed to fill a forty- to fifty-minute class period with sustained attention to the development of some concept or skill. Like a good story, the lesson has an introduction, a conclusion, and a consistent theme.

We can illustrate what we are talking about with this account of a fifth-grade Japanese mathematics class:

> The teacher walks in carrying a large paper bag full of clinking glass. Entering the classroom with a large paper bag is highly unusual, and by the time she has placed the bag on her desk the students are regarding her with rapt attention. What's in the bag? She begins to pull items out of the bag, placing them, one-by-one, on her desk. She removes a pitcher and a vase. A beer bottle evokes laughter and surprise. She soon

has six containers lined up on her desk. The children continue to watch intently, glancing back and forth at each other as they seek to understand the purpose of this display.

The teacher, looking thoughtfully at the containers, poses a question: "I wonder which one would hold the most water?" Hands go up, and the teacher calls on different students to give their guesses: "the pitcher," "the beer bottle," "the teapot." The teacher stands aside and ponders: "Some of you said one thing, others said something different. You don't agree with each other. There must be some way we can find out who is correct. How can we know who is correct?" Interest is high, and the discussion continues.

The students soon agree that to find out how much each container holds they will need to fill the containers with something. How about water? The teacher finds some buckets and sends several children out to fill them with water. When they return, the teacher says: "Now what do we do?" Again there is a discussion, and after several minutes the children decide that they will need to use a smaller container to measure how much water fits into each of the larger containers. They decide on a drinking cup, and one of the students warns that they all have to fill each cup to the same level—otherwise the measure won't be the same for all of the groups.

At this point the teacher divides the class into their groups (*han*) and gives each group one of the containers and a drinking cup. Each group fills its container, counts how many cups of water it holds, and writes the result in a notebook. When all of the groups have completed the task, the teacher calls on the leader of each group to report on the group's findings and notes the results on the blackboard. She has written the names of the containers in a column on the left and a scale from 1 to 6 along the bottom. Pitcher, 4.5 cups; vase, 3 cups; beer bottle, 1. 5 cups; and so on. As each group makes its report the teacher draws a bar representing the amount, in cups, the container holds.

Finally, the teacher returns to the question she posed at the beginning of the lesson: Which container holds the most water? She reviews how they were able to solve the problem and points out that the answer is now contained in the bar graph on the board. She then arranges the containers on the table in order according to how much they hold and writes a rank order on each container, from 1 to 6. She ends the class with a brief review of what they have done. No definitions of ordinate and abscissa, no discussion of how to make a graph preceded the example—these all became obvious in the course of the lesson, and only at the end did the teacher mention the terms that describe the horizontal and vertical axes of the graph they had made.

With one carefully crafted problem, this Japanese teacher has guided her students to discover—and most likely to remember—several important concepts. As this article unfolds, we hope to demonstrate that this example of how well-designed Asian class lessons are is not an isolated one; to the contrary, it is the norm. And as we hope to further demonstrate, excellent class lessons do not come effortlessly or magically. Asian teachers are not born great teachers; they and the lessons they develop require careful nurturing and constant refinement. The practice of teaching in Japan and China is more uniformly perfected than it is in the United States because their systems of education are structured to encourage teaching excellence to develop and flourish. Ours is not. We will take up the question of why and what can be done about this later in the piece. But first, we present a more detailed look at what Asian lessons are like.

COHERENCE BROKEN

Asian lessons almost always begin with a practical problem, such as the example we have just given, or with a word problem written on the blackboard. Asian teachers, to a much greater degree than American teachers, give coherence to their lessons by introducing the lesson with a word problem.

It is not uncommon for the Asian teacher to organize the entire lesson around the solution to this single problem. The teacher leads the children to recognize what is known and what is unknown and directs the students' attention to the critical parts of the problem. Teachers are careful to see that the problem is understood by all of the children, and even mechanics, such as mathematical computation, are presented in the context of solving a problem.

Before ending the lesson, the teacher reviews what has been learned and relates it to the problem she posed at the beginning of the lesson. American teachers are much less likely than Asian teachers to begin and end lessons in this way. For example, we found that fifth-grade teachers in Beijing spent eight times as long at the end of the class period summarizing the lessons as did those in the Chicago metropolitan area.

Now contrast the Japanese math lesson described above with a fifth-grade American mathematics classroom that we recently visited. Immediately after getting the students' attention, the teacher pointed out that today was Tuesday, "band day," and that all students in the band should go to the band room. "Those of you doing the news report today should meet over there in the corner," he continued. He then began the mathematics class with the remaining students by reviewing the solution to a computation problem that had been included in the previous day's homework. After this brief review, the teacher directed the students' attention to the blackboard, where the day's assignment had been written. From this point on, the teacher spent most of the rest of the period walking about the room monitoring the children's work, talking to individual children about questions or errors, and uttering "shushes" whenever the students began talking among themselves.

This example is typical of the American classrooms we have visited, classrooms where students spend more time in transition and less in academic activities, more time working on their own and less being instructed by the teacher; where teachers spend much of their time working with individual students and attending to matters of discipline; and where the shape of a coherent lesson is often hard to discern.

American lessons are often disrupted by irrelevant interruptions. These serve to break the continuity of the lesson and add to children's difficulty in perceiving the lesson as a coherent whole. In our American observations, the teacher interrupted the flow of the lesson with an interlude of irrelevant comments or the class was interrupted by someone else in 20 percent of all first-grade lessons and 47 percent of all fifth-grade lessons. This occurred less than 10 percent of the time at both grade levels in Sendai, Taipei, and Beijing. In fact, no interruptions of either type were recorded during the eighty hours of observation in Beijing fifth-grade classrooms. The mathematics lesson in one of the American classrooms we visited was interrupted every morning by a woman from the cafeteria who polled the children about their lunch plans and collected money from those who planned to eat the hot lunch. Interruptions, as well as inefficient transitions from one

activity to another, make it difficult to sustain a coherent lesson throughout the class period.

Coherence is also disrupted when teachers shift frequently from one topic to another. This occurred often in the American classrooms we observed. The teacher might begin with a segment on measurement, then proceed to a segment on simple addition, then to a segment on telling time, and then to a second segment on addition. These segments constitute a math class, but they are hardly a coherent lesson. Such changes in topic were responsible for 21 percent of the changes in segments that we observed in American classrooms but accounted for only 4 percent of the changes in segments in Japanese classrooms.

Teachers frequently capitalize on variety as a means of capturing children's interest. This may explain why American teachers shift topics so frequently within the lesson. Asian teachers also seek variety, but they tend to introduce new activities instead of new topics. Shifts in materials do not necessarily pose a threat to coherence. For example, the coherence of a lesson does not diminish when the teacher shifts from working with numerals to working with concrete objects, if both are used to represent the same subtraction problem. Shifting the topic, on the other hand, introduces variety, but at the risk of destroying the coherence of the lesson.

CLASSROOM ORGANIZATION

Elementary school classrooms are typically organized in one of three ways: the whole class is working as a unit; the class is divided into a number of small groups; or children work individually. In our observations, we noted when the child was receiving instruction or assistance from the teacher and when the student was working on his own. The child was considered to be receiving instruction whenever the teacher was the leader of the activity, whether it involved the whole class, a small group, or only the individual child.

Looking at the classroom in this manner led us to one of our most pronounced findings: Although the number of children in Asian classes is significantly greater than the number in American classes, Asian students received much more instruction from their teachers than American students. In Taiwan, the teacher was the leader of the child's activity 90 percent of the time, as opposed to 74 percent in Japan, and only 46 percent in the United States. No one was leading instruction 9 percent of the time in

Taiwan, 26 percent in Japan, and an astonishing 51 percent of the time in the United States (see Figure 1). Even American first graders actually spent more time on their own than they did participating in an activity led by the teacher.

One of the reasons American children received less instruction is that American teachers spent 13 percent of their time in the mathematics classes not working with any students, something that happened only 6 percent of the time in Japan and 9 percent in Taiwan. (As we will see later, American teachers have to steal class time to attend to the multitude of chores involving preparation, assessment, and administration because so little nonteaching time is available for them during the day.)

A much more critical factor in the erosion of instructional time was the amount of time American teachers were involved with individuals or small groups. American children spend 10 percent of their time in small groups and 47 percent of their time working individually. Much of the 87 percent of the time American teachers were working with their students was spent with these individual students or small groups, rather than with the class as a whole. When teachers provide individual instruction, they must leave the rest of the class unattended, so instructional time for all remaining children is reduced.

Children can learn without a teacher. Nevertheless, it seems likely that they could profit from having their teacher as the leader of their activities more than half of the time they are in the classroom. It is the incredibly large amounts of time that American children are left unassisted and the effect that unattended time has on the coherence of the larger lesson that is the problem.

When children must work alone for long periods of time without guidance or reaction from the teacher, they begin to lose focus on the purpose of their activity. Asian teachers not only assign less seatwork than American teachers, they also use seatwork differently. Chinese and Japanese teachers tend to use short, frequent periods of seatwork, alternating between group discussion of problems and time for children to work problems on their own. Seatwork is thereby embedded into the lesson. After they work individually or in small groups on a problem, Asian students are called upon to present and defend the solutions they came up with. Thus, instruction, practice, and evaluation are tightly interwoven into a coherent whole. In contrast, the average length of seatwork in American fifth-grade classrooms was almost twice as long as it was in

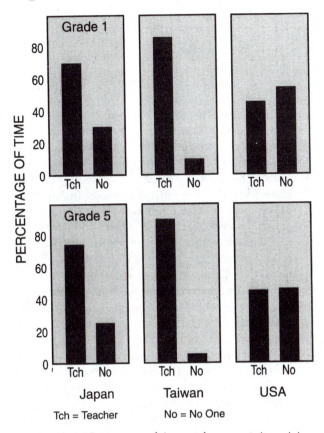

FIGURE 1   Percentage of time students spent in activity led by teacher and by no one.

Asian classrooms. And, instead of embedding seatwork into the ongoing back and forth of the lesson, American teachers tend to relegate it to one long period at the end of the class, where it becomes little more than a time for repetitious practice. In Chicago, 59 percent of all fifth-grade lessons ended with a period of seatwork, compared with 23 percent in Sendai and 14 percent in Taipei. American teachers often do not discuss the work or its connection to the goal of the lesson, or even evaluate its accuracy. Seatwork was never evaluated or discussed in 48 percent of all American fifth-grade classes we observed, compared to less than 3 percent of Japanese classes and 6 percent of Taiwan classes.

Since Asian students spend so much of their time in whole-group work, we need to say a word about that format. Whole-class instruction in the United States has gotten a somewhat bad reputation. It has become associated with too much teacher talk and too many passive, tuned-out students. But as we will see in more detail as we continue our description of Asian classrooms, whole-class instruction in Japan

HOW WE MADE SURE WE WERE LOOKING AT REPRESENTATIVE SCHOOLS

Frequent reports on television and in books and newspapers purport to depict what happens inside Japanese and Chinese classrooms. These reports usually are based on impressions gathered during brief visits to classrooms—most likely classrooms that the visitor's contacts in Asia have preselected. As a result, it is difficult to gauge the generality of what was seen and reported. Without observing large, representative samples of schools and teachers, it is impossible to characterize the teaching practices of any culture.

The descriptions that we present are based on two large observational studies of first- and fifth-grade classrooms that we conducted in Japan, Taiwan, China, and the United States. In contrast to informal observations, the strength of formal studies such as ours is that the observations are made according to consistent rules about where, when, and what to observe.

In the first study, our observers were in classrooms for a total of over four thousand hours—over a thousand class periods in 20 first- and fifth-grade classrooms in each of three cities: Sendai, Japan; Taipei, Taiwan; and Minneapolis, Minnesota.[1] Our second study took place in two hundred classrooms, forty each in Sendai and Taipei, plus forty in Beijing, China, and eighty in the Chicago metropolitan area of the United States.[2] Care was taken to choose schools that were representative. Our Chicago metropolitan area sample—the urban and suburban areas that make up Cook County—included schools that are predominantly white, black, Hispanic, and ethnically mixed; schools that draw from upper, middle, and lower socioeconomic groups; schools that are public and private; and schools that are urban and suburban.

Observers visited each classroom four times over a one- to two-week period, yielding a total of eight hundred hours of observations. The observers, who were residents of each city, wrote down as much as they could about what transpired during each mathematics class. Tape recordings made during the classes assisted the observers in filling in any missing information. These detailed narrative accounts of what transpired in the classrooms yielded even richer information than we obtained in the first study, where the observers followed predefined categories for coding behavior during the course of observations.

After the narrative records had been translated into English, we divided each observation into segments, which we defined as beginning each time there was a change in topic, materials, or activity. For example, a segment began when students put away their textbooks and began working on a worksheet or when the teacher stopped lecturing and asked some of the students to write their solutions to a problem on the blackboard.

Both studies focused on mathematics classes rather than on classes in subjects such as reading, where cultural differences in teaching practices may be more strongly determined by the content of what is being taught. For example, it is likely that the processes of teaching and learning about the multiplication of fractions transcend cultural differences, whereas teaching children how to read Chinese characters may require different approaches from those used to teach children to read an alphabetic language.

References

1. Stevenson, H. W., Stigler, J. W., Lucker, G. W., Lee, S. Y., Hsu, C. C., & Kitamura, S. (1987). Classroom behavior and achievement of Japanese, Chinese, and American children. In R. Glaser (Ed.), *Advances in instructional psychology.* Hillsdale NJ: Erlbaum.

2. Stigler, J. W., & Perry, M. (1990). Mathematics learning in Japanese, Chinese, and American classrooms. In Stigler, J. W., Shweder, R. A., & Herdt, G. (Eds.), *Cultural psychology: Essays on comparative human development.* Cambridge, Cambridge University Press. Pp. 328–356.

and China is a very lively, engaging enterprise. Asian teachers do not spend large amounts of time lecturing. They present interesting problems; they pose provocative questions; they probe and guide. The students work hard, generating multiple approaches to a solution, explaining the rationale behind their methods, and making good use of wrong answers.

HANDLING DIVERSITY

The organization of American elementary school classrooms is based on the assumption that whole-group instruction cannot accommodate students' diverse abilities and levels of achievement; thus, large amounts of whole-class time are given up so that the teacher can work individually with students. Asian educators are more comfortable in the belief that all children, with proper effort, can take advantage of a uniform educational experience, and so they are able to focus on providing the same high-quality experience to all students. Our results suggest that American educators need to question their long-held assumption that an individualized learning experience is inherently a higher-quality, more effective experience than is a whole-class learning experience. Although it may be true that an equal amount of time with a teacher may be more effective in a one-on-one situation than in a large-group situation, we must realize that the result of individualized instruction, given realistic financial constraints, is to drastically reduce the amount of teacher instruction every child receives.

Japanese and Chinese teachers recognize individual differences among students, but they handle that diversity in a very different way. First, as we will see in more detail later, they have much greater amounts of nonteaching time than do American teachers, and part of that time is available for working with individual students. They may spend extra time with slower students or ask faster students to assist them, but they focus their lesson on teaching all children regardless of apparent differences in ability or developmental readiness. Before we discuss how they do that in a whole-group setting, we need to first address the question of whether American classrooms are more diverse than Asian ones, thus potentially rendering whole-class instruction more difficult.

Whenever we discuss our research on teaching practices, someone in the audience inevitably reminds us that Japan and China are nations with relatively homogeneous populations while the United States is the melting pot of the world. How could we expect that practices used in Asian societies could possibly be relevant for the American context, where diversity is the rule in race, ethnicity, language, and social class?

What impedes teaching is the uneven preparation of children for the academic tasks that must be accomplished. It is diversity in children's educational backgrounds, not in their social and cultural backgrounds, that poses the greatest problems in teaching. Although the United States is culturally more diverse than Japan or China, we have found no more diversity at the classroom level in the educational level of American than of Asian students. The key factor is that, in the United States, educational and cultural diversity are positively related, leading some persons to the inappropriate conclusion that it is ethnic and cultural diversity, rather than educational diversity, that leads to the difficulties faced by American teachers.

It is true, for example, that there is greater variability in mathematics achievement among American than among Japanese children, but this does not mean that the differences are evident in any particular classroom. Variability in the United States exists to a large extent across neighborhoods and schools (rather than within them). Within individual classrooms, the variability in levels of academic achievement differs little between the United States and Japan, Taiwan, or China. It is wrong to argue that diversity within classrooms is an American problem. Teachers everywhere must deal with students who vary in their knowledge and motivation.

Tracking does not exist in Asian elementary schools. Children are never separated into different classrooms according to their presumed levels of intellectual ability. This egalitarian philosophy carries over to organization within the classroom. Children are not separated into reading groups according to their ability; there is no division of the class into groups differentiated by the rate at which they proceed through their mathematics books. No children leave the classroom for special classes, such as those designed for children who have been diagnosed as having learning disabilities.

How do teachers in Asian classrooms handle diversity in students' knowledge and skills? For one thing, they typically use a variety of approaches in their teaching, allowing students who may not understand one approach the opportunity to experience other approaches to presenting the material. Periods of recitation are alternated with periods in which children work for short periods on practice problems. Explanations by the teacher are interspersed with periods in which children work with concrete materials or struggle to come up with their own solutions to problems. There is continuous change from one mode of presentation, one type of representation, and one type of teaching method to another.

Asian teaching practices thrive in the face of diversity, and some practices can depend on diversity for their effectiveness. Asking students to suggest alternative solutions to a problem, for example, works best when students have had experience in generating a variety of solutions. Incorrect solutions, which are typically dismissed by the American teacher, become topics for discussion in Asian classrooms, and all students can learn from this discussion. Thus, while American schools attempt to solve the problems of diversity by segregating children into different groups or different classrooms, and by spending large amounts of regular class time working with individual students, Asian teachers believe that the only way they can cope with the problem is by devising teaching techniques that accommodate the different interests and backgrounds of the children in their classrooms.

Asian teachers also exploit the fact that the same instruction can affect different students in different ways, something that may be overlooked by American teachers. In this sense, Asian teachers subscribe to what would be considered in the West to be a "constructivist" view of learning. According to this view, knowledge is regarded as something that must be constructed by the child rather than as a set of facts and skills that can be imparted by the teacher. Because children are engaged in their own construction of knowledge, some of the major tasks for the teacher are to pose provocative questions, to allow adequate time for reflection, and to vary teaching techniques so that they are responsive to differences in students' prior experience. Through such practices, Asian teachers are able to accommodate individual differences in learning, even though instruction is not tailored to each student.

USE OF REAL-WORLD PROBLEMS AND OBJECTS

Elementary school mathematics is often defined in terms of mathematical symbols and their manipulation; for example, children must learn the place-value system of numeration and the operations for manipulating numerals to add, subtract, multiply, and divide. In addition, children must be able to apply these symbols and operations to solving problems. In order to accomplish these goals, teachers rely primarily on two powerful tools for representing mathematics: language and the manipulation of concrete objects. How effectively teachers use these forms of representation plays a critical role in determining how well children will understand mathematics.

One common function of language is in defining terms and stating rules for performing mathematical operations. A second, broader function is the use of language as a means of connecting mathematical operations to the real world and of integrating what children know about mathematics. We find that American elementary school teachers are more prone to use language to define terms and state rules than are Asian teachers, who, in their efforts to make mathematics meaningful, use language to clarify different aspects of mathematics and to intergrate what children know about mathematics with the demands of real-world problems. Here is an example of what we mean by a class in which the teacher defines terms and states rules:

> An American teacher announces that the lesson today concerns fractions. Fractions are defined and she names the numerator and denominator. "What do we call this?" she then asks. "And this?" After assuring herself that the children understand the meaning of the terms, she spends the rest of the lesson teaching them to apply the rules for forming fractions.

Asian teachers tend to reverse the procedure. They focus initially on interpreting and relating a real-world problem to the quantification that is necessary for a mathematical solution and then to define terms and state rules. In the following example, a third-grade teacher in Japan was also teaching a lesson that introduced the notation system for fractions.

> The lesson began with the teacher posing the question of how many liters of juice (colored water) were contained in a large beaker. "More than one liter," answered one child. "One and a half liters," answered another. After several children had made guesses, the teacher suggested that they pour the juice into some one-liter beakers and see. Horizontal lines on each beaker divided it into thirds. The juice filled one beaker and part of a second. The teacher pointed out that the water came up to the first line on the second beaker—only one of

the three parts was full. The procedure was repeated with a second set of beakers to illustrate the concept of one-half. After stating that there had been one and one-out-of-three liters of juice in the first big beaker and one and one-out-of-two liters in the second, the teacher wrote the fractions on the board. He continued the lesson by asking the children how to represent two parts out of three, two parts out of five, and so forth. Near the end of the period he mentioned the term "fraction" for the first time and attached names to the numerator and the denominator.

He ended the lesson by summarizing how fractions can be used to represent the parts of a whole.

In the second example, the concept of fractions emerged from a meaningful experience; in the first, it was introduced initially as an abstract concept. The terms and operations in the second example flowed naturally from the teacher's questions and discussion; in the first, language was used primarily for defining and summarizing rules. Mathematics ultimately requires abstract representation, but young children understand such representation more readily if it is derived from meaningful experience than if it results from learning definitions and rules.

Asian teachers generally are more likely than American teachers to engage their students, even very young ones, in the discussion of mathematical concepts. The kind of verbal discussion we find in American classrooms is more short-answer in nature, oriented, for example, toward clarifying the correct way to implement a computational procedure.

Teachers ask questions for different reasons in the United States and in Japan. In the United States, the purpose of a question is to get an answer. In Japan, teachers pose questions to stimulate thought. A Japanese teacher considers a question to be a poor one if it elicits an immediate answer, for this indicates that students were not challenged to think. One teacher we interviewed told us of discussions she had with her fellow teachers on how to improve teaching practices. "What do you talk about?" we wondered. "A great deal of time," she reported, "is spent talking about questions we can pose to the class—which wordings work best to get students involved in thinking and discussing the material. One good question can keep a whole class going for a long time; a bad one produces little more than a simple answer."

In one memorable example recorded by our observers, a Japanese first-grade teacher began her class by posing the question to one of her students: "Would you explain the difference between what we learned in yesterday's lesson and what you came across in preparing for today's lesson?" The young student thought for a long time, but then answered the question intelligently, a performance that undoubtedly enhanced his understanding of both lessons.

CONCRETE REPRESENTATIONS

Every elementary school student in Sendai possesses a "Math Set," a box of colorful, well-designed materials for teaching mathematical concepts: tiles, clock, ruler, checkerboard, colored triangles, beads, and many other attractive objects.

In Taipei, every classroom is equipped with a similar, but larger, set of such objects. In Beijing, where there is much less money available for purchasing such materials, teachers improvise with colored paper, wax fruit, plates, and other easily obtained objects. In all cases, these concrete objects are considered to be critically important tools for teaching mathematics, for it is through manipulating these objects that children can form important links between real-world problems and abstract mathematical notations.

American teachers are much less likely than Chinese or Japanese teachers to use concrete objects. At fifth grade, for example, Sendai teachers were nearly twice as likely to use concrete objects as the Chicago area teachers, and Taipei teachers were nearly five times as likely. There was also a subtle, but important, difference in the way Asian and American teachers used concrete objects. Japanese teachers, for example, use the items in the Math Set throughout the elementary school years and introduced small tiles in a high percentage of the lessons we observed in the first grade. American teachers seek variety and may use Popsicle sticks in one lesson, and in another, marbles, Cheerios, M&Ms, checkers, poker chips, or plastic animals. The American view is that objects should be varied in order to maintain children's interest. The Asian view is that using a variety of representational materials may confuse children, and thereby make it more difficult for them to use the objects for the representation and solution of mathematics problems. Having learned to add with tiles makes multiplication easier to understand when the same tiles are used.

Through the skillful use of concrete objects, teachers are able to teach elementary school children to understand and solve problems that are not introduced in American curricula until much later. An example occurred in a fourth-grade mathematics lesson we observed in Japan. The problem the teacher posed is a difficult one for fourth graders, and its solution is generally not taught in the United States until much later. This is the problem:

> There are a total of thirty-eight children in Akira's class. There are six more boys than there are girls. How many boys and how many girls are in the class?

This lesson began with a discussion of the problem and with the children proposing ways to solve it. After the discussion, the teacher handed each child two strips of paper, one six units longer than the other, and told the class that the strips would be used to help them think about the problem. One slip represented the number of girls in the class and the other represented the number of boys. By lining the strips next to each other, the children could see that the degree to which the longer one protruded beyond the shorter one represented 6 boys. The procedure for solving the problem then unfolded as the teacher, through skillful questioning, led the children to the solution: The number of girls was found by taking the total of both strips, subtracting 6 to make the strips of equal length, and then dividing by 2. The number of boys could be found, of course, by adding 6 to the number of girls. With this concrete visual representation of the problem and careful guidance from the teacher, even fourth graders were able to understand the problem and its solution.

STUDENTS CONSTRUCT MULTIPLE SOLUTIONS

A common Western stereotype is that the Asian teacher is an authoritarian purveyor of information, one who expects students to listen and memorize correct answers or correct procedures rather than to construct knowledge themselves. This may or may not be an accurate description of Asian high school teachers,[4] but, as we have seen in previous examples, it does not describe the dozens of elementary school teachers that we have observed.

Chinese and Japanese teachers rely on students to generate ideas and evaluate the correctness of the ideas. The possibility that they will be called upon to state their own solution as well as to evaluate what another student has proposed keeps Asian students alert, but this technique has two other important functions. First, it engages students in the lesson, increasing their motivation by making them feel they are participants in a group process. Second, it conveys a more realistic impression of how knowledge is acquired. Mathematics, for example, is a body of knowledge that has evolved gradually through a process of argument and proof. Learning to argue about mathematical ideas is fundamental to understanding mathematics. Chinese and Japanese children begin learning these skills in the first grade; many American elementary school students are never exposed to them.

We can illustrate the way Asian teachers use students' ideas with the following example. A fifth-grade teacher in Taiwan began her mathematics lesson by calling attention to a six-sided figure she had drawn on the blackboard. She asked the students how they might go about finding the area of the shaded region. "I don't want you to tell me what the actual area is, just tell me the approach you would use to solve the problem. Think of as many different ways as you can of ways you could determine the area that I have drawn in yellow chalk." She allowed the students several minutes to work in small groups and then called upon a child from each group to describe the group's solution. After each proposal, many of which were quite complex, the teacher asked members of the other groups whether the procedure described could yield a correct answer. After several different procedures had been suggested, the teacher moved on to a second problem with a different embedded figure and repeated the process. Neither teacher nor students actually carried out a solution to the problem until all of the alternative solutions had been discussed. The lesson ended with the teacher affirming the importance of coming up with multiple solutions. "After all," she said, "we face many problems every day in the real world. We have to remember that there is not only one way we can solve each problem."

American teachers are less likely to give students opportunities to respond at such length. Although a great deal of interaction appears to occur in American classrooms—with teachers and students posing questions and giving answers—American teachers generally pose questions that are answerable with a yes or no or with a short phrase. They seek a correct answer and continue calling on students until one produces it. "Since we can't subtract

8 from 6," says an American teacher, "we have to . . . what?" Hands go up, the teacher calls on a girl who says "Borrow." "Correct," the teacher replies. This kind of interchange does not establish the student as a valid source of information, for the final arbiter of the correctness of the student's opinions is still the teacher. The situation is very different in Asian classrooms, where children are likely to be asked to explain their answers and other children are then called upon to evaluate their correctness.

Clear evidence of these differing beliefs about the roles of students and teachers appears in the observations of how teachers evaluate students' responses. The most frequent form of evaluation used by American teachers was praise, a technique that was rarely used in either Taiwan or Japan. In Japan, evaluation most frequently took the form of a discussion of children's errors.

Praise serves to cut off discussion and to highlight the teacher's role as the authority. It also encourages children to be satisfied with their performance rather than informing them about where they need improvement. Discussing errors, on the other hand, encourages argument and justification and involves students in the exciting quest of assessing the strengths and weaknesses of the various alternative solutions that have been proposed.

Why are American teachers often reluctant to encourage students to participate at greater length during mathematics lessons? One possibility is that they feel insecure about the depth of their own mathematical training. Placing more emphasis on students' explanations necessarily requires teachers to relinquish some control over the direction the lesson will take. This can be a frightening prospect to a teacher who is unprepared to evaluate the validity of novel ideas that students inevitably propose.

USING ERRORS EFFECTIVELY

We have been struck by the different reactions of Asian and American teachers to children's errors. For Americans, errors tend to be interpreted as an indication of failure in learning the lesson. For Chinese and Japanese, they are an index of what still needs to be learned. These divergent interpretations result in very different reactions to the display of errors—embarrassment on the part of the American children, calm acceptance by Asian children. They also result in differences in the manner in which teachers utilize errors as effective means of instruction.

We visited a fifth-grade classroom in Japan the first day the teacher introduced the problem of adding fractions with unequal denominators. The problem was a simple one: adding one-third and one-half. The children were told to solve the problem and that the class would then review the different solutions.

After everyone appeared to have completed the task, the teacher called on one of the students to give his answer and to explain his solution. "The answer is two-fifths," he stated. Pointing first to the numerators and then to the denominators, he explained: "One plus one is two; three plus two is five. The answer is two-fifths." Without comment, the teacher asked another boy for his solution. "Two point one plus three point one, when changed into a fraction adds up to two-fifths." The children in the classroom looked puzzled. The teacher, unperturbed, asked a third student for her solution. "The answer is five-sixths." The student went on to explain how she had found the common denominator, changed the fractions so that each had this denominator, and then added them.

The teacher returned to the first solution. "How many of you think this solution is correct?" Most agreed that it was not. She used the opportunity to direct the children's attention to reasons why the solution was incorrect. "Which is larger, two-fifths or one-half?" The class agreed that it was one-half. "It is strange, isn't it, that you could add a number to one-half and get a number that is smaller than one-half." She went on to explain how the procedure the child used would result in the odd situation where, when one-half was added to one-half, the answer yielded is one-half. In a similarly careful, interactive manner, she discussed how the second boy had confused fractions with decimals to come up with his surprising answer. Rather than ignoring the incorrect solutions and concentrating her attention on the correct solution, the teacher capitalized on the errors the children made in order to dispel two common misperceptions about fractions.

We have not observed American teachers responding to children's errors so inventively. Perhaps because of the strong influence of behavioristic teaching that conditions should be arranged so that the learner avoids errors and makes only a reinforceable response, American teachers place little emphasis on the constructive use of errors as a teaching technique. It seems likely, however, that learning about what is wrong may hasten children's understanding of why the correct procedures are appropriate.

WHY NOT HERE?

Few who have visited urban classrooms in Asia would disagree that the great majority of Chinese and Japanese teachers are highly skilled professionals. Their dedication is legendary; what is often not appreciated is how thoughtfully and adroitly they guide children through the vast amount of material that they must master during the six years of elementary school. We, of course, witnessed examples of excellent lessons in American classrooms. And there are of course individual differences among Asian teachers. But what has impressed us in our personal observations and in the data from our observational studies is how remarkably well most Asian teachers teach. It is the *widespread* excellence of Asian class lessons, the high level of performance of the *average* teacher, that is so stunning.

The techniques used by Chinese and Japanese teachers are not new to the teaching profession—nor are they foreign or exotic. In fact, they are the types of techniques often recommended by American educators. What the Japanese and Chinese examples demonstrate so compellingly is that when widely implemented, such practices can produce extraordinary outcomes.

Unfortunately, these techniques have not been broadly applied in the United States. Why? One reason, as we have discussed, is the Asian belief that the whole-group lesson, if done well, can be made to work for every child. With that assumption, Asian teachers can focus on the perfection of that lesson. However, even if American educators shared that belief, it would be difficult for them to achieve anything near the broad-based high quality that we observed in Asian classrooms. This is not the fault of American teachers. The fault lies with a system that prepares them inadequately and then exhausts them physically, emotionally, and intellectually while denying them the collegial interaction that every profession relies upon for the growth and refinement of its knowledge base.

The first major obstacle to the widespread development and execution of excellent lessons in America is the fact that American teachers are overworked. It is inconceivable that American teachers, by themselves, would be able to organize lively, vivid, coherent lessons under a regimen that requires that they teach hour after hour every day throughout the school year. Preparing lessons that require the discovery of knowledge and the construction of understanding takes time. Teaching them effectively requires energy. Both are in very short supply for most American teachers.

Being an elementary school teacher in the United States at the end of the twentieth century is extraordinarily difficult, and the demands made by American society exhaust even the most energetic among them. "I'm dancing as fast as I can," one teacher summarized her feelings about her job, "but with all the things that I'm supposed to do, I just can't keep up."

The full realization of how little time American teachers have when they are not directly in charge of children became clear to us during a meeting in Beijing. We were discussing the teachers' workday. When we informed the Chinese teachers that American teachers are responsible for their classes all day long, with only an hour or less outside the classroom each day, they looked incredulous. How could any teacher be expected to do a good job when there is no time outside of class to prepare and correct lessons, work with individual children, consult with other teachers, and attend to all of the matters that arise in a typical day at school! Beijing teachers teach no more than three hours a day, unless the teacher is a homeroom teacher, in which case, the total is four hours. During the first three grades, the teaching assignment includes both reading and mathematics; for the upper three grades of elementary school, teachers specialize in one of these subjects. They spend the rest of their day at school carrying out all of their other responsibilities to their students and to the school. The situation is similar in Japan. According to our estimate, Japanese elementary school teachers are in charge of classes only 60 percent of the time they are at school.

The large amounts of nonteaching time at school are available to Asian teachers because of two factors. The first concerns the number of teachers typically assigned to Asian schools. Although class sizes are considerably larger in Asia, the student-to-teacher ratio within a school does not differ greatly from that in the United States. By having more students in each class and the same number of teachers in the school, all teachers can have fewer teaching hours. Time is freed up for teachers to meet and work together on a daily basis, to prepare lessons for the next day, to work with individual children, and to attend staff meetings.

The second factor increasing the time available to Japanese and Chinese teachers at school is that they spend more hours at school each day than do American teachers. In our study, for example, teachers in Sendai and Taipei spent an average of 9.5 and 9.1 hours per day, respectively, compared to only 7.3 hours for the American teachers. Asian teachers arrive at school early and stay late, which gives them time to meet together and to work with children who need extra help. Most American teachers, in contrast, arrive at school shortly before classes begin and leave not long after they end. This does not mean a shorter work week for American teachers. What it does mean is that they must devote their evenings to working alone on the next day's lessons, further increasing their sense of isolation.

LEARNING FROM EACH OTHER

The second reason Asian classes are so well crafted is that there is a very systematic effort to pass on the accumulated wisdom of teaching practice to each new generation of teachers and to keep perfecting that practice by providing teachers the opportunities to continually learn from each other.

Americans often act as if good teachers are born, not made. We hear this from both teachers and parents. They seem to believe that good teaching happens if the teacher has a knack with children, gets along well with them, and keeps them reasonably attentive and enthusiastic about learning. It is a commonly accepted truism in many colleges of education that teaching is an art and that students cannot be taught how to teach.

Perhaps because of this belief, students emerge from American colleges of education with little training in how to design and teach effective lessons. It is assumed that teachers will discover this for themselves. Courses in teaching methods are designed to serve a different purpose. On the one hand, they present theories of learning and cognitive development. Although the students are able to quote the major tenets of the theorists currently in vogue, the theories remain as broad generalizations that are difficult to apply to the everyday tasks that they will face as classroom teachers. At the opposite extreme, these methods courses provide education students with lists of specific suggestions for activities and materials that are easy to use and that children should enjoy (for example, pieces of breakfast cereal make handy counters for teaching basic number facts). Teachers are faced, therefore, with information that is either too general to be applied readily or so specific that it has only limited usefulness. Because of this, American teachers complain that most of what they know had to be learned by themselves, alone, on the job.

In Asia, graduates of teacher training programs are still considered to be novices who need the guidance and support of their experienced colleagues. In the United States, training comes to a near halt after

the teachers acquire their teaching certificates. American teachers may take additional coursework in the evenings or during summer vacations, or they may attend district or citywide workshops from time to time. But these opportunities are not considered to be an essential part of the American system of teacher training.

In Japan, the system of teacher training is much like an apprenticeship under the guidance of experienced colleagues. The teacher's first year of employment marks the beginning of a lengthy and elaborate training process. By Japanese law, beginning teachers must receive a minimum of twenty days of inservice training during their first year on the job.[5] Supervising the inservice training are master teachers, selected for their teaching ability and their willingness to assist their young colleagues. During one-year leaves of absence from their own classrooms, they observe the beginner in the classroom and offer suggestions for improvement.

In addition to this early tutelage in teaching techniques, Japanese teachers, beginners as well as seasoned teachers, are required to continually perfect their teaching skills through interaction with other teachers. One mechanism is through meetings organized by the vice principal and head teachers of their own school. These experienced professionals assume responsibility for advising and guiding their young colleagues. The head teachers organize meetings to discuss teaching techniques and to devise lesson plans and handouts. These meetings are supplemented by informal districtwide study groups and courses at municipal or prefectural education centers.[6]

A glimpse at what takes place in these study groups is provided in a conversation we recently had with a Japanese teacher. She and her colleagues spend a good deal of their time together working on lesson plans. After they finish a plan, one teacher from the group teaches the lesson to her students while the other teachers look on. Afterward, the group meets again to criticize the teacher's performance and to make suggestions for how the lesson could be improved. In her school, there is an annual "teaching fair." Teachers from other schools are invited to visit the school and observe the lessons being taught. The visitors rate the lessons, and the teacher with the best lesson is declared the winner.

In addition, national television in Japan presents programs that show how master teachers handle particular lessons or concepts. In Taiwan, such demonstrations are available on sets of videotapes that cover the whole curriculum.

Making use of lessons that have been honed over time does not mean that the Asian teacher simply mimics what she sees. As with great actors or musicians, the substance of the curriculum becomes the script or the score; the goal is to perform the role or piece as effectively and creatively as possible. Rather than executing the curriculum as a mere routine, the skilled teacher strives to perfect the presentation of each lesson. She uses the teaching techniques she has learned and imposes her own interpretation on these techniques in a manner that she thinks will interest and motivate her pupils.

Of course, teachers find it easier to share helpful tips and techniques among themselves when they are all teaching the same lesson at about the same time. The fact that Taiwan, Japan, and China each has a national curriculum that provides a common focus is a significant factor in teacher interaction. Not only do we have no national curriculum in the United States, but the curriculum may not be consistent within a city or even within a single school. American textbooks, with a spiral curriculum that repeats topics year after year and with a profusion of material about each topic, force teachers to omit some of each year's material. Even when teachers use the same textbook, their classes differ according to which topics they choose to skip and in the pace with which they proceed through the text. As a result, American teachers have less incentive than Asian teachers to share experiences with each other or to benefit from the successes and failures that others have had in teaching particular lessons.

Adding further to the sense of isolation is the fact that American teachers, unlike other professionals, do not share a common body of knowledge and experience. The courses offered at different universities and colleges vary, and even among their required courses, there is often little common content from college to college. Student teaching, the only other activity in which all budding teachers participate, is a solitary endeavor shared only with the regular classroom teacher and perhaps a few fellow student teachers.

Opportunities for Asian teachers to learn from each other are influenced, in part, by the physical arrangements of the schools. In Japanese and Chinese schools, a large room in each school is designed as a teachers' room, and each teacher is assigned a desk in this room. It is here that they spend their time away from the classroom preparing lessons, correcting students' papers, and discussing teaching techniques. American teachers, isolated in their own classrooms, find it much harder to discuss their work with colleagues. Their desk and teaching materials are in their own classrooms, and the only common space available to teachers is usually a cramped room that often houses supplies and the school's duplicating facilities, along with a few chairs and a coffee machine. Rarely do teachers have enough time in their visits to this room to engage in serious discussions of educational policy or teaching practices.

Critics argue that the problems facing the American teacher are unique and that it is futile to consider what Japanese and Chinese teaching are like in seeking solutions to educational problems in the United States. One of the frequent arguments is that the students in the typical Asian classroom share a common language and culture, are well disciplined and attentive, and are not distracted by family crises and their own personal problems, whereas the typical American teacher is often faced with a diverse, burdened, distracted group of students. To be sure, the conditions encountered by teachers differ greatly among these societies. Week after week, American teachers must cope with children who present them with complex, wrenching personal problems. But much of what gives American classrooms their aura of disarray and disorganization may be traced to how schools are organized and teachers are trained as well as to characteristics of the children.

It is easy to blame teachers for the problems confronting American education, and this is something that the American public is prone to do. The accusation is unfair. We cannot blame teachers when we deprive them of adequate training and yet expect that on their own they will become innovative teachers; when we cast them in the roles of surrogate parents, counselors, and psychotherapists and still expect them to be effective teachers; and when we keep them so busy in the classroom that they have little time or opportunity for professional development once they have joined the ranks of the teaching profession.

Surely the most immediate and pressing task in educating young students is to create a new type of school environment, one where great lessons are a commonplace occurrence. In order to do this, we must ask how we can institute reforms that will make it possible for American teachers to practice their profession under conditions that are as favorable for their own professional development and for the education of children as those that exist in Asia. *Note: The research described in this article has been funded by grants from the National Institute of Mental Health, the National Science Foundation, and the W.T. Grant Foundation. The research is the result of collaboration with a large group of colleagues in China, Japan, Taiwan, and the United States who have worked together for the past decade. We are indebted to each of these*

colleagues and are especially grateful to Shinying Lee of the University of Michigan who has been a major contributor to the research described in this article.

Questions

1. What are three classroom practices that are different in the US, Japan and China and how do these affect what children learn about mathematics in school?

2. How is instructional time eroded in the US classroom? What can be done to change this?

3. Stigler and Stevenson found that the use of real-world problems and objects helped children learn mathematics better than more abstract references. Why do you think real-world problems help students learn? What is it about the mind and how we learn that may be aided by such practical approaches?

References

1. The superior academic achievement of Chinese and Japanese children sometimes leads to speculation that they are brighter than American children. This possibility has been supported in a few reports that have received attention in the popular press and in several scientific journals. What has not been reported or widely understood is that, without exception, the studies contending that differences in intelligence are responsible for differences in academic performance have failed to meet acceptable standards of scientific inquiry. In fact, studies that have reported differences in I.Q. scores between Asian and American children have been flawed conceptually and methodologically. Their major defects are nonequivalent tests used in the different locations and noncomparable samples of children. To determine the cognitive abilities of children in the three cultures, we needed tests that were linguistically comparable and culturally unbiased. These requirements preclude reliance on tests translated from one language to another or the evaluation of children in one country on the basis of norms obtained in another country. We assembled a team with members from each of the three cultures, and they developed ten cognitive tasks falling into traditional "verbal" and "performance" categories. The test results revealed no evidence of overall differences in the cognitive functioning of American, Chinese, and Japanese children. There was no tendency for children from any of the three cultures to achieve significantly higher average scores on all the tasks. Children in each culture had strengths and weaknesses, but by the fifth grade of elementary school, the most notable feature of children's cognitive performance was the similarity in level and variability of their scores. [Stevenson, H. W., Stigler, J. W., Lee, S. Y., Lucker, G. W., Kitamura, S., & Hsu, C. C. (1985). Cognitive performance and academic achievement of Japanese, Chinese, and American children. *Child Development*, 56, 718–734.]

2. Stevenson, H. W. (1990). Adapting to school: Children in Beijing and Chicago. *Annual Report*. Stanford CA: Center for Advanced Study in the Behavioral Sciences. Stevenson, H. W., Lee, S., Chen, C., Lummis, M., Stigler, J., Fan, L., & Ge, F. (1990). Mathematics achievement of children in China and the United States. *Child Development*, 61, 1053–1066. Stevenson, H. W., Stigler, J. W., & Lee, S.Y (1986). Mathematics achievement of Chinese, Japanese, and American children. *Science*, 231, 693–699. Stigler, J. W., Lee, S. Y., & Stevenson, H. W. (1990). *Mathematical knowledge*. Reston, VA: National Council of Teachers of Mathematics.

3. Stevenson, H. W., Lee, S. Y., Chen C., Stigler, J. W., Hsu, C. C., & Kitamura, S. (1990). Contexts of achievement. *Monographs of the Society for Research in Child Development*. Serial No. 221, 55, Nos. 1–2.

4. Rohlen, T. P. (1983). *Japan's High Schools*. Berkeley: University of California Press.

5. Dorfman, C. H. (Ed.) (1987). *Japanese Education Today*. Washington, D.C.: U.S. Department of Education.

6. Ibid.

22

The Effect of Peer and Adult-Child Transactive Discussions on Moral Reasoning

ANN CALE KRUGER

Social interaction plays an important role in the development of morality. Discussions with others about moral issues create opportunities for children to consider moral views that are different from their own and thereby help them to develop their moral reasoning abilities. One question psychologists have raised about the process of moral development concerns the relative importance of moral discussions with peers versus those with adults. Whereas, as Piaget contends, peers may provide arguments that are closely matched to those of the child and therefore may be easier for that child to understand, others argue that adults may provide more mature models of morality and thereby facilitate growth. In the following paper, Ann Cale Kruger describes her research examining this question. Her results support Piaget's view that peer interaction may be more beneficial for enhancing moral reasoning in children than adult-child interaction.

Reprinted with permission from *Merrill-Palmer Quarterly*, *38*, 1992, 191–211. Copyright 1992 by Wayne State University Press.

A briefer version of this paper was presented at the meeting of the Society for Research in Child Development, Kansas City, MO, April 1989. The author thanks the mothers and children who made this research possible. The assistance of Sara Mannie and Steven Cole in data preparation is acknowledged with appreciation. The author is grateful to Michael Tomasello for his helpful comments on the manuscript. Correspondence may be sent to Ann Cale Kruger, Department of Psychology, Oglethorpe University, 4484 Peachtree Rd., Atlanta, GA 30319.

Piaget (1932) hypothesized that children's interactions with peers during middle childhood are essential to their moral reasoning development. To test this hypothesis, 48 female focal subjects (M age = 8.6 years) were paired with either a female agemate or their mother. All focal subjects were pretested and posttested for moral reasoning abilities. In the intervention, the adult-child and peer dyads engaged in consensus-seeking discussions of two moral dilemmas. Focal subjects' moral reasoning at pretest and posttest and their use of reasoning (transacts) in the intervention discussions were measured. As predicted, focal subjects paired with peers showed significantly more sophisticated moral reasoning subsequent to their discussions than did focals paired with adults. In addition, focals paired with peers used more active transacts in their discussions than did focals paired with adults. Styles of dyadic discussion that featured active transacts by focal subjects were positively correlated with the focals' moral reasoning at posttest, whether the focal subject was paired with a peer or an adult. The more sophisticated posttest reasoning by focals paired with peers was attributed to the greater use of active discussion styles in peer dyads.

Piaget (1932) hypothesized that peers are uniquely important in children's moral development because, during middle childhood, children's interactions with peers are egalitarian, marked by a symmetry of competence and influence. When peer interaction results in the conflict of egocentric, but equally valid points of view, the child is prompted to take another perspective into account and to use reasoning to integrate the perspectives. Piaget asserted that this process of conflict and resolution is crucial to development (1970), and he contended that opportunities to resolve sociomoral differences are a more frequent and more typical feature of peer interaction (1932).

Interactions with adults during this time are not as likely to foster this type of developmental process. Adults' greater authority and interpersonal power contribute to their social dominance in interactions with children. Piaget observed that when children and adults experience conflict, the children, acknowledging the asymmetry of the relationship, yield to the adult solution, which removes the child's motivation to use reasoning and to abstract new sociomoral rules. Thus, for Piaget (1932), it is the independent negotiation that children conduct with peers that is vital to moral development.

This hypothesis is untested, although one part of Piaget's idea has been supported by training studies,

most involving adult subjects. These studies suggest that interpersonal conflict resolved by consensus-seeking discussions results in change in moral reasoning. Neither personal consideration of moral dilemmas nor open-ended group discussion of them is as successful in promoting the developmental change in moral reasoning as is group discussion with the goal of resolution and consensus (Maitland & Goldman, 1974). Dyads who actively debate moral dilemmas to consensus change more than do those who passively listen to moral arguments (Arbuthnot, 1975), and the more conflict that dyads experience in their discussions, the more likely they are to change as a result (Berkowitz, Gibbs, & Broughton, 1980).

A fine-grained analysis of this developmental process of conflict and resolution was conducted by Berkowitz and Gibbs (1983). They compared moral discussions by adult dyads who showed subsequent developmental change to discussions by dyads who showed no change. Their results indicated that changing dyads, as opposed to unchanging dyads, are distinguished by the presence of transaction in their discussions. Berkowitz and Gibbs defined *transaction* as reasoning about reasoning: one individual uses reasoning that operates on the reasoning of the partner or that significantly clarifies his or her own ideas. Damon and Killen (1982) conducted a similar investigation of triads that were composed of children age 5 to 9 years. Like Berkowitz and Gibbs, they found that the children who advanced as a result of a moral discussion were those who both directed transforming (transacting) statements to their partners and received transactive statements from their partners.

Kruger and Tomasello (1986) applied this process analysis to investigate differences in the dialogues that children have with adults and with peers. To reflect the developmental level of the subjects and the process differences in adult-child and peer dialogues, they examined two aspects of transacts: the activity required for production (spontaneous transactive statements and questions vs. passive transactive responses) and the personal orientation of the transaction (reasoning about the listener's ideas vs. reasoning about the speaker's ideas). They showed that children who were paired with peers used transactive reasoning more often than did children paired with adults. Furthermore, the transacts between peers were more likely to be critiques of the listener's ideas, rather than clarifications of the speaker's ideas, and were produced more spontaneously. Children who were paired with adults were more passive and self-oriented in their use of reasoning because adult partners dominated the discussions by asking many questions.

It has been demonstrated, thus, that sociomoral conflict and its resolution lead to developmental change and that a key element in this process is transactive reasoning. It also has been demonstrated that discussions between peers feature more and qualitatively different transacts than do discussions between adults and children. However, the crucial assertions in Piaget's hypothesis remain untested. It is not known if indeed peer discussions produce greater changes in moral reasoning than do adult-child discussions. Nor is it known if the different use of reasoning in the process of adult-child and peer discussions is responsible for such changes. The purpose of the present study, therefore, was to test these hypotheses by comparing the moral reasoning of children before and after their moral discussions with either a peer or an adult. It was hypothesized that: (a) At posttest, focal subjects in peer dyads show greater moral reasoning as a result of their discussions than do focal subjects in adult-child dyads. (b) In their discussions, focal subjects in peer dyads, as compared to focals in adult-child dyads, use more transacts, use them more spontaneously, and focus their transacts on their partner's ideas, rather than their own. And (c) the use of spontaneous transacts in discussions, no matter the partner, is positively related to moral reasoning level at posttest.

METHOD

Subjects

Focal subjects were 48 middle-class females (45 white, 3 black) recruited from Girl Scout troops in metropolitan Atlanta. The mean age of the subjects was 8.6 years (range = 7.3 to 10.2 years). The sample was restricted to a single sex because of the preference for same-sex dyads and because of the greater availability of female adults as participants. All subjects were selected from a small set of comparable neighborhoods.

Subjects were recruited by mail. For a subject to be considered for participation, it was required that she receive parental permission and that her mother volunteer to participate in the study. It was further required that the subject nominate a friend (same-sex agemate) to participate with her. The parents of the nominated friends were contacted by mail and requested to allow their children to participate. From this pool of focal subjects, each with two potential partners (a parent volunteer and a peer volunteer), focal subjects were randomly assigned to participate with either their parent or their peer as a partner; the other partner was dropped from the study. This procedure yielded 24 adult-child dyads and 24 peer dyads.

Procedure

Each dyad met on one occasion in the focal child's home. This choice of setting has ecological validity because children's personal dilemmas are likely to be discussed with important others in comfortable environments. The outline of the procedure was: The pretest consisted of two private interviews, one between the experimenter and the focal subject and one between the experimenter and the partner subject (counterbalanced for order across conditions). This interview was followed by dyadic discussion (intervention) of two dilemmas between focal subject and partner. The procedure ended with a posttest interview between the experimenter and the focal subject.

PRETEST   The subjects were interviewed privately by the experimenter, a white adult female, using Damon's standard positive justice interview (1975, 1977, 1980). The interviews and all other components of the experiment were tape-recorded. In this pretest interview, the subjects were presented with a dilemma about fairness, sharing, and distributive justice. The dilemma was presented, illustrative drawings were provided, and a set of probing questions followed. The questions were designed to learn the subjects' solution to the problem and, more importantly, the reasoning process used to arrive at the solution. These were nondirective interviews. Although all subjects, including adult partners, were given the pretest, only the focal subjects' pretests were transcribed and scored.

A total of four positive justice dilemmas was used in the present study. All four addressed similar issues and were similar in structure. Dilemma 1 and Dilemma 4 were used as the pretest and posttest. Previous research has shown that the scores derived from interviews using Dilemma 1 and interviews using Dilemma 4 are highly correlated ($r = 86$; Damon, 1980). The order of the pretest interviews (focal subject or partner going first) and the dilemma used (1 or 4) were fully crossed and counterbalanced across conditions.

INTERVENTION   Following the pretest, the focal girl and partner subjects were reunited, and two dilemmas were presented. Dilemmas 2 and 3 were used in the intervention, always in the same order (2 followed by 3). The dilemmas were illustrated with line drawings. The experimenter read Dilemma 2 and the probe questions, but did not allow immediate discussion. Instead, the subjects were instructed to discuss competing solutions to the dilemma until they agreed on the best one. The possibility of a disagreement and the meaning of consensus were discussed. Subjects were encouraged to take their time and to consider all solutions to avoid a superficial discussion. The experimenter left the room immediately after providing instructions and was not present during the discussion. Following the discussion of Dilemma 2, Dilemma 3 was read and the same procedure was followed.

POSTTEST Following the intervention, the subjects were instructed that there was time left for one more story and that, for this final interview, the focal girl's name had been selected in advance by drawing straws. This mild deception appeared to satisfy the children's sense of fairness. The procedure for the posttest was identical to that of the pretest.

Scoring Procedure: Pretest and Posttest

Transcripts of the focals' pretests and posttests were scored according to Gerson and Damon's criteria (1975). The scoring procedure focused on the reasoning process used by the subjects, specifically, the nature of the considerations articulated by the subjects in arriving at solutions and how the considerations related to one another.

Damon's (1980) index of moral reasoning is an ordered, six-step sequence that has been validated for several populations of North America, Europe, Asia, and the Middle East in both longitudinal and cross-sectional studies. In scoring the interviews, each subject's responses were divided into "chunks" of reasoning. A *chunk* was a sentence, statement, or group of statements that corresponded to a characteristic of one of Damon's stages. For example, when asked, "Why do you share with Sally?" one child may respond, "Because she's a girl. I'm a girl, and I share with girls." This response corresponds to one characteristic of stage 0-B: an assertion of size, sex, or other physical characteristic as justification for a choice. Each chunk was scored as corresponding to a stage level.

All posttest interviews were scored prior to the scoring of the pretest interviews. A random sample of 20% of the pretests and posttests was independently rescored to assess scorer reliability. The ran-

dom selection was constrained so that a representative number of focal pretests and focal posttests were rescored. The obtained agreement was excellent, Cohen's kappa = .84.

For purposes of statistical analysis, subjects were assigned a weighted mean reasoning score for each interview. Assigned weights were: 10 points to each chunk scored as 0-B, 20 points to each chunk scored as 1-A, 30 for 1-B, 40 for 2-A, and 50 for 2-B. The assigned values were summed and averaged. Thus, the subject's score reflected the mean level of reasoning expressed in each interview. Similar weighting schemes have been used in previous training studies (Berkowitz et al., 1980).

Coding Procedure: Intervention Discussions

The 48 tape recordings of the intervention discussions were transcribed for coding. The unit of analysis was the conversational turn. Each time a subject spoke (uninterrupted) was considered one conversational turn. Turns ranged in length from one word to several sentences. Conversational turns were identified as either *nontransactive* (no code) or *transactive,* as defined by Berkowitz and Gibbs (1983) and adapted for younger subjects by Kruger and Tomasello (1986). Three specific types of transacts were coded, each with two orientations: transactive statements (self-oriented and other-oriented), transactive questions (self-oriented and other-oriented), and transactive responses (self-oriented and other-oriented).

Transactive statements were defined as spontaneously produced critiques, refinements, extensions, or significant paraphrases of ideas. Operations on the partner's ideas were labeled as *other-oriented.* (Example: "Your idea might get the little girl in trouble.") Spontaneously produced clarifications of one's own ideas were coded as *self-oriented.* (Example: "No, you see, my solution is only about the teacher.")

Transactive questions were defined as spontaneously produced requests for clarification, justification, or elaboration. Requests for such elaboration of the partner's ideas were coded as *other-oriented.* (Example: "Why do you think the class should use your solution?") Requests for evaluative feedback regarding one's own ideas were coded as *self-oriented.* (Example: "Do you think my idea is fair or unfair?")

Transactive responses were defined as clarifications, justifications, or elaborations of ideas given in answer to a transactive question. Responses that elaborated on the partner's ideas were coded as *other-oriented,* whereas those that elaborated on one's own ideas were coded as *self-oriented.* Response transacts were given only in response to and immediately following transactive questions. It should be noted that transactive statements and transactive questions were defined as actively self-generated by the subject. However, transactive responses were passive replies to requests and were not spontaneously produced.

A random sample of 20% of the transcripts, equally distributed between the groups, was independently recoded to assess coder reliability. Coders scored copies of the same unmarked transcripts, and the obtained agreement was excellent, Cohen's kappa = .87.

For purposes of statistical analysis, scores were assigned to subjects as follows: Each conversational turn in the intervention discussions was assessed independently. If a turn contained no transactive content, it received no code. If a turn was transactive, it was coded with one of the six mutually exclusive and exhaustive transact codes described earlier. Each turn received only one code. In no transcripts did a subject generate two or more of the six transacts in one turn.

Discussions varied in length, that is, in their total frequency of conversational turns (for the 48 dyads, $M = 47.25$, range = 15 to 94 turns). Consequently, the frequency of total transacts varied (for the 48 dyads, $M = 10.06$, range = 0 to 18 transacts). Because discussions varied, subjects' transactive reasoning in the intervention session was quantified as proportions. Each subject received a score for each of the six codes, computed as that code's frequency divided by that subject's total frequency of conversational turns. In addition to these six measures, each subject also received four summary scores: total transactive statements (self-orientation and other-orientation combined), total transactive questions (self-orientation and other-orientation combined), total transactive responses (self-orientation and other-orientation combined), and total transacts (all transacts combined). Each summary score

was calculated as a proportion, using total frequency of conversational turns as the divisor.

By definition, transacts reflect the context of the discussion. Coding transacts requires taking into consideration the content of the preceding turns. However, for statistical purposes, the transacts by the focal subjects and the transacts by the partner subjects were summarized separately. Therefore, for each dyad the coding procedure yielded 20 proportions, 10 proportional transacts (six individual measures and four summary measures) for each member of the dyad (focal subject and partner).

RESULTS

Group Differences in Reasoning at Posttest

Focals who were paired with peers and focals who were paired with adults were equal in their level of pretest reasoning, with means of 32.77 (focals with peers) and 31.97 (focals with adults), t = n.s. As predicted, focals who were paired with peers produced significantly higher levels of reasoning at posttest ($M = 35.34$, $SD = 4.44$) than did focals paired with adults ($M = 32.46$, $SD = 5.32$), $t(46) = 2.03$, $p = .025$ (one-tailed).[1]

Group Differences in Transacts

A 2 (Group: adult, peer) × 3 (Transact Type: statements, questions, responses) × 2 (Transact Orientation: self-orientation, other-orientation) mixed model analysis of variance (ANOVA) for repeated measures was calculated. This first analysis was based on data generated by focal subjects only. No significant main effect for group was found, $F(1, 46) = 2.94$, $p = .09$. There was no group difference in the proportions of focal girls' conversational turns that were coded as transactive across types and orientations (for focals with peers, $M = 0.214$, $SD = 0.122$; for focals with adults, $M = 0.158$, $SD = 0.103$). As expected, group

[1] Given the absence of pretest differences and the random assignment of subjects to experimental groups, posttest scores are the preferred outcome variable for the measurement of change in the present study (Achenbach, 1978; Cronbach & Furby, 1970; Linn & Slinde, 1977). Change scores as outcome variables are highly problematic, one of the often-noted problems being the regression to the mean. A negative correlation between pretest scores and change scores indicates that there has been such an effect (Borg & Gall, 1983). In the present study, the correlation between pretest and change was negative and significant, $r = -.373$, $p < .01$. Thus, change scores are unreliable and posttest scores are the preferred measure of change.

differences in the type and orientation of the transacts generated by focal girls were found.

As predicted, a significant three-way interaction was found (Group × Transact Type × Transact Orientation), $F(2, 92) = 5.40$, $p = .01$. Analyses of the six simple, simple main effects contained in this interaction (that is, analyses of the variability due to group alone for the six transacts) revealed that, as predicted, focal girls who were paired with adults produced proportionally more self-oriented responses ($M = 0.073$, $SD = 0.062$) than did focal girls who were paired with peers ($M = 0.018$, $SD = 0.037$), $F(1, 92) = 20.00$, $p < .001$. Also consistent with predictions, focals paired with peers produced proportionally more other-oriented statements ($M = 0.124$, $SD = 0.081$) than did focals paired with adults ($M = 0.030$, $SD = 0.045$), $F(l, 92) = 70.96$, $p < .001$. None of the remaining simple, simple main effects reached significance.

Thus, focals in the two groups generated the same proportional number of transacts, but those generated by focals with peers were more spontaneous (i.e., statements) and other-oriented, and those generated by focals with adults were more passive (i.e., responses) and self-oriented. Figure 1 is a graphic representation of the differences between the groups in the types and orientations of transacts generated by the focals.[2]

Also of interest were the transacts generated by the adult and peer partner subjects. A second ANOVA was calculated, based on the transact data generated by the partner subjects only. A 2 (Group) × 3 (Transact Type) × 2 (Transact Orientation) mixed model ANOVA for repeated measures was calculated. No significant main effect for group was found, $F(1, 46) = 0.96$, $p = .33$, indicating no difference between peer and adult partners in the proportions of their conversational turns that were identified as transactive across types and orientations (for peer partners, $M = 0.225$, $SD = 0.113$; for adult partners, $M = 0.257$, $SD = 0.115$). As predicted, a significant three-way interaction effect was found (Group × Transact Type × Transact Orientation), $F(2, 92) = 8.98$, $p < .0001$. Analyses of the six simple, simple

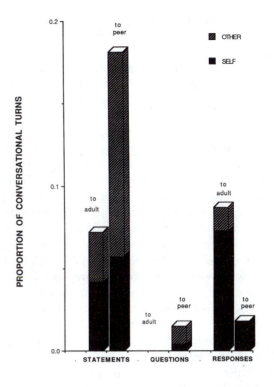

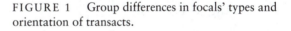

TRANSACTS BY FOCAL SUBJECTS

FIGURE 1   Group differences in focals' types and orientation of transacts.

main effects contained in this interaction indicated that, as predicted, adult partners produced proportionally more other-oriented questions ($M = 0.117$, $SD = 0.089$) than did peer partners ($M = 0.025$, $SD = 0.039$), $F(1, 92) = 62.71$, $p < .0001$. Also consistent with predictions, peer partners produced proportionally more other-oriented statements ($M = 0.146$, $SD = 0.072$) than did adult partners ($M = 0.109$, $SD = 0.068$), $F(1, 92) = 9.87$, $p < .01$. In addition, peer partners generated proportionally more self-oriented statements ($M = 0.043$, $SD = 0.050$) than did adult partners ($M = 0.017$, $SD = 0.032$), $F(1, 92) = 5.02$, $p < .05$. None of the

---

[2]Other results from this analysis, not directly addressed by the present hypotheses, were: no main effect for transact orientation was found, $F(1, 46) = 0.32$, $p = .57$. A significant main effect for transact type was found, $F(2, 92) = 35.79$, $p < .001$. A significant Group × Transact Type interaction effect occurred, $F(2, 92) = 19.58$, $p < .001$. A significant Group × Transact Orientation interaction effect was found $F(1, 46) = 22.06$, $p < .001$. A significant Transact Type × Transact Orientation interaction effect was found $F(2, 92) = 17.01$, $p < .001$.

remaining simple, simple main effects reached significance. Figure 2 is a graphic representation of group differences in the type of transacts produced by the partners.[3]

To summarize the foregoing analyses of the intervention discussions: All subjects, focals and partners, children and adults, generated the same proportional numbers of transacts in their conversations. However, consistent with predictions, group differences appeared in the nature of the transacts generated, that is, in the types and orientations used. Focals paired with peers produced more other-oriented statements than did focals paired with adults, and peer partners produced more other-oriented statements than did adult partners. Thus, peer dyads were characterized by their mutual use of other-oriented transactive statements. In contrast, focals paired with adults produced more self-oriented responses than did focals paired with peers. Adult partners produced more other-oriented questions than did peer partners. Therefore, adult-child dyads were characterized by a pattern of adult questions and child responses. These patterns are consistent with expectations and with previous findings (Kruger & Tomasello, 1986).

Relationships among Partner, Transacts, and Reasoning at Posttest

The differential use of transacts by subjects in the two conditions was predicted to be related to the differential posttest reasoning by those subjects. To assess this possibility, multiple regression analyses were made after a complete correlation matrix had been constructed. This correlation matrix (presented in Table 1) served as the basis for the selection of variables to be included in the multiple regressions, and it described the relationships between 20 transact measures (10 proportional scores for the 48 focal subjects and 10 proportional scores for the 48 partner subjects, both children and adults, as previously described) and focal posttest scores. Thus, for both

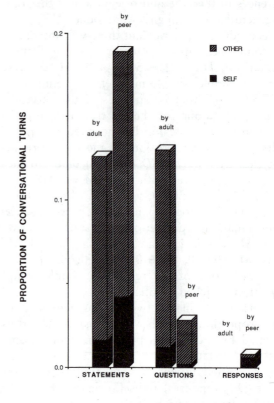

TRANSACTS BY PARTNER SUBJECTS

FIGURE 2   Group differences in partners' types and orientation of transacts.

the correlations and the multiple regressions, the focal posttest score was the outcome variable.[4]

Analysis of styles. The correlation matrix was calculated for the two experiment groups separately and for the total sample, and the results showed that specific types and orientations of transacts by focals in the intervention discussions correlated with reasoning at posttest. However, in addition to the focals' use of transacts, specific patterns in the

---

[3]Other significant effects from this analysis, not directly addressed by the present hypotheses, occurred: a main effect for transact type, $F(2, 92) = 57.74$, $p < .001$; a main effect for transact orientation, $F(1, 46) = 100.57$, $p < .001$; a Group × Transact Type interaction effect, $F(2, 92) = 17.01$, $p < .001$; a Group × Transact Orientation interaction effect, $F(1, 46) = 5.65$, $p < .05$; a Transact Type × Transact Orientation interaction effect, $F(2, 92) = 38.89$, $p < .001$.

[4] Due to the lack of reliability of change scores, their use can attenuate correlations between predictors and outcome, particularly when the correlation between pretest and posttest is high (Linn & Slinde, 1977). In the present study, the correlation between pretest and posttest is positive and highly significant, $r = .545$, $p < .001$. In this experiment, the null hypothesis states that the two treatments have the same effect; therefore, the crucial question is whether the posttest scores vary between the groups. Thus, the posttest score is the preferred criterion variable (Achenbach, 1978).

TABLE 1

Pearson Product Moment Correlations: Transacts and Posttest Scores

	Adult-Child	Peer	Total Sample
Focals			
Self-oriented statements	.230	.006	.144
Other-oriented statements	.445*[a]	−.050	.279*
Total statements	.436*	−.032	.281*
Self-oriented questions	.000	.322†	.253*
Other-oriented questions	.000	.298†	.268*
Total questions	.000	.346*	.293*
Self-oriented responses	−.070	.043	−.163
Other-oriented responses	−.028	.000	−.094
Total responses	−.064	.043	−.163
Total transacts	.263	.072	.244†
Partners			
Self-oriented statements	.167	−.537**	−.114
Other-oriented statements	.459*	−.181	.219†
Total statements	.561	−.382*	.118
Self-oriented questions	−.022	.223	−.029
Other-oriented questions	.085	.177	−.078
Total questions	.065	.243	−.076
Self-oriented responses	.000	.270	.233†
Other-oriented responses	.000	.223	.178
Total responses	.000	.297†	.250*
Total transacts	.378*	−.211	.067
Dyadic styles			
Egocentric	.268	−.306†	.045
Socratic	.023	.116	−.177
Egalitarian	.597***	−.139	.307*
Leadership		.337*	.284*

[a] All probability values are one-tailed.   *$p < .05$.   **$p < .01$.   ***$p < .001$.   †$p < .10$.

partners' transacts influenced focals' reasoning as well. These results suggested an influence of dyadic style on focal reasoning at posttest. A dyadic influence on reasoning is logical, given the interactional nature of the transact measures. Furthermore, dyadic style differences were found in the analyses of transacts previously reported and were suggested by patterns in the correlations. Therefore, four types of dyadic discussion style were described post hoc. The styles, conceptualized by combining the focal and partner transact measures that independently predicted focal posttest, represent four distinct interactional patterns observed and reflect transaction at the level of the dyad. However, for the purpose of hypothesis-testing, the four dyadic styles may be ranked hierarchically to reflect four degrees of transactive engagement with the partner from the focal subject's point of view.

Egocentric style is defined as the combination of self-oriented statements by the focal subject and self-oriented statements by the partner. It represents an absence of engagement with the partner and a focus on the self. Egocentric style was suggested by a pattern of negative correlations in the peer group.

Socratic style is defined as other-oriented questions by the partner combined with self-oriented responses by the focal subject. It represents the focal's passive engagement in the transactive dialogue and features the focal's compliance with the partner's requests for transacts. Socratic style was suggested by the question-and-response pattern typical of discussions by adult-child dyads reported earlier.

Egalitarian style, defined as the combination of other-oriented statements by the focal subject and other-oriented statements by the partner, represents the focal's active and spontaneous collaboration with the partner in the transactive dialogue. It features the focal's and partner's equal status, and was suggested by the pattern of transacts typical of discussions by peer dyads previously reported and by a pattern of significant positive correlations in the adult-child group.

Leadership style is defined as the total questions by the focal subject combined with total responses by the partner. It represents the focal's most active level of engagement in the transactive dialogue. Leadership style features the focal's spontaneous control of the interaction by way of questioning and passive compliance by the partner, and was suggested by a pattern of significant positive correlations in the peer group.

For these four specific discussion styles, scores were assigned to dyads by simply adding the individual proportional transact scores involved. Each dyad, then, received four style scores, one score for each of the four discussion styles. Thus, the dyads were not characterized as using one style as opposed to the other three. Instead, the proportional use of the four styles in each dyad's discussions was measured. There was no difference between the groups in the use of egocentric style (for the adult-child group, $M = 0.06$, $SD = 0.06$; for the peer group, $M = 0.10$, $SD = 0.09$; $t = $ n.s.). However, as suggested by the previously reported results, adult-child dyads featured more socratic style interaction ($M = 0.19$, $SD = 0.14$) than did peer dyads ($M = 0.04$, $SD = 0.07$), $t(46) = 4.44$, $p < .001$. Peer dyads featured

more egalitarian style interaction ($M = 0.27$, $SD = 0.12$) than did adult-child dyads ($M = 0.14$, $SD = 0.09$), $t(46) = 4.27$, $p < .001$. In addition, peer dyads featured more leadership style interaction ($M = 0.02$, $SD = 0.05$) than adult-child dyads ($M = 0.00$, $SD = 0.00$), $p = .02$ (Fisher's Exact Test). A Fisher's Exact Test was employed to compare the groups' use of leadership style due to a lack of variability in the adult-child group. The four discussion styles were correlated with focal posttest scores for the two groups separately and for the total sample (see Table 1), with one exception. The absence of variability in the use of leadership style in the adult-child group (zero evidence of its use) made a correlation coefficient inappropriate for that group. These correlations between the dyadic styles and focal posttest scores also served the selection of variables for the multiple regressions.

MULTIPLE REGRESSIONS   All measures significantly correlated with posttest reasoning were selected to enter the multiple regression equations with one exception: When two correlating measures were not mutually exclusive, such as other-oriented statements and total statements, the measure with the highest correlation coefficient was selected to enter the equation. This was done to eliminate the collinearity of the two predictors, protecting that assumption of multiple regression analysis.

For the total sample, the adult-child group, and the peer group, equations were calculated two ways, utilizing as predictors (a) the individual transact measures and (b) the discussion style transact measures. All variables competed to enter the equations. Results of the multiple regression analyses are presented in Table 2.

Two equations were written to describe the total sample. For the first equation, the following predictors were entered: focals' total statements, focals' total questions, partners' other-oriented statements, and partners' total responses. The equation created by the four individual transact variables was not successful in describing the entire sample, $F(4, 43) = 1.88$, $p = .13$, multiple $r^2 = .15$. The variables did not independently make significant contributions to the model.

In the second equation, egalitarian style and leadership style were selected for entry by the aforementioned criteria. The equation created by the two discussion styles accounted for 15% of the variance and the contribution was significant, $F(2, 45) = 4.05$, $p = .02$. The two variables contributed to the model at a marginally significant level (.06 and .09 for egalitarian and leadership, respectively), which was

TABLE 2

Multiple Regression Analyses

Model					Predictors' Contributions	
F	df	p	R^2	Predictors	t	p
				Total Sample		
1.88	4, 43	.13	.15	Partner—other-oriented statements	0.90	.37
				Focal—total statements	1.05	.30
				Focal—total questions	1.07	.29
				Partner—total responses	−0.30	.77
4.05	2, 45	.02	.15	Egalitarian	1.95	.06
				Leadership	1.76	.09
				Adult-Child Group		
5.55	2, 21	.01	.35	Focal—other-oriented statements	−1.00	.33
				Partner—total statements	2.18	.04
12.15	1, 22	.002	.36	Egalitarian	3.49	.00
				Peer Group		
3.91	3, 20	.02	.37	Focal—total questions	0.62	.54
				Partner—self-oriented statements	−2.82	.01
				Partner—total responses	0.20	.85
3.71	2, 21	.04	.26	Egocentric	−2.05	.05
				Leadership	2.18	.04

superior to the level of contribution of individual transact measures and suggests that the discussion style variables may be more powerful predictors than individual transact measures.

Two equations were written to describe the adult-child group. The first equation utilized individual transact measures. Focals' other-oriented statements and partners' total statements were entered. The equation successfully described the adult-child group, $F(2, 21) = 5.55$, $p = .01$, multiple $r^2 = .35$. Focals' other-oriented statements did not contribute significantly to the model ($p = .33$), but partners' total statements did ($p = .04$). The second equation utilized egalitarian style as a predictor and was highly successful, $F(1, 22) = 12.15$, $p = .002$, multiple $r^2 = .36$. Egalitarian style contributed significantly to the model ($p < .0001$).

Two equations were written to describe the peer group. The first equation utilized individual transact measures: focals' total questions, partners' self-oriented statements, and partners' total responses.

This equation successfully described the peer group, $F(3, 20) = 3.91$, $p = .02$, multiple $r^2 = .37$. However, only one variable, partners' self-oriented statements, contributed significantly to the model ($p = .01$), having a negative relationship with reasoning.

The second equation utilized discussion style variables, egocentric style and leadership style. This equation was significant, $F(2, 21) = 3.71$, $p = .04$, multiple $r^2 = .26$. Both variables contributed significantly to the model. Egocentric style made a significant contribution ($p = .01$), with a negative relationship with reasoning; leadership style contributed significantly ($p = .04$) with a positive relationship with reasoning.

The discussion styles that predicted outcome varied between the groups: Egalitarian style was predictive in the adult-child group; leadership style was positively predictive in the peer group; and egocentric style was negatively predictive in the peer group. This difference in predictors was tested for significance: First, the correlation between egalitarian style and focal posttest scores was calculated for the adult-child group and for the peer group (as reported in Table 1). The correlations for the two groups are significantly different, $z = 2.68$, $p < .01$. Second, the correlation between egocentric style and focal posttest scores was calculated for the two groups (Table 1); the correlations are significantly different, $z = 2.00$, $p < .05$. Third, the correlation between leadership style and focal posttest scores was calculated for the peer group (Table 1). It was inappropriate to calculate a correlation in the adult-child group because of zero evidence of leadership style use. Therefore, it was impossible to compare correlations between the adult-child and peer groups. However, given the absence of leadership style in the adult-child group, and given the significant correlation between leadership style and posttest scores in the peer group, it appears that the two groups varied meaningfully in the presence of a relationship between leadership style and outcome.[5]

To summarize the multiple regressions: For the sample as a whole, leadership style and egalitarian style were the best positive predictors of posttest reasoning. That is, those dyadic styles consisting of greater spontaneity and activity by focal subjects were most predictive of growth. For adult-child dyads considered alone, egalitarian style was predictive, and for peers considered alone, leadership style predicted reasoning.

DISCUSSION

These results support Piaget's hypothesis (1932) that interaction with peers during middle childhood is important to the development of moral reasoning. The findings of the present study indicated that children paired with peers for a discussion of sociomoral dilemmas produced more sophisticated moral reasoning, subsequent to the discussion, than did children paired with adults.

Other results of the present study confirmed another part of Piaget's hypothesis. As Piaget predicted, children who were paired with peers used reasoning (transacts) in their intervention discussions in a qualitatively different way then did children who were paired with adults. A pattern of activity in peer transaction and passivity in adult-child transaction was found in Kruger and Tomasello (1986) and here as well. Although Kruger and Tomasello also found quantitative differences in transacts, this finding was not replicated here in that form. In the present study, focal girls with adults generated as many transacts as did focal girls with peers overall, but they were of a different nature in the two situations. The transacts generated by focals paired with adults were passive, elicited by the adults and not spontaneously produced. The transacts produced by focals paired with peers were active in nature, spontaneously generated without prompting by the partner. The present finding of differences in the quality of transaction is of more crucial theoretical significance. The active quality of transaction, rather than the amount of transaction, is hypothesized to be related to reasoning development.

A third set of results here supported Piaget's contention of a causal link between the use of reasoning in discussions with peers and the greater reasoning level subsequent to peer interaction. In the present study, the use of spontaneous, self-generated transacts by focal girls was predictive of their subsequent reasoning. Dyadic styles that featured such activity by the focal girl, egalitarian and leadership, were predictive of posttest reasoning for the total sample. Whether a child was paired with a peer or an adult, active reasoning in dyadic discussions led to a more sophisticated reasoning at posttest.

Thus, this third set of results, when viewed in light of group differences in dyadic style, is critical to the Piagetian hypothesis. The differential level of reasoning subsequent to discussions with peers and adults may be attributed to the differential use of reasoning by the groups. Children who were paired with peers engaged in egalitarian- and leadership-style discussions more often than did children who were paired with adults. These two types of discussions were predictive of focal moral reasoning at posttest for the total sample. The interpretation of these findings is that the type, rather than the amount, of transactive discussion generated was important to subsequent reasoning and that the partner in the discussion, whether peer or adult, constrained the type of transacts produced. Peer symmetry of power

---

[5] Because there were trivial differences in pretest scores, partial correlations also were performed, measuring the relationship between discussion styles and posttest scores, controlling for pretest scores. The pattern of results was unchanged, but the degree of some relationships was affected.
Egalitarian style: adult-child group, $r = .442$, $p < .05$; peer group, $r = -.187$, n.s.; $z = 2.14$, $p < .05$.
Egocentric style: adult-child group, $r = .225$, n.s.; peer group, $r = -.305$, $p < .10$; $z = 1.75$, $p < .10$.
Leadership style: adult-child group, not measured (as before); peer group, $r = .290$, $p < .10$.

allowed greater activity of reasoning, from egalitarian co-construction to leadership, and this activity was critical to development.

In both groups, the type of focal transacts that were predictive of reasoning represented control and responsibility. Children paired with adults who engaged in active critiquing subsequently showed greater reasoning skills. Instead of a consistent pattern of compliance, they showed the ability to share control of the conversation and were willing to criticize the adult's thinking, to treat the adult as a peer. Children who were paired with peers generally engaged in shared control of the interaction and showed greater posttest scores than children who were paired with adults. Those focals in peer dyads who assumed an even greater share of responsibility were particularly likely to show improvement. That is, when children paired with peers acted as adults, assumed more control, and questioned the other, they developed in their reasoning.

Two considerations may limit the generality of the current findings. First, these data represent the effect of a single, brief experience by the subjects. Although the present intervention was brief, however, it was designed to enhance thinking in a specific content area, distributive justice, and this is what was measured at pre- and posttest. Furthermore, other training studies with brief interventions (e.g., Nelson & Aboud, 1985) have been effective and have recorded effects beyond the time of the experiment (e.g., Damon & Killen, 1982). Although it remains an empirical question, long-term interventions may promote the effectiveness of Socratic dialogue. At present, the importance of such adult-child interaction is undefined, but it has been demonstrated that, in general, moral discussions between children and adults can be related to changes in reasoning (Azrak, 1978; Grimes, 1974; Hoffman, 1970, 1980; Holstein, 1972; Parikh, 1980; Stanley, 1976). Second, observation may have affected adults and children differentially, but such differences in response to "performance pressure" may reflect similar differences between adults and children in their approaches to interaction in general. Often adults may feel motivated to regulate and guide children (Kaye & Charney, 1981; Martinez, 1987; Rogoff & Wertsch, 1984; Vygotsky, 1978), particularly in discussions of moral dilemmas (Youniss, 1980). Children, by contrast, may view such interactions less seriously, creating a looser, more playful experience.

The present study has demonstrated the importance of peer interaction in the development of the sociocognitive skill of moral reasoning. Other researchers have compared the effect of peer and adult-child interaction on cognitive tasks, such as planning, and have produced results that differ sharply from those presented here. It has been demonstrated that peer dyads and adult-child dyads differ in their problem solving style when engaged in a planning task (Gauvain & Rogoff, 1989), and adult-child interaction is more effective than peer interaction in fostering the development of planning skills (Radziszewska & Rogoff, 1988). Whether these different findings are attributable to different methodologies or whether, in fact, the beneficial social process in problem solving is dependent on the domain of the task involved remains an important empirical question.

It has been demonstrated previously that transacts are important to change in moral reasoning in training studies with adults (Berkowitz & Gibbs, 1983) and with children (Damon & Killen, 1982). It also has been established that children use transacts in qualitatively different ways with peers and adults (Kruger & Tomasello, 1986). In the present study, evidence is presented for the first time that peer discussions of moral dilemmas result in greater improvement in moral reasoning than do discussions between children and adults. In addition, these data indicate that a spontaneous, active use of reasoning is conducive to moral reasoning development.

Mutual engagement in transactive dialogue was predictive of posttest scores when it occurred between children and adults as well as when it occurred between peers. However, here, children in peer dyads had the freedom to use this important, active reasoning more often than did children paired with adults. The peers' equal status allowed a critical reciprocity that was infrequent in adult-child dyads. Thus, Piaget's contention (1932) that symmetry of power leads to greater moral reasoning development is supported, and the current study indicates that active reasoning is the essential element in the process.

Questions

1. What four types of dyadic discussions were identified in this research and which of these predicted the best outcomes for reasoning on the posttest? Why do you think these particular styles were most effective?

2. If transactions with peers help children develop moral reasoning, how might this be incorporated in the classroom to benefit development?

3. Have you ever had the experience that talking over a moral issue with a peer helped you understand the issue better? Would a similar discussion with someone significantly older have been as helpful? Explain.

References

Achenbach, T. M. (1978). *Research in developmental psychology: Concepts, strategies, and methods.* New York: The Free Press.

Arbuthnot, J. (1975). Modification of moral development through role playing. *Developmental Psychology, 11,* 319–324.

Azrak, R. (1978). Parental discipline and early adolescent moral development. *Dissertation Abstracts International, 39,* 2747A–2748A.

Berkowitz, M., & Gibbs, J. (1983). Measuring the developmental features of moral discussion. *Merrill-Palmer Quarterly, 29,* 399–410.

Berkowitz, M., Gibbs, J., & Broughton, J. (1980). The relation of moral judgment stage disparity to developmental effects of peer dialogues. *Merrill-Palmer Quarterly, 26,* 341–357.

Borg, W. R., & Gall, M. D. (1983). *Educational research: An introduction* (4th ed.). New York: Longman.

Cronbach, L. J., & Furby, L. (1970). How we should measure "change"—or should we? *Psychological Bulletin, 74,* 68–80.

Damon, W. (1975). Early conceptions of positive justice as related to the development of operational reasoning. *Child Development, 46,* 301–312.

Damon, W. (1977). *The social world of the child.* San Francisco: Jossey-Bass.

Damon, W. (1980). Patterns of change in children's social reasoning: A two-year longitudinal study. *Child Development, 51,* 1010–1017.

Damon, W., & KILLEN, M. (1982). Peer interaction and the process of change in children's moral reasoning. *Merrill-Palmer Quarterly, 28,* 347–367.

Gauvain, M., & Rogoff, B. (1989). Collaborative problem solving and children's planning skills. *Developmental Psychology, 25,* 139–151.

Gerson, R., & Damon, W. (1975). *Scoring manual for positive justice.* Unpublished manuscript, Clark University, Worcester, MA.

Grimes, P. (1974). Teaching moral reasoning to eleven year olds and their mothers: A means of promoting moral development. *Dissertation Abstracts International, 35,* 1498A–1499A.

Hoffman, M. L. (1970). Conscience, personality, and socialization techniques. *Human Development, 13,* 90–126.

Hoffman, M. L. (1980). Moral development in adolescence. In J. Adelson (Ed.), *Handbook of adolescent psychology.* New York: Wiley.

Holstein, C. B. (1972). The relation of children's moral judgement level to that of their parents and to communication patterns in the family. In R. C. Smart & M. S. Smart (Eds.), *Readings in child development and relationships.* New York: Macmillan.

Kaye, K., & Charney, R. (1981). Conversational asymmetry between mothers and children. *Journal of Child Language, 8,* 35–49.

Kruger, A. C. & Tomasello, M. (1986). Transactive discussions with peer and adults. *Developmental Psychology, 22,* 681–685.

Linn, R. L., & Slinde, J. A. (1977). The determination of the significance of change between pre- and posttesting periods. *Review of Educational Research, 47,* 121–150.

Maitland, K., & Goldman, J. (1974). Moral judgment as a function of peer group interaction. *Journal of Personality and Social Psychology, 30,* 699–704.

Martinez, M. A. (1987). Dialogues among children and between children and their mothers. *Child Development, 58,* 1035–1043.

Nelson, J., & Aboud, F. E. (1985). The resolution of social conflict between friends. *Child Development, 56,* 1009–1017.

Parikh, B. (1980). Development of moral judgment and its relation to family environmental factors in Indian and American families. *Child Development, 51,* 1030–1039.

Piaget, J. (1932). *The moral judgment of the child.* London: Kegan Paul.

Piaget, J. (1970). Piaget's theory. In P. Mussen (Ed.), *Carmichael's manual of child psychology* (Vol. 1). New York: Wiley.

Radziszewska, B., & Rogoff, B. (1988). Influence of adult and peer collaborators on children's planning skills. *Developmental Psychology, 24,* 840–848.

Rogoff, B., & Wertsch, J. V. (Eds.). (1984). *Children's learning in the "zone of proximal development."* San Francisco: Jossey-Bass.

Stanley, S. (1976). A curriculum to affect the moral atmosphere of the family and the moral development of adolescents. *Dissertation Abstracts International, 36,* 7221A–7222A.

Vygotsky, L. S. (1978). *Mind in society.* Cambridge, MA: Harvard University Press.

Youniss, J. (1980). *Parents and peers in social development: A Sullivan-Piaget perspective.* Chicago: University of Chicago Press.

23

Determinants of Complexity in Mexican-American and Anglo-American Mothers' Conceptions of Child Development

JEANNIE GUTIERREZ AND ARNOLD SAMEROFF

The following article investigates different mothers' views of child development in relation to their ethnic background and their extent of acculturation within the larger U. S. society. By comparing middle-class Mexican-American mothers who differ in their degree of acculturation with Euro-American mothers who are also from the middle class, Jeannie Gutierrez and Arnold Sameroff provide insight into the relationship between acculturation and traditional cultural values and its effect on how mothers think about how to raise their children.

Complexity of parental reasoning about child development was studied in mothers who varied in ethnic background and biculturalism. Middle-class mothers from Mexican-American and Anglo-American backgrounds were compared on their level of concepts of development on a scale from categorical to perspectivistic reasoning. Categorical mothers interpreted child development as being caused by single constitutional or environmental factors. Perspectivistic mothers interpreted development as the result of the dynamic interplay between constitution and environment over time

Reprinted with permission from *Child Development*, 61, 1990, 384–394. Copyright 1990 by The Society for Research in Child Development.

This research was completed in partial fulfillment of the requirements for the degree of Doctor of Philosophy at the University of Illinois at Chicago by the first author.

and accepted that the same developmental outcome could have multiple determinants. In a comparison among moderately acculturated Mexican-Americans, highly acculturated Mexican-Americans, and Anglo-Americans, the highly acculturated Mexican-American group scored as more perspectivistic than the other two groups, despite the fact that the Anglo-Americans were the most acculturated. When the 2 Mexican-American groups were subdivided into monocultural (Mexican or American) and bicultural subgroups and compared with the Anglo-American group, the bicultural subgroup of the highly acculturated Mexican-American mothers was the most perspectivistic. These results suggest a complex picture of diversity in Mexican-American mothers who retain values and beliefs from their own culture, as well as taking on values and beliefs of the American culture. Maternal intelligence and adherence to traditional cultural values were not found to correlate significantly with level of developmental reasoning.

Child development is regulated by patterns of child rearing. These patterns are influenced by parental beliefs and values (Goodnow, 1988), which vary from one culture to another and from one social status to another within cultures (Kohn, 1969). Although many find it easy to agree that culture influences social and perhaps emotional development, there is far less accord about social influences on cognitive processes. Wertsch, Minick, and Arns (1984) contrast individualistic theories of cognitive development as represented by Piaget (1950) with social theories as represented by Vygotsky (1978). Wertsch et al. (1984) suggest that in Vygotsky's view cognitive development is explained by sociocultural mediation and modes of activity. The intellectual outcome for any individual is the product of a dialectic between the constructivistic aspects of cognition and social patterns of activity.

The typical arena for studying such issues in cognitive development is in the classroom using concept-formation tasks. However, the social influence on the nature of thought may also be studied in the broader area of cognitions about human growth and development. Analogies to the parents' structuring of tasks for the child may be found in cultural structuring of how parents raise children. More specifically, this study is an investigation of cultural influences on how parents conceptualize child development.

The social context in which development occurs influences both parenting cognitions and how parents relate these cognitions to the characteristics of the child. Modern American culture is characterized by a great diversity of child-rearing practices, many of them rooted in the ethnic traditions of the family. Immigrants from more agrarian, less industrialized countries bring with them many child-rearing beliefs and practices that diverge from families that have been fully acculturated (Werner, 1979). The acculturation process has often been described as accommodation to the host culture in terms of giving up traditional forms of behavior and adopting modal behaviors of the host country (Garcia & Lega, 1979; Szapocznik, Scopetta, Kurtines, & Aranalde, 1978). An amplification of this view is that modern cultures permit and promote more diversity than traditional cultures, and thus acculturation would involve not just changing from one pattern of behavior to another but changing the way one thinks about behavior, changing one's concepts of development.

The concepts of development that parents hold will influence the way they understand the behavior of their children. Sameroff and Feil (1985) proposed a hierarchy of developmental concepts moving from a categorical belief that single causes were associated with single outcomes, to a compensating belief that outcomes could have multiple causes, to a perspectivistic belief that these multiple causes could interact and be transformed over time to produce alternative outcomes. To the extent that these concepts are flexible or perspectivistic, parents will be able to adapt to a variety of outcomes for their children. To the extent that these beliefs are rigid or categorical, parents will have difficulty adapting their rearing for children who differ from parent expectations in either appearance or behavior, especially if the children are handicapped. In a study of intellectual functioning in preschool children, it was found that the higher the level of the mother's concepts of development, the higher the IQ of the children at 4 years of age (Sameroff, Seifer, Barocas, Zax, & Greenspan, 1987). Furthermore, these concepts of development have great stability over many years. A high correlation ($r = .65$) was found between parents' scores on a concepts-of-development questionnaire given when their children were 4 and again when their children were 13 (Sameroff & Seifer, 1989).

Diversity in parenting cognitions both within and between ethnic groups must be interpreted within the socioeconomic and cultural context in which they exist. For Mexican-American families the cultural context includes socializing their children as part of a larger host culture. Exposure to a different cultural context can induce dramatic, often conflictual, changes within families. Part of what influences change in parenting values is the immigrant's belief system at the time of immigration, as well as the parenting values endorsed by the host culture. The immigrant may have come from a society or community with either a traditional, transitional, or contemporary value orientation (Karrer, 1986). Recently, acculturation has been viewed as a transactional process involving change in both the immigrant group and the host culture (Karrer, 1986; Padilla, 1980; Szapocznik & Kurtines, 1980). In many ways the acculturation process is an accommodation between the two groups that unfolds as a function of their reactions to each other and the cultural context of the society. The cultural context must include the process of acculturation, as well as the level of cultural evolution of the ethnic group at the time of immigration (Karrer, 1986).

In regard to beliefs about children, Gutierrez, Sameroff, and Karrer (1988) proposed that acculturation would move parents to more flexible concepts of development in which more possibilities for parent and child behavior would be entertained. By comparing mothers in different states of acculturation, they examined the relation between adaptation to a modern industrial culture and concepts of development. Gutierrez et al. (1988) compared higher- and lower-SES groups of Mexican-American and Anglo-American mothers. The Mexican-American mothers were selected to be at low, moderate, or high levels of acculturation ranging from recent immigrants who planned to return to Mexico to second- and third-generation parents who had less involvement in Mexican culture or language. SES was found to be a major correlate of the concepts of development score, with both Mexican-American and Anglo American low-SES mothers scoring as more categorical than high-SES mothers. The predicted acculturation effect was found only among the high-SES mothers, with the more acculturated Mexican-American mothers scoring as more perspectivistic than the less acculturated ones. A surprise, however, was that the highly acculturated Mexican-American mothers were even more perspectivistic than the SES matched Anglo-American mothers. In order to explain these results, Gutierrez et al. hypothesized that perspectivism was enhanced by the need for highly acculturated Mexican-Americans to operate in two cultures, as compared with Anglo-Americans or less acculturated Mexican-Americans who functioned predominantly in one culture, either American or Mexican. However, this hypothesis could not be tested because there was no individual assessment of the degree to which each mother was involved in one or two cultures, that is, the degree to which she was monocultural or bicultural.

Szapocznik and Kurtines (1980) have suggested that the concept of biculturalism be incorporated in acculturation models. According to this model, acculturation is a complex process of accommodation to a total cultural context that may be unidirectional or bidirectional depending upon the type of cultural context involved. Given that Mexican-Americans tend to function in both Mexican and American communities, they need to be able to participate in both cultural contexts. In this respect, it may be important for individuals both to take on values of the dominant culture and to retain values and characteristics of the culture of origin. Bicultural individuals who live in a bicultural context may be more likely to have additional flexibility for coping with their social environment.

The present study was designed to test this hypothesis by examining the relation of both acculturation level and biculturalism to mothers' levels of concepts of development. Specifically, we predicted that mothers who were bicultural—who lived comfortably in both Mexican and American cultural contexts—would be more perspectivistic in their beliefs about child development than mothers who were monocultural. Further, we predicted that biculturalism would be a more important influence on parental concepts of development than level of acculturation into the dominant culture.

METHOD

Subjects

The subjects were 60 middle-class, professional Mexican-American and Anglo-American mothers, divided into three groups; a group of 20 moderately acculturated Mexican-American mothers, a group of 20 highly acculturated Mexican-American mothers, and a group of 20 Anglo-American mothers. The three groups were matched for age and socioeconomic status (SES). Socioeconomic status was established using a modification of the Hollingshead (1957) Two-Factor Index of Social Position (ISP), which combines head of household's occupational and educational levels; the modification was that mothers' and fathers' educational levels were averaged before computing the ISP (Sameroff & Seifer, 1983). Only mothers' education and occupation were used in father-absent families. Only families in SES categories 1 and 2 (primarily professional employment and advanced educational status) were included in the study. Subjects were recruited into the three groups (moderately acculturated Mexican-American, highly acculturated Mexican-American, and Anglo-American) to maximize educational and occupational equivalence for the groups. This stringent condition made subject recruitment difficult due to the higher likelihood of finding Mexican-American mothers with less education and lower occupational status in the lower acculturation group. However, less acculturated, professional, educated Mexican-American mothers were successfully sought out who had equivalent occupational and educational experience to the more acculturated Mexican-American mothers. Table 1 presents demographic data on maternal occupation, education, age, number of children, and generation in the United States for the Mexican-American and Anglo-American mothers, subdivided into monocultural and bicultural subgroups (moderately acculturated monocultural Mexican-American, moderately acculturated bicultural Mexican-American, highly acculturated monocultural Mexican-American, highly acculturated bicultural Mexican-American, and monocultural Anglo-American). The categories for education and occupation are those used by Hollingshead. For example, the mothers' occupational categories were major professional (lawyer, accountant), lesser pro-

fessional (teacher, social worker), and minor professional (physical therapist). Only third-generation Anglo-American mothers who were not involved in any ethnic group and neither they nor their parents spoke another language were included in the study.

Measures

All interviews were conducted in the subjects' homes and in their preferred language. The measures were translated into Spanish using a back-translation technique (English into Spanish and Spanish back into English) until they were easily understandable to monolingual Spanish-speaking subjects.

CONCEPTS OF DEVELOPMENT   The Concepts of Development Vignettes (CODV) were used to assess the level of complexity at which mothers understood development (Sameroff & Feil, 1985). The instrument consists of six vignettes that depict developmental problems common to all cultures. The mothers were told the vignettes and asked to explain why the child or parent acted as described. Responses were

TABLE 1

Maternal Demographic Data for Monocultural
and Bicultural Subgroups of Mothers

| | Mexican-American | | | | |
| | Moderately Acculturated | | Highly Acculturated | | Anglo (Mono) |
	Mono	Bi	Mono	Bi	
n	10	10	8	12	20
Maternal age	36.4	41.2	34.0	34.5	35.3
Number of children *(M)*	1.9	2.4	2.0	1.9	2.2
Maternal occupation:					
Major professional	4	3	4	3	7
Lesser professional	6	7	4	9	12
Minor professional	0	0	0	0	1
Maternal education:					
Less than BA	1	2	0	3	2
College graduate	5	5	4	6	11
Postgraduate	4	3	4	3	7
Generation in United States:					
First	7	6	1	1	0
Second	3	4	5	8	0
Third	0	0	2	3	20

scored according to the detailed codebook given in Sameroff and Feil (1985) into six levels of complexity: transition to categorical (1.5), categorical (2.0), transition to compensating (2.5), compensating (3.0), transition to perspectivistic (3.5), and perspectivistic (4.0). Examples of responses coded at different levels of complexity to one of the vignettes are shown in Table 2 (for more examples see Gutierrez et al., 1988; Sameroff & Feil, 1985). Thirty vignettes were scored by two raters to determine reliability; there was perfect agreement on 80% and agreement within a half point on the remaining 20%.

ACCULTURATION   The Acculturation Rating Scale for Mexican Americans (ARSMA), developed by Cuellar, Harris, and Jasso (1980), was used to measure level of acculturation. The ARSMA consists of 20 items designed to assess acculturation such as language familiarity, usage, and reference; ethnic identity and generation; reading, writing, and cultural exposure; and ethnic interaction. Each item is scored on a 5-point Likert-type scale, and the cross-items average is used to categorize subjects into acculturation groups, from very "Mexicanized" to very "Anglicized."

TABLE 2

Sample of Responses to Concepts of Development Vignettes: Vignette 5

Mr. and Mrs. Raymond have two children: Billy, who is 5, and Mary, who is 3. Billy was a very demanding baby and still asks for a lot of attention from his parents. Billy would get very angry if he didn't get what he wanted from his parents. Lately, Mr. and Mrs. Raymond have had a lot of money problems because Mr. Raymond was laid off from his job. One evening at bedtime Mrs. Raymond heard Billy and Mary fighting over a toy. She stormed into the bedroom and began spanking Billy very hard and she wouldn't stop. Mr. Raymond had to pull her away from the boy and had a hard time calming her down.

How would you explain Mrs. Raymond's behavior?

2.0 *Categorical.* "It seems like Mrs. Raymond is having a lot of trouble dealing with the financial problems due to husband losing his job. Maybe they can't meet their bills and they might not have money saved to cover their current expenses. It seems that the problem doesn't have a whole lot to do with Billy. Instead of finding out who had the toy last she let out her emotions on him. It was the straw that broke the camel's back—the kids fighting over a menial toy. She just seems to be getting her anger out, it was the mounting pressure of not having enough money for the family." *Scoring criteria: (a)* environment is the singular causal agent.

3.0 *Compensating.* "I think her behavior is from built-up tension from lack of money due to husband being laid off and the 5-year-old who has always been demanding. Yes, she's releasing her pent-up anxiety over money problems on her son. Since he's very demanding and gets angry when he doesn't get what he wants from his parents, he probably magnifies or exacerbates their lack of money. She's probably dealt with incident over incident with the boy, so from this tension and the lack of money comes her frustration and then her hitting. Normally when kids fight over a toy you would take the toy away from both; here she focuses on him due to stress and his personality. He is headstrong; sometimes these kinds of kids don't change, they are just born like this. He seems to have the kind of personality that gets on people's nerves. Maybe Mrs. Raymond doesn't see other qualities he might have, like he might be good at playing games alone. Maybe if she saw his good points he wouldn't get on her nerves so much." *Scoring criteria: (a)* environmental and constitutional causal agents, and *(b)* parental perception of child can compensate for negative qualities.

4.0 *Perspectivistic.* "This is a complicated one; it seems like her behavior is coming from a position of anger, she's not so mad about the kids fighting, but other things she is unable to deal with, maybe that are coming from her. To begin with she has always had to give Billy a lot of attention; he may have been born with colic. Now she may resent him and even feel closer to him. You usually strike out at those you feel closer to. She may also feel angry toward husband for being laid off. They may not be talking about this very stressful situation, or they may not be reaching out to others. Mrs. Raymond may be feeling that she is not getting what she needs from her husband. I see a parallel in her son as he felt he had to take everything himself and maybe felt he wouldn't get what he needed. There seems to be a pattern in this family of reacting with their feelings to stress. Billy might have trouble as he gets older, because this kind of behavior will not be tolerated by his teachers. This family may need counseling or need to reach out to others." *Scoring criteria: (a)* environmental, constitutional, and psychological influences interact to determine outcome; *(b)* psychological process fully differentiated; *(c)* developmental consequences described; and *(d)* remediation suggested.

The mothers fell into two acculturation groups utilizing Cuellar's established cut-off points: (1) 20 mothers were assigned to a moderately acculturated (MA) Mexican-American group that included subjects with a score of 2.00–3.20 (M = 2.6), and (2) 20 mothers were assigned to a highly acculturated (HA) Mexican-American group that included subjects with a score of 3.21–3.90 (M = 3.5). Mothers were not included in the study if they scored lower than 2.00 (low acculturation). In addition, as in the previous study (Gutierrez et al., 1988), no Mexican-American mothers scored as extremely acculturated (ARSMA score above 4.00).

BICULTURALISM   The Bicultural Involvement Questionnaire (Szapocznik, Kurtines, & Fernandez, 1980) was used to assess biculturalism. The Bicultural Involvement Questionnaire (BIQ) measures the degree to which a person feels comfortable and involved in Hispanic and Anglo-American cultures independently of each other. Symmetrical items for each culture are rated on a 5-point Likert scale. The questionnaire measures a dimension of biculturalism that ranges from monoculturalism to biculturalism. An Americanism score is derived by summing all of the items reflecting involvement with American culture, while a Hispanicism score is obtained by summing all the items reflecting involvement with Hispanic culture. Scores on the biculturalism scale are derived by subtracting the Americanism score from the Hispanicism score. Scores close to zero indicate biculturalism and scores deviating from zero indicate monoculturalism. A positive-difference score reveals monoculturalism in the Hispanic direction, whereas a negative-difference score suggests monoculturalism in the Anglo direction.

INTELLIGENCE   Maternal intelligence was estimated by administering the vocabulary subtest of the Wechsler Adult Intelligence Scale-Revised (WAIS-R) or the equivalent form in Spanish, the Escala de Inteligencia Wechsler Para Adultos (EIWA), which was normed on a Spanish-speaking population (Wechsler, 1968). The vocabulary subtest of the WAIS-R correlates (.82–.85) highly with the full-scale score of the WAIS-R, as does the vocabulary subtest of the EIWA (.86) with the full-scale score of the EIWA, and these were considered satisfactory estimates of maternal intelligence.

The WAIS-R and EIWA vocabulary subtests were administered and scored as recommended in the WAIS-R and EIWA manuals. The subjects were presented with the word list, and the experimenter pointed to each word and asked its meaning. This process was discontinued after five consecutive failures. Each subject's full-scale IQ was estimated by converting the subject's raw vocabulary subtest score to a scale score and then multiplying by 11 to obtain an estimate of the sum-of-scales score. The subject's sum-of-scales score was then used to estimate the full-scale IQ. The scores ranged from 79 to 150 (M = 103.32 and SD = 16.19), with only one subject choosing administration of the vocabulary subtest in Spanish.

TRADITIONALISM   The Traditional Family Ideology Scale (TFIS) was used to assess endorsement of traditional values (Levinson & Huffman, 1955). The scale is composed of 12 six-point Likert-type items. A score of 1 indicated strong agreement with traditional values, and a score of 6 indicated strong disagreement with traditional values. The 12 items were averaged to obtain the subject's nonendorsement of traditional values. For example, a mother who agreed with the following type of items was judged to be more traditional, while a mother who disagreed with these items was judged to be less traditional: "some equality in marriage is a good thing, but by and large the husband ought to have the main say-so in family matters," and "a child should never be allowed to talk back to his parents, or else he will lose respect for them."

RESULTS

Acculturation Analyses

To determine if the two main findings of the Gutierrez et al. (1988) study could be replicated, several analyses were done. To see if Mexican-American mothers at higher levels of acculturation would score higher on concepts of development, a one-way analysis of variance comparing the effects of acculturation to mothers' conceptions of development was performed. Three groups of SES-matched mothers were examined: (1) moderately acculturated (MA) Mexican-American mothers, (2) highly acculturated (HA) Mexican-American mothers, and (3) Anglo-American mothers. The one-way analysis of variance produced a significant main effect for groups, $F(2,57)$ = 8.91, p < .01. The mean CODV scores for the groups are presented in Table 3.

To determine if more acculturated Mexican-American mothers scored higher on concepts of development than Anglo-American mothers, a mean comparison was done between the two groups. The

TABLE 3

Mean CODV Scores for the MA and HA
Mexican-American Mothers
and the Anglo-American Mothers and Correlations
Between CODV and Intelligence and Traditionalism

	Mexican-American		Anglo (AA)
	MA	HA	
n	20	20	20
Concepts of development	2.62	3.04	2.77
Correlations between CODV and intelligence	.05	−.36	.41
Correlations between CODV and traditionalism	.35	−.23	.14

HA Mexican-American mothers scored significantly higher on the CODV than did the Anglo-American mothers, $t(57) = 2.68$, $p < .01$. These data replicate the previous finding that HA Mexican-American mothers were more perspectivistic than their Anglo-American counterparts (Gutierrez et al., 1988).

Mean comparisons were also made between the MA Mexican-American and HA Mexican-American groups and between the MA Mexican-American and the Anglo-American groups. The HA Mexican-American group scored significantly higher than the MA Mexican-American group, $t(57) = 4.16$, $p < .001$. The MA Mexican-American and Anglo-American groups did not differ significantly from each other in terms of concepts of development.

Biculturalism Analyses

To test the prediction that bicultural mothers would be more perspectivistic in their concepts of development than mothers who were monocultural (either Mexican or American), the two Mexican-American groups were further subdivided into monocultural and bicultural subgroups and compared with the monocultural Anglo-American group. The subgroups were: (1) an MA monocultural group, (2) an MA bicultural group, (3) an HA monocultural group, (4) an HA bicultural group, and (5) a monocultural Anglo-American group.

COMPARISON OF THE MEXICAN-AMERICAN SUBGROUPS   A 2×2 analysis of variance comparing the effects of acculturation (MA. vs. HA) and biculturalism (monocultural vs. bicultural) to mothers' conceptions of development revealed significant main effects for acculturation, $F(1,39) = 52.91$, $p < .001$, and biculturalism, $F(1,39) = 120.73$, $p < .001$, and an acculturation ×215 biculturalism interaction effect, $F(1,39) = 16.14$, $p < .001$. As can be seen in Table 4, CODV scores did not vary along an acculturation dimension for the monocultural Mexican-American mothers; both monocultural Mexican-American groups tended to give lower CODV level responses. Concepts of development did vary with level of acculturation for the bicultural Mexican-American mothers. The HA bicultural Mexican-American mothers gave the highest CODV responses, followed by the MA bicultural mothers and then the HA and MA monocultural mothers.

COMPARISON OF THE HA MEXICAN-AMERICAN AND ANGLO-AMERICAN SUBGROUPS   Mean comparisons were made between the HA bicultural Mexican-American group, the HA monocultural Mexican-American group, and the monocultural Anglo-American group. As expected, all Anglo-American mothers scored as monocultural. The HA bicultural Mexican-American group scored significantly higher on concepts of development than did the HA monocultural Mexican-American and the monocultural Anglo-American groups. A significant difference was not found between the HA monocultural Mexican-American and monocultural Anglo-American groups.

Regression Analyses

We predicted that biculturalism would account for variance in concepts of development that was independent of the effects of acculturation and ethnicity. Specifically, within the Mexican-American mothers, biculturalism would be a more important influence on concepts of development than level of acculturation. In addition, when comparing Mexican-American and Anglo-American mothers, biculturalism would be a more important influence on concepts of development than the effects of ethnicity (membership in the Mexican or Anglo group).

To test these hypotheses, two hierarchical regressions were performed. The first hierarchical regression analysis was performed among the Mexican-American subjects. The predictor variables were entered in the following order: (1) years of maternal education, (2) maternal occupation,

TABLE 4

Means and Standard Deviations on Concepts of Development,
Biculturalism, Traditionalism, and Intelligence for the
Mexican-American and Anglo-American Monocultural
and Bicultural Subgroups

| | Mexican-American | | | | |
| | Moderately Acculturated | | Highly Acculturated | | |
	Mono	Bi	Mono	Bi	Anglo(Mono)
Concepts of development	2.44 (.16)	2.77 (.19)	2.61 (.14)	3.33 (.10)	2.77 (.32)
Biculturalism	68.77 (4.40)	79.45 (5.10)	64.00 (4.56)	80.16 (2.88)	50.70 (4.14)
Traditionalism	4.21 (.79)	4.35 (.96)	5.03 (.57)	4.73 (.45)	5.08 (.61)
Intelligence estimate	97.35 (14.18)	94.36 (11.60)	122.00 (22.16)	108.33 (12.73)	104.07 (14.15)

Note: Standard deviations are in parentheses.

(3) traditionalism, (4) intelligence, (5) acculturation, and (6) biculturalism. The first four categories of variables were entered first to control for the possible confounding effects of maternal background and attitudinal variables. Biculturalism was entered after acculturation to test the unique variance accounted for by this variable after the effects of acculturation were removed. The multicollinearity found between the two important predictor variables, acculturation and biculturalism, was minimal ($r = -.15$). This low and nonsignificant correlation suggests an empirically sound basis for utilizing a regression analysis to test the hypothesis. Table 5 presents the results expressed as cumulative R^2 and changes in R^2 as each variable is entered into the analysis.

Although the subjects were of equivalent SES backgrounds, some research has suggested that the component SES variables of maternal education and maternal occupation can affect maternal values differently (Kohn, 1969; Laosa, 1980). Maternal education and occupation each accounted for nonsignificant percentage of the variance. Traditionalism and intelligence were entered next, and each accounted for a nonsignificant percentage of the variance.

It was expected that acculturation would account for a significant portion of variance in concepts of development. This prediction was con-

firmed. The acculturation variable accounted for 11% of unique variance. The prediction that biculturalism would account for a larger portion of variance than acculturation was strongly confirmed.

TABLE 5

Percent Variance Accounted for by Maternal
Education, Occupation, Intelligence,
Traditionalism, Acculturation, and Biculturalism
as Predictors of Concepts of Development for
Subjects of Mexican Descent

Predictor Variable	R^2	R^2 Change
Maternal education	.0020	.0020
Maternal occupation	.0023	.0003
Traditionalism	.0702	.0679
Intelligence	.0703	.0001
Acculturation	.1849	.1147*
Biculturalism	.6592	.4742***
Total R^2	.6592**	

* $p < .05$.
** $p < .01$.
*** $p < .001$.

TABLE 6

Percent Variance Accounted for by Maternal Education, Occupation, Intelligence, Traditionalism, Ethnicity, and Biculturalism as Predictors of Concepts of Development for HA Mexican-American and Anglo-American Mothers

Predictor Variable	R^2	R^2 Change
Maternal education	.0027	.0027
Maternal occupation	.0037	.0010
Traditionalism	.0158	.0121
Intelligence	.0251	.0093
Ethnicity	.1538	.1267*
Biculturalism	.5429	.3891***
Total R^2	.5429**	

* $p < .05.$
** $p < .01.$
*** $p < .001.$

Biculturalism accounted for an additional 47% of unique variance in parental concepts of development. These results powerfully support the hypothesis that biculturalism would increase parental concepts of development for Mexican-American mothers.

The second hierarchical regression analysis was performed among the HA Mexican-American and Anglo-American subjects. The predictor variables were entered in the order as the previous hierarchical regression. Table 6 presents the results. Again, maternal education, occupation, traditionalism, and intelligence were not significant contributors to concepts of development.

It was expected that ethnicity would account for a significant amount of variance in parental reasoning. This prediction was confirmed, with ethnicity accounting for 12% of unique variance. The prediction that biculturalism would account for a larger portion of the variance than ethnicity was also confirmed. Biculturalism accounted for an additional 39% of unique variance in parental concepts of development. These results support the hypothesis that biculturalism would increase parental concepts of development.

IQ and Traditionalism Analyses

Several analyses were done to examine determinants of parental reasoning about development other than acculturation and biculturalism. One factor that might influence parental cognitions is intellectual capacity. For the entire sample, the correlation, $r(59) = .15$, between the WAIS-R estimated full-scale IQ and CODV was not significant, indicating that for this sample of middle-class professional mothers general intellectual capacity did not account for level of complexity in concepts of development.

The relation between general intelligence and concepts of development for each of the three groups was also examined. The correlation coefficients were $r(19) = .05$ for the moderately acculturated Mexican-American group, and $r(19) = .41$ for the Anglo-American group (see Table 3). General intelligence was not related significantly to parental reasoning about development for any of the three groups.

Another question was whether parental reasoning about development was related to endorsement of traditional values. For the entire sample, the correlation, $r(59) = .19$, between the TFIS and CODV was not significant, suggesting that a mother's ability to think in complex ways about development was not related to level of traditionalism. Traditionalism was not related to concepts of development for any of the three groups: the correlation for the moderately acculturated Mexican-American group was $r(19) = .35$, the correlation for the highly acculturated Mexican-American group was $r(19) = -.23$, and the correlation for the Anglo-American group was $r(19) = .14$ (see Table 3).

DISCUSSION

The Gutierrez et al. (1988) finding that complex developmental explanations are given by more acculturated rather than less acculturated Mexican-American mothers was replicated in the present study. The more acculturated Mexican-American mothers, like their counterparts in the previous study, were more perspectivistic than the Anglo-American mothers. Although acculturation is an important contributor to concepts of development, it alone cannot explain parental complexity (Gutierrez et al., 1988). Acculturation has typically referred to an individual's ability to function within the host culture value orientation. Karrer (1986) and Szapocznik and Kurtines (1980) have both emphasized bidirectional rather than unidirectional models of acculturation, that is, the ability of an individual to function both in the culture of origin and in the host culture. It has been suggested by Carringer (1974) that flexibility or complexity in thinking is related to biculturalism. For these reasons, parents at different levels of acculturation and biculturalism are likely to differ in their interpretation of the developmental process.

Biculturalism was found to be a correlate of complexity in Mexican-American mothers' concepts of development. The relative effects of acculturation and biculturalism were examined in a comparison of Mexican-American mothers who varied on both dimensions. There were separate effects of both factors, with more acculturated and more bicultural mothers scoring at higher levels of concepts of development. But when the two factors were combined, there was a synergistic interaction effect such that the Mexican-American mothers who were high on both acculturation and biculturalism had even higher scores than would be expected from the addition of the two factors. These mothers also scored significantly higher than the well acculturated third-generation Anglo-American mothers. The Anglo-American mothers' scores were the same as those of Mexican-American mothers who were high on acculturation and monocultural or low on acculturation and bicultural. In addition, biculturalism accounted for the largest amount of variance compared to acculturation or ethnicity. Intellectual capacity, level of traditionalism, and maternal occupation or education did not contribute significantly to maternal reasoning about development for any of these middle-class groups.

The concepts-of-development measure was designed to assess the level of complexity at which parents understood development. Parents who are environmentalists can score at the same level as parents who are constitutionalists. If they see environment or constitution as a singular causal agent for a specific child outcome, they would score at a low categorical level. If they see environmental or constitutional factors interacting, among themselves or with each other, they would score as more perspectivistic. The bicultural, highly acculturated Mexican-American mothers were the only group in which the average concepts-of-development score was above 3.0, that is, between the compensating and perspectivistic level. Their modal response was that at least two explanations were possible for every vignette. Every other group's modal response was between categorical and compensating levels where singular causes were the frequent explanation of developmental outcomes. More perspectivistic parents are seen as being more flexible in their interpretation of and reaction to variations in child behavior.

How can we explain the connection between biculturalism and perspectivism? Our findings are in accord with other studies that have shown a relation between cognitive flexibility and biculturalism

(Ben-Zev, 1977; Peal & Lambert 1962). The connection is not simply acculturation into a more complex society or the greater number of alterative behavioral styles found in modern societies. We found no significant correlation between concepts of development and traditionalism in any of the groups in the study. Mothers with categorical and perspectivistic reasoning endorsed both traditional and nontraditional values.

The connection to higher-level concepts of development is not through the higher intelligence that would be expected in more acculturated groups. We did find that the more acculturated Mexican-American mothers had higher IQs than less acculturated ones who were matched for both education and occupational level. However, the bicultural subgroups of mothers who scored higher on the concepts of development had lower IQ scores, emphasizing the lack of correlation found between concept-of-development scores and IQ.

The explanation we would propose is in the spirit of Vygotsky's belief in the social regulation of thought. Within any traditional culture there is a modal pattern of acceptable behavior and explanations and rationalizations for that behavior. It is in the necessity of integrating two cultures that an individual must transcend these rationalizations to appreciate that each culture has a different form of acceptable behavior. Such integrations require a perspectivism that appreciates the relativism of belief systems in each specific culture. Such perspectivism has been described by Bertalanffy (1968) as typifying the development of our understanding of history. For Bertalanffy, each historical epoch has a modal correct belief system that supplants the previous incorrect belief system. He sees a new perspectivistic philosophy now emerging in which belief systems are understood as contextually dependent, which means that there will always be new belief systems if contexts change.

It must be understood, however, that higher levels of concepts of development need not be better than lower levels when context is taken into account. Kohn (1969) identified a dimension of parental values in which conforming values were associated with lower-SES life and self-directing values were associated with higher-SES conditions. In his analysis, he did not argue that one orientation was better than another, but that each represented an appropriate adaptation to a subcultural context. Similarly, a parent's level of concepts of development reflects an adaptation to the cultural context. What we found is that bicultural contexts are related to more perspectivistic concepts of development because bicultural life requires an appreciation that each culture may differ in values and behavior.

In a society where a group is a minority in a larger majority culture, the worldview of the larger society either supports or acts to suppress certain values of the minority culture. The worldview of the immigrant group is also important in effecting the acculturation process. A group immigrating from a society with a traditional value orientation will have a different experience than a group immigrating from a society with a modern value orientation. It is important to be aware of the cultural and socio-economic contexts in which an ethnic group functions to obtain a clearer picture of that group. In previous studies (Gutierrez et al., 1988; Sameroff & Feil, 1985) we found strong relations between social class and concepts of development. In this study,

complexity in Mexican-American mothers' concepts of development was strongly related to where the mother was in terms of both acculturation and bi-culturalism.

The melting pot image of American society has given way in recent decades to the encouragement of cultural diversity within a common society. A variety of values have been attributed to the maintenance of ethnic roots within families. This study has identified another consequence of maintaining a biculturalism identification, that is, enhanced perspectivism and flexibility of thought about human development. The correlates of this flexibility are that parents may be more accepting of a variety of outcomes for their children and more flexible in their ability to react to such diversity, perhaps in the direction of encouraging and supporting adaptive functioning.

Questions

1. Why should developmental psychologists be interested in parental conceptions or beliefs about child development?

2. What is acculturation and how did it relate to child rearing practices or preferences among the Mexican-American mothers interviewed by Gutierrez and Sameroff?

3. Many studies have found biculturalism in Latinos to be related to more effective functioning on several dimensions. Why might a bicultural orientation help Latino children and adults in their life in the United States?

References

Ben-Zev, S. (1977). The influence of bilingualism on cognitive development. *Child Development*, 48, 1009–1018.

Bertalanffy, L. von. (1968). *Organismic psychology and systems theory*. Barre, MA: Clark University Press.

Carringer, D. A. (1974). Creative thinking abilities of Mexican youth. *Journal of Cross Cultural Psychology, 5,* 492–504.

Cuellar, I., Harris, L. C., & Jasso, R. (1980). An acculturation scale for Mexican-American normal and clinical populations. *Hispanic Journal of Behavioral Sciences, 2,* 199–217.

Garcia, M., & Lega, L. I. (1979). Development of a Cuban ethnic identity questionnaire. *Hispanic Journal of Behavioral Sciences, 1,* 247–261.

Goodnow, J. J. (1988). Parents' ideas, actions, and feelings: Models and methods from developmental and social psychology. *Child Development, 59,* 286–330.

Gutierrez, J., Sameroff, A. J., & Karrer, B. M. (1988). Acculturation and SES effects on Mexican-American

parents' concepts of development. *Child Development, 59,* 250–255.

Hollingshead, A. B. (1957). *Two-Factor Index of Social Position*. Unpublished manuscript.

Karrer, B. M. (1986). Families of Mexican descent: A contextual approach. In R. B. Birrer (Ed.), *Urban family medicine* (pp. 228–232). New York: Springer Verlag.

Kohn, M. L. (1969). *Class and conformity*. Chicago: London: University of Chicago Press.

Laosa, L. (1980). Maternal teaching strategies and cognitive styles in Chicano families. *Journal of Educational Psychology, 72,* 45–54.

Levinson, D., & Huffman, P. (1955). Traditional family ideology and its relation to personality. *Journal of Personality, 23,* 251–273.

Padilla, A. M. (1980). The role of cultural awareness and ethnic loyalty in acculturation. In A. M. Padilla (Ed.), *Acculturation: Theory, models, and some new findings* (pp. 47–84). Boulder, CO: Westview.

Peal, E., & Lambert W. E. (1962). The relation of bilingualism to intelligence. *Psychological Monographs, 76,* 1–23.

Piaget, J. (1950). *The psychology of intelligence.* New York: International Universities Press.

Sameroff, A. J., & Feil, L. A. (1985). Parental conceptions of development. In I. E. Sigel (Ed.), *Parental belief systems: The psychological consequences for children* (pp. 83–105). Hillsdale, NJ: Erlbaum.

Sameroff, A. J., & Seifer, R. (1983). Familial risk and child competence. *Child Development, 54,* 1254–1268.

Sameroff, A. J., & Seifer, R. (1989). *Social regulation of developmental continuities.* Paper presented at the annual meeting of the American Association for the Advancement of Science, San Francisco.

Sameroff, A. J., Seifer, R., Barocas, B., Zax, M., & Greenspan, S. (1987). IQ scores of 4-year-old children: Social-environmental risk factors. *Pediatrics, 79,* 343–350.

Szapocznik, J., & Kurtines, W. (1980). Acculturation, biculturalism and adjustment among Cuban Americans. In A. M. Padilla (Ed.), *Acculturation: Theory, models and some new findings* (pp. 139–159). Boulder, CO: Westview.

Szapocznik, J., Kurtines, W., & Fernandez, T. (1980). Bicultural involvement and adjustment in Hispanic-American youths. *International Journal of Intercultural Relations, 4,* 353–365.

Szapocznik, J., Scopetta, M., Kurtines, W., & Aranalde, M. A. (1978). Theory and measurement of acculturation. *International Journal of Psychology, 12,* 113–130.

Vygotsky, L. S. (1978). *Mind in society: The development of higher psychological processes.* Cambridge, MA: Harvard University Press.

Werner, E. E. (1979). *Cross-cultural child development: A view from the planet Earth.* Monterey, CA: Brooks/Cole.

Wertsch, J. V., Minick, N., & Arns, F. J. (1984). The creations of context in joint problem solving. In B. Rogoff & J. Lave (Eds.), *Everyday cognition: Its development in social context* (pp. 151–171). Cambridge, MA: Harvard University Press.

Wechsler, D. (1968). *Escala de Intelligencia Wechsler Para Adultos.* Copyright by the Psychological Corporation, San Antonio, TX.

24

Peer Rejection: Origins and Effects on Children's Development

JOHN D. COIE AND ANTONIUS H. N. CILLESSEN

One of the important realizations to emerge from research in the last few decades is the critical role that peers play in development. Psychologists are concerned both about the immediate effects of peer relations on the child and about possible long-term effects that may persist into adulthood. In the following article, John Coie and Antonius Cillessen explore the psychological risks for children who have been rejected by peers. In particular they examine whether and how poor peer relations as a child may lead to dysfunctional patterns later in life.

Research over the past 20 years has brought a growing consensus among developmentalists that peer relations are a very influential factor in child development. Entry into school marks the beginning of a significant increase in the amount of time children spend with peers. As important as the time a child spends with peers is the way these peers feel about that child. It is now widely accepted that adequate relations with peers form an important social context in which children acquire many of their social skills.

A significant number of children, however, lack access to a peer context that serves this developmental function. Consider Michael, for instance, an 8-year-old boy whose parents and school teacher have become very concerned about his frequent anger and aggression in interactions with other children. Michael tends to be bossy, dominating, and disrup-

Reprinted with permission from the authors and *Current Directions in Psychological Science, 2*, 1993, 89–92. Published by Cambridge University Press, New York. Copyright 1993 by the American Psychological Society.

Some of the research reported here was supported by Grants R01MH39140 and K05MH00797 from the Prevention Branch and Grant R01MH38765 from the Violence and Antisocial Behavior Branch of the National Institute of Mental Health.

tive. He also frequently starts fights with other children. Often, he gets angry and upset with other children without adequate reason. As a result of this behavior, Michael's classmates have started to dislike him, and as the school year progresses they consistently try to avoid him.

A second example is Sean, another 8-year-old boy in Michael's class. When other children come to school in an irritable mood, Sean is an easy victim for them to pick on. Other children do not seem to be very concerned when this happens. In fact, the other children often tease Sean and exclude him from their play. When Sean is around other children, he appears anxious and often says embarrassing things that make them uncomfortable being with him. For the most part, however, peers ignore Sean, and he is usually by himself on the playground.

Although their ways of interacting with peers are notably different, Michael and Sean have something important in common: Neither is well liked by peers. In fact, both are actively disliked by other children. Children who are rejected by their peers often lack the opportunity to acquire socially competent skills in their interactions with other children. Although we do not yet know all of the causal mechanisms involved, longitudinal data indicate that rejected children are at serious risk for various forms of social maladjustment in later life,[1] even when some antisocial characteristics of the children, such as aggression, are taken into account. Because of these findings, peer rejection in childhood has been given increasing research attention over the last two decades.

Peer social rejection typically is measured by sociometric methods, that is, by asking children to name three peers that they like the most, as well as three that they like the least.[2] These votes are summed across peers for each child. Those children who receive a high number of liked-least votes and a low number of liked-most votes are classified as rejected. Conversely, those children receiving many liked-most and few liked-least votes are considered popular. Although this is the essence of a sociometric method, several variations of this methodology have been introduced and investigated. One alternative to peer nominations is the use of Likert-type ratings children make of each other. Another important methodological development is the use of an unlimited number, instead of a fixed number, of peer nominations. Following these methodological changes, refinements have also taken place in the complex statistical procedures used to derive sociometric group classifications from the continuous liked-most and liked-least scores.[2]

The way peer rejection is assessed points to an important aspect of this concept: Social rejection is a statement of a relationship between an individual child and his or her school peers. While characteristics of the individual child, such as frequent aggressive behavior, may form a partial basis of that child's rejection by the group, being disliked is not simply a property of the individual. It is a response of the group to that individual and describes an aspect of the relationship between the individual and the group. There also is evidence that once an individual is rejected by a group, the group tends to maintain that perception. Two levels of analysis are thus involved in understanding social rejection. Individual characteristics usually are one essential factor in a child's being rejected by peers, but group dynamics play an important role in the maintenance of that rejected status. There is also some evidence that matches or mismatches between the characteristics of individuals and groups can be important determinants of rejection or acceptance by the group.

ORIGINS OF PEER REJECTION

Methods for resolving questions about the determinants of rejection have evolved dramatically over the past 20 years, from simple field studies in which observed behavior was correlated with peer status, to more complex experimental paradigms involving children being brought together for the first time so that video sequences of the acquaintance process can be analyzed. A common early method for studying the factors that are related to childhood peer rejection was to identify rejected children by means of classroom sociometric measures and then to observe these children in various school contexts in order to compare their behavior to that of children who were not rejected. Using this method, researchers related social rejection to aggression, disruptiveness, hyperactivity, social intrusiveness, bossiness, and anxious-withdrawn behavior. But behavioral differences discovered in this way do not necessarily mean that these differences cause peer rejection. The problem with this method is that it does not permit investigators to determine which behaviors contribute to rejection and which are the result of being rejected.

More recently, a number of investigators have studied peer rejection as it emerges in experimentally created peer groups of children who were previously unacquainted. Observations of these small groups have documented the negative peer consequences of aggressiveness, social intrusiveness, disruption, and, to some extent, social fearfulness. There is, in fact, some evidence for two general subcategories of rejected children; one of these subtypes is illustrated by the description of Michael, and the other is illustrated by Sean.

Several studies indicate that around 40% to 50% of rejected children are highly aggressive. Aggression seems to be more of a contributing factor to rejection among boys than girls, and as children move into later childhood and adolescence, other factors besides aggression begin to take prominence. Aggression has been studied as a basis for rejection more intensely than social withdrawal or other factors. Dodge and his colleagues have found several ways that aggressive-rejected children process social information differently than other rejected children or nonrejected children.[3] Aggressive-rejected children are more likely to impute hostile intentions to peers when having difficult social interactions with them than are nonaggressive-rejected or nonrejected children. They also are more inclined to overemphasize the functional value of aggressive solutions to social problems. More detailed observations of aggression episodes involving aggressive-rejected boys suggest that they are more punitive and less forgiving in such situations than aggressive boys who are not rejected by peers.[4]

Asher and his colleagues have argued that there is more to becoming rejected than is accounted for simply by categories of behavior such as aggression; they contend that it is the continuation of these behaviors along with deficits in important prosocial capacities that is critical.[5] Another way to think of this point is that some children who are highly aggressive may not be rejected by peers because their aggressiveness is balanced by socially redeeming characteristics. They can be fun to play with, be athletically gifted, or have important leadership skills, for example.

The search for an understanding of the origins of peer rejection has moved from an investigation of the behavior patterns leading to rejection to the study of early parenting influences.[6] Putallaz concluded that children of warm, positive parents develop a social orientation toward peers that is also warm and positive. Conversely, mothers who are disagreeable and controlling have children of lower social status. Parental influence on emotional development also has been related to early social status. Parents influence their children's ability to read and express emotion effectively, and this ability is related to peer status. In research on children's peer relations, the role of family variables is a relatively new area of investigation that is expected to expand in the future. Parallel to this trend, there also will be increased attention to the role of the family context in intervention programs for children who are rejected by their peers.

MAINTENANCE OF REJECTION

Although rejection by peers is not stable for some children, other children remain rejected over time, even when they move to a new peer group. In one study,[7] almost half the children rejected in fifth grade continued to be rejected when they were followed from year to year over a 5-year period. Some of this stability may be attributed to the stability of those personal behaviors and characteristics that lead a child to be rejected. However, there also is evidence that peer group dynamics contribute to the stability of peer rejection and that group processes play a role in maintaining existing social status distinctions.[8] In a study of the way children explain the behavior of other children, Hymel found that children made notably different causal attributions for rejected peers than for nonrejected peers. Children explained the negative behavior of a rejected child in terms of stable characteristics of that child. However, the same behaviors in a nonrejected child were said to be caused by more temporary characteristics. Children also held nonrejected peers less responsible than rejected children for negative outcomes. Thus, biased perceptions of a rejected peer lead children to interpretations of that peer's behavior that serve to maintain the negative feelings they have about him or her.

These biases are not limited to the level of children's social cognitions. They also operate on the level of actual social interactions. When children have negative expectations of another child, they act more negatively toward that child. This negative behavior then seems to trigger a reciprocally negative reaction from the target child that, in turn, fulfills the negative bias of the perceiving child. In this way, a self-fulfilling prophecy is created by some of the interactions between rejected children and their peers. By tracing children's expectations, behavioral exchanges, and interpretations over time, researchers have been able to document the existence of such self-perpetuating cycles of cognitions and behavior. It is now clear that children who are rejected repeatedly by peers over time are confronted with consistently negative expectations, behavioral initiatives, and interpretations of their behavior by their peers. This group process contributes to the stability of the rejected child's poor social reputation.

An important implication of these studies is that even if rejected children change their behavior, they still face a difficult time recovering accepted positions in the peer group. If their behavior is subject to negative interpretations by other children, they will be treated by these peers in ways that may challenge their motivation to try to behave positively with peers. Peer ridicule can also undermine the confidence necessary for them to try out newly acquired skills. There also is some very interesting research evidence suggesting that when rejected children think other children are going to like them, they behave more appropriately in subsequent interactions with new acquaintances and actually are more well liked by these new acquaintances. Consequently, it seems that in addition to changing the behavior of the rejected target child, intervention efforts may need to attack the biased perceptions of the child's peers.

CONSEQUENCES OF REJECTION

One major reason for the study of the origins and maintenance of peer rejection is that children who are rejected by their peers are at risk for a series of negative consequences, both immediately and over the course of a longer time period. For aggressive-rejected children like Michael, the immediate social consequences of their behavior may not be so obvious to them. Because their aggressiveness makes them a threat to peers, these peers may not give them direct feedback about their negative regard. Thus, they may not be rejected overtly. There is some evidence that they are not noticeably isolated from peers,[4] and they do not report being as lonely or as aware of peer dislike as are more submissive-rejected children.[5] The social consequences of rejection appear to be more immediate for the withdrawn or submissive children like Sean. These children recognize that other children do not like them, and they describe themselves as lonely and wanting help with friendships. Perry and his colleagues have found that a significant percentage of rejected children, like Sean, are the targets of peer bullying and abuse.[9]

In addition to these immediate social consequences, peer rejection has further negative effects emerging as early as the first year in school. Ladd found that children who are rejected by their peers after 2 months in kindergarten are at risk for adjustment problems by the end of that first school year.[10] Early rejection in this study predicted less favorable attitudes toward school, increased avoidance of school, and lower levels of performance over the course of kindergarten. Ladd argued that peer rejection interferes with children's early adjustment in school because it is a serious stressor in the early school environment.

The immediate negative consequences of rejection are related to research questions about the continuing negative consequences of peer rejection over the course of a child's school career and beyond. In fact, there is important evidence for long-term consequences of peer rejection, in line with its immediate consequences. These long-term negative consequences fall into three main categories: delinquency, school dropout, and psychopathology. aggressive-rejected children are the ones who are most at risk for delinquency problems and school dropout, although nonaggressive-rejected children also have more of these problems than nonrejected children. Less is known about psychopathology, but aggressive-rejected children show a similarly high prevalence of internalizing disorders as well as externalizing disorders.[1] Internalizing disorders are also an important category of long-term outcomes of peer rejection, and Rubin has evidence that some nonaggressive-rejected children are at high risk for depression.[11]

CONCLUSION

The long-term correlates of peer rejection suggest that it is an important factor to be considered in designing prevention programs for a variety of serious problems in adolescence. This is particularly true for aggressive-rejected children, although there is also evidence that nonaggressive-rejected children are at greater long-term risk than children who are neither rejected nor aggressive.[1] The immediate consequences of rejection, however, are obvious in nonaggressive-rejected children and call for some form of help for them, too. Their experience is painful. Perhaps because of this pain, many nonaggressive-rejected children may get help. Their pain may motivate them to change their behavior if help is offered, unlike their aggressive counterparts who create more pain for others. If, in fact, many of these nonaggressive children are successful in getting help in changing their peer relations, this may be one reason there is less strong evidence for serious adjustment problems in later life for this group of rejected children than for children who are both aggressive and rejected.

Questions

1. Why is the peer context so critical for children in learning social skills?

2. Peer rejection is a sad experience for children. Children respond to rejection with both internalizing reactions, such as lowered self esteem, and externalizing reactions, such as increased aggression. What interventions do you think might help rejected children to avoid such consequences?

3. What role can parents play in the development of social skills that may help protect children from being rejected by peers?

Notes

1. J. G. Parker and S. R. Asher, Peer relations and later personal adjustment: Are low-accepted children at risk? Psychological Bulletin, 102, 357–389 (1987); J. D. Coie, J. E. Lochman, R. Terry, and C. Hyman, Predicting early adolescent disorder from childhood aggression and peer rejection, Journal of Consulting and Clinical Psychology, 60, 782–792 (1992).

2. J. D. Coie, K. A. Dodge, and H. Coppotelli, Dimensions and types of social status: A cross-age perspective, Developmental Psychology, 18, 557–571 (1982); J. D. Coie and K.A. Dodge, Continuities and changes in children's social status: A five-year longitudinal study, Merrill-Palmer Quarterly, 29, 261–282 (1983); R. Terry and J. D. Coie, A comparison of methods for defining sociometric status among children, Developmental Psychology, 27, 867–880 (1991).

3. See K. A. Dodge and E. Feldman, Issues in social cognition and sociometric status, in Peer Rejection in Childhood, S. R. Asher and J. D. Coie, Eds. (Cambridge University Press, New York, 1990).

4. J. D. Coie, K. A. Dodge, R. Terry, and V. Wright, The role of aggression in peer relations: An analysis of aggression episodes in boys' play groups, Child Development, 62, 812–826 (1991).

5. S. R. Asher and G. A. Williams, Helping children without friends in home and school, in Children's Social Development: Information for Teachers and Parents (ERIC Clearing House on Elementary and Early Childhood Education, Urbana, IL, 1987); J. T. Parkhurst and S. R. Asher, Peer rejection in middle school: Subgroup differences in behavior, loneliness, and interpersonal concerns, Developmental Psychology, 28, 231–241 (1992).

6. M. Putallaz and A. H. Heflin, Parent-child interaction, in Peer Rejection in Childhood, S. R. Asher and J. D. Coie, Eds. (Cambridge University Press, New York, 1990); J. Cassidy, R. D. Parke, L. Butkovsky, and J. M. Braungart, Family-peer connections: The roles of emotional expressiveness within the family and children's understanding of emotions, Child Development, 63, 602–618 (1992).

7. Coie and Dodge, note 2.

8. S. Hymel, Interpretations of peer behavior: Affective bias in childhood and adolescence, Child Development, 57, 431–445 (1986); A. H. N. Cillessen and T. J. Ferguson, Self-perpetuation processes in children's peer relations, manuscript submitted for publication (1993); D. L. Rabiner and J. D. Coie, Effect of expectancy inductions on rejected children's acceptance by unfamiliar peers, Developmental Psychology, 25, 450–457 (1989).

9. D. G. Perry, S. J. Kusel, and L. C. Perry, Victims of peer aggression, Developmental Psychology, 24, 807–814 (1988).

10. G. W. Ladd, Having friends, keeping friends, making friends, and being liked by peers in the classroom: Predictors of children's early school adjustment? Child Development, 61, 1081–1100 (1990).

11. K.H. Rubin, L. J. LeMare, and S. Lollis, Social withdrawal in childhood: Developmental pathways to peer rejection, in Peer Rejection in Childhood, S. R. Asher and J. D. Coie, Eds. (Cambridge University Press, New York, 1990).

Recommended Reading

Asher, S. R., and Coie, J. D. (Eds.). (1990). *Peer Rejection in Childhood* (Cambridge University Press, New York).

PART V

Adolescence

25

Is Adolescence a Phenomenon of Modern Times?

VIVIAN C. FOX

Is adolescence a universal stage of human development? If it is a stage, has it historically always been so? Vivian C. Fox raises these issues in the following essay and by so doing provides an historical context for understanding adolescent development. She argues that particular historical circumstances have helped shape our current views of adolescence as a unique period of development.

Most of the recent discussions concerning the historical dimensions of adolescence place its conceptual origins in modern times—somewhere from the beginning to the close of the 19th century.[1] Thus, Phillipe Aries believes the first youth to portray the qualities of the modern adolescent was in the 19th century with Wagner's *Siefried*[2], while Tamara Hareven suggests the invention of adolescence evolved during the first half of the 19th century.[3] In an article entitled, "Adolescence in Historical Perspective," John and Virginia Demos maintain "the concept of adolescence, as generally understood and applied, did not exist before the last two decades of the nineteenth century" and point to G. Stanley Hall as the formulator of this modern concept.[4] John R. Gillis in *Youth and History*, places the emergence of adolescence in the period of 1870–1900.[5] Although it is clear that leading authorities such as these differ among themselves as to exactly when adolescence arose, they do adopt a common position that prior to modern times one cannot find what we know and identify as adolescence.

What seems to be central to their recognition of *when* adolescence occurs is that it is primarily to be recognized as a form of psychology and behavior exhibited by pre-adults and that it results from the peculiar social conditions which arose in the last century.

Among the personality traits most associated with adolescence by historians, social scientists, psychologists and psychoanalysts are an inner-turmoil, experienced during a time of "storm and stress," of

Reprinted with permission from *Journal of Psychohistory*, 5, 1977, 271–290. Copyright 1977 by Atcom, Inc.

uncertainty but of conformity with peers. It is a stage of life when the individual is seeking self-identity and in this process becomes inwardly absorbed, perhaps egoistic, sometimes cruel. However, it is also a most spontaneous, energetic and promising phase, one devoted to ideals and romanticizing, and is as concerned with the demonstration of physical and sexual prowess as it is characterized by laziness, unsteadiness, preoccupation with sex and possibly criminal acts. Adolescence, finally, is a phase of life when youth is most "pliable, plastic and formative."[6]

For Demos, as well as for Hareven, Gillis and Aries, the social phenomena for the necessary emergence of adolescence occurred during the 19th century, the time of modernization. What do they see as the characteristics of this period—the social conditions—which made it so uniquely capable of producing adolescence? For one, the expansion and extension of education led to a greater economic dependence on parental financial support as well as to a clearer separation of children from adults than had ever previously existed. The point is made over and over again that in preindustrial society children and youth were miniature adults: treated, dressed and identified with adults.[7] It is apparently central to their thesis that during the 19th century this changed, as seen, for example, in the segregation of youth by age groups in the school room which created a *de facto* distinction between adults and children. With the further introduction of school age-grading there grew even finer distinctions among the children themselves.[8] Nineteenth century education, therefore, is said to be a major force in bringing about a sharp preadult youth status, increased cohort segregation and a longer dependence on parents: in short a unique "adolescent experience."[9]

At about the same time, the 19th century's increased industrialization and urbanization also played an important role in the development of adolescence. These social processes brought more and more people, including youth, to the city to look for work. As a consequence, it is noted by historians that youth came to engage in a form of behavior which historical authorities identified as the "mark" of adolescence. Namely, they were attracted to join cohort groups, some of which appeared as gangs which became major social problems as a result of their criminal activity. Scholars have drawn our attention to the concern of authorities who questioned why so many young people seemed inclined to cause trouble.[10] Then, as now, there was the prevailing notion that previous generations of youths had not been as "bad" or dangerous.[11] Historians also note that concerned middle-class parents were alarmed by what they viewed as the increase in delinquency violence. Both parents and officials were

also apprehensive about the sexual changes that occurred during puberty. In the attempt to shield their offspring from these dangers of the adolescent period, parents and reform groups suggested school activities to help channel youthful energy feared to be sexual in nature.[12]

Another highly relevant characteristic of the 19th century was the new burgeoning middle class family which was having fewer children as a result of its increasing use of contraception. With fewer children, they were able to focus greater and greater attention on them. Indeed, according to Aries, parental concentration on children generated greater control, hence loss of "freedom" previously experienced when they were more neglected.[13]

School status, parental control, extended dependence on parents, creation of cohort groups or gangs, all conveyed, it is suggested, similar meaning to the youth: that they were pre-adults and not yet in control of their destiny. Confronted by this extended period of control, whether at school or with parents, facing an increasingly industrial complex and changing world, youth became bewildered and confused about the process of becoming an adult and thereby was spawned what historians identify as the unique psychological features of adolescence. A pillar of this psychology is the confrontation with one's identity and the accompanying commitment to ideals. Skolnick sums up the picture, "Thus, economic, familial, and cultural changes transformed the experience of growing up; adolescence became an important stage of the individual's biography. The opening of a gap between physical maturation and the attainment of social adulthood led to the psychological characteristics that have become known as the adolescent experience—the urge to be independent from the family: the discovery of the unique and private world of the self: the search for an identity: and the questioning of adult values and assumptions which may take the form of idealism, or cynicism, or both at the same time."[14]

These are the explanations for the recent emergence of adolescence. There is, however, reason to believe that adolescence is a far older phenomenon than is thus generally acknowledged, and this paper undertakes to re-examine the historic basis for asserting adolescence to be a product of modern times. It is not, however, the purpose of this paper to relocate the rise of adolescence to a different time in history. The more limited aim is simply to point out that we cannot rest satisfied with some historians' view that adolescence emerged in modern times. The re-examination reveals that:

1. Adolescent personality traits were identified and described in a manner similar to modern

characterizations of adolescence well before the modern era;

2. The adolescent years were seen as a period of transition to adulthood well before the modern era;

3. What is accepted today as social behavior that is typically adolescent was ascribed to youth well before the modern era; and

4. Well before the modern era, conceptions of a human developmental life cycle made explicit provision for a stage of adolescence.

Before outlining the evidence to support these propositions, the modern conception of adolescence may usefully be compared with the following:

> The young are in character prone to desire and ready to carry any desire they may have formed into action. Of bodily desires it is the sexual to which they are most disposed to give away, and in regard to sexual desire they exercise no self-restraint. They are changeful too and fickle in their desires, which are as transitory as they are vehement: for their wishes are keen without being permanent . . . They are passionate, irascible, and apt to be carried away by their impulses. They are slaves, too, of their passion as their ambition prevents their ever brooking a slight and renders them indignant at the mere idea of enduring an injury . . . They are charitable rather than the reverse, they are sanguine too, for the young are heated by Nature as drunken men by wine, not to say that they have not yet experienced frequent failures. Their lives are lived principally in hope, as hope is of the future and memory of the past; and while the future of youth is long, its past is short . . . They are inclined to be valorous, for they are full of passion, which excludes fear, and of hope, which inspires confidence . . . They are bashful, too, having as yet no independent standard of honor and having lived entirely in the school of conventional law . . . Youth is the age when people are most devoted to their friends or relations . . . if the young commit a fault, it is always on the side of excess and exaggeration . . . They regard themselves as omniscient and are positive in their assertions . . . [15]

This description of youth should sound familiar to us today even though it was written over 2,000 years ago by Aristotle. Aristotle was able to capture the emotional swings of this age, when he wrote youth

was bashful, yet assertive, fickle yet devoted to their friends. In the 19th century G. Stanley Hall, claimed by some to be the modern formulator of adolescence, appears more to echo Aristotle's observation of the emotional swings of the adolescent stage than to present views unheard before:

> Often those most tender and considerate, most prone to take pains, to prefer other's enjoyment to their own, and to renounce . . . and conquer the strongest natural desires . . . were those most liable occasionally to fall lowest in gloating self-gratification at the expense of others. [16]

In light of this one might well be ready to question whether the stage of adolescence was unknown or only vaguely known prior to the 19th century. The historical evidence appears to place a substantial appreciation of that stage well before that time.[17]

SEXUAL DEVELOPMENT AS A PROBLEM OF ADOLESCENCE

Inner-turmoil, the "storm and stress," are taken as signs that the adolescent stage is being experienced. Some of the stress has been seen to be a result of pubescent changes which spark sexual desire, but which, however, conflict with social values of sexual repression. Long before Freud recognized the struggles between the demands of civilization and the urges of the Id, St. Augustine in his *Confessions* described this new flood of feelings which caused him inner anguish throughout his adolescent period:

> I will now call to mind my past foulness, and the carnal corruptions of my soul . . . in which I was torn to pieces, while, turned away from Thee the One, I lost myself among many vanities . . . But what was it that I delighted in save to love and to be loved? But I held it not in moderation, mind to mind, the bright path of friendship, but out of the dark concupiscence of the flesh and the effervescence of youth exhalations came forth which obscured and overcast my heart, so that I was unable to discern pure affection from unholy desire. Both boiled confusedly within me.[18]

Other autobiographical material from 17th century England also confirms that there were acknowledgements of feelings of an inner turmoil generated by the onset of puberty and in sharp opposition to Christian morality. A youth leaving home for school, for example reported:

then did youthful lust and corruption begin to prevail over me, stronger in me than the grace of God.[19]

So, too, with a 17th century apprentice in London, burdened with recognition that "the corruption of my heart showed itself abundantly in lust." When he left his apprenticeship his anguish intensified. He recorded that on a journey to Rome,

> I began to be troubled with that nightly disease which we call the mare, which afterwards increased upon me very grievously that I was scarce any night free from it, and seldom it left me without nocturnal pollutions and visions. Oft-times I verily thought that I descended into Hell and there felt the pains of the damned, with many hideous things. Usually in my dreams me thought I saw my father always grievously angry with me.[20]

Youth in the past suffered from conflict and experienced guilt because sexual maturity affected their actions, which were in opposition to the values they identified with the adult world.

Most writers about adolescence accept the fact that puberty ushers in biological changes. But the psychological manifestations of these changes have not been acknowledged as more or less similar over time. Aristotle reported that Greek youth were primarily preoccupied with sexual gratification, and this has been similarly attested to by St. Augustine as well as by youth of the 17th century. The autobiographical material, however, provides additional psychological insight into inner conflict which the Aristotlian observation does not address. Perhaps this was because Aristotle's comment was about youth not from them. From his point of view, however, the stage of youth was inherently extreme, passionate, lacking moderation, a value cherished by the Greeks.

ADOLESCENCE AS A CONFLICT WITH ADULT VALUES: RELIGION AND EDUCATION

As the last section indicated, there is evidence that control of sexual urges has long been recognized by youth itself as a developmental hurdle to be surmounted during adolescent years. Similar recognition of the need to restrain certain aspects of adolescent development, among which sexuality was but one characteristic, can be found in the exhorta-tions of pre-modern authorities. Paramount among this group were religious and educational leaders, since much of what they identified as primary features of youth were in sharp conflict with the values they deemed significant.

Many of the writers during the early modern period were acutely aware of special personality traits associated with the adolescent stage of life. As Stephen Smith has pointed out in this *Journal*, in 17th-century London, religious and moral books can be found which painted youth as fickle, full of strength and vigor, as sinful, exuberant, immature, lustful, sensual, proud, vain, over-talkative, hasty, susceptible to peer pressure and so on.[21]

One can observe in the religious literature, for example, a pre-modern recognition of adolescence. The struggles to suppress and otherwise deal with these characteristics is strikingly close to the task described by modern psychologists such as G. Stanley Hall:

> The most critical revolution in life,
> to successfully accomplish which is to
> make catharses of our lower nature and
> to attain full ethical maturity without arrest
> of perversion; this is the very meaning of
> adolescence.[22]

At the same time, other authors thought youth to be a most unique and promising stage of life. In *Apples of Gold*, for example, Brooks wrote, "it is no small honor to you, who are in the spring and morning of your days, that the Lord hath left upon record several instances of his love and delight in young men."[23] Special lectures and sermons were directed especially to youth because of their promise, and also because of the concern for their particular adolescent vulnerabilities. In such a sermon given to youthful scholars at Eton, Thomas Horn urged that religious education should begin at an early age because,

> 1— it is the great foundation of wisdom; 2— it makes a person less liable to error in later life; 3— it is a preventative of sin and the best means of enabling a person to overcome temptation; 4— it makes a man more obedient and socially useful. [24]

The sermons, the books, the lectures were designed to help guide youth through their critical, stressful transition period, when the heat of man according to *The Anglia Notitia,* a 17th-century English encyclopedia, was at its height.[25]

New England Puritan religious leaders in the early 18th century shared similar anxieties concerning their youth. About this, N. Ray Hiner, also in this *Journal*, concludes:

> Scarcely a year passed that did not bring forth a large number of sermons and essays concerning youth, their behavior, their social and psychological characteristics, and their spiritual needs.[26]

The response of the religious community to the particular problems of youth resulted from the increased secularization of their society, from problems in recruiting youthful conversions, as well as from the extended period of youthful dependence. Sensuality and pride were the epithets characterizing youth, and the ones the religious community wanted to be redirected through conversion. Thus they called upon youth to follow the religious instruction of their elders, and not be influenced by the wanton ways of their peers. Yet, as their English religious colleagues had recognized a century before, American Puritan ministers described youth as a promising time, when their capabilities were most flourishing,[27] and beckoned them to resist temptation and maximize their spiritual and productive capabilities. Puritan ministers used techniques not different from those "developmental tasks of adolescence as described by modern psychologists."

> 1— self-control (sublimation and neutralization of libidinal and aggressive drives); 2— independence (detachment from infantile and object ties); and 3— identity (consolidation and integration of personality, and the organization of behavior into available social roles.)[28]

Thus it appears religious and moral leaders in 17th century England and in early 18th century America acknowledged youth as a recognizable group whom they must protect, while at the same time conceding that this group might itself pose special dangers to society if not subjected to appropriate controls. They became "youth watchers" because they were the guardians of morality of their society; and in the process were sensitized to this stage of life. They were, however, not the only ones in this surveillance role.

There existed another group of "youth watchers". These were pedagogues, educational theorists, humanists and teachers of youth, who believed that at each educational stage, an indelible imprint was left on the individual psyche.[29] Therefore, the nature of the education became a most important consideration, an obligation society should not ignore. It was with such considerations in mind that the humanist Thomas More wrote his *Utopia*, which was in effect a treatise on education. That More was so incensed at the false values and improper training accorded most youth clearly implies an awareness of the social significance of the adolescent stage:

> When you allow your youth to be badly brought up and their characteristics, even from early years, to become more and more corrupt, to be punished, when as grown-up men, they commit the crimes which from boyhood they have shown every prospect of committing, what else, I ask, do you do but first create thieves and then become the very agents of their punishments.[30]

Thomas More was but one among many humanist educators of his day who regarded the human growth process along a developmental, accumulative and irreversible path and as a result of this thinking he considered investment in youth a value society could not overlook.[31]

One group of educators, during the 16th century, was especially preoccupied with reaching humans at their "impressionable age" during their childhood and youth.[32] Each of these categories of pre-adulthood was viewed differently. German Protestant reformers, anxious to draw and keep a large group of citizens in their churches, made the conscious decision to achieve this goal by concentrating on the education of the young through the establishment of elementary and secondary schools, which were separate from one another. In order to determine the best curriculum to influence youth in the secondary schools, they drew upon a literary tradition which "supplied a ready made and coherent set of assumptions about the nature of children and young people." The literary tradition predicted the behavior and illustrated the possible responses of the adolescent period.[33] The reformers were, furthermore, aware of the ancient terms, *infantia*, *pueritia* and *adolescentia* which differentiated childhood from youthful development. Indeed, Jacob Wimpheling entitled his educational book, *Adolescentia*.[34] Among these reformers, consonant with the tradition which they read and absorbed, the ages 14–16 appeared to them to be the most vulnerable to corruption.

> Unrestrained by experience of consequence and with no care about the future, adolescents, in

the first flush of their physical powers, are driven to "natural" vices: lying, blasphemy, violence, and cruelty. Theft, disobedience of parents and disrespect towards their elders, idleness, gambling, recklessness and lack of shame, and "to come to the point-voluptuous desires which consume the body and mind" namely masturbation and sexual advances.[35]

One of the methods these reformers proposed to "re-direct" some of the natural proclivities of youth was to remove any kind of sexual stimulus until the flush of passion was reduced by education and/or age. Reformers such as Jean Gerson appealed to both secular and religious authorities to assist in restraining youth from the dangers which they recognized to be inherent at the adolescent stage.[36]

ADOLESCENT YOUTH AS A PERIOD OF TRANSITION IN PRE-MODERN TIMES

One of the commonly accepted indices of modern adolescence is its transitional nature. Both adult and youthful characteristics appear to coexist.

In early modern times youth was viewed as a transition between children's roles and responsibilities of adults; while they were being trained for some adult roles, mostly occupational, they were at the same time restricted from a premature assumption of other adult social roles.[37]

By the 17th century the period of apprenticeship had more or less begun to coincide with the period of adolescence. There is evidence that apprenticeship commonly terminated from between the ages of 21–24. As Smith argues, the fact that apprenticeship was a seven year period strongly suggests that adolescence was the transitional period when training for adult occupation was undertaken.[38] Yet it was also clear that during the transitional training time some adult roles were prohibited. Thus, during the year 1603 "three London apprentices were sent to jail for refusing to cut their hair and renounce the sartorial splendor that was causing distress among both their masters and local authorities."[39] Moreover, it was the duty of masters to watch that their charges did not prematurely enter adulthood by indulging in drink, gambling or sex. Nor were these pre-adults permitted the sort of mobility generally associated with adulthood. Curfew hours were established to keep servants and youth at home during the night hours.[40]

Apprenticeship was not the only occasion for the training of youth for some adult roles and the simultaneous denial of others. English youths attending schools, universities, the inns of court and those who worked as servants were subject to similar kinds of regulations.

Transition can be observed in another dimension as well, namely that of responsibility. If young children can be seen as having virtually no responsibility for controlling their behavior and adults as being fully responsible, there is much historical evidence to suggest that youth belongs to a middle area between childhood and adulthood. This middle area can best be illustrated by participation in a scheme of collective responsibility. Examples of this abound in pre-modern times. Whenever youths joined clubs or "fraternal orders" they were subject to strict rules and regulations of the group, such as, for example the rule of continence. In order to bind them to these rules each novice was subject to initiation rites.[41] In Germany, for example, during the 16th century, new students who were called *adolescens,* were hazed up until about a year, or at least until strenuous "moral and social" tests were passed.[42]

The principal theme underlying most of these controls centered around sexual regulations of youth during their years of pre-adulthood. The youth groups themselves had direct responsibility in controlling their members. Throughout preindustrial Europe most male and possibly female youths from about the age of 14 till marriage belonged to organizations which regulated sexual behavior of its participants. These "fraternal orders" often controlled access to the eligible females of the community, and at times acted as a collective morality to the community in which they lived. Thus, courting practices were composed and enforced by the youth themselves. Intruders into a community, and older men, were often cruelly deprived of the eligible females, and sometimes promiscuous girls found "their doorways decorated with the obscene symbol of the gorse bush."[42] The groups were called Abbeys of Misrule or in Germany and parts of Switzerland, *Bruderschaften.*[43] They all shared similar characteristics: they organized youth from puberty to marriage into a subculture and prohibited premarital sex among their members.

By assuming leadership of their community's as well as their own morality, this sub-culture of youth was preparing itself to enter the adult world. Simultaneously, during this transition period they learned a trade or trained for a profession. Most of these youths were attached to households as servants or apprentices and their masters shared in the responsibility for adhering to the rules. This stage of youth, as previously indicated, may have lasted until the mid-twenties, when apprenticeship ended and they became economically independent, or when they married and could then achieve full membership in their community.[44] It would thus appear that an extended preadult status is not an exclusive feature of modern life.[45]

ADOLESCENT SOCIAL BEHAVIOR OF PRE-INDUSTRIAL YOUTH

The kinds of tensions and energies generally ascribed to modern adolescence were also exhibited by preindustrial youth. For example, youthful frolic helped to release their energies, but was not always appreciated by the older generation. During the early modern era in England, for example, the hiring season was a time of frivolty allowing the youth in concert to behave like adolescents. Philip Stubbs describes one such event on Pack Rag Day at the end of the 16th century.

> All the wildheads of the parish, conventing together, choose them a grand captain (of all mischief) whom they enoble with the title of "my lord of Misrule", and him they crown with great solemnity, and adopt for their king . . . Then march these heathen company towards the church and churchyard, their pipers piping, their drummers thundering, their stump dancing, their bells jingling . . . They have also certain papers, wherein is painted some bablery or other of imagery worked, and these they call "my Lord of Misrule's badges." These they give to everyone that will give money for them to maintain them in their heathenry, devilry, whoredome, drunkenness, pride or what not.[46]

Compare the report of Philip Stubbs with the comments of a reformer in the 19th century:

> It must be confessed that an irreverent unruly spirit has come to be prevalent, an outrageous evil among young people.[47]

The equivalent of modern adolescent tensions between adolescents and adults was also found between masters and their apprentices. Despite society's efforts to look upon the master's household as a surrogate family and despite apprentices being told to be as obedient to their masters as to their fathers, apprentices were mistreated and complained. According to Steven Smith, "the records of the Middlesex Sessions of the Peace and of other Mayor's Court contain numerous cases of apprentices suing their masters as a result of mistreatment." The converse was also true. The literature of the times complained about "dishonest and rowdy apprentices."[48] The ideal relationship of obedient apprentices nurtured, watched over and trained by a stern but kindly master was just that, an ideal. Apprentices rebelled and misbehaved, and were not always treated with generative kindness.

A central feature of modern adolescence is its adherence to a set of ideals or values. Aspects of reform movements of the past demonstrate that youth often channeled their energy to an ideology and through it attempted to gain an identity. Herbert Moller's article,[49] "Youth as a Force in History" illustrated the extent to which youth from early modern times joined new ideologically motivated groups with which they could find identity. During the Reformation, for example, students were attracted to the religious ideas initiated by Luther. These youth rejected the older generation's religion, finding the new ideological outlook of Lutheran Protestantism more consonant with their "ideological mind", as Erikson phrased it, as well as a means to release their energy. The appeal that ideology had for youth is further evidenced by their involvement in the religious revolts of the 16th century:

> In several towns in Provence-Marseille, Toulon and elsewhere—Catholic Youths stoned Protestants to death and burned them. The reputation of the adolescents in Sens and Provens was so frightening that a member of a well-known Huguenot family was afraid to walk through the streets . . . In Toulouse, Catholic students had the university in an uproar, whistling and banging in lectures when the canon law or the "old religion" was mentioned. In Poitiers in 1559 and again in 1562, Protestant youngsters and students take the initiative in smashing statues and overturning altars. Indeed, youths are mentioned as a part of almost all the great iconoclastic disturbances—in the Netherland, in Rouen and elsewhere.[50]

In sum, there appears to be a plethora of evidence indicating that both the psychology and behavior of the 19th century adolescent are clearly observable in pre-modern youth. In the past, youth joined peer groups, frolicking, behaving irreverently and causing general disturbances. They identified with new ideological movements and, in the name of ideology, with their cohorts became violent and destructive, making people fear to walk in the streets. How representative was this of all youth in the past? It is difficult to tell. But on the other hand, it is far from clear that the descriptions of modern adolescents are truly representative either.[51]

More important, however, in an evaluation of the significance of the evidence which has been presented, is the role of the long-held beliefs about human growth and development.

ADOLESCENCE AS PART OF THE LIFE CYCLE

A concept of adolescence, as has been previously stated, was known as early as Greek times. It was an integral part of their perspective of the human life cycle which they believed to be developmental, because change and development were considered to be intrinsic to the nature *(physis)* of all living things. In order to comprehend the *physis* of man it was necessary to understand his successive stages of development, an understanding which encompassed man's origins and his ultimate purpose of "final cause" as Aristotle conceived it.[52] According to Aristotle, "a plant", or human being had "a development which consist[ed] of the determinable sequence of changes proceeding from its very structure and" was as 'necessary' to its being as any other intrinsic attribute."[53]

Skolnick's characterization of modern developmental psychology seems to suggest a similar philosophic perspective which appears to include all of the essential Greek developmental elements. "Although each [developmental psychological] theory selects a different aspect of the child as the key to understanding the process of development, they all agree on several things:

1. Development is self-propelled and teleological—that is, the "push" to change comes from within the organism, and the endpoint of development is implicit at the beginning. [Aristotle's idea of the structure or intrinsic attribute.]

2. The adult is categorically, or qualitatively different from the child. The different stages of childhood are also qualitatively different from each other. [The Greek idea of the successive stages of development.]

3. Developmental theories are organized around specific concepts of adult competence. For Freud, the endpoint of development is the genital, heterosexual adult, parent to children, with a

place in the occupational world. For Piaget, the endpoint of development is the stage of formal operational thinking—the ability to think hypothetically and abstractly." [Aristotle's Final Form or Cause.][54]

With the Greek idea of a developmental life cycle moving from stage to stage, it is not surprising, as we observed with Aristotle, that they were able to perceive what they considered to be both the inherent and universal nature of youth. Each stage of the life cycle moved on to the next because it contained dialectically its own specific characteristic while bearing the "seed" or internal attribute for the change into the next stage. Within childhood were the mechanisms for change into adolescence, specifically triggered by puberty.

The laws of Plato, for example, illustrate an educational appropriateness for different ages of the young and imply a reliance on a developmental sequential concept. His educational program began while the baby was still inside its mother;[55] for the years 0–3 nurses were told to try to distinguish between the cries of the babies, while not overindulging them; from 3–6, informal co-education began with spontaneous play under the careful supervision of nurses. At six, the sexes were to be separated but educated similarly if the female so desired. The purpose of their education was twofold: "training of the body and cultural education to perfect personality."[56] Thus, for example, from 10–13, literature should be studied, while at 13, the lyre was to be learned. Educational training, beginning in the womb, was to "re-direct . . . natural development along the right line."[57]

This paradigm of the life cycle, with its inherent developmental modes, has influenced Western thought ever since its inception. Strauss notes that:

> Augustine distinguishes between the nursing and the learning-to-speak phases of infancy, and between the *puer loquens,* who has just emerged from childhood helplessness, and a later condition of *puerita,* just preceding puberty, when reason begins to be active . . . There was no doubt about the significance of one . . . stage, adolescence coming at fourteen. It would be difficult to improve upon the picture of the inner storms and pressures, the restless longing and seeking for something not clearly perceived which is conveyed by Augustine in his *Confessions.*[58]

CONCLUSION

Basic to the question of adolescent's vintage is the matter of whether the conditions of any century or historical period can be identified as the cause for the emergence of adolescent psychology and behavior. An affirmative response to this query represents an extreme form of environmentalism, a position which the historians under discussion appear to have adopted. The implicit denial of the historically important role of inherent characteristics is not warranted. Certainly social conditions have varied greatly over time, but the evidence of adolescent behavior and psychology which has occurred so frequently in Western history must be explained, at least in part, by the influence of human biological development. For example, there are wide differences between the religious ideological commitment of youth in 16th-century France and Germany and the ideologically oriented uprisings in Western universities in the 1960's, but both may well be expressions of the same human developmental qualities of adolescence which has persisted through time.[59]

In light of this it seems paradoxical that many of the historians who contend adolescence to be a 19th-century phenomena also accept the developmental life cycle model. The terms they use in identifying adolescent behavior and the framework they apply to the life process comes from developmental psychology whose central assumption is that it is timeless.[60]

Adolescence thus appears not to be a product of modern times. In its most recognizable behavorial features it has been acknowledged and in its psychological manifestations it has been recorded at least since Greek times.

Questions

1. What personality traits have been historically associated with adolescence?

2. What effect has a prolonged period of adolescence, such as exists in industrialized societies, had on the possibilities and pitfalls of the adolescent period?

3. How might the way in which adolescence is experienced in a culture influence what is expected of a person once he or she enters adulthood?

References

1. Some social scientists place the emergence of adolescence earlier. Arlene Skolnick suggests the 18th century and identifies Rousseau as the possible initiator of this conception. See "The Limits of Childhood Conceptions of Child Development and Social Context" in *Law and Contemporary Problems* (Summer, 1975), p. 61, on the other hand, in the same volume see F. Raymond Marks, "Detours on the Road to Maturity: A View of the Legal Conception of Growing Up and Letting Go" places adolescence in the 20th century. "Adolescence—in a social sense—is largely a twentieth century creation", p. 78.

2. Philip Aries, *Centuries of Childhood* (New York, 1962), p. 30. Aries considers the 20th century "The Century of Adolescence."

3. Tamara K. Hareven, "Historical Adulthood and Old Age" *Daedalus*, No. 4 (Fall, 1976), p. 17. Hareven is included among the historians who locate adolescence in the 19th century, but her focus in this article is not on adolescence.

4. John and Virginia Demos, "Adolescence in Historical Perspective" in *The American Family in Social-Historical Perspective* edited by Michael Gordon (New York, 1973), p. 210.

5. John R. Gillis, *Youth and History* (New York, 1974), pp. 98–99.

6. This compilation of adolescent qualities can be observed in the following literature. See for example, Demos and Demos, pp. 211–218; Gillis, Chapters 3 and 4; Peter Blos, *On Adolescence: A Psychoanalytic Interpretation* (New York, 1962); Erik H. Erikson, "Youth: Fidelity and Diversity," *Daedalus* (Winter, 1962); G. Stanley Hall, *Adolescence* (New York, 1904), Vol. 2.

7. One wonders even if children and youth were treated as "miniature adults" if they felt like adults. See Ross W. Beales, Jr., "In Search of the Historical Child: Miniature Adulthood and Youth in Colonial New England" in *American Quarterly* 27 (1975) which presents a reexamination of this entire question of Miniature Adulthood. Beales looks at the law and the attitude of religious reformers and comes to the conclusion that children and youth were perceived and treated differently from adults.

8. For an account of the expansion of education see among others, Gillis, pp. 98–105 and Aries especially, Chapter IV and pp. 412–413; Skolnick, pp. 69–70.

9. See Skolnick, p. 63.

10. For an excellent discussion on the fears of reformers during the 19th century see Sanford J. Fox, "Juvenile Justice Reform: An Historical Perspective" in the *Stanford Law Review*, Vol. XXII (June 1970).

11. See for example, Demos and Demos, p. 211, and Gillis especially p. 134.

12. Demos and Demos suggest concern for sexual maturity and its effects on youthful behavior were muted because of Victorian sentiment, but discussions became more open after 1870; see p. 213. In England, however, the subject of "puberty" and its consequences was more open. See Gillis, pp. 112–115.

13. Aries, pp. 413–415.

14. Skolnick, p. 63.

15. Aristotle, quoted in Norman Keil, *The Universal Experience of Adolescence* (New York, 1964), pp. 18–19.

16. See G. Stanley Hall, Vol 2, pp. 75–90, quoted in D. Ross, G. Stanley Hall, *The Psychologist as Prophet* (The University of Chicago Press, 1972), p. 327.

17. Although the term adolescence was known and used from Greek times, for approximately the same years as youth, prior to the modern era youth was the word generally applied to pre-adults after the childhood stage. Even Demos and Demos acknowledge that the 19th century used the word youth rather than adolescence. But they add, "Lest it be imagined that Americans of the 19th century had no special concern whatsoever for the period which we now call adolescence (and which in their day was simply termed "youth"), p. 212. Then they go on to demonstrate that adolescent behavior existed in the 19th century. Thus, they implicitly acknowledge that the semantic usage of the word youth in the 19th century means adolescence. Yet, John Demos, in *A Little Commonwealth: Family Life in Plymouth Colony* (N.Y. 1970) seems to conflict with his view. Claiming that the widespread use of the word adolescence is only about seventy-five years and that in earlier times the word youth was used vaguely, he then goes on to say, "These semantic details point to a very substantial area of contrast in the developmental process then and now." p. 145. The semantic distinctions, however, are still unclear even seventy-five years after the word adolescence has gained widespread currency. In some of the modern literature on adolescence both words are used while the conceptual differences are not yet obvious. See for example, *Adolescence in the Life Cycle*, edited by Glenn H. Elder, Jr. (New York, 1975). On page 3 Elder states, with unusual clarity, "In this volume, adolescence and youth are employed interchangeably in reference to the years between 7th grade and (relatively) complete independence from the family of origin." This paper also uses the words adolescence and youth interchangeably. Puberty marks the beginning of this stage, while relatively complete economic independence or marriage is taken as the terminal point of adolescence and youth.

18. *The Confessions of St. Augustine*, translated by J. G. Pilkington, (New York, 1943), pp. 27–28.

19. Walter Pringle, "The Memoir of Walter Pringle," in *Selected Biographies* edited by W. K. Tweedie (Edinburgh, 1845) 1, p. 423, quoted in Steven R. Smith, "Youth in 17th Century England" in *History of Childhood Quarterly*, 2 (1975), p. 506.

20. Richard Norwood, *The Journal of Richard Norwood, Surveyor of Bermuda*, (New York, 1945), p. 26 in Smith, "Youth," pp. 507–508.

21. See for example, Smith, "Youth," pp. 498–501. Also, Steven Smith "The London Apprentices as Seventeenth Century Adolescents" in *Past and Present*, No. 61 (November, 1973), pp. 153–155.

22. Hall (2:337) in Ross, p. 331.

23. Thomas Brooks, *Apples of Gold in Young Men and Women and a Crown of Glory from Old Men and Women* (London, 1667), in Smith "Youth" p. 497.

24. Smith, "Youth," pp. 502–503.

25. E. Chamberlayne, *Anglia Notitia* (London, 1669) 15th edition ed. 1700. See Chapter V `Of Women, Children and Servants'. In this edition, the age 25 is considered a time when the "Heat of Youth is Somewhat Abayed." Thus it is not an unwarranted inference that youth was considered the time when the heat of man is at its height.

26. N. Ray Hiner, "Adolescence in Eighteenth Century America" *History of Childhood Quarterly* (1975), p. 254.

27. Hiner, p. 267.

28. Hiner, p. 272.

29. See Gerald Strauss, "The State of Pedagogical Theory c 1530: What Protestant Reformers Knew About Education" in Lawrence Stone, *ed., Schooling and Society, Studies in the History of Education* (The John Hopkins University Press, 1976), p. 75.

30. Thomas More, *Utopia* in the *Yale Edition of the Complete Works of St. Thomas More*, edited by Edward Surz and J. H. Hexter, (1967), p. 71.

31. See Strauss, pp. 77–89 who suggests these ideas are as old as the Greeks; see footnotes 29–32.

32. Strauss, p. 70.

33. Strauss, p. 70.

34. Strauss, p. 71, see also Aries, p. 21. The 17th century book, *The Office of Christian Parents* divided life into six stages, of which youth was 14 to 28 years, [n.a.] as quoted in Smith, "Youth," p. 495. See also forthcoming book by Vivian C. Fox and Martin H. Quitt, eds. *The Anglo-American Family Cycle 1500-1800* (Psychohistory Press) which delineates the stages of childhood: into infancy, childhood and youth.

35. Strauss, p. 76.

36. Strauss, p. 76.

37. Marks notes this as a characteristic of modern adolescence, "Although able to work, engage in mature sexual relations and make moral choices, he is denied full adult status", p. 78.

38. Smith, "Apprentices" p. 157.

39. Gillis, p. 22.

40. See for example, Smith, "Apprentices" p. 157; Ivy Pinchbeck and Margaret Hewitt, *Children in English Society, From Tudor Times to the Eighteenth Century,* (London 1969) Vol. I Chap. IX. Also Alan Macfarlene, *The Family Life of Ralph Josselin, a Seventeenth Century Clergyman: An Essay on Historical Anthropology* (Cambridge, 1970), especially pp. 205–210; Gillis, pp. 22–3.

41. Gillis, p. 23.

42. Gillis, p. 24.

43. Gillis, pp. 29–30; see also Natalie Z. David, "The Reasons of Misrule: Youth Groups and *Charvaris* in Sixteenth Century France," *Past and Present, No. 50* (February, 1971) also Natalie Z. Davis, "The Rites of Violence, Religious Riot in Sixteenth Century France," *Past and Present,* No. 59 (May, 1973).

44. See for example, Smith, "Apprentices," p. 157, also Peter Laslett, *The World We Have Lost, 2nd edition,* (London, 1971), p. 94.

45. The idea that adolescence is prolonged is in current vogue. See Kenneth Keniston in *The Uncommitted: Alienated Youth in American Society* (1965), pp. 196–200.

46. Philip Stubbs, *The Anatomie of Abuses* (1583) quoted in Gillis, p. 27.

47. Warren Burton, *Helps to Education* (Boston, 1863), pp. 38–39, quoted in Demos and Demos, p. 211.

48. Smith, "Apprentices," pp. 152–153.

49. Herbert Moller, "Youth as a Force in History," *Comparative Studies in Social History* 10 (1968), p. 238. Moller reports in 1519, when Luther, Carlstadt and Melancthon set out for Leipzig debate—nearly 2,000 students and other supporters joined.

50. Davis, "The Rites of Violence," p. 87.

51. See for example, Daniel Offer, *The Psychological World of the Teen-ager; A Study of Normal Adolescent Boys* (New York, 1969) and Frank Musgrove, "The Problem of Youth and the Structure of Society in England," in *Youth and Society,* Vol I (Sept. 1969). Musgrove states in the 1960's "An English empirical study . . . shows clearly that average 15 year old English boys and girls identify closely with their parents, rather than their peers," p. 41. Compare this with his book, *Youth and the Social Order* (Indiana University Press, 1964).

52. See for example, Robert A. Nisbet, *Social Change and History: Aspects of the Western Theory of Development* (Oxford University Press, 1969), especially Chapter 1, pp. 24–25. Also Arthur O. Lovejoy, *The Great Chain of Being: A Study of the History of An Idea* (Harper, 1936), Chapter 2. Also Werner Jaeger, *Paideia, The Ideals of Greek Culture,* Vol. I translated by Gilbert Highet (New York, 1944).

53. Nisbet, p. 39.

54. Skolnick, pp. 50–51. For an interpretation which claims that the Greek idea of development was not truly developmental; see, Louis Breger, *From Instinct to Identity: The Development of Personality* (Englewood Cliffs, N.J., 1974) Chapter 1. I am grateful to my colleague, Martin H. Quitt, for drawing my attention to this book.

55. Plato, *The Laws,* Penguin (1970), p. 227.

56. Plato, p. 281.

57. Plato, p. 298.

58. Strauss, p. 75; see also Aries, p. 21; also, Smith, "Youth," p. 495. Robert Nisbet's book traces the Greek idea of Life Cycle and Developmentalism up to the present day.

59. See S. N. Eisenstadt, "Archetypal Patterns of Youth" in *Youth: Change and Challenge,* ed. by Erik H. Erikson. (N.Y. 1963). Eisenstadt examines the "subtle dialectics" between the biological aspects of adolescence and cultural variations which help define the expression of the adolescent period.

60. See Skolnick, pp. 49–52, especially, p. 51, in which she says, "Developmental theories claim to be universal."

26

Trends in Cognitive and Psychosocial Gender Differences

MARCIA C. LINN AND JANET S. HYDE

There has been long-standing interest in whether males and females think differently, especially during the years of adolescence and beyond. One clear finding to emerge from cognitive developmental research on this topic is that such differences are actually quite small and are specific to certain types of thinking. Marcia Linn and Janet Hyde review the literature on gender differences in adolescent development and raise interesting questions as to why we, as a society, often assume that differences in the thinking processes of males and females are greater than they really are.

Mounting evidence suggests that gender differences on cognitive and psychosocial tasks were always small, that they have declined in the last two decades, and that differences arise in some contexts and situations but not in others. Meta-analysis, a technique of research synthesis, combined with process analysis, a technique for characterizing the cognitive skills used in complex tasks, allow more precise understanding of the nature and magnitude of gender differences. This paper summarizes trends and argues that explanations for gender differences in earning power and career access may lie in interactions among factors within societal control.

Reprinted with permission from the *Encyclopedia of Adolescence*, 1991, 139–150, edited by R. M. Lerner, A. C. Petersen, and J. Brooks-Gunn, New York: Garland Publishing, Inc.

This paper was supported in part by the National Science Foundation under grant No. MDR 8470514 to the first author and grant Nos. BNS 8508666 and BNS 8696128 to the second author. Any opinions, findings, and conclusions or recommendations expressed in this publication are those of the authors, and do not necessarily reflect the views of the National Science Foundation.

RESEARCH SYNTHESIS AND PROCESS ANALYSIS

Meta-analysis has become a powerful tool for synthesizing results from studies gender differences and analyzing what moderator variables are implicated. In current meta-analyses, the most commonly used statistic is d, (Cohen, 1969; Glass, McGaw, & Smith, 1981; Hedges & Olkin, 1985). In analyzing gender differences, d is computed as the difference between the female mean and the male mean, divided by the pooled within-group standard deviation. The measure d indicates how far apart the group means are in standard deviation units. In conducting a meta-analysis, researchers cumulate d values over many studies. Using corrections devised by Hedges (1982a, 1982b), d values can be used to estimate population values.

In performing meta-analyses, researchers often obtain d values that vary substantially from one study to the next. Hedges (1982a, 1982b) has developed techniques following the traditional analysis of variance and regression approaches that permit investigators to determine whether variation in values of d can be attributed to random sampling variation or to systematic effects. If systematic effects exist, then investigators can partition the studies on the basis of variables that might have contributed to the heterogeneity, and test whether the groups determined by the partitioning have homogeneous values of d.

Thus, meta-analytic methods allow the statistical accumulation of effects from different research investigations. It is possible to determine whether the accumulated values can be accounted for by a single underlying dimension or by a variety of different factors. By partitioning studies into groups hypothesized to be homogeneous, researchers can identify factors that influence the magnitude of gender differences.

Process analysis has helped researchers partition studies in meta-analysis into groups that require the same solution strategies. For example, mathematics tests may measure computation, or solving of problems involving multiplication, or planning solutions to complex problems. Each require some different processes.

COGNITIVE GENDER DIFFERENCES

In 1974 Maccoby and Jacklin, in a landmark analysis of cognitive gender differences, concluded that differences existed for (1) verbal ability, (2) quantitative ability, and (3) spatial ability. Studies conducted since 1974 suggest that these gender differences in cognitive abilities are declining. Meta-analyses suggest that differences are *not* uniform within these categories. Process analyses show that differences arise on only a few dimensions and are often reduced or eliminated by training. Figure 1 summarizes some of these results.

VERBAL ABILITY Hyde and Linn (1988) recently synthesized gender differences in verbal ability and concluded that they no longer exist. They found very small overall differences, with an average $d = +.11$. Since the overall effect was not homogeneous, Hyde and Linn partitioned the studies by type of test, age of subjects, cognitive process, and date of study. They found no systematic variation with age and found that the cognitive process analysis came closest to dividing the studies into homogeneous groups. Furthermore, the combined d for studies conducted since 1974 was .10, compared with the combined d for those conducted prior to 1974 of .24.

Several investigations support this decline. Feingold (1988) reported declines on tests given to national samples. Rosenthal and Rubin (1982) documented this decline in gender differences using studies published between 1966 and 1973 identified by Maccoby and Jacklin and meta-analyzed by Hyde (1981). Rosenthal and Rubin computed a correlation between recency of publication and degree of female superiority for three cognitive skills. The correlations, all significant, were .29 for verbal ability, .21 for quantitative ability, and .46 for visual-spatial ability. They concluded that differences are declining "faster than the gene can travel!" (Rosenthal & Rubin, 1982, p. 711).

Gender differences for the voluntary group of students taking the Scholastic Aptitude Test-Verbal (SAT-V) favor males slightly, with $d = -.11$. Studies reveal that more females than males take the SAT-V and that the females have less academic preparation, come overall from a lower socioeconomic group, and have a lower level of parental education. When these factors are considered, ETS reports that the gender differences on the SAT-V are reduced to $d = -.02$ (Burton & Lewis, 1988).

In summary, a variety of studies support the conclusion that gender differences in verbal ability have diminished and are now negligible.

SPATIAL ABILITY Spatial ability is a construct frequently hypothesized to explain gender differences in science and mathematics, although only correlational studies are available to test the hypothesis (e.g., Hyde, Geiringer, & Yen, 1975). Meta-analyses

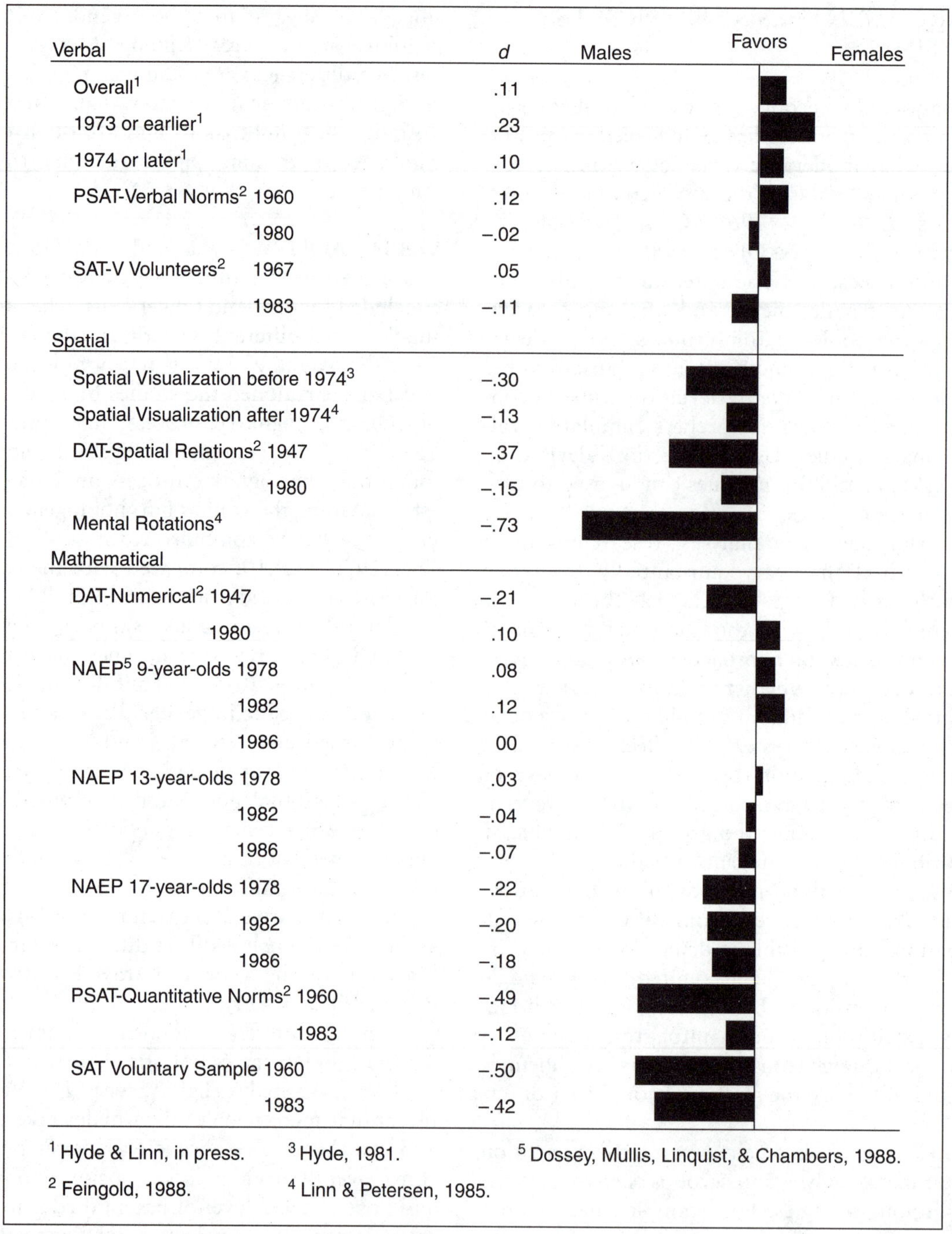

Verbal	d	Males Favors Females
Overall[1]	.11	
1973 or earlier[1]	.23	
1974 or later[1]	.10	
PSAT-Verbal Norms[2] 1960	.12	
1980	−.02	
SAT-V Volunteers[2] 1967	.05	
1983	−.11	
Spatial		
Spatial Visualization before 1974[3]	−.30	
Spatial Visualization after 1974[4]	−.13	
DAT-Spatial Relations[2] 1947	−.37	
1980	−.15	
Mental Rotations[4]	−.73	
Mathematical		
DAT-Numerical[2] 1947	−.21	
1980	.10	
NAEP[5] 9-year-olds 1978	.08	
1982	.12	
1986	00	
NAEP 13-year-olds 1978	.03	
1982	−.04	
1986	−.07	
NAEP 17-year-olds 1978	−.22	
1982	−.20	
1986	−.18	
PSAT-Quantitative Norms[2] 1960	−.49	
1983	−.12	
SAT Voluntary Sample 1960	−.50	
1983	−.42	

[1] Hyde & Linn, in press.   [3] Hyde, 1981.   [5] Dossey, Mullis, Linquist, & Chambers, 1988.
[2] Feingold, 1988.   [4] Linn & Petersen, 1985.

FIGURE 1   Trends in cognitive gender differences.

of gender differences in spatial abilities suggest that no evidence is forthcoming and, instead, reveal that (1) gender differences occur for some spatial processes but not others; (2) processes revealing gender differences respond to training; and (3) gender differences in spatial ability are declining.

Hyde meta-analyzed the studies of spatial ability reviewed by Maccoby and Jacklin in 1974 and found $d = -.45$ overall and a $d = -.30$ for spatial visualization tests such as embedded figures. Linn and Petersen (1985) conducted a meta-analysis of studies of spatial ability subsequent to those summarized by Maccoby and Jacklin in 1974. They found heterogeneous values of d and partitioned the studies by spatial process. For spatial visualization, requiring the process of reasoning about spatially presented information (e.g., the Paper Folding Test), they found a d of $-.13$ and concluded that gender differences no longer exist on this task. For mental rotations, involving the process of mentally rotating a complex figure through space, Linn and Petersen also found heterogeneous gender differences. They partitioned studies by whether the stimulus figures were simple or complex. They found large gender differences for complex figures ($d = -.94$) and small differences for simple figures ($d = -.26$). On this task gender differences reflect speed of mental rotation, not accuracy (Kail, Carter, & Pellegrino, 1979). Lohman (1988) reported that differences in speed of rotation diminish with training.

Consistent with the trend for verbal ability, gender differences in spatial ability are declining. For early studies there is a significant correlation between d and recency of publication. For spatial visualization, the effect has declined from $d = -.30$ before 1974 to $d = -.13$ recently. These trends are consistent with a decline from $d = -.37$ to $d = -.15$ in national norms for Differential Aptitude Test (DAT) spatial-visualization (Feingold, 1988).

In summary, gender differences in spatial ability are heterogeneous and declining. The largest differences arise on speed of mental rotations of complex figures, and these can be reduced or eliminated by training. The small differences that remain seem unlikely to influence quantitative ability. These differences have been hypothesized to arise in part from differential participation in athletics. Declines in gender differences in spatial ability accompany increases in female participation and success in athletics (Newcombe, 1981).

QUANTITATIVE ABILITY Large-scale studies of gender differences in quantitative ability reveal that (1) differences are declining; (2) problem context influences performance; (3) differences on complex problem solving are larger than differences on other measures; and (4) more males than females enroll in advanced high school mathematics. Gender differences in quantitative ability have recently been surveyed nationally (Dossey, Mullis, Lindquist, & Chambers, 1988).

Data from the National Assessment of Educational Programs (NAEP) items, Differential Aptitude Test (DAT) scales, and Preliminary Scholastic Aptitude Test-Mathematics (PSAT-M) indicate declines in quantitative gender differences over the last two decades. Consistent with studies of national samples conducted around 1970, Hyde (1981) found $d = -.43$ for studies identified by Maccoby and Jacklin in 1974, while NAEP, PSAT, and DAT report $d \leq .20$ recently. In addition, as mentioned above, Rosenthal and Rubin (1982)

meta-analyzed trends from 1966 to 1973, and found a significant decline in gender differences in quantitative ability.

Analyses reveal that gender differences are not homogeneous across items (Burton & Lewis, 1988; Chipman, 1988). There are large effects for the context of the items. Generally, males perform better than females on items having to do with measurement, sports, and science, whereas females outperform males on items having to do with typing, cooking, and sewing. As a result, it is possible to eliminate or to exaggerate gender differences simply by selecting items with contexts favoring particular groups.

Process analyses suggest that females outperform males at computation, whereas males excel at proportional reasoning and complex applications (Meehan, 1984). Enrollment patterns of males and females in calculus or precalculus are consistent with gender differences on complex applications. Nationally females in precalculus and calculus comprised 36% of the students in 1978, 45% in 1982, and 39% in 1986. In California females comprised 41% of the calculus students in 1983, 42% in 1987, and 41% in 1988. In enrollment in science, data from California high schools from 1983 to 1987 reveal that girls made up about 38% of physics students, 34% of advanced physics students, and 42% of chemistry students (Zimmerer and Bennett, 1987).

Compared with the declines on quantitative assessments administered to national samples, the large, consistent gender differences found for the voluntary SAT-M sample are anomalous. As mentioned for SAT-V, this is due in part to the decline in preparation of female volunteers relative to male volunteers. The main gender difference is in the proportion of those earning extremely high scores. For the June 1981 and May 1982 administration of the SAT, 96% of the individuals earning 800 on the SAT-M were male (Dorans & Livingston, 1987).

What processes might contribute? The processes required for success on the SAT include ability to solve word problems quickly. One popular SAT review course raises overall scores 150 points by teaching students to make rapid, intelligent guesses rather than engaging in lengthy computations (Robinson & Katzman, 1986).

Examination of a variety of items suggests that an important skill on the SAT-M is the ability to select a strategy that can be applied quickly and accurately to the problem. If, in addition, SAT-M items can be solved by strategies learned from gender-typed activities, differences in excess of these found for other mathematics assessments may arise. Furthermore, examination of precollege mathematics textbooks reveals that students taking algebra and geometry are not encouraged to take "shortcuts" or to reason backwards from the answers. In some classes students would be required to "show their work" and penalized if they used a more direct approach.

In summary, gender differences in quantitative ability are declining on most measures but remain for the SAT-M. Since the SAT-M reveals differences not detected in other assessments, caution should be used in interpreting scores on this test. Research is needed to clarify the processes that result in superior performance, and to determine how these processes are acquired.

SCIENCE, LANGUAGE, AND MECHANICAL REASONING Males and females enroll differentially in courses covering science, language, and mechanical reasoning, and gender differences persist in these areas. In science, several assessments reveal that males outperform females on science knowledge but not on science processes (Linn & Petersen, 1986; Zimmerer & Bennett, 1987). For grammar and mechanical reasoning, differences have declined since 1947 but in 1980 $d = -.40$ for language and $d = -.76$ for mechanical reasoning (Feingold, 1988).

SUMMARY OF COGNITIVE GENDER DIFFERENCES In summary, cognitive gender differences are more limited to specific processes than was previously thought and are declining. No differences remain for verbal ability, spatial visualization, and mathematics computation. Differences remain for high scores on SAT-M, for mental rotations, and for topics studied more by one sex than the other. These results suggest that gender differences in mathematics and science are related to opportunity to learn. Figure 2 provides some of this more recent information.

PSYCHOSOCIAL GENDER DIFFERENCES

Do trends for psychosocial gender differences parallel those found for cognitive gender differences? Maccoby and Jacklin concluded in 1974 that of psychosocial variables, only gender differences in aggression could be termed "well-established." Furthermore, they refuted common beliefs that girls were more social or suggestible than boys. Subsequent meta-analyses have (1) expanded and redefined the variables in the psychosocial domain,

adding nonverbal behavior; (2) demonstrated that differences are heterogeneous, influenced by many different situational and cultural factors; and (3) suggested that differences are declining in some areas and evolving in others, perhaps as the result of changing social roles.

AGGRESSION Maccoby and Jacklin (1974) concluded that gender differences in aggression were well-established. Subsequent analyses suggest that differences in aggression are heterogeneous, subject to situational influences, and declining. Hyde (1984, 1986) obtained a large sample of studies including those located by Maccoby and Jacklin and conducted a developmental meta-analysis. Hyde's (1986) results provided evidence of the specific nature of gender differences in aggression. The weighted mean effect size, over all studies, was $d = -.50$. However, there were significant differences in the magnitude of the gender difference depending on whether aggression was studied in an experimental setting ($d = -.29$) or a naturalistic, correlational setting ($d = -.56$). In addition, Hyde found that gender differences in aggression were larger for children, ($d = -.64$) than for adults ($d = -.29$). For all settings, though, males were more aggressive than females.

Eagly and Steffen (1986) meta-analyzed studies of adult (mostly college-age) subjects to test various predictions deriving from social role theory. Overall, they found the weighted mean effect size to be $-.29$. However, they found that the tendency for men to aggress more than women was larger in laboratory settings ($d = -.35$) than in field settings ($d = -.21$). Further, the gender difference in physical aggression ($d = -.40$) was significantly larger than the gender differences in psychological aggression ($d = -.18$). Looking further into the data, Eagly and Steffen also concluded that females were more likely to feel guilt and concern about possible harm to others in aggressive situations than were males. Overall, both Eagly and Steffen and Hyde concluded that gender differences in aggression were situation-specific.

The heterogeneity of the gender differences in aggression make it difficult to determine changes over time since they may be confounded with the situational factors studied. Hyde, using studies of children and adults, found $d = -.53$ for studies published from 1966 to 1973 and $d = -.41$ for studies published between 1978 and 1981. In contrast, Eagly and Steffen's (1986) meta-analysis of aggression in adult subjects found no relationship between the year of publication and the magnitude of the gender difference.

Social Influence[1]	N	d	Males	Favors	Females
Resists persuasion		−.06			
Resists group pressure		−.32			
Helping[2]					
Overall helping	99	−.34			
Laboratory setting	16	.18			
Off-campus setting	47	−.50			
Without surveillance	41	.02			
With surveillance	16	−.74			
With other helpers uncertain	42	−.20			
With other helpers available	57	−.42			
When requested	59	−.07			
When not requested	40	−.55			
Aggression					
Aggression at All Ages[3]					
Overall aggression	69	−.50			
Experimental	27	−.29			
Naturalistic	42	−.56			
Age 6 or less		−.58			
College students		−.27			
Aggression Among Adolescents and Adults[4]					
Overall aggression		−.29			
Field setting	13	−.21			
Laboratory setting	34	−.35			
Psychological aggression	20	−.18			
Physical aggression	30	−.40			

[1] Eagly & Carli, 1981.   [3] Hyde, 1986.

[2] Eagly & Crowley, 1986.   [4] Eagly & Steffen, 1986.

FIGURE 2   Gender differences in psychosocial domains.

SOCIAL INFLUENCE   Researchers have concluded that data do not support the common belief that females are more suggestible than males (Maccoby & Jacklin, 1974). Research suggests that social influence depends on situational factors and that differences are declining. Eagly and her colleagues (Eagly, 1978; Eagly, 1986; Eagly & Carli, 1981) located studies conducted since 1974 and, consistent with Maccoby and Jacklin, found small heterogeneous differences in social influence and group persuasion across all studies.

HELPING OTHERS   Maccoby and Jacklin (1974) examined altruism and nurturance and concluded that gender differences were heterogeneous. Eagly and Crowley (1986) focussed on a narrower domain—the extent to which males and females give and receive help—and found that gender differences were heterogeneous, and influenced by situational factors. Overall, the mean effect size was $d = −.34$. The factors that contributed to the magnitude of gender differences in helping behavior were the degree of danger involved in helping and the availability of others who could help instead. When there was no danger and no other available helpers, females were more likely to help than males. However, when the situation was dangerous, and where other possible helpers were available, females were less likely to help than males.

CONFIDENCE AND EXPECTATIONS Studies consistently report that males are more confident than females concerning their abilities in mathematics and science. These differences arise even when gender groups perform equally on mathematics or science assessments.

For mathematics, in the NAEP national sample in 1986 consistently fewer females report that they are "good at mathematics." For all 17-year-olds there has been an overall increase in confidence in the last two decades but the "confidence gap" between males and females has remained large. In 1978, 49% of females and 59% of males reported that they were good at mathematics ($d = -.27$). In 1982 it was 53% of the females and 63% of the males ($d = -.27$), and in 1986 it was 55% of the females and 66% of the males ($d = -.29$). Furthermore, during this period 1 to 2% of the females and 3 to 4.2% of the males report that "mathematics is more for boys than girls" (Dossey et al., 1988).

For science, a survey of all eighth-graders in California revealed that 39% of the boys and 12% of the girls ($d = -.92$) believe that boys understand science better than girls (Zimmerer & Bennett, 1987). Analysis of the processes contributing to these differences in confidence and expected success revealed that males expect to do better than females on science problems even when the two groups perform equally (Linn, 1986). Males overestimate their likelihood of success while females are realistic (Linn, De Benedictis, Delucchi, Harris, & Stage, 1987). We suspect that optimism is preferable and may be a factor in the greater persistence of males in mathematics and science courses.

NONVERBAL BEHAVIOR Hall (1984) identified nonverbal behavior as an area for the study of gender differences and found large, heterogeneous effects for smiling and gazing. Subsequently, Hall and Halberstadt (1986) partitioned these effects to achieve homogeneity. They found larger differences in smiling and gazing for adults than for children and in interpersonal situations than in isolated situations. It is possible that gender differences in smiling and gazing stem from the status differences between males and females that are more established for older individuals.

SUMMARY OF PSYCHOSOCIAL DIFFERENCES In summary, gender differences in the psychosocial realm are heterogeneous, small, and situation-specific. Interactions between these factors and cognitive gender differences may influence both persistence and success. Both aggressiveness and willingness to help may provide males with more feedback on their problem-solving activities, and contribute to greater use of estimation, shortcuts, and other unconventional problem-solving strategies. In contrast, responsiveness to social influence, lack of confidence, and expectations that males are more suited to mathematics and science than females may prevent females from getting the help they need and the respect they deserve. As a result, females may follow directions more and tend to keep innovative ideas to themselves.

DEVELOPMENTAL TRENDS AT ADOLESCENCE

Although gender differences in cognitive and psychosocial skills are small and declining, there still remains the possibility that these differences could increase at adolescence. Maccoby and Jacklin (1974) hypothesized that gender differences in verbal, mathematical, and spatial abilities emerge at the beginning of adolescence, based on empirical data. However, meta-analyses of the Maccoby and Jacklin studies combined with subsequent studies show no increase in gender differences at adolescence. The meta-analysis of verbal ability showed no gender differences at any point in the life span (Hyde & Linn, 1988). The analyses of mathematics ability showed no change at adolescence, although an increase in the gender difference for mathematical ability on problem-solving tasks emerged in the 15 to 18 age range. This may reflect differences in course participation that also emerge at this time. The meta-analysis of gender differences in spatial ability also showed no change at adolescence, although it has proven difficult to assess gender differences in mental rotations at ages below about 10. There are very few longitudinal studies of gender differences. One by Block and Block (1980) showed no changes in spatial ability at adolescence. In summary, the hypothesis that gender differences in cognitive tasks emerge at adolescence has not been supported.

Developmental trends for psychosocial abilities also do not support the emergence of any gender differences in adolescence, although situational influences change over the age range. For example, young children are more physically aggressive than older individuals, presumably because physical aggression is more acceptable among young individuals and more observable in field settings. Gender differences in confidence have been detected at all ages, although the majority of the data on confidence in mathematics and science has been collected among adolescents and adults.

Thus, the hypothesis that gender differences in cognitive and psychosocial abilities increase during adolescence has not been supported by meta-analyses. Changes across the life span are more likely among older individuals, possibly reflecting cohort differences.

CONCLUSIONS

Combining meta-analysis techniques with process and situational analyses has clarified the nature, magnitude, and developmental trends for gender differences on cognitive and psychosocial tasks. There have been declines in gender differences consistent with more equal participation in precollege courses, some convergence in social roles, and greater participation of females in the work place. Workers need more communication and technological skills as society moves from a manufacturing to an automation and service economy.

Researchers have clarified the processes and situations that evoke gender differences, revealing that differences are not general but specific and that many are responsive to training. The largest differences are speed of mental rotation of complex figures and mechanical reasoning, differences that decline and may disappear with training. Smiling in social situations is the next largest difference.

Although gender differences in cognitive skills have declined and those that remain are largely explained by differences in experience, there are still massive discrepancies between males and females in career access and earning power. General cognitive and psychosocial gender differences cannot account for these differences. What does explain them? Researchers should examine the interactions between cognitive and psychosocial differences to find explanations. Looking, for example, at the interaction between instruction in mathematics that emphasizes following procedures and the tendency of females to conform more to classroom practices than males may reveal that females are less likely to learn the shortcuts and estimation techniques useful for solving complex problems even though they get equivalent grades. There may also be interactions between communication practices and perception of success. In some fields, aggressive argumentation is taken as a sign of intelligence, yet it may be more comfortable for males than for females.

Questions

1. What is meta-analysis and why is it useful for the type of questions raised by Linn and Hyde?

2. What differences in thinking between males and females did the authors find? Were you surprised by these results? Why?

3. Despite the lack of major differences in the thinking of males and females, there remains a generally held belief that such differences exist. What effect do you think this belief has on the way males and females try to develop and use their thinking skills during the high school and college years?

References

Block, J., & Block, J. (1980). *Cognitive development from childhood to adolescence* (National Institute of Mental Health Grant MH16080). Unpublished manuscript.

Burton, N. W., & Lewis, C. (1988, April). *Modelling women's performance on the SAT.* Paper presented at the annual meeting of the American Educational Research Association, New Orleans, LA.

Chipman, S. F. (1988, April). *Cognitive issues in math test bias.* Paper presented at the annual meeting of the American Educational Research Association, New Orleans, LA.

Cohen J. (1969). *Statistical power analysis for the behavioral sciences.* New York: Academic Press.

Dossey, J. A., Mullis, I. V. S., Lindquist, M. M., & Chambers, D. L. (1988). *The mathematics report card. Are we measuring up?* (Trends and achievement based on the 1986 National Assessment, Report No. 17-M-01). Princeton, NJ: Educational Testing Service.

Dorans, N. J., & Livingston, S. A. (1987). Male-female differences in SAT-Mathematical ability. *Journal of Educational Measurement, 24,* 65–71.

Eagly, A. H. (1978). Sex differences in influenceability. *Psychological Bulletin, 85,* 86–116.

Eagly, A. H. (1986). Some meta-analytic approaches to examining the validity of gender difference research. In J. S. Hyde & M. C. Linn (Eds.), *The psychology of gender: Advances through meta-analysis* (pp. 159–177). Baltimore: Johns Hopkins University Press.

Eagly, A. H., & Carli, L. L. (1981). Sex of researchers and sex-typed communications as determinants of sex differences in influenceability: A meta-analysis of social influence studies. *Psychological Bulletin, 90,* 1–20.

Eagly, A. H., & Crowley, M. (1986). Gender and helping behavior: A meta-analytic review of the social psychological literature. *Psychological Bulletin, 100,* 283–308.

Eagly, A. H., & Steffen, V. J. (1986). Gender and aggressive behavior: A meta-analytic review of the social psychological literature. *Psychological Bulletin, 100,* 309–330.

Feingold, A. (1988). Cognitive gender differences are disappearing. *American Psychologist, 43*(2), 95–103.

Glass, G. V., McGaw, B., & Smith, M. L. (1981). *Meta-analysis in social research.* Beverly Hills, CA: Sage.

Hall, J. A. (1984). *Nonverbal sex differences: Communication accuracy and expressive style.* Baltimore: Johns Hopkins University Press.

Hall, J. A., & Halberstadt, A. G. (1986). Smiling and gazing. In J. S. Hyde & M. C. Linn (Eds.), *The psychology of gender: Advances through meta-analysis* (pp. 136–158). Baltimore: Johns Hopkins University Press.

Hedges, L. B. (1982a). Fitting categorical models to effect sizes from a series of experiments. *Journal of Educational Statistics, 7,* 119–137.

Hedges, L. B. (1982b). Fitting continuous models to effect size data. *Journal of Educational Statistics, 7,* 245–270.

Hedges, L. B., & Olkin, I. (1985). *Statistical methods for meta-analysis.* New York: Academic Press.

Hyde, J. S. (1981). How large are cognitive gender differences? A meta-analysis using omega squared and *d. American Psychologist, 36,* 892–901.

Hyde, J. S. (1984). How large are gender differences in aggression? A developmental meta-analysis. *Developmental Psychology, 20,* 722–736.

Hyde, J. S. (1986). Introduction: Meta-analysis and the psychology of gender. In J. S. Hyde & M. C. Linn (Eds.), *The psychology of gender: Advances through meta-analysis* (pp. 1–13). Baltimore: Johns Hopkins University Press.

Hyde, J. S., Geiringer, E. R., & Yen, W. M. (1975). On the empirical relation between spatial ability and sex differences in other aspects of cognitive performance. *Multivariate Behavioral Research, 10,* 289–310.

Hyde, J. S., & Linn, M. C. (1988). Gender differences in verbal ability: A Meta-analysis. *Psychological Bulletin, 104*(1), 53–69.

Kail, R., Carter, P., & Pellegrino, J. (1979). The locus of sex differences in spatial ability. *Perception and Psychophysics, 26,* 182–186.

Linn, M. C. (1986). Meta-analysis of studies of gender differences: Implications and future directions. In J. S. Hyde & M. C. Linn (Eds.), *The psychology of gender: Advances through meta-analysis* (pp. 210–231). Baltimore: Johns Hopkins University Press.

Linn, M. C., De Benedictis, T., Delucchi, K., Harris, A., & Stage, E. (1987). Gender differences in National Assessment of Educational Progress science items: What does "I don't know" really mean? *Journal of Research in Science Teaching, 24*(3), 267–278.

Linn, M. C., & Petersen, A. C. (1985). Emergence and characterization of sex differences in spatial ability: A meta-analysis. *Child Development, 56,* 1479–1498.

Linn, M. C., & Petersen, A. C. (1986). A meta-analysis of gender differences in spatial ability: Implications for mathematics and science achievement. In J. S. Hyde & M. C. Linn (Eds.), *The psychology of gender. Advances through meta-analysis* (pp. 67–101). Baltimore: Johns Hopkins University Press.

Lohman, D. F. (1988). Spatial abilities as traits, processes, and knowledge. In R. J. Sternberg (Ed.), *Advances in the psychology of human intelligence* (Vol. 4, pp. 181–248). Hillsdale, NJ: Lawrence Erlbaum Associates.

Maccoby, E. E., & Jacklin, C. N. (1974). *The psychology of sex differences.* Stanford University Press.

Meehan, A. M. (1984). A meta-analysis of sex differences in formal operational thought. *Child Development, 55,* 1110–1124.

Moore, M., & Newcombe, N. (1987). The role of experience in spatial test performance: A meta-analysis. In N. Newcombe (Chair), *Sex-related differences in spatial ability: Recent meta-analyses and future directions.* Symposium conducted at the annual Meeting of the Society for Research in Child Development, Baltimore.

Newcombe, N. (1981). Spatial representation and behavior: Retrospect and prospect. In L. Liben, A. Patterson, & N. Newcombe (Eds.), *Spatial representation and behavior across the life span: Theory and application* (pp. 373–388). New York: Academic Press.

Robinson, A., & Katzman, J. (1986). *Cracking the system.* New York: Villard Books.

Rosenthal, R., & Rubin, D. C. (1982). Further meta-analytic procedures for assessing cognitive gender differences. *Journal of Educational Psychology, 74,* 708–712.

Yen, W. M. (1975). Sex-linked major-gene influences on selected types of spatial performance. *Behavior Genetics, 5,* 281–298.

Zimmerer, L. K., & Bennett, S. M. (1987, April). *Gender differences on the California Statewide Assessment of Attitudes and Achievement in Science.* Paper presented at the annual meeting of the American Educational Research Association, Washington, DC.

27

Prosocial Development in Adolescence: A Longitudinal Study

NANCY EISENBERG, PAUL A. MILLER, RITA SHELL,
SANDRA MCNALLEY, AND CINDY SHEA

An important aspect of developing morality is the development of prosocial behaviors, that is behaviors that benefit others. Nancy Eisenberg and colleagues have studied the development of prosocial moral reasoning during early to mid-adolescence. In the study reported here, they examine the relationship between prosocial reasoning, empathy, perspective taking, and prosocial behavior over the teen years, and by so doing help to clarify how children become mature, responsible, moral beings.

Change in prosocial moral reasoning over an 11-year period, gender differences in prosocial reasoning in adolescence, and the interrelations of moral reasoning, prosocial behavior, and empathy-related emotional responses were examined with longitudinal data and data from adolescents *interviewed for the first time. Hedonistic reasoning declined in use until adolescence and then increased somewhat (primarily for boys). Needs-oriented reasoning, direct reciprocity reasoning, and approval and stereotypic reasoning increased until midchildhood or early adolescence and then*

Reprinted with permission from the authors and *Developmental Psychology* 27, 1991, 849–857. Copyright 1991 by the American Psychological Association.

This research was supported by National Science Foundation Grant BNS8807784 and National Institute of Child Health and Development Career Development Award K04 HDO0717 to Nancy Eisenberg. We thank the mothers and students in our longitudinal samples and the principals, students, and teachers at Connolly Junior High School and Tempe High School for their participation.

declined. Several modes of higher level reasoning emerged in late childhood or adolescence. Girls' overall reasoning was higher than boys'. Consistent with expectations, there was some evidence of high level prosocial reasoning being associated with prosocial behavior and empathy and of a relation between sympathy or empathy and prosocial behavior.

The roles of cognition and affect in morality have been a topic of discussion for centuries (e.g., Hume, 1777/1966; Kant, 1797/1964). In recent years, psychologists such as Kohlberg (1981) have argued that cognition is the foundation of morality, whereas others such as Batson (1990) or Hoffman (1987) have emphasized the role of sympathy and empathy in moral behavior, particularly in altruism. In recent research and writings, the role of each has been acknowledged (e.g., Hoffman, 1987; Underwood & Moore, 1982).

The cognitive process most closely linked with morality, including prosocial behavior, is moral reasoning. Cognitive developmentalists have argued that developmental advances in the sociocognitive skill of perspective taking underlie age-related changes in moral reasoning and that the quality of individuals' thinking about moral issues affects the maturity of their moral functioning. In support of this view, higher level moral reasoning or self-attributions have been associated with frequency of prosocial behavior and with higher quality (e.g., more altruistic) behavior (Bar-Tal, 1982; Eisenberg, 1986; Underwood & Moore, 1982).

Although most researchers studying moral judgment have focused on reasoning about moral dilemmas in which rules, laws, authorities' dictates, and formal obligations are central (Kohlberg, 1981; Rest, 1983), some investigators have studied issues related to positive morality (e.g., Damon, 1977; Eisenberg, 1986; Gilligan & Attanucci, 1988). One type of reasoning that investigators have explored is prosocial moral reasoning, that is, reasoning about moral dilemmas in which one person's needs or desires conflict with those of another (or others) in a context in which the role of prohibitions, authorities' dictates, and formal obligations is minimal.

In cross-sectional research on the prosocial moral reasoning of children and adolescents in industrialized cultures, age-related changes in prosocial moral judgment have been delineated. These changes are, in general, consistent with Kohlberg's (1969, 1981) view that the capability for complex perspective taking and for understanding abstract concepts is associated with advances in moral reasoning. However, levels of prosocial moral reasoning are not viewed as hierarchical, integrated structures (with the result that individuals' reasoning is primarily at one stage) or as being invariant in sequence and universal (Eisenberg, 1986). Specifically, young children tend to use primarily hedonistic reasoning or needs-oriented (primitive empathic) reasoning. In elementary school, children's reasoning begins to reflect concern with approval and enhancing interpersonal relationships as well as the desire to behave in stereotypically good ways, although such reasoning also appears to decrease in use from the elementary to high school years. Contrary to initial expectations, direct reciprocity reasoning, which reflects an orientation to self-gain, has been found to increase in the elementary school years, perhaps because of the cognitive sophistication involved in thinking about reciprocity over time. In late elementary school and beyond, children begin to express reasoning reflecting abstract principles, internalized affective reactions (e.g., guilt or positive affect about the consequences of one's behavior for others or living up to internalized principles), and self-reflective sympathy and perspective taking. Nonetheless, even in adolescence people frequently verbalize other, less mature modes of reasoning, although hedonistic reasoning decreases with age (Eisenberg-Berg, 1979a; see Eisenberg, 1986).

In the limited longitudinal research on prosocial reasoning, change in moral reasoning has been examined from age 4–5 years to 11–12 years (Eisenberg, Lennon, & Roth, 1983; Eisenberg et al., 1987). A longitudinal study of prosocial moral reasoning was initiated because intraindividual change can be examined only with longitudinal data and because longitudinal procedures overcome the confound between developmental change and cohort inherent in cross-sectional research. In this research, we have for the most part replicated the aforementioned findings in the cross-sectional research for preschool and elementary school children. However, consistent with Gilligan's (Gilligan & Attanucci, 1988) argument that females use more care-oriented reasoning than do males, we found that the initial increase in self-reflective other-oriented modes of reasoning in late elementary school was primarily for girls. Because no longitudinal study has included participants older than age 12, the declines in some modes of reasoning (e.g., stereotypic, approval oriented) noted during adolescence in cross-sectional research have not been replicated with a longitudinal design; nor has the developmental course of direct reciprocity reasoning (primitive other-oriented reasoning, which increases during elementary school) or needs-oriented reasoning (which has been found to increase into the mid-elementary school years and then to level off in usage) been adequately delineated. Furthermore, some of the higher level modes of reasoning that seem to emerge in adolescence have not been examined longitudinally, even though sociocognitive changes during this age period are substantial (Colby, Kohlberg, Gibbs, & Lieberman, 1983; Hoffman, 1987; Selman, 1980).

Thus, the primary purpose of this study was to examine change in prosocial moral reasoning during early and midadolescence (i.e., at ages 13–14 and 15–16). The subjects in this study have been followed since age 4–5 years for 11 years. Because of the changes in early and midadolescence in logical reasoning, perspective-taking skills (Selman, 1980), and Kohlbergian moral reasoning (Colby et al., 1983), it seemed reasonable to expect the development of more abstract and morally sophisticated modes of reasoning during this period of development. Moreover, changes in the complexity of the child's social environment as he or she moves into adolescence might be expected to stimulate perspective taking and, consequently, moral reasoning (see Kohlberg, 1981). In addition, given the debate over the possible existence of a gender difference in moral reasoning in adolescence and adulthood (Gilligan & Attanucci, 1988; Walker, 1984), we were also interested in determining whether the sex difference in the emergence of other-oriented modes of reasoning found at age 11–12 persisted into adolescence.

The second purpose of this study was to examine the relations among prosocial moral reasoning, prosocial behavior, and empathy-related emotional reactions in adolescence. Few investigators have examined prosocial reasoning or empathy in adolescence, and even studies of adolescents' prosocial behavior are relatively few in number (Eisenberg, 1990). Indeed, the prosocial side of morality in adolescence has been neglected by researchers.

Theorists such as Kohlberg (1981) and Rest (1983) have argued that moral reasoning influences individuals' moral decisions and behavior. Consistent with this view, moral reasoning, including prosocial moral judgment, does seem to be correlated with the performance of prosocial behaviors, although the empirical associations generally are modest (Eisenberg, 1986; Underwood & Moore, 1982). Specifically, elementary school children's prosocial behavior generally has been positively related to needs-oriented reasoning and negatively

related to hedonistic reasoning (Eisenberg, 1986; Eisenberg et al., 1987). In one of the only studies on this topic involving adolescents, Eisenberg-Berg (1979b) found that the level of moral judgment was positively correlated with helping behavior, but only for males. In this study, we sought to further examine the relation of prosocial moral reasoning to prosocial behavior in early and midadolescence. Investigators have hypothesized that the relation between reasoning and behavior increases with age because higher level reasoning is associated with the "progressive stripping away of bases for justifying behavior that are extrinsic to principle" (Rholes & Bailey, 1983, p. 104), resulting in a stronger motive to maintain consistency between attitudes and behaviors at higher stages of development. Thus, we hypothesized that helping behavior in adolescence would be positively correlated with other-oriented modes of reasoning, as well as with overall level of reasoning, and negatively related to hedonistic reasoning.

The relation of empathy to prosocial moral reasoning has been studied very infrequently, although some modes of moral reasoning explicitly reflect cognitive role taking, empathy, and sympathy. Indeed, investigators have suggested that sympathy (concern for others based on the apprehension of another's state) and empathy (an emotional reaction elicited by and congruent with another's state) stimulate the development of internalized moral principles reflecting concern for others' welfare (Hoffman, 1987) and prime the use of preexisting moral cognitions reflecting concern for others (Eisenberg, 1986).

The very limited empirical data are consistent with the argument that there is an association between empathy and prosocial moral reasoning. In the last two follow-ups of our longitudinal research, we found that scores on Bryant's (1982) empathy scale were positively related to needs-oriented and higher level moral reasoning and negatively related to hedonistic reasoning. However, the associations generally were stronger at age 9–10 years than at age 11–12 years. Thus, it was unclear whether the association would continue into adolescence, although level of prosocial reasoning was associated with global empathy in one study of high school students (Eisenberg-Berg & Mussen, 1978).

In addition, in previous research on the relation of prosocial reasoning to vicarious emotional responding, only the association of empathy to moral reasoning has been examined. However, researchers have found that it is important to differentiate among various emotionally based reactions that often stem from empathy, including sympathy and personal distress (i.e., a self-oriented aversive response to another's state; Batson, 1987). Sympathy, which is viewed as stemming from perspective taking (e.g., Batson, 1987; Hoffman, 1987) and as leading to other-oriented, altruistic motivations (Batson, 1987), has been positively related to altruistic behavior (e.g., Batson, 1987, 1990). In contrast, personal distress appears to be associated with egoistic motives and behavior (Batson, 1987; Eisenberg & Fabes, 1991), particularly with the motive to alleviate one's own negative emotional state. Thus, at the most recent follow-up, we examined the relations of sympathy and personal distress, as well as perspective taking, to prosocial moral reasoning.

The positive relation between empathy and prosocial behavior has been documented more frequently than has the relation between empathy and moral reasoning (see Barnett, 1987; Eisenberg & Miller, 1987). Indeed, empathy and sympathy are viewed by many theorists as important motivators of altruism (Batson, 1990; Hoffman, 1987; Staub, 1978). Consistent with this view and with the finding of weaker relations in childhood than during adulthood (Eisenberg & Miller, 1987), in our longitudinal research empathy was associated with prosocial behavior at age 11–12 years but not 10–11 years. In other studies, there does seem to be some positive relation between empathy and prosocial behavior in adolescence (Eisenberg & Miller, 1987; Underwood & Moore, 1982); however, the research on this association in adolescence is quite limited, and no one, to our knowledge, has published research concerning the relations of sympathy and personal distress to adolescents' prosocial behavior. Thus, another goal of this study was to examine the aforementioned relations at two ages during adolescence.

Finally, in any study in which moral development is assessed with self-report data one must be concerned with the possibility that responses are contaminated by self-presentational concerns. Thus, in this study we examined the relation of social desirability to our other moral indexes.

In summary, the purposes of this study were to examine change in prosocial moral reasoning in adolescence and the interrelations among moral reasoning, prosocial behavior, and empathy-related responses at that stage of life. To do so, we conducted two longitudinal follow-ups of children studied since the age of 4–5 years, one at age 13–14 years and one at age 15–16 years, and also tested additional students at each age.

METHOD

Subjects

Three groups of middle-class children participated in this study. The primarily longitudinal cohort (C1) consisted of 16 girls and 16 boys (all White except 2) who had been interviewed five times previously, at ages 4–5, 5½–6½, 7–8, 9–10, and 11–12 (at 108, 90, 72, 48, and 24 months before the first assessment in this study); the seven testing sessions henceforth are referred to as T1 through T7. The mean ages of the children at T6 and T7 were 163 months (range = 154–171 months; approximately 13–14 years of age) and 187 months (approximately 15–16 years of age). No children have been lost since T3 (in 8 years); 1 was lost in the past 9.5 years and 5 have been lost over the 11-year period (3 boys and 2 girls; the original sample was 37 children).

The second sample (C2) consisted of 39 eighth graders from a middle-class, predominantly White neighborhood (20 girls and 19 boys; mean age = 164 months, range = 154–176 months). These children attended a school in the suburban city in which the longitudinal subjects lived at the beginning of the study. They were interviewed for the first and only time at T6. A similar group (C3) of 34 tenth graders (17 of each sex) was interviewed for the first and only time at T7 (mean age 189 months, range = 180–199 months).

Instruments

Children's prosocial moral reasoning was assessed with the same four moral reasoning stories used in prior follow-ups (see Eisenberg et al., 1983, 1987), although a few words were changed to make the stories sound less childlike (e.g., "birthday party" was changed to "birthday celebration"). However, an additional story previously used with school-aged children and adolescents in another study (concerning going into the hospital to donate a rare type of blood at a cost to the self; Eisenberg-Berg, 1979a) was also used in these two follow-up sessions. This story was added because the costs of helping in some of the other stories appeared to be rather low for adolescents (e.g., missing a birthday celebration), whereas the costs of helping in the giving-blood story would likely be substantial for adolescents (losing time at work and school).

As at T4 and T5, subjects at T6 in C1 and C2 were also administered Bryant's (1982) 22-item Empathy scale (αs = .78 and .69) and Crandall's 47-item Social Desirability (SD) Scale for children (αs = .92 and .87, respectively; Crandall, Crandall, & Katkovsky, 1965). To assess social desirability at T7, children in C1 and C3 completed 25 items from the Marlowe-Crowne Social Desirability Scale (αs = .86 and .74, respectively; Crowne & Marlowe, 1964), which appeared to be more age-appropriate for adolescents than the Crandall et al. index. To assess capabilities related to empathy, students in C1 and C3 at T7 were also administered three subscales of Davis's Interpersonal Reactivity Scale: Sympathy (α = .83), Perspective Taking (.73), and Personal Distress (.74). In addition, at both T6 and T7, children filled out a 23-item adapted version of Rushton, Chrisjohn, and Fekken's (1981) self-report Altruism scale (αs = .86 and .90 at T6 and T7, respectively). Children indicated on a 5-point scale (ranging from *never* to *very often*) how frequently they engaged in 23 behaviors such as giving money to charity or volunteer work. Finally, children at T6 and T7 were given an opportunity to assist the experimenter by filling out some additional questionnaires and returning them in a stamped, addressed envelope.

Mothers of children in C1 also filled out the modified Rushton et al. Altruism scale; however, they filled it out in regard to their child rather than themselves. Because they were given the additional option of "don't know," alphas could not be computed for these scales (due to the fact that items with this response were considered missing, resulting in few mothers with all items completed).

For all of the aforementioned questionnaires, scores for the various items were summed (after reversing their direction, if necessary). For mothers' reports of children's prosocial behavior, this sum was divided by the number of items the mothers answered. Two indexes of helping behavior were computed: whether the students returned the questionnaires and whether all parts of the questionnaires were completed.

Procedures

C1 Interviews for C1 took place in the home or at the university. In either case, mother and child were interviewed in different rooms, the mother by a woman and the child by a man (at T6) or a woman (at T7) who had not been involved in any previous follow-ups. For the children, the prosocial dilemmas were presented first in random order; they were read to the children while the children read along (re-sponses were taped). Children repeated dilemmas to check for comprehension, and a standard sequence of questioning was followed (Eisenberg et al., 1983). The moral reasoning task was always administered first because it was considered most important and we did not want to influence the children's responses by having it follow other procedures.

Subsequent to the moral interview, the children completed the measures of empathy, social desirability, and self-reported prosocial behavior (presented in random order). The students were told that their responses were confidential. Next, after the children were paid for their participation ($5 at T6 and $10 at T7), the experimenter told the students that he or she would appreciate their filling out a few more forms at home, but that they need not do so if they did not want to. If the student agreed to take the questionnaires (all did), they were given the forms and a stamped envelope.

C2 AND C3 C2 and C3 students were individually administered the procedures at their schools. Their mothers were not present. Tapes for moral interviews of 4 C2 students were lost due to mechanical difficulties.

Scoring

PROSOCIAL REASONING STORIES Scoring of prosocial reasoning was done in two ways. First, the children's judgments were coded into the categories of reasoning outlined by Eisenberg et al. (1983, 1987; Eisenberg-Berg, 1979a). Those used by children with any frequency were as follows:

HEDONISTIC REASONING (a) *hedonistic gain to the self* (orientation to gain for oneself), (b) *direct reciprocity* (orientation to personal gain because of direct reciprocity or lack of reciprocity from the recipient of an act), and (c) *affectional relationship* (orientation to the individual's identification or relationship with another or liking for the other);

PRAGMATIC (orientation to practical concerns that are unrelated to selfish considerations);

NEEDS-ORIENTED (orientation to the physical, material, or psychological needs of the other person; e.g., "He needs blood," or "He's sad");

STEREOTYPES OF A GOOD OR BAD PERSON (orientation to stereotyped images of a good or bad person);

APPROVAL AND INTERPERSONAL ORIENTATION (orientation to others' approval and acceptance in deciding what is the correct behavior;

SELF-REFLECTIVE EMPATHIC ORIENTATION (a) sympathetic orientation (expression of sympathetic concern and caring for others), (b) role taking (the individual explicitly takes the perspective of the other or has the story protagonist do so), (c) internalized positive affect related to consequences (orientation to internal positive affect as a result of a particular course of action because of the consequences of one's act for the other person), and (d) internalized negative affect related to consequences (the same as [c] but for negative affect);

INTERNALIZED AFFECT BECAUSE OF LOSS OF SELF-RESPECT AND NOT LIVING UP TO ONE'S VALUE (a) positive (orientation to feeling good, often about oneself, as a consequence of living up to internalized values), (b) negative (concern with feeling bad as a consequence of not living up to internalized values);

INTERNALIZED LAW, NORM, AND VALUE ORIENTATION (orientation to an internalized responsibility, duty, or need to uphold the laws and accepted norms or values);

OTHER ABSTRACT OR INTERNALIZED TYPES OF REASONING (a) generalized reciprocity (orientation to indirect reciprocity in a society, that is, exchange that is not one-to-one but eventually benefits all or a larger group), (b) *concern with the condition of society* (orientation to improving the society or community as a whole), (c) *concern with individual rights and justice* (orientation to protecting individual rights and preventing injustices that violate another's rights), and (d) *equality of people* (orientation to the principle of the equal value of all people).

Children were assigned scores indicating the frequency with which they used each of the various types of reasoning when discussing both the pros and cons of helping the needy other in the story dilemma (1 = no use of category; 2 = vague, questionable use; 3 = clear use of a mode of reasoning; and 4 = a major type of reasoning used). Next, the scores for each category were summed across the stories. At each time period, two coders scored either half or all the data; interrater reliabilities for T1, T2, T3, T4, and T5 have been presented in previous articles (Eisenberg et al., 1983, 1987; Eisenberg-Berg & Roth, 1980). For all time periods, the primary coder was the same person, whereas five persons have

served as reliability coders over the 7 time periods. To prevent bias in scoring, the coders were blind to the identity of the children. The primary coder was also blind to any information regarding the subjects' scores on other measures (e.g., prosocial behavior and empathy); this was usually the case for the reliability coder. Interrater reliabilities (Pearson product-moment correlations) computed for each reasoning category at T6 and T7 (using data for all subjects at T6 and for half the subjects at T7) ranged from .81 (for positive affect-self at T6) to 1.00, with most being above .85. (These reliabilities are for four stories; those for five stories were very similar.)

As was just noted, the primary coder for the moral reasoning protocols was the same person who scored the data at all previous follow-ups. This procedure was used to prevent differences across different coders at different times being interpreted as age-related changes in reasoning. To determine if there was any change in the primary coder's scoring over the years (and to prevent the primary coder from knowing the age of subjects being coded), five protocols from each of the previous follow-ups were mixed together with the various protocols from T6 and T7 and were rescored by the primary coder to determine if there was any change in her scoring over the years (the coder was blind to which protocol was from which follow-up). Scoring of the data from earlier sessions was highly similar to the original scores for the same data (agreement on codings within one point was 75% or higher on all categories; correlations were .89 and higher).

The categories of reasoning are viewed as representing components of developmental levels of prosocial moral reasoning; these levels were derived from the results of cross-sectional research (Eisenberg-Berg, 1979a; see Eisenberg, 1986). Briefly, the levels are as follows: Level 1, hedonistic, self-focused orientation; Level 2, needs of others orientation; Level 3, approval and interpersonal orientation and stereotyped orientation; Level 4, self-reflective, empathic orientation; and Level 5, strongly internalized orientation. On the basis of these levels, a score representing level of moral judgment was computed for each child. The level score was constructed in a manner similar to that used to score Kohlbergian reasoning; that is, subjects were assigned composite scores by weighing the proportion of the child's reasoning at each level (see Eisenberg et al., 1983, for more detail). Because it is debatable whether Level 5 is more moral than Level 4 and because Levels 4 and 5 were weighted equally in previous follow-ups, they were weighted equally in the analyses presented in this article (although the data changed little if Level 5 was weighted higher).

RESULTS

Age Changes in Moral Judgment

To examine age changes in moral reasoning for C1 over the 11 years, multivariate analyses of variance (MANOVAs) and univariate trend analyses of variance (ANOVAs) were computed with one within-subjects factor (time, adjusted for unequal time gaps when appropriate) and one between-subjects factor (sex). On the basis of prior research and theoretical formulations in which types of reasoning involving more complex perspective taking and abstract concepts are expected to increase with age (Eisenberg, 1986; Kohlberg, 1981), we expected the self-reflective and internalized-abstract modes of reasoning to increase with age into adolescence. In contrast, direct reciprocity, approval, and stereotypic modes of reasoning, which increased in childhood, were expected to decrease in usage in adolescence, whereas levels of needs-oriented and hedonistic reasoning were not expected to change much in adolescence (although the latter modes of reasoning do exhibit dramatic change in childhood).

Different MANOVAs had to be computed for groups of reasoning that emerged at different ages because of the linear dependencies in the data that occur if a particular mode of reasoning is not used at more than one time period (and because quadratic trends could occur if a type of reasoning was not used much in childhood and then emerged in adolescence). Only categories of reasoning used with some frequency during at least one time period were included in the analyses. Because types of reasoning that were used infrequently tended to be positively skewed, a logarithmic transformation was performed on the data (although the means presented in Table 1 and in the text are nontransformed means). Linear, quadratic, and cubic trends were examined when possible because from early childhood to adolescence some categories of reasoning were expected to show both increases and decreases in usage, sometimes with a period of relative stability in use (which could result in a cubic trend analysis, for example, when a period of little use of a type of reasoning was followed by an increase in use during midchildhood and then a decline in its use in adolescence). In the first analysis, the categories of reasoning were those that had been used with some frequency (by at least one sex) at six or more time periods (i.e., hedonistic, needs-oriented, pragmatic, direct reciprocity, approval-oriented, and stereotypic; see Eisenberg et al., 1987). Scores were computed from the four stories used at all seven follow-ups. The multivariate Fs

for the linear, quadratic, and cubic effects of time were highly significant, Fs$(7, 24)$ = 40.86, 9.60, and 4.58, ps < .001, .001, and .002, respectively. For hedonistic reasoning, the univariate Fs for the linear and quadratic trends were highly significant, Fs$(1, 30)$ = 116.72 and 53.58, ps < .001, respectively. Hedonistic reasoning decreased sharply with age until 11–12 years and then increased slightly in adolescence (see Table 1). Interestingly, perusal of the means indicated that the scores in hedonistic reasoning for girls changed little in adolescence (Ms = 4.56, 4.56, and 4.62 for T5, T6, and T7, respectively), whereas such reasoning clearly increased during adolescence for boys (Ms = 4.81, 4.94, and 5.28 for T5, T6, and T7, respectively). For needs-oriented reasoning, there was a highly significant quadratic trend and weaker (but highly significant) linear and cubic trends, Fs$(1, 30)$ = 47.04, 11.89, and 10.02, ps < .001, .002, and .004, respectively; needs-oriented reasoning increased with age until 7–8 years, was relatively stable from 7–8 to 11–12 years (with a small decrease at age 9–10 followed by a small increase at age 11–12, and declined somewhat through early to midadolescence; see Table 1). According to a highly significant linear trend and weaker quadratic and cubic trends, Fs$(1, 30)$ = 49.02, 4.13, and 20.93, ps < .001, .051, and .001, respectively, direct reciprocity reasoning was used with little frequency until age 9–10, increased in use until early adolescence (13–14 years), and then started to decline. Similarly, stereotypic and approval-oriented judgments exhibited strong linear trends, Fs$(1, 30)$ = 42.24 and 25.20, ps < .001, respectively, and weaker cubic trends, Fs$(1, 30)$ = 4.52 and 4.29, ps < .042 and .047, respectively; these types of reasoning were used infrequently until mid to late elementary school, increased in use until age 13–14, and then decreased slightly in use in midadolescence. Finally, pragmatic reasoning increased in a linear fashion with age, $F(1, 30)$ = 34.20, p < .001, whereas affectional relationship reasoning fluctuated in amount of use in elementary school (but was never used much) and then increased somewhat at T7, cubic $F(1, 30)$ = 8.73, p < .006.

A second 2 (sex) × 5 (time) trend analysis was computed for those higher level categories of reasoning used with any frequency at T3 or T4 (sympathetic, role taking, internalized positive affect about consequences, internalized negative affect about consequences, internalized positive affect about values, internalized negative affect about values, and internalized law, norm, or value orientation reasoning). The multivariate F for the linear effect of time was significant, $F(7, 24)$ = 5.28, p < .001. Role taking, positive affect/consequences, and internalized norm,

TABLE 1
Moral Reasoning Categories: Means for Cohort

Reasoning Category	1	2	3	4	5	6	7
Hedonistic	12.12	8.66	6.31	5.88	4.69	4.75	5.28
Direct reciprocity	4.00	4.09	4.09	4.31	5.38	5.91	4.88
Affectional relationship	4.03	4.38	4.00	4.25	4.19	4.09	4.53
Pragmatic	4.12	4.47	4.28	5.03	5.25	5.81	6.28
Needs-oriented	8.53	11.59	13.62	13.12	13.59	12.25	12.00
Stereotypic	4.50	4.31	4.68	5.12	5.62	6.72	6.47
Approval-interpersonal	4.00	4.06	4.22	4.44	4.88	5.34	4.97
Sympathetic	4.00	4.03	4.00	4.19	4.38	4.06	4.19
Role taking	4.00	4.00	4.06	4.59	4.62	5.12	5.81
Positive affect—simple or related to consequences	4.00	4.00	4.09	4.56	4.78	5.09	5.53
Negative affect—simple or related to consequences	4.00	4.00	4.00	4.16	4.28	4.22	4.44
Positive affect regarding self-respect	4.00	4.00	4.09	4.03	4.00	4.19	4.28
Negative affect regarding self-respect	4.00	4.00	4.00	4.06	4.00	4.09	4.06
Internalized law, norm, or value orientation	4.00	4.00	4.03	4.00	4.00	4.16	4.47
Generalized reciprocity	4.00	4.00	4.00	4.00	4.00	4.03	4.38
Condition of society	4.00	4.00	4.00	4.00	4.00	4.03	4.16
Individual rights	4.00	4.00	4.00	4.00	4.12	4.16	4.03
Equality of individuals	4.00	4.00	4.00	4.00	4.03	4.00	4.25

Note: Means are based on the nontransformed data.

rule, and law reasoning increased in usage with age, Fs$(1, 30) = 13.37, 31.77$, and 6.46, ps $< .001, .001$, and $.016$, respectively.

Although the multivariate Fs for sex and for Sex × Time (ps $< .12$ and $.92$, respectively) were not significant, it is important to look at the univariate Fs because of the gender differences in trends noted in some of these types of reasoning at T5. None of the Sex × Time interactions were significant, although across all time periods, girls used more role-taking and positive affect/values reasoning than did boys, Fs$(1, 30) = 4.41$ and 4.21, ps $< .044$ and $.049$, respectively.

In a third 2 (sex) × 3 (time) analysis, we examined age changes in the use of categories of reason-

ing that emerged only in adolescence (generalized reciprocity, concern with society, rights and justice, and equality of people reasoning). These categories of reasoning were used quite infrequently (see Table 1); nonetheless, the multivariate F for time was marginally significant, $F(7, 24) = 2.40$, $p < .075$, and there was a linear increase with age in generalized reciprocity reasoning, $F(1, 30) = 4.97$, $p < .033$.

In a summary analysis, we examined change in C1 students' moral reasoning composite scores from the follow-up preceding the two reported in this article, that is, T5 to T6 and T7. According to a 2 (sex) × 3 (time) trend analysis, there were main effects of both sex and the linear trend, $F(1, 30 = 12.00$ and 11.29, ps $< .002$, respectively. Girls scored higher than boys on the composite scores, and scores increased with age (*Ms* = 227, 241, and 254 for T5, T6, and T7, respectively).[1]

It is also of interest to examine intraindividual patterns of change. However, given that children frequently used a variety of types of moral reasoning (reflecting different levels of moral judgment) and higher levels of reasoning were weighted more heavily, a composite score at a given level did not necessarily indicate the predominance of a given mode of reasoning. For example, a score of 200 was obtained when subjects verbalized all needs-oriented reasoning or when they used half hedonistic reasoning and half stereotypic reasoning.

Nonetheless, we examined whether individuals' composite scores dropped considerably at any point in development (in comparison to any prior point). A drop of 50 points is roughly equivalent to a change of half a stage (because all hedonistic reasoning equals a score of 100, all needs-oriented reasoning equals a score of 200, etc). Nine children exhibited a drop of 50 points or more (3 dropped about 100 points) at one point in their development. Thus, although reasoning generally increased in sophistication with age, there were sizable declines in some children's reasoning at various points in their development.

According to additional analyses using the five (instead of four) moral reasoning stories at T6 and T7 (with the scores multiplied by .8 to adjust for the number of stories), the findings were generally the same or stronger. Moreover, the age trends in the children's reasoning did not seem to be the result of repeated testing. If they were, one would not expect the reasoning for C1 to be similar to that of children of the same age interviewed for the first time at T6 or T7 (C2 or C3). However, at T6, the only difference in reasoning between C1 and C2 was that C1 used more direct reciprocity reasoning, $t(65) = -2.32$, $p < .032$. At T7, the only differences were that C1 used more affectional relationship and role-taking reasoning, $t(64) = -2.25$ and -2.11, $ps < .028$ and .039, respectively, whereas C3 used more rights/justice reasoning, $t(64) = 2.28$, $p < .026$. Affectional relationship and rights/justice reasoning were used infrequently by both groups, and there were clear age trends for these types of reasoning. Thus, it seems unlikely that the repeated testing significantly affected the results of the analyses.[2]

Consistency of Indexes from T6 to T7

Most of the measures for C1 were fairly consistent from T6 to T7. The Bryant empathy scale from T6 (*M* = 33.28) was positively related to Davis' measures of sympathy (*M* = 27.39) and perspective taking at T7 (*M* = 23.74), but not to personal distress (*M* = 18.38), $rs(30) = .48$ and .45, $ps < .006$ and .01, respectively.[3] Social desirability, although measured with different scales at the two time periods (*Ms* = 60.63 and 34.35 at T6 and T7, respectively), was also consistent over time, $r(30) = .37$, $p < .037$, as were the children's (*Ms* = 62.28 and 71.75 at T6 and T7, respectively) and mothers' reports (*Ms* = 2.71 and 3.00 at T6 and T7, respectively) of prosocial behavior (on the modified Rushton et al., 1981, scale), $rs(30)$ and $(29) = .59$ and .51, $ps < .001$ and .003, respectively. Similarly, whether subjects helped was positively correlated from T6 to T7 (percentage of subjects helping at T6 and T7 were 46% and

---

[1] For the entire sample of longitudinal and cross-sectional subjects, there was not a significant sex difference in the moral reasoning composite scores at T6 (although girls were somewhat higher), whereas at T7 girls scored higher than boys on the composite scores composed of both four and five stories, $ps < .008$ and .006. For the entire sample at T7, girls scored higher than boys on stereotypic and positive affect/self-reasoning, $ps < .047$ and .024, respectively, whereas boys scored higher on hedonistic reasoning, $p < .03$ (*ps* are for five stories; those for four stories are similar).

[2] On the basis of a small replication sample of 10 children interviewed six times between 4–5 and 13–14 years of age (a younger sample than C1; four girls, six boys; *M* age = 139 months at T5 and 163 months at T6), hedonistic reasoning decreased with age, $F(1, 8) = 20.40$, $p < .024$, whereas needs-oriented and approval-oriented reasoning increased with age, $F(1, 8) = 8.11$ and 16.42, $ps < .022$ and .004, respectively. Stereotypic reasoning increased with age until 13–14 years and then dropped in use at age 15–16; linear and quadratic trends were $F(1, 8) = 12.76$ and 10.24, $p < .007$ and .013, respectively. Finally, according to Linear and Sex × Time quadratic trends for direct reciprocity reasoning, $F(1, 8) = 7.16$ and 10.24, $ps < .028$ and .015, respectively; direct reciprocity reasoning increased steadily with age for boys but increased for girls until age 13–14 (*M* = 5.00) and dropped off in use at age 15–16 (*M* = 4.00).

[3] Nineteen C1 subjects also returned the Davis perspective-taking, sympathy, and personal distress scales as part of the helping task at T6. For them, sympathy, perspective-taking, and personal distress were highly correlated from T6 to T7, $rs(17) = .72, .48$, and .63, $ps < .001, .039$, and .004, respectively.

53%, respectively), $r(30) = .41$, as was the composite index of helping, $r(30) = .37$, $p < .038$ (see next section); whether subjects completed all questions was nonsignificantly positively related ($r = .23$; 33% and 48% of subjects at T6 and T7, respectively, completed all parts). The only correlations that dropped substantially when sex was partialed out were those between the Bryant scale at T6 and the Sympathy and Perspective-Taking scales at T7; nonetheless, these correlations were still marginally significant, partial $rs(29) = .32$ and $.34$, $ps < .083$ and $.059$, for sympathy and perspective taking, respectively.

Interrelations of Prosocial Indexes

The two indexes of helping—whether subjects returned the questionnaires and whether all parts were completed (those who did not return anything were coded as not completing the questionnaires)—were highly intercorrelated at both T6 and T7 (using C1 and either C2 or C3), rs (69) and (64) = .58 and .91, $ps < .001$, respectively. Thus, the two indexes of helping were standardized and combined at both T6 and T7; these composite scores were then used in subsequent analyses.

At T6, the composite index of helping was significantly related to mothers' reports of children's prosocial behavior, $r(29) = .51$, $p < .003$, but not with children's reports on the modified Rushton self-report scale. Mothers' and children's reports of prosocial behavior were significantly, positively related, but only for boys, $r(13) = .53$, $p < .041$. At T7, the composite index of helping was not significantly correlated with either mothers' or children's reports of helpfulness; nor were mothers' and children's reports of prosocial behavior significantly related.

Relation of Sex to Prosocial Behavior, Empathy and Related Constructs, and Social Desirability

T tests were performed to determine whether there were sex differences in scores for the indexes of prosocial behavior, empathy, and social desirability at either T6 or T7. In these and all subsequent analyses, data from C2 and C3, as well as C1, were used when possible. At T6, girls scored higher than boys on the empathy scale and the composite index of helping, $ts(69) = 6.89$ and 2.17, $ps < .001$ and $.037$, respectively. At T7, girls also scored higher on the empathy-related scales, that is, on sympathy, perspective taking, and personal distress, $ts(64) = 5.11, 2.27$, and

2.52. $ps < .001, .027$, and $.014$, respectively, as well as on students' and mothers' reports of prosocial behavior, $t(64) = 2.56$ and $t(30) = 2.38$, $ps < .013$ and $.024$, respectively. This pattern of findings is, of course, consistent with sex role stereotypes.

Relation of Social Desirability to Moral Judgment, Moral Behavior, and Empathy

In these and subsequent analyses involving moral judgment, results for the composite scores based on all five stories are reported because composite scores based on more stories are generally assumed to be more reliable (Rushton, Brainerd, & Pressley, 1983) and the new story was considered to be more age-appropriate than some of the other four stories. However, the findings based on these composite scores generally were very similar to those based on data from the four stories.

At T6 and T7, the Social Desirability scale was not significantly related to the moral judgment composite scores. In addition, social desirability was not significantly correlated with any moral reasoning category used with some frequency at T6 (i.e., those categories in the first 2 MANOVAs conducted for C1 in *the Age Changes in Moral Judgment* section; only these categories of reasoning were used in any correlational analyses). At T7, the Social Desirability scale was negatively related to sympathy reasoning, $r(64) = -.29$, $p < .017$.

Children's social desirability was unrelated to helping at either T6 or T7, although their self-reported prosocial behavior was positively related to social desirability at T7, $r(64) = .37$, $p < .002$. In addition, social desirability was significantly, positively related to most of the various indexes of empathy-related reactions. At T6, the Empathy scale was positively correlated with social desirability, $r(69) = .29$, $p < .015$, although this relation was due solely to the correlation for boys, $r(33) = .42$, $p < .012$; $r(34) = -.01$ for girls. At T7, social desirability was positively related to the Sympathy and Perspective-Taking scales, $rs(64) = .38$ and $.51$, $ps < .002$ and $.001$, respectively, and these correlations were substantial for both sexes. Because of the aforementioned relations between social desirability or sex and some of our measures (particularly empathy-related indexes and the modified Rushton helping scale), partial correlations controlling for social desirability and sex were computed in addition to zero-order correlations in subsequent analyses. In addition, we note when the pattern of findings was markedly different for boys and girls.

Relation of Moral Reasoning to Prosocial Behavior

At T6, the helping composite index was not significantly related to the moral reasoning composite scores. However, consistent with findings in prior follow-ups, helping was negatively related to hedonistic reasoning, $r(67) = -.28$, $p < .023$; partial $r(63) = -.25$, $p < .048$, controlling for sex and social desirability. Children's self-reported prosocial behavior was unrelated to moral reasoning; mothers' reports of children's prosocial behavior were positively related to children's pragmatic moral reasoning, $r(29) = .45$, $p < .001$; partial $r(27) = .52$, $p < .004$.

At T7, the helping behavior was positively related to higher scores on the moral reasoning composite score, $r(64) = .30$, $p < .015$; partial $r(62) = .25$, $p < .049$. Mothers' and children's reports of the children's prosocial behavior were not significantly related to the moral judgment composite score, although children's reports of prosocial tendencies were negatively related to hedonistic reasoning, $r(64) = -.38$, $p < .002$; partial $r(62) = -.30$, $p < .017$, particularly for boys, $r(31) = -.45$, $p < .009$; $r(31) = -.11$ for girls).

Relations of Moral Reasoning to Empathy and Related Constructs

At T6, the Bryant empathy index was not significantly related to the moral judgment composite scores, although it was negatively related to hedonistic moral reasoning, $r(65) = -.43$, $p < .001$; partial $r(63) = -.41$, $p < .001$, controlling sex and social desirability. At T7 there were more relations between empathy-related indexes and moral judgment, although the relations were nearly always due to the boys' data. Scores for perspective taking were positively related to the composite judgment scores, $r(64) = .28$, $p < .022$; partial $r(62) = .27$. The correlation between perspective taking and the composite reasoning score was due primarily to the data for boys, $r(30) = .44$, $p < .01$. In addition, sympathy and perspective taking were negatively related to hedonistic reasoning, $rs(64) = -.40$ and $-.35$, $ps < .001$ and .004, respectively, whereas sympathy was positively related to needs-oriented reasoning, $r(64) = .32$, $p < .008$, and these correlations remained significant when sex and social desirability were partialed, partial $rs(62) = -.29, -.28$, and $.35$, $ps < .019, .027$, and .005, respectively. Again, however, these relations were due to the boys' data: $rs(31) = -.46, -.43$, and $.44$, $ps < .008, .012$, and .011, respectively, and partialing social desirability had virtually

no effect on these correlations ($rs = -.06, -.17$, and $.17$ for girls). Moreover, when sex and social desirability were partialed, scores on perspective taking tended to be positively correlated with sympathetic moral reasoning, partial $r(62) = .28$, $p < .027$; partial $r(30) = .49$, $p < .004$, for boys; $r = .08$ for girls. None of the relations for personal distress were significant when social desirability was partialed from the correlations.

Relation of Prosocial Behavior to Empathy and Related Constructs

At T6, helping was positively correlated with Bryant empathy scores, $r(71) = .33$, $p < .006$, although this correlation dropped somewhat when the effects of sex and social desirability were partialed, partial $r(67) = .22$, $p < .068$. Similarly, children's self-reported prosocial behavior was positively related to Bryant empathy scores, $r(69) = .27$, $p < .023$; partial $r(67) = .24$, $p < .043$. At T7, the empathy-related indexes were unrelated to helping behavior. However, children's reported prosocial behaviors (but not maternal reports) were positively related to both sympathy and perspective taking, $rs(64) = .52$ and $.57$, $ps < .001$, respectively; partial $rs(62) = .34$ and $.43$, $ps < .006$ and .001.

DISCUSSION

Several important findings were obtained in this study. First, we clarified the pattern of some modes of prosocial moral reasoning that previously were unclear. For example, we obtained the first longitudinal data indicating that approval and stereotypic prosocial moral reasoning start to decline in use in midadolescence. With this finding, we can reconcile the potentially discrepant findings that such reasoning increases in the elementary school years (Eisenberg et al., 1987) but that it has been found to decrease in use in a cross-sectional study of elementary and high school students (Eisenberg-Berg, 1979a). Moreover, the pattern obtained in this study for approval and stereotypic reasoning is consistent with that for Kohlbergian moral reasoning (Colby et al., 1983). However, given the relatively weak cubic trends obtained for approval and stereotypic reasoning (due to either periods of no change or minor fluctuations, followed by an increase and then a drop in usage), it is important to examine the further development of these modes of reasoning in late adolescence.

In addition, the developmental course of direct reciprocity reasoning has been clarified somewhat. Direct reciprocity reasoning, which is scored as a low level of prosocial moral judgment, increased significantly with age in elementary school and then decreased in use in adolescence. The initial increase with age in this mode of reasoning may be because it involves cognitive concepts of exchange and coordination between people and consequently is more sophisticated cognitively than merely a focus on what the self desires (e.g., hedonistic reasoning). Thus, direct reciprocity reasoning seems to be a relatively sophisticated mode of self-oriented reasoning, but one that decreases in use in mid-adolescence.

Moreover, in these follow-ups, we were able to observe the emergence of some of the higher level modes of reasoning (e.g., internalized norm, rule, and law reasoning and generalized reciprocity) during adolescence. An additional finding of interest was that although role taking and sympathetic reasoning emerged earlier for girls than for boys (i.e., at age 11–12; Eisenberg et al., 1987), the developmental curves for these modes of reasoning were very similar in adolescence. Girls did use somewhat higher levels of reasoning overall; however, there was little evidence of girls using more of the other-oriented modes of reasoning after age 11–12. Thus, it appears that girls used other-oriented, self-reflective modes of reasoning earlier than did boys, but boys caught up in their use of these modes of reasoning within 2 years.

The fact that girls exhibited a higher level of reasoning overall was probably due in part to the modest increase in boys' hedonistic reasoning in adolescence (which had decreased in use until adolescence), as well as to the tendency for girls to use somewhat more of some higher level modes of reasoning. Consistent with our data, Ford, Wentzel, Wood, Stevens, and Siesfeld (1989) found that high school boys made fewer socially responsible choices on a questionnaire index than did girls and their choices were more a function of self-interested emotions. As Ford et al. concluded, perhaps issues concerning responsibility for others are more problematic for adolescent boys than girls.

Another important finding is that we obtained some evidence of relations between moral reasoning and adolescents' prosocial behavior. At T6, helping was negatively related to hedonistic reasoning; at T7, helping was positively related to overall level of moral reasoning. Thus, as at younger ages, children's level of prosocial moral judgment seemed to be reflected in actual behavior (although the direction of causality is unclear). These relations are impres-

sive given that the index of helping was fairly weak (i.e., did not involve much cost to the helper).

Adolescents' moral reasoning also was related to their empathy (at T6) and sympathy and perspective taking (at T7), although the relations at T7 held primarily for boys. The reason for the sex difference in the patterns of relations at T7 is unclear; global empathy was positively related to level of moral reasoning for both sexes in a previous study conducted with adolescents (Eisenberg-Berg & Mussen, 1978). The lack of a relation for girls' sympathy at T7 could be due to the restricted range of their responses (mean for sympathy was 30.30 out of a range of 7–35; for boys, $M = 24.48$); recall that girls scored higher on both sympathy and perspective taking. However, a ceiling effect was not evident for perspective-taking scores (means for girls and boys were 25.15 and 22.33) and the standard deviations for boys' and girls' sympathy and perspective taking were not markedly different. Although social desirability was significantly, positively related to both boys' and girls' sympathy ($rs = .38$ and $.47$, $ps < .029$ and $.005$, respectively) and perspective taking ($rs = .41$ and $.60$, $ps < .017$ and $.001$, respectively), these relations were somewhat stronger for girls—a finding that suggests that the indexes of sympathy and perspective taking were slightly more valid for boys. Whatever the reason, the data for T6 and for boys at T7 are consistent with the view that other-oriented concerns and perspective-taking tendencies are intimately involved in moral reasoning (Eisenberg, 1986; Hoffman, 1987).

The findings in regard to the relations between empathy-related responses and prosocial behavior were mixed, albeit all findings were in the predicted direction. Empathy-related reactions were significantly, positively related to helping behavior only at T6. At T7, children's reports of sympathy and perspective taking were positively related to their reported helping behavior; however, the validity of the students' self-reported prosocial behavior is questionable because of the relation of these indexes to social desirability and the lack of their relation to actual helping behavior. Given the relations of indexes of empathy-related reactions with social desirability, it would be useful in the future to replicate the positive relations between adolescents' prosocial actions and empathy-related responses by means of non-self-report indexes. Moreover, given the relatively small number of subjects in this study, replication of these findings with larger samples would be useful.

In summary, in this study we obtained longitudinal data confirming, for the most part, the predicted pattern of development for prosocial moral reasoning in adolescence. In addition, prosocial moral reasoning, prosocial behavior, and empathy/sympathy and perspective taking were interrelated in theoretically meaningful ways, although sex differences in the relations of sympathy and perspective taking to moral reasoning merit further attention.

Questions

1.   In this study by Eisenberg et al., what types of moral reasoning increased in adolescence and what types declined?

2.   What role does the ability to think in a more complex manner play in the development of moral reasoning skills during adolescence?

3.   Although psychologists are interested in moral *reasoning* in adolescence, they are also concerned about moral *behavior.* How are moral reasoning and moral behavior related?

References

Bar-Tal, D. (1982). Sequential development of helping behavior: A cognitive-learning approach. *Developmental Review, 2,* 101–124.

Barnett, M. A. (1987). Empathy and related responses in children. In N. Eisenberg & J. Straver (Eds), *Empathy and its development* (pp. 146–162). Cambridge, England: Cambridge University Press.

Batson, C. D. (1987). Prosocial motivation: Is it ever truly altruistic? In L. Berkowitz (Ed.), *Advances in experimental social psychology* (Vol. 20, pp. 65–122). New York: Academic Press.

Batson, C. D. (1990). How social an animal? The human capacity for caring. *American Psychologist, 45,* 336–346.

Bryant, B. K. (1982). An index of empathy for children and adolescents. *Child Development, 53,* 413–425.

Colby, A.. Kohlberg. L., Gibbs, J., & Lieberman, M. (1983). A longitudinal study of moral judgment. *Monographs of the Society for Research in Child Development, 48(1–2,* Serial No. 200).

Crandall, V. C., Crandall. V. J., & Katkovsky, W. (1965). A child's social desirability questionnaire. *Journal of Consulting Psychology, 29,* 27–36.

Crowne, D. P.. & Marlowe, D. (1964). *The approval motive.* New York: Wiley.

Damon, W. (1977). *The social world of the child.* San Francisco: Jossey-Bass.

Eisenberg, N. (1986). *Altruistic emotion, cognition and behavior.* Hillsdale, NJ: Erlbaum.

Eisenberg, N. (1990). Prosocial development in early and mid adolescence. In R. Montemayor, G. R. Adams, & T. P. Gullotta (Eds.), *From childhood to adolescence: A transitional period? Advances in adolescence* (Vol. 2. pp. 240–269). Newbury Park, CA: Sage.

Eisenberg, N., & Fabes. R. A. (1991). Prosocial behavior and empathy: A multimethod, developmental perspective. In P. Clark (Ed.). *Review of personality and social psychology* (pp. 34–61). Newbury Park, CA: Sage.

Eisenberg, N., Lennon, R., & Roth, K. (1983). Prosocial development: A longitudinal study. *Developmental Psychology, 19,* 846–855.

Eisenberg, N., & Miller, P A. (1987). The relation of empathy to prosocial and related behavior. *Psychological Bulletin, 101,* 91–119.

Eisenberg, N., Shell, R., Pasternack, J., Lennon, R., Beller, R., & Mathy, R. M. (1987). Prosocial development in middle childhood: A longitudinal study. *Developmental Psychology, 23,* 712–718.

Eisenberg-Berg, N. (1979a). Development of children's prosocial moral judgment. *Developmental Psychology, 15,* 128–137.

Eisenberg-Berg, N. (1979b). The relationship of prosocial moral reasoning to altruism, political liberalism, and intelligence. *Developmental Psychology, 15,* 87–89.

Eisenberg-Berg, N., & Mussen, P. (1978). Empathy and moral development in adolescence. *Developmental Psychology, 14,* 185–186.

Eisenberg-Berg, N., & Roth, K. (1980). The development of children's prosocial moral judgment: A longitudinal follow-up. *Developmental Psychology, 16,* 375–376.

Ford, M. E., Wentzel, K. R., Wood, D., Stevens, E., & Siesfeld, G. A. (1989). Processes associated with integrative social competence: Emotional and contextual influences on adolescent social responsibility. *Journal of Adolescent Research, 4,* 405–425.

Gilligan, C., & Attanucci, J. (1988). Two moral orientations: Gender differences and similarities. *Merrill-Palmer Quarterly 34,* 223–238.

Hoffman, M. L. (1987). The contribution of empathy to justice and moral judgment. In N. Eisenberg & J. Strayer (Eds), *Empathy and its development* (pp. 47–80). Cambridge, England: Cambridge University Press.

Hume, D. (1966). *Enquiries concerning the human understanding and concerning the principles of morals* (2nd ed.). Oxford, England: Clarendon Press. (Original work published 1777).

Kant, I. (1964). *The doctrine of virtue*. New York: Harper & Row. (Original work published 1797).

Kohlberg, L. (1969). Stage and sequence: The cognitive-developmental approach to socialization. In D. A. Goslin (Ed), *Handbook of socialization theory and research* (pp. 325–480). Chicago: Rand McNally.

Kohlberg, L. (1981). *The philosophy of moral development: Moral stages and the idea of justice*. San Francisco: Harper & Row.

Rest, J. R. (1983). Morality. In P. Mussen (Ed.), *Handbook of child psychology. Vol. 3. Cognitive development* (pp. 556–629). New York: Wiley.

Rholes, W. S., & Bailey, S. (1983). The effects of level of moral reasoning in consistency between moral attitudes and related behaviors. *Social Cognition, 2*, 32–48.

Rushton, J. P., Brainerd, C. J., & Pressley, M. (1983). Behavioral development and construct validity: The principle of aggregation. *Psychological Bulletin, 94*, 18–38.

Rushton, J. P., Chrisjohn, R. D., & Fekken, G. C. (1981). The altruistic personality and the self-report altruism scale. *Personality and Individual Differences, 2*, 1–11.

Selman, R. L. (1980). *The growth of interpersonal understanding*. San Diego, CA: Academic Press.

Staub, E. (1978). *Positive social behavior and morality: Social and personal influences (Vol. 1)*. New York: Academic Press.

Underwood, B. & Moore, B. (1982). Perspective-taking and altruism. *Psychological Bulletin, 91*, 143–173.

Walker, L. (1984). Sex differences in the development of moral reasoning: A critical review. *Child Development, 55*, 677–691.

28

A Developmental Perspective on Antisocial Behavior

GERALD R. PATTERSON, BARBARA DEBARYSHE, AND ELIZABETH RAMSEY

Violence toward other people and willful destruction of property are disturbing crimes that shatter our trust in one another, regardless of the age of the perpetrators. However, when such acts are committed by youth, they strike an especially deep chord. What are the explanations for and origins of these behaviors? Developmental psychologists have examined these questions from many perspectives, including the role of peer relations, academic experience, and poverty. But by far the largest portion of research on this topic has focused on the role of family relations, especially parent-child interaction, as a determining factor in the development of conduct disorders. The research by Gerald R. Patterson and colleagues that is described in the following article offers a rich framework for understanding how parent-child interaction may influence the organization and development of delinquency.

A developmental model of antisocial behavior is outlined. Recent findings are reviewed that concern the etiology and course of antisocial behavior from early childhood through adolescence. Evidence is presented in support of the hypothesis that the route to chronic delinquency is marked by a reliable developmental sequence of experiences. As a first step, ineffective parenting practices are viewed as determinants for childhood conduct disorders. The general model also takes into account the contextual variables that influence the family interaction process. As a second step, the conduct-disordered behaviors lead to academic failure and peer rejection. These dual failures lead, in turn, to increased risk for depressed mood and involvement in a deviant peer group. This third step usually

Reprinted with permission from the authors and *American Psychologist*, 44, 1989, 329–335. Copyright 1989 by the American Psychological Association.

    We gratefully acknowledge the support of National Institute of Mental Health Grants 2 RO1 MH 37940 and 5 T32 MH 17126 in the preparation of this article.

occurs during later childhood and early adolescence. It is assumed that children following this developmental sequence are at high risk for engaging in chronic delinquent behavior. Finally, implications for prevention and intervention are discussed.

In 1986, more than 1.4 million juveniles were arrested for nonindex crimes (e.g., vandalism, drug abuse, or running away) and almost 900,000 for index crimes (e.g., larceny-theft, robbery, or forcible rape; Federal Bureau of Investigation, 1987). The United States spends more than $1 billion per year to maintain our juvenile justice system. The yearly cost of school vandalism alone is estimated to be one-half billion dollars (Feldman, Caplinger, & Wodarski, 1981). These statistics are based on official records and may represent only a fraction of the true offense rate. Data on self-reported delinquent acts indicate that police records account for as little as 2% of the actual juvenile law violations (Dunford & Elliott, 1982).

Of course, not all costs can be counted in dollars and cents. Antisocial children are likely to experience major adjustment problems in the areas of academic achievement and peer social relations (Kazdin, 1987; Walker, Shinn, O'Neill, & Ramsey, 1987; Wilson & Herrnstein, 1985). Follow-up studies of antisocial children show that as adults they ultimately contribute disproportionately to the incidence of alcoholism, accidents, chronic unemployment, divorce, physical and psychiatric illness, and the demand on welfare services (Caspi, Elder, & Bem, 1987; Farrington, 1983; Robins, 1966; Robins & Ratcliff, 1979).

Antisocial behavior appears to be a developmental trait that begins early in life and often continues into adolescence and adulthood. For many children, stable manifestations of antisocial behavior begin as early as the elementary school grades (see Farrington, Ohlin, & Wilson, 1986; Loeber, 1982; and Olweus, 1979, for reviews). As Olweus noted, stability coefficients for childhood aggression rival the figures derived for the stability of IQ. Findings that early behaviors such as temper tantrums and grade school troublesomeness significantly predict adolescent and adult offenses suggest the existence of a single underlying continuum. If early forms of antisocial behavior are indeed the forerunners of later antisocial acts, then the task for developmental psychologists is to determine which mechanisms explain the stability of antisocial behavior and which control changes over time.

From a policy standpoint, a serious social problem that is predictable and understandable is a viable target for prevention. The purpose of this article is to present an ontogenic perspective on the etiology and developmental course of antisocial behavior from early childhood through adolescence. Evidence is presented in support of the notion that the path to chronic delinquency unfolds in a series of predictable steps. This model is presented in detail by Patterson, Reid, and Dishion (in press). In this model, child behaviors at one stage lead to predictable reactions from the child's social environment in the following step. This leads to yet further reactions from the child and further changes in the reactions from the social environment. Each step in this action-reaction sequence puts the antisocial child more at risk for long-term social maladjustment and criminal behavior.

A DEVELOPMENTAL PROGRESSION FOR ANTISOCIAL BEHAVIOR

Basic Training in the Home

There is a long history of empirical studies that have identified family variables as consistent covariates for early forms of antisocial behavior and for later delinquency. Families of antisocial children are characterized by harsh and inconsistent discipline, little positive parental involvement with the child, and poor monitoring and supervision of the child's activities (Loeber & Dishion, 1983; McCord, McCord, & Howard, 1963).

Two general interpretations have been imposed on these findings. Control theory, widely accepted in sociology (Hirschi, 1969), views harsh discipline and lack of supervision as evidence for disrupted parent–child bonding. Poor bonding implies a failure to identify with parental and societal values regarding conformity and work. These omissions leave the child lacking in internal control. Several large-scale surveys provide correlational data consistent with this hypothesis. The correlations show that youths who have negative attitudes toward school, work, and authority tend to be more antisocial (Elliott, Huizinga, & Ageton, 1985; Hirschi, 1969). The magnitude of these correlations tends to be very small. Because the dependent and independent variables are often provided by the same agent, it is difficult to untangle the contribution of method variance to these relations.

In contrast, the social–interactional perspective takes the view that family members directly train the child to perform antisocial behaviors (Forehand, King, Peed, & Yoder, 1975; Patterson, 1982; Snyder, 1977; Wahler & Dumas, 1984). The parents tend to be noncontingent in their use of both positive reinforcers for prosocial and effective punishment for deviant behaviors. The effect of the inept parenting practices is to permit dozens of daily interactions with family members in which coercive child behaviors are reinforced. The coercive behaviors are directly reinforced by family members (Patterson, 1982; Snyder, 1977; Snyder & Patterson, 1986). While some of the reinforcement is positive (attend, laugh, or approve), the most important set of contingencies for coercive behavior consists of escape-conditioning contingencies. In the latter, the child uses aversive behaviors to terminate aversive intrusions by other family members. In these families, coercive behaviors are functional. They make it possible to survive in a highly aversive social system.

As the training continues, the child and other family members gradually escalate the intensity of their coercive behaviors, often leading to high-amplitude behaviors such as hitting and physical attacks. In this training, the child eventually learns to control other family members through coercive means. The training for deviant behaviors is paralleled by a lack of training for many prosocial skills. Observations in the homes of distressed families suggest that children's prosocial acts are often ignored or responded to inappropriately (Patterson, 1982; Patterson, Reid, & Dishion, in press; Snyder, 1977). It seems that some families produce children characterized by not one, but two problems. They have antisocial symptoms and they are socially unskilled.

A series of structural equation modeling studies by Patterson and his colleagues support the theory that disrupted parent practices are causally related to child antisocial behavior. They used multiple indicators to define parental discipline and monitoring practices, child coercive behavior in the home, and a cross-situational measure of the child antisocial trait. In four different samples, involving several hundred grade school boys, the parenting practices and family interaction constructs accounted for 30-40% of the variance in general antisocial behavior (Baldwin & Skinner, 1988; Patterson, 1986; Patterson, Dishion, & Bank, 1984; Patterson et al., in press). Forgatch (1988) used a quasi-experimental design based on data from families referred for treatment of antisocial boys. She showed that changes in parental discipline and monitoring were accompanied by significant reductions in child antisocial behavior. There were no changes in antisocial child behavior for those families who showed no changes in these parenting skills.

Social Rejection and School Failure

It is hypothesized that coercive child behaviors are likely to produce two sets of reactions from the social environment. One outcome is rejection by the social environment. One outcome is rejection by members of the normal peer group, and the other is academic failure.

It is consistently found that antisocial children show poor academic achievement (Hawkins & Lishner, 1987; Wilson & Herrnstein, 1985). One explanation for this is that the child's noncompliant and undercontrolled behavior directly impedes learning. Classroom observations of antisocial children show they spend less time on task than their nondeviant peers (Shinn, Ramsey, Walker, O'Neill, & Steiber, 1987; Walker et al., 1987). Earlier classroom observation studies showed that they were also deficient in academic survival skills (e.g., attending, remaining in seat, answering questions) necessary for effective learning (Cobb, 1972; Cobb & Hops, 1973; Hops & Cobb, 1974). Two studies showed a significant covariation between antisocial behavior and failure to complete homework assignments (Dishion, Loeber, Stouthamer-Loeber, & Patterson, 1983; Fehrmann, Keith, & Reimers, 1987).

The association between antisocial behavior and rejection by the normal peer group is well documented (Cantrell & Prinz, 1985; Dodge, Coie, & Brakke, 1982; Roff & Wirt, 1984). Experimental studies of group formation show that aggressive behavior leads to rejection, not the reverse (Coie & Kupersmidt, 1983; Dodge, 1983). Rejected children are also deficient in a number of social-cognitive skills, including peer group entry, perception of peer group norms, response to provocation, and interpretation of prosocial interactions (Asarnow & Calan, 1985; Dodge, 1986; Putallaz, 1983).

It is often suggested that academic failure and peer rejection are causes rather than consequences of antisocial behavior. However, a stronger case may be made that antisocial behavior contributes to these negative outcomes. For example, some investigators have predicted that successful academic remediation will lead to a reduction in antisocial behavior (e.g., Cohen & Filipczak, 1971). However, it has been repeatedly demonstrated that programs improving the academic skills of antisocial youths have not achieved reductions in other antisocial symptoms (Wilson & Herrnstein, 1985); similar findings have been obtained for social skills training (Kazdin, 1987).

Deviant Peer Group Membership

Antisocial behavior and peer group rejection are important preludes to deviant peer group membership (Dishion, Patterson, & Skinner, 1988; Snyder, Dishion, & Patterson, 1986). These analyses also suggest that lax parental supervision also accounts for unique variance to the prediction of deviant peer affiliation.

A large number of studies point to the peer group as the major training ground for delinquent acts and substance use (Elliott et al., 1985; Hirschi, 1969; Huba & Bentler, 1983; Kandel, 1973). Peers are thought to supply the adolescent with the attitudes, motivations, and rationalizations to support antisocial behavior as well as providing opportunities to engage in specific delinquent acts. There are, however, only a small number of studies designed to investigate the hypothesized training process. One study in an institutional setting showed that delinquent peers provided considerable positive reinforcement for deviant behavior and punishment for socially conforming acts (Buehler, Patterson, & Furniss, 1966).

It seems, then, that the disrupted family processes producing antisocial behavior may indirectly contribute to later involvement with a deviant peer group. This particular product may function as an additional determinant for future antisocial behavior. In effect, the deviant peer group variable may be thought of as a positive feedback variable that contributes significantly to maintenance in the process. Common adult outcomes for highly antisocial youths include school dropout, uneven employment histories, substance abuse, marital difficulties, multiple offenses, incarceration, and institutionalization (Caspi et al., 1987; Huesmann, Eron, Lefkowitz, & Walder, 1984; Robins & Ratcliff, 1979).

Figure 1 depicts the relation among the concepts discussed up to this point.

SOME IMPLICATIONS OF THE DEVELOPMENT PERSPECTIVE

Early Versus Late Starters

Boys starting their criminal career in late childhood or early adolescence are at the greatest risk of becoming chronic offenders (Farrington, 1983; Loeber, 1982). Studies of prison populations have shown that recidivists are generally first arrested by age 14 or 15, whereas one-time offenders are first arrested at a later age (Gendreau, Madden, & Leipciger, 1979). Farrington found that boys first arrested between 10 and 12 years of age average twice as many convictions as later starters (Farrington, Gallagher, Morley, St. Ledger, & West, 1986); this comparison holds into early adulthood.

One implication of the aforementioned developmental perspective is that early forms of age-prototypic antisocial behavior may be linked to the early onset of official juvenile offenses. Following this logic, the child who receives antisocial training from the family during the preschool and elementary school years is likely to be denied access to positive socialization forces in the peer group and school.

On the other hand, the late starter would be someone committing his or her first offense in middle to late adolescence. This individual lacks the early training for antisocial behaviors. This implies that he or she has not experienced the dual failure of rejection by normal peers and academic failure.

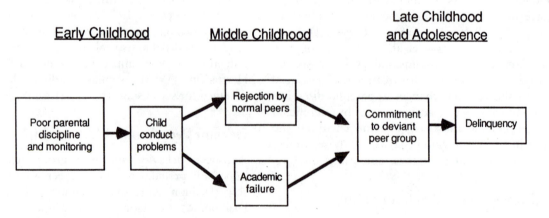

FIGURE 1   A developmental progression for antisocial behavior.

Only about half the antisocial children become adolescent delinquents, and roughly half to three quarters of the adolescent delinquents become adult offenders (Blumstein, Cohen, & Farrington, 1988; Farrington, 1987; Robins & Ratcliff, 1979). At some point in late adolescence, the incidence of delinquent acts as a function of age group begins to drop; the drop continues into the late 20s. One interpretation of these data is that many of the delinquent offenders drop out of the process. We assume that many of these dropouts are late starters, but more research is clearly needed to specify what factors determine the probability of an individual's dropping out of the antisocial training process. A proper developmental theory of antisocial behavior must delineate not only the variables that lead a child into the process but those that cause some of them to drop out of it.

CONTEXTUAL VARIABLES FOR FAMILY DISRUPTION

Because parent–child interaction is a central variable in the etiology of antisocial behavior, it is important to determine why a minority of parents engage in highly maladaptive family management practices. A number of variables, which shall be referred to as disruptors, have negative effects on parenting skill. These variables also correlate with the probability of children's antisocial behavior. Thus, the effect of disruptors on children's adjustment is indirect, being mediated through perturbations in parenting. Potential disruptors include a history of antisocial behavior in other family members, demographic variables representing disadvantaged socioeconomic status, and stressors—such as marital conflict and divorce—that hamper family functioning.

Antisocial Parents and Grandparents

There is a high degree of intergenerational similarity for antisocial behavior (Farrington, 1987; Robins & Ratcliff, 1979). As a predictor of adult antisocial personality, having an antisocial parent places the child at significant risk for antisocial behavior; having two antisocial parents puts the child at even higher risk (Robins & Earls, 1985). Concordance across three generations has also been documented (Elder, Caspi, & Downy, 1983; Huesmann et al., 1984; Robins, West, & Herjanic, 1975).

There is considerable evidence that parental discipline practices may be an important mediating mechanism in this transmission. Our set of findings shows that antisocial parents are at significant risk for ineffective discipline practices. Ineffective discipline is significantly related to risk of having an antisocial child. For example, Elder et al. (1983) found a significant relation between retrospective accounts of grandparental explosive discipline and paternal irritability. Irritable fathers tended to use explosive discipline practices with their own children who tended to exhibit antisocial behavior. Patterson and Dishion (1988) also found a significant correlation between retrospective reports of grandparental explosive reactions in the home and parental antisocial traits. Furthermore, the effect of the parents' antisocial trait on the grandchildren's antisocial behavior was mediated by parental discipline practices.

Family Demographics

Demographic variables such as race, neighborhood, parental education, income, and occupation are related to the incidence of antisocial behavior, particularly in its more severe forms (Elliott et al., 1985; Rutter & Giller, 1983; Wilson & Herrnstein, 1985). We presume that the effect of social class on child adjustment is mediated by family management practices.

The empirical findings linking social class to parenting practices are not consistent. But, in general, middle-class parents seem more likely to use reasoning and psychological methods of discipline, allow their children more freedom of choice and self-direction, show egalitarian parenting styles, express positive affect toward their children, verbalize, and support cognitive and academic growth (Gecas, 1979; Hess, 1970). Lower class parents are more likely to use physical discipline, be controlling of their child's behavior, exhibit authoritarian parenting styles, and engage in less frequent verbal and cognitive stimulation.

The findings from the at-risk sample at the Oregon Social Learning Center are in keeping with the trends in the literature (Patterson et al., in press). Uneducated parents working in unskilled occupations were found to be significantly less effective in discipline, monitoring, problem solving, positive reinforcement, and involvement.

Family Stressors

Stressors impinging on the family such as unemployment, family violence, marital discord, and divorce are associated with both delinquency (Farrington,

1987) and child adjustment problems in general (Garmezy & Rutter, 1983; Hetherington, Cox, & Cox, 1982; Rutter, 1979). Although stressors may well have direct and independent effects on child behavior, we assume that the major impact of stress on child adjustment is mediated by family management practices. If the stressors disrupt parenting practices, then the child is placed at risk for adjustment problems. For example, in the case of divorce, postseparation behavior problems occur with diminished parental responsiveness, affection, and involvement, and increased parental punitiveness and irritability (Hetherington et al., 1982; Wallerstein & Kelley, 1981). Structural equation modeling using data from a large sample of recently separated families provided strong support for the relation among stress, disrupted discipline, and antisocial behavior for boys (Forgatch, Patterson, & Skinner, in press).

We assume that antisocial parents and parents with marginal child-rearing skills are perhaps most susceptible to the disrupting effects of stressors and socioeconomic disadvantage. Elder, Caspi, and Nguyen (in press) described this interaction as an *amplifying effect*. External events are most disabling to those individuals who already exhibit negative personality traits or weak personal resources because stressors amplify such problems in adjustment. The interaction between the aforementioned disruptors and parental susceptibility is presented in Figure 2.

When antisocial parents or parents with minimal family management skills are faced with acute or prolonged stress, nontrivial disruptions in family management practices are likely to occur. It is these disruptions that are thought to place the child at risk for adjustment problems. A recent study by Snyder (1988) provided strong support for the mediational hypothesis. Roughly 20 hours of observation collected in the homes of three mother–child dyads showed significant covariation across days between stress and both disrupted maternal discipline and maternal irritability. Days characterized by high stress prior to the observation showed higher rates of disrupted behavior for the mother and increased child problem behaviors. A similar covariation was shown in the study by Wahler and Dumas (1984).

Is Prevention a Possibility?

Reviews of the literature summarizing efforts to intervene with antisocial adolescents invariably lead to negative conclusions (Kazdin, 1987; Wilson & Herrnstein, 1985). At best, such interventions produce short-term effects that are lost within a year or two of treatment termination. For example, efforts to apply behavior modification procedures in a halfway house setting (Achievement Place) showed no treatment effects after youths returned to their homes and communities (Jones, Weinrott, & Howard, 1981).

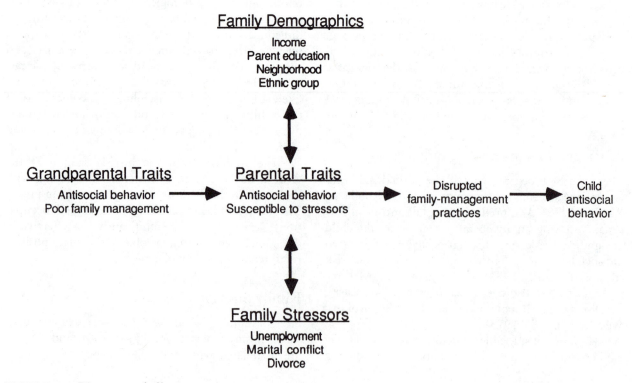

FIGURE 2   Disruptors of effective parenting.

Similarly, systematic parent training for families of delinquent adolescents produced reductions in offenses, but this effect did not persist over time (Marlowe, Reid, Patterson, Weinrott, & Bank, 1988).

Successful intervention appears to be possible for preadolescents, with parent-training interventions showing the most favorable outcomes (Kazdin, 1987). Parent training refers to procedures in which parents are given specific instructions in ways to improve family management practices (e.g., Forehand, Wells, & Griest, 1980; Patterson, Reid, Jones, & Conger, 1975). As shown in the review by Kazdin (1987), the parent-training programs have been evaluated in a number of random assignment evaluation studies including follow-up designs (six-month to four-year intervals). In general, the findings support the hypothesis that parent training is effective when applied to younger antisocial children. That several major studies failed to show a treatment effect led most investigators to conclude that parent training techniques *and* soft clinical skills are necessary for effective treatment. Current intervention studies have expanded their scope to include teaching academic and social-relational skills in addition to parent training. In order to alter both the problem child's lack of social skills and his or her antisocial symptoms, it seems necessary to design these more complex interventions.

We believe that prevention studies are now feasible. It seems reasonable to identify children in the elementary grades who are both antisocial and unskilled. Successful programs would probably include three components: parent training, child social-skills training, and academic remediation.

Questions

1. How does stress effect parents' ability to manage children's behavioral problems and how might this affect the development of antisocial behavior?

2. What factors, possibly passed across generations in a family, may affect the development of antisocial behavior in children?

3. How might socioeconomic or social status, together with family factors, be related to the incidence of antisocial behavior?

References

Asarnow, J. R., & Calan, J. R. (1985). Boys with peer adjustment problems: Social cognitive processes. *Journal of Consulting and Clinical Psychology, 53,* 80–87.

Baldwin, D. V., & Skinner, M. L. (1988). *A structural model for antisocial behavior: Generalization to single-mother families.* Manuscript submitted for publication.

Blumstein, A., Cohen, J., & Farrington, D. P. (1988). Criminal career research: Its value for criminology. *Criminology, 26,* 1–35.

Buehler, R. E., Patterson, G. R., & Furniss, J. M. (1966). The reinforcement of behavior in institutional settings. *Behavior Research and Therapy, 4,* 157–167.

Cantrell, V. L., & Prinz, R. J. (1985). Multiple predictors of rejected, neglected, and accepted children: Relation between sociometric status and behavioral characteristics. *Journal of Consulting and Clinical Psychology, 53,* 884–889.

Caspi, A., Elder, G. H., & Bem, D. J. (1987). Moving against the world: Life course patterns of explosive children. *Developmental Psychology, 23,* 308–313.

Cobb, J. A. (1972). The relationship of discrete classroom behavior to fourth grade academic achievement. *Journal of Educational Psychology, 63,* 74–80.

Cobb, J. A., & Hops, H. (1973). Effects of academic skill training on low achieving first graders. *Journal of Educational Research, 63,* 74–80.

Cohen, H. L., & Filipczak, J. (1971). *A new learning environment.* San Francisco: Jossey Bass.

Coie, J. D., & Kupersmidt, J. B. (1983). A behavioral analysis of emerging social status in boys' groups. *Child Development, 54,* 1400–1416.

Dishion, T. J., Loeber, R., Stouthamer-Loeber, M., & Patterson, G. R. (1983). Social skills deficits and male adolescent delinquency. *Journal of Abnormal Child Psychology, 12,* 37–54.

Dishion, T. J., Patterson, G. R., & Skinner, M. L. (1988). *Peer group selection processes from middle childhood to early adolescence.* Manuscript in preparation.

Dodge, K. A. (1983). Behavioral antecedents of peer social status. *Child Development, 54,* 1386–1399.

Dodge, K. A. (1986). A social information processing model of social competence in children. In M. Perlmutter (Ed.), *Minnesota symposium on child psychology* (Vol. 18, pp. 77–125). Hillsdale, NJ: Erlbaum.

Dodge, K. A., Coie, J. D., & Brakke, N. P. (1982). Behavior patterns of socially rejected and neglected preadolescents: The roles of social approach and aggression. *Journal of Abnormal Child Psychology, 10,* 389–410.

Dunford, F. W., & Elliott, D. S. (1982). *Identifying career offenders with self-reported data* (Grant No. MH27552). Washington, DC: National Institute of Mental Health.

Elder, G. H., Jr., Caspi, A., & Downey, G. (1983). Problem behavior in family relationships: A multigenerational analysis. In A. Sorensen, F. Weinert, & L. Sherrod (Eds.), *Human development: Interdisciplinary perspective* (pp. 93–118). Hillsdale, NJ: Erlbaum.

Elder, G. H., Jr., Caspi, A., & Nguyen, T. V. (in press). Resourceful and vulnerable children: Family influences in stressful times. In R. K. Silbereisen & K. Eyferth (Eds.), *Development in context: Integrative perspectives on youth development.* New York: Springer.

Elliott, D. S., Huizinga, D., & Ageton, S. S. (1985). *Explaining delinquency and drug use.* Beverly Hills, CA: Sage.

Farrington, D. P. (1983). Offending from 10 to 25 years of age. In K. T. Van Dusen & S. A. Mednick (Eds.), *Prospective studies of crime and delinquency* (pp. 17–37). Boston: Kluwer-Nijhoff.

Farrington, D. P. (1987). Early precursors of frequent offending. In J. Q. Wilson & G. C. Loury (Eds.), *From children to citizens: Vol. III. Families, schools, and delinquency prevention* (pp. 27–51). New York: Springer-Verlag.

Farrington, D. P., Gallagher, B., Morley, L., St. Ledger, R. J., & West, D. J. (1986). *Cambridge study in delinquent development: Long term follow-up.* Unpublished annual report, Cambridge University Institute of Criminology, Cambridge, England.

Farrington, D. P., Ohlin, L. E., & Wilson, J. Q. (1986). *Understanding and controlling crime: Toward a new research strategy.* New York: Springer-Verlag.

Federal Bureau of Investigation. (1987). *Crime in the United States: Uniform crime reports, 1986,* Washington, DC: Government Printing Office.

Fehrmann, P. G., Keith, T. Z., & Reimers, T. M. (1987). Home influences on school learning: Direct and indirect effects of parental involvement in high school grades. *Journal of Educational Research, 80,* 330–337.

Feldman, R. A., Caplinger, T. E., & Wodarski, S. S. (1981). *The St. Louis conundrum: Presocial and antisocial boys together.* Unpublished manuscript.

Forehand, R., King, H. E., Peed, S., & Yoder, P. (1975). Mother-child interactions: Comparison of a non-compliant clinic group and a nonclinic group. *Behaviour Research and Therapy, 13,* 79–85.

Forehand, R., Wells, K., & Griest, D. (1980). An examination of the social validity of a parent training program. *Behavior Therapy, 11,* 488–502.

Forgatch, M. S. (1988, June). *The relation between child behaviors, client resistance, and parenting practices.* Paper presented at the Earlscourt Symposium on Childhood Aggression, Toronto.

Forgatch, M. S., Patterson, G. R., & Skinner, M. (in press). A mediational model for the effect of divorce on antisocial behavior in boys. In E. M. Hetherington (Ed.), *The impact of divorce and step-parenting on children.* Hillsdale, NJ: Erlbaum.

Garmezy, N., & Rutter, M. (Eds,). (1983). *Stress, coping, and development in children.* New York: McGraw Hill.

Gecas, V. (1979). The influence of social class on socialization. In W. R. Burr, R. Hill, F. I. Nye, & I. L. Reiss (Eds.), *Contemporary theories about the family* (Vol. 1, pp. 365–404). New York: Free Press.

Gendreau, P., Madden, P., & Leipeiger, M. (1979). Norms and recidivism rates for social history and institutional experience for first incarcerates: Implications for programming. *Canadian Journal of Criminology, 21,* 1–26.

Hawkins, J. D., & Lishner, D. M. (1987). Schooling and delinquency. In E. H. Johnson (Ed.), *Handbook on crime and delinquency prevention* (pp. 179–221). New York: Greenwood Press.

Hetherington, E. M., Cox, M., & Cox, R. (1982). Effects of divorce on parents and children. In M. Lamb (Ed.), *Nontraditional families* (pp. 233–288). Hillsdale, NJ: Erlbaum.

Hess, R. D. (1970). Social class and ethnic influences on socialization. In P. H. Mussen (Ed.), *Charmichael's manual of child psychology* (Vol. 2, pp. 457–558). New York: Wiley.

Hirschi, T. (1969) *Causes of delinquency.* Berkeley, CA: University of California Press.

Hops, H., & Cobb, J. A. (1974). Initial investigations into academic survival-skill training, direct instruction, and first-grade achievement. *Journal of Educational Psychology, 66,* 548–553.

Huba, G. J., & Bentler, P. M. (1983). Causal models of the development of law abidance and its relationship to psychosocial factors and drug use. In W. S. Laufer & J. M. Day (Eds.), *Personality theory, moral development and criminal behavior* (pp. 165–215). Lexington, MA: Lexington Books.

Huesmann, L. R., Eron, L. D., Lefkowitz, M. M., & Walder, L. O. (1984). Stability of aggression over time and generations. *Developmental Psychology, 20,* 1120–1134.

Jones, R. R., Weinrott, M. R., & Howard, J. R. (1981). *The national evaluation of the Teaching Family Model.* Unpublished manuscript, Evaluation Research Group, Eugene, OR.

Kandel, D. B. (1973). Adolescent marijuana use: Role of parents and peers. *Science, 181,* 1067–1081.

Kazdin, A. E. (1987). Treatment of antisocial behavior in children: Current status and future directions. *Psychological Bulletin, 102,* 187–203.

Loeber, R. (1982). The stability of antisocial and delinquent child behavior: A review. *Child Development, 53,* 1431–1446.

Loeber, R., & Dishion, T. J. (1983). Early predictors of male delinquency: A review. *Psychological Bulletin, 94,* 68–99.

Marlowe, H. J., Reid, J. B., Patterson, G. R., Weinrott, M. R., & Bank, L. (1988). Treating adolescent multiple offenders: A comparison and follow up of parent training for families of chronic delinquents. Manuscript submitted for publication.

McCord, W., McCord, J., & Howard, A. (1963). Familial correlates of aggression in nondelinquent male children. *Journal of Abnormal and Social Psychology, 62,* 79–93.

Olweus, D. (1979). Stability of aggressive reaction patterns in males: A review. *Psychological Bulletin, 86,* 852–875.

Patterson, G. R. (1982). *A social learning approach: 3. Coercive family process.* Eugene, OR: Castalia.

Patterson, G. R. (1986). Performance models for antisocial boys. *American Psychologist, 41,* 432–444.

Patterson, G. R., & Dishion, T. J. (1988). Multilevel family process models: Traits, interactions, and relationships. In R. Hinde & J. Stevenson-Hinde (Eds.), *Relationships within families: Mutual influences* (pp. 283–310). Oxford: Clarendon Press.

Patterson, G. R., Dishion, T. J., & Bank, L. (1984). Family interaction: A process model of deviancy training. *Aggressive Behavior, 10,* 253–267.

Patterson, G. R., Reid, J. B., & Dishion, T. J. (in press). *Antisocial boys.* Eugene, OR: Castalia.

Patterson, G. R., Reid, J. B., Jones, R. R., & Conger, R. E. (1975). *A social learning approach to family intervention: Vol 1. Families with aggressive children.* Eugene, OR: Castalia.

Putallaz, M. (1983). Predicting children's sociometric status from their behavior. *Child Development, 54,* 1417–1426.

Robins, L. N. (1966). *Deviant children grown up: A sociological and psychiatric study of sociopathic personality.* Baltimore: Williams & Wilkins.

Robins, L. N., & Earls F. (1985). A program for preventing antisocial behavior for high-risk infants and preschoolers: A research prospectus. In R. L. Hough, P. A. Gongla, V. B. Brown, & S. E. Goldston (Eds.), *Psychiatric epidemiology and prevention: The possibilities* (pp. 73–84). Los Angeles: Neuropsychiatric Institute.

Robins, L. N., & Ratcliff, K. S. (1979). Risk factors in the continuation of childhood antisocial behavior into adulthood. *International Journal of Mental Health, 7*(3–4), 96–116.

Robins, L. N., West, P. A., & Herjanic, B. L. (1975). Arrests and delinquency in two generations: A study of black urban families and their children. *Journal of Child Psychology and Psychiatry, 16,* 125–140.

Roff, J. D., & Wirt, R. D. (1984). Childhood aggression and social adjustment as antecedents of delinquency. *Journal of Abnormal Child Psychology, 12,* 111–116.

Rutter, M. (1979). Protective factors in children's responses to stress and disadvantage. In M. W. Kent & J. E. Rolfe (Eds.), *Primary prevention of psychopathology: 3. Social competence in children.* Hanover, NH: University Press of New England.

Rutter, M., & Giller, H. (1983). *Juvenile delinquency: Trends and perspectives.* New York: Penguin Books.

Shinn, M. R., Ramsey, E., Walker, H. M., O'Neill, R. E., & Steiber, S. (1987). Antisocial behavior in school settings: Initial differences in an at-risk and normal population. *Journal of Special Education, 21,* 69–84.

Snyder, J. J. (1977). Reinforcement analysis of interaction in problem and nonproblem families. *Journal of Abnormal Psychology, 86,* 528–535.

Snyder, J. J. (1988). *An intradyad analysis of the effects of daily variations in maternal stress on maternal discipline and irritability: Its effects on child deviant behaviors.* Manuscript in preparation.

Snyder, J. J., Dishion, T. J., & Patterson, G. R. (1986). Determinants and consequences of associating with deviant peers during preadolescence and adolescence. *Journal of Early Adolescence, 6*(1), 20–43.

Snyder, J. J., & Patterson, G. R. (1986). The effects of consequences on patterns of social interaction: A quasi-experimental approach to reinforcement in natural interaction. *Child Development, 57,* 1257–1268.

Wahler, R. G., & Dumas, J. E. (1984). Family factors in childhood psychopathology: Toward a coercion neglect model. In T. Jacob (Ed.), *Family interaction and psychopathology.* New York: Plenum Press.

Walker, H. M., Shinn, M. R., O'Neill, R. E., & Ramsey, E. (1987). Longitudinal assessment and long-term follow-up of antisocial behavior in fourth-grade boys: Rationale, methodology, measures, and results. *Remedial and Special Education, 8,* 7–16.

Wallerstein, J. S., & Kelley, J. B. (1981). *Surviving the breakup: How children and parents cope with divorce.* New York: Basic Books.

Wilson, J. Q., & Herrnstein, R. J. (1985). *Crime and human nature.* New York: Simon & Schuster.

29

Adolescent Sexual Behavior

JEANNE BROOKS-GUNN AND FRANK F. FURSTENBERG, JR.

Few developmental topics receive more attention in the popular press than teenage sexuality. Although biological changes initiate development of sexual interest, social and cognitive factors are also associated with adolescent sexual activity. In the following article, Jeanne Brooks-Gunn and Frank F. Furstenberg, Jr. review historical patterns in this area of development and discuss social and cognitive changes that directly influence adolescent sexual behavior. Certainly, no discussion of adolescent sexuality is complete without some attention to applied concerns such as contraceptive use and sexually transmitted diseases. How these issues are addressed, both publicly and privately, is critical for securing and maintaining not only adolescents' health, but babies' health as well, in the world today.

What is known about adolescent sexual behavior is reviewed. First, the onset of sexual behavior in the teenage years is considered as a function of cohort, gender, and ethnic differences. Omissions in the research on sexual behavior other than intercourse are highlighted. Possible biological, social, and social cognitive processes underlying teenage sexual behavior are then considered. Next, demographic trends in the use of contraceptives and antecedents of regular birth control use are reviewed. Finally, some of the successful program initiatives directed toward altering sexual and contraceptive practice are discussed, keeping in mind the importance and relative lack of well-designed and carefully evaluated programs.

The tension between sexuality as pleasure and sexuality as reproduction is probably a universal human

Reprinted with permission from the authors and *American Psychologist*, 44, 1989, 249–257. Copyright 1989 by the American Psychological Association.

   The current support of the Robert Wood Johnson Foundation, the Ford Foundation, and the Office of Adolescent Pregnancy Programs (Department of Health and Human Services) is greatly appreciated. The Russell Sage Foundation, where we are visiting scholars, also is thanked for their assistance. Roberta Paikoff, Laurie Zabin, Lindsay Chase-Lansdale, and Brent Miller deserve special thanks for their critical reading of this article. We are grateful for help in manuscript preparation from R. Deibler and F. Kelly.

condition. All societies attempt to manage sexuality in order to regulate fertility. This task is both necessary and difficult because sexual desire guarantees species perpetuation. Typically, efforts to control fertility and arousal emerge during puberty, as the child is transformed into a reproductively mature adult. Chaperonage, seclusion, bride-price, and residence with the bridegroom's family prepubertally are mechanisms in traditional societies for managing fertility prior to marriage. These practices have been linked to the economic value of the female reproductive potential in societies where high birth rates were necessary given agricultural work and childhood mortality (Paige, 1983). Today's concern over teenage sexuality also is often couched in political and economic terms, as evidenced by discussions of the societal and individual cost of teenage parenthood (the proportion of Aid to Families with Dependent Children payments going to families of young childbearers and the reduced prospects of employment and education for teenage mothers). As sexuality, marriage, and childbearing have become less closely linked during the last quarter century, societal strategies for regulating sexuality have been revised accordingly, which is the focus of this article. First, we take a brief historical tour of teenage sexual behavior as studied by social scientists, in order to highlight the sometimes glaring research omissions. Then we turn to what is known about fertility management, keeping in mind that other aspects of sexual behavior have been woefully understudied. The onset of sexual behavior is considered in light of historical, gender, and ethnic changes that have occurred in the last 20 years. Possible biological, social, and social cognitive processes underlying teenage sexual behavior are examined in an effort to go beyond a mere listing of known antecedents. This is followed by a look at patterns of contraceptive use and their antecedents, since fertility may be controlled by delaying the onset of intercourse or by practicing birth control. Finally, within the small universe of well-designed and carefully evaluated programs, successful initiatives directed toward altering sexual or contraceptive practices are examined.

SOCIAL SCIENCE AND THE STUDY OF TEENAGE SEXUAL BEHAVIOR

Perhaps the best known and most influential work on sexual behavior was conducted by Kinsey and his colleagues in the 1940s and 1950s (Kinsey, Pomeroy, & Martin, 1948; Kinsey, Pomeroy, Martin, & Gebhard, 1953). Documenting increases in premarital intercourse since World War I led to speculation on the role of sex in mate selection. In the 1950s and 1960s, as Gagnon (1987) suggested, most studies were quite delicate in their handling of such topics, focusing on attitudes and, when behavior was the emphasis, on the age of first intercourse. A few exemplary studies (Gagnon & Simon, 1973; Jessor & Jessor, 1975, 1977; Reiss, 1960) in the late 1960s embedded sexuality in the adolescent experience, collecting data on other adolescent behavior.

However, subsequent research did not provide broader perspectives for the study of sexuality; nor did it provide theoretical models to explain sexual desires and behavior. One source of this limited vision can be traced to the rising concern about teenage fertility in the late 1960s and early 1970s. Given the increase in out-of-wedlock births and the decrease in age of intercourse, research focused almost solely on fertility control (sexual onset and contraceptive use). What sexuality means to adolescents, how it relates to other aspects of teenage life, and what strategies teens use to manage or incorporate it into their lives have not been studied in any detail. Particular specific research omissions (in both the adolescent and adult literature) include the following: (a) frequency of behaviors other than intercourse and variations in type and frequencies of sexual behavior by gender, ethnicity, age, social class, and sex of partner; (b) pubertal education aimed at boys on topics such as ejaculation and condom use (many young men today still learn about ejaculation from magazines, locker room jokes, or their first nocturnal emission; Gaddis & Brooks-Gunn, 1985); (c) same-sex preferences and behavior; (d) the relation of sexual behavior to other adolescent behavior and life events (as an exception, see Jessor & Jessor, 1977); (e) the meaning of eroticism in adolescents' sex lives; (f) the influence of social contexts (school and community environments) on the regulation and expression of social behaviors; (g) differences between younger and older adolescents in all of the above; and (h) comparisons of fertility regulation and onset of sexual activity in other cultures.

TRANSITION TO SEXUAL BEHAVIOR

Historical Trends

Perhaps reflective of our society's ambivalence about teenage sexuality, national survey data on age of intercourse were not collected until 1971. Earlier estimates were based on selective samples, such as that of Kinsey. Dramatic increases in the number of teenage girls having intercourse have taken place in the last 50 years. In 1938 to 1950, approximately 7% of White females had intercourse by age 16 (Kinsey et al., 1948). By 1971, one third of never-married White girls 16 years of age had had intercourse, with the figure rising to 44% by 1982 (Hofferth & Hayes, 1987; Zelnik & Kantner, 1980). Trends have been carefully documented in the 1970s and 1980s. The proportion of all never-married girls ages 15 to 19 who have had intercourse is illustrated in Figure 1 by race and by time (1971 to 1982). Large increases occurred between 1971 and 1979, after which time the percentage of sexually active girls remained stable or perhaps even declined. Black girls had significantly higher rates of intercourse than White girls at all time points, although the difference had dropped to only 13% by 1982.

Historically, boys were much more likely to make their sexual debut as teenagers than girls. Estimates of selected samples from the 1940s to 1960s are that one third to two thirds of male teenagers were sexually active (Hofferth & Hayes, 1987). Data comparable to that just reported for teenage girls in the 1970s and 1980s do not exist for boys, perhaps reflective of the fact that fertility regulation is considered a female, not a male, issue. The rises in teenage sexual behavior are probably not as pronounced for boys as for girls, since many more of the former engaged in intercourse in previous decades. What has happened is that the gap between male and female teenagers narrowed as more and more girls became sexually active. Cumulative percentages using the National Longitudinal Survey of Youth by age of initiation, sex, and race in 1983 tell the story (Hofferth & Hayes, 1987). Sixty percent of

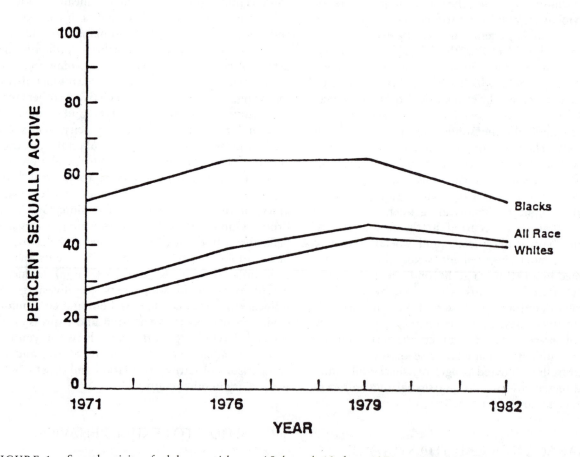

FIGURE 1   Sexual activity of adolescent girls ages 15 through 19, from 1971 to 1982. Note: Data are from "Sexual Activity, Contraceptive Use and Pregnancy Among Metropolitan Area Teenagers: 1971–1979" by M. Zelnick and J. F. Kantner, 1980. *Family Planning Perspectives, 12(5)*, pp. 230–237, Copyright 1980 by Alan Guttmacher Institute, NY; "The Use of Family Planning Services by Sexually Active Teenagers" by W.F. Pratt and G.E. Hendershot, 1984, *Population Index, 50(3)*, pp. 412–413. Copyright 1984 by Office of Population Research, Princeton University, Princeton, NJ; and *Risking the Future: Adolescent Sexuality, Pregnancy, and Childbearing* (Vol. 1, p. 41), edited by C.D. Hayes, 1987, Washington, DC: National Academy Press. Reprinted by permission.

White male teens had intercourse by age 18, and 60% of White girls just a year later, by age 19. Greater gender disparities are evident for Black teenagers: 60% of Black male teens had intercourse by age 16, and 60% of Black girls two years later, by age 18. Racial differences for boys are greatest at early adolescence. Indeed, in 1983, 42% of Black boys had had intercourse by age 15 or earlier; in some male subgroups, prepubertal initiation is common.

We have much less information on aspects of sexual behavior other than intercourse: Information on percentages of teenage girls who have had intercourse only once, frequency of intercourse, number of partners, and relationship with first partner is sparse. The little available information on the patterns of sexual activity suggests that many youth have intercourse only very occasionally when they initiate coitus. It is not uncommon for a teen to have first intercourse at age 14 or 15 and then not to have sexual relations again for a year or two. Age at intercourse may be a relatively poor proxy for risk of pregnancy under these circumstances.

Antecedents of Sexual Behavior

Most teens do not consciously plan to become sexually active, and they often do not foresee their first sexual experience. As such, it frequently is not experienced as a decision but rather as something that "happened" (Chilman, 1983). Studies on the antecedents of sexual activity in adolescence show that some but not all of the factors associated differ for Blacks and Whites and for boys and girls (see Hofferth & Hayes, 1987).

BIOLOGICAL PERSPECTIVES Of the biological changes associated with puberty, hormonal factors are thought to account in some part for the onset of sexual activity, either by effects occurring prenatally or activation effects that change hormonal levels at puberty. Hormonal activation may influence behavior directly by increasing arousal or indirectly by the social stimulus associated with physical changes. The fact that levels of testosterone are associated with sexual activities in boys, independent of secondary sexual development, is evidence for a direct effect (Udry, Billy, Morris, Groff, & Raj, 1985). In girls, sexual interests, but not behavior, are associated with testosterone levels, suggesting that social factors may play a greater role in their coital behavior (Udry, Talbert, & Morris, 1986). However, whether engagement in sexual intercourse increases androgen level or vice versa is not known.

In addition, contextual effects, if entered into the equation, might account for more of the variation in sexual activity than hormonal levels. Initiation of sexual behavior is highly associated with what is perceived as normative in one's peer group (Furstenberg, Moore, & Peterson, 1986), so it is likely that while very early sexual initiations may be in part hormonally mediated, by the time that behavior is normative, social factors may account for sexual initiation (see Gargiulo, Attie, Brooks-Gunn, & Warren, 1987, for a similar argument about dating behavior). Thus, even when hormonal effects are demonstrated, they must be evaluated relative to social factors before assuming direct or large hormonal-sexual behavior associations (Brooks-Gunn & Warren, 1989). Race differences in the initiation of intercourse prior to puberty also speak to the importance of social and contextual factors on sexual behavior.

The developing body acts as a stimulus for behavior change regardless of hormonal status. (No one-to-one correspondence exists between hormonal levels and secondary sexual characteristics.) For example, more physically mature girls seem to elicit more freedom from parents, perhaps making it more likely that they engage in dating and ultimately early sexual behavior. At the same time, pubertal children expect to be granted more autonomy in terms of friends and curfews than prepubertal children. Early-maturing girls are more likely to have older friends, which is associated with intercourse, smoking, and drinking (Brooks-Gunn, 1988; Magnusson, Strattin, & Allen, 1985). Such facts may in part explain associations between early maturation and intercourse beyond the potential influence of hormonal factors.

PARENTAL INFLUENCES Parental influences on sexual behavior are believed to be strong, although research is surprisingly sparse (Ooms, 1981). Teens who rate perceived communication with their parents as poor are more likely to initiate sex early; they also are likely to begin smoking and drinking early (Jessor & Jessor, 1977). Close relationships with parents as well as feelings of connectedness and supportiveness seem to be associated with later onset of intercourse (Inazu & Fox, 1980; Jessor & Jessor, 1977). However, as Hofferth and Hayes (1987) suggest, familial communication prior to first intercourse is usually not measured; nor are different aspects of communication, the age at which discussions occur, or the context in which it is embedded. Parents are often uncomfortable discussing sexual topics associated with reproduction with their post-pubertal children, as are their children (the exception being mothers and daughters about menarche; Brooks-Gunn & Ruble, 1982). The cultural acceptance of sexuality in boys but not girls also may influence the nature of communication; for example, in one study, mother–daughter communication was associated with later intercourse, as was mother–son communication. However, sons' discussions with the father and earlier sexual activity were linked (Kahn, Smith, & Roberts, 1984). Fathers may condone sexual activity in their sons, given the sexual script of male potency. Parental supervision also is associated with later onset of intercourse. These associations are in part mediated by neighborhood influences as well as residence in single-parent households (Hogan & Kitagawa, 1985; Newcomer & Udry, 1987).

More process-oriented research directed at how parents may influence their teens' sexual behavior is sorely needed. Several approaches may be profitable. Certain styles of family interactions enhance social cognitive abilities, such as role taking, decision making, and moral judgments (Cooper, Grotevant, & Condon, 1983). Ego development and autonomy also are associated with interaction styles characterized as enabling, authoritative, and legitimating (Brooks-Gunn & Zahaykevich, in press; Grotevant & Cooper, 1986; Hauser et al., 1984). More autonomous adolescents who are able to consider situations from several perspectives and make well-informed decisions may be more likely to delay the onset of sexual behavior or to use contraceptives more effectively. At the same time, the parental styles just mentioned may promote greater feelings of self-efficacy, which in turn could influence sexual behavior (Bandura, 1982; Strecher, McEvoy, Becker, & Rosenstock, 1986). Such premises await further testing.

PEER INFLUENCES As pointed out by Hofferth and Hayes (1987), beliefs about the importance of peers in the initiation of sexual behavior are much stronger than the actual research evidence. Perceptions about what one's peers are doing or what is normative in one's peer group are more strongly associated with sexual behavior than actual behavior, which is not frequently measured (Cvetkovich & Grote, 1980). Friendship choices may be predicated in part by sexual activity, at least for some subgroups. In addition, age may also mediate peer effects; it is thought that younger adolescents are more susceptible to peer pressure, although little research exists on this point.

Not surprisingly, early dating and early intercourse are associated. Of more interest are differences in sexual norms associated with precoital sexual activity, often seen in the context of dating. For example, White teenagers are more likely to engage in a predictable series of behaviors prior to first intercourse than are Black teenagers. Black girls, who are more likely to move from necking to intercourse without intermediate steps, may be less likely to be prepared for intercourse, in the sense that there is little time to think about and obtain contraceptives (Smith & Udry, 1985).

ACADEMIC PERSPECTIVES Teenagers who are not doing well in school and have lower educational aspirations are more likely to have sex during adolescence than those faring better in school (Hofferth & Hayes, 1987). School functioning itself is mediated by education, job, and welfare status of the mother (Furstenberg, Brooks-Gunn, & Morgan, 1987). It is no surprise, then, that children in poverty are clearly at risk for school failure and early sexuality.

It is important to place the association between academic failure and early sexuality into the context of the school experience, especially for young adolescents. Entrance into middle school is considered one of the most difficult educational transitions and often results in drops in academic performance (Hamburg, 1986). Providing support for the transition to middle school, especially for vulnerable children, seems essential, both to avoid increases in school failure experiences and to promote health behaviors.

SOCIAL COGNITIVE PERSPECTIVES Social cognitive abilities often associated with sexual decision making provide yet another and largely unexplored perspective for understanding sexual transitions among adolescents. We know that the abilities to integrate domain-specific knowledge into a coherent system, to understand the nature of social relationships, to consider the future, and to anticipate consequences of decisions all increase during adolescence (Damon & Hart, 1982; Harter, 1983). The sparse literature on social cognitive abilities and sexual behavior is illustrative. Using a Piagetian approach to study the understanding of "where babies come from," concrete operational responses give way to more formal operational ones during childhood and early adolescence: Formal operations are characteristic of the majority of 11- to 12-year-olds, whereas they are rare in younger children (Bernstein & Cowan, 1975). In a cross-sectional study, North American adolescents were slower in attaining formal abilities related to "where babies come from" than their peers in England, Sweden, and Australia (Goldman & Goldman, 1982). These authors suggest that the North Americans are lagging because of the cultural context (teenage sexual activity being less acceptable in the United States than other Western countries) and education (sex education being later, less complete, and less accepted in the United States). Recently, four stages of reasoning about sexual behavior have been proposed, following other cognitive developmental stage models. These stages are related to age and ego development during adolescence and young adulthood but not in later adulthood (Gfellner, 1986). Whether such reasoning is associated with sexual behavior has not been studied.

Other social cognitive processes might be applied to the study of teenage sexual behavior including self-definitions, self-efficacy, and social comparisons (Bandura, 1982; Higgins, Ruble, & Hartup, 1983). For example, at the time of menarche, girls construct a self-definition of what it means to be a mature, reproductive woman based on actual experiences, information seeking, and interactions with others (Brooks-Gunn, 1987).

CONTRACEPTIVE USE

Rates of sexual activity among teens in the United States are not notably higher than the rates in several countries in Western Europe. Yet, the incidence of adolescent pregnancy and childbearing in the United States, especially among younger teens, exceeds the level of most other industrialized nations (Jones et al., 1985; Westoff, Calot & Foster, 1983). This is partly due to poor contraceptive use among American teenagers. Case studies by the Alan Guttmacher Institute suggest that American youth are exposed to mixed messages about contraception and that birth control services are not effectively delivered to the teenage population (Jones et al., 1985). When considering the difficulties adolescents have in using contraceptives, it is important to recognize that many American adults are poor contraceptive users as well. Indeed, the most widely used method of contraception among married adults in their 30s is sterilization (Bachrach, 1984; Jones et al., 1988). Presumably, mature adults resort to sterilization because they have many of the same apprehensions and problems with contraception that teenagers do.

Initiating the Use of Contraceptives

About one half of all teenagers do not use contraceptives the first time they have sexual relations (Zelnik & Shah, 1983). Younger adolescents are much less likely to use contraceptives than are older adolescents. In addition, more Whites than Blacks have used birth control methods during the first intercourse, although these racial differences largely disappear after controlling for age of initiation (Zelnik, Kantner, & Ford, 1981). Little comparable data on use of contraceptives by gender exist. In one study, more than half of the White teenage boys and almost three quarters of the Black teenage boys had not used a method of birth control during first intercourse: This compared to a little less than half of the White teenage girls and a little more than half of the Black teenage girls not having used contraception during the first intercourse (Zelnik & Shah, 1983).

Of those who use a method, male methods seem to be the overwhelming choice, as reported by both boys and girls, Blacks and Whites. For example, two thirds to three quarters of all White teenagers and Black teenage boys reported using a male method; in contrast, approximately 45% of Black girls reported using a male method, in that they were much more likely to use a female prescription method than the other three groups. In addition, among both boys and girls, those who planned first intercourse were much more likely to have used contraception than those who did not plan the first intercourse. Reasons for not having used a method at first intercourse were provided in this same survey. The reasons, in descending order of their being mentioned, were as follows: Intercourse was not planned, they did not know about intercourse, they did not want to use contraceptives, they did not think about using contraceptives, contraceptives were not available, and pregnancy was thought to be impossible. White teenagers were more likely than Black teenagers to state that contraception was not available, and more Black than White teenagers said that they did not know about contraception (Zelnik & Shah, 1983).

Contraceptive Use After Sexual Initiation

Failure to use contraception the first time intercourse occurs is unfortunately not a one-time event. The percentage of teenagers who use birth control only occasionally or not at all is substantial. These delays have serious consequences. One half of all first pregnancies occur in the first six months following intercourse, and one fifth in the first month (Zabin, Kantner, & Zelnik, 1979). In a study of 1,200 teenagers attending a family planning clinic for the first time, one third came to the clinic because of a possible pregnancy, and 14% came prior to the initiation of intercourse. Of the remaining young women, only 8% found their way to the clinic within three months of sexual initiation (Zabin &

Clark, 1981). However, three quarters of those coming to the clinic had used some form of contraception previously. Most conspicuous among the many reasons for not coming to a family planning clinic earlier were procrastination and ambivalence as well as fear that parents would find out. Many teens believed, incorrectly, that parental consent or notification was necessary for clinic attendance. Clearly, this finding has important implications for altering perceptions about clinics among sexually active teenagers. It also underscores the lack of communication between parents and children about matters associated with sexuality.

Antecedents of Girls' Contraceptive Use

Antecedents of contraceptive use have been studied extensively. The following is a brief summary of these findings (Chilman, 1986; Morrison, 1985). In general, the characteristics of early sexual initiation are similar to those for irregular contraceptive use. Irregular contraceptive use is associated with lower social class, nonattendance of college, and fundamentalist Protestant affiliation. Situational determinants include not having a steady partner, having never had been pregnant, infrequent intercourse, and no access to free confidential family planning. Familial correlates include little communication with parents, perceived troubled relationship with parents, and lack of knowledge of parents' contraceptive experience. Peer influences include having friends who become parents. Academically, low educational achievement and aspirations are associated with irregular contraceptive use. From a personality perspective, high levels of anxiety, low self-esteem, and feelings of fatalism, powerlessness, and alienation are associated with poor contraceptive use.

Lack of knowledge about the safe time of the month also contributes to poor contraceptive use. However, we have little information about sexual knowledge and its relation to sexual behavior more generally. A few relevant surveys suggest that knowledge of contraception and abortion increases during adolescence, which is often attributed to education. However, taking a sex education course does not guarantee adequate knowledge (only one third of 15- to 19-year-olds were able to identify the cycle phase in which risk of pregnancy was the greatest; Zelnik & Kantner, 1977). It appears that knowledge is a necessary but insufficient determinant of effective contraceptive use.

The social cognitive perspective so relevant to understanding the onset of sexual behavior could be applied equally well to contraceptive use and unplanned pregnancy. Almost all girls report being surprised at finding themselves pregnant (Shah, Zelnik, & Kantner, 1975). What accounts for their surprise? Reasons include (a) the belief that they could not become pregnant because of cycle phase (although the majority of adolescents are unable to identify the time at which ovulation occurs); (b) the misperception that they did not have sex often enough, had used withdrawal, had not had an orgasm, or were too young; (c) even while knowing the risk, believing they would not get "caught"; and (d) procrastination or forgetting to use birth control, perhaps indicating a denial of personal responsibility for their behavior. Unfortunately, most of these studies surveyed only pregnant girls or girls obtaining a pregnancy test, so it is unclear whether these reasons constitute post hoc explanations or rationalizations. Furthermore, although contraceptive use has been attributed to self-insight and future orientation, this assumption has not been directly examined. Theoretical models for contraceptive use should include social cognitive and motivational processes (Morrison, 1985).

Male Contraceptive Use

We know very little about boys' attitudes about contraceptive use or distinguishing characteristics of regular and irregular contraceptive users. Approximately 40% of girls rely on male methods and therefore depend on the "vigilance" of their male partner. Like girls, boys know very little about reproduction, even the time during the menstrual cycle when conception is likeliest to occur. Boys also may be less knowledgeable about specific contraceptives and may have even more reservations about contraceptive use than girls.

Sexual Activity and Other Adolescent Behaviors

Teenage sexual activity and contraceptive use must be considered in light of other adolescent experiences. For example, teenage sexual behavior is generally associated with alcohol and drug use as well as declines in school achievement and interest. Adolescents may engage in such behaviors for many different reasons, including (a) efforts to achieve what seem to be unavailable goals, (b) a way of coping with personal frustrations and anticipated failure, (c) an expression of opposition to conventional society, and (d) membership in peers' subcultures (Hamburg, 1986; Jessor & Jessor, 1977). Just describing demographic trends in sexual behavior and antecedent factors does not offer much insight into why adolescents engage in sexual activity or other behaviors. Intervention efforts have been hampered by the lack of research on the context in which sexuality occurs, the possible personal correlates of certain behavior patterns, and the interaction of the two.

It is important to consider differences between older and younger adolescents' goals and motivations. For example, sexual behavior is more likely to be termed problem behavior for younger than older adolescents. Whether the motivations of young adolescents are different from those of older adolescents has not been studied. From a developmental perspective, it is not known whether early engagement in sexual behavior and other risk-taking behaviors truncates the process of adolescent development, making it less likely that these teens achieve autonomy and a healthy sense of self. However, it is clear that the young adolescents' life course trajectory might be more likely to be negatively affected by early engagement in sexual behavior, as reflected in school problems, early pregnancy, and poor job prospects, than the adolescent who has already completed high school. (For more discussion of these issues, see our companion article on pregnancy and childbearing in this issue.)

SEXUALLY TRANSMITTED DISEASES

Adolescents are at high risk for sexually transmitted diseases (STDs). Excluding homosexual men and prostitutes, female teenagers have the highest rates of gonorrhea, cytomegalovirus, chlamydia cervicitis, and pelvic inflammatory diseases of any age group (Cates & Rauh, 1985; Mosher, 1985). Risk factors for STDs include early age of intercourse and no or irregular contraceptive use.

Of pressing concern is the incidence of the acquired immune deficiency syndrome (AIDS). Although few adolescents have been reported to have AIDS, the numbers have been doubling in recent years. In addition, one fifth of all cases have occurred in 20- to 29-year-olds, and the virus has a long incubation period, suggesting that many of these cases may have originated in the late adolescent years (Curran et al., 1988). If the proportion of reported cases increases in the heterosexual population, as many expect it will, adolescents may be at relatively high risk for infection, given their current rates of other STDs and their contraceptive histories (Brooks-Gunn, Boyer, & Hein, 1988). Educational programs about STDs generally and AIDS in particular are becoming more commonplace in school sex educational programs. In a recent national survey by Harris, virtually all parents wanted AIDS education

in the schools (Meade, 1988). Many of the preventative strategies discussed in the next section could be tailored to include behavioral interventions aimed at reducing the incidence of STDs and AIDS by increasing the use of condoms, advocating the practice of less risky sexual behaviors, reducing the use of intravenous drugs, and minimizing the sharing of needles among intravenous drug users. These are behavior changes advocated for adults as well as for adolescents (Koop, 1988; see review of adolescent AIDS by Brooks-Gunn et al., 1988).

PREVENTION STRATEGIES

Several preventative strategies have been proposed and implemented: offering access to contraception, providing knowledge about sexuality and contraception, influencing sexual attitudes, and enhancing life options (Dryfoos, 1984). The majority of programs offer services (family planning) or knowledge (sex education); fewer attempt to change motivational constructs such as strengthening competing goals (school achievement), providing alternative means of achieving goals (intimacy without sexual behavior or with regular contraceptive use), or altering peer group norms (making early sexual activity less desirable; Hamburg, 1986). What follows is a very brief review of some of the preventative strategies currently being used. (See Hofferth & Hayes, 1987, for a more complete discussion, especially of interventions that have not been systematically evaluated or are currently being evaluated, such as programs to delay first intercourse or abstain from sexual activity.) Family life and sex education, media programs, family planning services, and school-based clinic programs are reviewed. Other approaches using more specific social psychological principles include decision making, peer counseling, peer resistance training, behavioral skills training, and decreases in risk-taking behavior generally (Botvin, 1986; Perry, 1984). Systematic application of such approaches to sexual behavior is rare. Most prevention strategies focus on females.

Family Life and Sex Education

The primary purpose of family life and sex education is to provide information about human reproduction and, increasingly, about contraceptive use. Once believed to be exclusively in the province of the family, responsibility for sex education has shifted in part to the school. A vast majority of parents, other adults, and adolescents support sex education in the schools (Norman & Harris, 1981). In the early 1980s, three quarters of all school districts provided some sex education and three quarters of adolescents in national surveys reported having had some sex education (Zelnik & Kim, 1982). Only one state currently prohibits instruction on reproductive topics. However, the timing, extensiveness, and intensiveness of sex education programs are widely divergent. Almost all school districts include decision making about sexual behavior as a goal of their sex education programs. Three quarters include reproductive knowledge, and a scant one quarter include reduction of sexual activity and teenage childbearing as goals. Most programs are short (10 hr or less), and perhaps less than 10% of all students have taken comprehensive programs (40 hr or more; Kirby, 1984). Elementary school programs seem to be rare, although pubertal education is provided in many fifth and sixth grades (no systematic review of these programs exists). Junior high school programs focus on puberty, reproduction, and dating, but typically not on contraception. High school coverage is more inclusive: Three quarters of all programs include family planning, contraceptive methods, and abortion, and one half include masturbation and homosexuality as topics (Hofferth & Hayes, 1987; Orr, 1982).

Several tests of the efficacy of sex education have been performed in recent years. Generally, knowledge about reproduction increases after such programs, especially in younger adolescents. Of more interest is whether such programs alter behavior. The fear that sex education would promote early sexuality is largely unfounded (Furstenberg et al., 1986; Zelnik & Kim, 1982). Such programs may promote contraceptive use among sexually active teens, but evidence is mixed (Kirby, 1984). Because sex education is part of the adolescent experience in the United States today, it is clear that more evaluation is needed as well as design of new approaches. Peer counseling and parent-adolescent communication programs have been developed, although little is known about their effectiveness.

SCHOOL-BASED CLINICS Such clinics are perhaps the most major programmatic effort, and the most hotly debated one, to be initiated in the 1970s and 1980s. In the most well-known program in St. Paul, Minnesota, fertility rates dropped from 79 per thousand to 26 per thousand from 1973 to 1984; continuation rate for contraceptive use was high (more than 80% over a two-year period); dropout rates for girls with babies dropped from 45% to 10% from 1973 to 1976-1977 (Edwards, Steinman,

Arnold, & Hakanson, 1980). Another innovative program has recently been evaluated in Baltimore, where a health clinic was opened adjacent to a junior high and a high school. Using a pre-post, comparison-treatment design, first intercourse was delayed by seven months for girls who were exposed to the program for three years, clinic attendance increased for girls prior to first intercourse, and many boys attended. Most impressive, conceptions dropped in the program schools during the three-year period while increasing in the comparison schools (Zabin, Hirsch, Smith, Strett, & Hardy, 1986). However, not all program evaluations have yielded such positive results.

Media

Information provided in the media is a way to reach almost all teens and their families. However, television executives have been hesitant to address issues related to sexual behavior and contraceptive use in regular programming and in advertisements. Public health messages and advertisements about sexuality and contraception also do not make their way into the major networks with any frequency. In 1985, the three major networks refused to place public service announcements on teenage pregnancy, although they have done so subsequently with no negative public response. In 1987, all three networks rejected a public education message about oral contraceptive use as too controversial. In 1988, even though public health service messages on condom use to prevent AIDS were aired, network executives state that they would turn down identical advertisements by condom manufacturers; public service announcements on contraceptives not linked to disease prevention are still not being aired by the three major networks (although a few local stations do so).

Family Planning Services

Family planning services play a major role in teenagers' fertility regulation, especially since three quarters of teenage girls using contraception use prescription methods (primarily oral contraceptives). One half of all teenage girls obtaining services use family planning clinics and one half use private physicians. A disproportionate number of clinic users are young, Black, and poor (Pratt & Hendershot, 1984). About two thirds of family planning clinics' funds are provided through federal grants (Title X, Maternal and Child Health Grants, Medicare Funds, and State Block Grants). Issues under study include how to encourage regular scheduled visits, how to decrease the time between first intercourse and first clinic visits, and how effective family planning clinics have been in reducing unwanted pregnancies. Little effort is directed toward bringing male teenagers into the system; for example, less than 1% of all patients served by family planning clinics are male.

CONCLUSION

In 1987, the National Academy of Sciences Panel on Early Childbearing recommended that the rate and incidence of unintended pregnancy among adolescents be reduced. Recommended programs included ones to enhance life options (school performance, role models, and employment opportunities), delay sexual initiation, and encourage contraception after the sexual debut. The panel urged that sex education include sections on contraceptive use, decision making, and assertiveness training; that medical and community services work together to provide integrative, continuous services; that the media be discouraged from glorifying sex; that the media be encouraged to promote contraceptive advertising; and that more school-bill clinics be designed and evaluated (Hayes, 1987). Many of these policy initiatives have been suggested before or are being attempted in select communities, but no large-scale efforts have been undertaken yet.

Perhaps ironically, directing research to girls' fertility, although arising from what is clearly an important policy issue, may have made it difficult to design effective interventions; that is, in the absence of data on the meaning and frequency of different sexual behaviors, program development occurs in what seems to be a social science vacuum. Often untested assumptions have driven program initiatives, some of which have turned out to be good bets and others unfortunate guesses. Our lack of knowledge is all the more distressing given the haunting specter of AIDS and the rapid rise of STDs in adolescents. How do we alter sexual practices among homosexual teenagers or in intravenous drug users (the two groups at greatest risk for AIDS) if we do not know how many there are, where they are located, or what their current sexual practices are? How might teens be encouraged to use condoms (the most effective protection against human immunodeficiency virus infection known today) when almost no information exists as to how teens initiate sexual activity, how they view and use the condom, what they know about proper use of the condom, how they discuss condom use with a partner, and so on? Clearly, we are limited in what may be said about every aspect of sexuality except fertility control, specifically age of intercourse onset and (girls') contraceptive use. Although a critical concern, in that teenage parenthood extracts a cost to the young mother, the young father, and their children (see our companion piece in this issue, Furstenberg, Brooks-Gunn, & Chase-Lansdale, pp. 313–320), other concerns are not addressed by social scientists generally or psychologists in particular.

Questions

1. How has sexual activity of adolescent boys and girls changed over the last two decades?

2. How do parents and peers influence adolescent sexual behavior?

3. It is clear that education reduces the incidence of pregnancy and sexually transmitted diseases among teens. What type of education is needed and what type is generally available?

References

Bachrach, C. A. (1984). Contraceptive practice among American women, 1973-1982. *Family Planning Perspectives, 16*, 253–259.

Bandura, A. (1982). Self-efficacy mechanism in human agency. *American Psychologist, 37*, 122–147.

Bernstein, A. C., & Cowan, P. A. (1975). Children's concepts of how people get babies. *Child Development, 46*, 77–91.

Botvin, G. J. (1986). Substance abuse prevention research: Recent developments and future directions. *Journal of School Health, 56(9)*, 369–374.

Brooks-Gunn, J. (1987). Pubertal processes and girls' psychological adaptation. In R. Lemer & T. T. Foch (Eds.), *Biological-psychosocial interactions in early adolescence: A life-span perspective* (pp. 123–153). Hillsdale, NJ: Erlbaum.

Brooks-Gunn, J. (1988). Antecedents and consequences of variations in girls' maturational timing. *Journal of Adolescent Health Care, 9(5),* 1–9.

Brooks-Gunn, J., Boyer, C. B., & Hein, K. (1988). Preventing HIV infection and AIDS in children and adolescents: Behavioral research and intervention strategies. *American Psychologist, 43,* 958–964.

Brooks-Gunn, J., & Ruble, D. N. (1982). The development of menstrual-related beliefs and behaviors during early adolescence. *Child Development, 53,* 1567–1577.

Brooks-Gunn, J., & Warren, M. P. (in press). Biological contributions to affective expression in young adolescent girls. *Child Development.*

Brooks-Gunn, J., & Zahaykevich, M. (in press). Parent–daughter relationships in early adolescence: A developmental perspective. In K. Kreppner & R. Lerner (Eds.), *Family systems and life-span development.* Hillsdale, NJ: Erlbaum.

Cates, W., Jr., & Rauh, J. L. (1985). Adolescents and sexually transmitted diseases: An expanding problem. *Journal of Adolescent Health Care, 6,* 1–5.

Chilman, C. S. (1983). *Adolescent sexuality in a changing American society: Social and psychological perspectives for the human services professions* (2nd ed.). New York: Wiley.

Chilman, C. S. (1986). Some psychosocial aspects of adolescent sexual and contraceptive behaviors in a changing American society. In J. B. Lancaster & B. A. Hamburg (Eds.), *School-age pregnancy and parenthood: Biosocial dimensions* (pp. 191–217). New York: Aldine De Gruyter.

Cooper, C., Grotevant, H., & Condon, S. (1983). Individuality and connectedness in the family as a context for adolescent identity formation and role-taking skill. *New Directions for Child Development, 22,* 43–60.

Curran, J. W., Jaffe, H. W., Hardy, A. M., Morgan, W. M., Selik, R. M., & Dondero, T. J. (1988). Epidemiology of HIV infection and AIDS in the United States. *Science, 239,* 610–616.

Cvetkovich, G., & Grote, B. (1980). Psychological development and the social problem of teenage illegitimacy. In C. Chilman (Ed.), *Adolescent pregnancy and childbearing: Findings from research* (pp. 15–41). Washington, DC: U.S. Department of Health and Human Services.

Damon, W., & Hart, D. (1982). The development of self-understanding from infancy through adolescence. *Child Development, 53,* 841–864.

Dryfoos, J. G. (1984). A new strategy for preventing unintended teenage childbearing. *Family Planning Perspectives, 16,* 193–195.

Edwards, L., Steinman, M., Arnold, K., & Hakanson, E. (1980). Adolescent pregnancy prevention services in high school clinics. *Family Planning Perspectives, 12,* 6–14.

Furstenberg, F., Jr., Brooks-Gunn, J., & Chase-Lansdale, L. (1989). Teenaged pregnancy and childbearing. *American Psychologist. 44,* 313–320.

Furstenberg, F. F. Jr., Brooks-Gunn, J., & Morgan, S. P. (1987). *Adolescent mothers in later life.* New York: Cambridge University Press.

Furstenberg, F. F., Jr., Moore, K. A., & Peterson, J. L. (1986). Sex education and sexual experience among adolescents. *American Journal of Public Health, 75,* 1221–1222.

Gaddis, A., & Brooks-Gunn, J. (1985). The male experience of pubertal change. *Journal of Youth and Adolescence, 14(1),* 61–69.

Gagnon, J. H. (1987). *Some notes on aspects of sexual conduct relevant to the AIDS epidemic.* Unpublished manuscript.

Gagnon, J., & Simon, W. (1973). *Sexual conduct: The social sources of human sexuality.* New York: Aldine de Gruyter.

Gargiulo, J., Attie, I., Brooks-Gunn, J., & Warren, M. P. (1987). Dating in middle school girls: Effects of social context, maturation, and grade. *Developmental Psychology, 23(5),* 730–737.

Gfellner, B. M. (1986). Concepts of sexual behavior: Construction and validation of a developmental model. *Journal of Adolescent Research, 1(3),* 327–347.

Goldman, R. J., & Goldman, J. D. G. (1982). How children perceive the origin of babies and the roles of mothers and fathers in procreation: A cross-national study. *Child Development, 53,* 491–504.

Grotevant, H. D., & Cooper, C. R. (1986). Individuation in family relationships. *Human Development, 29,* 82–100.

Hamburg, B. A. (1986). Subsets of adolescent mothers: Developmental, biomedical, and psychosocial issues. In J. B. Lancaster & B. A. Hamburg (Eds.), *School-age pregnancy and parenthood: Biosocial dimensions* (pp. 115–145). New York: Aldine De Gruyter.

Harter, S. (1983). Developmental perspectives on the self-system. In E. M. Hetherington (Ed.), *Socialization, personality, and social development: Vol. 4. Handbook of child psychology* (4th ed.). New York: Wiley.

Hauser, S., Powers, S. I., Noam, G. G., Jacobson, A. M., Weiss, B., & Follansbee, D. J. (1984). Familial contexts of adolescent ego development. *Child Development, 55,* 195–213.

Hayes, C. D. (Ed.). (1987). *Risking the future: Adolescent sexuality, pregnancy, and childbearing* (Vol. 1). Washington, DC: National Academy Press.

Higgins, E. T., Ruble, D. N., & Hartup, W. W. (1983). *Social cognition and social development: A sociocultural perspective.* New York: Cambridge University Press.

Hofferth, S. L., & Hayes, C. D. (Eds.). (1987). *Risking the future: Adolescent sexuality, pregnancy, and childbearing: Vol. 2. Working papers and statistical reports.* Washington, DC: National Academy Press.

Hogan, D. P., & Kitagawa, E. M. (1985). The impact of social status, family structure, and neighborhood on the fertility of Black adolescents. *American Journal of Sociology, 90,* 825–855.

Inazu, J. K., & Fox, G. L. (1980). Maternal influence on the sexual behavior of teenage daughters. *Journal of Family Issues, 1,* 81–102.

Jessor, R., & Jessor, S. L. (1977). *Problem behavior and psychosocial development.* New York: Academic Press.

Jessor, S. L., & Jessor, R. (1975). Transition from virginity to nonvirginity among youth: A social-psychological study over time. *Developmental Psychology, 11(4),* 473–484.

Jones, E., Forrest, J. D., Goldman, N., Henshaw, S., Lincoln, R., Rosoff, J., Westoff, C., & Wulf, D. (1985). Teenage pregnancy in developed countries: Determinants and policy implications. *Family Planning Perspectives, 17(2),* 53–63.

Jones, E., Forrest, J. D., Henshaw, S. K., Silverman, J., & Torres, A. (1988). Unintended pregnancy, contraceptive practice and family planning services in developed countries. *Family Planning Perspectives, 20(2),* 53–67.

Kahn, J., Smith, K., & Roberts, E. (1984). *Familial communication and adolescent sexual behavior* (Final report to the office of adolescent Pregnancy Programs). Cambridge, MA: American Institutes for Research.

Kinsey, A. C., Pomeroy, W. B., & Martin, C. E. (1948). *Sexual behavior in the human male.* Philadelphia: W. B. Saunders.

Kinsey, A. C., Pomeroy, W. B., Martin, C. E., & Gebhard, P. H. (1953). *Sexual behavior in the human female.* Philadelphia: W. B. Saunders.

Kirby, D. (1984). *Sexuality education: An evaluation of programs and their effects.* Santa Cruz, CA: Network Publications.

Koop, C. E. (1988). *Understanding AIDS.* Rockville, MD: The Surgeon General and the Centers for Disease Control, U.S. Public Health Service.

Magnusson, D., Strattin, H., & Allen, V. L. (1985). Biological maturation and social development: A longitudinal study of some adjustment processes from mid-adolescence to adulthood. *Journal of Youth and Adolescence, 14(4),* 267–283.

Meade, J. (1988). What parents should know when AIDS comes to school. *Children Magazine,* pp. 59–65.

Morrison, D. M. (1985). Adolescent contraceptive behavior: A review. *Psychological Bulletin, 98(3),* 538–568.

Mosher, W. D. (1985). Reproductive impairments in the United States, 1965–1982. *Demography, 22,* 415–430.

Newcomer, S., & Udry, J. R. (1987). Parental marital status effects on adolescent sexual behavior. *Journal of Marriage and the Family, 49,* 235–240.

Norman, J., & Harris, M. (1981). *The private life of the American teenager.* New York: Rawson Wade.

Ooms, T. (Ed.). (1981). *Teenage pregnancy in a family context: Implications for policy.* Philadelphia: Temple University Press.

Orr, M. (1982). Sex education and contraceptive education in U.S. public high schools. *Family Planning Perspectives, 14,* 304–313.

Paige, K. E. (1983). A bargaining theory of menarcheal responses in preindustrial cultures. In J. Brooks-Gunn & A. C. Petersen (Eds.), *Girls at puberty: Biological and psychosocial perspectives* (pp. 301–322). New York: Plenum Press.

Perry, C. L. (1984). Health promotion at school: Expanding the potential for prevention. *School Psychology Review, 13(2),* 141–149.

Pratt, W. F., & Hendershot, G. E. (1984). The use of family planning services by sexually active teenagers. *Population Index, 50(3),* 412–413.

Reiss, R. L. (1960). *Premarital sexual standards in America.* New York: Free Press.

Shah, F., Zelnik, M., & Kantner, J. (1975). Unprotected intercourse among unwed teenagers. *Family Planning Perspectives. 7,* 39–44.

Smith, E. A., & Udry, J. R. (1985). Coital and non-coital sexual behaviors of white and black adolescents. *American Journal of Public Health, 75,* 1200–1203.

Strecher, V. J., McEvoy, B., Becker, M. H., & Rosenstock, I. M. (1986). The role of self-efficacy in achieving health behavior change. *Health Education Quarterly, 13(1),* 73–91.

Udry, J. R., Billy, J. O. G., Morris, N. M., Groff, T. R., & Raj, M. H. (1985). Serum androgenic hormones motivate sexual behavior in boys. *Fertility and Sterility, 43(1),* 90–94.

Udry, J. R., Talbert, L., & Morris, N. M. (1986). Biosocial foundations for adolescent female sexuality. *Demography, 23(2),* 217–230.

Westoff, C. F., Calot, G., & Foster, A. D. (1983). Teenage fertility in developed nations: 1971–1980. *Family Planning Perspectives, 15(3),* 105–110.

Zabin, L. S., & Clark, S. D., Jr. (1981). Why they delay: A study of teenage family planning clinic patients. *Family Planning Perspectives, 13(5),* 205–217.

Zabin, L. S., Hirsch, M. B., Smith, E. A., Strett, R., & Hardy, J. B. (1986). Evaluation of a pregnancy prevention program for urban teenagers. *Family Planning Perspectives, 18,* 119–126.

Zabin, L. S., Kantner, J. F., & Zelnik, M. (1979). The risk of adolescent pregnancy in the first months of intercourse. *Family Planning Perspectives, 11(4),* 215–222.

Zelnik, M., & Kantner, J. F. (1977). Sexual and contraceptive experience of young unmarried women in the United States, 1976 and 1971. *Family Planning Perspectives, 9,* 55–71.

Zelnik, M., & Kantner, J. F. (1980). Sexual activity, contraceptive use and pregnancy among metropolitan area teenagers: 1971–1979. *Family Planning Perspectives, 12(5),* 230.

Zelnik, M., Kantner, J. E., & Ford, K. (1981). *Sex and pregnancy in adolescence* (Sage Library of Social Research, Vol. 133). Beverly Hills: Sage.

Zelnik, M., & Kim, Y. J. (1982). Sex education and its association with teenage sexual activity, pregnancy and contraceptive use. *Family Planning Perspectives, 14(3),* 117–126.

Zelnik, M., & Shah, R. K. (1983). First intercourse among young Americans. *Family Planning Perspectives, 15(2),* 64–70.